Maharishi Mahesh Yogi
on the
Bhagavad-Gītā

A rediscovery to fulfil the need of our time

Maharishi Mahesh Yogi
on the
Bhagavad-Gītā

A NEW TRANSLATION AND COMMENTARY
WITH SANSKRIT TEXT

Chapters 1 to 6

Maharishi University of Management Press

First published by International SRM Publications 1967
Published by Penguin Books 1969
Published by Maharishi International University Press 1976
Published by Arkana 1990
This new edition published by Maharishi University of Management Press 2015

British spelling and style conventions are used in this Maharishi University of Management Press edition, as in earlier editions of this book. For Sanskrit transliteration, a convention has been adopted based on Maharishi's later books, which enables those without formal Sanskrit training to pronounce the Sanskrit words and expressions more accurately.

Maharishi University of Management Press
Fairfield, Iowa 52557 USA
Website: mumpress.com

Hardcover Edition ISBN 978-0-923569-64-8
Paperback Edition ISBN 978-0-923569-65-5

Contents

Preface 9

Introduction 19

Chapter I 23

Chapter II 73

Chapter III 175

Chapter IV 247

Chapter V 323

Chapter VI 381

Appendix

The Holy Tradition 469

The *Transcendental Meditation®* Technique:
The Main Principle 470

Cosmic Law, The Basic Law of Creation 471

The Six Systems of Indian Philosophy 472

Index 495

Contact Information
for Maharishi's Global Programs 539

TO

THE LOTUS FEET OF SHRI GURU DEV,

HIS DIVINITY

BRAHMANANDA SARASWATI,

JAGADGURU, BHAGWAN SHANKARACHARYA

OF JYOTIR MATH, HIMALAYAS,

AND

AS BLESSINGS FROM HIM

TO THE LOVERS OF LIFE

DESIROUS OF ENJOYING ALL GLORIES,

WORLDLY AND DIVINE

Preface

THE Vedas are the lighthouse of eternal wisdom leading man to salvation and inspiring him to supreme accomplishment.

The omnipresence of eternal Being, unmanifested and absolute; Its status as That, even in the manifested diversity of creation; and the possibility of the realization of Being by any man in terms of himself — these are the great truths of the perennial philosophy of the Vedas.

The Vedas reveal the unchanging Unity of life which underlies the evident multiplicity of creation, for Reality is both manifest and unmanifest, and That alone is. 'I am That, thou art That, and all this is That', is the Truth; and this is the kernel of the Vedic teaching, which the *Ṛishis* extol as teaching 'worthy of hearing, contemplating, and realizing'.

The truth of Vedic wisdom is by its very nature independent of time and can therefore never be lost. When, however, man's vision becomes one-sided and he is caught by the binding influence of the phenomenal world to the exclusion of the absolute phase of Reality, when he is thus confined within the ever-changing phases of existence, his life loses stability and he begins to suffer. When suffering grows, the invincible force of Nature moves to set man's vision right and establish a way of life which will again fulfil the high purpose of his existence. The long history of the world records many such periods in which the ideal pattern of life is forgotten and then restored to man.

Veda Vyāsa, the sage of enlightened vision, records the growth of unrighteousness in the families of those who ruled the people about five thousand years ago. It was then that Lord Kṛishṇa came to remind man of the true values of life and living. He restored that direct contact with the transcendental Being which alone can give fullness to every aspect of life. He brought to light absolute Being as the basic Reality of life and established It as the foundation of all thinking, which in turn is the basis of all doing. This philosophy of Being, thinking, and doing is the true philosophy of the integrated life. It not only helps the doer to gain success in his undertaking, but, at the same time, sets him free from the bondage of action, bringing fulfilment at every level. Such is the teaching of eternal Truth, given by Lord Kṛishṇa to Arjuna in the Bhagavad-Gītā.

Gradually this teaching came to be forgotten, so that two thousand years later even the principle of Being as the absolute Reality, the source and basis of all creation, was overshadowed by misguided beliefs which glorified only the relative aspects of life. 'The long lapse of time', says Lord Kṛishṇa, is the reason for such a loss of wisdom.

When the philosophy of the integrated life restored by Lord Kṛishṇa was lost from view, the idea grew that everything which life can offer is present on the obvious levels of existence, and that therefore it would be useless to aspire to anything that might lie deeper than external appearances. Society became dominated by this superficial outlook, insight into Reality was lost, the right sense of values forgotten, and the stability of life destroyed. Tension, confusion, superstition, unhappiness, and fear prevailed.

Lord Buddha came to remedy this situation. Finding the field of action distorted, He came with a message of right action. Speaking from His level of consciousness established in Being, in eternal freedom (*Nirvāṇa*), Lord Buddha taught the philosophy of action in freedom. He advocated meditation in order to purify the field of thought through direct contact with Being and bring about the state of right action in society. Lord Buddha's message was complete because He incorporated the fields of Being, thinking, and doing in His theme of revival. But because His followers failed to correlate these different fields of life in a systematic manner through the practice of Transcendental Meditation, realization of Being as the basis of a good life became obscured. The whole structure of Lord Buddha's teaching not only became distorted but was also turned upside down. The effect was mistaken for the cause. Right action came to be regarded as a means to gain *Nirvāṇa*, whereas right action is in fact the result of this state of consciousness in freedom.

It has been the misfortune of every teacher that, while he speaks from his level of consciousness, his followers can only receive his message on their level; and the gulf between the teaching and understanding grows wider with time.

The teaching of right action without due emphasis on the primary necessity of realization of Being is like building a wall without a foundation. It sways with the wind and collapses before long. Within three or four hundred years all real connection between the essential teachings of Lord Buddha and the daily life of His followers had disappeared. Insight into the principle of the integrated life was again lost. Having forgotten the prime importance of realizing Being, society became immersed once more in the superficialities of life.

Nature will not allow humanity to be deprived of the vision of Reality for very long. A wave of revival brought Shankara to re-establish the basis of life and renew human understanding. Shankara restored the wisdom of the Absolute and established It in the daily life of the people, strengthening the fields of thought and action by the power of Being. He brought the message of fulfilment through direct realization of transcendental Being in the state of Self-consciousness, which is the basis of all good in life.

Shankara's emphasis on Self-realization stems from the eternal philosophy of the integrated life expressed by Lord Kṛishṇa in the Bhagavad-Gītā when He asks Arjuna first to 'Be without the three *Guṇas*' and then to perform actions while thus established in Being. That all men should at all times live the Bliss Consciousness of absolute Being, and that they should live the state of fulfilment in God Consciousness throughout all thought, speech, and action: this is the essence of Shankara's message, as it is the essence of Lord Kṛishṇa's and of the entire Vedic philosophy.

The greatest blessing that Shankara's teaching has offered to the world is the principle of fullness of intellectual and emotional development in the state of enlightenment, based on transcendental pure consciousness, in which the heart is so pure as to be able to flow and overflow with waves of universal love and devotion to God, while the mind is so refined as to enjoy awareness of the divine nature as separate from the world of action.

The spontaneous expressions of Shankara's mind and heart in this state of freedom and fulfilment have been a source of inspiration both to those who live by the heart and those who live by the mind. His consciousness exemplified the highest state of human development; his heart expressed supreme transcendental devotion to God (*Parā Bhakti*), while his mind expressed awareness of the Self as separate from the field of action (*Gyān*). This it was that led Shankara's speech to flow into ecstasies of devotion and at the same time into clear expressions of knowledge, the dry and hard-headed truths concerning divine nature as detached from the world. These are the two aspects of the living reality of a life in complete fulfilment.

Shankara not only revived the wisdom of integrated life and made it popular in his day, but also established four principal seats of learning in four corners of India to keep his teaching pure and to ensure that it would be propagated in its entirety generation after generation. For many centuries his teaching remained alive in his followers, who lived the ideal state of knowledge with devotion (*Gyān* and *Bhakti*). But in spite of all his foresight and endeavours, Shankara's message inevitably suffered with time the same misfortunes as those of the other great teachers.

If the occupants of a house forget the foundations, it is because the foundations lie underground, hidden from view. It is no surprise that Being was lost to view, for It lies in the transcendental field of life.

The state of Reality, as described by the enlightened, cannot become a path for the seeker, any more than the description of a destination can replace the road that leads to it. When the truth that Being forms the basis of the state of enlightenment became obscured, Shankara's statements about the nature of the goal were mistaken for the path to realization.

This misunderstanding was increased by the very beauty of Shankara's eloquence. His expressions of deep devotion made in the state of complete surrender and oneness with God, and his intellectual clarifications made in the state of awareness of the divine nature, are both so full and complete in themselves that, seen from the ordinary level of consciousness, they appeared to present two independent paths to enlightenment: the path of knowledge and the path of devotion.

This is the tragedy of knowledge, the tragic fate that knowledge must meet at the hands of ignorance. It is inevitable, because the teaching comes from one level of consciousness and is received at quite a different level. The knowledge of Unity must in time shatter on the hard rocks of ignorance. History has proved this again and again. Shankara's teaching could not prove an exception to the rule.

The idea of two paths became more predominant owing to the carelessness of the custodians of Shankara's teaching. Since they followed the recluse way of life, they were naturally concerned with thoughts of the separateness of the Divine from the world; and, with the continuance of this situation generation after generation, the aspect of knowledge began to dominate Shankara's tradition while the aspect of devotion gradually lost its importance. The teaching became one-sided and, deprived of its wholeness, eventually lost its universal appeal. It came to be regarded as *Māyāvāda*, a philosophy of illusion, holding the world to be only illusory and emphasizing the detached way of life.

As the principle of Being began more and more to disappear from view, the paths of devotion and knowledge became more and more separate, and finally the link between them was lost. The principle of full development of heart and mind through one process (Transcendental Meditation) was lost. The integral nature of realization was lost. The true wisdom of life's fulfilment, which lies in the simultaneous development of heart and mind, was lost. The idea that devotion and knowledge are necessarily separate was the greatest blow to Shankara's teaching.

In the absence of the moon, the stars take over and provide as much light as they can. When Shankara's high ideal of transcendental devotion disappeared from sight, Rāmānuja, Madhva, and other teachers upheld the path of devotion, even though without its proper basis in Being. People followed them, and thus there arose many devotional sects all on the level of emotion and every one founded on the comfortable basis of hope that 'some day our prayer will be heard, some day He will come to us and call us to Him'. Indeed a comfort to the heart but, alas, such devotion is on the imaginary plane of feeling! It is far, far away from the reality of actual contact between the devotee and his God. Awareness in the state of Being alone makes the whole field of devotion real.

All these sects hold that transcendental devotion is the last stage of a devotee's achievement. But Shankara's principle of devotion is founded on Transcendental Consciousness from the very beginning. The first step for Shankara is the last step for these devotional sects, a step which according to their understanding is far above the reach of the ordinary man.

The idea that devotion must start from Transcendental Consciousness having been lost by the guardians of Shankara's wisdom, entrance into the field of devotion was closed. Seekers of God remained seeking in thin air, and lovers of God remained weeping for Him without finding Him.

As devotion remained merely on the level of thinking and of assuming an attitude of feeling (mood-making), so knowledge met with the same fate once the direct way to the realization of Transcendental Consciousness had been lost. Understanding of the Unity of life cannot be significant until one has thoroughly understood, by direct experience, that one's inner divine nature is separate from the world of action. If a man has not gained consciousness in Being through the practice of Transcendental Meditation, he continues to live in ignorance and bondage. Because he has not yet opened himself to the experience of the separateness of the Divine from the world, the thought of Unity has no practical use for such a man. He has nothing to unite.

On the fertile field of Transcendental Consciousness both knowledge and devotion find their fulfilment. But this principle once forgotten and the technique for developing Transcendental Consciousness lost, many, many generations have died without seeing the Light of God and without gaining fulfilment. That has been the situation for more than a thousand years. Misunderstanding itself has taken the shape of a tradition, unfortunately known as Shankara's tradition. This great loss to human life can hardly be compensated; but that has been the course of history. Time cannot be recaptured. It is no use repenting the past.

In our review of the rise and fall of Truth, we must not lose sight of the great impact that Shankara produced on Indian life. It was the perfection of his presentation that caused Shankara's teaching to be accepted as the core of Vedic wisdom and placed it at the centre of Indian culture. It became so inseparable from the Indian way of life that when, in course of time, this teaching lost its universal character and came to be interpreted as for the recluse order alone, the whole basis of Indian culture also began to be considered in terms of the recluse way of life, founded on renunciation and detachment.

When this detached view of life became accepted as the basis of Vedic wisdom, the wholeness of life and fulfilment was lost. This error of understanding has dominated Indian culture for centuries and has turned the principle of life upside down. *Life* on the basis of detachment! This is a complete distortion of Indian philosophy. It has not only destroyed the path of realization but has led the seekers of Truth continuously astray. Indeed it has left them without the possibility of ever finding the goal.

Not only was the path to enlightenment lost, but the entire art of living disappeared in the clouds of ignorance which obscured every phase of life. Even religion became blind to itself. Instead of directly helping people to gain God Consciousness and act rightly on that basis, religious preachers began to teach that right action is in itself a way to purification and thereby to God Consciousness.

Without Being, confusion of cause and effect invaded every field of understanding. It captured even the most practical field of the philosophy of Yoga. *Karma Yoga* (attainment of Union by way of action) began to be understood as based on *Karma* (action), whereas its basis is Yoga, Union, Transcendental Consciousness. The Yoga philosophy of Patanjali was itself misinterpreted and the order of stages on its eightfold path reversed. The practice of Yoga was understood to start with *Yama*, *Niyama*, and so on (the secular virtues), whereas in reality it should begin with *Samādhi*. *Samādhi* cannot be gained by the practice of *Yama*, *Niyama*, and so on. Proficiency in the virtues can only be gained by repeated experiences of *Samādhi*. It was because the effect was mistaken for the cause that this great philosophy of life became distorted and the path to *Samādhi* was blocked.

With the loss of insight into Yoga, the other five classical systems of Indian philosophy lost their power. They remained on the theoretical level of knowledge, for it is through Yoga alone that knowledge steps into practical life.

Thus we find that all fields of religion and philosophy have been misunderstood and wrongly interpreted for many centuries past. This has blocked the path to the fullest development of heart and mind, so precisely revived by Shankara.

Interpretations of the Bhagavad-Gītā and other Indian scriptures are now so full of the idea of renunciation that they are regarded with distrust by practical men in every part of the world. Many Western universities hesitate to teach Indian philosophy for this reason. The responsibility for this loss of Truth to the whole world lies with the interpreters of Shankara's teaching; missing the essence of his wisdom, they have been unable to save the world from falling ever deeper into ignorance and suffering.

This age has, however, been fortunate. It has witnessed the living example of a man inspired by Vedic wisdom in its wholeness and thus able to revive the philosophy of the integrated life in all its truth and fullness. His Divinity Brahmananda Saraswati, the inspiration and guiding light of this commentary on the Bhagavad-Gītā, adorned the seat of the Shankarāchārya of the North and, glowing in divine radiance, embodied in himself the head and heart of Shankara. He expounded the Truth in Its all-embracing nature. His quiet words, coming from the unbounded love of his heart, pierced the hearts of all who heard him and brought enlightenment to their minds. His message was the message of fullness of heart and mind. He moved as the living embodiment of Truth and was addressed as Vedānt Incarnate by that great Indian philosopher, now President of India, Dr Radhakrishnan.

It was the concern of Guru Dev, His Divinity Brahmananda Saraswati, to enlighten all men everywhere that resulted in the foundation of the worldwide Spiritual Regeneration Movement in 1958, five years after his departure from us.

India is a country where Truth matters most and Indians are a people to whom God matters most. Indian soil has witnessed many times the revival of life's true philosophy. The people of India have never hesitated to return once more to the right path whenever it was convincingly pointed out to them that their way of life had taken a wrong course. This receptiveness to Truth of the Indian people has always been a source of inspiration and a signal of hope to all movements aiming at the revival of true life and living.

May the present commentary on the Bhagavad-Gītā produce the desired effect in response to the historical necessity of today.

The purpose of this commentary is to restore the fundamental truths of the Bhagavad-Gītā and thus restore the significance of its teaching. If this teaching is followed, effectiveness in life will be achieved, men will be fulfilled on all levels, and the historical need of the age will be fulfilled also.

MAHARISHI MAHESH YOGI

The Old Manor, Aldbourne,
Wiltshire, England
12 January 1965

Introduction

THE Bhagavad-Gītā is the Light of Life, lit by God at the altar of man, to save humanity from the darkness of ignorance and suffering. It is a scripture which outlives time, and can be acknowledged as indispensable to the life of any man in any age. It is the encyclopedia of life, and this commentary provides an index to it.

There will always be confusion and chaos in the relative fields of life and man's mind will always fall into error and indecision. The Bhagavad-Gītā is a complete guide to practical life. It will always be there to rescue man in any situation. It is like an anchor for the ship of life sailing on the turbulent waves of time.

It brings fulfilment to the life of the individual. When society accepts it, social well-being and security will result, and when the world hears it, world peace will be permanent.

The Bhagavad-Gītā presents the science of life and the art of living. It teaches how to be, how to think, and how to do. Its technique of glorifying every aspect of life through contact with inner Being is like watering the root and making the whole tree green. It surpasses any practical wisdom of life ever cherished by human society.

The Bhagavad-Gītā has a greater number of commentaries than any other known scripture. The reason for adding one more is that there does not seem to be any commentary which really brings to light the essential point of the whole teaching.

Wise commentators, in their attempt to fulfil the need of their times, have revealed the truth of the teaching as they found it. By so doing they have secured a place in the history of human thought. They stand out as torch-bearers on the long corridor of time. They have fathomed great depths of the ocean of wisdom. Yet with all their glorious achievements they have not brought out the central point of the Bhagavad-Gītā. It is unfortunate that the very essence of this ancient wisdom should have been missed.

The Bhagavad-Gītā needs a commentary which restates in simple words the essential teaching and technique given by Lord Kṛishṇa to Arjuna on the battlefield. There are commentaries to extol the wisdom of the paths of knowledge, devotion, and action in the Bhagavad-Gītā, but none to show that it provides a master-key to open the gates of all these different highways of human evolution simultaneously. No commentary has yet shown that through one simple technique proclaimed in the Bhagavad-Gītā, any man, without having to renounce his way of life, can enjoy the blessings of all these paths.

This commentary has been written to present that key to mankind and preserve it for generations to come.

The Bhagavad-Gītā is the Scripture of Yoga, the Scripture of Divine Union. Its purpose is to explain in theory and practice all that is needed to raise the consciousness of man to the highest possible level. The marvel of its language and style is that every expression brings a teaching suitable to every level of human evolution.

Fundamentally there are four levels of consciousness on each of which the nature of the practice changes: the waking state, Transcendental Consciousness, Cosmic Consciousness, and God Consciousness. Every teaching of the Bhagavad-Gītā has its application on each of these planes of development. Every expression must therefore be interpreted in four different ways to explain, both in theory and in practice, the ascending progression of the discourse on each of these four different levels. Thus it is obvious that the Bhagavad-Gītā as a whole must also be interpreted in four different ways so that the whole path of God-realization may be explained clearly.

As the Bhagavad-Gītā has not yet been interpreted in this manner, the true message of the scripture has remained dormant. It is highly important that these four commentaries should be written, not only to do justice to the scripture but also to present a straight path to the seeker and bring him the profound wisdom of this practical philosophy.

Thorough knowledge of any subject requires that its validity be substantiated by the criteria provided by the six systems of Indian philosophy: Nyāya, Vaisheshik, Sāṁkhya, Yoga, Karma Mīmāṁsā, and Vedānt.

In order to be complete, every aspect of the theory and practice at any stage of development must be verifiable by all these six systems simultaneously. It follows therefore that six interpretations of each of the four commentaries mentioned above are necessary to bring to light the complete significance of the Bhagavad-Gītā.

The present commentary should be regarded as a general basis for these twenty-four commentaries. If time allows, these commentaries will be written. But because the world is in such urgent need of the basic principle of spiritual development, it has been thought necessary to bring out the present commentary without further loss of time.

It will be of interest to the reader to know that this commentary is being brought out only after the technique has been verified in the lives of thousands of people of different nationalities throughout the world, under the auspices of the Spiritual Regeneration Movement founded with the sole purpose of spiritually regenerating the lives of all men in every part of the world. It presents a truth that is timeless and universal, a truth of life equally suited to all men, irrespective of differences of faith, culture, or nationality.

The overall conception of this commentary is supplementary to the unique vision and profound wisdom of the great Shankara, as set forth in his Gītā-Bhāshya. The wisdom is a gift from Guru Dev. All glory to Him! It presents the Light of Life and sets the stream of life to find its fulfilment in the ocean of eternal Being, in devotion to God, and in the bliss of God Consciousness.

May every man make use of the practical wisdom given in the 45th verse of the second chapter, and thereby glorify all aspects of his life and gain eternal freedom in divine consciousness.

Chapter I

A Vision of the Teaching in Chapter I

Verse 1. The chapter opens with a question that demands detailed knowledge of the battlefield of life and the whole range of human evolution.

Verse 2. The answer begins with words that can be interpreted to explain the whole philosophy of the integration of life: not only the philosophy of Yoga, or Divine Union, but all the six systems of Indian philosophy, of which Yoga is only one. The most systematic knowledge of the whole range of life and evolution is here presented in one verse.

Verse 3. The necessity for recognizing that opposing forces on the battlefield of life are one's own creation.

Verses 4–6. An account of the forces that support good.

Verses 7–11. An account of the forces that support evil.

Verses 12–13. Evil rejoices in challenging good.

Verses 14–19. Good responds to the challenge of evil.

Verses 20–24. The seeker of Truth takes his stand between the opposing forces of good and evil.

Verse 25. His consciousness is raised by a wave of love divinely inspired.

Verses 26–8. He sees the reality of the battlefield of life; he sees the conflict of opposing forces as the very core of life.

Verses 29–46. He probes deep and finds sixteen fundamental problems that form the basis of all conflicts. He seeks for a solution so that life may be lived free from problems.

Verse 47. His appreciation of the fundamental problems inherent in life is so intense that he becomes completely identified with them. He stands silent, deeply absorbed, seeking for a solution on the level of impossibility, where no solution exists.

This is the most extreme situation that could confront a seeker of Truth. Resolving this extreme situation, the Scripture of Divine Union provides one simple solution to all problems in life.

THIS chapter prepares the ground and sets the scene for the glorious dialogue of the Lord's Song, the Bhagavad-Gītā. Although it does not contain the actual discourse of the Lord, which really begins in the second chapter, it presents the basic problems of life and gives Lord Kṛishṇa the chance to propound the philosophy and practice which enable man to live life free from suffering. It is of great value for its contribution to the science of living.

It serves as a petition from the representative of humankind to the Incarnation of the Divine — a petition to say that, even though we try our best to live a life of righteousness, suffering does not appear to leave us. The demand is: give us a life free from suffering.

There is one short sentence in this chapter spoken by Lord Kṛishṇa to Arjuna on the battlefield. The first word that falls from the lips of the Lord fills Arjuna with love and raises his heart to the elevated plane of his mind. Arjuna's heart and mind, thus established on a high level of alertness, gain a state of such self-sufficiency that communication between them is almost lost, and with it is lost the spur to activity. But inwardly Arjuna's consciousness is raised to that high level of suspension which purifies his heart and mind of all stain and enables him to receive, within a short time, the wisdom of the Absolute, the timeless message of life for the good of all.

Duryodhana, seeing his own army and the army opposing it drawn up on the battlefield, gives the signal for battle. And Arjuna, the greatest archer of his time, thoughtful and conscientious, resolved to oppose evil yet overflowing with a wave of love, visualizes the consequences of war and reaches a state of suspension between the dictates of his heart and mind. This situation, where consciousness is in a state of suspension, where both the mind and the heart are on the highest level of alertness, provides the ideal occasion for the divine intelligence to overtake and shape the destiny of man.

Life is a battlefield of opposing forces. He who, like Arjuna, has recourse to divine intelligence receives the light and shares the cosmic purpose of fulfilment both for himself and others. But he who is trapped by temptation, like Duryodhana, becomes a drag upon life; he retards his own evolution and also hinders the progress of others.

This chapter presents the mechanics of Nature and reveals the fundamentals of life and society. While remaining on the human level, it portrays the heights of human consciousness through which the Divine descends on earth. It provides a firm foundation for the edifice of Lord Kṛishṇa's teaching — the wisdom of eternal freedom in life.

The chapter opens with Dhṛitarāshtra in his royal palace at Hastināpur asking Sanjaya to tell him about the battle.

VERSE 1

धृतराष्ट्र उवाच
धर्मक्षेत्रे कुरुक्षेत्रे समवेता युयुत्सवः
मामकाः पाराडवाश्चैव किमकुर्वत संजय

Dhṛitarāshtra uvācha
Dharmakshetre Kurukshetre samavetā yuyutsavaḥ
māmakāḥ Pāṇdavāsh chaiva kim akurvata Sanjaya

Dhṛitarāshtra said:
Assembled on the field of Dharma, O Sanjaya, on the field of the Kurus, eager to fight, what did my people and the Pāṇdavas do?

'*Dharma*' is that invincible power of Nature which upholds existence. It maintains evolution and forms the very basis of cosmic life. It supports all that is helpful for evolution and discourages all that is opposed to it.

Dharma is that which promotes worldly prosperity and spiritual freedom. In order to understand the role of *Dharma* in life, we have to consider the mechanics of evolution.

When life evolves from one state to another, the first state is dissolved and the second brought into existence. In other words, the process of evolution is carried out under the influence of two opposing forces — one to destroy the first state and the other to give rise to a second state. These creative and destructive forces working in harmony with one another maintain life and spin the wheel of evolution. *Dharma* maintains equilibrium between them. By maintaining equilibrium between opposing cosmic forces, *Dharma* safeguards existence and upholds the path of evolution, the path of righteousness.

Man's life is so highly evolved that he enjoys freedom of action in Nature. This enables him to live in any way he desires, either for good or for evil. As he behaves, so he receives. When the good increases in life and the positive forces tend to overbalance the normal state of existence, then the process of *Dharma*, restoring equilibrium, results in feelings of happiness in the heart and satisfaction in the mind. In the same way, when evil increases in life and the negative forces predominate, the power of *Dharma*, restoring the balance, produces sensations of pain and suffering.

Life is as we want it — either suffering or joy. When we allow the positive and negative forces to remain in their normal state of equilibrium, we live through normal periods of life. Assisting the growth of negative forces results in suffering; when we help the positive forces to increase we share the joy of life. 'As you sow, so shall you reap' expresses the role of *Dharma* in practical life.

Calamities, crises, and catastrophes in a community or country are caused by the increase of negative forces resulting from the evil deeds of a majority of their people. A high degree of concentration of negative forces, without positive forces to balance them, ends in suffering and destruction of life. Similarly, a high degree of concentration of positive forces fails to maintain life in its normal state. The life of an individual under the influence of increasing positive forces enters into a field of increasing happiness and is eventually transformed into Bliss Consciousness, in which state it gains the status of cosmic existence, eternal life.

In this way, we find that the increase of negative forces ends in passivity or extinction of life, whereas the increase of positive forces results in life eternal. Our individual life moves backwards and forwards automatically as we direct it under the influence of *Dharma*. Positive and negative forces, as we develop them, play their role on the field of *Dharma* and shape the destiny of life.

The two armies of the Kauravas and Pāṇdavas on the battlefield of Kurukshetra represent the negative and positive forces on the field of *Dharma*. This is what made Dhṛitarāshtra say: 'Assembled on the field of *Dharma*, on the field of the Kurus'.

Dhṛitarāshtra, as an old experienced head of the royal family, knows that the battlefield of Kurukshetra lying within the Dharmakshetra, the land between the rivers Yamunā and Saraswatī, always maintains its sanctity and brings victory to the righteous.

He is anxious to hear details of the happenings and curious to find out whether the good influence of the land has had any effect on the destructive tendencies of his evil-minded sons; or whether it stimulated the righteousness of the Pāṇdavas and encouraged them to forgive the evildoers.

This is the only time that Dhṛitarāshtra speaks in the text of the Bhagavad-Gītā. He only appears in order to ask this question.

The 'Kurus' are the members of the Kuru family, a leading clan of the time.

'The field of the Kurus' is a vast plain near Hastināpur in the neighbourhood of Delhi. As it belonged to the Kurus at the time of this battle it is called Kurukshetra.

'My people and the Pāṇdavas': Dhṛitarāshtra was the blind king of the Kuru family. His younger brother Pāṇdu was managing the affairs of the kingdom for him. When Pāṇdu died, Dhṛitarāshtra wanted to give the reins of the kingdom to Yudhishthira, the eldest of the five sons of Pāṇdu, who was called Dharmarāj, the embodiment of righteousness, for his noble qualities; but Duryodhana, the eldest of the hundred evil-minded sons of Dhṛitarāshtra, by trick and treachery secured the throne for himself and began attempting to destroy Yudhishthira and his four brothers.

Lord Kṛishṇa, as head of the Yādava clan, tried to bring

about a reconciliation between the cousins; but when all his attempts failed and the treachery of Duryodhana continued and increased, war between the Kauravas and Pāṇḍavas became inevitable. It brought kings and warriors from all over the globe to take sides, according to the level of their consciousness, with the righteous Pāṇḍavas or the evil-minded Kauravas. The good and evil of the whole world formed the two armies. Lord Kṛishṇa's main mission, which was to destroy evil and give protection to righteousness, had been simplified.

'Sanjaya' is the charioteer of the blind king Dhṛitarāshtra. The word, however, means one who has conquered the senses and the mind. Sanjaya was asked to narrate the details of the battle because he was clairvoyant and clairaudient and at the same time impartial. The whole of the Bhagavad-Gītā is Sanjaya's answer to Dhṛitarāshtra.

VERSE 2

संजय उवाच
दृष्ट्वा तु पाण्डवानीकं व्यूढं दुर्योधनस्तदा
आचार्यमुपसंगम्य राजा वचनमब्रवीत्

Sanjaya uvācha
Dṛishtwā tu Pāṇḍavānīkaṁ vyūdhaṁ Duryodhanas tadā
āchāryam upasaṁgamya rājā vachanam abravīt

Sanjaya said:
Then Duryodhana the prince, seeing the army of
the Pāṇḍavas drawn up in battle array, approached
his master and spoke these words:

'Master' is one who understands the meaning of the scriptures, teaches it to others, and practises the teaching[1] himself. The master here is Droṇāchārya, who had taught the art of war to both Kauravas and Pāṇḍavas.

It is a crucial moment, so it is natural for Duryodhana to approach his master, Droṇāchārya, for blessings and strength.

1 See Appendix: The Six Systems of Indian Philosophy.

VERSE 3

पश्यैतां पाण्डुपुत्राणामाचार्य महतीं चमूम्
व्यूढां द्रुपदपुत्रेण तव शिष्येण धीमता

Pashyaitāṁ Pāṇḍuputrāṇām āchārya mahatīṁ chamūm
vyūdhāṁ Drupadaputreṇa tava shishyeṇa dhīmatā

Behold, O Master, this great army of the sons of Pāṇdu,
arrayed by your wise pupil, the son of Drupada.

'The son of Drupada', Dhṛishtadyumna, is the commander-in-chief of the Pāṇdavas' army.

Duryodhana points out to his master that the opposing army is certainly large and powerful but that this does not matter because his own army is graced by the master, while the other is supported only by the disciple. Although wise, he remains after all a disciple, and since he is so ready to fight against his master, his morale will be weak and his strength will fail him. At the same time, by saying 'your wise pupil', Duryodhana creates an effect to excite the master's mind against the disciple who has organized the front against him.

VERSE 4

अत्र शूरा महेष्वासा भीमार्जुनसमा युधि
युयुधानो विराटश्च द्रुपदश्च महारथः

Atra shūrā maheshwāsā Bhīmārjunasamā yudhi
Yuyudhāno Virātash cha Drupadash cha Mahārathaḥ

Here are men of valour, mighty archers, the equals
of Bhīma and Arjuna in battle — Yuyudhāna, Virāta,
and Drupada, the Mahārathī.

'Bhīma' is the second son of Pāṇdu, the mightiest warrior of the Pāṇdavas' army and virtually in control of it, even though the office of commander-in-chief is held by Dhṛishtadyumna.

'Arjuna', the hero of the Mahābhārat, is the third son of Pāṇdu. He is the greatest archer of his time and a close friend of Lord Kṛishṇa.

'Mahārathī' means a great warrior proficient in military science who, single-handed, can fight ten thousand archers.

'Yuyudhāna' is Lord Kṛishṇa's charioteer, also called Sātyaki.

'Virāta' is the prince in whose territory the Pāṇdavas lived for some time in disguise after losing a dice match with Duryodhana.

VERSE 5

धृष्टकेतुश्चेकितानः काशिराजश्च वीर्यवान्
पुरुजित्कुन्तिभोजश्च शैब्यश्च नरपुंगवः

Dhṛishtaketush Chekitānaḥ Kāshirājash cha vīryavān
Purujit Kuntibhojash cha Shaibyash cha narapuṁgavaḥ

Dhṛishtaketu, Chekitāna, and the valiant king of Kāshī,
also Purujit, Kuntibhoja, and Shaibya, chief among men.

'Dhṛishtaketu' is the king of the Chedis.

'Chekitāna' is a famous warrior in the army of the Pāṇdavas.

'Purujit' and 'Kuntibhoja' are two brothers.

'Shaibya' is a king of the Shibi tribe.

VERSE 6

युधामन्युश्च विक्रान्त उत्तमौजाश्च वीर्यवान्
सौभद्रो द्रौपदेयाश्च सर्व एव महारथाः

Yudhāmanyush cha vikrānta Uttamaujāsh cha vīryavān
Saubhadro Draupadeyāsh cha sarva eva Mahārathāḥ

Yudhāmanyu, the brave; the valiant Uttamaujas; also the son of
Subhadrā and the sons of Draupadī — all of them Mahārathīs.

Duryodhana seems to accomplish several aims in naming these great warriors in the opposing army. It strengthens his own mind, awakens a deep sense of responsibility in the mind of his master, and produces alertness in all those who are listening to him.

Having created these effects, this atmosphere, Duryodhana, in the following verse, draws the attention of his master to the great heroes of his own army.

VERSE 7

अस्माकं तु विशिष्टा ये तान्निबोध द्विजोत्तम
नायका मम सैन्यस्य संज्ञार्थं तान्ब्रवीमि ते

Asmākaṁ tu vishishtā ye tān nibodha Dwijottama
nāyakā mama sainyasya saṁgyārthaṁ tān bravīmi te

Know well, O noblest of the twice-born, those who are pre-eminent among us. I speak to you of the leaders of my army that you may know them.

'Twice-born' is a term that Duryodhana uses in addressing the master, Droṇāchārya. This is to flatter him and at the same time to arouse in him a sense of responsibility, so that he shall remain true to the cause that he has undertaken.

The term 'twice-born' is generally used for one born in a *Brāhmaṇa* family, although other castes are also eligible for the ceremony of purification according to Vedic rites.

A *Brāhmaṇa* is said to be twice-born because after his birth, when he is about eight years old, he undergoes a Vedic ceremony of purification, and this qualifies him for the study of the Vedas — the main function of a *Brāhmaṇa*. Thus the ceremony is referred to as the second birth.

This second birth is important in life because it gives a man, born of flesh, entry into the field of spirit. This is the main purpose of the study of the Vedas, which opens the door to the inner kingdom of man and enables him to see the Light of God.

By recalling to his master the names of the heroes of his army, Duryodhana reviews his own strength and creates an awareness of the mighty power which belongs to him and to everyone who is there to support him.

VERSE 8

भवान्भीष्मश्च कर्णश्च कृपश्च समितिंजयः
अश्वत्थामा विकर्णश्च सौमदत्तिस्तथैव च

Bhavān Bhīshmash cha Karṇash cha Kṛipash cha samitiṁjayaḥ
Ashwatthāmā Vikarṇash cha Saumadattis tathaiva cha

Thyself and Bhīshma and Karṇa and Kṛipa, victor in battle;
Ashwatthāmā and Vikarṇa and also the son of Somadatta.

'Bhīshma' is the grandsire (grandfather's step-brother) of both the Kauravas and Pāṇdavas. He brought up Dhṛitarāshtra and Pāṇdu. He is the most experienced of all the assembled warriors. On him, Duryodhana chiefly relies.

'Karṇa' is half-brother to Arjuna.

'Kṛipa' is the brother-in-law of Droṇāchārya.

'Ashwatthāmā' is the son of Droṇāchārya.

'Vikarṇa' is the third of the hundred sons of Dhṛitarāshtra.

'Somadatta' is the king of the Bāhīkas.

VERSE 9

अन्ये च बहवः शूरा मदर्थे त्यक्तजीविताः
नानाशस्त्रप्रहरणाः सर्वे युद्धविशारदाः

Anye cha bahavaḥ shūrā madarthe tyaktajīvitāḥ
nānāshastrapraharaṇāḥ sarve yuddhavishāradāḥ

And many other heroes there are, armed with
various weapons, all skilled in warfare, who
have risked their lives for me.

Having recounted the names of the heroes of his own army, Duryodhana stresses their might and in the following verse compares the strength of the two sides.

VERSE 10

अपर्याप्तं तदस्माकं बलं भीष्माभिरक्षितम्
पर्याप्तं त्विदमेतेषां बलं भीमाभिरक्षितम्

Aparyāptaṁ tad asmākaṁ balaṁ Bhīshmābhirakshitam
paryāptaṁ twidam eteshāṁ balaṁ Bhīmābhirakshitam

Unlimited is that army of ours commanded by Bhīshma,
whereas this their army commanded by Bhīma is limited.

Duryodhana had to rouse his own commander, Bhīshma, against the mighty Bhīma, chief of the Pāṇdavas' army. At the same time he reminded Bhīshma that, as commander, victory or defeat was his responsibility.

Having proclaimed that he is more powerful than his opponent, Duryodhana, in the following verse, pronounces his final order of battle.

VERSE 11

अयनेषु च सर्वेषु यथाभागमवस्थिताः
भीष्ममेवाभिरक्षन्तु भवन्तः सर्व एव हि

Ayaneshu cha sarveshu yathābhāgam avasthitāḥ
Bhīshmam evābhirakshantu bhavantaḥ sarva eva hi

Therefore, stationed in your respective positions on all
fronts, support Bhīshma alone, all of you!

This verse brings out Duryodhana's shrewdness. He knows that most of the warriors assembled on his side are not there primarily for his sake but because of their love for Bhīshma. This is why he speaks as he does; and by so doing he wins their sympathy and confidence along with that of Bhīshma.

VERSE 12

तस्य संजनयन्हर्षं कुरुवृद्धः पितामहः
सिंहनादं विनद्योच्चैः शङ्खं दध्मौ प्रतापवान्

Tasya saṁjanayan harshaṁ Kuruvṛiddhaḥ pitāmahaḥ
siṁhanādaṁ vinadyochchaiḥ shankhaṁ dadhmau pratāpavān

The aged Kuru, the glorious grandsire (Bhīshma),
gave a loud roar like a lion and blew his conch, gladdening
the heart of Duryodhana.

Having heard the words of Duryodhana, Bhīshma, encouraging him, begins to give the signal for battle.

The following verse describes how the whole army of Duryodhana joined Bhīshma in making an uproar to show their readiness to fight.

VERSE 13

ततः शङ्खाश्च भेर्यश्च पणवानकगोमुखाः
सहसैवाभ्यहन्यन्त स शब्दस्तुमुलोऽभवत्

Tataḥ shankhāsh cha bheryash cha paṇavānakagomukhāḥ
sahasaivābhyahanyanta sa shabdas tumulo 'bhavat

Then quite suddenly conches, horns, kettledrums, tabors, and
drums blared forth, and the sound was tumultuous.

'Quite suddenly' gives expression to the way in which Nature functions. Nature ensures great flexibility for the growth of good or evil in the atmosphere. But when an influence grows beyond elastic limits, Nature will no longer sustain it; suddenly the breaking-point is reached. The sudden burst of the lion roar of Bhīshma and the tumultuous noise produced by the whole army symbolized the great cry of Nature announcing the breaking-point of the immeasurable evil that Duryodhana and his supporters had accumulated for themselves.

Wars in history have resulted from the cumulative effect of aggression on the innocent; individuals continue to oppress others, not knowing that aggression is growing in the atmosphere, eventually to break upon them as their own disaster. One reaps the consequences of one's own actions.

The following verses describe the effect of this upon the opposing army.

Verse 14

ततः श्वेतैर्हयैर्युक्ते महति स्यन्दने स्थितौ
माधवः पाण्डवश्चैव दिव्यौ शङ्खौ प्रदध्मतुः

Tataḥ shwetair hayair yukte mahati syandane sthitau
Mādhavaḥ Pāṇdavash chaiva divyau shankhau pradadhmatuḥ

Then, seated in a great chariot yoked to white horses,
Mādhava (Lord Kṛishṇa) and the son of Pāṇdu (Arjuna)
also blew their glorious conches.

In this verse the word 'then' has a special significance, for it shows that the Pāṇdavas — Arjuna and his party — are not taking the lead in the battle but are only responding to the Kauravas' actions.

This is the natural behaviour of righteous people — they are never aggressive. If they appear to be so, they are only playing their role as instruments of the divine plan. The Pāṇdavas are challenged, and they have to accept the invitation as it comes; but they do not give the first signal for war. Only when they have received the signal from the other side are they obliged to answer it. And when they do answer, their reply is more powerful because it has the power of righteousness behind it.

The word 'chariot' has a special metaphysical connotation. The 'chariot' is the physiological structure, the body. It stands on the battlefield of life as a vehicle for the natural process of evolution. The senses are the horses to which the body-chariot is yoked.

'Yoked to white horses': 'white' symbolizes '*Sattwa*', or purity, meaning thereby that the chariot was driven under the influence of purity or righteousness. When the Self guides, the body moves under the influence of *Sattwa*. Lord Kṛishṇa symbolizes the Self, and the chariot He drives must be yoked to white horses. The very appearance of the chariot expresses its purpose. It stands and moves to safeguard and protect purity and righteousness.

'Mādhava' means Lord of fortune and also slayer of the demon Madhu. The use of this name indicates Lord Kṛishṇa's power over Nature. It indicates that He will prove to be the Lord of fortune to those who are supporting positive forces and the slayer of demons to those who are promoting evil. Lord Kṛishṇa stands neutral between the two armies, blowing His conch to proclaim that He is there for anyone to derive advantage from His presence.

VERSE 15

पाञ्चजन्यं हृषीकेशो देवदत्तं धनंजयः
पौण्ड्रं दध्मौ महाशङ्खं भीमकर्मा वृकोदरः

Pānchajanyaṁ Hṛishīkesho Devadattaṁ Dhananjayaḥ
Pauṇdraṁ dadhmau mahāshankhaṁ Bhīmakarmā vṛikodaraḥ

Hṛishīkesha (Lord Kṛishṇa) blew Pānchajanya,
Dhananjaya (Arjuna) blew Devadatta, Bhīma of
powerful deeds blew his great conch Paundra.

'Hṛishīkesha' has two meanings, according to the two different ways in which the word may be derived from the root. It means the Lord of the senses and also one with long hair. Both meanings are significant. Long hair has to do with control of the senses. Cutting the hair produces some subtle energy which tends to release the senses from control. So the word reveals not only the appearance of Lord Kṛishṇa on the battlefield but also the inner strength of the charioteer who, being the Lord of the senses, can control any situation.

'Pānchajanya' is the conch made from the bone of the demon Panchajana.

'Devadatta' means given by God — this conch was received by Arjuna from his divine Father, Indra.

'Dhananjaya' means the winner of wealth, Arjuna.

The words 'Hṛishīkesha blew Pānchajanya' reveal many significant points. They convey first that Lord Kṛishṇa's breath was absorbed by the demon element in the conch which produced the sound. This left Lord Kṛishṇa neutral in the battle, as He had promised.

Lord Kṛishṇa was revered both by the Kauravas and the Pāṇḍavas. He was approached for help at the same time both by Arjuna and Duryodhana, when each was preparing for war. As Lord Kṛishṇa could not say yes to either in the presence of the other, He resolved the situation by asking them to decide between themselves.

Lord Kṛishṇa said: 'I will be on one side, and my army will be on the other, but I shall not fight, though my army will. Now decide between yourselves who would like to have me and who would like my army.'

The first choice was given to Duryodhana, who preferred to take the army. Lord Kṛishṇa thus came out to help Arjuna, but as He had promised not to fight He became Arjuna's charioteer and guided the destiny of the battle.

The Lord of the senses blowing the signal for war through the demon's conch has a further meaning. It indicates that Lord Kṛishṇa created a powerful demoniac force against the devilish Kauravas. The reason is that the force of righteousness is always positive. It is always creative and constructive; it cannot destroy. Destruction can be brought about only by negative forces. Because they had the power of righteousness, it was hard for the Pāṇḍavas to destroy the Kauravas. So Lord Kṛishṇa, through the sound of Pānchajanya, excited the negative powers in all those present in both armies. The excitement of the negative forces in the Pāṇḍavas' army gave that army much more power to destroy evil because of the support from the great power of righteousness, whereas the excitement of the negative forces in the Kauravas' army hastened their destruction owing to an over-concentrated negative element without the support of any positive force.

There is yet another implication. Lord Kṛishṇa blew Pānchajanya to declare aloud that the Pāṇdavas' response to the war signal did not belong to their righteousness. It was only the resonance of the devilish uproar of the Kauravas echoing from Pānchajanya. It was a devil echoing the voice of a devil, and if there was anything original in the sound, it was Pānchajanya's sigh for the pain and iniquities which the Pāṇdavas had suffered for many long years under the Kauravas' oppression.

The Lord of the senses did not use His senses: He only breathed out through Pānchajanya. The occasion was too far beneath the divinity of Lord Kṛishṇa for Him to respond. The Lord of the senses is neutral, ever established in His eternal state of Being, while all things around Him react to the prevailing atmosphere. As the Lord of the senses, His status transcends the highest righteousness, and the Kauravas were on the lowest level of evil. It was because of the great difference between Lord Kṛishṇa's status and the level of the Kauravas' consciousness that He promised at the beginning that He would not fight in the battle.

All these implications are contained in the first phrase of this verse. It is the glory of Vyāsa, the sage of enlightened vision who wrote down the Bhagavad-Gītā, that the implications of any one word in it are inexhaustible.

The recounting of the names of warriors and of the conches that they blew continues through the next three verses.

VERSE 16

अनन्तविजयं राजा कुन्तीपुत्रो युधिष्ठिरः
नकुलः सहदेवश्च सुघोषमणिपुष्पकौ

Anantavijayaṁ Rājā Kuntīputro Yudhishthiraḥ
Nakulaḥ Sahadevash cha Sughoshamaṇipushpakau

Prince Yudhishthira, the son of Kuntī, blew his conch Anantavijaya; Nakula and Sahadeva blew Sughosha and Maṇipushpaka.

'Kuntī' is the mother of the five Pāṇdavas, the sons of Pāṇdu.

'Yudhishthira' is the eldest of the five Pāṇdavas.

'Nakula' is the fourth, skilled in the art of training horses.

'Sahadeva' is the fifth and youngest, skilled in the management of cattle.

'Anantavijaya' means eternal victory.

'Sughosha' means sweet-toned.

'Maṇipushpaka' means gem-flowered.

Verse 17

काश्यश्च परमेष्वासः शिखण्डी च महारथः
धृष्टद्युम्नो विराटश्च सात्यकिश्चापराजितः

Kāshyash cha parameshwāsaḥ Shikhaṇḍī cha Mahārathaḥ
Dhṛishtadyumno Virātash cha Sātyakish chāparājitaḥ

The King of Kāshī, the great archer, and Shikhandī,
the Mahārathī, Dhṛishtadyumna and Virāta and
Sātyaki, the unsubdued.

Verse 18

द्रुपदो द्रौपदेयाश्च सर्वशः पृथिवीपते
सौभद्रश्च महाबाहुः शङ्खान्दध्मुः पृथक्पृथक्

Drupado Draupadeyāsh cha sarvashaḥ Pṛithivīpate
Saubhadrash cha mahābāhuḥ shankhān dadhmuḥ pṛithak pṛithak

Drupada, as well as the sons of Draupadī,
and the mighty-armed son of Subhadrā,
O Lord of earth, all blew their different conches.

'O Lord of earth': Sanjaya is addressing Dhṛitarāshtra, the king.

VERSE 19

स घोषो धार्तराष्ट्राणां हृदयानि व्यदारयत्
नभश्च पृथिवीं चैव तुमुलो व्यनुनादयन्

Sa ghosho Dhārtarāshtrāṇāṁ hṛidayāni vyadārayat
nabhash cha pṛithivīṁ chaiva tumulo vyanunādayan

That tumultuous uproar, reverberating through earth and sky, rent the hearts of Dhṛitarāshtra's men.

The Pāṇdavas announced their readiness for war by the blowing of the conches, which thrilled the air and vibrated through everything in earth and sky. A stir was created in the universe.

A cosmic process is revealed here. The evil doings of the Kauravas had saturated the atmosphere and had, as it were, pervaded everything with an evil influence. This evil influence was shaken when righteousness, having gained strength, rose to accept its challenge. The force of destruction in the world was to be destroyed by the rising wave of life.

VERSE 20

अथ व्यवस्थितान्दृष्ट्वा धार्तराष्ट्रान्कपिध्वजः
प्रवृत्ते शस्त्रसंपाते धनुरुद्यम्य पाण्डवः

Atha vyavasthitān dṛishtwā Dhārtarāshtrān kapidhwajaḥ
pravṛitte shastrasaṁpāte dhanur udyamya Pāṇdavaḥ

Then, seeing the sons of Dhṛitarāshtra drawn up in battle order, as missiles were about to fly, the son of Pāṇdu (Arjuna), whose banner bore the image of Hanumān, took up his bow.

'The sons of Dhṛitarāshtra drawn up in battle order' represents evil prepared to annihilate righteousness.

When Arjuna 'took up his bow', he expressed the readiness of righteousness to resist evil and restore harmony on earth.

This is a cosmic process. Whenever evil arises and threatens to overtake life, Nature moves to balance it. A wave of righteousness rises to neutralize the evil. Those who are the medium through which vice enters the world perish from the rise of such a wave, and those who have borne suffering under the influence of evil, becoming the instrument of righteousness, begin to enjoy.

'Banner bore the image of Hanumān': Hanumān symbolizes devotion and service to the supreme Lord. Arjuna's life was dedicated to the divine cause. His skill and art of archery were useful for the cause of righteousness. Therefore his chariot had a sign which bore the image of Hanumān.

VERSE 21

हृषीकेशं तदा वाक्यमिदमाह महीपते
सेनयोरुभयोर्मध्ये रथं स्थापय मेऽच्युत

Hṛishīkeshaṁ tadā vākyam idam āha Mahīpate
senayor ubhayor madhye rathaṁ sthāpaya me 'chyuta

Then, O Lord of earth, he spoke these words to
Hṛishīkesha (Lord Kṛishṇa): Draw up my chariot
between the two armies, O Achyuta,

'Lord of earth': through this expression Sanjaya draws Dhṛitarāshtra's attention to the fact that he had the influence to intervene and stop the two armies from involving themselves in destruction. Already in verse 18 Sanjaya has addressed Dhṛitarāshtra as 'Lord of earth'. The repeated expression indicates that he wants to make Dhṛitarāshtra see the seriousness of the situation — both the armies have declared their readiness to fight, and now Arjuna is moving to the forefront. Every moment is vital and significant. The destruction seems inevitable.

'Achyuta' means immovable. Arjuna calls Lord Kṛishṇa 'Achyuta'. He wants the immovable to start moving for him! 'Achyuta' also means one who has never fallen. Thereby Arjuna wants to suggest to Lord Kṛishṇa that He will never fail him.

Arjuna asks for the chariot to be placed between the two

armies, so that both himself and Lord Kṛishṇa shall be there. By placing Lord Kṛishṇa midway, Arjuna desires to present a picture on the screen of time — absolute Being present between the opposing forces — a picture expressing the inner mechanics of Nature which will explain the fundamentals of life and clarify the basic principles of war and peace for the generations to come.

Lord Kṛishṇa symbolizes the absolute Being, which is the field of *Dharma* and which, by remaining between the negative and positive powers in Nature, balances them. Although remaining neutral, It always supports righteousness. Although Lord Kṛishṇa is neutral, He is with Arjuna, who enjoys His support.

In the following verse Arjuna explains why he himself wishes to be placed between the two armies.

VERSE 22

यावदेतान्निरीक्षेऽहं योद्धुकामानवस्थितान्
कैर्मया सह योद्धव्यमस्मिन्रणसमुद्यमे

Yāvad etān nirīkshe 'haṁ yoddhukāmān avasthitān
kair mayā saha yoddhavyam asmin raṇasamudyame

So that I may observe those who stand here eager for battle
and know with whom I should fight in this toil of war.

The skill of battle lies first in locating the strategic points of the enemy line.

Arjuna's power of concentration was so great that if he correctly located the positions of the enemy leaders his arrows would fly straight at them.

'Eager for battle' shows that Arjuna wanted carefully to pick off only those who were eager for battle. He would not concern himself with those who were not eager to fight. This illustrates Arjuna's bravery and self-confidence; it also expresses his readiness for battle.

VERSE 23

योत्स्यमानानवेक्षेऽहं य एतेऽत्र समागताः
धार्तराष्ट्रस्य दुर्बुद्धेर्युद्धे प्रियचिकीर्षवः

Yotsyamānān avekshe 'haṁ ya ete 'tra samāgatāḥ
Dhārtarāshtrasya durbuddher yuddhe priyachikīrshavaḥ

Let me look on those who are assembled here ready to fight, eager to accomplish in battle what is dear to the evil-minded son of Dhṛitarāshtra.

The tone of this voice shows the strength of Arjuna's indignation against the evil which the supporters of Duryodhana wish to accomplish by fighting. The contempt is so great that Arjuna does not even speak Duryodhana's name — and by naming his father, Dhṛitarāshtra, he brings shame on him also.

Arjuna is sure of his position, sure that he is making a stand to safeguard virtue and resist corruption. He does not think that all those assembled in the opposing army are evil in themselves, but they are supporters of evil.

In verse 21 Sanjaya addressed Dhṛitarāshtra as 'Lord of earth', yet here he reports Arjuna's insinuation that Dhṛitarāshtra is being brought to shame by the actions of his sons. This shows that, as father of his evil-minded sons, Dhṛitarāshtra is ultimately responsible for the threatened destruction of the whole community.

When the collective *Karma* (action) threatens national destruction, it is beyond the power of the individual to check it; this is even more true when it has reached the ultimate limit and is about to break into catastrophe. Therefore it is wise for people of every generation to be cautious and not to tolerate an increase of wrong-doing in their surroundings, but to nip it in the bud. For it is the cumulative influence of these small wrongs done by individuals in their own little spheres of activity that produces national and international tensions and leads to catastrophe.

There is a way of Transcendental Meditation,[2] taught by Lord Kṛishṇa, to be practised by each individual daily in order

2 See II, 45, and Appendix: The *Transcendental Meditation* Technique.

to infuse the transcendental divine consciousness into his own mind, so that by nature man may become freed from wrong tendencies and may become the source of good influence in all spheres of life.

Had Dhṛitarāshtra, as a king, educated his sons in the art of transcending and gaining divine consciousness, the royal family of the Kauravas would not have been the cause of this great war, which brought disaster on the civilization of the time.

This is a message which should be heeded in every generation. It is for the world's rulers and for those in public life, who have the welfare of mankind at heart, to organize education in such a way that everyone has an opportunity of learning how to cultivate divine consciousness. No generation should be allowed to leave behind an evil influence, the accumulated consequences of which will be reaped by future generations.

VERSE 24

संजय उवाच
एवमुक्तो हृषीकेशो गुडाकेशेन भारत
सेनयोरुभयोर्मध्ये स्थापयित्वा रथोत्तमम्

Sanjaya uvācha
Evam ukto Hṛishīkesho Gudākeshena Bhārata
senayor ubhayor madhye sthāpayitwā rathottamam

Sanjaya said:
O Bhārata, thus invoked by Gudākesha (Arjuna),
Hṛishīkesha (Lord Kṛishṇa), having drawn up the
magnificent chariot between the two armies,

Sanjaya is reporting to Dhṛitarāshtra what is happening on the battlefield. Here he is addressed as 'Bhārata', descendant of the great king of Bhārata — greater India.

Arjuna, the hero of the Mahābhārat, drives out between the two armies to see with whom he has to fight. Sanjaya here uses the name Gudākesha to refer to him. This is to symbolize an essential quality of Arjuna's, for Gudākesha means the Lord of sleep, one who has mastery over sleep, over dullness of mind. Arjuna's one-pointedness of mind is thus expressed. As an unfailing archer, Arjuna has a mind which is fully alive; Sanjaya uses the word 'Gudākesha' to depict the character and quality of the hero.

Such is Vyāsa's narrative skill; he uses exact and concise expressions with great fullness of meaning to tell the story. It only needs a mind to understand them in order to enjoy his writings and derive the maximum from them.

Vyāsa has used the adjective 'magnificent' to describe Arjuna's chariot. This one word, which in the Sanskrit text reads '*uttamam*', conveys a world of glory. It indicates magnificence, comfort, stability, lightness, and strength; in fact, all the qualities of a chariot that is designed to meet the fiercest enemy there could be. Again, the chariot is magnificent not only for its quality but also for its charioteer and the hero within it. Hṛishīkesha, the Lord of the senses, is the charioteer and Gudākesha, the conqueror of sleep, is the hero.

VERSE 25

भीष्मद्रोणप्रमुखतः सर्वेषां च महीक्षिताम्
उवाच पार्थ पश्यैतान्समवेतान्कुरूनिति

Bhīshmadroṇapramukhataḥ sarveshāṁ cha mahīkshitām
uvācha Pārtha pashyaitān samavetān Kurūn iti

Before Bhīshma and Droṇa and all the rulers of the earth,
said: Pārtha (Arjuna)! Behold these Kurus gathered together.

Lord Kṛishṇa had seen that Arjuna was outraged.[3] Anger is a great enemy;[4] it reduces one's strength. And his charioteer does not like to see Arjuna's strength waning. Lord Kṛishṇa is required to do something to restore Arjuna to his normal stature. But this alone will not suffice; something more is necessary to make Arjuna really strong. Anger in him indicates that he is

3 See verse 23.
4 See III, 37, commentary.

not really strong, for anger is a sign of weakness. Lord Kṛishṇa knows that Arjuna, although the greatest archer of his time, has not been given the real secret of warfare. He has been taught the art of archery, but he has not been trained to shoot his arrows while remaining firm in himself. If an archer shoots while he is angry, his anger will make him weak.

Arjuna has called Lord Kṛishṇa 'Achyuta',[5] which means firm and unmoved. This is what Lord Kṛishṇa has to teach Arjuna to be. But wisdom cannot be given to a man unless he asks for it and shows his readiness to receive it. It is therefore necessary for Lord Kṛishṇa to arouse in Arjuna the need and desire to learn.[6] It would have been demoralizing if Arjuna had been told on the battlefield that he needed to know the art of being firm. He had to recognize this for himself; only then could Lord Kṛishṇa help him. To produce the desired result in Arjuna, the Lord speaks one short sentence:

'Pārtha! Behold these Kurus gathered together.' This is the first utterance of Lord Kṛishṇa in the Bhagavad-Gītā, the first word of advice to Arjuna on the battlefield.

The miracle it produced in Arjuna has for centuries escaped the attention of practically every commentator, and in consequence Arjuna is portrayed as a confused mental wreck. A close study of the commentary on the following verses will reveal the true nature of Arjuna's condition.

Lord Kṛishṇa addresses Arjuna as 'Pārtha', the son of Pṛithā. With this expression He reminds Arjuna of his mother and thereby creates a warm wave of love in his heart, the warmth of love that connects son and mother. It is this tender bond of love that develops into all family and social relationships, that maintains a family, a society, a nation, and a world.

Having created this wave of love in Arjuna's heart, Lord Kṛishṇa desires to strengthen it; and for this He says: 'Behold these Kurus gathered together.' This quickens all the ways of the heart, where different relationships are held in different shades of love. Seeing all his dear ones 'together' in one glance, his whole heart swells with love.

5 See verse 21.
6 See II, 7.

Verse 26

तत्रापश्यत्स्थितान्पार्थः पितृनथ पितामहान्
आचार्यान्मातुलान्भ्रातृन्पुत्रान्पौत्रान्सखींस्तथा

Tatrāpashyat sthitān Pārthaḥ pitṛīn atha pitāmahān
āchāryān mātulān bhrātṛīn putrān pautrān sakhīṁs tathā

The son of Pṛithā (Arjuna) saw there before him uncles and grandfathers, teachers, maternal uncles, brothers, sons and grandsons, and many friends as well.

'The son of Pṛithā saw' indicates that when Arjuna gazed on the opposing army his vision was coloured by love and not by enmity or bravery. Had he seen with the vision of the 'scorcher of enemies', this is what he would have been called.

This indicates the power of control that Lord Kṛishṇa possesses. He said, 'Pārtha behold', and Arjuna became as a son before his mother, full of love and reverence.

Verse 27

श्वशुरान्सुहृदश्चैव सेनयोरुभयोरपि
तान्समीक्ष्य स कौन्तेयः सर्वान्बन्धूनवस्थितान्

Shwashurān suhṛidash chaiva senayor ubhayor api
tān samīkshya sa Kaunteyaḥ sarvān bandhūn avasthitān

Fathers-in-law and well-wishers also in both the armies. Then that son of Kuntī (Arjuna), seeing all these kinsmen thus present,

Arjuna stands up to behold his opponents but he fails to see opponents; instead he sees his dear ones. This is because his vision has been coloured with love by Lord Kṛishṇa's calling him Pārtha. With this the whole scene takes a critical turn. Arjuna, who was about to go into battle, is overtaken by pity, as the following verses show.

VERSE 28

कृपया परयाविष्टो विषीदन्निदमब्रवीत्
दृष्ट्वेमं स्वजनं कृष्ण युयुत्सुं समुपस्थितम्

Kṛipayā parayāvishto vishīdann idam abravīt
dṛishtwemaṁ swajanaṁ Kṛishṇa yuyutsuṁ samupasthitam

Possessed by extreme compassion, spoke this in grief:
Seeing these my kinsmen, O Kṛishṇa, gathered, eager to fight,

This verse presents the basis of the problems that Arjuna is going to lay before Lord Kṛishṇa.

He expresses his thoughts aloud to Lord Kṛishṇa, who is close at hand. One thinks aloud with someone who is close to one's heart and mind and wise enough to further the thought. Lord Kṛishṇa is like this to Arjuna. He can share his thoughts and feelings and think intimately with Him.

'Possessed by extreme compassion' and 'kinsmen' indicate the basic principle of 'grief'. It is born of the condition of the individual and his relationship with others.

This verse not only depicts Arjuna's condition but lays open the fundamental principle of suffering in human society and seeks a solution to it.

Compassion is among the most glorious qualities of the heart. 'Extreme compassion' expresses fullness of heart. But once dissociated from the qualities of the mind, the heart as such can no longer be effective in supporting action in life. Even good qualities of heart or of mind fail to uphold life in the absence of coordination between them. This verse proclaims 'extreme compassion' as the source of all the problems confronting Arjuna, a most balanced man of noble character.

The whole discourse of Lord Kṛishṇa in the Bhagavad-Gītā is designed to give the wisdom of life and the technique of living which enable man to live all the good qualities of life with full coordination of heart and mind. By this wisdom and this technique the individual is raised to a high level of consciousness where he gains eternal contentment within himself. He lives a life in fulfilment, useful to himself and society. Such a life supports surrounding Nature; all becomes harmonious, resulting in ideal relationships with others.

Here is the glory of the Bhagavad-Gītā — it records for all time and for the use of all men the wisdom of life and the technique of living. So that everyone may live a life free from suffering, it selects the most noble character, Arjuna, leading the most balanced life, and places that life completely under the influence of the most cherished qualities of heart and mind. On this high level of glory and grace, where heart and mind are at their best, it locates the basic cause of all suffering at a point between the heart and mind. The heart is full of feeling, saturated with love; the mind is completely alert, full of the sense of righteousness and the call of duty. Both are at their full stature. No suffering can possibly touch either of them taken separately, but as the Upanishad says: '*Dwitīyād vai bhayaṁ bhavati*' — 'Certainly fear is born of duality'. Whenever and wherever there is a sense of two, fear or suffering can exist.

Within man there is mind and there is heart. These, by their very existence as two, hold the possibility of suffering. When they are united, when there is harmony between a heart and mind full of righteousness and noble inspiration, suffering cannot arise. But when there is a lack of coordination or a conflict between them, suffering automatically results. Arjuna's 'grief' is born of the basic difference between the heart and the mind.

Religious scriptures prescribe a mode of conduct to save man from falling into error and suffering. They induce man to do good and to spurn evil.

The Bhagavad-Gītā, the scripture of the eternal religion of realization, in its diagnosis of suffering is not satisfied by the rejection of evil or the acceptance of virtue alone; it finds that suffering can result even from two good qualities. For a life to be free from suffering, it is not enough for heart and mind to be free from the stain of sin and established in righteousness.

The Bhagavad-Gītā undertakes to solve the problem of suffering completely. It locates the ultimate cause of suffering and provides a means to eliminate it. The seed of suffering in life is located in the duality inherent in the characteristic difference between the qualities of heart and mind. The Bhagavad-Gītā therefore takes Arjuna, already most noble, sinless, and most highly developed in both heart and mind, and sets him down in an environment which further stimulates his heart[7] and his mind.[8] As both continue to grow more active in their respective domains, the basic difference in their structure becomes greater. When heart and mind are both at their best, each is full in itself and is no longer concerned with the other; there is no link left between them. The heart, fully saturated with love, naturally becomes sufficient unto itself and oblivious to the decisions of the mind. Likewise, the mind becomes oblivious to the cry of the heart. Separately they are each in a state of fulfilment. But because there is no communication between them, both cease to contribute to activity in life. That is why Arjuna is in a state of suspension without activity.

Activity starts with the flow of desire. When the heart feels the lack of something and the mind responds to it, or when the mind feels the lack and the heart responds, then a stream of desire arises from between them and flows towards the object in view, engaging different faculties of heart, mind, and body as well as the available material in the surroundings. This makes it clear that communication between heart and mind must exist for desire to arise. And if the flow of desire is in the direction of the natural current of evolution, it is further supported by the invisible influence of Nature and will find fulfilment.

Arjuna is in a state where the mind and heart are held high in the fullness of their respective qualities with no link between them. In the fullness of heart and mind, where both are contented in themselves, neither feels the lack of anything, and hence there exists no room for desire to arise. Absence of desire leaves Arjuna in a state of suspension in which the entire personality loses its dynamic structure and is faced with seemingly insuperable problems whenever the need for action arises in any sphere of life.

Thus the Bhagavad-Gītā portrays a situation in which life can be full of problems, even while it is established in fulfilment

7 See verses 26–35.

8 See verses 36–46.

of heart and mind. By resolving such an extreme situation, it brings to light the wisdom and technique of living life without suffering at any level. It establishes that life must be without suffering. No one should ever suffer in life: this is the teaching of the Bhagavad-Gītā.

Duality is the fundamental cause of suffering. But when the entire field of life is dual in nature, how can life be free from suffering? This has always been a serious problem of metaphysics and indeed of practical life as well. The solution lies in the infusion into the field of duality of a non-dual element which blesses man's life with a status unaffected by suffering, even while he remains in the field where suffering is possible. This will be appreciated as the discourse advances.

Arjuna starts placing his problems before Lord Kṛishṇa.

Verse 29

सीदन्ति मम गात्राणि मुखं च परिशुष्यति
वेपथुश्च शरीरे मे रोमहर्षश्च जायते

Sīdanti mama gātrāṇi mukhaṁ cha parishushyati
vepathush cha sharīre me romaharshash cha jāyate

My limbs fail and my mouth is parched,
my body quivers and my hair stands on end.

A great strength of noted warriors lies in their concern for their fellow men, which has moved them to become the saviours of their societies. Arjuna was filled with a concern for others which enabled him to accept the challenge of his time when evil threatened. Because this concern for others formed the basis of his acceptance of battle, it comes as no surprise that the power of love overwhelms his heart and brings it to fullness. In this state of self-contentedness the heart becomes oblivious to the need of the mind — the call of duty. Arjuna is caught between the power of love and the call of duty. He finds he cannot yield to either.

The call of righteousness and the tide of love rising in the heart — both are dear to him because life, as he understands it, is all love of righteousness.

But as he is placed now, suspended between the heart and mind, he is not in a position to undertake activity. Even if, by some miracle, he tries to initiate action, he is faced with a terrible situation. If he follows the call of righteousness, he must rebel against love and kill all his dear ones assembled for battle. And if he follows the call of love, he must sacrifice the cause of righteousness and yield to evil. From this viewpoint we find that Arjuna is divided between the two forces which have so far been the essential components of his life. He stands like a child who is being called with love by his mother and at the same time is being summoned by his father from the other side. If he goes towards one, the other pulls him. He swings both ways. That is why he begins to feel shaken in body and mind.

When one is deeply absorbed in thinking, the attention no longer remains outside on the level of the senses, and the coordination of the body and mind becomes weak. If at this time the heart is not supported by the mind, that coordination is weakened still further. If this process goes far enough, the body does not function properly. This is why Arjuna felt his limbs failing, his mouth parched, his body quivering. His physical state indicates that the power of love is dominating Arjuna and challenging the call of duty by throwing his body out of balance. The consequences of a further rise in this power of love are described in the following verses.

VERSE 30

गाण्डीवं स्रंसते हस्तात्त्वक्चैव परिदह्यते
न च शक्नोम्यवस्थातुं भ्रमतीव च मे मनः

Gāṇḍīvaṁ sraṁsate hastāt twak chaiva paridahyate
na cha shaknomyavasthātuṁ bhramatīva cha me manaḥ

Gāṇḍīva (the bow) slips from my hand and even
my skin burns all over; I am unable to stand and
my mind seems to whirl.

'Gāṇḍīva slips from my hand': Arjuna's fast grip on Gāṇḍīva has been in response to the call of righteousness. His mind was completely dominated by the call of duty, and it was this which made him hold Gāṇḍīva fast. But now, after the wave of love created by Lord Kṛishṇa, the power of love has filled his heart and in its fullness equals the power of his mind. They balance each other, and therefore the power of mind no longer remains dominant. Consequently, his grip becomes loose, and Gāṇḍīva slips from his hand. Never before had the bow slipped from Arjuna's hand. The wave of love causes this to happen.

'My skin burns': Arjuna has been overwhelmed with the power of love. The warmth of love is soothing and comforting. What then burns his skin? We have seen that the power of *Dharma* upholds existence and evolution. As long as love is on the level of *Dharma* or on the path of righteousness, it helps evolution, supports life, and is soothing and comforting. But when the innocent power of love stands without supporting the path of righteousness, it is influenced by negative forces and becomes a means of destruction, misery, and suffering. In thinking that he could avoid fighting, Arjuna is deserting the cause of righteousness, and so he feels his skin burning in the warmth of love.

'Unable to stand': love with the power of righteousness makes a man strong but without it leaves him weak. Arjuna has been overcome with love, which threatens to overthrow the cause of righteousness. Therefore it is no surprise that he feels weak, 'unable to stand'.

'Mind seems to whirl': Arjuna is overtaken by the qualities of the heart. But Arjuna's mind is strong. It has the essential qualities of a brave man. Even when his heart is overwhelmed by the force of love, his mind is active and alert. The alert mind puts out a great force to change the course of the heart. It is as if the car of Arjuna's life were being driven with great speed on the road of love, and there came a great force of mind to reverse the direction. This attempt at reversing the flow of the life-stream produces the impression that his mind is whirling.

VERSE 31

निमित्तानि च पश्यामि विपरीतानि केशव
न च श्रेयोऽनुपश्यामि हत्वा स्वजनमाहवे

Nimittāni cha pashyāmi viparītāni Keshava
na cha shreyo 'nupashyāmi hatwā swajanam āhave

And I see adverse omens, O Keshava (Lord Kṛishṇa),
nor can I see good from killing my kinsmen in battle.

Arjuna in this verse gives expression to the feeling of the whole of Nature at that perilous moment of war.

'Killing my kinsmen' is an expression which contains the cry of both Arjuna's heart and mind. 'Killing' comes from the mind, for it is dedicated to Truth and righteousness and the destruction of evil. 'My kinsmen' is the cry of the heart. Arjuna's heart, full of love, allows him to see his opponents only as his 'kinsmen' and not as the aggressor and the enemy. Seeing them thus, he is right in saying: 'nor can I see good from killing my kinsmen in battle'.

In his present state of deep concern, Arjuna feels love for all his kinsmen standing before him and, at the same time, grief for their destruction in battle. His heart is torn between these two feelings. Deep within himself, immersed in feeling the situation and its consequences, he visualizes 'adverse omens'. The cries of anguish and the terrible sufferings that follow destruction in war flash through his mind. Arjuna's vision of omens reveals the purity of his heart and the deep state of concentration of his mind.

The future casts its image on the sanctuaries of pure hearts.

'Good' here means spiritual comfort. The Sanskrit word used is '*Shreyas*', which means evolution or fulfilment — the security and accomplishment that lies in spiritual freedom. Arjuna sees that spiritual comfort does not lie in killing his kinsmen. But this is the act that awaits him. Under the circumstances he finds he can do nothing but reject all that could possibly be desired.

VERSE 32

न कांक्षे विजयं कृष्ण न च राज्यं सुखानि च
किं नो राज्येन गोविन्द किं भोगैर्जीवितेन वा

Na kāṁkshe vijayaṁ Kṛishṇa na cha rājyaṁ sukhāni cha
kiṁ no rājyena Govinda kiṁ bhogair jīvitena vā

I desire not victory, O Kṛishṇa, nor a kingdom,
nor pleasures. Of what avail will a kingdom be
to us, or enjoyments, or even life, O Govinda?

Desire presents no problem if it is allowed to flow freely. Problems arise when a desire is checked or encounters resistance. Arjuna's words express this fact. He challenges the validity of victory, pleasures, kingdom, and even life in which desire has no chance of fulfilment.

The desire of a great man rises to support others and rejoices in the happiness that others derive from such support.

Having found the cause of battle to be damaging to body,[9] mind,[10] and surroundings,[11] Arjuna now looks at the situation from the point of view of usefulness to his own aims in life. He finds that nothing in the outside world is of interest to him personally because, as he sees life, it is for others. So, from this point of view also, he sees no reason for fighting.

Arjuna raises his voice against the corrupting influences of a kingdom, pleasure, and power. He has seen in the case of Duryodhana how they can blind a man's vision and cause the destruction of a whole civilization.

In the previous verse Arjuna has said that he can see no good from killing his kinsmen. Here he gives expression to the possible advantages that could come from the battle and weighs them in terms of their validity in life. This shows his presence of mind and the unbiased manner in which he is analysing the situation. He rejects the validity of victory, a kingdom, and pleasures if

9 See verse 29.
10 See verse 30.
11 See verse 31.

they are for selfish ends. He expresses not only indifference but positive aversion towards them. He makes it clear that 'even life' has no significance for him.

Arjuna uses the word 'us', which can imply either that he wants to verify his views with Lord Kṛishṇa, or that he is sure that Lord Kṛishṇa's views are in accord with his own.

'Govinda' means master of the senses. In using this word Arjuna is also silently suggesting that Lord Kṛishṇa, as master of the senses, naturally also has little use for the objects of the senses and the pleasures derived from them.

In his present state of deep contemplation, what Arjuna finds significant is a dedicated way of life. In the next verse he says clearly that his whole life is dedicated to others.

VERSE 33

येषामर्थे कांक्षितं नो राज्यं भोगाः सुखानि च
त इमेऽवस्थिता युद्धे प्राणांस्त्यक्त्वा धनानि च

Yeshām arthe kāṁkshitaṁ no rājyaṁ bhogāḥ sukhāni cha
ta ime 'vasthitā yuddhe prāṇāṁs tyaktwā dhanāni cha

Those for whose sake we desire a kingdom, enjoyments, and comforts are here on the battlefield, having resigned their lives and riches.

This brings to light the greatness of Arjuna's heart and mind. His vision is clear: he views the situation with a serene and deep insight. His logic is profound. His thought is balanced and noble. His feeling is for others: when he thinks, it is in terms of others; if he wants to fight and gain sovereignty, it is for the sake of others; if he wants to amass enjoyments and pleasures, it is for the sake of others; if he wants to live, it is for others. Such is his developed consciousness, devoid of any thought of self-interest. This is the status of truly great men — living, they live for others; dying, they die for others.

The question may be asked: If Arjuna's character shows such greatness of heart and mind, why does he come on to the battlefield prepared to fight? A close study of Arjuna's utterances reveals that he is bent upon resisting evil; he is not interested in killing people. He wants to destroy the evil without destroying the evil-doer. It is a noble ideal. His aim is to destroy the evil on earth, if possible without bringing down upon society the untold suffering and destruction of war. Only a man of such an ideal character can speak as does Arjuna in the next two verses.

VERSE 34

आचार्याः पितरः पुत्रास्तथैव च पितामहाः
मातुलाः श्वशुराः पौत्राः श्यालाः संबन्धिनस्तथा

Āchāryāḥ pitaraḥ putrās tathaiva cha pitāmahāḥ
mātulāḥ shwashurāḥ pautrāḥ shyālāḥ saṁbandhinas tathā

Teachers, uncles, sons, and likewise grandfathers,
maternal uncles, fathers-in-law, grandsons, brothers-in-law,
and other kinsmen.

This portrays the state of Arjuna's heart. It is full of love, full of life. From all sides he finds different channels of love pouring life into his heart and leaving it full. When love is full, life is full like the ocean. It is full like a silent ocean, for it ceases to flow in any direction. It just is. It is free from any desire. That is why Arjuna could only mention the names of relationships to portray the different fields of love and give expression to the condition of his heart.

This verse, coming in the midst of verses which express many problems, presents a vast field of life in love and silently proclaims that there are no problems in this field. The field of love is an innocent field of life. Problems arise when attachment[12] or detachment[13] overshadows pure love.

12 See verse 33.
13 See verse 35.

VERSE 35

एतान्न हन्तुमिच्छामि घ्नतोऽपि मधुसूदन
अपि त्रैलोक्यराज्यस्य हेतोः किं नु महीकृते

Etān na hantum ichchhāmi ghnato 'pi Madhusūdana
api trailokyarājyasya hetoḥ kiṁ nu mahīkṛite

O Madhusūdana (Lord Kṛishṇa), these I do not wish to kill — though killed myself — even for the sake of sovereignty of the three worlds, how much less for this world.

'Madhusūdana' means the slayer of the demon Madhu. By using this name, Arjuna suggests to Lord Kṛishṇa that, as the slayer of the demon, He may rise to kill the Kauravas if he finds that they are demoniacal; but as far as he himself is concerned, he finds that they are dear relatives and noble elders whom he would do anything to protect. Whatever the cost of letting them live, he cannot think of killing them. Arjuna speaks as only a conscientious, deeply thoughtful, and brave man will speak. This is his character. He stands for principle. Nothing can tempt him to deny the high ideals of life. This is why his thinking is so uncompromising.

The words 'even for the sake of sovereignty of the three worlds' indicate that Arjuna's vision was not restricted to the field of man's life on earth. Only such a man as he could challenge the value of sovereignty over the three worlds. Such is the height of human consciousness which upholds Arjuna even at this hour of his great concern.

VERSE 36

निहत्य धार्तराष्ट्रान्नः का प्रीतिः स्याज्जनार्दन
पापमेवाश्रयेदस्मान्हत्वैतानाततायिनः

Nihatya Dhārtarāshtrān naḥ kā prītiḥ syāj Janārdana
pāpam evāshrayed asmān hatwaitān ātatāyinaḥ

What happiness could come to us from slaying the sons of Dhṛitarāshtra, O Janārdana (Lord Kṛishṇa)? Only sin would come upon us through killing these aggressors.

This verse presents another change in Arjuna's vision. In the opposing army, he has been seeing just his own kinsmen; now, once again, they are the 'sons of Dhṛitarāshtra', 'these aggressors'. Arjuna has so far looked at the situation from the aspect of love but has arrived at no solution to his problem. He therefore decides to consider it from the mind — with discrimination and intuition — yet cannot suddenly abandon the fullness of love in his heart. Maintaining that fullness of heart, he begins to make more use of his mind.

As he gives himself over to reason, the call of duty begins to gain ground. With this his vision changes. He begins to see his kinsmen as 'aggressors'; the reality begins to dawn. Seeing them in this light, Arjuna asks: 'What happiness could come to us from slaying the sons of Dhṛitarāshtra?' And when he starts thinking in these terms, he finds killing is sin.

The act of killing does not produce life-supporting influences for anyone at any time. Killing is a sin for all time. No matter who is killed, killing is sin. The pain and suffering caused in the act of killing produce negative influences in creation, and the reaction recoils on the killer. So Arjuna says: 'Only sin would come upon us'.

The killing of aggressors is supposed to be a right action. The aggressor's life is put to an end, and thereby he is prevented from producing more negative influences for himself and others. But this justification of killing arises from a completely different consideration. The act of killing as such is sinful. And this is

Arjuna's main concern here.

Arjuna can see killing as sin even when he is on the battlefield. This indicates that his mind is clear and his vision not obstructed either by feelings of the heart or by the call of duty. He is deep in thought, evaluating the situation from every side. Arjuna is at a high pitch of mental and emotional activity. Both his alertness of mind and fullness of heart are displayed in the innocent utterance of truth: 'Only sin would come upon us through killing these aggressors.'

The expressions: 'What happiness could come to us' and 'Only sin would come upon us' indicate that happiness and suffering are considered as well as sin and virtue. For suffering results from sin, and happiness from virtue.

VERSE 37

तस्मान्नार्हा वयं हन्तुं धार्तराष्ट्रान्स्वबान्धवान्
स्वजनं हि कथं हत्वा सुखिनः स्याम माधव

Tasmān nārhā vayaṁ hantuṁ Dhārtarāshtrān swabāndhavān
swajanaṁ hi kathaṁ hatwā sukhinaḥ syāma Mādhava

Therefore it would not be right for us to kill the sons of
Dhṛitarāshtra, our own kinsmen. How should we be happy
after killing our own people, O Mādhava?

Arjuna's arguments have gone further. Previously it was only his 'wish' not to kill, but now he finds that it is not 'right' for him to engage in killing.[14]

In this verse Arjuna seems to weigh the killing of his kinsmen in terms of the happiness which could be derived from it: could any happiness remain after killing them? This does not mean that happiness is the criterion of action for Arjuna. He only wants to emphasize that he does not even see any happiness to justify it.

Happiness has certainly to be taken into account while considering the performance of any action, because the aim of any

14 See verse 31, commentary.

action is the increase of happiness — the very purpose of creation and of evolution is expansion of happiness. So if happiness does not result from an action, then that action defeats the very purpose of action, and its performance cannot be justified. That is why Arjuna says killing 'would not be right for us'.

Verse 38

यद्यप्येते न पश्यन्ति लोभोपहतचेतसः
कुलक्षयकृतं दोषं मित्रद्रोहे च पातकम्

Yadyapyete na pashyanti lobhopahatachetasaḥ
kulakshayakṛitaṁ doshaṁ mitradrohe cha pātakam

Although, their minds clouded by greed, they see no wrong in bringing destruction to the family, and no sin in treachery to friends,

Verse 39

कथं न ज्ञेयमस्माभिः पापादस्मान्निवर्तितुम्
कुलक्षयकृतं दोषं प्रपश्यद्भिर्जनार्दन

Kathaṁ na gyeyam asmābhiḥ pāpād asmān nivartitum
kulakshayakṛitaṁ doshaṁ prapashyadbhir Janārdana

How should we not know to turn away from this sin, we who clearly see the wrong in bringing destruction upon the family, O Janārdana?

'Know' shows Arjuna's chief concern at this moment. He tries to understand why he is unable to take a right course of action when he sees the truth of the situation and, even more so, when he knows what is right.

Arjuna expresses his concern over the influence of greed that has blinded the vision of his kinsmen and has prevented them from seeing 'the wrong'. This again shows that Arjuna's vision is clear.

The tone of the verse indicates that he does not give as much importance to the actual 'destruction' as to 'the wrong' that will result from it. But, for all his purity and clarity of vision, Arjuna fails to see the right way out of this sin of killing that awaits him. He turns to the Lord to receive the light.

Such moments in life make a man fall at the feet of God — moments when he sees and yet does not see, moments when he wants to act yet is unable to act.

When we investigate the invisible mechanics of Nature, we find that everything in the universe is directly connected with everything else. Everything is constantly being influenced by everything else. No wave of the ocean is independent of any other. Each certainly has its individuality, but it is not isolated from the influence of other waves. Every wave has its own course to follow, but this course is dependent on that of every other wave. The life of any individual is a wave in the ocean of cosmic life, where every wave constantly influences the course of every other.

Certainly man is the master of his own destiny. He has free will — the greatest of God's gifts to him — whereby he has complete freedom of action. But having performed an action he has to bear its consequence, for reaction is always equal to action.

When people behave rightly, a corresponding atmosphere is naturally produced, and when such an influence is dominant, the individual's tendencies are affected by it. If in such an atmosphere of grace and glory an individual is tempted to follow a wrong path, he is protected by the unseen influence of righteousness which surrounds him. Similarly when a man fails in his efforts, the unseen working of Nature is behind that failure. No amount of intellectual analysis can reveal to him why the failure occurs. He must rise to another level and realize the working of Nature and the power behind it. He must rise to understand the Laws of Nature and the Cosmic Law which underlies all of them.

Arjuna fails to understand why his decision to refrain from battle produces no result, and he continues to be drawn into the battle. It is not because he is in a state of confusion, but because no amount of intellectual clarity can provide anyone with insight into the complex workings of diverse Nature.

Arjuna, although his consciousness is pure, has not yet fathomed the absolute Being which is the field of the Cosmic Law. This is why he fails to see that he is living in an atmosphere saturated with evil influence, in which it is not possible for virtue to survive for long. Arjuna is trying to refrain from fighting out of consideration for family and caste *Dharmas*; he is not aware of the absolute state of *Dharma* whose power is leading him to fight. In consequence he fails to see why he is unable to act according to his feelings.

The following verse presents Arjuna's argument on how the path of evolution becomes extinct and bears witness to his concern for society.

VERSE 40

कुलक्षये प्रणश्यन्ति कुलधर्माः सनातनाः
धर्मे नष्टे कुलं कृत्स्नमधर्मोऽभिभवत्युत

Kulakshaye praṇashyanti kuladharmāḥ sanātanāḥ
dharme nashte kulaṁ kṛitsnam adharmo 'bhibhavatyuta

The age-old family Dharmas are lost in the destruction of a family. Its Dharma lost, adharma overtakes the entire family.

'*Dharmas*', the plural of *Dharma*, signifies the different powers of Nature upholding different avenues of the way of evolution. They take expression as specific modes of activity or different ways of righteousness, which keep the whole stream of life in harmony — every aspect of life being properly balanced with every other aspect — and moving in the direction of evolution. As these specific modes of activity are passed on from generation to generation, they form what we call traditions. It is these traditions which are referred to here as family *Dharmas*.

'*Adharma*' means absence of *Dharma*. When *adharma* prevails, the great power of Nature, which maintains the equilibrium between positive and negative forces, is lost, and the process of evolution is thereby obstructed.

Arjuna uses the word 'age-old' because the ideals of life that have withstood the test of time represent the genuine path of evolution, the upward current in Nature. Nothing that is against evolution lasts long. Therefore the tradition which has survived the ages has certainly proved itself to be the right one, the one nearest to the Truth, which is Life Eternal. That is why Arjuna is afraid to break this path of evolution for the generations to come.

In the process of analysing the quality of the act of fighting, Arjuna shows great foresight and a highly developed mind. It is clear that his thinking is extremely logical and correct, and that it certainly does not come from the superficial level of consciousness. Its basis is *Dharma*, the basic power of evolution. Arjuna's vision is not restricted; the boundaries of his foresight lie far in the future.

As a great man of his time, Arjuna, before entering upon an undertaking, gauges its influence on succeeding generations. Only such a heightened state of consciousness could inspire the dawn of great wisdom on earth.

Arjuna's chief concern is the preservation of the path of evolution. With this in view he places great value on *Dharma* and on the conduct of society, which supports it and is upheld by it.

Arjuna continues his argument in the following verse.

VERSE 41

अधर्माभिभवात्कृष्ण प्रदुष्यन्ति कुलस्त्रियः
स्त्रीषु दुष्टासु वार्ष्णेय जायते वर्णसंकरः

Adharmābhibhavāt Kṛishṇa pradushyanti kulastriyaḥ
strīshu dushtāsu Vārshṇeya jāyate varṇasaṁkaraḥ

When adharma prevails, O Kṛishṇa, the women of the family become corrupt, and with the corruption of women, O Vārshṇeya, intermixture of castes arises.

A mother's life is the expression of the creative power of Nature. Creative intelligence has to be pure in order to be effective.

Impurity brings ineffectiveness, and when ineffectiveness increases, destruction is the result. For the creation of more effective people, the purity of the mother's life is of great concern.

'Intermixture of castes' is of concern to Arjuna because he understands how difficult and dangerous it is to shift from one boat to another in a fast current. All beings, under the tremendous influence of the mighty force of Nature, are held fast in the current of evolution. Each has his own specific course to follow. If a man deviates from his own natural course, his own *Dharma*, then it is like changing boats in a fast current. He has to struggle hard to maintain life — a struggle which is experienced as sorrow and suffering and which gives rise to all problems on the path of evolution.

The answer to every problem is that there is no problem. Let a man perceive this truth and then he is without problems. This is the strength of knowledge — the strength of Sāṁkhya — the strength of the wisdom that offers instantaneous realization. This is the knowledge that Lord Kṛishṇa is going to reveal to Arjuna in answer to all the basic problems of life that Arjuna is posing in these verses 28 to 46.

VERSE 42

संकरो नरकायैव कुलघ्नानां कुलस्य च
पतन्ति पितरो ह्येषां लुप्तपिण्डोदकक्रियाः

Saṁkaro narakāyaiva kulaghnānāṁ kulasya cha
patanti pitaro hyeshāṁ luptapiṇḍodakakriyāḥ

This intermixture leads only to hell, both for the family and its destroyers. Their forefathers fall as well, when the offerings of the Piṇdodaka cease.

Purity of blood is at the basis of long life for a family and a society. And this purity depends upon the preservation of ancient family traditions. Destruction of the social order is the greatest loss to a nation. Arjuna is viewing the battle with this vital consideration in mind, taking into account the life of many future generations. His vision is perfect and his concern is genuine. The depth of his thought, his foresight, and love for human life and society inspire Lord Kṛishṇa to strengthen him with the wisdom of eternal liberation. Lord Kṛishṇa quietly listens to what he is saying in order to prepare him more thoroughly for this great blessing.

Every sentiment expressed by Arjuna, every doubt raised by him, and every inquiry of his into the field of knowledge is being sympathetically received by Lord Kṛishṇa and will be answered by Him to Arjuna's satisfaction.

'*Piṇdodaka*': according to the Vedic *Karma Kāṇda*, the exposition of *Karma*, or action, sons and grandsons are expected to perform certain rites and ceremonies in the name of their departed father and grandfather. The performance of these rites by the direct blood relations, according to the law of affinity, brings goodwill, peace, and satisfaction to the departed forefathers wherever they may be in the field of evolution. Not only this, but as a child receives blessings and comforts from his parents, so the departed also bless their children. The Vedic performance of the *Piṇdodaka* connects the departed parents with their children on earth and serves as a channel through which the blessings flow.

Having shown his concern for the life of individuals, Arjuna, in the following verse, again expresses his concern for the path of evolution and for the whole of society.

VERSE 43

दोषैरेतैः कुलघ्नानां वर्णसंकरकारकैः
उत्साद्यन्ते जातिधर्माः कुलधर्माश्च शाश्वताः

Doshair etaiḥ kulaghnānāṁ varṇasaṁkarakārakaiḥ
utsādyante jātidharmāḥ kuladharmāsh cha shāshwatāḥ

Through the wrongs done by the destroyers of the family
in causing the intermixing of castes, the immemorial
Dharmas of caste and family become extinct.

The laws maintaining the well-being of the whole body consist of a collection of the laws maintaining its different parts, together with others added to coordinate different limbs. The laws of the evolution of the body likewise are the sum total of those governing the evolution of different limbs, along with those coordinating them.

In a similar way, there are *Dharmas* governing individual evolution and there are *Dharmas* which connect and coordinate different individuals. These latter are said primarily to govern the evolution of the society or caste. In verse 40 Arjuna was thinking in terms of the *Dharma* of the family. In this verse he is considering the *Dharma* of the caste, that is, a collection of families upholding similar *Dharmas*.

The intermixing of castes destroys the ideals preserved by the immemorial traditions and has the direct result of upsetting the social equilibrium. What happens to a life which is not based on ancient traditions is shown in the following verse.

VERSE 44

उत्सन्नकुलधर्माणां मनुष्याणां जनार्दन
नरके नियतं वासो भवतीत्यनुशुश्रुम

Utsannakuladharmāṇāṁ manushyāṇāṁ Janārdana
narake niyataṁ vāso bhavatītyanushushruma

Men whose family Dharmas have lapsed, so we have heard,
O Janārdana (Lord Kṛishṇa), necessarily live in hell.

'Family *Dharmas*' are the powers of different principles which uphold the coordination between different members of a family, at the same time enabling every member, consciously or unconsciously, to help every other member on his path of evolution. Such family *Dharmas* are, for example, those that go to make the relationship of a mother with her son or daughter, or of a brother with his brother or sister, and so on. Family *Dharmas* are maintained in the family traditions. If the family traditions are broken, people living together do not know how to live in such a manner that their way of life naturally helps each of them to evolve. The result is the loss of the path of evolution and the increase of disorder and chaos in the family. Life in such a family is a life in hell, and those fallen into such a degenerate pattern of life remain off the path of evolution and continue to mould their destinies in wretchedness. This is what Arjuna means when he says 'necessarily live in hell'.

Here is a great teaching of vital importance which has been missed for centuries. It sets a standard for any society.

'Family *Dharma*' is an established tradition where people born in a particular family engage in the profession of that family. Because of their parental heritage they work efficiently, produce better material for society, and improve in their profession. Working with all ease and comfort in their profession, they do not exhaust themselves in work and find time to be regular in their practice for spiritual unfoldment, which is the basis of all success in life. This is how family *Dharmas* and traditions help both the individual and society.

Arjuna addresses Lord Kṛishṇa as 'Janārdana', which is a reminder that He established law and order by destroying the demon Jana. Now, as a result of battle, greater chaos will prevail, for family *Dharmas* will be lost — the world will become hell.

Arjuna's concern over the destruction of *Dharmas* indicates that he is reviewing the whole situation from the point of view of the working of Nature.

This verse establishes a fundamental principle of action: the action should be such that it does not stray from the invisible power of *Dharma*.

The following verse indicates how one's wisdom could fail one and wrong decisions result.

VERSE 45

अहो बत महत्पापं कर्तुं व्यवसिता वयम्
यद्राज्यसुखलोभेन हन्तुं स्वजनमुद्यताः

Aho bata mahat pāpaṁ kartuṁ vyavasitā vayam
yad rājyasukhalobhena hantuṁ swajanam udyatāḥ

Alas! We are resolved to commit great sin in that we are prepared to slay our kinsmen out of greed for the pleasures of a kingdom.

Arjuna feels sorrowful because he is going to sacrifice a greater end for a smaller gain — family and caste *Dharmas* are going to be sacrificed for the sake of his individual *Dharma*.

Arjuna calls it a great sin because he is aware that the establishment of righteousness, the Kingdom of God on earth, is a cooperative enterprise. All men have to play their part in it, and this can be done only when family and caste *Dharmas* are properly maintained by the individuals firmly established in their individual *Dharmas*. The loss of family and caste *Dharmas* is a calamity for the social order, a destruction of righteousness; it is a sin against God. That is why Arjuna calls it 'great sin'.

Arjuna begins in the following verse to express the line of action he would like to take.

VERSE 46

यदि मामप्रतीकारमशस्त्रं शस्त्रपाणयः
धार्तराष्ट्रा रणे हन्युस्तन्मे क्षेमतरं भवेत्

Yadi mām apratīkāram ashastraṁ shastrapāṇayaḥ
Dhārtarāshtrā raṇe hanyus tan me kshemataraṁ bhavet

It were better for me if the sons of Dhṛitarāshtra, weapons in hand, should slay me, unresisting and unarmed in battle.

Arjuna sees that he would be committing great sin by fighting. As a warrior, once having come on to the battlefield he can neither hold back from fighting nor can he flee; but if he fights, there remains that fear of great sin. He sees no way of escape from this situation, so he says that he were better killed in battle. Because he cannot be killed while armed and alert, he wishes to be unarmed and unresisting. In this way he will not incur great sin against God. This is the faultless mind of the greatest archer of all time; this is bravery and nobility of character. Arjuna considers it better to die than to commit sin.

VERSE 47

संजय उवाच
एवमुक्त्वार्जुनः संख्ये रथोपस्थ उपाविशत्
विसृज्य सशरं चापं शोकसंविग्नमानसः

Sanjaya uvācha
Evam uktwārjunaḥ saṁkhye rathopastha upāvishat
visṛijya sasharaṁ chāpaṁ shokasaṁvignamānasaḥ

Sanjaya said:
Having spoken thus at the time of battle, casting away
arrow and bow, Arjuna sat down on the seat of the chariot,
his mind overwhelmed with sorrow.

'Having spoken thus': in the previous verses, Arjuna has described the consequences of battle as they presented themselves to his developed heart and mind. Now, still unable to decide his course of action, he becomes aware of himself standing with bow and arrow in his chariot, apparently prepared for war. Arjuna may have thought that by standing armed for battle he did not allow himself to be impartial in his consideration and so decided to cast away arrow and bow, abandon his battle posture, and sit down to reflect more deeply in order to find an answer which would satisfy both sides of his problem — love for dear ones and the demand of duty.

Arjuna's mind was 'overwhelmed with sorrow': the hour of

duty was at hand, but his heart prevented him from responding. With his clear mind he could visualize the far-reaching effects of the destruction the battle would bring. This overwhelmed his thought with sorrow. Fortunate are they whose minds are distressed for the misfortunes of others. More fortunate still are they who are able to relieve the misfortunes of others, themselves remaining undisturbed.

In the following chapter, Arjuna will receive the light which will enable him, without a trace of distress and established in the blissful freedom of God Consciousness, to alleviate the evil overshadowing the world.

ॐ तत्सदिति श्रीमद्भगवद्गीतासूपनिषत्सु ब्रह्मविद्यायां योगशास्त्रे
श्रीकृष्णार्जुनसंवादे अर्जुनविषादयोगो नाम प्रथमोऽध्यायः

Oṁ tat sad iti Shrīmad Bhagavadgītāsūpanishatsu Brahmavidyāyāṁ Yogashāstre Shrīkṛishṇārjunasaṁvāde Arjunavishādayogo nāma prathamo 'dhyāyaḥ

Thus, in the Upanishad of the glorious Bhagavad-Gītā, in the Science of the Absolute, in the Scripture of Yoga, in the dialogue between Lord Kṛishṇa and Arjuna, ends the first chapter, entitled: The Yoga of the Despondency of Arjuna.

Chapter II

A Vision of the Teaching in Chapter II

Verse 1. The seeker of Truth is held in a state of suspension, for he sees no solution to the basic problems of life.

Verses 2–3. From the point of view of the Divine, problems do not exist. Impurity overshadows the dignity that naturally belongs to life.

Verses 4–9. This statement about the nature of life appears meaningless to one who clearly knows that problems do exist at the basis of individual and social life. As a practical man, he does not wish to turn a blind eye to them.

Verses 10–38. To him the teaching comes, giving insight into life. There are two aspects of life, the changing body and the unchanging Self, whose real nature is absolute Being. Until Being is realized, life is without a stable foundation and remains based solely on the fundamental problems of existence, even though it may be in accord with almighty Nature and the force of evolution. Knowledge of the Self and Being brings equanimity of mind.

Verses 39–44. Equanimity is made permanent by gaining absolute consciousness: the mind gains absolute consciousness naturally and easily, but the man who is immersed in sensory enjoyment misses it.

Verses 45–8. The technique lies in allowing the mind to arrive naturally at absolute consciousness and then, having become acquainted with the fullness of life, to engage in action.

Verses 49–52. The advantages are improved efficiency and greater success in all fields of life, relief from problems, and complete liberation from bondage.

Verses 53–72. A description of life established in equanimity and of precautions to safeguard that blessed state of freedom in divine consciousness.

THIS chapter is the soul of the Bhagavad-Gītā, while all those that follow form the body. Hope and fulfilment are the blessings of this glorious chapter. It gives a direct way to peaceful, energetic, and successful life in the world, together with spiritual comfort and freedom from bondage.

The chapter expounds *Brahma Vidyā* in its completeness — the wisdom of the Absolute both in its theoretical and practical aspects — and presents the central idea of the entire theme of the Bhagavad-Gītā. It has seed ideas which are developed in all the following chapters.

At the same time this chapter is self-contained. It is in itself powerful enough to uplift any mind, however low its level. It presents a complete philosophy of life, starting from the state of a seeker and ending in the state of fulfilment.

The thought of the first chapter continues to flow into the early part of this one. The potential force underlying Arjuna's state of suspension finds an outlet in the ocean of the eternal wisdom of Lord Kṛishṇa.

Arjuna's condition, which inspired Lord Kṛishṇa to reveal the secret wisdom of integrated life, is portrayed at the beginning of the chapter, and the key to this wisdom is revealed in the 45th verse.

VERSE 1

संजय उवाच
तं तथा कृपयाविष्टमश्रुपूर्णाकुलेक्षणम्
विषीदन्तमिदं वाक्यमुवाच मधुसूदनः

Sanjaya uvācha
Taṁ tathā kṛipayāvishtam ashrupūrṇākulekshaṇam
vishīdantam idaṁ vākyam uvācha Madhusūdanaḥ

Sanjaya said:
To him thus overcome by compassion, full of sorrow,
his eyes distressed and filled with tears, Madhusūdana
(Lord Kṛishṇa) spoke these words:

'Madhusūdana': the slayer of the demon Madhu. The use of this word indicates that a mighty power is rising to put an end to Arjuna's paralysing state of suspension.

Even a mind as highly alert and intelligent as was Arjuna's had become caught in a situation which was out of control. His heart could not be reconciled with his mind — his love of kinsmen with the call of duty to destroy evil. On the practical level, this is like wanting to remain in darkness and yet be in the light. Arjuna has set himself a task which is impossible unless he attains a state of consciousness which will justify any action of his and will allow him even to kill in love, in support of the purpose of evolution.

Arjuna could not reconcile killing and loving. This is no weakness on his part and does not detract from his greatness. Any man of similar high development would arrive at this state of suspension between heart and mind.

Arjuna was a man of dynamic nature. His heart was full of love, yet he could not at this time love his dear ones. His mind was clear, alert, and full of purpose, yet he could not at this time act according to its dictates. Held in suspension as he was, he could not fight and satisfy his mind, nor could he love his dear ones and satisfy his heart. For this reason he was 'full of sorrow'.

Arjuna was not confused, as commentators in general have

portrayed him. His heart and mind were at the height of alertness, but they could not show him a line of action to fulfil their contradictory aspirations. Even this could not throw Arjuna off his balance, for Sanjaya says: 'eyes distressed and filled with tears'. Had he been off his balance, his eyes would have been vacant. But they had life in them: distress is seen in them, and they express the heart through tears. The 'distress' seen in the eyes gives expression to his great concern, and this shows mental alertness.

The sequence of the expressions used in this verse is of great significance in arriving at the truth of Arjuna's condition. 'Overcome by compassion' shows that his heart is filled with compassion alone. The expression that follows is 'full of sorrow'. If the heart is full of compassion, then there is no place in it for an emotion of such a dissimilar quality as sorrow. This makes it clear that the phrase 'full of sorrow' does not refer to Arjuna's heart. It does not describe an emotion, but only the state of his mind.

Thus Arjuna's heart was full of compassion and his mind full of sorrow. His state should not be misunderstood as indicating weakness or confusion. This verse shows Arjuna in his full stature, at the height of his intelligence, sensitivity, and alertness, and at the same time without any line of action to follow.

This condition of suspension is of value, for it provides a real basis for divine intelligence. At first sight it appears to be the result of circumstances, but it is in fact produced by the first word of Lord Kṛishṇa on the battlefield.[1] The purity of Arjuna's life, receiving a wave of love from Lord Kṛishṇa, developed into a state of suspension and prepared the ground for the divine wisdom to dawn.

Here is the picture of a man of the world who is going to receive the greatest divine wisdom ever revealed to man. In order to find the real Arjuna on whom the blessing came, we must look beyond the appearance of tears and distress. The outer structure of tears and distress serves to protect the inner glory of consciousness in a state of suspension. It is like the bitter skin of an orange which contains sweet juice within it. The apparent phenomenal phase of the world is not so attractive, but within it is the altar of God whose light sustains our life.

1 See I, 25, commentary.

Lord Kṛishṇa will not allow even the outer aspect of Arjuna's life to look 'sorrowful'. He will improve the appearance also. And with that in view He shocks Arjuna as He begins His speech.

VERSE 2

श्रीभगवानुवाच
कुतस्त्वा कश्मलमिदं विषमे समुपस्थितम्
अनार्यजुष्टमस्वर्ग्यमकीर्तिकरमर्जुन

Shrī Bhagavān uvācha
Kutas twā kashmalam idaṁ vishame samupasthitam
anāryajushtam aswargyam akīrtikaram Arjuna

The Blessed Lord said:
Whence has this blemish, alien to honourable men,
causing disgrace and opposed to heaven, come upon
you, Arjuna, at this untimely hour?

Problems are not solved on the level of problems. Analysing a problem to find its solution is like trying to restore freshness to a leaf by treating the leaf itself, whereas the solution lies in watering the root.

Arjuna, in the previous twenty-one verses, has raised, basically, all the problems that may confront any life at any time. When the Lord begins to answer, He does not devote a moment to Arjuna's arguments. He simply dismisses everything that Arjuna has said without analysing it, because by analysing each statement it would not be possible to resolve the situation.

All problems of life arise from some weakness of mind. All weakness of mind is due to the mind's ignorance of its own essential nature, which is universal and the source of infinite energy and intelligence. This ignorance of one's own self is the basis of all problems, sufferings, and shortcomings in life. In order to root out any problem of life it is only necessary to be brought out of ignorance, to be brought to knowledge.

In order to bring anyone to knowledge, it is first necessary to bring him to a state of mind where he will listen. Arjuna being in a state of suspension, the Lord said something to him which would shake his mind and make him capable of hearing and understanding.

In this verse the Lord appraises Arjuna's situation in words which suggest its solution. The first word spoken by Lord Kṛishṇa in this discourse expresses the whole philosophy of life, the whole of Vedānt: the world of forms and phenomena in its ever-changing nature, and the absolute never-changing Reality of transcendental nature, both are full — '*Pūrṇam adaḥ pūrṇam idam*'. Whence then has come this blemish of ignorance, which causes sorrow? Again, as the present is composed of the two 'fulls', the blemish does not belong to any present time; that is why it is 'untimely' at any 'hour'.

Arjuna has presented his problems in verses 28 to 46 of the first chapter; how Lord Kṛishṇa sees the situation and disapproves of it is clear from the expressions of this verse.

'Whence' indicates the baselessness of the whole argument. This word runs parallel to verse 28, which provides a basis for Arjuna's argument.

'Blemish' refers to the content of verses 29–31.

'Alien to honourable men' expresses the nature of verses 32–5.

'Causing disgrace' refers to verses 36–9.

'Opposed to heaven' refers to verses 40–6.

The Lord exclaims to Arjuna: 'Whence has this blemish ... come upon you?' He speaks with surprise and uses the word 'blemish' to epitomize Arjuna's overall state and way of thinking. The word 'blemish', accompanied by 'alien to honourable men, causing disgrace and opposed to heaven' and 'untimely hour', hit Arjuna hard. His alert mind and heart received a severe shock, which jolted him out of the state of suspension. Immediately he lost confidence in the way he was thinking. This made him look to the Lord.

The following verse brings another shock to Arjuna and strengthens the effect produced by this verse. The Lord implies that, whether surroundings and circumstances are favourable or unfavourable, men of honour and grace always act in a way that leads them to glory here on earth and in heaven.

VERSE 3

क्लैब्यं मा स्म गमः पार्थ नैतत्त्वय्युपपद्यते
क्षुद्रं हृदयदौर्बल्यं त्यक्त्वोत्तिष्ठ परंतप

Klaibyaṁ mā sma gamaḥ Pārtha naitat twayyupapadyate
kshudraṁ hṛidayadaur balyaṁ tyaktwottishtha Paraṁtapa

Pārtha! Yield not to unmanliness. It is unworthy of you. Shake off this paltry faintheartedness. Stand up, O scorcher of enemies!

Again this verse shows psychological skill in handling a problem. Here the Lord uses the word 'unmanliness', at the same time reminding Arjuna of his honourable heritage by calling him 'Pārtha', the son of Pṛithā. This is to neutralize in Arjuna what Lord Kṛishṇa calls 'faintheartedness'.

Lord Kṛishṇa realized that when He first addressed him as Pārtha, asking him to behold the Kurus assembled in the battle,[2] He awoke in him the love of his mother Pṛithā, and He knew that the great wave of love instilled by Him in Arjuna's heart was responsible for his present state of suspension. Therefore, to bring Arjuna back to his initial preparedness to fight, it was necessary to expand the one-sided nature of the love produced by the word 'Pārtha'. This is the reason why Lord Kṛishṇa here again uses 'Pārtha' and associates it with 'faintheartedness'.

Having produced this effect in the heart, it was at once necessary to direct the flow of Arjuna's mind away from the state of suspension towards action; so the Lord tells him to 'stand up'. In this way, the Lord sets up an impulse in his mind towards fighting and immediately supplements it by reminding him of his status as a 'scorcher of enemies'.

The Lord wants to stop Arjuna at once from thinking in a manner that will lead him nowhere. He tells Arjuna that this way does not belong to him, for he has always been a dynamic personality — 'It is unworthy of you.'

This saying of the Lord's also has a deeper meaning. 'It is

2 See I, 25.

unworthy of you' reminds Arjuna of his essential nature. 'That Thou Art', declare the Upanishads — unbounded eternal Being. You should breathe universal life and not fall prey to 'faintheartedness', for that belongs to the field of ignorance.

Asking him to shake off his 'faintheartedness', the Lord qualifies it by 'paltry'. By this He means to encourage Arjuna: the weakness he has to overcome is not great but just a failing of the heart. Lord Kṛishṇa wants to convey to Arjuna that when love grows in man's heart, his outlook becomes more universal, and he should become stronger and more dynamic, but that in his case this has not happened. Arjuna has not gained a universal outlook.

This expresses a great metaphysical truth: ignorance has no material substance. It is just an illusion which should be easy to shake off. Unfortunately this ignorance has deprived Arjuna of the strength that the wave of love should naturally bring.

Certainly, as a great warrior, Arjuna is brave by nature. That is why the Lord seems only to remind him of what he is: unbounded and eternal in his absolute nature and the 'scorcher of enemies' in his relative nature, in his human form.

A close study of these two verses, which form the Lord's first exhortation, shows that they contain in essence the entire teaching of the Bhagavad-Gītā.

VERSE 4

अर्जुन उवाच
कथं भीष्ममहं संख्ये द्रोणं च मधुसूदन
इषुभिः प्रतियोत्स्यामि पूजार्हावरिसूदन

Arjuna uvācha
Kathaṁ Bhīshmam ahaṁ saṁkhye Droṇaṁ cha Madhusūdana
ishubhiḥ pratiyotsyāmi pūjārhāvarisūdana

Arjuna said:
How shall I fight Bhīshma and Droṇa with arrows on the battlefield, O Madhusūdana? Worthy of reverence are they, O slayer of enemies!

Arjuna addresses Lord Kṛishṇa as Madhusūdana, slayer of the demon Madhu, while recounting the names of Bhīshma and Droṇa. Thereby he silently suggests to Lord Kṛishṇa: You are the slayer of demons; how can you ask me to slay these noble elders? You are the slayer of enemies; how can you ask me to kill those who are worthy of reverence?

This shows Arjuna's alertness of mind even in this state of suspension. If one is alert and awake in heart and mind, there is always hope of rising above any time of trial.

Arjuna presses his point further in the next verse.

Verse 5

गुरूनहत्वा हि महानुभावान्
श्रेयो भोक्तुं भैक्ष्यमपीह लोके
हत्वार्थकामांस्तु गुरूनिहैव
भुञ्जीय भोगान्रुधिरप्रदिग्धान्

Gurūn ahatwā hi mahānubhāvān
shreyo bhoktuṁ bhaikshyam apīha loke
hatwārthakāmāṁs tu gurūn ihaiva
bhunjīya bhogān rudhirapradigdhān

It is surely better to live even on alms in this world than to slay these noble-minded masters; for though they are desirous of gain, having killed them I should enjoy only blood-stained pleasures in this world.

This shows Arjuna's greatness, nobility of character, and far-sightedness. It shows the quality of his human heart. Arjuna, as a great archer, was aware of the pathetic records of blood-stained conquests in history. He could foresee great damage to the civilization of his time. He could picture in his mind ruins of war everywhere; he could hear within himself the cries of children and lamentations of women, tales of calamity and oppression. Arjuna, a hero with a good human heart, would do anything to hold back from the situation that seems imminent. He goes so far as to say that it is 'better to live even on alms in this world than to slay these noble-minded masters' and 'enjoy only blood-stained pleasures'.

In the following verse he continues his argument.

VERSE 6

न चैतद्विद्मः कतरन्नो गरीयो
यद्वा जयेम यदि वा नो जयेयुः
यानेव हत्वा न जिजीविषामस्
तेऽवस्थिताः प्रमुखे धार्तराष्ट्राः

Na chaitad vidmaḥ kataran no garīyo
yad vā jayema yadi vā no jayeyuḥ
yān eva hatwā na jijīvishāmas
te 'vasthitāḥ pramukhe Dhārtarāshtrāḥ

We do not know which is better for us: that we should conquer them or they should conquer us. The sons of Dhṛitarāshtra stand face to face with us. If we killed them we should not wish to live.

This shows Arjuna's selfless view of life. If he is to enjoy the kingdom, he wants the joy of it to be shared by all those who are dear to him; and if he cannot share it with them, he prefers to forgo the kingdom altogether. The verse brings to light the way of thinking of a man of evolved consciousness. Arjuna, realizing the gravity of the situation, is concerned over the responsibility that rests upon him. He thinks about the consequences of victory or defeat and finds no justification even for a victory of his own side, if that will deprive him of his dear ones.

Placed in a helpless situation, Arjuna decides that it cannot be resolved on any level of human thinking or feeling. He therefore looks to the Lord for divine guidance.

The following verse records the helplessness of the greatest archer of all time, the most innocent and sincere feelings of surrender of a great and wise man.

VERSE 7

कार्पण्यदोषोपहतस्वभावः
पृच्छामि त्वां धर्मसंमूढचेताः
यच्छ्रेयः स्यान्निश्चितं ब्रूहि तन्मे
शिष्यस्तेऽहं शाधि मां त्वां प्रपन्नम्

Kārpaṇyadoshopahataswabhāvaḥ
pṛichchhāmi twāṁ dharmasaṁmūdhachetāḥ
yach chhreyaḥ syān nishchitaṁ brūhi tan me
shishyas te 'haṁ shādhi māṁ twāṁ prapannam

My nature smitten with the taint of weakness, confused in mind about Dharma, I pray Thee, tell me decisively what is good for me. I am Thy disciple; teach me for I have taken refuge in Thee.

Arjuna has persisted in his attitude, and when he has gone as far as he possibly can in that direction, he suddenly feels unable to think any more. He stops, his intellect rebounds, and he falls at the feet of the Lord.

It generally happens that as long as a man feels that he can think and do for himself, he sees no need to listen to others. When he is at his wits' end, he looks for refuge. If he finds a refuge, he approaches it in all humility and puts his trust in it. When he has surrendered himself completely, it takes full care of him. This is the impartial divine nature: I am to them as they are to Me.

'Tell me decisively' reveals Arjuna's character. He is a practical man who does not want to remain on the level of idealistic talk. He asks for a clear line of action, which he can follow without doubt and which will prove to be right for him, his aim being the good of all. If a man has dedicated his life to the service of others and is conscientious about his responsibilities, he has all the greater need to be right in the course of action he adopts.

This situation does not in any way reflect on Arjuna's character. It is the integrity of his inner life that makes him see weakness in himself. His greatness is revealed when he says: 'confused in mind about *Dharma*'. On one side he has his family *Dharma* (duty of a householder) impelling him to protect and love his kinsmen, and on the other his caste *Dharma* (duty of a *Kshatriya*, protector of society) demanding that he kill the aggressors. He is not able to decide for himself which *Dharma* to follow and looks upon this as his weakness. In reality it is the circumstances that are responsible. No man of heart and mind would consider it to be Arjuna's weakness; but he calls it his weakness. His greatness of character makes him too humble in analysing his condition before Lord Kṛishṇa.

When Arjuna surrenders himself to gain wisdom as a disciple, the Lord accepts him, and it is from this point that Lord Kṛishṇa's teaching commences. This is really the beginning of the Bhagavad-Gītā.

It is an established natural law that action and reaction are equal to one another. In order that the reaction may take place, the action has first to begin. In the same way, in order that the teaching may begin, the pupil has first to approach the teacher. When he has done this he is considered serious, and the teacher feels a responsibility to teach him.

As long as Arjuna was talking to Lord Kṛishṇa on a friendly basis, Lord Kṛishṇa answered in the same manner. But when Arjuna became serious and said: I submit myself to you as a disciple, show me the way, guide me to the light, for I am unable to see for myself — when Arjuna became quiet and turned completely to Lord Kṛishṇa, then the Lord took him seriously and began to enlighten him with the practical wisdom of life.

When a patient will not keep still, the surgeon cannot start the operation; only when the patient submits himself to the surgeon to do as he wishes does he feel free to operate.

This is a great secret of success when guidance is sought from another in any walk of life. And the wisdom of peace and happiness in life, the wisdom of success in the world and freedom from bondage, is the greatest secret of life. It is *Brahma Vidyā*, the knowledge of the Ultimate. Naturally it can be imparted only to those who are at least willing to receive it. Their willingness is judged by their readiness to receive, and this in turn by their one-pointed attention in faithful devotion to the master.

Faith makes the student a good assimilator of knowledge. Devotion sets him free from resistance and at the same time influences the heart of the master, whence the spring of wisdom pours forth. Devotion on the part of the disciple creates affection in the heart of the master. When a calf approaches its mother, the milk begins to flow from her udder, ready for the calf to drink without effort. Such is the glory of devotion and faith in a disciple. He surrenders at the feet of the master and cuts short the long path of evolution.

The result of Arjuna's sincere surrender to Lord Kṛishṇa was seen without delay. By His teaching, both theoretical and practical, He helped Arjuna to free himself from his state of suspension. At the end of a short discourse on a battlefield, Arjuna had become a *Yogī*,[3] a *Bhakta*,[4] and a *Gyānī*.[5] He had become established in the fullness of resolute intellect, in great skill in action, and in the eternal freedom of existence.

To reach that state, Arjuna had only to surrender at the feet of the Lord. Surrender does not mean blind passivity. Throughout the Bhagavad-Gītā, Arjuna continues to ask questions, for the student gains complete freedom to ask anything, once he has impressed the master with his sincerity. In a relationship of this quality between the teacher and the taught, the task of both becomes easy and free from resistance. Wisdom flows spontaneously from one to the other.

Having surrendered himself, Arjuna, in the next verse, shows clearly the present state of his mind. The path of surrender does not allow any reservations.

3 An integrated man.
4 A devotee of God.
5 An enlightened man.

VERSE 8

न हि प्रपश्यामि ममापनुद्याद्
यच्छोकमुच्छोषणमिन्द्रियाणाम्
अवाप्य भूमावसपत्नमृद्धं
राज्यं सुराणामपि चाधिपत्यम्

Na hi prapashyāmi mamāpanudyād
yach chhokam uchchhoshaṇam indriyāṇām
avāpya bhūmāvasapatnam ṛiddhaṁ
rājyaṁ surāṇām api chādhipatyam

Indeed I do not see what could dispel the grief that dries up my senses, though I should obtain an unrivalled and prosperous kingdom on earth and even lordship of the gods.

'Dries up my senses': by reason of Arjuna's state of suspension, the coordination between the mind and the senses is lost. A plant becomes dry because it has received no nourishment from the root, and there is no way of giving it nourishment from outside. Without coordination with the mind, the senses have no chance of remaining alert and cannot enjoy even the greatest pleasures on earth.

If the surrender described in the previous verse had been complete, Arjuna should have been silent about his grief from that moment. But he expresses it even after declaring that he has surrendered. This shows that even the sense of surrender cannot immediately free him. It can happen that even the ocean fails to subdue a volcanic eruption. Nothing in the outer world can dispel the grief in Arjuna's mind, for he is overtaken by a suspension so profound that it renders him incapable of action.

Study of this verse brings out a fundamental principle of spiritual life. The true state of surrender does not leave one suffering; one casts off all difficulties, and the relief brings one to silence.

This and the previous four verses summarize the basic problems of life that Arjuna put before the Lord in verses 28 to 46 of Chapter I.

VERSE 9

संजय उवाच
एवमुक्त्वा हृषीकेशं गुडाकेशः परंतपः
न योत्स्य इति गोविन्दमुक्त्वा तूष्णीं बभूव ह

Sanjaya uvācha
Evam uktwā Hṛishīkeshaṁ Gudākeshaḥ paraṁtapaḥ
na yotsya iti Govindam uktwā tūshṇīṁ babhūva ha

Sanjaya said:
Gudākesha, oppressor of the foe, having spoken thus
to Hṛishīkesha, said to Govinda (Lord Kṛishṇa):
'I will not fight' and fell silent.

Arjuna has been called 'Gudākesha' (the conqueror of sleep) and 'oppressor of the foe'. These expressions indicate that at this point, when Arjuna says: 'I will not fight', he is free from dullness and his strength is not failing him.

The use of 'Hṛishīkesha' or 'Govinda', the lord and master of the senses, expresses Lord Kṛishṇa's position in relation to Arjuna. With all his strength and alertness of mind, Arjuna stands as a child before the greatness of Lord Kṛishṇa. His words: 'I will not fight', are like the words of a child who says: 'I will not go there', and yet looks to his father to find out his intentions. Once Arjuna has surrendered[6] himself at the feet of the Lord, he becomes as a child before Him.

Arjuna is justified in saying that he will not fight, because he has surrendered himself. Arjuna is a warrior; when he says he has surrendered, he means it and begins to behave accordingly. Now his heart, body, and mind all belong to Lord Kṛishṇa; therefore he cannot fight or do anything unless he receives orders. He knows that the problem must be expressed clearly, and then the solution will come easily. Arjuna has had his say; now Lord Kṛishṇa will speak.

6 See verse 7.

VERSE 10

तमुवाच हृषीकेशः प्रहसन्निव भारत
सेनयोरुभयोर्मध्ये विषीदन्तमिदं वचः

Tam uvācha Hṛishīkeshaḥ prahasann iva Bhārata
senayor ubhayor madhye vishīdantam idaṁ vachaḥ

To him, O Bhārata (Dhṛitarāshtra), sorrowing in the midst of the two armies, Hṛishīkesha smilingly spoke these words:

'Hṛishīkesha smilingly spoke': this expression is used to indicate that lifting Arjuna out of his state of silence and hesitancy and releasing him from the benumbed condition of the senses was not a big task for one who is the Lord of the senses. 'Smilingly' may also be understood as indicating the technique of enlightening a disciple by encouraging him at the very start.

The disheartened seeker becomes encouraged by the first sign of the master's smile, which shows him without a word that his problems are neither so serious as he thinks nor so difficult as to be insurmountable. The contrast brought out is significant. It shows Arjuna in despair, while Lord Kṛishṇa smiles in His usual divine, playful, blissful mood. The two aspects of existence are represented here: on the one hand, unmanifested absolute Bliss Consciousness, symbolized by Lord Kṛishṇa; and on the other, the height of human consciousness represented by Arjuna. The darkness is on the point of being illumined by the celestial light; the silence of Arjuna is about to be broken and made melodious by the celestial song, as his grief is transformed into the smile of the Lord.

The word 'smilingly' also refers to the unshakeable nature of Lord Kṛishṇa. Anyone but the Lord would have been overwhelmed to find that, with the two great armies drawn up ready to fight, the hero on his side was sinking into despair.

In the following verse Lord Kṛishṇa begins his glorious discourse. But it should be noted again[7] that He does not enter

7 See verse 2, commentary.

into Arjuna's arguments; He dismisses them all with the first word that He speaks.

VERSE 11

श्रीभगवानुवाच
अशोच्यानन्वशोचस्त्वं प्रज्ञावादांश्च भाषसे
गतासूनगतासूंश्च नानुशोचन्ति पण्डिताः

Shrī Bhagavān uvācha
Ashochyān anvashochas twaṁ pragyāvādāṁsh cha bhāshase
gatāsūn agatāsūṁsh cha nānushochanti paṇḍitāḥ

The Blessed Lord said:
You grieve for those for whom there should be no grief, yet speak as do the wise. Wise men grieve neither for the dead nor for the living.

The Lord tells Arjuna that he speaks in the language of the wise, and in saying this He also shows him how wise men think. The first mark of such men is that they do not grieve over anything, for they know that everything is in its essence everlasting. From the point of view of real existence, Bhīshma and Droṇa and all those for whom Arjuna is concerned have infinite life. It is wrong for Arjuna to grieve for them. Can there be grief in the mind of a wise man either for the living or for the dead? He does not grieve over the past, nor can anything in the present make him unhappy, for he is established in Truth, the unchangeable Reality.

This verse reveals the wisdom of the master: he makes the aspirant aware of his own position and at the same time makes clear to him his goal. Lord Kṛishṇa makes Arjuna see his present state of mind, in which he is grieving over nothing, and his goal, the state of wisdom, in which he would not grieve over anything.

This also illustrates a principle of the relationship between master and pupil: the master is only concerned with taking the disciple from his present state to the goal. The Lord does not bring Himself into the picture here; He only describes Arjuna's present position and the state to which He wishes to lead him. He has only hinted at the goal but has made Arjuna clearly aware of his condition, His purpose being to bring Arjuna to that complete dependence which will enable him to receive His skilful guidance to the fullest advantage. The disciple is not asked to be alert and listen, yet this effect is produced in his mind at the beginning of the discourse by making him aware of his position.

This verse begins the first part of Lord Kṛishṇa's discourse, which is known as 'Sāṁkhya'. From here to verse 38, Lord Kṛishṇa gives Arjuna this wisdom of full life, the wisdom of both the absolute and the relative aspects of existence, which He calls Sāṁkhya.

A close study suggests that the questions raised by Arjuna in five verses[8] are answered by the five expressions contained in this verse:

1. You grieve for those for whom there should be no grief.
2. Yet speak as do the wise.
3. Neither for the living nor for the dead.
4. Grieve not.
5. Wise men.

VERSE 12

न त्वेवाहं जातु नासं न त्वं नेमे जनाधिपाः
न चैव न भविष्यामः सर्वे वयमतः परम्

Na twevāhaṁ jātu nāsaṁ na twaṁ neme janādhipāḥ
na chaiva na bhavishyāmaḥ sarve vayam ataḥ param

There never was a time when I was not, nor you, nor these rulers of men. Nor will there ever be a time when all of us shall cease to be.

8 II, 4–8. These verses, in turn, contain in essence all the questions Arjuna had put in I, 28–46.

Here the Lord presents to Arjuna the permanent nature of the inner man, the inner Reality of individual life. The nature of this spirit in man is imperishable. Despite the continual change of bodies in the past, present, and future, it ever remains the same. The permanent nature of the inner aspect of life, the Self, is an abstract conception and so, in order to make it as concrete as possible, the Lord speaks about it in terms of Himself, Arjuna, and those present. This illustrates an important aspect of teaching: abstract theories are explained by concrete illustrations.

The Lord says we shall all continue to exist even after the death of these bodies, for the Self is eternal — life continues to be, it is everlasting. Here follows an illustration which illumines the wisdom of Sāṁkhya.

VERSE 13

देहिनोऽस्मिन्यथा देहे कौमारं यौवनं जरा
तथा देहान्तरप्राप्तिर्धीरस्तत्र न मुह्यति

Dehino 'smin yathā dehe kaumāraṁ yauvanaṁ jarā
tathā dehāntaraprāptir dhīras tatra na muhyati

As the dweller in this body passes into childhood, youth,
and age, so also does he pass into another body.
This does not bewilder the wise.

The wise are not taken aback by changes of the body; the death of the body is like the change that takes place when children become grown-up, or when the young become old. Phenomenal changes continue to take place, while the never-changing Reality of life, the dweller in the body, remains ever the same.

It is not possible for a man who knows this to feel great concern about the death of the body, but even with this knowledge he still feels heat and cold, pleasure and pain. How this situation should be met is explained in the next verse.

These verses express the vital content of the wisdom of Sāṁkhya.

VERSE 14

मात्रास्पर्शास्तु कौन्तेय शीतोष्णसुखदुःखदाः
आगमापायिनोऽनित्यास्तांस्तितिक्षस्व भारत

Mātrāsparshās tu Kaunteya shītoshṇasukhaduḥkhadāḥ
āgamāpāyino 'nityās tāṁs titikshaswa Bhārata

Contacts (of the senses) with their objects, O son of Kuntī,
give rise to (the experience of) cold and heat, pleasure and pain.
Transient, they come and go. Bear them patiently, O Bhārata!

Firmly established in the understanding of the unchangeable, the wise are never affected by the changing conditions of the body during life or after death. The experience of the objects of the senses and their effects, the experience of pleasure and pain, are just phenomena which come and go. Here the Lord wants to show Arjuna that things which are not of a permanent nature should not weigh heavily. It is as if He were saying: Take it lightly, for things will naturally go in the same way in which they came. Your life should be based on something which is of lasting nature, Arjuna! Do not give importance to the consideration of the fleeting and impermanent phases of life. Rise to the understanding that the permanent Reality of existence will continue to be, while that which is temporary will go on changing. So take life as it comes. This alone befits you, for you are called Bhārata, the descendant of the great Bharata, who was established in the light, the Reality of life.

The result of remaining even-minded in pleasure and pain is shown in the following verse.

VERSE 15

यं हि न व्यथयन्त्येते पुरुषं पुरुषर्षभ
समदुःखसुखं धीरं सोऽमृतत्वाय कल्पते

Yaṁ hi na vyathayantyete purushaṁ Purusharshabha
samaduḥkhasukhaṁ dhīraṁ so 'mṛitatwāya kalpate

That man indeed whom these (contacts) do not disturb,
who is even-minded in pleasure and pain, steadfast,
he is fit for immortality, O best of men!

The Lord emphasizes to Arjuna that, once a man has become established in the understanding of the permanent Reality of life as explained in verse 13, his mind rises above the influence of pleasure and pain. Such an unshakeable man passes beyond the influence of death and lives in the permanent phase of life; he attains eternal life. It is the Lord's purpose that Arjuna shall gain this state where he will be above all considerations in the relative field, even death, and all problems of life and death.

The unlimited state of the ocean is not affected either by the inflow of rivers or the process of evaporation. In the same way, a man established in the understanding of the unlimited abundance of absolute existence is naturally free from influence of the relative order. This is what gives him the status of immortal life.

At the present time it is generally found that people try to make a mood of equanimity in pleasure and pain, in loss and gain — they try to create a mood of equable behaviour and unaffectedness while engaged in the diverse activities of the world. But trying to make a mood on the basis of understanding is simply hypocrisy. Many seekers become trapped in such an attitude. This will become clearer as we proceed.

The understanding does not become ripe as a result of mood-making. It is only necessary to understand the meaning of this and the previous three verses once, in order to live the Reality of the relationship between the inner eternal life and the outer ever-changing phases of existence. When once a man knows that he is king and the state belongs to him, he immediately begins to make use of his relationship with the state, begins to behave as a king. He is not required to cultivate kingship by practice and by constant thought about his position, just as a child is not required to remember always that his mother is his mother. He just knows it once and lives the relationship at all times. So simple is the path of understanding which results in freedom from bondage.

The whole truth of life is that there is nothing substantial to bind the never-changing to the ever-changing sphere of life. And nothing to keep them bound together. It is only ignorance of the natural state of freedom existing between these spheres that results in binding them together. This ignorance, and the bondage born of it, keep life in motion — the inner aspect remaining never-changing and the outer ever-changing. The outer ever-changing aspect continues eternally by virtue of the inner. Thus life flows onward in the natural state of eternal freedom — on the basis of ignorance!

The knowledge contained in these verses — the wisdom of Sāṁkhya — cuts asunder the bonds of ignorance and allows life to be in its natural state of eternal freedom.

The following verses further expound this wisdom.

Verse 16

नासतो विद्यते भावो नाभावो विद्यते सत:
उभयोरपि दृष्टोऽन्तस्त्वनयोस्तत्त्वदर्शिभि:

Nāsato vidyate bhāvo nābhāvo vidyate sataḥ
ubhayor api dṛishto 'ntas twanayos tattwadarshibhiḥ

The unreal has no being; the real never ceases to be.
The final truth about them both has thus been perceived
by the seers of ultimate Reality.

The indestructibility of human essence is explained here. Ultimate Reality has been defined as that which never changes. Opposed to it is the unreal, which is ever-changing; for clearly that which always changes has no substance, no real existence.

Here in this verse the Lord brings Arjuna to see the Reality at the basis of the multiplicity of creation. This is the next step, following logically upon that of the previous verse. Here the seer of Truth perceives clearly the difference between the permanent, never-changing absolute state of life and its ever-changing states of diversified phenomenal existence. It is this which gives him that stability and heightened state of consciousness by which he rises above the binding influence of activity in the phenomenal world.

Arjuna is being led step by step towards the vision of a realized man.

VERSE 17

अविनाशि तु तद्विद्धि येन सर्वमिदं ततम्
विनाशमव्ययस्यास्य न कश्चित्कर्तुमर्हति

Avināshi tu tad viddhi yena sarvam idaṁ tatam
vināsham avyayasyāsya na kashchit kartum arhati

Know That to be indeed indestructible by which all this is pervaded. None can work the destruction of this immutable Being.

The Lord presents to Arjuna the indestructibility of the inner Reality, the Being of the phenomenal objective world, which pervades everything.

It may be made clear here that the omnipresent Being and the spirit within man are not two different entities. They are found to be different because of the different individual nervous systems. As the same sun appears as different when shining on different media, such as water and oil, so the same omnipresent Being, shining through different nervous systems, appears as different and forms the spirit, the subjective aspect of man's personality. When the nervous system is pure, Being reflects more and the spirit is more powerful, the mind more effective. When the nervous system is at its purest, then Being reflects in all its fullness, and the inner individuality of the spirit gains the level of unlimited eternal Being. Thus it is clear that in its essential nature the spirit is undying and omnipresent. This explains the universality of individuality.

In the previous verses, step by step, and each a step of profound wisdom, the everlasting nature of the spirit was brought home to Arjuna. In this verse its indestructible nature is stressed. In the verses which follow, the impermanence of phenomenal life will be emphasized and with it the principle that the phenomenal world is just the manifested phase of eternal unmanifested Being. The conclusion is that, from both points of view — that of the permanence of Being and that of the impermanent level of life — Arjuna's duty is not to worry about anything, but to rise up and do what he has to do.

VERSE 18

अन्तवन्त इमे देहा नित्यस्योक्ताः शरीरिणः
अनाशिनोऽप्रमेयस्य तस्माद्युध्यस्व भारत

Antavanta ime dehā nityasyoktāḥ sharīriṇaḥ
anāshino 'prameyasya tasmād yudhyaswa Bhārata

These bodies are known to have an end; the
dweller in the body is eternal, imperishable, infinite.
Therefore, O Bhārata, fight!

It is obvious that at every moment the body is changing. The body of a child is not the body of a youth; and the body of a youth is not the body of an old man. So if death is inevitably going on, even during what is said to be life, nothing new seems to happen when one body dies and another body is taken. There is no point therefore in lamenting the death of the body — and even less in lamenting it in anticipation.

'Dweller in the body': this verse brings out a distinction between the body and the spirit that dwells within it. There is no aim here of classifying the different aspects of the spirit within, but only of drawing a line between the unchangeable inner content of life and the destructible nature of the outer body.

It can, however, be explained that the inner spirit may be understood in two ways: first, as the ego, together with the mind and senses, which constitutes the doer and the experiencer, the enjoyer and the sufferer; secondly, as the 'dweller in the body', which is the individual aspect of cosmic existence, of eternal Being, and which is known in Sanskrit terminology as *Jīva*.

Jīva, then, is individualized cosmic existence; it is the individual spirit within the body. With its limitations removed, *Jīva* is *Ātmā*, transcendent Being.

When the individuality of the *Jīva* and the universality of the transcendent Self, the *Ātmā*, are united and found together on one level of life, then there is *Brahman*, the all-embracing cosmic life.

As the individual *Jīva* in its essence is *Ātmā*,[9] it is here called 'eternal, imperishable, infinite'.

VERSE 19

य एनं वेत्ति हन्तारं यश्चैनं मन्यते हतम्
उभौ तौ न विजानीतो नायं हन्ति न हन्यते

Ya enaṁ vetti hantāraṁ yash chainaṁ manyate hatam
ubhau tau na vijānīto nāyaṁ hanti na hanyate

He who understands him to be the slayer, and he who
takes him to be the slain, both fail to perceive the truth.
He neither slays nor is slain.

It has been made clear that the self, or spirit, in its essential nature, knows no change or variation, is free from any attributes, is neither the doer nor the doing. All attributes belong to the relative, the manifested field of life; therefore the spirit cannot be regarded as either the subject or the object of any action. The activity assumed by an ignorant man to belong to himself — to the subjective personality that he calls himself — does not belong to his real Self, for this, in its essential nature, is beyond activity. The Self, in its real nature, is only the silent witness of everything. That is why the Lord says: 'He who understands him to be the

9 See verse 17, commentary.

slayer, and he who takes him to be the slain, both fail to perceive the truth.'

VERSE 20

न जायते म्रियते वा कदाचि-
न्नायं भूत्वा भविता वा न भूयः
अजो नित्यः शाश्वतोऽयं पुराणो
न हन्यते हन्यमाने शरीरे

Na jāyate mriyate vā kadāchin
nāyaṁ bhūtwā bhavitā vā na bhūyaḥ
ajo nityaḥ shāshwato 'yaṁ purāṇo
na hanyate hanyamāne sharīre

He is never born, nor does he ever die; nor once having been, does he cease to be. Unborn, eternal, everlasting, ancient, he is not slain when the body is slain.

The eternal unmanifested absolute nature of the spirit, or self, is ever unaffected by happenings in the relative field. It is ever the same, beyond the limits of time, space, and causation. Without beginning or end, it knows no birth or death. Whether in this or that body, the Self continues to be. The immutable eternal life remains through the ever-changing phases of the bodies which it takes.

VERSE 21

वेदाविनाशिनं नित्यं य एनमजमव्ययम्
कथं स पुरुषः पार्थ कं घातयति हन्ति कम्

Vedāvināshinaṁ nityaṁ ya enam ajam avyayam
kathaṁ sa purushaḥ Pārtha kaṁ ghātayati hanti kam

One who knows him to be indestructible, everlasting, unborn, undying, how can that man, O Pārtha, slay or cause anyone to slay?

In these verses Lord Kṛishṇa provides the intellectual conception of that state to which He wants Arjuna to rise — the state where he will be established in his real, eternal Self. Once established in It, he will attain to the Reality of existence and thus rise above the influence of the action of fighting and, indeed, of all actions in life. For action is in the field of ever-changing existence, and his consciousness will be established in the changeless existence of Being. Therefore he will quite naturally be above the influence of action.

The discourse is presented with marvellous skill. Since the Lord wants to give Arjuna the intellectual conception of Reality, not only does He continue to describe that which has no attributes, but He also questions Arjuna to attract his attention and to awaken his wits so that the description will be more clearly understood. It is obvious, the Lord tells him, that anyone who knows the Reality of life as never-changing eternal Being would not — how could he? — attribute to It anything of the perishable order.

VERSE 22

वासांसि जीर्णानि यथा विहाय
नवानि गृह्णाति नरोऽपराणि
तथा शरीराणि विहाय जीर्णा-
न्यन्यानि संयाति नवानि देही

Vāsāṁsi jīrṇāni yathā vihāya
navāni gṛihṇāti naro 'parāṇi
tathā sharīrāṇi vihāya jīrṇā-
nyanyāni saṃyāti navāni dehī

As a man casting off worn-out garments takes other new ones, so the dweller in the body casting off worn-out bodies takes others that are new.

This is an illustration to make clear the idea contained in the previous verse. It presents a picture of the unchanging nature of the dweller in the body, the spirit or *Jīva*, which is enlarged upon in the following verse.

VERSE 23

नैनं छिन्दन्ति शस्त्राणि नैनं दहति पावकः
न चैनं क्लेदयन्त्यापो न शोषयति मारुतः

Nainaṁ chhindanti shastrāṇi nainaṁ dahati pāvakaḥ
na chainaṁ kledayantyāpo na shoshayati mārutaḥ

Weapons cannot cleave him, nor fire burn him;
water cannot wet him, nor wind dry him away.

The intention here is to bring home to Arjuna the immortality, the never-changing nature of the self, and to make him see clearly that nothing can possibly affect it in any way. One thing was deep-rooted in Arjuna's mind: the feeling that his sharp arrows would pierce and mutilate the bodies of those he held dear and slay them. That is why the Lord begins by making him understand that their existence would not, in the real sense, be destroyed by his weapons. Reality is one, omnipresent, devoid of any duality, without components — that is why It cannot be slain. The body is composed of different parts — that is why it can be slain.

To make the idea still clearer, the Lord explains that even the elements of air, water, and fire, which are much more refined and powerful than Arjuna's weapons, are unable to disturb the Self. The Lord mentions weapons, fire, air, and water as symbolic of the entire creation. His aim is to show Arjuna that the Self, being transcendental, remains ever untouched by anything in this relative field. This idea is developed in the verses that follow, so as to leave Arjuna in no doubt regarding the permanent nature of the self.

VERSE 24

अच्छेद्योऽयमदाह्योऽयमक्लेद्योऽशोष्य एव च
नित्यः सर्वगतः स्थाणुरचलोऽयं सनातनः

Achchhedyo 'yamadāhyo 'yam akledyo 'shoshya eva cha
nityaḥ sarvagataḥ sthāṇur achalo 'yaṁ sanātanaḥ

He is uncleavable; He cannot be burned; He cannot be wetted, nor yet can He be dried. He is eternal, all-pervading, stable, immovable, ever the same.

The teacher may start, as in this verse, by explaining Reality in terms of the negation of common experience. When the mind of the pupil begins to rise to something abstract, beyond the sphere of his present experience, he is then told of what may be called the positive attributes of Reality. It is true that absolute Reality is without any attribute, but even so, expressions have to be used to convey some sense of It.

Here the Lord uses both means of enlightenment, negation and affirmation, beautifully in one stroke. The teacher has to be alert enough not to miss a single reaction of the pupil's mind to every word he speaks. Only by striking at the right moment are the desired results achieved.

The sequence of words is important: being eternal, Reality is all-pervading; being all-pervading, It is stable; being stable, It is immovable; and being immovable, It is ever the same.

VERSE 25

अव्यक्तोऽयमचिन्त्योऽयमविकार्योऽयमुच्यते
तस्मादेवं विदित्वैनं नानुशोचितुमर्हसि

Avyakto 'yam achintyo 'yam avikāryo 'yam uchyate
tasmād evaṁ viditwainaṁ nānushochitum arhasi

He is declared to be unmanifest, unthinkable, unchangeable; therefore knowing Him as such you should not grieve.

It was essential for Lord Kṛishṇa to impart to Arjuna a vivid intellectual conception of the soul, the real Self, transcendent and without attributes, and He had to do this when Arjuna's mind was 'full of sorrow'. It was therefore all the more necessary to present the conception of the unknowable through attributes of the already known world.

Arjuna had to be given this clear intellectual conception of Reality in order to prepare him for the state of enlightenment. He could not be given the direct vision but had to be shown the intellectual conception first and then be led to experience step by step. Otherwise Arjuna could not have understood that behind obvious phenomenal existence there lies eternal Being, and that he himself is That, and everything is That.

VERSE 26

अथ चैनं नित्यजातं नित्यं वा मन्यसे मृतम्
तथापि त्वं महाबाहो नैवं शोचितुमर्हसि

Atha chainaṁ nityajātaṁ nityaṁ vā manyase mṛitam
tathāpi twaṁ Mahābāho nainaṁ shochitum arhasi

Even if you think of him as constantly taking birth and constantly dying, even then, O mighty-armed, you should not grieve like this.

Up to this stage in the dialogue, the Lord has explained life from the viewpoint of the indestructibility of the self. In this verse He begins on a different argument.

Even if Arjuna remains unconvinced of the immortality of the dweller in the body, this does not justify his grieving; even if the dweller in the body is seen as repeatedly dying with the death of the body and repeatedly being born with the birth of the body, Arjuna still has no need to grieve.

So perfect is the Lord's logic that one argument is given and a statement established, and then, even when quite contrary reasoning is applied, the same conclusion is reached. This is the glory that belongs to the teaching of the Absolute: It is found to be the same whatever one's angle of vision. Only the Absolute can be known in this manner.

While this is the glory of the Absolute, it is also the glory of the master's mind that can deduce the same conclusion from two diametrically opposed lines of reasoning. If Arjuna is not convinced by one line of reasoning, the Lord does not leave him to his fate but tries to convince him through another. This is the situation between Arjuna and the Lord that was created by his surrender[10] at His feet.

VERSE 27

जातस्य हि ध्रुवो मृत्युर्ध्रुवं जन्म मृतस्य च
तस्मादपरिहार्येऽर्थे न त्वं शोचितुमर्हसि

Jātasya hi dhruvo mṛityur dhruvaṁ janma mṛitasya cha
tasmād aparihārye 'rthe na twaṁ shochitum arhasi

Certain indeed is death for the born and certain is birth for the dead; therefore over the inevitable you should not grieve.

Change is inevitable in the field of relative existence; it is going on even in the present, as it was in the past and will be in the future. Therefore birth and death are natural events about which one should not feel much concern.

The phenomenon of birth and death is the expression of the eternal process of evolution, which in its turn expresses the purpose of creation. Life evolves with a view to the realization of perfection. Development through change is the natural course of this cosmic process. Every change is significant, for it provides a step to perfection. The manner in which change takes place is also in line with the cosmic purpose of evolution, for it too is governed by the eternal laws of cause and effect. This is how, through birth and death, the plan of life finds its fulfilment.

Man has freedom of action; thereby he can adopt any channel, good or bad, through which he wants the course of his life to flow. This is in his hands. But change is inevitable, and it is for

10 See verse 7.

the sake of life that this is so: 'therefore over the inevitable you should not grieve'. On the contrary, change should be welcomed for it opens new vistas of life towards fulfilment.

VERSE 28

अव्यक्तादीनि भूतानि व्यक्तमध्यानि भारत
अव्यक्त निधनान्येव तत्र का परिदेवना

Avyaktādīni bhūtāni vyaktamadhyāni Bhārata
avyaktanidhanānyeva tatra kā paridevanā

Creatures are unmanifest in the beginning, manifest
in the middle state, and unmanifest again at the end,
O Bhārata! What grief is there in this?

Here again, and from yet another angle, the same conclusion is reached: the phenomenal presents the manifested state of life, while Being is of unmanifested transcendental nature.

According to the findings of modern physics, all matter has only phenomenal existence and is in reality formless energy. Both in its previous state and in its present obvious form, matter is nothing but pure energy, and on dissolution of the present form it will remain the same energy. Similarly, the present phenomenal phase of existence is seen to have no permanent significance, and it is this that the Lord is impressing upon Arjuna.

VERSE 29

आश्चर्यवत्पश्यति कश्चिदेनम्
आश्चर्यवद्वदति तथैव चान्यः
आश्चर्यवच्चैनमन्यः शृणोति
श्रुत्वाप्येनं वेद न चैव कश्चित्

Āshcharyavat pashyati kashchid enam
āshcharyavad vadati tathaiva chānyaḥ
āshcharyavach chainam anyaḥ shriṇoti
shrutwāpyenaṁ veda na chaiva kashchit

One sees him as a wonder, another likewise speaks of him as a wonder, and as a wonder another hears of him. Yet even on (seeing, speaking, and hearing) some do not understand him.

Because the self is of unmanifested nature, and because man's life is always in the field of the manifested, it is not to be wondered at if some people hear about it with great surprise and others are not able to understand it at all. The purpose of this verse is simply to give a picture of the dissimilar nature of the ephemeral and eternal aspects of life. Although Arjuna is obviously unfamiliar with eternal Reality, it is not the Lord's aim to stress the difficulty of understanding It. It is a wonder to some because, although omnipresent, It is found as the individual self, and although eternal, It is found dying and being born. That is why it is difficult to comprehend Its full nature by mere intellectual process. It needs a direct experience for the abstract Reality to be properly understood.

There is yet another implication. Up to this verse, the Lord has been trying in different ways to make Arjuna understand that he should not grieve. But he is not free from grief, and therefore, as an additional step in the task of enlightening him, the Lord points out that his response to what he has heard is a feeling of strangeness. In order to encourage him, the Lord seems to be saying that this feeling of strangeness does not matter, for it is natural with regard to knowledge of eternal life. Many marvel at it and find it a wonder.

One can take a different point of view and conclude that the Lord means to show that Reality is difficult to attain, for many having heard of It and spoken about It are not able to understand It. Nevertheless it is wiser to hold that the purpose of the verse is not to convince Arjuna of the difficulty of attainment, but to give him hope that, although many find it difficult, it is going to prove easy for him.

This verse speaks of eternal Reality, which is strange to many in many different ways, because everyone looks at It from his own level of consciousness. For this reason, many who seek It find It impossible to attain on the level of the senses and the intellect, since these are concerned only with the temporary, phenomenal phases of life.

The next verse brings to an end the intellectual description of the two aspects of life, the ever-changing and the never-changing.

VERSE 30

देही नित्यमवध्योऽयं देहे सर्वस्य भारत
तस्मात्सर्वाणि भूतानि न त्वं शोचितुमर्हसि

Dehī nityam avadhyo 'yaṁ dehe sarvasya Bhārata
tasmāt sarvāṇi bhūtāni na twaṁ shochitum arhasi

He who dwells in the body of everyone is eternal
and invulnerable, O Bhārata; therefore you should
not grieve for any creature whatsoever.

This is the conclusion of all that has been said by the Lord from the eleventh verse onwards. Every creature is on the path to perfection. Through births and deaths of bodies, everyone is progressing towards fulfilment. No one should grieve over the death of another. Arjuna, having acquired understanding of the permanent nature of the dweller in the body and the impermanence of the body, should respond to the call of duty, for that alone will help his own evolution and that of others.

The following verse begins the argument on the level of duty.

This is to deepen the understanding of life after the absolute and relative aspects of existence have been made clear.

VERSE 31

स्वधर्ममपि चावेक्ष्य न विकम्पितुमर्हसि
धर्म्याद्धि युद्धाच्छ्रेयोऽन्यत्क्षत्रियस्य न विद्यते

Swadharmam api chāvekshya na vikampitum arhasi
dharmyād dhi yuddhāch chhreyo 'nyat kshatriyasya na vidyate

Even if you consider your own Dharma you should not waver, for there is nothing better for a Kshatriya than a battle in accord with Dharma.

The event of war is a natural phenomenon. It is a process of restoring the balance between the negative and positive forces of Nature. To rise to the call of a war to establish righteousness is to respond to the cosmic purpose, the Will of God. To live and die to maintain law and order in society, thereby remaining a faithful instrument in the hand of God, is the privilege of a man born in a *Kshatriya* family.

The Lord's purpose is to convince Arjuna that, from the point of view of his duty, the only worthwhile course is to shake off his reluctance to fight and face up to the action for which he is born. Having explained to him in the previous verse that from the viewpoint of life's eternal existence he need not grieve either for the living or for the dead, He wants to bring home to Arjuna that to him, born a *Kshatriya*, fighting is natural; it is his normal duty in life. To do 'battle in accord with *Dharma*' and establish righteousness for the good of the world is the most glorious and justifiable way of fulfilling the life of a *Kshatriya*, who is born to protect *Dharma* at any cost.

Dharma[11] maintains the stream of evolution in life. The *Kshatriya* who does not accept a just fight wavers from this natural stream of evolution.

11 See I, 1, commentary.

VERSE 32

यदृच्छया चोपपन्नं स्वर्गद्वारमपावृतम्
सुखिनः क्षत्रियाः पार्थ लभन्ते युद्धमीदृशम्

Yadṛichchhayā chopapannaṁ swargadwāram apāvṛitam
sukhinaḥ kshatriyāḥ Pārtha labhante yuddham īdṛisham

Happy are the Kshatriyas, O Pārtha, who find, unsought,
such a battle — an open door to heaven.

'Open door to heaven': by following his *Dharma*, a *Kshatriya* serves to uphold law and order in society and maintains the stream of his own evolution. If he dies while fighting in this cause, he is a hero of cosmic life and gains the highest happiness in heaven.

This verse makes a general statement proclaiming the good fortune of a *Kshatriya* who gains an opportunity for such a battle. At the same time, by calling him 'Pārtha', the son of Pṛithā, Lord Kṛishṇa reminds Arjuna that he is a *Kshatriya*.

When a *Kshatriya* has a chance of battle he feels happy, because he gains whether he wins or loses:[12] victorious, he achieves glory on earth; dying in battle, he gains heaven.

What will happen if Arjuna does not participate in the battle?

VERSE 33

अथ चेत्त्वमिमं धर्म्यं संग्रामं न करिष्यसि
ततः स्वधर्मं कीर्तिं च हित्वा पापमवाप्स्यसि

Atha chet twam imaṁ dharmyaṁ saṁgrāmaṁ na karishyasi
tataḥ swadharmaṁ kīrtiṁ cha hitwā pāpam avāpsyasi

Now, if you do not engage in this battle, which is in accord
with Dharma, then casting away your own Dharma and
good fame, you will incur sin.

'Casting away your own *Dharma*' means falling out of the path

12 See verse 37.

of evolution, and that in itself is a positive sin.

'Sin' is that through which a man strays from the path of evolution. It results in suffering.

Having reminded Arjuna of his great good fortune in being given this opportunity for battle, the Lord immediately impresses upon him the danger of not accepting it. To abstain from fighting, and so neglect his *Dharma*, would bring loss of fame and would plainly be sinful.

Dharma and fame are placed together in this verse. The connection between them is clarified in the commentary on the following verse.

In the 31st verse the Lord began the argument on the basis of duty. Having enlightened Arjuna about his duty, his *Dharma*, which maintains the natural stream of evolution, He now wants to make clear also the nature of duty from the level of social consideration.

It may be mentioned that the moral code of conduct in any society has *Dharma* at its basis, whether or not the people in that society are aware of the inner workings of Nature guided by the invincible force of *Dharma*. The fundamentals of social behaviour in every society on earth are based on this principle which governs the laws of evolution. Therefore the Lord wants to analyse the nature of duty in the light of its influence on society. How others think of one's life, how others are affected by one's actions, and how others talk about one are here the main concern. The word 'fame' covers all these points.

The following three verses are devoted to this consideration, which will complete the wisdom of Sāṁkhya.

VERSE 34

अकीर्तिं चापि भूतानि कथयिष्यन्ति तेऽव्ययाम्
संभावितस्य चाकीर्तिर्मरणादतिरिच्यते

Akīrtiṁ chāpi bhūtāni kathayishyanti te 'vyayām
saṁbhāvitasya chākīrtir maraṇād atirichyate

Moreover men will ever tell of your disgrace, and to a man of honour ill fame is worse than death.

Those who are esteemed are they who, living for themselves, live for others and, dying, die for others. Their lives are justified in the degree to which others recognize them. Their happiness in life is in proportion to the goodwill accorded to them. Therefore if those who have enjoyed goodwill and fame in society lose it, they suffer shame and misery, which is worse than death. Loss of renown for a once famous man is more than death to him. Arjuna was the most famous archer of his time; that is why Lord Kṛishṇa makes this telling point about the nature of a famous man.

The underlying principle of good fame in society is that when a man constantly does good he becomes a centre of harmonious vibrations which, enjoyed by the people around him, naturally create warmth and love in their hearts. That is why he is described in glowing terms by all. In this way the good fame of a man is the criterion of his goodness, and ill fame the criterion of his badness. No one who is good could possibly acquire ill fame. It is the vibrations spreading from a man's actions that induce people to speak well of him or otherwise. The Lord particularly wants to bring home this truth to Arjuna.

The way to uplift a man is first to remind him of the glorious aspects of his character and so gain a sympathetic response. The second step is to point out at once some delicate feature in the situation. The Lord does this in the next verse by saying that the brave will attribute cowardice to Arjuna. A close study of this verse in relation to preceding and subsequent verses will make the point clear.

The Lord lays stress on the importance of fame, not for the sake of fame itself but to call Arjuna's attention to a principle of life: if he behaves in a way that will bring him ill fame, he will become a centre of something unrighteous, and this will impair his personal evolution. It is primarily the principle of personal evolution that is the subject of this consideration of life from the point of view of Sāṁkhya.

VERSE 35

भयाद्रणादुपरतं मंस्यन्ते त्वां महारथाः
येषां च त्वं बहुमतो भूत्वा यास्यसि लाघवम्

Bhayād raṇād uparataṁ maṁsyante twāṁ mahārathāḥ
yeshāṁ cha twaṁ bahumato bhūtwā yāsyasi lāghavam

The great warriors will think you fled from battle out of fear, and they who held you in esteem will belittle you.

The Lord now speaks to Arjuna of the great humiliation which awaits him if he does not fight. For a man of honour and repute this is a very telling point. Arjuna is being reminded of the different implications of ill fame. Lord Kṛishṇa is helping him to break through the state of suspension by raising points that will touch his heart and mind and induce him to fight.

VERSE 36

अवाच्यवादांश्च बहून्वदिष्यन्ति तवाहिताः
निन्दन्तस्तव सामर्थ्यं ततो दुःखतरं नु किम्

Avāchyavādāṁsh cha bahūn vadishyanti tavāhitāḥ
nindantas tava sāmarthyaṁ tato duḥkhataraṁ nu kim

Your enemies will speak many ill words of you and will deride your strength. What greater pain than this!

The Lord shows Arjuna exactly how he will be put to shame in the eyes of the world.[13]

Having demonstrated in the previous verses the validity of fighting from the point of view of its social implications, and having made it quite clear in the present verse that pain awaits him if he does not fight, the Lord, in the following verse, shows Arjuna the rewards that fighting will bring him both in this life and hereafter.

13 See verse 34, commentary.

VERSE 37

हतो वा प्राप्स्यसि स्वर्गं जित्वा वा भोक्ष्यसे महीम्
तस्मादुत्तिष्ठ कौन्तेय युद्धाय कृतनिश्चयः

Hato vā prāpsyasi swargaṁ jitwā vā bhokshyase mahīm
tasmād uttishtha Kaunteya yuddhāya kṛitanishchayaḥ

Slain, you will reach heaven; victorious, you will enjoy the earth.
Therefore, O son of Kuntī, stand up, resolved to fight!

This verse considers the performance of duty from the point of view of gain.

The Lord says to Arjuna: You should realize that, whether you die on the battlefield or whether you survive, you stand to gain,[14] because fighting is in accordance with the natural course of your evolution. And if you are established on that course, then you are automatically on the path of increasing fortune in this life and hereafter. Therefore without losing more time, come, make up your mind to fight.

This places the teaching of Sāṁkhya on the most practical level of life. It is not right to associate this teaching with the life of the recluse only.

VERSE 38

सुखदुःखे समे कृत्वा लाभालाभौ जयाजयौ
ततो युद्धाय युज्यस्व नैवं पापमवाप्स्यसि

Sukhaduḥkhe same kṛitwā lābhālābhau jayājayau
tato yuddhāya yujyaswa naivaṁ pāpam avāpsyasi

Having gained equanimity in pleasure and pain,
in gain and loss, in victory and defeat, then come
out to fight. Thus you will not incur sin.

Having made clear to Arjuna in the last verse that he stands to

14 See verse 32.

gain whether he dies or wins the battle, the Lord now wishes to convince him that he should waste no more time in the consideration of victory or defeat. Whatever the consequences, he should be prepared to fight, because at least one thing is certain: by fighting he will not incur sin. If, on the other hand, he refuses to fight, he is certain to fall into sin.

Arjuna was convinced that, whether he won or lost the battle, by killing he would in fact incur great sin. That is why, in this verse, bringing to an end the intellectual aspect of His discourse, the Lord says to him: I am not asking you to fight with a view to this or that loss or gain, but because by fighting you will not incur sin.

Unfortunately, for the last few centuries this part of Lord Kṛishṇa's teaching has been interpreted as indicating that a mood of equanimity should be cultivated during the experience of either loss or gain. In fact, the Lord means that right or wrong, virtue or sin, should be the primary consideration when deciding upon the validity of an action. It should not be decided on the basis of loss or gain. In judging the validity of an action, the first consideration should be its nature — whether or not it will in any way be sinful.

It is the purpose of the action that creates its need. Once the need for an action is felt, the first step is to make sure that it is not in any way sinful. To consider the loss or gain is only the second step. If it is an action leading to the fulfilment of one's mission in life, or an action which it would be sinful to leave undone, then its performance becomes a necessity. In such a case the consideration of a temporary loss or gain becomes all the more unimportant.

In this verse the Lord is clearly saying to Arjuna: First rise to the wisdom of life given so far (11–37). Established in this wisdom, come out to fight. Thus you will not incur sin.

'You will not incur sin': this is the guarantee that the Lord offers. One becomes uninvolved in sin as a result of 'having gained equanimity in pleasure and pain, in gain and loss, in victory and defeat'. This state of equanimity is born of the wisdom so far given to Arjuna, starting from verse 11 — the wisdom of Sāṁkhya, as the Lord names it in the verse that follows.

To sum up, this wisdom of Sāṁkhya comprises:

1. Understanding of the perishable and imperishable phases of life (11–30).
2. Understanding of *Dharma* (31–3).
3. Understanding of one's relationship with others (33–6).
4. Understanding of the results of actions (36–7).
5. Understanding of the nature of the doer as uninvolved with action, giving rise to equanimity in loss and gain.

Knowledge of the perishable and imperishable aspects of life broadens the vision and makes a man see beyond the mundane and limited sphere of daily life. This, when supplemented by knowledge of *Dharma*, induces in him a natural tendency to act rightly. His life becomes more useful to himself and to others. Through the understanding of his relationship with others, he rises above selfish ends to more and more universal aspects of life. This growing universal outlook, enriched by the proper understanding of the results of action, helps a man to develop and make progress on all levels of life. And finally, with the understanding of the nature of the doer as uninvolved, he gains equanimity,[15] rises above the influence of dualities, lives a life free from sin and suffering, and enjoys eternal freedom.

The following verse begins the teaching of Yoga, whereby the mind will rise above the binding influence of action — the teaching whereby the intellect, cultured by the wisdom of Sāṁkhya, will be eternally established in the oneness of life, in the oneness of absolute Being, the eternal liberation in divine consciousness here and now.

15 See verse 15.

VERSE 39

एषा तेऽभिहिता सांख्ये बुद्धिर्योगे त्विमां शृणु
बुद्ध्या युक्तो यया पार्थ कर्मबन्धं प्रहास्यसि

Eshā te 'bhihitā sāṁkhye buddhir yoge twimāṁ shṛiṇu
buddhyā yukto yayā Pārtha karmabandhaṁ prahāsyasi

This which has been set before you is understanding in terms of Sāṁkhya; hear it now in terms of Yoga. Your intellect established through it, O Pārtha, you will cast away the binding influence of action.

Yoga, the path of Union, is a direct way to experience the essential nature of Reality. This Reality is described and understood intellectually by a system which the Lord calls Sāṁkhya, and which has been set forth in the previous verses.

The Sāṁkhya of the Bhagavad-Gītā presents the principles of all the six systems of Indian philosophy, while the Yoga of the Bhagavad-Gītā presents their practical aspects.

This verse illustrates the technique of intelligent teaching. The subject is introduced and its result made clear in one stroke so that, seeing both the scale of the subject and the possibility of achieving the desired goal, the disciple is eager to begin the practice. For the Lord assures him that he will 'cast away the binding influence of action'[16] as a result of his intellect becoming established in Yoga.

Intellectual understanding of Reality convinces a man of the existence of a nobler and more permanent field of life that lies beyond and underlies the ordinary level of phenomenal existence. That has been the purpose of the discourse up to this point. Now Lord Kṛishṇa wishes to introduce Arjuna to the practice whereby his intellect will become established in Reality. This is to give him that positive experience of the truth of existence which will bring him to a state where he is unaffected by the binding influence of action.

The direct experience of transcendental bliss gives a man

16 See verse 50, commentary.

such great contentment that the joys of the relative world fail to make a deep impression on him, and he rises above the binding influence of action, just as a contented businessman, having achieved great wealth, is not affected by small losses or gains.

By using the word 'intellect', the Lord makes it clear that the mind, purified or settled by the wisdom of Sāṁkhya, becomes established in the Self through the practice of Yoga.

As has already been shown in the commentary on verse 15, no practice is involved in gaining the understanding of life through Sāṁkhya. If one wants to practise, one should turn to Yoga. The use of the words 'intellect established' indicates that it is the intellect that accomplishes Yoga, not the wandering mind. The suggestion is that the mind should be raised to the state of intellect through the wisdom of Sāṁkhya and then be turned to Yoga to become established in the Self. This presents Sāṁkhya and Yoga as complementary, a point which is developed in Chapter V.

It is interesting to note that the essence of the wisdom of Sāṁkhya was given in four verses (12–15) and that the essence of Yoga is also given in four verses (45–8). These two groups of four verses expound the essential wisdom of the Bhagavad-Gītā. All other verses are simply an extension of them.

In the following verse, the Lord conveys to Arjuna the simplicity and effectiveness of the technique which he is about to give him and which will establish him in complete contentment, the state of eternal freedom from the bondage of action.

VERSE 40

नेहाभिक्रमनाशोऽस्ति प्रत्यवायो न विद्यते
स्वल्पमप्यस्य धर्मस्य त्रायते महतो भयात्

Nehābhikramanāsho 'sti pratyavāyo na vidyate
swalpam apyasya dharmasya trāyate mahato bhayāt

In this (Yoga) no effort is lost and no obstacle exists.
Even a little of this Dharma delivers from great fear.

'Obstacle': the Sanskrit word '*pratyavāya*' also means any reversal of progress or any adverse effect.

'*Dharma*' signifies the path of evolution. The practice of Yoga is a direct way to evolution. Through it, the individual mind gains the state of cosmic intelligence — that unbounded state of universal Being which is the summit of evolution. *Dharma* is natural to man, and so is this practice of Yoga, for it is in accordance with the very nature of the mind and brings fulfilment to life. That is why this Yoga is the *Dharma* of everyone.

Lord Kṛishṇa's wonderful teaching in this verse brings great hope to mankind. On the way to eternal freedom 'no effort is lost'. Any effort on this path results in the goal; the process, having started, cannot stop until it has reached its goal. This is so in the first place because the flow of the mind towards this state is natural, for it is a state of absolute bliss, and the mind is always craving for greater happiness. Therefore as water flows down a slope in a natural way, so the mind flows naturally in the direction of bliss.

Secondly, 'no effort is lost' because, for the mind to become blissful, no effort is needed! If effort were necessary, then the question of effort being lost would arise. When an action is being performed, one stage of the process leads to another, which in turn gives rise to a further stage, so that when one stage has been reached, the previous stage is a thing of the past. In the performance of every action, therefore, some stage is lost, some energy is lost, some effort is lost. When the Lord says here that no effort is lost, it can only be because no effort is required. This means that Lord Kṛishṇa's technique of establishing the intellect in the Absolute is based on the very nature of the mind.[17] We must therefore inquire how the mind, motivated by its own nature, succeeds in gaining divine consciousness without effort.

When a man is listening to music and a more beautiful melody begins to come from another source, his whole mind will turn to enjoy it. No effort is needed to shift the attention to the more charming melody; the process is automatic. There is no loss of energy between starting to listen and enjoying the music with rapt attention. This is the Lord's meaning: since the field of eternal freedom is absolute bliss, the process of uniting the mind with it, once having begun, comes to completion without loss of

17 See verse 45, commentary.

energy or effort. It does not stop until the experience is full, for 'no obstacle exists'.

Seen from this angle, the very beginning of the process is its fulfilment, for it is the movement of the mind to bliss. The end is found in the beginning. The very start of the process brings the mind to the goal because, according to the Lord, there is no resistance on the way, there is 'no obstacle' to surmount. It is a path of no resistance, a pathless path, a path whose goal is omnipresent. That is why 'a little of this' 'delivers from great fear'.

Following the path of no resistance means that the technique of establishing the mind in the Absolute has only to be started, and from that point deliverance from suffering follows. The very start in this direction relieves a man 'from great fear' in life.

To establish the mind in the Absolute, says the Lord, very little — if anything — has to be done. This is because not even the natural direction of the mind has to be changed. The mind wanders from object to object, and it wanders, not for the sake of the object itself, but for the possibility of happiness that the object provides. Thus it does not actually wander from object to object but moves from a point of lesser happiness to a point of greater happiness. Since the greatest happiness is its goal, and the flow of the mind is already in the direction of greater happiness, the direction need not be changed. And since there is no need even to change the direction of the mind, it appears that nothing need be done to realize the goal.

But the Lord says 'a little of this' practice. This shows that something has to be done. What is necessary is only to begin to experience the increasing charm on the way to transcendental absolute bliss. As in the case of diving, one has only to take a correct angle and let go — the whole process is accomplished in an automatic manner. This is what the Lord means by 'a little of this'.

Just as the first ray of the sun dispels the darkness of the night, so the first step in this practice dispels the darkness of ignorance and fear. But although the first ray of the rising sun is able to dispel the darkness of the night, the sun still continues to rise, because its nature is not only to remove darkness, leaving the atmosphere dimly lighted, but also to shine forth in splendour and illumine the whole earth. The glory of the sun is its full midday light.

The Lord clearly means that the path of divine unfolding is so simple and natural that the process, once having been consciously started, encounters no obstacles. Quickly it produces an effect strong enough to enlighten the mind and release a man from all negativeness in life, from fear of the cycle of birth and death.

This is a noble way of enlightening the aspirant. There is a confident assurance of results from the very beginning of the practical teaching. Arjuna is told the nature of the technique and the results that will follow from its practice so that he may know in advance what it involves. Realization is not something that comes from outside: it is the revelation of the Self, in the Self, by the Self.

This revelation cannot occur unless a man gives himself completely to it, and then it happens by itself. But in order to be able to give himself completely to it, he has to know at least two things: first, that it is within his power to accomplish, and secondly, that its accomplishment will be of use to him. This is why Lord Kṛishṇa speaks the words of this verse. Arjuna is being prepared for the direct experience of Reality which wipes out all uncertainties and brings stability to life. The Lord proclaims to him the simplicity of the approach to the Divine and at the same time describes its result.

Why is it that in the modern world this spiritual practice has faded into the background of life? The answer lies in the wrong interpretation of verses such as this and the consequent spread of a misguided view of Reality which has persisted for many centuries.

Having explained the simplicity and effectiveness of the principle of establishing the intellect in the Divine, the Lord, in the following verses, introduces the technique for its accomplishment.

VERSE 41

व्यवसायात्मिका बुद्धिरेकेह कुरुनन्दन
बहुशाखा ह्यनन्ताश्च बुद्धयोऽव्यवसायिनाम्

Vyavasāyātmikā buddhir ekeha Kurunandana
bahushākhā hyanantāsh cha buddhayo 'vyavasāyinām

In this Yoga, O joy of the Kurus, the resolute intellect is one-pointed, but many-branched and endlessly diverse are the intellects of the irresolute.

'In this Yoga': in this path to bliss. When the mind moves towards bliss, it experiences increasing charm at every step, as when one proceeds towards the light, the intensity increases continuously. When the mind experiences increasing happiness, then it does not wander; it remains focused in one direction, unwavering and resolute. Such is the state of the mind moving in the direction of bliss, and when it arrives at the direct experience of bliss, it loses all contact with the outside and is contented in the state of transcendental Bliss Consciousness. When the mind comes out of this state into the field of action again, it remains contented and therefore maintains its resolute state to a greater or lesser degree. Through practice this state becomes established. This is what the Lord means when He says that 'In this Yoga … the resolute intellect is one-pointed'.

The minds of those who do not practise this Yoga are constantly in the field of sensory experience. This fails to provide the mind with that great joy which alone can satisfy its thirst for happiness. That is why the minds of such people continue to search and wander endlessly.

The Lord here further clarifies verse 38. Arjuna is advised to rise to the state of resolute intellect. For only in this state will he be able to win that evenness of mind in pleasure and pain, loss and gain, victory and defeat, which the Lord makes the prerequisite for battle.

It may appear that there is something negative in this approach to Reality, for although the purpose is to establish Arjuna in the resolute state of mind, in this verse the characteristics of the irresolute mind are emphasized. This is significant. If a man on a mountain peak, wishing to guide another who is only half-way up, keeps shouting directions about where he himself is standing, it will not help the other man to arrive at the top. The direct way of guiding him up is first to tell him where he is and describe his surroundings, thus making him aware of his own position, and then to guide him to the peak. Arjuna is in a state of irresoluteness, and the Lord's intention is to bring him to the resolute state by first showing him all about the irresolute state of his mind, and then guiding him to the resolute state.

Having pointed out these two states of mind, the Lord, in the following three verses, explains the conditions under which the mind continues to remain irresolute. After this He will direct Arjuna to rise from that state and become resolute, so that his mind may be established in Reality.

VERSE 42

यामिमां पुष्पितां वाचं प्रवदन्त्यविपश्चितः
वेदवादरताः पार्थ नान्यदस्तीति वादिनः

Yām imāṁ pushpitāṁ vāchaṁ pravadantyavipashchitaḥ
Vedavādaratāḥ Pārtha nānyad astīti vādinaḥ

The undiscerning who are engrossed in the letter of the Veda, O Pārtha, and declare that there is nothing else, speak flowery words.

The Vedas are authentic expositions of the path of evolution. They elucidate, step by step, the gradual process of the integration of life and teach the knowledge by which a man may quickly rise through all levels of evolution and attain final liberation.

To enable a man to profit by this great wisdom of life, the Vedas advocate a course of disciplined action and thought. The discipline of action is dealt with in those chapters collectively called *Karma Kāṇda*, which means pertaining to action, while discipline of mind is set forth in the chapters called *Upāsana*

Kāṇda, which means pertaining to the mind in relation to Reality.

The nature of the supreme Reality and of life's fulfilment forms the subject of the chapters collectively called *Gyān Kāṇda*, which means pertaining to knowledge.

The purpose of the Vedic *Karma Kāṇda* is to establish a code of action that will bring success and prosperity in this life and hereafter. It deals with the rites and rituals necessary to establish coordination between the different aspects of individual life: coordination between man and other creatures, between man and the different forces in Nature, between man and angels, and between man and God in heaven.

It is great practical wisdom of the highest order; it deals with innumerable types of action and the unfathomable nature of their influence. When those who are learned in this field begin to enlighten others, their discourse is both fascinating and positive. Their exposition of the theory and practice of the rites and rituals is so complete in itself and so decisive and precise in its nature as to be completely authoritative.

The *Karma Kāṇda* of the Vedas lays down specific conditions for the attainment of specific results. It is a clear, practical exposition of the Laws of Nature governing cause and effect in creation.

Innumerable are the aspirations of man, innumerable the objects to be attained. Innumerable also are the ways and means of acting to attain these ends. The purpose of the *Karma Kāṇda* is to bring about the coordination of the mind with the body and with the forces of Nature in such a way that it results in progress to a higher level and an improved quality of life.

The purpose of the *Upāsana Kāṇda* is to bring about the coordination of the mind with the inner forces of Nature and the ultimate transcendental Being in such a way that it results in the integration of life.

In this and the following two verses, the Lord refers to the *Karma Kāṇda*, and then in the 45th verse He brings out the glorious practical aspect of the *Upāsana Kāṇda* — that of bringing the diffused mind to a resolute state, in order that it may be established in Reality and may live It, thereby fulfilling the purpose of the *Gyān Kāṇda* of the Vedas. This is what makes the Bhagavad-

Gītā the essence of the Vedas and the highway to the fulfilment of the Vedic way of life.

VERSE 43

कामात्मानः स्वर्गपरा जन्मकर्मफलप्रदाम्
क्रियाविशेषबहुलां भोगैश्वर्यगतिं प्रति

Kāmātmānaḥ swargaparā janmakarmaphalapradām
kriyāvisheshabahulāṁ bhogaishwaryagatiṁ prati

Filled with desires, with heaven as their goal, (their words) proclaim birth as the reward of action and prescribe many special rites for the attainment of enjoyment and power.

This verse speaks of the tendency of man to resort to Vedic rites for the sake of a better life and greater worldly joys. The result of being engrossed in wordly desires is that one remains in the cycle of birth and death. For the joys of the senses can never satisfy; they involve man more and more and thus keep him in bondage. There being no chance of lasting contentment, the cycle of birth and death continues.

The following verse reveals the loss that occurs when the mind becomes entangled in these joys which enrich life only with material gains.

VERSE 44

भोगैश्वर्यप्रसक्तानां तयापहृतचेतसाम्
व्यवसायात्मिका बुद्धिः समाधौ न विधीयते

Bhogaishwaryaprasaktānāṁ tayāpahṛitachetasām
vyavasāyātmikā buddhiḥ samādhau na vidhīyate

The resolute state of intellect does not arise in the mind of those who are deeply attached to enjoyment and power and whose thought is captivated by those (flowery words).

It does not necessarily follow that a man who has great knowledge of relativity cannot also have the wisdom of the Absolute. If even an illiterate man can enjoy the absolute bliss which is his own Being, why not the man of learning? The verse objects not to worldly enjoyment and power, not to the Vedic wisdom of action, which is a way of gaining such enjoyment and power, but to the mental state of being engrossed in them that is produced by hearing the glory of Vedic rites proclaimed in flowery words.

It is not surprising that those always occupied in the field of action should proclaim that every attainment is possible through action — and specifically through the Vedic way of action, which undoubtedly provides a direct path to the attainment of anything whatsoever. This point of view, while quite valid in the relative field of life, obviously does not concern itself with the Being of the Absolute. The manifested and the unmanifested fields of life together comprise the whole of Reality. But those who only possess the wisdom of the Vedic *Karma Kāṇda* aspire within the manifested field alone. Their wisdom of action does not directly give them the wisdom of the unmanifested field of Reality.

Owing to lack of knowledge of the unmanifested Absolute, such people are heard proclaiming in flowery language that there is nothing beyond the field of Vedic action (verse 42).

In the 43rd verse, the Lord has depicted the mind held fast in the grip of action. Fascinated by the flowery language which proclaims the glory of action, it becomes involved in vigorous and manifold activities. Such an ever-active mind naturally remains outside the realm of the resolute intellect.

Wordly joys, together with a sense of progress through action and effort, keep the mind engaged in outside activities. It is difficult for such a mind to converge towards the resolute state by itself; activity engages the mind in diversity and by so doing is clearly opposed to the process of convergence, which leads to the resolute state. Only if the intention is there and guidance is received can the mind gain one-pointedness, and that even in the midst of 'enjoyment and power'.

In the following verse, the Lord gives the principle of the technique for bringing such a diffused mind to a resolute state.

VERSE 45

त्रैगुण्यविषया वेदा निस्त्रैगुण्यो भवार्जुन
निर्द्वन्द्वो नित्यसत्त्वस्थो निर्योगक्षेम आत्मवान्

Traiguṇyavishayā vedā nistraiguṇyo bhavārjuna
nirdwandwo nityasattwastho niryogakshema Ātmavān

The Vedas' concern is with the three Guṇas.
Be without the three Guṇas, O Arjuna, freed from duality, ever firm in purity, independent of possessions, possessed of the Self.

This is the technique of instantaneous realization. The Lord shows Arjuna a practical way of converging the many-branched mind into the one-pointedness of the resolute intellect. Here is an effective technique for bringing the mind to a state where all differences dissolve and leave the individual in the state of fulfilment.

Everything that has so far been said by Lord Kṛishṇa is to prepare Arjuna to understand this practice of bringing his mind from the field of multiplicity to that of eternal Unity. This practice is to brighten all aspects of his life by bringing his mind to Transcendental Consciousness, the limitless source of life, energy, wisdom, peace, and happiness. It is to raise him to that cosmic status which harmonizes all the opposite forces of life.

Modern psychological theories investigate causes in order to influence effects. They grope in darkness to find the cause of darkness in order to remove it. In contradistinction, here is the idea of bringing light to remove darkness. This is 'the principle of the second element'. If you wish to produce an effect on the first element ignore that element, do not seek its cause; influence it directly by introducing a second element. Remove the darkness by introducing light. Take the mind to a field of happiness in order to relieve it of suffering.

However, even if we accept that by investigating the cause it is easy to influence the effect, we shall find that this verse will serve our purpose, for it provides a technique by which the ultimate cause of all human life can be investigated. If knowledge of the cause can help to influence the effect, then knowledge of the ultimate cause of life will effectively put an end to all suffering.

The greatness of Lord Kṛishṇa's teaching lies in its direct practical approach and its completeness from every point of view. The idea of introducing a second element and the idea of investigating the cause in order to influence its effect represent two principles distinctly opposed to each other, yet both of them are fulfilled in one technique. It is this completeness of practical wisdom that has made the Bhagavad-Gītā immortal.

Lord Kṛishṇa commands Arjuna: 'Be without the three *Guṇas*'; be without activity, be your Self. This is resolute consciousness, the state of absolute Being, which is the ultimate cause of all causes. This state of consciousness brings harmony to the whole field of cause and effect and glorifies all life.

Arjuna's main problem was to reconcile love of kinsmen with the necessity to root out evil. He was desperately seeking a formula of compromise between righteousness and evil. But on any plane of relative life these are irreconcilable. That is why, having explored all the avenues of his heart and mind, Arjuna could not find any practical solution, could not decide on any line of action. Lord Kṛishṇa, however, shows him the field where righteousness and love merge in eternal harmony, the eternal life of absolute Being.

The Lord makes clear to Arjuna that all influences of the outside world, and their consequences as well, will cling to him and affect him so long as he is out of himself, so long as he allows himself to remain in the sphere of relativity and under its influence. Once out of that sphere, he will find fulfilment in his own Self.

It is difficult for a man to improve his business affairs while he himself is constantly immersed in all their details. If he leaves them for a little while, he becomes able to see the business as a whole and can then more easily decide what is needed. Arjuna has a deep belief in *Dharma*; his mind is clear about considerations of right and wrong. But the Lord asks him to abandon the whole field of right and wrong for the field of the Transcendent. There, established in a state beyond all duality, beyond the influence of right and wrong, he will enjoy the absolute wisdom of life, from which springs all knowledge of the relative world. And the Lord says to Arjuna: The field of that absolute wisdom is not outside you. You have not to go out anywhere to acquire it. It is within you. You have only to be within yourself, 'possessed of the Self', ever firm in the purity of your Being.

Here indeed is the skill of bringing light to remove darkness. Arjuna is not asked to come or go anywhere; he is only asked to 'Be without the three *Guṇas*'. This instruction serves as a direct means to take man to the absolute state of his consciousness. It is enough for the Lord to say: 'Be without the three *Guṇas*, O Arjuna, freed from duality'.

The entire creation consists of the interplay of the three *Guṇas* — *Sattwa*, *Rajas,* and *Tamas* — born of *Prakṛiti*, or Nature. The process of evolution is carried on by these three *Guṇas*. Evolution means creation and its progressive development, and at its basis lies activity. Activity needs *Rajo-guṇa* to create a spur, and it needs *Sato-guṇa* and *Tamo-guṇa* to uphold the direction of the movement.

The nature of *Tamo-guṇa* is to check or retard, but it should not be thought that when the movement is upwards *Tamo-guṇa* is absent. For any process to continue, there have to be stages in that process, and each stage, however small in time and space, needs a force to maintain it and another force to develop it into a new stage. The force that develops it into a new stage is *Sato-guṇa*, while *Tamo-guṇa* is that which checks or retards the process in order to maintain the state already produced so that it may form the basis for the next stage.

This explains why the three *Guṇas* have inevitably to be together. No one *Guṇa* can exist in isolation without the presence of the other two. It is for this reason that the Lord asks Arjuna to be out of all the three *Guṇas*, to be entirely out of the influence of the forces that constitute life in the relative field.

While giving him the wisdom of Sāṁkhya, the Lord has told Arjuna that there are two aspects of life, perishable and imperishable. The perishable is relative existence, and the imperishable is absolute Being. All life in the relative field is under the sway of the *Guṇas*. Therefore, in order to give Arjuna the direct experience of the absolute state of life, He asks him to 'Be without the three *Guṇas*'.

There are gross planes of creation, and there are subtle planes. When the Lord says 'Be without the three *Guṇas*', He means that Arjuna should bring his attention from the gross planes of experience, through the subtle planes and thus to the subtlest plane of experience; transcending even that subtlest plane, he will be completely out of the relative field of life, out of the three *Guṇas*. So the Lord's words: 'Be without the three *Guṇas*', reveal the secret of arriving at the state of pure consciousness.[18]

When you say to someone: 'Come here', you imply by these two words that he must get up and begin to put one foot before the other, and that this walking on both feet will bring him to you. When the Lord says: 'Be without the three *Guṇas*', He obviously means that in whichever field of the three *Guṇas* you have your stand, from there you are to begin moving towards subtler planes of the *Guṇas* and, arriving at the subtlest, come out of it, transcend it, be by yourself, 'possessed of the Self' — 'freed from duality', 'ever firm in purity', 'independent of possessions'.

Lord Kṛishṇa, in this verse, has really given the technique of Self-realization. Arjuna was held in suspension between the dictates of his heart and mind. The Lord suggests to him that he should come out of the conflict and he will then see his way clear. That is why, having said: 'Be without the three *Guṇas*', He immediately adds: 'freed from duality', freed from the field of conflicts. The relative field of life is full of conflicting elements: heat and cold, pleasure and pain, gain and loss, and all the other pairs of opposites which constitute life. Under their influence life is tossed about as a ship on the rough sea from one wave to another. To be freed from duality is to be in the field of non-duality, the absolute state of Being. This provides smoothness and security to life in the relative field. It is like an anchor to the ship of life in the ocean of the three *Guṇas*. One gains steadiness and comfort.

Arjuna was highly sensitive to right and wrong. For this reason the Lord, after saying: 'freed from duality', at once adds: 'ever firm in purity'. He wants to assure Arjuna that this state

18 See Appendix: The *Transcendental Meditation* Technique.

will always prove right, in accordance with *Dharma*, ever furthering the process of evolution for the good of all. Nothing wrong can possibly result from it, because that is the state of fulfilment.

To convey this idea of fulfilment the Lord says: 'independent of possessions'. The Sanskrit word used in the text is '*Niryogakshema*', which carries the meaning that in this state one is not required to think of gaining what one does not have or of preserving what one has. Duryodhana's desire to possess and preserve possessions is the cause of the battle. Even in the ordinary life of man, it is his tendency to possess that tempts him to go the wrong way. So the Lord tells Arjuna that he will transcend this cause of transgression in life. Thereby He also reminds Arjuna that Duryodhana could take the wrong path because he gained kingdom, pleasure, and power but did not gain the wisdom of remaining 'independent of possessions'. That is why possessions kept him bound to themselves and he lost his sense of proportion.

By using this expression: 'independent of possessions', the Lord is providing the answer to Arjuna's own words in verse 32 of Chapter I: 'I desire not victory, O Kṛishṇa, nor a kingdom, nor pleasures.' Arjuna had seen how pleasure and power may ruin a man's life by blinding him to the cause of righteousness. Here Lord Kṛishṇa is educating him in the art of independence in the midst of possessions, for after the battle Arjuna is going to be placed in a position of great wealth and power.

Having said: 'freed from duality, ever firm in purity, independent of possessions', the Lord then adds: 'possessed of the Self'. This is to indicate to Arjuna that this blessed state of life is not far distant from him. It is within himself and therefore always within his reach. And moreover, it is his own Self, nothing other than his own Self.

There is great presence of mind, great skill in enlightening the ignorant, and the height of perfection in the style of this discourse. If you are told by someone: 'I will take you to the field of great wisdom and abundance of life', without some indication of where that field lies, you may well be puzzled about many things — about the distance, the difficulties on the way, your own ability to get there. That is why the Lord uses the words:

'possessed of the Self'. Let yourself be possessed by your Self. Once you are possessed by your Self the purpose of all wisdom has been achieved. There the Vedas end. That is the end of the journey of life, that is the state of fulfilment. For this reason, 'possessed of the Self' stands at the end of the verse.

Here is a technique that enables every man to come to the great treasure-house within himself and so rise above all sorrows and uncertainties in life. From this verse onwards, the entire teaching of the Bhagavad-Gītā proclaims the glory of achieving the state of the Transcendent.

It is this transcendental state of Being which enables a man to become a *Karma Yogī*, one who is successful on the path of action. It is this that enables a man to become a *Bhakta*, one who is successful on the path of devotion, and it is this that enables a man to become a *Gyānī*, one who is successful on the path of knowledge. This is the highway to the fulfilment of life's purpose.

If a man wants to be a true devotee of God, he has to become his pure Self; he has to free himself from those attributes which do not belong to him, and then only can he have one-pointed devotion. If he is enveloped by what he is not, then his devotion will be covered by that foreign element. His devotion will not reach God, and the love and blessings of God will not reach him. For his devotion to reach God, it is necessary that he should first become purely himself, covered by nothing. Then the process of devotion will connect him directly with the Lord, thereby bestowing on him the status of a devotee. Only when he has become himself can he properly surrender to the Great Self of the Lord. If he remains in the field of the three *Guṇas*, in the many sheaths of gross and subtle nature, then it is these sheaths that prevent direct contact with the Lord.

Therefore the first step towards Union through devotion is to be oneself. This, likewise, is the first step on the path of *Gyān Yoga*, the path of Union through knowledge, and also on the path of Union through action, *Karma Yoga*; because it is the state of Transcendental Consciousness that is the state of *Gyān*, or knowledge, and that delivers from the bondage of *Karma*. This state is also the basis of success in any field of life. The field of the three *Guṇas* is enlivened by the light of the absolute Being beyond the *Guṇas*.

The following verse shows that the purpose of all activity is fulfilled in this state of Being.

VERSE 46

यावानर्थ उदपाने सर्वतः संप्लुतोदके
तावान्सर्वेषु वेदेषु ब्राह्मणस्य विजानतः

Yāvān artha udapāne sarvataḥ saṁplutodake
tāvān sarveshu Vedeshu brāhmaṇasya vijānataḥ

To the enlightened Brāhmaṇa all the Vedas are of no more use than is a small well in a place flooded with water on every side.

'Enlightened *Brāhmaṇa*': one who has gone through the study and practice of the *Karma Kāṇda*, *Upāsana Kāṇda,* and *Gyān Kāṇda* of the Vedas. That is, one who knows the secret of action, dedication, and knowledge.

While every action has the aim of happiness, the actions prescribed by the Vedas at the same time help a man to evolve beyond his present level. But a *Jīvan-mukta*, a man of Cosmic Consciousness, finds himself at the ultimate fulfilment of all the duties prescribed for him. He knows Reality with such great fullness that he becomes established in That, in the state of absolute Bliss Consciousness. This is how, having gained the final aim of the whole Vedic way of life, such a man rises above the field of Vedic injunctions about right and wrong and also above the need for Vedic rituals; he rises above the need of the Vedic guidance.

The state of realization is like a reservoir full of water, from which people quite naturally draw to satisfy all their needs instead of getting their water from many small ponds. Therefore the Lord asks Arjuna to 'Be without the three *Guṇas*' and not waste his life in planning and achieving small gains in the ever-changing field of the three *Guṇas*, to be a self-contained whole instead of trying to achieve a little here and there.

Not only does the state of realization fulfil the overall purpose of man's craving for greater and greater happiness, it also brings the mind naturally to the highest degree of mental development. It brings a realized man to a state where, by virtue of a high development of mental strength and harmony with the Laws of Nature, he finds that his thoughts naturally become fulfilled without much effort on his part. A man in this state has given such a natural pattern to his existence that he enjoys the full support of almighty Nature for life. He is in direct attunement with Cosmic Law, the field of Being, which forms the basis of all the Laws of Nature.[19]

VERSE 47

कर्मण्येवाधिकारस्ते मा फलेषु कदाचन
मा कर्मफलहेतुर्भूर्मा ते सङ्गोऽस्त्वकर्मणि

Karmaṇyevādhikāras te mā phaleshu kadāchana
mā karmaphalahetur bhūr mā te sango 'stwakarmaṇi

You have control over action alone, never over its fruits. Live not for the fruits of action, nor attach yourself to inaction.

There is a marvellous sequence of instruction here. This verse demonstrates once more the awareness of Lord Kṛishṇa and His clear and deep insight into Arjuna's mind.

As Arjuna was instructed to 'Be without the three *Guṇas*' in verse 45 and in the next verse was told that as a result he would fulfil all his aspirations in the relative field, he might very well infer that he was not required to do anything more. Therefore in order that Arjuna might not develop an aversion to action, the Lord says in this verse: 'You have control over action alone'. This should bring Arjuna to feel that he is to concern himself with nothing but action. He should be so completely absorbed in the action itself as to become oblivious of everything else, even of its

19 See Appendix: Cosmic Law, The Basic Law of Creation.

fruits. For this reason the Lord adds: 'never over its fruits'.

This does not mean that Arjuna is not to fight for the sake of winning the battle; it does not mean that the action should be done without caring for its result. That would be hypocrisy.

It is the anticipated fruit of an action that induces a man to act. It is desire for a result that makes him begin to act and enables him to persist in the process of action. The Lord wishes to show that the result of the action will be greater if the doer puts all his attention and energy into the action itself, if he does not allow his attention and energy to be distracted by thinking of results. The result will be according to the action, there is no doubt about that.

If a student thinks the whole time about passing an examination, the progress of his study will be hampered, and this will jeopardize the result. It is to ensure the greater success of an action that the doer is asked not to concern himself with results during the course of the action. But this does not imply that he should be indifferent to results. If he becomes consciously indifferent to results, the process of action will certainly become weak, and this will also weaken the results.

It would be absurd to infer from this verse that a man has no right to the fruits of his action. Only the technique for achieving the maximum result from an action is given here. The doer has every right to enjoy the fruits of his action; the Lord says that he has no control over the fruits because the fruits will inevitably be according to the action. Having fixed the objective, having begun to act, and having become intimately engrossed in the process of action, he should fulfil the action with such complete devotion and undivided attention that he is oblivious even of its fruits. Only in this way will he achieve the maximum results from what he does.

The teaching of non-anticipation of the fruit of action has an even deeper, cosmic significance in that it is supported by the very process of evolution. If a man is held by the fruit of action, then his sole concern is centred on the horizontal plane of life. Seeing nothing higher than the action and its fruit, he loses sight of the Divine, which pervades the action and is the almighty power at its basis leading it to ultimate fulfilment. He thus loses direct contact with the vertical plane of life, on which the process of evolution is based.

Thus it is clear that the Lord's teaching on the one hand supports activity and on the other upholds evolution and freedom.

The following verse indicates that it is possible for everyone to live the values of the Divine in the world.

VERSE 48

योगस्थः कुरुकर्माणि सङ्गं त्यक्त्वा धनंजय
सिद्ध्यसिद्ध्योः समो भूत्वा समत्वं योग उच्यते

Yogasthaḥ kuru karmāṇi sangaṁ tyaktwā Dhananjaya
siddhyasiddhyoḥ samo bhūtwā samatwaṁ yoga uchyate

Established in Yoga, O winner of wealth, perform actions having abandoned attachment and having become balanced in success and failure, for balance of mind is called Yoga.

'Established in Yoga' means established in Cosmic Consciousness.[20]

Yoga, or Union of the mind with the divine intelligence, begins when the mind gains Transcendental Consciousness; Yoga achieves maturity when this transcendental Bliss Consciousness, or divine Being, has gained ground in the mind to such an extent that, in whatever state the mind finds itself, whether waking or sleeping, it remains established in the state of Being. It is to this state of perfect enlightenment that the Lord refers in the beginning of the verse when He says: 'Established in Yoga'. Towards the end of the verse He defines 'Yoga' with reference to action as 'balance of mind'. This balanced state of mind is the result of the eternal contentment which comes with Bliss Consciousness. It cannot be gained by creating a mood of equanimity in loss and gain, as commentators have generally thought.

Yoga is the basis of an integrated life, a means of bringing into harmony the inner creative silence and the outer activity of life, and a way to act with precision and success. Established in Yoga,

20 See verse 51, commentary.

Arjuna will be established in the ultimate Reality of life, which is the source of eternal wisdom, power, and creativity.

Part of the training for one who wishes to become a good swimmer is the art of diving. When one is able to maintain oneself successfully in deep water, then swimming on the surface becomes easy. All action is the result of the play of the conscious mind. If the mind is strong, then action is also strong and successful. The conscious mind becomes powerful when the deeper levels of the ocean of mind are activated during the process of Transcendental Meditation,[21] which leads the attention from the surface of the conscious mind to the transcendental field of Being. The process of diving within is the way to become established in Yoga.

When the Lord says that having been through this process Arjuna should come out and act, He gives him the mechanics of successful action. To shoot an arrow successfully it is first necessary to draw it back on the bow, thus giving it great potential energy. When it is brought back to the fullest possible extent, then it possesses the greatest dynamic power.

Unfortunately the art of action, which Lord Kṛishṇa expounded to Arjuna in this discourse, seems to have disappeared from practical life today. This is because for many centuries, owing to the lack of proper interpretation of these verses, it has been considered difficult to lead the mind to the Self and become established in Yoga. It is, in fact, perfectly easy to lead the attention to the field of Being: one has only to allow the mind to move spontaneously from the gross field of objective experience, through the subtle fields of the thought-process to the ultimate transcendental Reality of existence. As the mind moves in this direction, it begins to experience increasing charm at every step until it reaches the state of transcendental Bliss Consciousness.

The reward of bringing the mind to this state is that the small individual mind grows to the status of the cosmic mind, rising above all its individual shortcomings and limitations. It is like a small businessman becoming wealthy and reaching the status of a multimillionaire. The losses and gains of the market, which

21 See Appendix: The *Transcendental Meditation* Technique.

before used to influence him, now have no effect upon him and he rises quite naturally above their influence.

The Lord wants Arjuna to act, but He wants him, before beginning the action, to gain the status of cosmic mind. This is His kindness. When a wealthy man wants his son to start a business, he does not usually wish him to begin in a small way, because he knows that in that way small losses and gains will influence his dear son and make him miserable or happy over trivialities. Therefore he gives him the status of a wealthy man and then asks him to start business from that level. Lord Kṛishṇa, like a kind and able father, advises Arjuna to attain the state of cosmic intelligence and then to act from that high state of freedom in life.

A man cannot remain balanced in loss and gain unless he is in a state of lasting contentment. Here the Lord is asking Arjuna to get to that state of lasting contentment by a direct experience of transcendental eternal bliss. He is not advising a mere mood of equanimity.

The state of transcendental bliss in eternal Being is so self-sufficient that, in its structure, it is absolute. It is fullness of life, perfection of existence, and therefore completely unattached to anything in the relative field, completely free from the influence of action. When the Lord says: 'having abandoned attachment', He means having gained this state of eternal Being, which is wholly separated and detached from activity. And when He says: 'having become balanced in success and failure', He means having reached stability in this state of eternal Being.

The regular practice of Transcendental Meditation is the direct way of rising to the state of transcendental Being and stabilizing it in the very nature of the mind, so that irrespective of the mind's engagements in the conflicts inherent in the diversities of life, the structure of Unity in eternal freedom is naturally maintained and life is not lost to itself.

Here is the definition of Yoga for which the ground was prepared by the words 'Be without the three *Guṇas*' in verse 45: Yoga is that eternally balanced and never-changing state of Transcendental Consciousness which, remaining transcendent while yet grounded in the very nature of the mind, sets the mind free to participate in activity without becoming involved in it.

The following verses extol the glory of this Yoga, the balanced state of mind, and make clear its usefulness in raising the dignity of action and bringing eternal freedom to the doer.

VERSE 49

दूरेण ह्यवरं कर्म बुद्धियोगाद्धनंजय
बुद्धौ शरणमन्विच्छ कृपणाः फलहेतवः

Dūreṇa hyavaraṁ karma buddhiyogād Dhananjaya
buddhau sharaṇam anvichchha kṛipaṇāḥ phalahetavaḥ

Far away, indeed, from the balanced intellect is the action devoid of greatness, O winner of wealth. Take refuge in the intellect. Pitiful are those who live for the fruits (of action).

'Balanced intellect' (*Buddhi Yoga*): the balanced state of mind as explained in the last verse.

Here the Lord makes clear the distinction between the action in which the intellect becomes involved and that in which it remains uninvolved. He says that the action performed without gaining balance of mind, or Yoga, is of an inferior nature — it is ineffective and weak, 'devoid of greatness'. He asks Arjuna to rise to the uninvolved state of intellect, so that his action may acquire greatness and he may be enabled at the same time to gain the state of freedom.

The Lord derides the fate of those who are unable to rise to this state of action in non-attachment. He says that they are 'pitiful' who seek only to enjoy the outer field of life, who do not live the fullness of the inner and outer glories of life by developing the balanced state of mind described in the previous verse.

The Lord says: 'Take refuge in the intellect', thereby asking Arjuna first to turn within and 'Be without the three *Guṇas*' ('*Nistraiguṇyo bhava-Arjuna*', verse 45) and then, remaining established in the state of Yoga, in the Self, to perform actions ('*Yogasthaḥ kuru karmāṇi*', verse 48).

The Lord wants Arjuna, before he begins to act, to establish himself in Yoga. He has defined Yoga as 'balance of mind', a state of fullness which is a state of natural equanimity. In this state a man is not affected by success or failure. It is not that he consciously tries to treat loss and gain as the same, but that he is naturally unaffected by them — a really good and desirable state which is reached through the practice of Transcendental Meditation referred to in the 45th verse. The endeavour to preserve equanimity of mind without gaining this state, merely by trying to view all things as alike, may be called hypocrisy or self-deception.

The Lord is certainly not telling Arjuna to cultivate a mood of equanimity or maintain a conscious indifference towards results during the process of an action. Any such attempt to maintain equanimity on the thinking level can only lead to tension and dullness of mind. The emphasis here, as in the previous verse, is on gaining pure intelligence, or Being. It is the state of Being which cultures the mind to be one-pointed, thus improving its effectiveness during action.

It is unfortunate that, for many centuries past, this and similar verses spoken by Lord Kṛishṇa on the Yoga of action have been misinterpreted, for this has caused people to lose their vigour and perseverance in action in the name of non-attachment. The result has been idleness, impotence, and the weakening of the very structure of both individual and social life.

Here is a dynamic philosophy which is meant to inspire a disheartened man and strengthen a normal mind. Instead, owing to general misinterpretation, it has become a means to incapacitate man in all fields of activity; it has become a dragging influence on human endeavour.

The whole philosophy of *Karma*, or action, is clearly explained to Arjuna so that he may become an integrated and dynamic person.

The Lord says: 'Pitiful are those who live for the fruits' of action — those who look forward to the results of their actions are to be pitied. This statement in particular has been much misunderstood by commentators. They have advised people to work but not to aim at a result. It is certain, however, that an action must be done to achieve some result. No action can be performed without some clear result in view. The Lord here only means to show Arjuna a principle of raising the value of action by raising the level of the mind and enabling it to rise to the state of unbounded consciousness in eternal freedom.

When an arrow is to be shot, the first step is to pull it back on the bow. If, instead, in the hurry of things, the arrow is shot forward without being pulled back on the bowstring, then the aim will not be achieved, the target will not be reached, the action will be without force, and the actor will remain unfulfilled.

The Lord means that pitiable are those who are in such a hurry to achieve the fruit of action that they begin to act without adequate preparation to make the action forceful. They are not pitiable because they aim at the fruit of action, as so many commentators wrongly declare, but because they fail to achieve the full fruit of their action. They are pitiable because they do not know how to make their actions yield the maximum result and bring fulfilment to their aspirations.

They are pitiable because they care nothing for the cause, they care only for the effect. In this way they lose opportunities for improvement and greater gain. The intellect is the source or cause of action. Therefore the Lord says: 'Take refuge in the intellect' and 'Far away, indeed, from the balanced intellect is the action devoid of greatness'.

Unless his mind is withdrawn and brought back to the absolute state of intellect, a man's deeds in the world will be weak, and that is why he is called pitiable. Pitiable is he, says the Bṛihad-Āraṇyak Upanishad, who fails to commune with the inner divine consciousness. He is pitiable because he is neither able to enjoy the full result of his actions nor to overcome their binding influence.

Action is performed on the level of the senses but has its origin at the inception of the thinking process. A thought starts from the deepest level of the mind; it is appreciated on the thinking level, where it takes the form of a desire; desire, in its turn, expresses itself in the form of action. This is why the Lord says that the 'balanced intellect' and the field of action are far apart. One is on the level of absolute life-energy; the other is on a weak and diffused level of energy because, as the process of manifestation of a thought develops into action, the concentration of energy becomes weaker. For this reason the Lord declares that they are pitiable who tend towards action alone, rather than towards a resolute state of intellect first and then to action later.

He who practises Transcendental Meditation and becomes acquainted with the inner divine consciousness truly enjoys the greatest fruit of action in the world. At the same time he grows increasingly free from bondage and eventually achieves integration of life.

This is the purpose of Lord Kṛishṇa's teaching: 'Take refuge in the intellect.' It introduces the ideal principle for the integration of life and provides a simple technique for its achievement.

The Lord wants Arjuna to have a deep conviction and a clear conception of the relationship between the state of Yoga and action, and also between Yoga and the doer.

VERSE 50

बुद्धियुक्तो जहातीह उभे सुकृतदुष्कृते
तस्माद्योगाय युज्यस्व योगः कर्मसु कौशलम्

Buddhiyukto jahātīha ubhe sukṛitadushkṛite
tasmād yogāya yujyaswa yogaḥ karmasu kaushalam

He whose intellect is united (with the Self) casts off both good and evil even here. Therefore, devote yourself to Yoga. Yoga is skill in action.

Here the Lord contrasts the opposing characteristics of Yoga and *Karma* (action). Yoga is pulling the arrow back; *Karma* is shooting the arrow forward.

One who tries to shoot the arrow without first pulling it back on the bow is said to have a poor sense of action. His shot will not be strong, and his arrow will not go far because it will not be carried forward with force. Wise in the skill of action are those who first pull the arrow back before they proceed to shoot it ahead.

As the mind becomes established in Transcendental Consciousness, the state of Being becomes infused into the very nature of the mind, which thus gains the status of cosmic intelligence. Coming out of the transcendental state of consciousness, a man regains individuality, by virtue of which he is able to act in the relative field of life, but he now acts infused with Being. Such a person is as naturally above the influence of right and wrong as the wealthy businessman is above loss and gain.

In this verse, the Lord emphasizes that the effect of Yoga is to raise a man to his real stature of eternal freedom in divine consciousness, where he will ever remain untouched by the influence of action, be it good or bad. This is not because he should be deprived of the good and bad fruits of his action, but because it is his due that, while enjoying the fruits of his actions, he should enjoy the state of eternal freedom as well.

It is not the action or its fruits that bind a man; rather it is the inability to maintain freedom which becomes a means of bondage. Yoga removes this inability. It is the glory of Yoga that it increases the power of both the action and the actor, bringing dignity to life in all its aspects.

Bondage certainly lies in the field of action, but it is not born of action: it is born of the weakness of the actor. When a small businessman incurs a loss, his mind is profoundly affected by it. This creates a deep impression, which comes to the surface again as a desire for gain when favourable conditions present themselves. An impression on the mind is the seed of the desire which leads to action. Action in turn produces an impression on the mind, and thus the cycle of impression, desire, and action continues, keeping a man bound to the cycle of cause and effect, the cycle of birth and death. This is commonly called the binding influence of action, the bondage of *Karma*.

When the Lord says that Arjuna will transcend the binding influence of right and wrong, He immediately makes it clear that this will not be the result of inaction but will be due to 'skill in action'.

What is 'skill in action'? It is the technique of performing an action so that the whole process becomes easy. The action is completed with the least effort, leaving the doer fresh enough to enjoy fully the fruits of his action while at the same time remaining untouched by its binding influence. And not only this — the action is performed quickly so that the doer begins to enjoy the results immediately. 'Skill in action' does not allow any negative influence from outside to hinder the performance of action, nor does it produce any negative influence either upon the doer or upon anyone anywhere; on the contrary, the influence it creates is wholly positive.

The process of action, if carried out with what is here called 'skill in action', produces good results in all directions and enables the doer to derive maximum benefit from it. At the same time, it fails to produce a binding influence on him. This is because it influences the doer in such a way that its fruits do not leave an impression in the mind deep enough to form the seed of future action, the doer being established in the Self, the eternal Being, and ever unattached to the field of activity.

Verse 51

कर्मजं बुद्धियुक्ता हि फलं त्यक्त्वा मनीषिणः
जन्मबन्धविनिर्मुक्ताः पदं गच्छन्त्यनामयम्

Karmajaṁ buddhiyuktā hi phalaṁ tyaktwā manīshiṇaḥ
janmabandhavinirmuktāḥ padaṁ gachchhantyanāmayam

The wise, their intellect truly united with the Self, having renounced the fruits born of their actions and being liberated from the bonds of birth, arrive at a state devoid of suffering.

'Liberated from the bonds of birth': birth marks a step on the long road of evolution. Births continue one after the other until the goal of evolution is reached. Individual life reaches its highest state of evolution when it finds itself established on the level of cosmic life, on the level of unbounded and eternal Being.

In this verse, Arjuna is made to realize that by establishing his mind in transcendental Being he will rise to a state separate from and unattached to the sphere of action. The Lord tells him that because they are established in Being, which is naturally unattached to activity, the wise live in eternal freedom and are not bound by the fruit of action. Fully established in the divine intelligence, they break the shackles of bondage and are free even while remaining in the field of action, for they are ever in the state of the eternal unchanging existence of absolute Being.

It is a wonderful way of enlightenment. The Lord asks Arjuna to come completely out of the field of action: 'Be without the three *Guṇas*, O Arjuna' (verse 45). He thereupon bids him act with full force (verse 47). Then, combining these two commands, the Lord tells Arjuna to act while remaining established in Self-consciousness (verses 48–50). And in the present verse, He demonstrates that action of this kind leads to Cosmic Consciousness — liberation from all suffering and bondage during lifetime here on earth. Arjuna is given a systematic and direct way to the highest state of human evolution.

The first step is to bring the mind to the Transcendent. Through Transcendental Meditation,[22] the attention is brought from gross experience to subtler fields of expcrience until the subtlest experience is transcended and the state of Transcendental Consciousness is gained. The march of the mind in this direction is so simple as to be automatic; as it enters into experience of a subtler nature, the mind feels increased charm because it is proceeding towards absolute bliss. Once the mind reaches Transcendental Consciousness it no longer remains a conscious mind; it gains the status of absolute Being. This state of transcendental pure consciousness, also known as Self-consciousness, Self-awareness, *Samādhi*, represents the complete infusion of cosmic Being into the individual mind.

When, after this infusion, the mind comes out again into the field of relativity, then, being once more the individual mind, it acts while established in Being. Such action is called *Karma Yoga*; it is by virtue of *Karma Yoga* that transcendent Being is lived in the field of activity. And when complete fullness of Being has begun to be lived in the field of activity, the relative field of life, then one gains all-embracing eternal life in absolute freedom. That is Cosmic Consciousness, *Jīvan-mukti*. That is the state of which the Lord says: 'their intellect truly united with the Self'.

We may say that there is only one step on the path to this state of Cosmic Consciousness: a step out of the field of action into

22 See Appendix: The *Transcendental Meditation* Technique.

the Transcendent and back to action again. Thus we find a man reaches his highest evolution on the plane where he is already. He has only to take himself to a field which is outside action and come back again to his normal field of activity. One dives into the ocean, reaches the bottom, gathers the pearls, and comes out of the water to enjoy their value — the whole act is done in one dive. The technique of diving lies only in taking a correct angle and then letting go; reaching the bottom and coming up with the pearls follows automatically.

What a seeker of Truth has to do is only to learn how to take a correct angle for the dive within. This will quite naturally result in Self-consciousness, which in its turn develops into Cosmic Consciousness in the most natural way; the whole process goes by itself.

The state of Cosmic Consciousness is inclusive of Transcendental Consciousness as well as of consciousness of the relative order; it brings cosmic status to the individual life. When the individual consciousness achieves the status of cosmic existence then, in spite of all the obvious limitations of individuality, a man is ever free, unbounded by any aspect of time, space, or causation, ever out of bondage. This state of eternal freedom, set out here in principle, is a result of establishing the mind in the state of Transcendental Consciousness.

The Lord tells Arjuna that when he becomes established in the eternal freedom of divine intelligence, his life will become naturally full of meaning. That is why he need no longer seek the meaning of all the words of wisdom that he may hear or may have already heard, as the following verse makes clear.

VERSE 52

यदा ते मोहकलिलं बुद्धिर्व्यतितरिष्यति
तदा गन्तासि निर्वेदं श्रोतव्यस्य श्रुतस्य च

Yadā te mohakalilaṁ buddhir vyatitarishyati
tadā gantāsi nirvedaṁ shrotavyasya shrutasya cha

When your intellect crosses the mire of delusion, then will you gain indifference to what has been heard and what is yet to be heard.

Arjuna is caught up in what he has learnt about right and wrong. All his knowledge of the scriptures has not prevented him from falling into a state of suspension, or saved him from becoming inactive. He is still held in the state of suspension. This he will overcome only when his intellect rises above duality and reaches the field of pure Transcendental Consciousness.

The state of realization is beyond the limitations of thought, speech, and action; having reached it one truly rises above doubt and delusion.

The Lord is here summarizing all that he has so far told Arjuna. He has described to him the real state of Yoga, a state which satisfies both the intellect and the heart because, bringing fulfilment to both, it leaves no room for doubt or discontent in the domain of either. The emphasis in this verse is on the practice of arriving at Transcendental Consciousness and allowing the intellect to gain purity. This will mean the fulfilment of all the wisdom of life, of what has been heard in the past and what is worthy of being heard in the future. 'What has been heard and what is yet to be heard' will be superseded by the experience of Reality, for all hearing about Truth gains fulfilment in Its direct experience.

This verse takes one to a level of life that is free from problems. It makes clear the state in which one will 'gain indifference', and thereby shows a way to 'abandon attachment', as demanded by verse 48.

VERSE 53

श्रुतिविप्रतिपन्ना ते यदा स्थास्यति निश्चला
समाधावचला बुद्धिस्तदा योगमवाप्स्यसि

Shrutivipratipannā te yadā sthāsyati nishchalā
samādhāvachalā buddhis tadā yogam avāpsyasi

When your intellect, bewildered by Vedic texts, shall stand unshaken, steadfast in the Self, then will you attain to Yoga.

'Vedic texts': this refers to verses 42 to 44.

The Vedas expound the wisdom of right and wrong at various levels of evolution. They lay open the whole field of life, leaving a man to make his choice as to how he wants to proceed on the path of his evolution. Therefore it is quite possible that the mind influenced by Vedic learning, finding such a vast range of knowledge at its disposal, may become bewildered. But when once it has recourse to its own nature, the mind stands 'unshaken'. In this resolute state, when it transcends the whole field of relative life, it gains Self-consciousness, or pure awareness; and when this pure state of consciousness is never lost under any influence, then Yoga, or skill in action, is achieved.

Vedic wisdom comprises various expressions of Reality, as seen from different points of view and taught by different schools of thought. These manifold theories are meant to satisfy the different levels of human understanding, the purpose of the Vedas being to enlighten people of all types.

When one sees the different perspectives in Vedic Literature, one may be confused by the differences of opinion about the path of realization. But when the mind comes to *Samādhi*, or Transcendental Consciousness, the goal of all paths is reached. This resolute state of the mind in attainment stands completely clear, free from any confusion about the path towards it.

From the centre of Reality the whole circumference of life is seen to be completely harmonious, for when the centre is found it becomes clear that the innumerable radii all converge from the circumference towards a single point. If the centre is not found, then the various radii will be regarded as separate from one another with no common meeting-point. That is why the Lord stresses the importance of the direct experience of *Samādhi*, pure consciousness. This alone can dispel the uncertainties of the mind.

The purpose of the present verse is to strengthen the teaching given by the Lord in the 45th verse; it is in no way to refute the validity of the knowledge contained in the Vedic texts, without which intellectual satisfaction would not be possible. Scriptural knowledge becomes significant once Reality has been directly experienced.

Yoga here means 'skill in action', as defined in verse 50. The Lord makes it very plain to Arjuna that unless his mind first arrives at Transcendental Consciousness, and unless the intellect is then unshakeably established in this state of pure consciousness, that is to say, unless Cosmic Consciousness is attained, he cannot obtain Yoga, or skill in action.

In order to understand more thoroughly how Transcendental Consciousness is compatible with action and gives rise to skill in action, Arjuna, in the following verse, asks a very practical question.

VERSE 54

अर्जुन उवाच
स्थितप्रज्ञस्य का भाषा समाधिस्थस्य केशव
स्थितधीः किं प्रभाषेत किमासीत व्रजेत किम्

Arjuna uvācha
Sthitapragyasyạ kā bhāshā samādhisthasya Keshava
sthitadhīḥ kiṁ prabhāsheta kim āsīta vrajeta kim

Arjuna said:
What are the signs of a man whose intellect is steady, who is absorbed in the Self, O Keshava? How does the man of steady intellect speak, how does he sit, how does he walk?

Arjuna's question shows that the discourse up to this point has been very clearly understood by him and that his mind is attuned to Lord Kṛishṇa's thought.

'Keshava': one with long hair, Lord Kṛishṇa. When Arjuna asks for the outward 'sign' of the man of steady intellect, he addresses Lord Kṛishṇa by a name which refers to His outward appearance. Arjuna wants to know the distinctive characteristics of a man of steady intellect both when he is deep within himself, withdrawn from activity, and when he is active.

There are two ways of life: that of a householder and that of a recluse. *Karma Yoga* is the way of the householder, while Sāṁkhya, the way of knowledge, is for the recluse. Both types of men achieve the state of steady intellect and, having attained it, rise above the limitations of life and of society. Their lives present a synthesis of individual and cosmic existence. The freedom that they live and the universal outlook that they hold inspire the society to which they belong. Their lives are an expression of those ultimate values which are the foundation of social values of all time. Wherever they are, busy in the marketplace or silent in a Himālayan cave, they are the guiding light of the human race. Arjuna asks for some signs, some distinguishing marks of such souls. Being a practical man he wants to know the outward signs of a life of inner fulfilment.

The question shows that his mind is clearer at this moment than it was at the beginning of this chapter, when he could not think decisively. It also indicates the power of the teaching of Sāṁkhya and Yoga to clarify a man's mind and raise his consciousness.

Arjuna has been quietly listening to Lord Kṛishṇa. A discourse of forty-three verses (11–53) has turned his state of suspension to thoughts of a concrete nature. No longer occupied with thoughts of sorrow, his mind now rises to ask about the practical aspect of the integrated state of life. And this transformation has taken place within five to ten minutes, the time required to speak these verses.

His question is answered in the following eighteen verses, which present the characteristics of realized men who have gained steady intellect, whether by renouncing action through the knowledge of Sāṁkhya, or by way of *Karma Yoga*.

VERSE 55

श्रीभगवानुवाच
प्रजहाति यदा कामान्सर्वान्पार्थ मनोगतान्
आत्मन्येवात्मना तुष्टः स्थितप्रज्ञस्तदोच्यते

Shrī Bhagavān uvācha
Prajahāti yadā kāmān sarvān Pārtha manogatān
Ātmanyevātmanā tushtaḥ sthitapragyas tadochyate

The Blessed Lord said:
When a man completely casts off all desires that have gone (deep) into the mind, O Pārtha, when he is satisfied in the Self through the Self alone, then is he said to be of steady intellect.

Here Lord Kṛishṇa addresses Arjuna as 'Pārtha'. This is to maintain the tide of love created by the use of the same word when He spoke to Arjuna for the first time on the battlefield. Now that the Lord finds Arjuna's mind thinking on a more practical level, He still wants the qualities of Arjuna's heart to remain at their height and not be overshadowed by those of the mind.

This verse presents the 'steady intellect' in the state of *Samādhi*, or Transcendental Consciousness, and also in the state of *Nitya-samādhi*, or Cosmic Consciousness; in both cases the mind gains that state in which it 'completely casts off all desires that have gone (deep) into the mind'.

When, through the practice of Transcendental Meditation, the mind gains Transcendental Consciousness, it is completely out of the field of desires. This is the 'steady intellect' in the state of *Samādhi*.

How then is the 'steady intellect' maintained in *Nitya-samādhi*, when the mind, established in pure consciousness, is yet engaged in the field of action? Because in this state the mind has become transformed into Bliss Consciousness, Being is permanently lived as separate from activity. Then a man realizes that his Self is different from the mind which is engaged with thoughts and desires. It is now his experience that the mind, which had been identified with desires, is mainly identified with the Self.

He experiences the desires of the mind as lying outside himself, whereas he used to experience himself as completely involved with desires. On the surface of the mind desires certainly continue, but deep within the mind they no longer exist, for the depths of the mind are transformed into the nature of the Self. All the desires which were present in the mind have been thrown upward, as it were — they have gone to the surface, and within the mind the finest intellect gains an unshakeable, immovable status. '*Pragyā*'[23] is anchored to '*Kūtastha*'.[24] This is the 'steady intellect' in the state of *Nitya-samādhi*, Cosmic Consciousness.

Thus the wavering intellect gains a very stable basis, and as a result the field of activity is managed with great efficiency. It is quite wrong to think that one who has gained this state remains slumped in inertia and does not engage in action. This state of life is such that it maintains the freedom of the inner Being, keeping It uninvolved with activity, and at the same time deals with all actions most efficiently and successfully.

The word 'when' is very important. It indicates that one is said to be of 'steady intellect' only when one has gained Transcendental Consciousness, the state of separation from activity; or when one has gained Cosmic Consciousness, the state where one naturally maintains Self-consciousness even together with consciousness of the waking, dreaming, or sleeping states, and where the Self, or Being, remains unshadowed by any experience whatsoever.

It is wrong to conclude that only a recluse, who has given up all worldly desires, can attain this state of 'steady intellect'. It can be gained by anyone through the practice of Transcendental Meditation.[25]

The recluse way of life does not necessarily produce a condition where 'a man completely casts off all desires that have gone (deep) into the mind'. The state described by this phrase has nothing to do with any particular way of life. Lord Kṛishṇa is clearly referring to a state in which one is free from desires and 'satisfied in the Self'. And this is easily attained by anyone who

23 '*Pragyā*': intellect.

24 '*Kūtastha*': the Immovable, the Rocklike. See VI, 8.

25 See Appendix: The *Transcendental Meditation* Technique.

knows how to meditate and transcend relativity, whether he be recluse or householder, whether he meditate in a palace or a cave.

Shankara, the great exponent of the philosophy of integrated life, says in his commentary on this verse: 'By direct experience of the blissful nectar of the transcendent Reality the steady intellect holds itself absolutely without anything other than itself.'[26] And again he defines the man of steady intellect in the following words: 'He whose intellect, born of realization of the distinction between the ultimate and non-ultimate, is settled; he is a man of steady intellect.'[27] The intellectual understanding gained by the analysis of, and discrimination between, the ultimate and non-ultimate aspects of life does not produce the state of steady intellect. Such practices, remaining as they do on the level of thinking, can at best create moods of the mind; they certainly will not produce the state of mind called 'steady intellect'. This results only from direct experience of pure consciousness to such a degree of clarity that the difference between the 'ultimate' and the 'non-ultimate' is clearly cognized and appreciated on the intellectual level as well.

Thus Shankara plainly holds that this state of steady intellect is produced by the practice of transcending relativity, as expressed in verse 45, and not by merely spinning words about it or merely trying to understand it. The process of experience is very different from that of intellectual discrimination of Reality and non-Reality.[28]

This should be sufficient to remove the misunderstanding created by commentators or translators of the Bhagavad-Gītā who hold that the steady intellect can only be gained by recluses, a view which is responsible for spiritual decadence in modern society. Unfortunately, Shankara's own view has been misrepresented by commentators who undertook to propagate his philosophy. They seem to have missed the central part of spiritual life — Transcendental Consciousness and the direct way to its realization. As a result, everything which aimed at clarifying the process of transcending has been held to belong

26 '*Paramārtha-darshana-amṛita-rasa-lābhena anyāsmād alaṁ-pratyayavān sthitapragyaḥ.*'
27 '*Sthitā pratishthitā ātmānātma-vivekajā pragyā yasya saḥ sthitapragyaḥ.*'
28 See verse 40, commentary.

to the path of renunciation and attributed to the recluse way of life. This lack of insight into principle cast the centre of spiritual life on to the recluse order, thus debarring the householder from the gains of spirituality, and throwing the whole of humanity out of joint.

This verse does not record any outer sign of the man whose intellect is steady and who is established in the Self, because there cannot be any outer sign to show that a man is absorbed deep within himself. The inner state of such a man cannot be judged by outer signs. It cannot be said that he sits like this or like that or closes his eyes in any particular manner. No such external signs can serve as criteria of this state.

A man may sit in any style and go deep within himself and be in Bliss Consciousness. It may be said that when someone goes into *Samādhi* his face becomes serene and more glowing, but this is not something that can be gauged by any fixed standard. For this reason the Lord does not enter into any such description. The signs recounted here are only subjective. They concern the inner condition of the mind as indicated by 'casts off all desires' and 'is satisfied in the Self'.

This verse brings to light the basis of the steady intellect: the realization of Being in Transcendental Consciousness or in Cosmic Consciousness. The next verse presents the nature of the man who has gained steady intellect. Verse 57 describes the nature of the means whereby he acts in the state of steady intellect: non-attachment. Verse 58 explains the nature of his activity in this state: his senses are withdrawn from their objects. Finally, verse 59 points to the influence of the Unseen on the steady intellect.[29] It shows that not merely are the senses withdrawn from their objects, but even their taste for these objects vanishes when the Supreme unfolds Itself to them in Its unbounded grandeur — when the Supreme comes to be lived on the sensory level of existence. These five verses taken together reveal the essentials of the 'steady intellect'.

29 The basis, the doer, the means, activity, and Providence are the five factors for the accomplishment of any action, as given in XVIII, 14.

VERSE 56

दुः खेष्वनुद्विग्नमनाः सुखेषु विगतस्पृहः
वीतरागभयक्रोधः स्थितधीर्मुनिरुच्यते

Duḥkheshwanudwignamanāḥ sukheshu vigataspṛihaḥ
vītarāgabhayakrodhaḥ sthitadhīr muniruchyate

He whose mind is unshaken in the midst of sorrows, who amongst pleasures is free from longing, from whom attachment, fear, and anger have departed, he is said to be a sage of steady intellect.

'A sage' (*Muni*) is defined in this verse.

The Lord begins to answer Arjuna's question about the man of steady intellect, who quite naturally maintains balance of mind while he continues to act in the field of relative existence. The verse does not provide any signs of an objective nature, but it describes the subjective aspect of a man of steady intellect.

Just as a millionaire who has great wealth remains unaffected by the rise and fall of the market, so the mind which has gained the state of Bliss Consciousness through Transcendental Meditation remains naturally contented on coming out from the transcendental state to the field of activity. This contentment, being grounded in the very nature of the mind, does not allow the mind to waver and be affected in pleasure or pain, nor allow it to become affected by attachment or fear in the world. This natural equanimity of the mind, even while it is actively engaged, is the state of steady intellect.

'Sorrows' arise in the mind through want of understanding. When one understands only so much and no more of life, lacking vision of the whole span of life, then one feels sorrow. But the man who understands both the unchanging eternal phase of life and the unending nature of the ever-changing cycle of life and death will recognize the ephemeral nature of sorrow and not be overwhelmed by it.

The feeling of sorrow in the heart, as distinct from the mind, is due to lack of fulfilment, lack of love, lack of happiness. One who practises Transcendental Meditation experiences the bliss which fills the heart and brings eternal contentment, which leaves no room for any negative emotion, for sorrow, depression, fear, or the like. Neither does it leave room for waves of joy or other positive emotions because the heart is by nature full and contented. It is like the heart of a grown man remaining unaffected by the toys which create great emotions in the hearts of children.

The experience of Transcendental Consciousness raises a man's consciousness to a level where he finds his Self completely separate from all activity, and naturally his values will change. The values of life are different at different levels of evolution. This is why, when the normal behaviour of a man of steady intellect, established on the level of divine consciousness, is seen from the ordinary level of human consciousness, it appears different and more than normal — unshaken by pleasure and pain, fear and anger.

The basis of such a detached state of life is explained in the following verse.

VERSE 57

यः सर्वत्रानभिस्नेहस्तत्तत्प्राप्य शुभाशुभम्
नाभिनन्दति न द्वेष्टि तस्य प्रज्ञा प्रतिष्ठिता

Yaḥ sarvatrānabhisnehas tat tat prāpya shubhāshubham
nābhinandati na dweshti tasya pragyā pratishthitā

He who has no undue fondness towards anything, who
neither exults nor recoils on gaining what is good or bad,
his intellect is established.

The man whose mind is established in the Unity of Bliss Consciousness knows by experience that his Self is separate from all activity. He acts in the field of relativity, but experience cannot make any deep impression. This is why he naturally remains consistent in his outlook and behaviour with others, even while experiencing the diverse nature of the world.

Many a commentator upon these verses has introduced the idea that in order to achieve the state of established intellect one should try to be dispassionate and detached. But in the field of behaviour and experience the strain of attempting to be dispassionate and detached, of trying to make a mood of equanimity in pleasure and pain, only puts unnatural, undue stress on the mind, resulting in the development of an unnatural and warped state of the inner personality. This kind of practice has helped to bring dullness, artificiality, and tension to life in the name of spiritual growth; it has spoiled the brilliance of many a genius in every generation for centuries past. As a consequence, there has grown up in intelligent levels of society throughout the world a kind of fear of the spiritual life, which has gone so far that young and energetic people today find even discussion about spiritual practices embarrassing.

In his reply to Arjuna's question, the Lord wants to bring home to him that through the practice of Transcendental Meditation the mind becomes infused with divine intelligence and bliss. Thereafter, even while one acts in the world, the state of equanimity is naturally maintained.

This verse can never be interpreted in terms of mood-making, or of controlling the mind in an attempt to live evenness intellectually. It brings out that the man of steady intellect is by nature grounded in non-attachment.

Unfortunately some interpreters have gone so far in misrepresenting the truth of this verse as to disapprove even of enjoying a flower in full bloom or rejecting a faded one. And this way of making life cold and devoid of heart has been recommended as a way of gaining established intellect. What cruelty to life!

It is a mistake to copy the behaviour of a realized man while remaining in the unrealized state. If a poor man puts up the sign of a wealthy man and tries to behave like one, this can only result in tension. By superficially copying the behaviour of a rich man, he cannot possibly become rich. Similarly, the behaviour of a man of steady intellect provides no standard for one whose intellect is not steady. If he tries to go that way, his life will become cold, deprived of the qualities of heart and mind. This has been the destiny of many a sincere seeker of Truth down the ages.

Misguided interpretations of verses like this, which are found in almost all scriptures, are responsible for the spiritual plight of innumerable generations.

It must not be forgotten that there are two ways of life, that of a householder and that of a recluse. Men from both ways who meditate and arrive at the state of steady intellect will continue in their respective ways of life. The householder, by nature habituated to the field of activity with all the diversity of phenomenal existence, continues to act in the world, while the recluse continues in his detachment from worldly affairs. The state of steady intellect simply brings them fulfilment. They rise above attachment and detachment, finding their life on the level of eternity, unbounded by any limitation of time, space, and causation, far above the boundaries of any social bond or obligation. Their life is one of Cosmic Consciousness. They are above the distinction of day and night: waking or sleeping they are established in the oneness of divine intelligence and bliss. This world of joys and sorrows, of man's great enterprise and ambition, is for them like a world of dolls and toys with which children play and amuse themselves. Toys are a source of great excitement for children, but grown-ups remain untouched by them. The man of established intellect remains even and does not rejoice or recoil 'on gaining what is good or bad'.

'Has no undue fondness' means is not too emotionally attached. But this does not imply that the man of established intellect is cold and without warmth of heart. On the contrary, he alone is a man of full heart. He is an unbounded ocean of love and happiness. His love and his happiness flow and overflow for everyone in like manner; that is why he has no 'undue fondness towards anything'.

It may be stated that the detached and unshakeable nature of a man of established intellect, described in the previous verse, is based on the principle of non-attachment, as taught in this verse. Such non-attachment develops naturally with the growth of awareness of the Self as separate from activity. This same natural state of non-attachment is at the basis of activity in the state of steady intellect even when the senses remain 'withdrawn' from their objects, as shown in the following verse.

VERSE 58

यदा संहरते चायं कूर्मोऽङ्गानीव सर्वशः
इन्द्रियाणीन्द्रियार्थेभ्यस्तस्य प्रज्ञा प्रतिष्ठिता

Yadā saṁharate chāyaṁ kūrmo 'ngānīva sarvashaḥ
indriyāṇīndriyārthebhyas tasya pragyā pratishthitā

And when such a man withdraws his senses from their objects, as a tortoise draws in its limbs from all sides, his intellect is established.

This verse pictures the state of the senses of a man of established intellect by drawing a comparison with the indrawn limbs of a tortoise that from the outside seems to have no limbs at all. By this example the Lord also implies that it is not possible correctly to express the outward signs or distinguishing marks of a man of established intellect. But at least one thing is clear — his senses are drawn in, they are not turned in an outward direction.

It may appear that the man of steady intellect referred to in this verse is only he who is in the state of Transcendental Consciousness, for in this state alone are the senses completely withdrawn from their object. But 'withdraws his senses' does not necessarily mean that the senses do not experience outside objects, as in the state of Transcendental Consciousness. The senses can be involved with outer experiences and yet not be totally engrossed in them to the extent that they transfer to the mind impressions deep enough to become the seed of future desires. It is very important to understand the verse in this way; otherwise, the man of steady intellect would have to remain forever outside the domain of sensory activity, which is physically impossible. The established intellect has, in fact, little to do with the activity or non-activity of the senses; its basis lies in the natural state of non-attachment described in the previous verse. It is plain, therefore, that the present verse refers not to Transcendental Consciousness alone but also to Cosmic Consciousness, where it is possible for the senses to be in a state of non-attachment even while they are active.

The Lord is here emphasizing that in the state of established intellect the senses, being free from attraction towards their objects, remain as though withdrawn from them. When the mind is mainly identified with the inner Being, the senses do not identify themselves with their objects. Moreover the next verse shows that when the senses are exposed to the unbounded grandeur of the Supreme, they lose even the taste for their objects. This makes it clear that when the transcendent Being fills the mind and begins to be lived on the sensory level, then the intellect is established.

This is a very different state from mere non-indulgence of the senses, which is certainly no absolute criterion of the established intellect. A man who, because of some circumstance, does not enjoy the objects of sense may appear to be like an indrawn tortoise, although the mind within may be active, quietly absorbed in the thought of the joys of the senses. Such a state of mind is obviously not the resolute state; it is not established intellect.

Thc principle here brought out does not depend on whether or not the senses are active. It reveals the inner condition of non-attachment, on the sensory level, in the state of established intellect.

VERSE 59

विषया विनिवर्तन्ते निराहारस्य देहिनः
रसवर्जं रसोऽप्यस्य परं दृष्ट्वा निवर्तते

Vishayā vinivartante nirāhārasya dehinaḥ
rasavarjaṁ raso 'pyasya paraṁ dṛishtwā nivartate

The objects of sense turn away from him who does
not feed upon them, but the taste for them persists.
On seeing the Supreme even this taste ceases.

'Taste for them persists' means that the mind continues to experience objects through the finer levels of the senses. In thus distinguishing between the gross and subtle fields of sensory perception, the Lord means to convey that in the state of steady intellect even the finer faculties of the senses remain unattached to objects.

This verse presents a challenge to the whole philosophy of control of the senses. It shows clearly that the senses cannot be controlled from their own level.

In the field of the senses, the senses predominate. They drag the mind towards their objects, towards the joys of the world. None of the objects of the senses, however, is able to satisfy the longing of the mind for happiness. Therefore the mind is ever found wandering in the field of the senses. Only when the state of established intellect is gained and the mind ceases to wander, can the senses be controlled.

It is wrong to assume that unless the senses are controlled one cannot realize the Truth. As a matter of fact, the converse is true: according to this verse, the senses come under complete control only with the light of realization — only when the transcendent Self, or Being, comes to be appreciated on the level of the senses.

Wrong interpretations of this and other verses have led many genuine seekers of Truth to undertake rigorous and unnatural practices in order to control the senses, thus wasting their lives and benefiting neither themselves nor others. Mastery of the senses is gained only through the state of established intellect, for in this state where man is established in awareness of the Self as separate from activity, his behaviour is quite naturally unaffected by the otherwise overpowering influence of the senses. At the end of this chapter, the Lord concludes that when behaviour in the sensory field does not in any way disturb the state of established intellect, and established intellect behaves as master of the senses, the highest state of human evolution has been reached.

'On seeing the Supreme': when the intellect goes beyond the field of the three *Guṇas* and cognizes the transcendent Reality, that is, gains Transcendental Consciousness. When this state of Transcendental Consciousness is maintained even while the senses are active, then a situation is created in which the Transcendent comes to be lived naturally on the level of sensory perception. And when the Transcendent comes to be appreciated on the sensory level, then a man is said to have truly gained established intellect.

VERSE 60

यततो ह्यपि कौन्तेय पुरुषस्य विपश्चितः
इन्द्रियाणि प्रमाथीनि हरन्ति प्रसभं मनः

Yatato hyapi Kaunteya purushasya vipashchitaḥ
indriyāṇi pramāthīni haranti prasabhaṁ manaḥ

The turbulent senses, O son of Kuntī, forcibly carry away the mind even of a discerning man who endeavours (to control them).

Here the Lord describes to Arjuna the nature of the senses. Being the instruments which enable the mind to enjoy the glory of the diversity of creation, they are in duty bound to draw it towards objects of pleasure. Their main purpose is to bring the greatest possible happiness to the mind. And this they will continue to do so long as the mind has not become eternally contented in the bliss of the Absolute.

How to make best use of the senses in order to come to the experience of eternal bliss is described in the following verses.

VERSE 61

तानि सर्वाणि संयम्य युक्त आसीत मत्परः
वशे हि यस्येन्द्रियाणि तस्य प्रज्ञा प्रतिष्ठिता

Tāni sarvāṇi saṁyamya yukta āsīta matparaḥ
vashe hi yasyendriyāṇi tasya pragyā pratishthitā

Having brought them all under control, let him sit united, looking to Me as Supreme; for his intellect is established whose senses are subdued.

The previous verse explained the nature of the senses and their overpowering influence on the mind, while the verses that follow depict the dangers which result from their indulgence when the level of the Transcendent is not maintained. In this verse the

Lord holds out hope by showing that it is possible to control the senses and that 'his intellect is established whose senses are subdued'.

The Lord says: 'Having brought them all under control, let him sit united, looking to Me as Supreme'. This opens up a way, for when the attention has been brought to the Transcendent, the activity of the senses ceases and they will be automatically controlled. In this state of life, says the Lord, 'let him sit united, looking to Me as Supreme'.

The technique of bringing them 'all' under control is to engage any one sense in providing increasing happiness for the mind on the path of transcending — that is, to begin the practice of Transcendental Meditation. In this process the mind, using a particular sense for passing through the finer levels of experience and transcending the subtlest experience, also transcends the field of that sense and the fields of all the senses. Gaining Bliss Consciousness in this way, the mind wins automatic control over all the senses.

'Let him sit united, looking to Me as Supreme': the man who sits united is one whose self is united with the Self, or Being, even though he is engaged in action. Through the repeated practice of Transcendental Meditation he has realized Being to such fullness that no activity can overshadow It; that is to say, he has realized Being as separate from activity. Having gained this state, says the Lord, let him maintain it and in that state be devoted to Me, the Lord of all creation, who presides over both the absolute and relative phases of existence.

The teaching is that, having gained Cosmic Consciousness and having thereby created a situation where mind and senses remain naturally organized, using their full potential to fulfil desires that further the good of the world, a man should devote himself to God and let the heart flow and overflow in love for Him, the great Lord of all. He alone can be someone to whom life in Cosmic Consciousness can turn; for, being omnipotent and omniscient, He ranks higher than life in Cosmic Consciousness. The purpose of this teaching of devotion to God on that high level where man has reached his full potentiality is to enable him to experience the great waves of bliss in the ocean of

Cosmic Consciousness — experience that joyfulness of eternal life which brings complete fulfilment to his existence.

VERSE 62

ध्यायतो विषयान्पुंसः सङ्गस्तेषूपजायते
सङ्गात्संजायते कामः कामात्क्रोधोऽभिजायते

Dhyāyato vishayān puṁsaḥ sangas teshūpajāyate
sangāt saṁjāyate kāmaḥ kāmāt krodho 'bhijāyate

Pondering on objects of the senses, a man develops
attachment for them; from attachment springs up desire,
and desire gives rise to anger.

This verse depicts one who is not turned towards the Divine, but towards the objects of the senses. The Lord shows how such a man gradually sinks deeper and deeper into the mire of delusion until he perishes.

Thought is a great force in man. It develops into desire, which in turn translates itself into action, bringing glory or disgrace. 'Anger' arises from weakness or inability to fulfil one's desires, although it is generally attributed to obstacles in the way of such fulfilment. And thus desire is said to be the direct cause of anger.[30]

VERSE 63

क्रोधाद्भवति संमोहः संमोहात्स्मृतिविभ्रमः
स्मृतिभ्रंशाद्बुद्धिनाशो बुद्धिनाशात्प्रणश्यति

Krodhād bhavati saṁmohaḥ saṁmohāt smṛitivibhramaḥ
smṛitibhraṁshād buddhināsho buddhināshāt praṇashyati

From anger arises delusion; from delusion unsteadiness of
memory; from unsteadiness of memory destruction of intellect;
through the destruction of the intellect he perishes.

30 See III, 37, commentary.

Anger excites the mind, which loses its balance and power of discrimination; it loses proper vision and foresight and a right sense of values. This state of 'delusion' obscures the track of memory, and thereby one feels as if disconnected from the harmonious rhythm of life. Wisdom fails, and the intellect ceases to function. The boat of life is left with nobody in control; it meets with disaster as a matter of course.

The intellect is the finest aspect of one's subjective nature. As long as the intellect is intact there is every hope of the advancement and fulfilment of life. That is why the Lord says that the destruction of the intellect results in a man's ruin.

VERSE 64

रागद्वेषवियुक्तैस्तु विषयानिन्द्रियैश्चरन्
आत्मवश्यैर्विधेयात्मा प्रसादमधिगच्छति

Rāgadweshaviyuktais tu vishayān indriyaish charan
ātmavashyair vidheyātmā prasādam adhigachchhati

But he who is self-disciplined, who moves among the objects of the senses with the senses freed from attachment and aversion and under his own control, he attains to 'grace'.

'Grace' here means delight and wholeness, resulting from the state of pure consciousness.

This verse contrasts with the two preceding verses. Having explained to Arjuna the plight of those who surrender themselves to the call of desire without possessing control of the senses, the Lord, in this verse, shows him the reward gained by the man who disciplines himself before plunging into worldly life.

The Lord here explains the status of the integrated man. He is established in the Self, and by virtue of this, even when he acts in the field of the senses and experiences their objects, he is not lost in them; maintaining his status in Being, he quite naturally maintains evenness of mind. His sense of values is balanced. Acting in the world, he is not lost in it. He is above attachment and detachment, contented in himself, not bound by anything.

The results of reaching this state of blissful freedom are described in the verses that follow.

VERSE 65

प्रसादे सर्वदुःखानां हानिरस्योपजायते
प्रसन्नचेतसो ह्याशु बुद्धिः पर्यवतिष्ठते

Prasāde sarvaduḥkhānāṁ hānir asyopajāyate
prasannachetaso hyāshu buddhiḥ paryavatishthate

In 'grace' is born an end to all his sorrows. Indeed the intellect of the man of exalted consciousness soon becomes firmly established.

The experience of pure Bliss Consciousness puts an end to all suffering; filling the heart with happiness it brings perfect tranquillity to the mind.

The principle is that if freedom from suffering, lasting peace, health, and fulfilment are desired, it is necessary to gain Bliss Consciousness.

VERSE 66

नास्ति बुद्धिरयुक्तस्य न चायुक्तस्य भावना
न चाभावयतः शान्तिरशान्तस्य कुतः सुखम्

Nāsti buddhir ayuktasya na chāyuktasya bhāvanā
na chābhāvayataḥ shāntir ashāntasya kutaḥ sukham

He who is not established has no intellect, nor has he any steady thought. The man without steady thought has no peace; for one without peace how can there be happiness?

The glory of the established intellect is brought out here. When the mind is established in the Self, then it is in tune with cosmic intelligence, and then only has it what the Lord calls 'intellect', the faculty of discrimination. Unless one is in tune with cosmic intelligence there is no wisdom, no steadiness, no peace, no happiness in the real sense.

The verse may also be interpreted as showing the stages through which a worldly mind passes on the way to Bliss Consciousness. Confused in the world as the mind is, it has to become peaceful in order to have a steady thought, which then converges into a state of one-pointedness called 'intellect', which then becomes established in Being.

When, during meditation, the mind enters into the experience of subtle levels of thought, it becomes more collected, more steady, with every step and therefore feels itself entering a field of increasing charm. This process ends in the absolute happiness of the Transcendent.

If the mind is more steady, it is in a better position to experience greater happiness. As on a calmer surface of water the sun reflects more clearly, so a calmer mind receives a clearer reflection of the omnipresent bliss of the absolute Being. As the mind fathoms finer fields of thinking during meditation, the metabolism is simultaneously reduced. This establishes the nervous system in degrees of ever-increasing peace. Eventually, when the entire nervous system comes to a completely peaceful state, it reflects Being, and this gives rise to Bliss Consciousness.

The state of Transcendental Consciousness cannot be gained unless the nervous system is completely peaceful. This is the truth revealed by the words 'for one without peace how can there be happiness?' The bliss is already there; it is only necessary to calm down the wanderings of the mind.

A question arises here. If the wanderings of the mind are due to its search for happiness, could it not be said: unless there is happiness how can there be peace? But no, the expression 'unless there is happiness' is completely wrong; it could not have been framed by Lord Kṛishṇa because it is not true. For bliss is omnipresent and eternal, while happiness is the expression of the reflection of the omnipresent bliss on the mind. Absolute bliss being always there, the experience of happiness thus depends upon the degree of steadiness of the mind. If the mind is more collected, more peaceful, it experiences more happiness.

During meditation the mind, entering the subtle phases of a

thought, becomes more collected and more peaceful;[31] that is why it proceeds that way automatically. This truth is expressed by the Upanishads when they declare that happiness varies in different states of creation, at different levels of evolution. As the mind evolves to higher levels of consciousness during meditation, it experiences increasing degrees of happiness, until it comes to absolute bliss in the most highly evolved state of pure Transcendental Consciousness.

VERSE 67

इन्द्रियाणां हि चरतां यन्मनोऽनुविधीयते
तदस्य हरति प्रज्ञां वायुर्नावमिवाम्भसि

Indriyāṇāṁ hi charatāṁ yan mano 'nuvidhīyate
tad asya harati pragyāṁ vāyur nāvam ivāmbhasi

When a man's mind is governed by any of the wandering senses, his intellect is carried away by it as a ship by the wind on water.

The mind by nature thirsts for greater happiness. Let us suppose it is enjoying experience through a particular sense. In its eagerness to enjoy the utmost which that sense can provide, it becomes absorbed in the process of enjoying, and in this one-sided absorption loses the power of discrimination, which is the main faculty of the intellect. This is what the Lord means when He says the senses rob a man of intellect.

The mind is prepared to accept anything that can tempt it with the promise of happiness. Any sensory object which promises happiness is capable of taking possession of the mind. This is not to the discredit of the mind, for its nature is to enjoy.

If the senses draw the mind to the joys of their objects, this similarly is no discredit to the senses. They are the machinery through which the mind enjoys and, like a ready servant, are waiting to serve the mind.

As a ship is carried away by the wind, so is the mind com-

31 See verse 70.

pletely carried away by the senses in the outward direction of gross creation, the direction of the objects of the senses. It loses the power of concentration, for it travels as if in a diverging beam, a course naturally opposed to the concentrated state of intellect.

The following verse advises control over the senses for safety's sake.

VERSE 68

तस्माद्यस्य महाबाहो निगृहीतानि सर्वशः
इन्द्रियाणीन्द्रियार्थेभ्यस्तस्य प्रज्ञा प्रतिष्ठिता

Tasmād yasya Mahābāho nigṛihītāni sarvashaḥ
indriyāṇīndriyārthebhyas tasya pragyā pratishthitā

Therefore he whose senses are all withdrawn from their objects, O mighty-armed, his intellect is established.

This verse, which is almost a repetition of verse 58, presents the conclusion of the last six verses. It gives the quintessence of the entire scheme of fulfilment in life, which is to channel the mind into regions of experience more blissful than the ordinary gross fields of sensory life.

'Therefore' refers back to the words of verse 66: 'for one without peace how can there be happiness?' It indicates that if happiness is sought, peace has to be created, the nervous system has to be brought to a state of restful alertness. For this to happen, the activity of the senses must cease. That is why the Lord says: 'whose senses are all withdrawn from their objects'.

The verse establishes that the senses lose their relationship to their objects when the intellect is resolute, when it is established in the Self.

The senses function on different levels. On the gross level they enable the mind to enjoy the external aspects of their objects. Functioning on subtler levels, they enable it to experience the more subtle aspects of objects; and joys arising from the experience of the subtler states of objects are greater than those arising from their gross states.

When, during meditation, the mind begins to experience the

subtler aspects of a thought, it experiences increasing charm and thus is naturally attracted to the experience of the subtlest aspect of the thought. The experience of this finest state of thought, which is on the subtlest level of creation, provides the mind with the greatest joy in the field of relativity, but even this joy is not permanent, is not of absolute nature.

Arjuna is being directed to bring his mind to a state beyond the greatest joy of relativity, so that he can free himself from dependence upon the transitory relative joys of life and become established in the bliss of the Absolute. To reach this eternal bliss, the Lord asks him to leave completely the field of sensory perception, both gross and subtle. Thus he will come to established intellect, intellect established in the Transcendent. To live this principle in daily life is simple, for one need only know how to allow the mind to come quite naturally out of the field of the senses and reach the state of established intellect.[32]

Thus in this verse, the principle that has already been explained from the point of view of the mind is illustrated from that of relative sensory perception.

The following verse distinguishes between the fields of life of the enlightened and the ignorant.

VERSE 69

या निशा सर्वभूतानां तस्यां जागर्ति संयमी
यस्यां जाग्रति भूतानि सा निशा पश्यतो मुनेः

Yā nishā sarvabhūtānāṁ tasyāṁ jāgarti saṁyamī
yasyāṁ jāgrati bhūtāni sā nishā pashyato muneḥ

That which is night for all beings, therein the self-controlled is awake. That wherein beings are awake is night for the sage who sees.

'Sage' (*Muni*): not necessarily a recluse, but rather a man of calm, far-seeing prudence and wisdom.

'Sees' means sees the Truth.

Here the Lord shows Arjuna the difference between the state

32 See II, 45, commentary.

of the ignorant man and that of the realized: one exists in darkness, the other in light. Or the night of the one is the day of the other, for the realized man is awake in the light of the Self, while the ignorant is awake in the light of the senses. The realized man is awake in the light of absolute bliss, the ignorant in the light of relative joys of perishable nature.

The Lord says that the light in which the established intellect behaves is not perceived by the ignorant, and the light in which the ignorant behave is looked upon as darkness by the enlightened.

Verse 70

आपूर्यमाणमचलप्रतिष्ठं
समुद्रमापः प्रविशन्ति यद्वत्
तद्वत्कामा यं प्रविशन्ति सर्वे
स शान्तिमाप्नोति न कामकामी

Āpūryamāṇam achalapratishthaṁ
samudram āpaḥ pravishanti yadvat
tadvat kāmā yaṁ pravishanti sarve
sa shāntim āpnoti na kāmakāmī

He whom all desires enter as waters enter
the ever-full and unmoved sea attains peace,
and not he who cherishes desires.

When a man has risen to this lasting state of consciousness, the state where his Self is detached from and not overshadowed by the relative states of life — waking, dreaming, and deep sleep — then his state is like that of an ever-full and steady ocean. This, being the state of absolute bliss, is the goal of all desires in life.

Desires arise from a particular want, from a lack of happiness; the mind is ever seeking a field of greater happiness. Thus desires are always flowing towards eternal Bliss Consciousness, as rivers to the ocean.

Once Bliss Consciousness is permanently attained, desires have served their purpose and therefore cravings do not arise. This is a state of true contentment, a state of lasting peace.

The Lord says that lasting peace is never achieved by one who is not complete in himself and still craves worldly things. However, this does not mean that in order to attain peace in life a man should cease to desire and to aspire. It is the desires that lead a man to greater happiness and to fulfilment — not the control and killing of desires, which has been widely advocated through the ages.

This verse too has been wrongly interpreted, with a consequent increase in dullness and inefficiency, particularly in the lives of young people in India. The undue stress laid on fatalism has proved disastrous for their physical well-being and for the material progress of society. Thinking that to desire and to aspire will not lead to peace, people begin to abstain from enterprise and cease to open the gates of progress. This is simply a wrong understanding of the Lord's teaching.

The verse shows Arjuna very clearly that the Self-awareness of the realized is like an ocean, which will accept any stream of desires and will satisfy it without being affected.

The ocean accepts the river as it comes and denies no stream rushing in, yet its status remains unaffected. Such is the state of established intellect, which cannot be affected by anything. It is a state of eternal peace.

The following verse gives the technique of maintaining such a permanent state of peace in the midst of activity.

Verse 71

विहाय कामान्यः सर्वान्पुमांश्चरति निःस्पृहः
निर्ममो निरहंकारः स शान्तिमधिगच्छति

Vihāya kāmān yaḥ sarvān pumāṁsh charati niḥspṛihaḥ
nirmamo nirahaṁkāraḥ sa shāntim adhigachchhati

When a man acts without longing, having relinquished all desires, free from the sense of 'I' and 'mine', he attains to peace.

'Having relinquished all desires' does not mean that the mind no longer entertains any desires, because this would not be possible for a living being. It means that the Self has been realized as detached from activity, as was made clear in the commentary on verse 55. Because a man in this state acts while remaining 'free from the sense of "I" and "mine"', it is quite natural that activity does not in any way disturb his state of established intellect. He has gained that eternal freedom in life where the status of one's Being remains unaffected by any activity. The following verse throws more light on this.

To have 'relinquished all desires' means to have gained transcendental divine consciousness permanently. This happens through meditation.

When, after meditation, the mind comes out infused with the transcendental divine nature, the individual acts in the world, and this action is quite naturally free from the narrowness of petty individuality, from the short-sightedness of selfish attachment, which previously held him imprisoned. Everything moves according to the cosmic plan,[33] and although the individual ego continues to function, the action is that of divine intelligence working through the individual who is living cosmic existence.

Such a life is a very natural expression of cosmic intelligence in the world. It represents the state of eternal freedom here on earth. Nothing in the world is able to overshadow or disturb this state, because it is inclusive of all that lies between two extremes of life — the transcendental divine nature of the Absolute and human nature in relative existence.

VERSE 72

एषा ब्राह्मी स्थितिः पार्थ नैनां प्राप्य विमुह्यति
स्थित्वास्यामन्तकालेऽपि ब्रह्मनिर्वाणमृच्छति

Eshā brāhmī sthitiḥ Pārtha naināṁ prāpya vimuhyati
sthitwāsyām antakāle 'pi Brahmanirvāṇam ṛichchhati

This is the state of Brahman, O Pārtha. Having attained it, a man is not deluded. Established in that, even at the last moment, he attains eternal freedom in divine consciousness.

33 See Appendix: Cosmic Law, The Basic Law of Creation.

The state of life described in the previous verse, says the Lord, is the state of Cosmic Consciousness. If a man is to attain to this state, it is necessary for him to gain stability of Self-consciousness in the midst of activity. This entails culturing the nervous system, the seat of consciousness, in such a way that it becomes capable of maintaining Self-consciousness, which in its nature is transcendental, along with the waking, dreaming, or sleeping states of consciousness. The process of refining the nervous system is a delicate one and takes its own time, depending upon the various factors of individual life.

When the mind transcends during Transcendental Meditation, the metabolism reaches its lowest point; so does the process of breathing, and the nervous system gains a state of restful alertness which, on the physical level, corresponds to the state of Bliss Consciousness, or transcendent Being. In order that the consciousness of the waking state may be maintained along with transcendental Bliss Consciousness, it is essential for the nervous system not to lose this state of restful alertness corresponding to Bliss Consciousness. At the same time, the nervous system should maintain a metabolic rate corresponding to the activity taking place in the waking state.

For this to come about, regular and continued practice of such meditation as leads to Transcendental Consciousness is necessary. This has to be followed by activity, because activity after meditation brings an infusion of transcendental Being into the nature of the mind and through it into all aspects of one's life in the relative field. With the constant practice of meditation, this infusion continues to grow, and when it is full-grown Cosmic Consciousness will have been attained.

Once this state is attained, to fall from it is impossible. It holds Transcendental Consciousness intact in the field of all the relative states, waking, dreaming, and deep sleep. Thus, in 'the state of *Brahman*', the state of eternal life, the activity or the silence of relative existence belongs to the absolute Being.

Having reached this state, a man's life is really the expression of divine life. The divine life is found in the individual life, the absolute Being on the human level, eternal freedom within the limitations of individuality: time, space, and causation. It would be wrong to estimate the state of Cosmic Consciousness in a man by anything he displays in the field of action, because this state accepts every activity, great or small, and at the same time retains complete stillness. His state cannot, in principle, be judged by what he does. There are no outer signs of a man who has risen to this state of *Brahman*.

Those seekers of Truth who have accepted a life of renunciation naturally continue to abstain from all activities of life even when they attain Cosmic Consciousness. This is due to their long-established habit of non-indulgence in activity. In the same way, when men of the world, actively engaged in many phases of life, reach the state of Cosmic Consciousness through Yoga, they continue to act, mainly from force of habit. But whether involved in activity or leading a quiet life, a soul evolved to this cosmic state is eternally contented.

This state is ever the same, whether the mind is active in the waking or dreaming state, or inactive in deep sleep. It is a state of eternal liberation during life here on earth. The Lord's words 'even at the last moment' provide a firm assurance that the fulfilment of life's purpose will be achieved through the teaching of this chapter. Arjuna has been given all that he needs to enable him to rise to 'eternal freedom in divine consciousness'.

ॐ तत्सदिति श्रीमद्भगवद्गीतासूपनिषत्सु ब्रह्मविद्यायां योगशास्त्रे
श्रीकृष्णार्जुनसंवादे सांख्ययोगो नाम द्वितीयोऽध्यायः

Oṁ tat sad iti Shrīmad Bhagavadgītāsūpanishatsu
Brahmavidyāyām̐ Yogashāstre Shrīkṛishṇārjunasam̐vāde
Sām̐khyayogo nāma dwitīyo 'dhyāyaḥ

Thus, in the Upanishad of the glorious Bhagavad-Gītā, in the Science of the Absolute, in the Scripture of Yoga, in the dialogue between Lord Kṛishṇa and Arjuna, ends the second chapter, entitled: The Yoga of Knowledge, Sām̐khya Yoga.

CHAPTER III

A VISION OF THE TEACHING IN CHAPTER III

Verses 1–4. Equanimity, the basis of all success and salvation in life, is gained and made permanent in two ways: by the path of knowledge and the path of action.

Verses 5–16. Both paths culture the mind and reorientate the functioning of the senses. By the practice of gaining Transcendental Consciousness and then engaging in action, the infusion of Being into the nature of the mind enables it to maintain equanimity and sets the senses spontaneously to perform actions which are natural and useful to evolution.

Verses 17–20. When, through practice, Transcendental Consciousness becomes permanent, the purpose of all action is accomplished. In this state of fulfilment action that is right must be performed, because it brings perfection in life and good to the world.

Verse 21. One should be careful of one's actions, because others follow one's example.

Verses 22–6. The Lord of Creation, Himself remaining uninvolved, is engaged in constant activity. So a man living in the Light of God should engage in action, remaining himself uninvolved, inspiring others to perform their natural duty.

Verses 27–9. All actions are performed by the forces of Nature. But, through ignorance, man takes their authorship upon himself and becomes bound by them. The enlightened man knows the truth and enjoys freedom even while engaged in activity.

Verses 30–5. The enlightened man should help to raise the consciousness of the ignorant. The technique for raising consciousness is to surrender all action to God. Control does not accomplish anything, because everything is worked out according to Nature. The criterion of right action is not like and dislike, but natural duty.

Verses 36–43. The excitement born of desire and anger is opposed to the practice of gaining equanimity. The seat of desire and anger is in the senses, mind, and intellect. By raising awareness above these and becoming established in Transcendental Consciousness, one becomes capable of spontaneously performing right action in the state of freedom. When Transcendental Consciousness is developed to coexist with the waking state of consciousness, then the inner state of no problems coexists with the outer world of problems. Man lives in freedom while acting in the field of bondage. This is the glory of the path of action.

THE second chapter has presented *Brahma Vidyā* — the wisdom of the full life, the wisdom of the Absolute and the relative — in both its aspects, theoretical and practical. The theoretical aspect is called the wisdom of Sāṁkhya; it brings *understanding* of the absolute and the relative fields of life as separate, one from another. The practical aspect is called Yoga, and it brings *direct experience* of these two fields of life in separation.

The nature of this experience gained through the practice of Yoga and its application to life in the world are unfolded in this third chapter. The aim is to make permanent the state of absolute Bliss Consciousness, so that it will not be lost even when the mind is engaged in the activity of the relative field. This alone can give full experience of life, for life is relative and absolute simultaneously.

This third chapter presents a practical application of the second. It describes in detail the role of the 'established intellect' in practical life, so as to provide those occupied in the marketplace of the world with a direct way of evolution and eternal liberation. Its teaching is applicable to everyone, whatever his vocation.

This chapter develops the seed thought contained in the first three words of verse 48 of the second chapter: '*Yogasthaḥ kuru karmāṇi*' — 'established in Yoga, perform actions'. This doctrine of *Karma Yoga*, the Yoga of action, forms the chapter's main theme.

Karma is in the field of diversity, and Yoga is Unity. Therefore in order to understand *Karma Yoga* one must be as familiar with the Unity of life as with the field of diversity; only by being at home in both fields can one understand the link between them. The teaching of the third chapter is designed to bring this about. But it is important for the student of *Karma Yoga* to remember that an intellectual understanding of the teaching of this chapter, without personal experience of the real nature of Unity, can never bring the fruits of *Karma Yoga*. The technique of directly contacting the transcendental divine consciousness, as brought out in verse 45 of the second chapter, has to be practised; only on the basis of that personal experience is it possible to attain fulfilment in life through *Karma Yoga*. The practice of Transcendental Meditation is essential if the wisdom of this chapter is to be put to practical use.

VERSE 1

अर्जुन उवाच
ज्यायसी चेत्कर्मणस्ते मता बुद्धिर्जनार्दन
तत्किं कर्मणि घोरे मां नियोजयसि केशव

Arjuna uvācha
Jyāyasī chet karmaṇas te matā buddhir Janārdana
tat kiṁ karmaṇi ghore māṁ niyojayasi Keshava

Arjuna said:
If Thou considerest knowledge superior to action, O Janārdana,
why dost Thou spur me to this terrible deed, O Keshava?

Arjuna's question, with which this chapter opens, does not indicate that he was confused and had missed the import of the Lord's discourse in the second chapter, as commentaries have often suggested. Such interpretations show the commentators' own inability to follow the sequence of the Lord's words. They have clearly failed to understand the aptness of Arjuna's questions in helping to develop the Lord's theme. His questions represent the glorious links between the teachings which precede and follow them in the ascending order of the Lord's discourse.

A close examination of the context will reveal that Arjuna's questions present themselves in a natural way. This is due not only to the skill of the Lord's teaching and Arjuna's promptness in following it, but also to the nature of the subject under consideration. The teaching about life deals with many points, even points opposed to each other, for it deals with the unlimited fields of the relative and absolute phases of existence. These lie so far apart that in their essential nature there exists no link between them. The mind, however, can serve as such a link, because it is able to remain in activity and in the state of absolute Being at the same time. Moreover it uses activity as a means to end activity and thus to make possible the state of Transcendental Consciousness. *Karma* thus becomes a means to Yoga.

Such are the apparently self-contradictory phases of the teaching about life to which Arjuna's questions draw attention. It is obvious, therefore, that his questions are pertinent and arise out of his right understanding of the discourse. The relevance of the questions asked by the pupil reveals the success of the teaching. The teacher even creates an opportunity for the pupil to ask each question, thus sustaining his interest and making sure that he is properly following the discourse. And when the teaching advances in this manner, by way of question and answer, it unfolds the whole of wisdom for the pupil.

'If Thou considerest knowledge': in order to probe deep into the nature of Arjuna's understanding about 'knowledge', it is necessary to analyse the teaching of the sccond chapter.

Life has two aspects, relative and absolute.[1] The relative aspect is perishable and the absolute is imperishable. In order to give meaning to life, it is first necessary to bring the perishable aspect into living harmony with the imperishable. This is achieved through action according to one's *Dharma*,[2] which maintains existence in a way that furthers one's own evolution and that of others. In order to set the whole stream of life flowing naturally in the ascending current of *Dharma*, it is necessary to cultivate the resolute intellect.[3] This will ensure that both aspects of man's life, perishable and imperishable, the body and the Self, will naturally maintain their *Dharma* and be in perfect harmony, the Self remaining in Its state of eternal freedom in absolute Being and the mind entertaining activity which will naturally be in tune with the process of evolution.

In order to cultivate the resolute intellect, one has to be 'without the three *Guṇas*',[4] completely out of the field of activity, established in the transcendental state of Being. When, through

1 See II, 11–38.

2 See II, 31.

3 See II, 41.

4 See II, 45.

constant practice in gaining the state 'without the three *Guṇas*', the mind gains fixity in Being, one becomes aware of the Self, or Being, as separate from activity. In this state one acts in the world while established in the eternal contentment and freedom of divine consciousness.

Therefore, although knowledge begins with the intellectual understanding of the two aspects of life, perishable and imperishable, it becomes a living Reality only when, through the practice of Transcendental Meditation, one becomes directly aware of the Self as separate from activity. This awareness is the state of knowledge, the state of established intellect.[5]

Arjuna has rightly understood all that the Lord has spoken about knowledge. But he demands confirmation that his understanding is correct. The word 'if' brings out this meaning.

'Knowledge superior to action': Arjuna asks his question not because he has failed to grasp the principle of action in the state of knowledge,[6] but because he has thoroughly understood that 'when a man acts without longing, having relinquished all desires, free from the sense of "I" and "mine", he attains to peace'.[7] He has understood that by fighting he will not incur sin.[8] But for that great heart of Arjuna's, merely to escape from sin is not a sufficient reason for plunging into action. He judges the action of fighting at its face-value and finds that to kill his dear ones would be a 'terrible deed'. He raises the question whether, on the strength of knowledge, he could after all avoid the 'terrible deed' of battle. Having reached this high state of established intellect, should not a man have freedom to act or not to act? This is Arjuna's question from his high state of consciousness. Arjuna here silently uses the Lord's teaching about the freedom which knowledge gives, in favour of freedom to choose what actions he wishes to perform. He probes deep into the Lord's teaching and finds that this point has not yet been answered.

This question further indicates that Arjuna has understood not only the relationship between action and knowledge, but also that between action and *Dharma*. He has understood the

5 See II, 55–8, 61.
6 See II, 48.
7 See II, 71.
8 See II, 38.

Lord's teaching about *Dharma*.[9] He has understood that one's own *Dharma* is the best criterion for judging the appropriateness of an action, and that, for a *Kshatriya*, a battle such as this is in accord with *Dharma*.

But the stress that the Lord has put on knowledge gives Arjuna an opportunity to question Him about the relationship between knowledge and *Dharma*, which has not yet been made clear and without which the teaching about action remains incomplete. Arjuna wants to know whether knowledge can override *Dharma* to the extent of permitting one to forego a particular 'deed'; whether knowledge gives a man sufficient freedom to enable him to make his own choice about action. Arjuna implies that if it does he would like to choose to forego 'this terrible deed'.

The question that Arjuna raises is of deep significance and has great value in furthering the theme of the Lord's discourse. It is this question of Arjuna's that brings forth a complete doctrine of action from the lips of the Lord.

Commentators in general have missed the great depth of understanding from which Arjuna was speaking and asking questions, because they have misunderstood his position right from the first chapter.

Arjuna, from his high level of consciousness, is able to distinguish the finest points of the Lord's discourse and to weigh them up in terms of practical life. His alert mind locates many contradictory statements in the teaching so far, and he makes mention of these in the verse which follows.

This explains how apt is Arjuna's question and how well it serves to unfold the wisdom of action in the light of knowledge, which forms the main subject of this chapter.

VERSE 2

व्यामिश्रेणेव वाक्येन बुद्धिं मोहयसीव मे
तदेकं वद निश्चित्य येन श्रेयोऽहमाप्नुयाम्

Vyāmishreṇeva vākyena buddhiṁ mohayasīva me
tad ekaṁ vada nishchitya yena shreyo 'ham āpnuyām

---

9 See II, 31–7.

With these apparently opposed statements Thou dost, as it were, bewilder my intelligence. So, having made Thy decision, tell me the one by which I may reach the highest good.

The tone of this verse brings to light Arjuna's intimacy with the Lord and his good understanding of the teaching. It also further reveals the alertness of Arjuna's mind in evaluating different aspects of the discourse.

'Apparently opposed': in verse 38 of the preceding chapter, the Lord enjoined Arjuna to 'come out to fight'. But in verse 45 He said to him, 'Be without the three *Guṇas*', which means: come out of the field of activity. Again, in verse 47, He said: 'You have control over action alone', do not 'attach yourself to inaction'. Then, in verse 48, He expressed the synthesis of action and the established intellect in the words: 'Established in Yoga, O winner of wealth, perform actions'. In verse 49, however, he went on to destroy the very principle of this synthesis by declaring: 'Far away, indeed, from the balanced intellect is the action devoid of greatness'.

Arjuna wants to verify whether 'these apparently opposed statements' point to some hidden principle which has not yet been expressed, or whether there exists some hidden link joining them together.

In the seventh verse of Chapter II, Arjuna had surrendered himself to the Lord, saying: 'tell me decisively what is good for me'. Now he finds that he is being provided with two boats, each apparently going in an opposite direction. He is asked simultaneously to come on to this and to get into that. So he stands bewildered and asks: Tell me which boat to take, this or that, for if I start in two boats I am sure to drown. His question is a pertinent one.

The words 'apparently opposed' indicate Arjuna's modesty. Wishing to draw attention to the fact that Lord Kṛishṇa is offering him statements that oppose each other, he softens the expression by adding 'apparently'. And again, when he wants to convey that the Lord is bewildering his intelligence, he shows his modesty by adding 'as it were'.

Arjuna needed some intellectual jolt, some means of quickly shaking the intellect to bring him out of the state of suspension.

To this end the Lord showered Arjuna with apparently opposed statements of Truth. Thus Lord Kṛishṇa succeeded in bringing Arjuna's mind to the level where he could think in a practical manner. He became so practical as to say: 'Thou dost . . . bewilder my intelligence.' Now the Lord begins the second course of His teaching, the most glorious aspect of the wisdom of practical life.

VERSE 3

श्रीभगवानुवाच
लोकेऽस्मिन्द्विविधा निष्ठा पुरा प्रोक्ता मयानघ
ज्ञानयोगेन सांख्यानां कर्मयोगेन योगिनाम्

Shrī Bhagavān uvācha
Loke 'smin dwividhā nishthā purā proktā mayānagha
gyānayogena sāṁkhyānāṁ karmayogena yogināṁ

The Blessed Lord said:
As expounded by Me of old, O blameless one, there are in this world two paths: the Yoga of knowledge for men of contemplation and the Yoga of action for men of action.

In this verse the word 'Yoga' is common to both *Gyān Yoga*, the Yoga of knowledge, and *Karma Yoga*, the Yoga of action. The state of Transcendental Consciousness is the state of Yoga, or Union, where the mind remains so completely united with the divine nature that it becomes It. When this Union is naturally maintained, irrespective of the modes of the mind in the waking, dreaming, and sleeping states, then that state of consciousness is said to be Cosmic Consciousness.

When the state of Transcendental Consciousness, or Yoga, is supplemented by the process of thinking and discrimination in order to develop it into Cosmic Consciousness, the way is called the Yoga of knowledge, *Gyān Yoga*; whereas when the state of Transcendental Consciousness is supplemented by action on the sensory level in order to develop it into Cosmic Consciousness, the way is called *Karma Yoga*, the Yoga of action. These two types of Yoga fulfil the needs of all men, whether contemplative or active.

The experience of the Transcendent during meditation is

realization of only one aspect of Reality — the unmanifested, absolute aspect. For realization of the complete Truth, this experience has to go hand in hand with the experience of the manifested aspect, which is the relative phase of existence.

In order that transcendental Bliss Consciousness may be lived at all times, it is necessary that it should not be lost when the mind comes out of meditation and engages in activity. For this to be possible the mind has to become so intimately familiar with the state of Being that It remains grounded in the mind at all times, through all the mental activity of thinking, discriminating, and deciding, and through all phases of action on the sensory level. For this in turn, it is necessary that the process of gaining Transcendental Consciousness through meditation and that of engaging in activity should be alternated, so that Transcendental Consciousness and the waking state of consciousness may come close together and finally merge into one another to give rise to the state of Cosmic Consciousness, the state in which one lives Bliss Consciousness, the inner awareness of Being, through all the activity of the waking and dreaming states and through the silence of the deep sleep state.

As there are two types of people, men of thought and men of action, so there are two ways of life, the way of the recluse for the man of thought and the way of the householder for the man of action. The man of thought, after meditation, engages in the mental activity of contemplation and thereby achieves the integration of the transcendental and waking states of consciousness; whereas a man of action, after meditation, engages in the field of action and thereby accomplishes the same goal.

Thus the *Gyān Yoga* of the recluse and the *Karma Yoga* of the householder differ from one another only in the phase of activity. One type of man devotes himself to the mental activity of thinking, discriminating and deciding about the nature of the world and the Divine; the other devotes himself to action without making the process of thinking a means of fulfilment. In this way, both engage in activity after gaining Transcendental Consciousness.

The Lord says to Arjuna that these two ways of realization have been handed on from generation to generation, from time immemorial. They are two distinct paths for the two distinct types of people who lead two distinct ways of life.

Unfortunately a muddle has been created in the understanding of this principle of realization, the highway of evolution. If the householder adopts the outlook of the Yoga of knowledge, then he falls into the world of thought and becomes less practical. Similarly, if a recluse embraces the outlook of the Yoga of action, he loses the opportunity of impartial discrimination and the constant flow of contemplation. He falls into the field of action, into the marketplace of life.

Both paths are equally valid for developing Cosmic Consciousness. *Karma Yoga* and *Gyān Yoga* each presents a direct way to fulfilment, but the path chosen should suit the way of life and the natural tendencies of the aspirant. A householder should not try to realize through Sāṁkhya or *Gyān Yoga*: let him adopt the path of *Karma Yoga* and, fulfilling the aspirations of a life in the world, he will gain Cosmic Consciousness in a natural and harmonious manner. Similarly, a recluse, or *Sanyāsī*, should not aspire to adopt the path of *Karma Yoga*. He should follow the Sāṁkhya teaching, or *Gyān Yoga*, and fulfilling the aspirations of a recluse way of life, he also will attain Cosmic Consciousness in a natural and harmonious manner.

Those interested in spiritual progress have for centuries adopted an outlook suited only to the recluse way of life. While perfectly valid for the few who retire from the world, such an outlook has no place in the lives of the vast majority of mankind who lead the householder's way of life. The path of *Karma Yoga* does not, like the path of knowledge, proceed by way of thinking or intellectual understanding; it is the innocent path of action, supplemented by Transcendental Meditation. Thinking of the divine Self or of God has no place on the path of *Karma Yoga*. Those who try to keep their mind on God while they are engaged in action neither succeed in taking the mind to God Consciousness at the level of transcendental Divinity, nor do they properly succeed in the field of action, because action becomes weak when the mind is divided and not fully given to it. This amounts to a loss in both directions. They neither fully become men of God nor succeed as men of the world.

For those who want to be successful both in the field of the

Divine and in the world, the path is that of *Karma Yoga* — a few minutes of meditation in the morning and in the evening and normal activity during the rest of the day. The meditation, however, should be of a kind that takes the mind directly to Transcendental Consciousness, and the activity during the day should be undertaken with ease and without strain.

It must be borne in mind that the practice of meditation is essential for both the recluse and the householder. At the same time, it is essential for enlightenment that after the practice both should engage in activity — whether the activity is of the intellect, as in the case of the recluse, or of the senses, as in the case of the householder, is immaterial.

A recluse is provided with a particular code of thinking which serves to keep him fixed to his path of renunciation. The householder likewise is provided with a code of action to keep him fixed to his path of action. This activity after meditation is important for the integration of the waking and transcendental states of consciousness, but the actual content of the thinking of the recluse and the action of the householder does not in any way help to bring about the integration of the two states of consciousness. It is the activity as such, physical or mental, which is of value in bringing about integration. The content of thought and action certainly has its value in the two ways of life but it does not touch the field of Being.

The purpose of both paths is to establish a man on a level of consciousness where he will enjoy a meaningful life, established in the eternal freedom of Bliss Consciousness. Such a man becomes more powerful and successful in his own way of life — the activity of the householder and the seclusion of the recluse are fully protected and brought to fulfilment.

VERSE 4

न कर्मणामनारम्भान्नैष्कर्म्यं पुरुषोऽश्नुते
न च संन्यसनादेव सिद्धिं समधिगच्छति

Na karmaṇām anārambhān naishkarmyaṁ purusho 'shnute
na cha saṁnyasanād eva siddhiṁ samadhigachchhati

Not by abstaining from action does a man achieve non-action;
nor by mere renunciation does he attain to perfection.

'Non-action' is the nearest translation of the Sanskrit word '*Naishkarmya*', which expresses a specific quality of the doer, a quality of non-attachment whereby he enjoys freedom from the bondage of action even during activity. It expresses a natural and permanent state of the doer. Whether he is engaged in the activity of the waking or dreaming state or in the inactivity of deep sleep, he retains inner awareness. It is a state of life where Self-consciousness is not overshadowed by any of the three relative states of consciousness — waking, dreaming, or sleeping. In this state of *Naishkarmya*, the doer has risen to the fourth state of consciousness, *Turīya*; this, in its essential nature, is Self-consciousness, the pure absolute state of Bliss Consciousness — *Sat-chid-ānanda* — but yet is inclusive of the three relative states of consciousness.

The Lord began to explain 'non-action', in verse 48 of Chapter II, in terms of abandonment of attachment. In the present verse He explains it without any reference to attachment. In verse 30 He will explain it with reference to Himself — surrender of all actions to God. But in every case the direct experience of Being forms the basis of non-action.

'By abstaining from action' one merely falls into a state of idleness or the inactivity of sleep. This is far removed from the state of non-action, where the mind, deep within itself, remains attuned to absolute Being even when activity is maintained on the surface, where the two fields of Being and activity are cognized as separate from one another.

'Renunciation': a state of non-attachment where the doer remains separate from the field of activity; the state of non-action.

The blessing of the state of renunciation, or non-action, is that the Self finds Itself separate from the field of activity. But the awareness of separation from activity resulting in the total loss of activity for the self will not bring 'perfection'. Perfection demands not only separation from activity, but positive Union with God. It means that the individual self, detached from activity on the level of individual life, comes to unite itself with cosmic Being, God, who is detached from activity on the level of cosmic life. Cosmic Consciousness, the permanent state of Self-consciousness, rises to the state of God Consciousness; the state of non-action rises to the state of God's action.

VERSE 5

न हि कश्चित्क्षणमपि जातु तिष्ठत्यकर्मकृत्
कार्यते ह्यवशः कर्म सर्वः प्रकृतिजैर्गुणैः

Na hi kashchit kshaṇam api jātu tishthatyakarmakṛit
kāryate hyavashaḥ karma sarvaḥ prakṛitijair guṇaiḥ

No one, indeed, can exist even for an instant without performing action; for everyone is helplessly driven to activity by the Guṇas born of Nature.

In all the states of waking, dreaming, and deep sleep, which constitute relative life, outward and inward physical activity continues. Everything in creation evolves, and the process of evolution is always through activity. This is what the Lord means when he says: 'No one, indeed, can exist even for an instant without performing action'.

'Nature': this is the nearest English rendering of the word '*Prakṛiti*'. The ultimate aspect of creation is transcendental unmanifested absolute Being. Its 'nature' consists of the three '*Guṇas*',[10] whose various permutations and combinations constitute all phenomenal existence. Their activity continues unceasingly in all fields of creation, and that is why the Lord says that 'everyone is helplessly driven to activity by the *Guṇas*'. It is only in the transcendental field of existence that no activity is found.

This verse, by establishing activity as universal, demonstrates the impossibility of gaining the state of 'non-action' through non-engagement in activity.

10 See II, 45, commentary.

Verse 6

कर्मेन्द्रियाणि संयम्य य आस्ते मनसा स्मरन्
इन्द्रियार्थान्विमूढात्मा मिथ्याचारः स उच्यते

Karmendriyāṇi saṁyamya ya āste manasā smaran
indriyārthān vimūdhātmā mithyāchāraḥ sa uchyate

He who sits, restraining the organs of action, and dwelling in his mind on the objects of sense, self-deluded, he is said to be a hypocrite.

The previous verse established activity as absolutely necessary for life in the relative field. The present verse makes it clear that even thinking belongs to the sphere of activity. This leads to the conclusion that, if action binds, one becomes subject to its binding influence even if one has entertained only a thought of action.

The Lord says that it is wrong to sit 'restraining the organs of action' while the mind is dwelling on the objects of the senses. Here is a definite negation of the principle of sense-control. It silently suggests that the technique of controlling the senses does not lie in direct restraint; it lies, rather, in the field of the mind, in the sphere of mental activity. The teaching of this verse is: do not create strain by attempting directly to bridle the senses. The actual technique is given in the following verse.

'A hypocrite' is he who is neither true to himself nor true to others. He hides his true nature.

Verse 7

यस्त्विन्द्रियाणि मनसा नियम्यारभतेऽर्जुन
कर्मेन्द्रियैः कर्मयोगमसक्तः स विशिष्यते

Yas twindriyāṇi manasā niyamyārabhate 'rjuna
karmendriyaiḥ karmayogam asaktaḥ sa vishishyate

But he who, controlling the senses by the mind, without attachment engages the organs of action in the Yoga of action, he excels, O Arjuna.

The Yoga of action, or *Karma Yoga*, is performance of action with a skill that does not allow the senses of perception to register deep impressions of experiences. The organs of action[11] remain at work during activity; the senses of perception[12] also continue to experience, but the manner of their activity is such that, while experiencing fully, they do not register deep impressions of experiences. The man who is able to experience in this manner is described here as acting 'without attachment'.

Karma Yoga is that state where the senses of perception are functioning in an organized and controlled manner, while the organs of action are active. How do the senses remain organized and controlled? The Lord says that it is by virtue of a particular state of mind. How the mind arrives at this state is not explained here, for it has already been made clear to Arjuna in the 45th verse of the preceding chapter — the mind has to be established in the absolute bliss of divine consciousness, through Transcendental Meditation. This is the simple technique by which the senses of perception are automatically controlled and organized; to become a *Karma Yogī*, nothing need be done save to infuse the mind with Transcendental Consciousness. When the senses of perception are active while the mind is in this state of pure consciousness, then this is called *Karma Yoga*: the senses remain on their objects and the mind remains established in Being.

The technique of controlling the senses by the mind is elaborated in verses 42 to 43: one has to transcend the fields of mind and intellect or, as the Lord puts it in verse 45 of Chapter II, one has to 'Be without the three *Guṇas*'.

11 The five organs of action: hands, feet, tongue, organs of reproduction and elimination.

12 The five senses of perception: sight, hearing, smell, taste, and touch.

VERSE 8

नियतं कुरुकर्म त्वं कर्म ज्यायो ह्यकर्मणः
शरीरयात्रापि च ते न प्रसिद्ध्येदकर्मणः

Niyataṁ kuru karma twaṁ karma jyāyo hyakarmaṇaḥ
sharīrayātrāpi cha te na prasiddhyed akarmaṇaḥ

Do your allotted duty. Action is indeed superior to inaction. Even the survival of your body would not be possible without action.

'Allotted duty' is that which it is natural for one to do, that for which one was born — natural action in accordance with the Laws of Nature, action according to one's own *Dharma*, action which is in line with the natural stream of evolution, action which is an innocent link between Self-consciousness and Cosmic Consciousness, action which serves as a way to achieve God Consciousness, the fulfilment of life.

An important aspect of natural duty is that it is imperative for a man; if he does not perform his allotted duty, he will be engaging in actions which lie outside the path of his own evolution.

Allotted duty comprises all actions which enable a man to survive and to evolve. The rightness of such actions lies in this: that in performing them a man feels no strain; they are not a burden in life; in one stroke they maintain life and lead to evolution.

It is equally essential to understand that action which is not natural will inevitably produce strain and tension both in the doer and in the atmosphere around him. If the process of action is strained, it interferes with the harmony between the doer and his work, the subject and the object; this in turn hinders the infusion of the divine nature into the field of activity, and resistance is created to the development of Cosmic Consciousness. That is why the Lord particularly mentions 'allotted duty'.

The question arises of finding out what is one's allotted duty. In those parts of the world where natural divisions of society still exist, a man's duty is apparent by virtue of his birth in a particular family. Thus, Arjuna is born a *Kshatriya* and it is natural for him to fight. But in the complexities of the mixed civilizations and mixture of traditions in the world today, it seems hard to discover one's 'allotted duty'.

If, in the absence of any scriptural authority or tradition, a criterion of natural duty has to be found, it may be said on the basis of common sense that an action which is necessary and does not produce any undue tension or strain in the doer and his surroundings is his natural duty. It is true that there may be many flaws in a criterion based only on common sense. Meditation, however, smooths the flow of life and naturally sets the stream of life in accordance with the Laws of Nature, upholding it on the way to higher evolution. Therefore in the absence of any other means to discover one's allotted duty, it would be wise to accept Transcendental Meditation as a means to direct one towards a natural way of life.

It may be recalled that when the Lord began to instruct Arjuna in the art of spontaneous right action, He advised him to come out of the field of relativity and take his stand in the field of the Absolute;[13] he would thereby rise to that state of life — Cosmic Consciousness — where one becomes capable of performing actions in complete accordance with the Laws of Nature, thus fulfilling one's *Dharma* and serving the cosmic purpose.

The Lord says: 'Action is indeed superior to inaction', and He then adds: 'Even the survival of your body . . .' These words contain great wisdom about the integration of life and a supreme secret of evolution by way of action. The word 'even' is of deep significance. If survival of the body is the least result that the Lord attributes to action, what then is the greatest? It is the attainment of God Consciousness, the highest state of human evolution. The Lord means that, without action, not only would the body not survive, but the heights of evolution would not be attained. It must therefore be understood how action is necessary for attaining God Consciousness.

When, during Transcendental Meditation, the mind goes so deep within that it transcends the subtlest state of relativity, it attains the transcendental absolute state of Being. This is the state of pure awareness, or consciousness of the Self. When the

13 See II, 45.

mind, having been in that state, is subjected to action, the transcendental divine nature of the Self is brought out to be lived in the field of relativity. First the worldly mind of the waking state is led to the inner divine nature by the inward stroke of meditation, which is a withdrawal from activity; then, by virtue of embracing activity through the outward stroke of meditation, the inner divine nature is brought out into the world.

It should be noted that, in stressing the indispensability of action for the maintenance of life and the attainment of its purpose, the Lord is careful to qualify the action to which He refers. He does not say: Do your duty. He says: 'Do your alloted duty', your natural duty. How this commandment of the Lord's may be brought to bear on life can be expressed in one word: meditate.

Meditation is the key to the performance of one's allotted duty. It is a direct way to make glorious every aspect of life, for it transforms a life of bondage in the world into the divine life of eternal freedom in Cosmic Consciousness, where one experiences the Self as separate from activity.

Cosmic Consciousness in turn develops into God Consciousness through devotion, the most highly refined type of action, which unites in the Light of God the two separate aspects of Cosmic Consciousness, the Self and activity. This is the blessing of action, that it leads one from the waking state of consciousness to transcendental pure consciousness, thence to Cosmic Consciousness, and finally to God Consciousness, the highest state of human evolution.

Verse 9

यज्ञार्थात्कर्मणोऽन्यत्र लोकोऽयं कर्मबन्धनः
तदर्थं कर्म कौन्तेय मुक्तसङ्गः समाचर

Yagyārthāt karmaṇo 'nyatra loko 'yaṁ karmabandhanaḥ
tadarthaṁ karma Kaunteya muktasangaḥ samāchara

Excepting actions performed for Yagya, this world is in bondage to action. For the sake of Yagya engage in action free from attachment.

'Engage in action free from attachment': having stabilized the state of Bliss Consciousness and thereby clearly realized the Self as separate from activity, engage in action, do your 'allotted duty', as enjoined in the previous verse.

The process of action brings the doer out of himself; action is a direct way to bring the Self out into the field of relativity. This limits the unlimited absolute Self, and the effect is called the binding influence of action. Here the Lord gives Arjuna a technique whereby action itself may be used to take the individual back to his eternal status of absolute Being.

'*Yagya*' is action which helps evolution. Any action in the world which tends towards absolute Being helps to free man from bondage; actions in any other direction result in bondage.

When the Lord begins, in this chapter, to teach the theory of action, He naturally draws a distinction between those actions which are a means of liberation and those which lead to bondage.

The word '*Yagya*' commonly means a religious performance or a holy ritual, a sacrificial ceremony in which gifts are offered to the presiding deity and are consumed in fire. But here the Lord means the act of going to the transcendental Being — bringing the attention from the gross external experience of the world to the state of the Transcendent, allowing all thoughts and desires to converge upon the Transcendent, as objects of oblation consumed in the sacrificial fire.

In the light of this verse, *Yagya* is not confined to the narrow limits of particular ceremonies. It is a way of life which furthers evolution.

The interpretation of *Yagya* in terms of Transcendental Consciousness does not in any way undermine the validity of the Vedic rites performed to please different gods. Whatever a man does by way of activity after the practice of Transcendental Meditation, it helps him to integrate Transcendental Consciousness with the waking state of consciousness and thereby to develop Cosmic Consciousness. If, during such activity, he cherishes the act of pleasing the higher powers in Nature, the gods, this in no way hinders his progress; on the contrary, it brings him greater accomplishment through the support he receives from these powers in Nature.

Yagya is the subject of the Vedas. The Vedas are divided into various branches, called *Shākhās*. Each *Shākhā* expounds its *Yagya*, covering the whole range of life, relative and Absolute, and aiming at glorifying life in all its aspects, gross, subtle, and transcendent. Every *Shākhā* has three sections. One section, called '*Karma Kāṇda*' (Chapter of Action), deals with the gross aspect of *Yagya*, which is designed to improve the gross aspect of life, the body and all that relates to it in the world. The gross aspect of *Yagya* establishes the duties of men belonging to different levels of evolution, living in different times, in different places, and under different circumstances, so that they do not act against the Laws of Nature. This helps a man to evolve by virtue of whatever he does or experiences on the gross levels of life.

The second section of the *Shākhā* is called '*Upāsana Kāṇda*' (Chapter of Worship) and deals with the subtler aspects of *Yagya*, which win the blessings of the higher powers of Nature, the Vedic gods. This section has its own gross and subtle aspects. The gross aspect deals with ritualistic performances to please different Vedic gods and win their blessings, while the subtle aspect deals with training the mind to contact higher powers and receive their blessings upon all achievements in life.

The main purpose of this section is to connect man with the more evolved beings in creation so that he may receive their goodwill, their blessings, and their help in improving every aspect of his life.

The third section of each *Shākhā* is called '*Gyān Kāṇda*' (Chapter of Knowledge), and it contains the wisdom of eternal life. The Upanishads belong to this section. Each *Shākhā* has its own Upanishad to show the way of contacting *Brahman*, the ultimate Reality, for all those people to whom traditionally the teaching of that *Shākhā* applies. The wisdom of the Absolute and the way to transcend the relative fields of life and thereby infuse the divine nature into all spheres of human existence are dealt with in this section of each *Shākhā*.

In this way, each Vedic *Shākhā* contains wisdom to shape the entire field of human life in such a way that all its aspects, physical, mental, and spiritual, are perfectly coordinated with each other on every level and at the same time are in perfect harmony with the entire scheme of evolution. The aim is to lead every soul to the state of perfection, the highest and most exalted state of existence, God Consciousness. Such is the comprehensive scope of *Yagya*.

Verse 10

सहयज्ञाः प्रजाः सृष्ट्वा पुरोवाच प्रजापतिः
अनेन प्रसविष्यध्वमेष वोऽस्त्विष्टकामधुक्

Sahayagyāḥ prajāḥ srishtwā purovācha Prajāpatiḥ
anena prasavishyadhwam esha vo 'stwishtakāmadhuk

In the beginning, having created men along with Yagya,
the Lord of Creation said: By this Yagya shall ye prosper
and this shall bring forth the fulfilment of desires.

Yagya has been defined as action which helps evolution. It follows, therefore, that *Yagya* ultimately leads man to the highest state of evolution, to realization of God. Every step of evolution is connected with *Yagya*. *Yagya* thus upholds life from its beginning to its ultimate goal. This is what the Lord means when he says 'having created men along with *Yagya*'.

God is the source of all creation, and man's link with Him is through pure Transcendental Consciousness. Creation came out of this absolute level of Life, and the Creator proclaimed that It would be forever the source of all prosperity and advancement in life. By attuning the mind with It, one finds great intelligence, energy, happiness, and harmony and, possessed of these, no limit to the fulfilment of desires.

In this verse the Lord points to the prosperity of the individual as one result of *Yagya*; in the following verse He goes on to show another of its advantages.

VERSE 11

देवान्भावयतानेन ते देवा भावयन्तु वः
परस्परं भावयन्तः श्रेयः परमवाप्स्यथ

Devān bhāvayatānena te devā bhāvayantu vaḥ
parasparaṁ bhāvayantaḥ shreyaḥ param avāpsyatha

Through Yagya you sustain the gods and those gods will sustain you. By sustaining one another, you will attain the highest good.

The various types of *Yagya* expounded by the Vedas connect the individual with the entire process of cosmic evolution. *Yagya* thus has various levels of influence, ranging from the grossest to the subtlest states of creation, but always pointing towards the ultimate goal of God Consciousness.

This verse explains the mechanics of the vast influence which one's actions create throughout the universe — all the Laws of Nature on the level of the doer react to every action.

Yagya is regarded as the means to that complete success in life which consists of all possible achievements in the world together with freedom from bondage. *Yagya*, in fact, is a means to accomplish perfection of life. It brings the blessings of the powers which control and direct the evolution of the entire creation, wins the favour of almighty Nature, and ultimately brings fulfilment in God Consciousness.

Yagya is a process of bringing the individual into harmony with the stream of evolution, which enjoys the favour of all the forces of Nature engaged in the advancement of life, individual and cosmic.

The 'gods' mentioned here are the deities presiding over the innumerable Laws of Nature, which are present everywhere throughout relative life. They are the powers governing different impulses of intelligence and energy, working out the evolution of everything in creation. The existence of gods may be understood by an analogy: each of the myriad cells in the human body has its own level of life, energy, and intelligence; together, these innumerable lives produce human life. A human being is like a god to all these small impulses of energy and intelligence, each with its own form, tendencies, sphere of activity and influence, working for the purpose of evolution.

The Lord wishes that by way of *Yagya*, the act of coming to the Transcendent, men should simultaneously please the world of gods. This is possible only if the means of gaining Transcendental Consciousness is such that the influence produced by it supports the stream of evolution and wins the favour of the deities presiding over the Laws of Nature, the gods. We take a sound which produces such an influence of harmony in creation and experience its subtle states until the mind transcends even the subtlest and gains the state of Transcendental Consciousness. This is how the Lord wants us to create and maintain a mutual harmony with the higher powers of Nature on the way to becoming one with the transcendental eternal Divine.

When, through the practice of Transcendental Meditation, activity is realized as separate from the Self, then all of life's activity is said to have been given over as an offering to the gods. This means that activity continues in its sphere of relative life, over which the gods preside, while the Self remains in the freedom of the Absolute. This is the way to please all the gods through every activity at all times. A situation is created in which every activity automatically becomes a *Yagya*.

This manner of offering actions to the gods does not imply surrender to them or coming under their subjugation. The Self in this state becomes completely free from all the influences of relative life, including the gods.

'Highest good': the ritualistic aspect of *Yagya* produces effects in the relative field of life; its highest attainment is heaven, the summit of the relative world, where life is free from suffering. The technique of transcending through the process of *Yagya*, on the other hand, leads the individual to transcendental Bliss Consciousness, the state of eternal freedom in life, and thence to God Consciousness, which is the 'highest good' of all — higher than the highest in the relative sphere of life.

VERSE 12

इष्टान्भोगान्हि वो देवा दास्यन्ते यज्ञभाविता:
तैर्दत्तानप्रदायैभ्यो यो भुङ्क्ते स्तेन एव स:

Ishtān bhogān hi vo devā dāsyante yagyabhāvitāḥ
tair dattān apradāyaibhyo yo bhunkte stena eva saḥ

Satisfied by the Yagya, the gods will certainly bestow the enjoyments you desire. But he who enjoys their gifts without offering to them is merely a thief.

'Without offering to them': without forgoing possession in their favour, without performing the act of transferring ownership to them. The fruit of every action is the response of Nature to that action and is therefore nothing but the gift of the powers of Nature, the gods. How is it possible to forgo possession of everything that we gain in life? It is possible only by putting into effect the teaching of verse 48 of Chapter II and realizing the Self as separate from the field of activity. When a man has become established in the state where he is aware that all things are separated from the Self, he has, in effect, given over all things completely to Nature, or to the powers of Nature, the gods. In this way, he has risen above the charge of theft made by this verse and is able to enjoy the advantage shown in the following verse.

To create a mood of offering is to make a mockery of 'offering'. The teaching of this discourse is a teaching of practical life — it is a discourse of *Yoga Shāstra*, the Scripture of Yoga, the science of Divine Union. Its truth is far removed from imagination or mood-making. Unfortunately, owing to superficial interpretations current for many centuries, the essential teaching of this whole discourse has been greatly distorted, and society stands today surrounded by superstitions and lacking a proper sense of the values of life.

The prosperity and happiness that arise from the blessings of the gods, gained by means of *Yagya*, should not cause a man to become engrossed in enjoyment to the extent of forgetting the source of his prosperity. The Lord says that he who undermines the higher forces in Nature by possessing himself of the field of action, which actually belongs to them, acts like a thief. This is because he has not realized his Self as detached from activity. Anyone who has not gained fixity in Being automatically remains involved with activity; he assumes authorship of action and obtains ownership of its fruit, which in reality belong to Nature or to the gods, the powers of Nature. That is why such a man is called a 'thief', a usurper of possessions belonging to others.

A thief commonly enjoys the wealth of other men but makes no attempt to grow wealthier by his own efforts. Here is the warning that the Lord gives: one should not be satisfied only with the growth of material prosperity, wisdom, and creativity in the relative field of life, but should aspire to go beyond this and achieve oneness with the eternal life of absolute Being in God Consciousness. This is how one becomes established at the level of life underlying all creation and automatically produces life-supporting influences for all the powers of Nature and, indeed, for everything that exists throughout all the gross and subtle strata of creation. Thus one begins to live the basic teaching of this verse.

VERSE 13

यज्ञशिष्टाशिनः सन्तो मुच्यन्ते सर्वकिल्बिषैः
भुञ्जते ते त्वघं पापा ये पचन्त्यात्मकारणात्

Yagyashishtāshinaḥ santo muchyante sarvakilbishaiḥ
bhunjate te twaghaṁ pāpā ye pachantyātmakāraṇāt

The righteous, who eat the remains of the Yagya,
are freed from all sins. But the unrighteous, who
prepare food for themselves alone, truly, they eat sin.

'Remains of the *Yagya*': that which is left over after the performance of a *Yagya* has come to an end.

Yagya is action which furthers evolution, from the waking

state of consciousness to Transcendental Consciousness, from Transcendental Consciousness to Cosmic Consciousness, from Cosmic Consciousness to God Consciousness. These are the different states which develop through different types of practices. Each practice in itself is a performance of *Yagya*. Evolution finds ultimate fulfilment in God Consciousness, and once this is gained the goal of *Yagya* has been attained. That is why 'the remains of the *Yagya*' in its highest sense refers to the state of God Consciousness.

The state of Cosmic Consciousness, which forms the basis of God Consciousness, may also be said to be the remains of a *Yagya*. So may the state of Transcendental Consciousness, which forms the basis of Cosmic Consciousness.

That which is left over after the performance of the *Yagya* of Transcendental Meditation is Bliss Consciousness. This is the remains of the first and fundamental *Yagya* on the path to God Consciousness and forms the basis of Cosmic Consciousness and God Consciousness; he who partakes of it is 'righteous', says the Lord, because in this state his life is transformed into a life without wrong, a life that is wholly righteous. It is in this state that through every thought, word, and action, he creates life-supporting influences for himself and for the whole creation, because he is established in eternal Being, the basis of all life in creation.

Transcendental Consciousness being the remains of the fundamental *Yagya*,Transcendental Meditation is the most important of the *Yagyas*.

The wise man, established in Bliss Consciousness, is free from any sinful attitude because of the inner contentment which he experiences in the state of Absolute-consciousness. In contrast, the Lord describes those who concern themselves only with the affairs of their petty individuality and do not attempt to gain the unbounded status of the Absolute. Moved by their selfish thought, they forgo the chance of higher evolution; blinded by selfishness, their joys are only in the field of the senses. The Lord says they commit sin who do not work for their connection with the higher powers of Nature or for their own evolution.

Here is the technique for rising above the influence of all sin.

It is, as Lord Kṛishṇa put it, to 'eat the remains of the *Yagya*'. This is a metaphor explaining that the states of Transcendental Consciousness, Cosmic Consciousness, and God Consciousness should be made use of in daily life, so that actions may be free from sin. The Lord means that if the mind has not completed the course of *Yagya* — if it has not taken a dive into the Self and has not become connected with absolute Being, if it has not realized the Self as separate from activity, if it has not attained God Consciousness — then it is not attuned to cosmic Being and its activity is not attuned to the cosmic purpose. Therefore actions are not wholly in harmony with the process of evolution. Under the circumstances there is no certainty that a man's activity will be wholly right; there is always the possibility of an element of sin.

Even in the state of Cosmic Consciousness, before God Consciousness has been attained, every action fulfils the cosmic purpose and serves as a *Yagya*. But if one has not yet attained Cosmic Consciousness and created a situation where the Self is lived as separate from activity, then one's activity will not be graceful; it will be gripped by individuality, it will not have been set free to become universal. Such activity does not belong to the dignity of cosmic life. When those who have not realized Being as separate from activity engage in action, they appropriate the action to themselves and in so doing are taking something which does not belong to them, something which belongs to a realm outside the self, belongs to cosmic life. They fall within the category of thieves (verse 12) and partake of what, in the present verse, is called 'sin'.

The self, then, has no right to usurp activity, because activity belongs to cosmic life. There is also a further consideration. Activity thus usurped will actually damage the self by overshadowing its nature. The overshadowing of the true nature of the self, Bliss Consciousness, is the basis of all suffering, and that which causes suffering is called sin. For this reason the present verse also speaks of the association of the self with activity as 'sin' — ignorance is sin.

Only when a man has become permanently established in the eternal freedom of absolute Being is he 'freed from all sins'.

Such a man alone is a 'righteous' man, a man who is always right. Through all his activity he produces life-supporting influences in Nature because, having gained freedom from activity, his actions belong to the dignity of cosmic life. They fulfil the cosmic purpose of evolution; that is why they never fall into the realm of sin. This is what the Lord means when he uses the word 'righteous'.

If a man has not become 'righteous', if he has not placed his life in tune with the cosmic life of absolute Being, then he may be committing sin in everything he does. The only way out of the field of sin, or the binding influence of *Karma*, is to come under the influence of the eternal freedom of absolute Being. This is the subtlest level of the message of this verse. At its more obvious levels it refers to the gross fields of life, which demand ritualistic performances of *Yagya* for their development.

The quality of the mind depends upon the qualities of various factors, such as food and environment and the experiences, past and present, which have an effect upon it. The quality of food directly affects the quality of the mind. It depends on many factors, such as the materials themselves and the manner in which they were earned, whether this was legal or illegal, and also the manner of cooking and its purpose. Here the Lord lays emphasis on the purpose of cooking the food. He says that if the food is cooked to be offered to God and eaten by a man after the offering has been performed, then the man enjoys the blessings of God by means of that food; and thus the mind produced by such food will be pious, progressive, and graceful. Such a mind will certainly be quite naturally outside the sphere of sin. The contrary will be true, however, if the food is prepared without the purpose of making the offering, but with the sole intention of satisfying the man's own hunger.

In the following verse the Lord gives a graded sequence of creation.

Verse 14

अन्नाद्भवन्ति भूतानि पर्जन्यादन्नसंभवः
यज्ञाद्भवति पर्जन्यो यज्ञः कर्मसमुद्भवः

Annād bhavanti bhūtāni parjanyād annasaṁbhavaḥ
yagyād bhavati parjanyo yagyaḥ karmasamudbhavaḥ

From food creatures come into being; from rain is produced food; from Yagya comes forth rain and Yagya is born of action.

'From food creatures come into being': the Lord says that individual life is born of food, implying that it has little to do with divine Being, which is the Self of all; it is born of food, of nourishment that does not belong to the field of Being. Ego, intellect, mind, senses, and body belong to the relative field of existence.

'Food' likewise is born of rain, which again has little to do with divine Being.

'*Yagya*' has been considered in the previous verses as the process whereby the Self comes to be experienced as separate from activity. In this state of realization, activity is completely natural and perfectly attuned to the cosmic purpose of creation and evolution. As such, it produces a life-supporting influence in every field of creation and as a result the whole of Nature remains harmonious. The sun shines in due time, rain falls in due time, and all the seasons remain regular. This is how *Yagya* comes to be regarded as a cause of rain which, in turn, is responsible for the production of food.

'*Yagya* is born of action': it is through action that a *Yagya* is performed. *Yagya* is a performance or an activity of a specific nature whereby one becomes united with cosmic Being. This is the true meaning of *Yagya* in the present context of a discourse on Yoga. But this interpretation should not be understood as detracting from the truth of Vedic action, the performance of the Vedic rites, known as *Yagya*. The Vedas prescribe certain ritualistic performances by certain competent people to produce certain life-supporting influences in Nature. This also results in gaining the sympathy of the Laws of Nature by creating an influence of harmony in the atmosphere and maintaining the rhythm of Nature, so that rain comes in due time for the production of food. Naturally this type of *Yagya* too 'is born of action' — has action for its basis.

The more gross aspect of *Yagya*, that is, performance of rites and rituals to please the higher forces of Nature for the sake of material well-being, needs action in the gross field of life for its accomplishment. Likewise, the more subtle aspect of *Yagya*, which is the process of contacting the transcendental divine Absolute, needs action in the subtle fields. This action in the subtle aspect of life is the process of Transcendental Meditation whereby the mind travels through all the subtler levels of existence and transcends the subtlest level of manifested life to reach the state of absolute Being.

This explains why the glory of action[14] is emphasized here.

VERSE 15

कर्म ब्रह्मोद्भवं विद्धि ब्रह्माक्षरसमुद्भवम्
तस्मात्सर्वगतं ब्रह्म नित्यं यज्ञे प्रतिष्ठितम्

Karma Brahmodbhavaṁ viddhi Brahmāksharasamudbhavam
tasmāt sarvagataṁ Brahm nityaṁ yagye pratishthitam

Know action to be born of Brahmā (the Veda). Brahmā springs from the Imperishable. Therefore the all-pervading Brahmā is ever established in Yagya.

It has been said in the previous verse that '*Yagya* is born of action'. Here the Lord says that action (*Karma*) and all knowledge of it is contained in the Vedas, and that the Vedas are an expression of eternal life.

The Vedas expound the theory of action and everything pertaining to it, its causes and its effects. This is the first reason why the Lord says that action arises out of the Veda. The second is understood when we discover the origin of the Veda in the unmanifested transcendental divine Being.

14 See verse 19, commentary.

The first manifestation of creation is the self-illuminant effulgence of life. This is the field of established intellect, or the individual ego in its own established state. This self-illuminant effulgence of life is called the Veda. The second step in the process of manifestation is the rise of what we call vibration, which brings out the attributes of *Prakṛiti*, or Nature — the three *Guṇas*. This point marks the beginning of the *functioning* of the ego. Here experience begins in a very subtle form: the trinity of the experiencer, the experienced, and the process of experience comes into existence. This is the beginning of action in the process of creation. Just before the beginning of action, just before the beginning of the subtlest vibration, in that self-illuminant state of existence, lies the source of creation, the storehouse of limitless energy. This source of creation is the Veda, the field of almost absolute intelligence which underlies and pervades all activity responsible for the creation and evolution of life. This, being the source of all creation, is said to be *Brahmā*, the Creator. *Brahmā*, or the Veda, is naturally the source of all activity. That is why the verse says: 'Know action to be born of *Brahmā*.'

Yagya is that which helps evolution. It is a way to all accomplishment in life. Extending the meaning of *Yagya* to the fields of common life, it could be said that any action that helps evolution can be called *Yagya*. Thus we find that every *Yagya* is permeated with, and gives rise to, some degree of divine consciousness. In its higher aspect, *Yagya* is the way to Cosmic Consciousness and ultimately to fulfilment of life in God Consciousness; in its lower, it is the performance of rites and rituals to win the favour of the gods. This is the complete conception of *Yagya*.

Certainly the Divine is omnipresent and is therefore present in a latent form even in those things which are opposed to evolution. But the Lord says here that divine consciousness, *Brahmā*, is present in *Yagya*. He does not say that divine consciousness is present in actions other than *Yagya*.

Every orange is meant to contain juice, but a shrivelled orange does not yield any. So it is said that juice is present in a fresh orange. Even a shrivelled orange has juice, but because this cannot be extracted, such an orange is not considered when juice is wanted. Likewise divine consciousness can be developed through those types of action which help evolution. It cannot be developed through sinful or impious actions, which tend to make the mind coarse and lead to inertia. This robs the mind of its ability to transcend relativity and attain divine consciousness.

That is why the Lord says that actions which fall into the category of *Yagya* carry divine consciousness in them.

Verse 16

एवं प्रवर्तितं चक्रं नानुवर्तयतीह यः
अघायुरिन्द्रियारामो मोघं पार्थ स जीवति

Evaṁ pravartitaṁ chakraṁ nānuvartayatīha yaḥ
aghāyur indriyārāmo moghaṁ Pārtha sa jīvati

He who in this life does not follow the wheel thus set revolving, whose life is sinful, whose contentment lies in the senses, he lives in vain, O Pārtha.

'The wheel thus set revolving': life passes through different spheres of existence, gross and subtle, and by this means the process of evolution is carried out. The beginning of life is in the unmanifested pure consciousness, 'the Imperishable' of the previous verse. If a man remains always in the field of the senses and fails to reach the source of his being, if his mind does not travel from gross to subtle in order to realize that Imperishable, the ultimate source of all creation, 'he lives in vain'. He has not made use of the opportunity of enjoying that great happiness which lies beyond the range of the senses; he has not traversed the whole field of life; he has not gone from origin back to origin; he 'does not follow the wheel thus set revolving'. He has committed sin against himself and sin against God, because he has failed to rise to fulfilment. Therefore the Lord says that his 'life is sinful'.

One who has realized life through all the subtle and gross layers of existence and lives the ultimate Being through all actions, who lives fulfilment in God Consciousness, can be said to have followed the 'wheel' of creation — he has gone to That whence he came.

In the following verses, the Lord brings out in detail the state of one who is enjoying this full life.

VERSE 17

यस्त्वात्मरतिरेव स्यादात्मतृप्तश्च मानवः
आत्मन्येव च संतुष्टस्तस्य कार्यं न विद्यते

Yas twātmaratir eva syād Ātmatṛiptash cha mānavaḥ
Ātmanyeva cha saṁtushtas tasya kāryaṁ na vidyate

But the man whose delight is in the Self alone, who is content in the Self, who rejoices only in the Self, for him there is no action that he need do.

'The man': one who is firmly established in the Self, the eternal Being, and is not involved with anything else; who has realized Being as separate from the field of activity and is always detached from everything other than his own Self; who, despite any activity on the surface of life, eternally remains in the awareness of the Self; who, living through the relative states of consciousness, waking, dreaming, and sleeping, is ever established in the absolute state of consciousness, the state of Being, the awareness of Self.

All actions that a man performs are prompted by the desire to accomplish something and to enjoy it. When he reaches the field of absolute Bliss Consciousness, that state which is the fulfilment of all desires, he becomes filled with lasting contentment, for the purpose of all desires and actions is achieved. This is why the Lord says that 'for him there is no action that he need do'.

Does he then cease to act? The Lord answers in the following verse.

VERSE 18

नैव तस्य कृतेनार्थो नाकृतेनेह कश्चन
न चास्य सर्वभूतेषु कश्चिदर्थव्यपाश्रयः

Naiva tasya kṛitenārtho nākṛiteneha kashchana
na chāsya sarvabhūteshu kashchid arthavyapāshrayaḥ

Neither has he any profit to gain in this life from the actions he has done or from the actions he has not done; nor is there any living creature on whom he need rely for any purpose.

The man who is thus contented in himself certainly continues to act in the world, but his behaviour has become natural behaviour. It is no longer motivated by selfish desires, nor is its effectiveness disturbed by any shortcomings that might arise from dullness on his part.

This comes about because he has fulfilled the purpose of all possible desires and all possible actions in his life. He now engages himself in actions motivated not by selfish individuality but by cosmic purpose. Through him works the divine intelligence, for he has become a fitting instrument to carry out the divine plan in the world. Such a life is a natural life. It is the result of the established intellect.

This verse has generally been thought to advocate desireless action arrived at by creating a mental sense of disinterestedness in action but this interpretation is wrong. Such a sense of disinterestedness has no bearing on the realization of either Self-consciousness, Cosmic Consciousness, or God Consciousness, nor does it in any way add to effectiveness in life. It can only weaken all phases of life, material, mental, and spiritual. In the next verse the Lord emphasizes the validity of action for the integration of life.

VERSE 19

तस्मादसक्तः सततं कार्यं कर्म समाचर
असक्तो ह्याचरन्कर्म परमाप्नोति पूरुषः

Tasmād asaktaḥ satataṁ kāryaṁ karma samāchara
asakto hyācharan karma param āpnoti pūrushaḥ

Therefore, remaining unattached, always do the action worthy of performance. Engaging in action truly unattached, man attains to the Supreme.

Therefore, says the Lord, uninvolved as you are, detached as you are, forever separated as you naturally are from the field of action, perform 'action worthy of performance'.

The Lord demands action in the state of freedom and proclaims that freedom is there, natural to man — man's life is already in liberation. No effort is needed for the attainment of freedom; it is already there.

The doctrine of *Karma Yoga*, then, only asks man to be in his natural and normal state of Self-consciousness, to be in his own nature. The Lord, indeed, advises him to act, and this advice is in order to cultivate liberation in God Consciousness.

The mind, moved by its own nature to enjoy more, flows towards the subtler fields of experience during Transcendental Meditation and most spontaneously attains the state of Being. Activity after this state of Being is gained is likewise spontaneously carried out by Nature. Therefore the development of Cosmic Consciousness, which forms the basis of the supreme attainment of God Consciousness, is a natural process, free from effort.

'The Supreme': God, presiding over the relative and the Absolute in the fullness of both. This verse reminds us of the 47th verse of the second chapter. The Lord reveals the significance of unrestricted natural action on the way to the realization of God Consciousness. The previous verses brought out man's ability to act in a natural manner by virtue of possessing Cosmic Consciousness. The present verse shows that performance of action in an unstrained, natural manner is a means of realizing 'the Supreme'. In the state of Cosmic Consciousness the validity of action is accepted for the sake of developing God Consciousness. This verse should be studied very carefully in order to understand the means by which God Consciousness may be attained. The means should not be confused with the end. Cosmic Consciousness, in which the Self is experienced as separate from activity, is not the end, not the final state of development; it is a means to God Consciousness.

When, through meditation, the mind has reached transcendental Self-consciousness and then returns from the field of absolute Being, it becomes necessary for it to engage in activity. In this way the nature of transcendental Being, infused into the mind, has an opportunity of maintaining itself even when the mind is engaged in experiencing the relative field of life through the senses. This is how one remains permanently established in Self-consciousness and thereby enjoys life in Cosmic Consciousness.

This is how, by virtue of action, the transcendental divine nature is infused into practical life, making a man fully integrated, so that he acts in the relative field of existence while remaining established in absolute Being. In this state of contentment his actions are natural and normal, 'worthy of performance'.

When, in the state of Cosmic Consciousness, the Self has been realized as separate from all activity, 'the action worthy of performance' is action in devotion to God.[15] The activity of devotion is the highest and most refined type of activity, for it directly raises the awareness of separateness of Being from activity, as experienced in the state of Cosmic Consciousness, to a unified state of awareness of God alone. The awareness of Self and of activity, the awareness of the two, gives way to oneness in the awareness of God, in God Consciousness. The duality of the Self and activity finds itself pervaded by God. He alone remains. He alone dominates life, and in the light of Him, permeated by Him, the Self stands in Unity with Him and with the whole field of action dominated by Him. In Him are found united forever both the Self and the activity of Cosmic Consciousness.

15 See II, 61, commentary.

This is the state of life in the oneness of God Consciousness expressed by the words 'attains to the Supreme' in this verse which extols action in the state of Cosmic Consciousness.

Action worthy of performance may be considered on five different levels of life: one, during the ordinary waking state of consciousness; two, when Self-consciousness has been gained and is developing into Cosmic Consciousness; three, action in the state of Cosmic Consciousness; four, action which helps Cosmic Consciousness to develop into God Consciousness; and five, action in the state of God Consciousness. This verse is concerned with the last three levels of action. The expression 'worthy of performance' lays emphasis upon the quality of the action which is helpful for gaining the higher states of consciousness.

One who has realized the Self in Transcendental Consciousness, who has realized the Self as completely separate from activity in Cosmic Consciousness, and who has gained fulfilment by realizing the Self in Union with God in God Consciousness, has reached the state where the purpose of all[16] activity has been fulfilled. Because his self is fixed in the universal Self, there is nothing that he could gain from another. His Self is uninvolved in every way — it is uninvolved with activity (verse 17) and it is uninvolved with the selves of individual beings (verse 18). His own Self is the Self of all beings.

VERSE 20

कर्मणैव हि संसिद्धिमास्थिता जनकादयः
लोकसंग्रहमेवापि संपश्यन्कर्तुमर्हसि

Karmaṇaiva hi saṁsiddhim āsthitā Janakādayaḥ
lokasaṁgraham evāpi saṁpashyan kartum arhasi

By action alone, indeed, Janaka and others gained perfection. Moreover, even looking to the welfare of the world, you should perform action.

16 See IV, 23.

This verse extols action for its value to the world and as a means to eternal liberation from bondage. At the same time it illustrates with concrete examples the abstract principles of *Karma Yoga* and their effects.

It was the glory of action that brought integration of life in God Consciousness to 'Janaka and others' and enabled them to do good to the world.

Integration of life depends upon the mind passing in a cycle between the field of the Absolute and the field of activity. The mind goes to the unmanifest and comes back to the manifest, thus experiencing both fields of life, absolute and relative. This is the state of the integrated man in Cosmic Consciousness.

When King Janaka and others like him were found to be established in Reality while fully active in the world, the secret did not lie in their continuous outward activity. It lay in the fact that such activity was supplemented by their experience of the Transcendent through the inward activity of meditation. If we consider the march of the mind from gross outward activity to the Transcendent, we can say that it is activity in the direction of putting an end to activity that gives the mind the status of the Absolute. Meditation itself is an activity. In view of this, it can certainly be held that it is 'action[17] alone' that brings perfection.

The Self is omnipresent and eternal. It does not need anything to realize Itself. Man loses It by remaining in the field of activity. Therefore in order to realize It, he has simply to come out[18] of activity, to engage himself in subtler fields of activity until he is completely out of the field of activity, in the field of the Transcendent. This explains the principle of enlightenment through action.

As a direct result of this inward activity of meditation, outward activity in the world becomes more successful, more perfect. This is what the Lord means when He says: 'By action alone, indeed, Janaka and others gained perfection.'

Every action starts from the subtlest stratum of relative life, which is almost one with the level of the Absolute, with pure Being. It starts as a thought. The thought itself passes through

17 See verse 19, commentary.
18 See II, 45.

many stages from the subtle to the gross. At a certain stage it reaches that level of the mind where it is consciously appreciated as a thought, and it may then be translated into speech or action.

Through the practice of Transcendental Meditation, the thought begins to be appreciated at a subtler level. Here it is more powerful and results in more successful action. Thus, by direct experience of transcendental Being through the inward stroke of action during meditation, a man not only gains spiritual freedom but also greater success in the world.

The contentment and serenity gained through this action of meditation produce harmonious and life-supporting influences for the whole world. By raising man's consciousness, they fill his heart with universal love, which induces him to work for 'the welfare of the world' in a most natural way.

It should be remembered that it does not need a long time of silent meditation to reach transcendental Being: just a dive within the Self for a few minutes and the mind is infused with the nature of pure consciousness, which keeps it enriched through all the activities of the day. This is the way to live the spiritual life, which makes glorious even the physical and material aspects of life in the world.

VERSE 21

यद्यदाचरति श्रेष्ठस्तत्तदेवेतरो जनः
स यत्प्रमाणं कुरुते लोकस्तदनुवर्तते

Yad yad ācharati shreshthas tat tad evetaro janaḥ
sa yat pramāṇaṁ kurute lokas tad anuvartate

Whatsoever a great man does, the very same is also done by other men. Whatever the standard he sets, the world follows it.

A great man is he who lives the awareness of Being in his daily life and has gained a state in which he naturally maintains his high status of eternal Being even when engaged in activity and in doing good to others.

This verse describes the tendency of the masses to follow the example of evolved men. At the same time, it touches Arjuna's pride. In this lies the great skill of the discourse. Although indirectly stated, the idea is conveyed to Arjuna that he is venerated in society, and that people will follow his example. Therefore he has a responsibility which extends beyond the limits of his own interest.

For the evolution of his own soul, Arjuna is expected to stand up and engage in activity. And even should he not care about his own evolution, it behoves him to embrace activity for the sake of others.

The following verses throw more light on this.

VERSE 22

न मे पार्थास्ति कर्तव्यं त्रिषु लोकेषु किंचन
नानवाप्तमवाप्तव्यं वर्त एव च कर्मणि

Na me Pārthāsti kartavyaṁ trishu lokeshu kiṁchana
nānavāptam avāptavyaṁ varta eva cha karmaṇi

In the three worlds there is no action which I need do,
O Pārtha; nor is there for Me anything worth attaining
unattained; even so I am engaged in action.

Having mentioned 'Janaka and others' in verse 20, the Lord here points to Himself as an example to illustrate the principle affirmed in verse 21. He speaks from His absolute state of eternal contentment.

Having brought to light the importance of action in man's evolution, and having shown the authenticity of this principle by citing the example of men who lived perfection in life through action, the Lord now reveals the validity of action in the pure field of the Divine, which is completely free from activity in the relative field. It may be explained that whereas man in the state of enlightenment lives fully both activity and divine consciousness because his life has two aspects, relative and absolute, there is no trace of relativity in the pure transcendent divine field of the Lord. Nevertheless, the Lord says that He is 'engaged in action'.

The supreme Lord of creation, presiding over the absolute and the relative fields of life and the refuge of both, is 'engaged in action' — the divine activity that underlies the continuity of ever-changing creation.

When the Lord speaks about Himself and the three worlds, He addresses Arjuna as 'Pārtha' to maintain the fine bond of love between Himself and Arjuna. This is skill in teaching. Arjuna should see Lord Kṛishṇa as close to himself and not far off as a high ideal beyond his reach.

By 'the three worlds' is meant the entire field of relative existence.

VERSE 23

यदि ह्यहं न वर्तेयं जातु कर्मरयतन्द्रितः
मम वर्त्मानुवर्तन्ते मनुष्याः पार्थ सर्वशः

Yadi hyahaṁ na varteyaṁ jātu karmaṇyatandritaḥ
mama vartmānuvartante manushyāḥ Pārtha sarvashaḥ

What if I did not continue unwearyingly in activity,
O Pārtha? Men in every way follow My example.

The Lord means to convince Arjuna of the truth of the great principle that there can be no escape from duty without setting a sinful example in which the whole of society will be involved.

Moreover, the Lord points out that His own incessant activity lies at the root of all life. The entire creation is the manifested aspect of His unmanifested Being. Remaining unmanifested, He manifests Himself, and this action of manifestation expresses itself as creation. His continued activity is responsible for the maintenance and evolution of everything that exists; without it the entire creation would be reduced to nothingness.

This is how the Lord explains His perpetual activity, quoting it as an example to be followed by others.

VERSE 24

उत्सीदेयुरिमे लोका न कुर्यां कर्म चेदहम्
संकरस्य च कर्ता स्यामुपहन्यामिमाः प्रजाः

Utsīdeyur ime lokā na kuryāṁ karma ched aham
saṁkarasya cha kartā syām upahanyām imāḥ prajāḥ

If I did not engage in action, these worlds would perish and I would be the cause of confusion and of the destruction of these people.

The principle elaborated in the previous three verses is again emphasized, and a point is brought out similar to that raised by Arjuna in the 39th to the 45th verses of the first chapter. In these verses Arjuna had said that by fighting he would be causing the disruption of society.

In this verse, the Lord, by referring to Himself, turns the tables on Arjuna. He brings home clearly to him by His own example that if he does not engage in action he will corrupt the whole of society, and that his bad example will be responsible for allowing its values to be destroyed.

The conclusion is that even if a man has gained fulfilment in his own life, it behoves him to act for others. This idea is brought out very clearly in the following verse.

VERSE 25

सक्ताः कर्मण्यविद्वांसो यथा कुर्वन्ति भारत
कुर्याद्विद्वांस्तथासक्तश्चिकीर्षुर्लोकसंग्रहम्

Saktāḥ karmaṇyavidwāṁso yathā kurvanti Bhārata
kuryād vidwāṁs tathāsaktash chikīrshur lokasaṁgraham

As the unwise act out of their attachment to action, O Bhārata, so should the wise act, but without any attachment, desiring the welfare of the world.

The Lord shows Arjuna that there is absolutely no difference between the action of an ignorant man and that of one who is enlightened; action is action whether performed by the ignorant or the enlightened. The difference is found only in the result.

The result of an ignorant man's action is enjoyed by himself and concerns mainly himself, because he is attached to it; when the doer is attached to the action, the result of the action is naturally attached to the doer. But when the doer is not attached to the action, the results are not attached to him.

The ignorant man acts and benefits from the results of his actions; since he is attached to these results, they make a deep impression on him. The effects of the enlightened man's actions spread out in the world and everything benefits from them; the impression of the result passes him by, leaving him free from the bondage of action because he has realized the Self as separate from activity and acts from the basis of eternal contentment. His actions are in response to the needs of the time; they fulfil the demands of their surroundings. The wise are tools in the hands of the Divine; they innocently carry out the divine plan. Their actions arise from their desire for 'the welfare of the world'.

VERSE 26

न बुद्धिभेदं जनयेदज्ञानां कर्मसङ्गिनाम्
जोषयेत्सर्वकर्माणि विद्वान्युक्तः समाचरन्

Na buddhibhedaṁ janayed agyānāṁ karmasanginām
joshayet sarvakarmāṇi vidwān yuktaḥ samācharan

Let not the wise man create a division in the minds of the ignorant, who are attached to action. Established in Being, he should direct them to perform all actions, duly engaging in them himself.

'Let not the wise man create a division in the minds of the ignorant': the state of a realized man is the result of many years of inner development founded on right values in life. This causes his life to flow naturally in right channels of conduct. Although his Being is above the realms of right and wrong, his actions are quite naturally right actions. He is advised in this verse to allow the ignorant man to do his duty. He should refrain from telling him that the state of enlightenment is free from both good and evil, and that the whole field of relativity is just the play of the three *Guṇas*, which do not belong to his Being.

It is perhaps even more important that the wise man should not confuse the ignorant by telling him about the uninvolved nature of the Self. The intellect of the man who is not realized is wholly involved with activity. The realized should not create a division in such a man's mind. He should not talk to him of the separateness of the Self from activity, otherwise the ignorant man may lose interest in practical life, and if this happens he will never be able to gain realization. It is not the intellectual understanding of the separateness of the Divine and of activity, but rather the experience of this state which brings a man enlightenment. In order that one may gain this experience and become established in it, conscious activity both in the gross and subtle fields of life is necessary. The Lord exhorts the wise: Teach Transcendental Meditation to the ignorant man so that he may engage himself in subtler phases of activity and thereby realize the transcendent Being, the Self, in Its true nature as devoid of any activity. Teach him that, having gained this realization, he should continue to act in daily life so that it may become firmly established in the very nature of his mind. And then set him an example by 'duly engaging' in actions yourself.

'All actions': every type of activity is necessary for life in the world, activity of the ego, intellect, mind, and body. All activity, gross and subtle, in every field of life, has its place in the scheme of one's evolution.

Activity at more subtle levels is the activity of the thought-process. During meditation, the process of experience becomes at every moment more and more refined, and eventually the mind transcends the finest level of activity. The Lord implies that this finer activity also should not be ignored in the midst of the gross activity of thinking, speaking, and acting. It is given to the wise to see that all activity, gross and subtle, is undertaken by every man in society in due proportion — the activity of daily life should be supplemented by morning and evening meditations.

'All actions' should not be taken to include wrong actions. This has been shown in verses 8 and 9.

The following verses present Lord Kṛishṇa's justification for the performance of all right activity by the ignorant.

Verse 27

प्रकृतेः क्रियमाणानि गुणैः कर्माणि सर्वशः
अहंकारविमूढात्मा कर्ताहमिति मन्यते

Prakṛiteḥ kriyamāṇāni guṇaiḥ karmāṇi sarvashaḥ
ahaṁkāravimūdhātmā kartāham iti manyate

Actions are in every case performed by the Guṇas of Nature. He whose mind is deluded by the sense of 'I' holds 'I am the doer'.

This verse reveals the doer of all actions and provides a graceful answer to the question which naturally presents itself when, through the practice of Transcendental Meditation, one begins to live in Bliss Consciousness, begins to feel self-contained. How can action, which is always motivated by some desire, be possible in the state of complete contentment? The answer to this question is: 'Actions are in every case performed by the *Guṇas*'.

Sattwa, *Rajas*, and *Tamas* are the three *Guṇas* of Nature (*Prakṛiti*). *Prakṛiti* is the primal motive force. It is the essential constituent of manifested creation and is at the basis of all activity. This is what the Lord means when He says that all actions and all happenings in creation arise out of the three *Guṇas* and their permutations and combinations.

How the *Guṇas* interact may be made clear by an example. It is a natural law that when a vacuum is created somewhere in the atmosphere, at once a flow begins from an area of greater pressure. But while the flow starts from the area of greater pressure, the cause lies in the vacuum. It is the vacuum that creates the situation. Similarly, the currents of the three *Guṇas* flow in order to keep a balance among themselves. They continually flow from one field of existence to another and in this way create and maintain various activities in a natural way. The entire phenomenal world is nothing but the interplay of the three *Guṇas*.

The *Guṇas* find an expression, for instance, in the metabolic processes of the body, and on their basis feelings of hunger and thirst arise. The need for food and water is in the physiological sphere, but the ego feels 'I am hungry', 'I am thirsty'. The *Guṇas* are responsible in a similar way for all experience. They are the basis of all events and activities, but the ego takes these upon itself and feels 'I am acting'.

As long as the Self has not been experienced as separate from activity, the mind remains 'deluded' about its own status and its relationship with activity; associating itself with the nature of the *Guṇas*, it assumes the authorship of action, which actually belongs to the *Guṇas*. This is how, through ignorance of his own Self, man falls into the bondage of action.

VERSE 28

तत्त्ववित्तु महाबाहो गुणकर्मविभागयोः
गुणा गुणेषु वर्तन्त इति मत्वा न सज्जते

Tattwavit tu Mahābāho guṇakarmavibhāgayoḥ
guṇā guṇeshu vartanta iti matwā na sajjate

But he who knows the truth about the divisions of the Guṇas and their actions, O mighty-armed, knowing that it is the Guṇas which act upon the Guṇas, remains unattached.

This verse, in contrast to the preceding verse, shows the state of mind of the man who is realized, and at the same time provides insight into the process of realization through knowledge of the three *Guṇas*.

There are three *Guṇas* which constitute *Prakriti*. *Prakṛiti* is eightfold.[19] This gives rise to the twenty-four basic divisions in the field of the *Guṇas*. Knowledge of these twenty-four divisions and their actions liberates man from the bondage of action by

19 See VII, 4.

showing how both the subjective and objective aspects of our life emanate from the *Guṇas*, and how the Self is eternally uninvolved with anything in the manifested field of life.

The path of liberation from bondage here laid out has the following significant features:

1. The knowledge has to be thorough and comprehensive, for the Lord says: 'he who knows the truth'.
2. The knowledge has to be about
   (a) 'the *Guṇas*',
   (b) their 'divisions',
   (c) their 'actions'.
3. The knowledge has also to be about the interplay of the *Guṇas*; one has to know that the *Guṇas* are themselves the subject, are themselves the object, and are themselves the subject–object relationship; and that they constitute the entirety of phenomenal existence. For the Lord says: 'It is the *Guṇas* which act upon the *Guṇas*'.

Having, in the previous verse, attributed the authorship of action to the three *Guṇas*, the Lord, in this verse, says that he who knows the truth about the *Guṇas* and their actions 'remains unattached'.

The question may be asked: Is intellectual understanding of the *Guṇas* sufficient to bring freedom? If intellectual understanding could fulfil the conditions of knowledge given above, then, according to this verse, it could certainly make a man sufficiently 'unattached' to become completely free. But it is doubtful if the 'truth' about the three *Guṇas* and their interplay can be known only on the level of intellectual understanding, without directly comprehending the nature of the *Guṇas* at the subtlest level of creation.

The question then arises: What is the way to such direct comprehension? The answer is simple. The *Guṇas* are the finest aspect of creation. Therefore if a man could take his attention to the subtlest level of creation, it would be possible for him to know what the *Guṇas* are, their divisions, and all details concerning their actions. In fact, all this knowledge is gained during Transcendental Meditation when the mind is about to transcend the subtlest state of the object of attention. Consequently, the Lord's saying: 'he who knows the truth about ... the *Guṇas*' may be said to include in its scope the teaching: 'Be without the three *Guṇas*', for this is the way of knowing 'the truth' at the subtlest level of creation.

Once established in Transcendental Consciousness, the state without the three *Guṇas*, the knower of Reality knows by experience that the realm of action lies at the surface of his life and is separate from his real existence. Thus 'he who knows the truth' does not mean only he who knows 'the divisions of the *Guṇas* and their actions', but also he who has realized the Self as separate from activity. This natural state of separation from action, gained through the practice of Transcendental Meditation, is the basis of his remaining 'unattached'. When the state of Being, or pure consciousness, is firmly established in the very nature of the mind, one lives quite naturally this state of pure existence separated from the field of activity, even while ego, intellect, mind, and senses are engaged in action. One finds that the field of activity remains in the province of the three *Guṇas* and is no longer intimately connected with one's existence. This is how one naturally 'remains unattached' in the midst of activity. This state of knowledge fills the whole field of one's understanding. That is why the Lord says: 'knowing that it is the *Guṇas* which act upon the *Guṇas*, remains unattached'.

The present verse speaks of action in terms of freedom through the knowledge of Sāṁkhya, but as this knowledge gains completeness only through the process of direct experience, it is inclusive of the technique and philosophy of Yoga. Therefore the Lord, in this verse, brings together the philosophies of Sāṁkhya and Yoga, described separately in the second chapter, and initiates a principle of liberation from the bondage of *Karma* resulting from the combined effect of the two teachings. This provides the basis of *Karma Yoga* and the essentials for its fulfilment.

The whole purpose of this verse, even though it speaks in terms of the *Guṇas*, is to throw light on the state of fullness of life in absolute Bliss Consciousness—*Jīvan-mukti*.

VERSE 29

प्रकृतेर्गुणसंमूढाः सज्जन्ते गुणकर्मसु
तानकृत्स्नविदो मन्दान्कृत्स्नविन्न विचालयेत्

Prakṛiter guṇasaṁmūdhāḥ sajjante guṇakarmasu
tān akṛitsnavido mandān kṛitsnavin na vichālayet

Those deluded by the Guṇas of Nature are attached to the actions of the Guṇas. Let not him who knows the whole disturb the ignorant who know only the part.

Again the Lord warns the enlightened man not to thrust his understanding of life upon the unenlightened. The reason for this is that the enlightened man, established in Being, has a permanent ground on which to stand; from this he sees the world as the interplay of the three *Guṇas* and knows by experience that the effects of *Sattwa*, *Rajas,* and *Tamas* have no bearing on him. But if an ignorant man tries to copy the state of the enlightened in his own life, then he will create confusion in his behaviour, and his action may fall into a pattern in which the validity of good and evil in the field of practical life is undermined. Such a man will prove useful neither to himself nor to others. After committing a theft, the unenlightened man might say that it was only the three *Guṇas* reacting among themselves, while his Self was uninvolved, so that he is not responsible. He has not done anything! This is why the Lord warns the enlightened not to reveal the inner state of their mind to the ignorant.

The inference is that if the enlightened man wants to bless one who is ignorant, he should meet him on the level[20] of his ignorance and try to lift him up from there by giving him the key to transcending, so that he may gain Bliss Consciousness and experience the Reality of life. He should not tell him about the level of the realized, because it would only confuse him.

20 See verse 35, commentary.

VERSE 30

मयि सर्वाणि कर्माणि संन्यस्याध्यात्मचेतसा
निराशीर्निर्ममो भूत्वा युध्यस्व विगतज्वरः

Mayi sarvāṇi karmāṇi saṁnyasyādhyātmachetasā
nirāshīr nirmamo bhūtwā yudhyaswa vigatajvaraḥ

Surrendering all actions to Me by maintaining your consciousness in the Self, freed from longing and the sense of 'mine', fight, delivered from the fever (of delusion).

As the whole of creation is the play of the three *Guṇas*, the Lord tells Arjuna to contact the source of the three *Guṇas*. By bringing the attention to Transcendental Consciousness and becoming established in that field of Being, He says, you will be freed from all activities and their influence. In that state of freedom and contentment, stand up and fight.

This verse is complementary to verse 28 because the knowledge of relativity gains fulfilment in the realization of the Supreme. Furthermore, even for the complete knowledge of the three *Guṇas*, which form the basis of the whole creation, a thorough intimacy with the Creator is essential.

'Fever (of delusion)': the Lord reminds Arjuna of the bewilderment which he expressed in verse 2.

'Freed from longing': because one has gained fulfilment in life (verses 17 and 18).

'Freed from ... the sense of "mine"': when one has gained Union with Being and disunion from the field of activity (verses 27 and 28), the 'I' ceases to assume authorship of actions and therefore ceases to be bound by their fruits. All action is automatically passed on to the Lord of creation.

During the inward stroke of meditation, one gains a clear experience of transcendent Being. With repeated practice of transcending, one experiences one's Self as aloof from activity and recognizes It as non-doer, even though one is engaged in action. In this state one attributes all activity to the power of the Almighty underlying the *Guṇas*, their divisions, and their actions (verse 28). One remains fixed in the Self, while the Lord is recognized as the author of all actions, carrying them out through the agency of the *Guṇas*.

The steps by which this state is attained are as follows: through the practice of Transcendental Meditation one first experiences the Self, or Being, and then, as a result of this experience becoming deeper and clearer, one experiences the separateness of Being from activity. Again, as this experience of separateness becomes deeper and clearer, one is enlightened by knowledge about the mechanics of activity (verses 23, 24, 27, 28). This knowledge reveals one's own true position in the scheme of things and one's relationship with activity and with the Lord of all creation. This provides one with a sound basis for eternal life in God Consciousness. The glory of the present discourse is this: direct connection with God is established forever by virtue of one's having gained proficiency in the art of action.

Surrender of all actions to God is the living Reality of one's life. It is not a fanciful thought or a mood of surrender. It is the Truth of one's life in activity.

The range of surrender is not restricted to any one aspect of life: it comprehends all spheres of one's existence, physical, mental, and spiritual. Therefore it certainly includes the mind and the intellect. But to regard this state of surrender of action to God as merely an act of the mind, a thought or feeling, will be to do injustice to the principle brought to light by this verse.

'Maintaining your consciousness in the Self' means maintaining Self-consciousness while performing action. Maintenance of transcendental Self-consciousness along with activity in the waking state of consciousness requires coexistence of the two states of consciousness. The ability of man's nervous system, which is the physical machinery through which consciousness expresses itself, has to be developed to express these two states simultaneously. This is brought about by regularly interrupting the constant activity of the waking state of consciousness with periods of silence in Transcendental Consciousness. When, through this practice, the nervous system has been permanently conditioned to maintain these two states together, then the consciousness remains always centred in the Self. The Lord explains that this centring of consciousness in the Self is the way of 'surrendering all actions to Me'.

VERSE 31

ये मे मतमिदं नित्यमनुतिष्ठन्ति मानवा:
श्रद्धावन्तोऽनसूयन्तो मुच्यन्ते तेऽपि कर्मभि:

Ye me matam idaṁ nityam anutishthanti mānavāḥ
shraddhāvanto 'nasūyanto muchyante te 'pi karmabhiḥ

Those men who are possessed of faith, who do not find fault, and always follow this teaching of Mine, they too are liberated from action.

The teaching of the previous verse was directed to Arjuna himself, for the Lord said to him: 'fight'. The present verse extends the teaching to all men at all times.

'Possessed of faith' means that faith is unwavering, that it is permanent. When a man has become fixed in faith, he is freed from doubt and therefore ceases to find fault.

Not finding fault and not speaking ill of others is counted an essential prerequisite to the realization of God and freedom from bondage. When a man speaks ill of others, he partakes of the sins of those of whom he speaks. Such a man thus draws more and more bad influence to himself; that is, he falls deeper into impurity. Here the Lord means: Those who are devoted and who feel full in themselves do not find fault with Me or My teaching; they are released from bondage.

The benefits of the teaching are gained only when one begins to practise it. The teaching of the Lord in the previous three verses is so complete that its practice can result in nothing less than the fulfilment of life. It may be that one is not able to grasp the scope and significance of the teaching intellectually, but those who practise it faithfully, even without understanding it, 'they too are liberated from action' — they too realize that eternal contentment in Bliss Consciousness which establishes the Self as separate from activity and thereby brings fulfilment in God Consciousness.

VERSE 32

ये त्वेतदभ्यसूयन्तो नानुतिष्ठन्ति मे मतम्
सर्वज्ञानविमूढांस्तान्विद्धि नष्टानचेतसः

Ye twetad abhyasūyanto nānutishthanti me matam
sarvagyānavimūdhāṁs tān viddhi nashtān achetasaḥ

But those who find fault and do not follow My teaching: know them to be deluded about all knowledge, doomed and senseless.

The Lord's words are plain and effective.

'Those who find fault' do so because, failing to understand, they begin to misunderstand.

They 'do not follow My teaching' means that they do not understand it and do not put it into practice; they do not investigate the nature of the three *Guṇas* or the Reality which lies beyond.

'Deluded about all knowledge' means confused about the knowledge of relative existence and about the nature of absolute Reality.

'All knowledge': knowledge about the divisions of the *Guṇas* and their actions (verses 27 and 28), knowledge about the Self as separate from the field of action (verses 17 and 18), knowledge about the great Lord of all creation presiding over the absolute field of the Self, or Being, and over the relative field of the *Guṇas* (verses 30 and 31), and knowledge about the activity of the Lord (verses 22 and 23).

'Doomed': the purpose of their life is lost. They cannot find worldly fulfilment and they are lost to the Divine. They fail to live Bliss Consciousness and so remain in suffering.

'Senseless': without proper values in life and devoid of pure consciousness. They have not attained the state of Being. They have not experienced the Self as separate from activity; their self is involved in activity, it is not in its own nature. For this reason the Lord says that they are 'senseless', as if without life, without consciousness.

In this verse the Lord declares that realization of the state of all knowledge is the only way to salvation and success in life; there is no other way.

VERSE 33

सदृशं चेष्टते स्वस्याः प्रकृतेर्ज्ञानवानपि
प्रकृतिं यान्ति भूतानि निग्रहः किं करिष्यति

Sadṛishaṁ cheshtate swasyāḥ prakṛiter gyānavān api
prakṛitiṁ yānti bhūtāni nigrahaḥ kiṁ karishyati

Creatures follow their own nature. Even the enlightened man acts according to his own nature. What can restraint accomplish?

This verse brings out the truth that freedom from bondage is gained in a natural manner. The Lord denies the validity of control on the path of enlightenment. He means to introduce a natural way of life for fulfilment. In the field of activity it is not desirable to create stress and strain by attempting control either from within or from without. Let everyone proceed naturally, complementing the state of Transcendental Consciousness gained during meditation with the activity of daily routine, and so be sure to win fulfilment.

Because the natural tendency of the mind is towards greater happiness, it will inevitably find contentment in the supreme happiness that is transcendental Bliss Consciousness and will rise above 'attachment' (verse 34), which is the basis of bondage. In condemning 'restraint', the Lord, in this verse, advises Arjuna to take things easily[21] and not strain even to follow the teaching.[22] Restraint, being unnatural, cannot bring about that natural state of life where the Self stands by Itself in the state of non-attachment, uninvolved with activity.

Having said in the previous verse: 'know them to be deluded about all knowledge', the Lord, in this verse, gives the clue to all knowledge: in order to be 'liberated from action' (verse 31) it is not necessary to use 'restraint'; it is only necessary to raise

21 See II, 40.
22 See verse 29, commentary.

the level of one's consciousness by the experience of Being, it is only necessary to become 'enlightened'. 'Restraint' offered to activity does not 'accomplish' the goal because, as the next verse explains, the natural seat of bondage does not lie with the mind or the senses, which alone could be influenced by restraint. Attachment, the seat of bondage, does not lie within; it is located outside, in the region of the object of experience. Therefore non-attachment cannot be gained by restraining the mind or senses; keeping them away from activity does not create a state of non-attachment; non-attachment cannot be gained by non-activity (verse 4) or by any kind of restraint. It can only be gained by realizing the Self (verse 17) and by realizing Its separateness from activity (verse 28). There is no other way, because creatures must 'follow their own nature'. They must be engaged in activity according to their own level of consciousness, and therefore enlightenment, if it is to be of universal application, must be possible irrespective of the kind of activity in which one is engaged. That is why the state of enlightenment, the state of knowledge, cannot be gained through restraint, which discriminates between different kinds of activity. It must be on the level of absolute Being, on the level of realization of the Self and completely regardless of the activity that a man undertakes 'according to his own nature'.

The next verse throws more light on this.

VERSE 34

इन्द्रियस्येन्द्रियस्यार्थे रागद्वेषौ व्यवस्थितौ
तयोर्न वशमागच्छेत्तौ ह्यस्य परिपन्थिनौ

Indriyasyendriyasyārthe rāgadweshau vyavasthitau
tayor na vasham āgachchhet tau hyasya paripanthinau

The attachment and aversion of each sense are located in the object of that sense; let no man come under their sway, for both indeed are enemies besetting his path.

The Lord means to point out that all is well and wisely set: let everything remain in its place. The attachment and aversion of each sense are located in 'the object of that sense'. Let them remain in that field and let the field of the Self remain free from them.

This verse supplements the previous verse, for even the idea of restraint engages the mind in the objects of the senses: in order to forget them, the mind continues to think of them. And the moment the mind comes in contact with the object through the senses, it is influenced by attachment or aversion, which is present in the object. Therefore it is wrong to think in terms of abstinence from the activity of experience as the means of gaining a state of permanent freedom from attachment and aversion, because it is not physically possible to remain without activity at all times.

The teaching is: realize Being in Its fullness, realize It as separate from activity; and this will automatically maintain the Self as aloof from attachment or aversion in the midst of all activity and in the presence of all objects of the senses.

In the previous verse, the Lord asked Arjuna not to follow the way of 'restraint'. In this verse, he puts attraction and aversion on one level: 'both indeed are enemies besetting his path'.

This leads to a remarkable conclusion in the following verse.

VERSE 35

श्रेयान्स्वधर्मो विगुणः परधर्मात्स्वनुष्ठितात्
स्वधर्मे निधनं श्रेयः परधर्मो भयावहः

Shreyān swadharmo viguṇaḥ paradharmāt swanushthitāt
swadharme nidhanaṁ shreyaḥ paradharmo bhayāvahaḥ

Because one can perform it, one's own Dharma, (though) lesser in merit, is better than the Dharma of another. Better is death in one's own Dharma: the Dharma of another brings danger.

Life has different stages of evolution. For the process of evolution to advance, it is necessary that one stage should give rise to the next, and in this process each successive stage is of vital importance. The Lord gives expression to this truth by laying down a principle which has its significance at every level of evolution: 'Because one can perform it, one's own *Dharma*, (though) lesser in merit, is better than the *Dharma* of another.'

There are people at various levels of evolution, and each level has a guiding principle, a standard of its own. The guiding principle, or *Dharma*, of a higher level will be suitable and practical for that level, but will not be so for men of lesser development. The Lord emphasizes that a person should go by his own level of consciousness, because only by following that will he make sure of reaching the next stage of evolution. So far as the process of evolution of life is concerned, one's own *Dharma* is the most suitable even though it may appear 'lesser in merit' when compared with the *Dharma* of another. The true merit of *Dharma* lies in its usefulness in promoting evolution in the most effective manner.

Life at one stage, when promoted by the *Dharma* of that stage to a higher stage, begins to be governed by the *Dharma* of that higher stage. This is how, stage by stage, life evolves through the *Dharma* of different stages of evolution. The comparative merit of the *Dharma* of one's present state may be less than the *Dharma* of a higher state, but its merit in its own place is greater by far. The First English Reader is certainly inferior to Milton's Paradise, but it is more valuable for the student of the first grade because it is more suited to him.

If a man were to try to follow a *Dharma* suitable for one of higher development, he would not be able to put it into practice successfully and thus would waste his time and energy. This may go so far as to entail loss of the path of his evolution. Following his own *Dharma*, should he die, he would naturally rise to a higher state of life; but if he were to die while trying to practise the *Dharma* of another, he would die dislocated from his own level of development, in utter confusion about the path of his evolution.

The Lord says: 'Better is death in one's own *Dharma*', and the reason which He gives is that 'the *Dharma* of another brings danger'. It is evident from this that there is a yet greater danger to life than the phenomenon of death.

Death as such only causes a temporary pause in the process of evolution. A pause like this is no real danger to life because, with a new body taken after the pause, more rapid progress of life's evolution becomes possible. A greater danger will be something that actually retards the process of evolution.

In following the *Dharma* of another, one certainly produces some effect in one's life, but it will not have any bearing on one's present level of evolution, for this is solely concerned with one's own *Dharma*. The *Dharma* of another belongs to a level of evolution different from one's own. Because man has freedom of action, he is certainly capable of trying to assume the role of action belonging to different levels of evolution. This means that he is capable of attempting to perform actions suitable to the *Dharma* of another. But if he performs such actions, he loses the continuity of progress on the level from which he could evolve. This is the greatest danger to life: that one lives life, time goes by, without any progress on the path of evolution.

The Lord teaches that everyone should live according to the level of his own *Dharma*, for this will ensure steady progress on the path of evolution. Certainly there are ways to enhance one's progress, but each of them starts by raising the present level and not by abruptly abandoning it.

The present teaching being a discourse on *Yoga Shāstra*, it is necessary to consider *Dharma* not only on the level of relative life, the level of the three *Guṇas* and their activity, but also on the level of Being, which is devoid of activity. The *Dharma* of the Self is eternal, while *Dharma* in the relative field has its different values at different levels of activity. Life is inclusive of both these types of *Dharma* — the eternal *Dharma* of the unchanging Self and the changing states of *Dharma* on different levels of life in the relative field.

The teaching of this verse on its highest level is this: it is better to remain established in the *Dharma* of the Self, which is absolute Bliss Consciousness, than to partake of the *Dharma* of the three *Guṇas* and come under the sway of attachment and aversion. For when a man is established in his own *Dharma*, the *Dharma* of the Self, his activity is carried on under the direct influence of almighty Nature and enjoys Its full support; whereas if he partakes of the *Dharma* of another, the *Dharma* of the three *Guṇas*, he loses the support and patronage of almighty Nature in cosmic life, and his activity becomes limited by the limitations of individual life.

As this principle is true for the *Dharma* of the Self, it is equally true for the *Dharma* of the three *Guṇas*. Let not the field of activity usurp the field of the Self. Only thus can a man naturally live both the *Dharma* of the Self and *Dharma* in the field of activity at every level of evolution. The field of the Self and the field of activity will be forever maintained in their full stature. Man will live eternal freedom in the midst of all success in the different spheres of life's activity, individual and social.

When the body of a realized man meets with death and the nervous system finally ceases to function, the Self remains establised in Its own *Dharma*, the eternal *Dharma* of Being, while the sphere of the three *Guṇas* continues in its *Dharma* of continuous change, transforming the dead body into its different component elements. In such a case, death only amounts to the cessation of individual activity, leaving the Self in Its unbounded state of eternal freedom. Such a death is just a silent declaration of no return — no return to the cycle of birth and death. When the Lord says: 'Better is death in one's own *Dharma*', He is not extolling death; He is only establishing a principle of gaining that state of eternal Being in which death loses its miserable significance.

This, then, is the Lord's answer to all the concern that Arjuna has shown regarding *Dharma* in verses 40 to 45 of the first chapter. Whereas Arjuna considered *Dharma* mainly on the level of behaviour, on the level of the gross aspect of relative life, the Lord's consideration of *Dharma* comes from the very basis of life, from the level of Being, the basis of the three *Guṇas*. Considered from this fundamental level of life, *Dharma* will provide a solution to any problem at any stage of life's evolution.

VERSE 36

अर्जुन उवाच
अथ केन प्रयुक्तोऽयं पापं चरति पूरुषः
अनिच्छन्नपि वार्ष्णेय बलादिव नियोजितः

Arjuna uvācha
Atha kena prayukto 'yaṁ pāpaṁ charati pūrushaḥ
anichchhann api Vārshṇeya balād iva niyojitaḥ

Arjuna said:
What is it that impels a man to commit sin, even involuntarily, as if driven by force, O Vārshṇeya?

'Vārshṇeya': Lord Kṛishṇa, a member of the Vṛishṇi family belonging to the Yādava clan.

It is an essential and practical question that Arjuna asks; he wants to know what force it is that is driving on Duryodhana and his supporters and may cause him personally to commit the great sin of killing his kinsmen.

A thief knows that he is committing a sin and that this will result in punishment. Yet he is not able to resist. Why is this?

Having heard the deep philosophy of the separateness of the inner divine Self from the field of activity, and having clearly understood from the previous verse that it is dangerous for the Self to fall from Its *Dharma* of eternal existence into the sphere of *Dharma* in the ever-changing nature of the three *Guṇas*, it amazes Arjuna to see that this truth of the separateness of the Self and activity, which is the natural state of life, is not manifest in the daily lives of the people. It is this which makes him ask the question in the present verse. He wants to understand the force that robs man of the Reality of his existence.

Verse 37

श्रीभगवानुवाच
काम एष क्रोध एष रजोगुणसमुद्भवः
महाशनो महापाप्मा विद्ध्येनमिह वैरिणम्

Shrī Bhagavān uvācha
Kāma esha krodha esha rajoguṇasamudbhavaḥ
mahāshano mahāpāpmā viddhyenam iha vairiṇam

The Blessed Lord said:
It is desire, it is anger, born of Rajo-guṇa, all-consuming and most evil. Know this to be the enemy here on earth.

'*Rajo-guṇa*': *Rajas*, one of the three *Guṇas* of Nature. It is responsible for motion and energy.

It is desire that establishes contact of the senses with their objects and thereby influences the Self by way of attachment or aversion (verse 34), which in turn create a spur to activity involving the self.

Self-consciousness, unmanifested pure consciousness, manifests as vibration — consciousness vibrates and becomes conscious mind, and a thought arises. The process of manifestation continues, and the thought develops into a desire. Desire is vibrating consciousness set in motion and channelled in a particular direction. It is all motion superimposed on ever-motionless pure consciousness; and this is by virtue of *Rajo-guṇa*.

When the flow of a particular desire is obstructed by another flow, energy is produced at the point of collision, and this flares up as anger, which disturbs, confuses, and destroys the harmony and smooth flow of the desire. Thus confusion is created in the manifested field of Reality, and the purpose of manifestation, which is the expansion of happiness, is marred; the very purpose of creation is thwarted.

That is why anger is called 'the enemy' by the Lord. It is like a whirlpool in a river which threatens to upset the smooth flow of everything passing along it. It is like fire which burns up everything in its path. Anger is said to be the great evil, mutilating the very purpose of creation.

Here desire and anger both stand accused. Whereas anger destroys the purpose of creation, desire keeps the mind floating in the field of sensory experience and is therefore responsible for the mind's involving the Self with action unless the self has gained stability in its own nature. And thus the natural eternal freedom of the Self is overshadowed. Desire in the state of ignorance overshadows the pure nature of the self, which is absolute Bliss Consciousness, and this keeps the life in bondage and suffering.

'All-consuming': this expression is preceded by 'born of *Rajo-guṇa*'. This implies that since *Rajo-guṇa* is responsible for the functioning of *Sattwa* and *Tamas*[23] — since *Rajo-guṇa* lies at the basis of all the constructive and destructive forces of Nature — desire, having its source in *Rajo-guṇa*, also has the natural capacity of either supporting the whole field of the three *Guṇas* or overthrowing their entire purpose. The Lord here does not discuss the upholding and supporting aspect of desire, because in the present context He is analysing its very nature as bringing the Self out of Itself. As such, it is 'all-consuming and most evil', for it overshadows the real nature of the Self and so obscures absolute Bliss Consciousness, the true nature of life eternal.

The nature of desire, as brought to light here by the Lord, applies only so long as one has not gained enlightenment. It is only true of a seeker, an ignorant man, and not of a realized man. When one gains realization of the Self as separate from activity, desire ceases to be 'the enemy here on earth', because it is then upheld only by the three *Guṇas*, while the Self remains completely free from its influence.

In the remainder of this chapter the Lord continues to reflect upon the nature of anger and desire, and eventually shows a way to conquer these enemies of life.

23 See II, 45, commentary.

VERSE 38

धूमेनाव्रियते वह्निर्यथादर्शो मलेन च
यथोल्बेनावृतो गर्भस्तथा तेनेदमावृतम्

Dhūmenāvriyate vahnir yathādarsho malena cha
yatholbenāvṛito garbhas tathā tenedam āvṛitam

As fire is covered by smoke, as a mirror by dust, as an embryo is covered by the amnion, so is This covered by that.

'This covered by that': pure consciousness is overlaid by desires.

There are three metaphors in this verse, each with its own significance.

Smoke arises from fire and covers it: desire arises from pure consciousness and veils it.

The mirror is covered by dust, which comes from outside it. The source of desire lies outside the field of Being in the field of the *Guṇas*. This outer stimulus creates a desire and covers pure Being. So it can be said that the desire coming from outside covers Being as dust covers a mirror.

As the amnion covering the embryo supports it and keeps it alive, so does the desire overshadowing Being support and give life to beings, nourish them, and keep them alive.

Therefore it is desire which in every way veils the uninvolved nature of the Self and leaves It involved, as it were, and as if bound by activity.

VERSE 39

आवृतं ज्ञानमेतेन ज्ञानिनो नित्यवैरिणा
कामरूपेण कौन्तेय दुष्पूरेणानलेन च

Āvṛitaṁ gyānam etena gyānino nityavairiṇā
kāmarūpeṇa Kaunteya dushpūreṇānalena cha

Wisdom is veiled by this insatiable flame of desire which is the constant enemy of the wise, O son of Kuntī.

'Wisdom': see verse 32.

Desire, as defined in the 37th verse, is like an unquenchable fire, because the flow of desire in a particular direction, kept moving by the experience of happiness or the search for it, continues to flow from point to point, there being no point in the field of relativity to satisfy finally its craving for greater happiness.

This is how the ceaseless activity of desire continues to maintain a close tie of association between the self and the outside world, thus keeping the self bound, as it were, to the field of action. Desire does not allow the self to remain uninvolved with the field of action, even though all activity is in reality carried on by the three *Guṇas*.

'The wise' in this context are they who know 'the truth about the divisions of the *Guṇas* and their actions' and who know 'that it is the *Guṇas* which act upon the *Guṇas*', as explained in verse 28. The wise are they who, established in the knowledge of the three *Guṇas*, remain uninvolved with the field of action. When the Lord says in this verse that desire 'is the constant enemy of the wise', He is warning students of Sāṁkhya that mere intellectual understanding of the three *Guṇas* is not sufficient to establish the Self as uninvolved with action and its fruits. It is necessary to rise above the influence of desire. But as long as life continues, it has to be in the field of desires. No practical man could ever be without desires. When the Lord says: 'Wisdom is veiled by this insatiable flame of desire which is the constant enemy of the wise', He does not intend to lay down the principle that desire has to be eradicated, because this is not physically possible. Any attempt in that direction will only make life dull, useless, or tense.

The Lord's purpose is to lay the facts before Arjuna, and then to give him a technique by which he can rise with ease above the binding influence of desire and make his life brighter, more successful, and fulfilled on every level. The Lord explains clearly the mechanics of bondage, so that Arjuna may be better able to realize that to rise above this bondage and live a life of eternal freedom is not difficult but easy. The great emphasis in this verse upon the enmity of desires implicitly shows that the Lord is going to lead Arjuna to a way that will transform the influence of desire from enmity to usefulness. Desires will cease to be the 'enemy of the wise'; they will prove to be supporters of the wise and will bring them fulfilment on every side.

The Lord, out of His great kindness, is going to give Arjuna a simple technique of transforming the whole machinery that gives rise to desire, of transforming the mind and heart so that the rising up of desires and all their activities will serve as tidal waves of love and bliss in the unbounded ocean of the oneness of God Consciousness. This involves giving a pattern to the machinery that creates desire — senses, mind, and intellect — so that even while remaining in the field of desire, it remains free from the impact of desire. This allows the Self to remain uninvolved, leaving the desires to be taken care of by the three *Guṇas*, by virtue of which they arise, grow, and have their play.

The following verse analyses the machinery which gives rise to desires, and the remaining verses of this chapter are devoted to bringing out the basic and at the same time most highly advanced teaching of the technique whereby one passes out of the binding influence of desires.

VERSE 40

इन्द्रियाणि मनो बुद्धिरस्याधिष्ठानमुच्यते
एतैर्विमोहयत्येष ज्ञानमावृत्य देहिनम्

Indriyāṇi mano buddhir asyādhishthānam uchyate
etair vimohayatyesha gyānam āvṛitya dehinam

The senses, the mind, and the intellect are said to be its seat. Overshadowing wisdom by means of these, it deludes the dweller in the body.

Having thus far explained that the loss of wisdom is due mainly to the mind's incessant engagement in the field of activity, to desire, the Lord now begins to describe a way whereby the subjective aspect of one's life, which is responsible for all desire and activity, can be influenced in such a manner that, on the one hand, it does not permit desires to overshadow Being and, on the other, it brings fulfilment to them, thus bringing both success and salvation to life.

The Lord first describes the subjective machinery responsible for making concrete the abstract essence of desire. Through the intellect, mind, and senses, abstract desire in the form of a thought takes on a concrete shape. As a result, the Self becomes as if involved with the field of activity. This is how the uninvolved nature of the Self is deluded, as it were. The wisdom that holds the Self to be uninvolved and out of bondage is overshadowed by the senses, mind, and intellect coming into action under the sway of desire.

Having shown the senses to be the direct means through which desires function, the Lord, in the following verse, stresses the necessity of conditioning the senses to become free from the overshadowing nature of desires.

VERSE 41

तस्मात्त्वमिन्द्रियाण्यादौ नियम्य भरतर्षभ
पाप्मानं प्रजहि ह्येनं ज्ञानविज्ञाननाशनम्

Tasmāt twam indriyāṇyādau niyamya Bharatarshabha
pāpmānaṁ prajahi hyenaṁ gyānavigyānanāshanam

Therefore, having first organized the senses, O best of Bhāratas, shake off this evil, the destroyer of knowledge and realization.

'Organized': the Sanskrit word used in the text is '*niyamya*', which means literally having introduced law and order, having organized something to function in an orderly manner. Even the word 'organize' is inadequate to convey the accurate meaning, but it has been chosen to avoid the sense of control and restraint which has generally been implied by commentators and which has only resulted in mutilating the whole meaning and purpose of the teaching.

This verse brings out a fundamental principle showing how to make life free from 'this evil' of desire, leaving it in fullness of wisdom and freedom in divine consciousness.

The previous verse has declared the senses, mind, and intellect to be the 'seat' of desire. In teaching Arjuna how to regulate and organize the flow of desire so that it may cease to overshadow the essential nature of the Self, the Lord begins with a consideration of the field of the senses; for the senses are the fountainhead from which all the streams of desire flow.

In a mountain, various underground currents of water flow from all directions and all of them find a common outlet in a spring. The only way to organize all these underground currents is to organize the outlet. Desires in the fields of intellect and mind are like currents underground. The field of the senses is like the outlet from which the currents emerge into the open air. By controlling the outlet, it is quite possible to use the whole outflow of water to advantage. According to this verse, organizing the outlet, organizing the senses, is the way to make the best use of the underground currents of desire.

The advice here is not to abandon or kill desires, not to control desires as such, but to control the outlet of desires by organizing the senses. The purpose is to give a pattern to the functioning of the senses so that their activity will always, as a matter of course, be in accordance with the Laws of Nature conducting the process of evolution. This is the simple and effective means to 'shake off this evil, the destroyer of knowledge and realization'.

Organizing the senses lies at the root of all real accomplishments in life. The verses which follow expound the technique.

VERSE 42

इन्द्रियाणि पराण्याहुरिन्द्रियेभ्यः परं मनः
मनसस्तु परा बुद्धिर्यो बुद्धेः परतस्तु सः

Indriyāṇi parāṇyāhur indriyebhyaḥ paraṁ manaḥ
manasas tu parā buddhir yo buddheḥ paratas tu saḥ

The senses, they say, are subtle; more subtle than
the senses is mind; yet finer than mind is intellect;
that which is beyond even the intellect is he.

After emphasizing in the previous verse the necessity of organizing the senses, the Lord now indicates the sequence of the subtler aspects of subjective life which lie beyond the senses. This is to find the key to organizing the senses.

If one has difficulty in dealing with an officer, one should seek out his superior in rank. In the field of inner life, the Lord says, he who is beyond the intellect is the highest authority of all.

The next verse makes clear that by contacting him, the senses are naturally subdued.

VERSE 43

एवं बुद्धेः परं बुद्ध्वा संस्तभ्यात्मानमात्मना
जहि शत्रुं महाबाहो कामरूपं दुरासदम्

Evaṁ buddheḥ paraṁ buddhwā saṁstabhyātmānam ātmanā
jahi shatruṁ Mahābāho kāmarūpaṁ durāsadam

Thus, having known him who is beyond the intellect, having stilled the self by the Self, O mighty-armed, slay the enemy in the form of desire, difficult to subdue.

'Having known him': this means having known the indweller of the body in his true nature as Being, separate from the whole field of activity of the body,[24] senses, mind, and intellect. The expression implies that this is the way to 'slay the enemy in the form of desire'.

'Difficult to subdue': subduing of desires will be difficult by any attempt that aims directly to subdue them. Desires are the impulses of the mind. Unless the mind turns to Being it is naturally engaged in desire. As this is the natural relation of the mind to desires, and as the mind is the basis of the existence of desires, the only way to subdue them is to turn the mind to Being.

This is the great wisdom of life, the essence of the doctrine of *Karma Yoga*. The Lord makes a fundamental statement about cause and effect: influence the cause to modify the effect, go to the realm of Being in order to modify the nature of the intellect,

24 See II, 18–26, 29–30.

mind, and senses. Go to the absolute ultimate Reality, and all levels of relativity will cease to be a burden. Be illumined, and life will ever be in freedom and fullness, away from the darkness of ignorance.

The Lord says: Realization of the Ultimate is within your easy reach. You have the power to realize the Supreme, provided you do not undermine that power. It only amounts to being what you are. Being what you are, you will find the whole field of existence set in eternal harmony. Intellect, mind, and senses, all will function in accord, none will overpower the others, and no side of life will be impaired. Life will be lived in fullness.

This is a reaffirmation of the Lord's words in the 45th and 46th verses of the second chapter. It is an approach which does away with the need for controlling the senses by any unnatural or strenuous austerity. It makes unnecessary any practice of detachment or renunciation for the sake of cultivating the state of enlightenment.

A very practical method of realization is provided, whether one is on the path of *Gyān Yoga*, the way of knowledge, or of *Karma Yoga*, the way of action. Irrespective of one's way of life, that of a householder or that of a recluse, this is a direct approach to fulfilment.

Unfortunately it is commonly held that desires should be subdued in order to attain enlightenment. This is completely wrong. The misunderstanding has grown during the last few hundred years, and in consequence the task of those who seek the Truth has become more difficult than ever before. Here the Lord says: Go to the state of enlightenment in order to come out of the bondage of *Karma*, bring the light in order to remove the darkness. It is this which is the underlying principle of the verse; not that one should try to remove the darkness in order to come into the light.

So that Arjuna may be released from the bondage of *Karma*, the Lord wishes him to leave the whole field of *Karma*. He wants him to know the transcendental Reality and thereby build up his mind to such a degree that it will rise above the binding influence of desires and actions. This is a direct way of realizing the state of integration and of eternal freedom during one's lifetime here on earth.

This, being the last verse of the chapter, sums up the Lord's answer to Arjuna's questions in verses 1, 2, and 36.

This chapter, which expounds the science of action, advocates transcending desire as a technique of subduing desires and also of bringing fulfilment to them; useless desires will be subdued while useful ones will find their fulfilment. The principle of maintaining the life of a tree is to go beyond the tree. If one attends to the area surrounding the root, to the transcendental field of the tree, it is easy to bring nourishment to all its parts. If one attends to the field of the Transcendent one can make the whole tree of life healthy and fruitful.

The blessing of this chapter is the principle of transcending the field of action in order to bring fulfilment to action. It upholds and supports both the life of a householder and the life of a recluse.

ॐ तत्सदिति श्रीमद्भगवद्गीतासूपनिषत्सु ब्रह्मविद्यायां योगशास्त्रे
श्रीकृष्णार्जुनसंवादे कर्मयोगो नाम तृतीयोऽध्यायः

Oṁ tat sad iti Shrīmad Bhagavadgītāsūpanishatsu Brahmavidyāyāṁ Yogashāstre Shrīkṛishṇārjunasaṁvāde Karmayogo nāma tṛitīyo 'dhyāyaḥ

Thus, in the Upanishad of the glorious Bhagavad-Gītā,
in the Science of the Absolute, in the Scripture of Yoga,
in the dialogue between Lord Kṛishṇa and Arjuna, ends
the third chapter, entitled: The Yoga of Action, Karma Yoga.

Chapter IV

A Vision of the Teaching in Chapter IV

Verses 1–8. This path of action for gaining success in the world and freedom in Divine Consciousness has a long tradition. In its content it is eternal. Even if in time its purity is lost and it is forgotten by man, each time it is restored in the world by a wave of revival that comes from God.

Verses 9–10. Knowledge of the Divine as separate from activity, and knowledge of the Lord's birth and actions as divine, raise man's consciousness to that purity which places him on the divine level.

Verses 11–12. Divine reaction to man depends upon man's action towards the Divine. Success is born of action in the world of men.

Verses 13–15. Having known the Divine as Creator and yet as unattached to activity, the seekers of liberation follow this example and engage in action.

Verses 16–22. The course of action being unfathomable, performance of proper action is only possible with knowledge of the divine nature. This knowledge is fully gained in Divine Consciousness, in which inner freedom and outer activity are simultaneously maintained.

Verses 23–33. Gaining Divine Consciousness, man rises to oneness of life, and in this state all activity is in the Light of God. All actions culminate in the knowledge of God.

Verses 34–8. Established in this knowledge, a man sees all beings in himself and finds himself in God. This supreme state of purity in God Consciousness puts an end to ignorance and all bondage of action.

Verses 39–42. The light of this knowledge is kindled in one who is full of faith, intent of purpose, and has his senses subdued. It brings abiding peace without delay.

Gain the state of non-attachment and freedom from doubts; be established in the Self and action will not bind.

THIS chapter springs from the same breath of the Lord as Chapter III. Verse 48 of Chapter II contains the seed thoughts which give rise to both chapters: 'Established in Yoga ... perform actions' to Chapter III, and 'having abandoned attachment and having become balanced in success and failure' to Chapter IV. These two chapters together are therefore sufficient to bring enlightenment to a seeker. They give him, in so far as words can, the desired experience and full understanding of it.

The second chapter presented the doctrine of liberation. It analysed life in its relative and absolute aspects and promised liberation through knowledge of these.

Knowledge in its entirety comprises both understanding and experience. Therefore in order to gain fulfilment a man must necessarily acquire both understanding and experience of the relative and the Absolute, irrespective of whether his path is that of a householder or a recluse. It follows that the wisdom of Sāṁkhya, which brings liberation through *understanding* of the relative and the Absolute, and the practice of Yoga, which brings liberation by providing direct *experience* of these two spheres of existence, are both paths to enlightenment. All this teaching is contained in the second chapter.

The third chapter presented a doctrine of action designed to make permanent the experience of the Absolute first mentioned in the 45th verse of the second chapter.

When this experience of the Absolute has become permanent, Self-awareness is naturally maintained through all the waking, dreaming, and deep-sleep states of consciousness. One experiences oneself as separate from activity. As one lives this life of non-involvement, of natural non-attachment, one's intellect begins to inquire: 'Is this the truth of life? Has this sense of separateness or non-attachment anything to do with real life, or is it an escape from life? Is the reality of life a duality — the duality of Being and activity?' Such doubts are removed by the knowledge given in the fourth chapter.

This chapter, dedicated to the knowledge of renunciation, analyses the nature of action and the nature of the actor on both the individual and cosmic levels — on the level of man and on the level of God — and then proclaims the result of this systematic and rational analysis: action and actor are independent of one another; there exists a natural state of separation between them at every level. This state of non-attachment, or renunciation, provides on the one hand a solid foundation of eternal freedom for the actor, and on the other the maximum possible success in action with most glorious fruits. It is this state of renunciation that provides the eternal playground for the Divine and for man. Ignorance of this natural basis of life is the cause of bondage and all suffering. Knowledge of it results in eternal freedom. To unfold this knowledge is the purpose of the fourth chapter.

The most fascinating aspect of this chapter is that, in bringing out knowledge of the renunciation of action, it explains the whole field of action, showing how the stream of life advances towards the higher spheres of existence (verse 10) and towards the higher forces in Nature (verse 12), until it merges with the ocean of eternal freedom in God Consciousness (verse 9).

This chapter of knowledge is of the utmost importance to a seeker, for it explains the most valuable experience on the path to enlightenment, the experience of the separateness of the Self and activity. As his practice advances, every seeker must necessarily reach this experience; and if he is to proceed smoothly on his path, unhindered by doubts, he must possess this knowledge.

In order to bring out the complete knowledge of the separation, or the state of renunciation, that exists between the Self and activity, this chapter explains the two spheres of life, relative and absolute. In so doing, it proclaims the philosophy of two fullnesses found in the Upanishads: this is full and That is full, '*Pūrṇam adaḥ pūrṇam idam*' — That transcendental unmanifested absolute eternal Being is full, and this manifested relative ever-changing world of phenomenal existence is full. The Absolute is eternal in its never-changing nature, and the relative is eternal in its ever-changing nature.

This living Reality of two fullnesses in Cosmic Consciousness finds its consummation in the grand Unity of God Consciousness. In expounding this unified philosophy of the two fullnesses, this chapter presents the core of the wisdom contained in this Scripture of Yoga, and for this reason the Lord begins by giving Arjuna an account of the tradition of this Yoga.

VERSE 1

श्रीभगवानुवाच
इमं विवस्वते योगं प्रोक्तवानहमव्ययम्
विवस्वान्मनवे प्राह मनुरिक्ष्वाकवेऽब्रवीत्

Shrī Bhagavān uvācha
Imaṁ Vivaswate yogaṁ proktavān aham avyayam
Vivaswān Manave prāha Manur Ikshwākave 'bravīt

The Blessed Lord said:
I proclaimed this imperishable Yoga to Vivaswat,
Vivaswat declared it to Manu, and Manu told it to Ikshwāku.

'This imperishable Yoga': the preceding chapters have been devoted to Yoga — *Sāṁkhya Yoga* and *Karma Yoga*. By saying: 'this ... Yoga', the Lord speaks of them both as one. This is to bring home to Arjuna that, although they have been declared to be different, they have the same basis and yield the same results. The basis is: 'Be without the three *Guṇas*', which brings fulfilment both to the wisdom of Sāṁkhya and to the practice of *Karma Yoga*.[1] Thus the word 'Yoga' in this verse stands for both Sāṁkhya and *Karma Yoga*.

The Yoga expounded by Lord Kṛishṇa is imperishable because it brings to light the wisdom of the Absolute and the wisdom of the relative. The relative and the Absolute, both these are eternal; and so is Yoga, which expounds the truth of both,

1 See III, 28, commentary.

the truth of life in its fullness. It is eternal because it serves the cosmic purpose and is natural to the mind of man.

The Lord says that He taught this eternal Yoga to Vivaswat in the beginning of creation in order to infuse strength into the *Kshatriyas*[2] and to enable them to maintain law and order and preserve the path of righteousness for the well-being of society. Vivaswat revealed it to his son Manu,[3] the law-giver to the world. And Manu gave it to his son Ikshwāku, who ruled at Ayodhyā as the first king of the Solar Dynasty.

The Bhagavad-Gītā is the highest expression of divine intelligence understandable by man. Dealing with the unseen aspects of life, it also touches on the past and present of the world of our daily life. Furthermore, the Bhagavad-Gītā, while expounding universal Truth, is itself a historical record and relates incidents that took place five thousand years ago.

In order to understand the historical significance of the Bhagavad-Gītā, one must be familiar with the Indian conception of history and time.

The study of history has a definite purpose and a place in the life of the individual. Its aim is to educate the mind of the present with information from the past in order to ensure a better present and a better future. In this way each generation takes advantage of the achievements of the past and advances towards greater wisdom in life.

But it is not knowledge of the chronological order of events that educates students of history; it is the value of events that is important, and this is the aspect of history on which Indian historians have concentrated. They have put on record, for all generations to read, only such instances in the great span of time as can help to integrate men's lives. Their purpose is to inspire men both as individuals and as members of society.

The sage of enlightened vision, Veda Vyāsa, had before him a vast span of time to take into account. As a conscientious and fully integrated man, he could not write the history of this

2 It is interesting to note that the ancient wisdom was given to the *Kshatriyas*, the warriors.

3 Manu: the seventh Manu, being the son of Vivaswat, is called Vaivaswat Manu. He is said to be the progenitor of the present human race.

immeasurable period as a sequence of days and years. He could only select particular happenings and record them in such a way as to inspire and guide people of all times on the path of evolution and educate them in the integration of their life. This is why no chronological order is to be found in Indian histories. Vyāsa thought it absurd to pin every event down chronologically just for the sake of establishing each link on the long road of time.

Moreover, it is not physically possible to write the history of millions of years in chronological sequence. In the case of small countries with a few thousand years of civilization, it is quite practicable for historians, with a vision of that small area and that small span of time, to maintain chronological order. But Vyāsa had a clear vision of the whole span of time beginning from the day of creation. Such a mind would not and could not assign any value to chronology.

The Indian conception of time, as set out below, will clearly show the situation that confronted Vyāsa and other writers of Indian history.

Time is a conception to measure eternity. Indian historians base their conception of time on eternal Being; for them eternity is the basic field of time.

To arrive at some conception of the eternal, the best measure will be the life-span of something that has the greatest longevity in the relative field of creation. This, according to the enlightened vision of Vyāsa, is the Divine Mother, the Universal Mother, who is ultimately responsible for all that is, was, and will be in the entire cosmos.

The eternity of the eternal life of absolute Being is conceived in terms of innumerable lives of the Divine Mother, a single one of whose lives encompasses a thousand life-spans of Lord Shiva. One life of Lord Shiva covers the time of a thousand life-spans of Lord Vishṇu. One life of Lord Vishṇu equals the duration of a thousand life-spans of Brahmā, the Creator. A single life-span of Brahmā is conceived in terms of one hundred years of Brahmā; each year of Brahmā comprises 12 months of Brahmā, and each month comprises thirty days of Brahmā. One day of Brahmā is called a *Kalpa*. One *Kalpa* is equal to the time of fourteen *Manus*. The time of one *Manu* is called a *Manwantara*. One *Manwantara* equals seventy-one *Chaturyugīs*. One *Chaturyugī* comprises the total span of four *Yugas*, i.e. *Sat-yuga*, *Tretā-yuga*, *Dwāpara-yuga* and *Kali-yuga*. The span of the *Yugas* is conceived in terms of the duration of *Sat-yuga*. Thus the span of *Tretā-yuga* is equal to three quarters of that of *Sat-yuga*; the span of *Dwāpara-yuga* is half that of *Sat-yuga*, and the span of *Kali-yuga* one quarter that of *Sat-yuga*. The span of *Kali-yuga* equals 432,000 years of man's life.[4]

Now consider the time of creation: for how many billion trillion years the world has been! Even if the account of one year were to occupy a page or even a single line, how could anyone possibly read such a history and apply its lesson to his life? This is why chronological order was not maintained by Indian historians. Apart from being impracticable, it was considered to be unnecessary, useless, and damaging to the very purpose of history.

All this should be borne in mind by those modern historians who tend to reject as non-history any series of events for which they fail to find a proper chronological order. It is deplorable that such precious accounts of life on the highest human level as are to be found in the historical material of ancient India should have been regarded as myth. They should, on the contrary, be recognized as a most useful history of the highest civilization that has ever existed on earth.

The Bhagavad-Gītā forms the central core of the most authentic record of Indian history, the Mahābhārat. This cannot be dismissed as mythology just because the narrow vision of modern historians, tied to rigid chronology, fails to understand it as a historical record and puts it in the compartment of imaginative literature.

It is regrettable that some modern commentators on the Bhagavad-Gītā have followed in the footsteps of modern historians and refused to admit its historic authenticity. It is to be hoped that the light will dawn and truth will be recognized as truth.

When Lord Kṛishṇa recalls for Arjuna that the great wisdom

4 This elaboration of the conception of time also serves as a commentary to verse 17 of Chapter VIII.

of the Bhagavad-Gītā was given to Vivaswat in the beginning of this *Kalpa*, He does not enumerate in detail all the custodians of this supreme knowledge. To satisfy Arjuna about the original source of the teaching, it is sufficient to give him the idea of this eternal wisdom being handed on from generation to generation.

VERSE 2

एवं परंपराप्राप्तमिमं राजर्षयो विदुः
स कालेनेह महता योगो नष्टः परंतप

Evaṁ paraṁparāprāptam imaṁ rājarshayo viduḥ
sa kāleneha mahatā yogo nashtaḥ Paraṁtapa

Thus having received it one from another, the royal sages knew it. With the long lapse of time, O scorcher of enemies, this Yoga has been lost to the world.

The Lord says that this technique of integration of life was handed on to the philosopher-kings, men who led active lives and had great responsibilities in the world. In those days the rulers were held responsible for every aspect of the development of their people, physical, mental, and spiritual. They gave this wisdom of Yoga to the people in general. In the modern democratic world each man has to look after his own affairs. Thus it is in keeping with our times that each man should feel responsible for his own development.

As spiritual development is the basis of all other forms of development, it is necessary that this great science and art of successful living should now be handed on to every man everywhere in the world.

The Lord says: 'having received it one from another'. By this, He brings an unquestionable authenticity to this system of Yoga. It has been since the beginning of history. Again He says: 'the royal sages knew it', showing it to be a precious doctrine followed by those in positions of great responsibility.

The reason for its loss, the Lord says, is 'the long lapse of time'. But in the first verse He has spoken of this Yoga as 'imperishable'. This implies that while its principle is imperishable its practice needs periodic revival, according to the changed conditions of living from age to age. Because it awakens man's consciousness to extreme purity, this system of Yoga is equally suitable for people in every age. Sometimes, however, it is not followed in its pure form; then the desired results are not achieved and this eventually leads to indifference towards its practice. Thus this great principle of life becomes lost from time to time. But it cannot be lost forever because, as the Truth of existence, it must be brought to light again and again. Nature helps to restore it. From time to time great teachers come with the proper inspiration to reveal the path once more. They renew the tradition which maintains the teaching. The renewed tradition remains dominant so long as it continues to inspire the people. But when it fails to respond to the need of the age new teachers arise. This cycle is repeated again and again.

Some who come to revive the tradition honour the ancient line of teachers; others, failing to relate the traditional solutions to their present need, break away from the established tradition. Their teachings form new branches of the old trunk.

The custodians of the ancient tradition of Vedic wisdom act as the guardians of the main trunk, from which different branches have sprung from time to time in the form of different religions, faiths, philosophies, and cultures in different parts of the world.

Today the most cherished tradition of Vedic wisdom is the Shankarāchārya tradition which, in its present shape, began about 2,500 years ago[5] with the teaching of the first Shankarāchārya. He revived the forgotten Truth. By his faithful interpretation of the essence of Vedic Literature, he re-established the principle of the Unity of all-pervading Being in the midst of the diversities of life. He established the unified philosophy of the two fullnesses as the essential teaching of Vedānt. His commentaries on the Brahma Sūtra, the Upanishads, and the Bhagavad-Gītā are extolled for their depth of wisdom and magnificent exposition

5 According to the records kept by the *Maths* or monasteries of the Shankarāchārya tradition, though some modern scholars assign the life of Shankara to the ninth century A.D. They have perhaps confused an illustrious successor with Shankara himself, because all his successors are known as Shankarāchāryas; the name has become a title.

of the Reality of life.

Strange how the truth of a teaching becomes distorted with the passage of time! The truth of Shankara's teaching has been so misrepresented by his interpreters that modern writing about his thought retains little of his spirit. The *Sanyāsī*, or recluse orders, of Shankara's tradition have been interpreting Shankara-Vedānt as being completely closed to the householders, who form the main section of society, and open only to themselves. This has resulted in spiritual decadence and in the moral downfall of Indian society.

Such decay is nothing new. It happens, says Lord Kṛishṇa, 'with the long lapse of time'. The Truth is overshadowed, and distorted interpretations take its place. But when these depart so far from the Truth that the principle itself is in danger of extinction, then a revival comes to save it.

The Holy Tradition of great Masters,[6] which is responsible for reviving the teaching after every lapse, has captured the minds and hearts of lovers of Truth in every age. It is not merely held in high regard, but has come to be actually worshipped by seekers of Truth and knowers of Reality. A verse[7] recording the names of the greatest and most highly revered Masters has not only inspired seekers, but has been a joy even to the fulfilled hearts of realized souls passing through the long corridor of time.

'Scorcher of enemies': by using this expression, the Lord indicates to Arjuna that this Yoga has been lost through falling into the hands of the weak, and that now, by finding its way into the strong hands of Arjuna, it will prove its worth and help the world to restore and maintain the path of righteousness.

The Lord's expression also indicates to Arjuna that he will not prove unworthy of this great blessing.

In the following verse He gives further reasons for teaching this wisdom to Arjuna.

6 See Appendix: The Holy Tradition.

7 See Appendix: The Holy Tradition.

Verse 3

स एवायं मया तेऽद्य योगः प्रोक्तः पुरातनः
भक्तोऽसि मे सखा चेति रहस्यं ह्येतदुत्तमम्

Sa evāyaṁ mayā te 'dya yogaḥ proktaḥ purātanaḥ
bhakto 'si me sakhā cheti rahasyaṁ hyetad uttamam

This same age-old Yoga, which is indeed the supreme secret,
I have today declared to you because you are My devotee and friend.

'Age-old Yoga' indicates that the teaching has withstood the test of time, and that it cannot but prove useful. The Lord is not trying out any new method; He is only restoring the old tradition. Such has been the declaration of all the great masters from time immemorial; they never claimed that their teaching was new, but rather that they were bringing out the forgotten wisdom of life. They spoke only of restoration because the truth of any useful principle continues to exist in time.

The Lord here mentions two qualities of Arjuna's which entitle him to receive this great secret wisdom: 'friend' and 'devotee'. And also two qualities of the system of Yoga: 'supreme' and 'secret'. That which is secret can be passed on to a friend, but that which is supreme can be passed on only to a devotee. A devotee never questions his master. In order to allow Arjuna the freedom to question, Lord Kṛishṇa calls him His friend.

Arjuna makes use of this freedom in the following verse.

Verse 4

अर्जुन उवाच
अपरं भवतो जन्म परं जन्म विवस्वतः
कथमेतद्विजानीयां त्वमादौ प्रोक्तवानिति

Arjuna uvācha
Aparaṁ bhavato janma paraṁ janma Vivaswataḥ
katham etad vijānīyāṁ twam ādau proktavān iti

Arjuna said:
Later was Thy birth and earlier the birth of Vivaswat:
how am I to understand this saying that Thou didst
proclaim it in the beginning?

This question shows Arjuna's alertness to every word that the Lord speaks to him, his vigilance and careful scrutiny of every point. Such is the mind of a good seeker of Truth. A good master is only encouraged by such questions.

In the previous verse, Lord Kṛishṇa, through Himself, has connected the far distant past with the present. Now Arjuna isolates Him in time and states his difficulty in understanding the eternity of time in Him.

Lord Kṛishṇa's answer is plain and simple.

VERSE 5

श्रीभगवानुवाच
बहूनि मे व्यतीतानि जन्मानि तव चार्जुन
तान्यहं वेद सर्वाणि न त्वं वेत्थ परंतप

Shrī Bhagavān uvācha
Bahūni me vyatītāni janmāni tava chārjuna
tānyahaṁ veda sarvāṇi na twaṁ vettha Paraṁtapa

The Blessed Lord said:
Many births have passed for Me and for you also, O Arjuna.
I know them all but you know them not, O scorcher of enemies.

This verse may be said to exemplify what verses 12 and 22 of the second chapter spoke of in principle: bodies change in time, but time changes in the Self, in Being, which continues to be, regardless of past, present, or future. As the embodied self remains unchanged when the body passes into the changing states of childhood, youth, and old age,[8] so does the Self continue unchanged in the eternity of time.

The Lord says: 'I know them all but you know them not'. This

8 See II, 13.

points to a difference between the life of man and the Incarnation of God. Man is born as a result of his past actions, good and bad, so that his vision remains coloured or obstructed by those influences. The nature of the divine Incarnation is ever pure eternal unbounded intelligence. His vision is absolutely clear; that is why for Him the eternity of knowing is maintained and the factor of time fails to obstruct it.

The Lord's Being is the playground of the time which He creates. It comes and goes, but He, steadfast in His eternal Being, forever and ever continues to be. He is the ocean of life, while time rises and falls as the tide on the surface of the ocean. Though the tidal waves draw on the depths they can never fathom the unfathomable abyss.

The life of man is like a wave which rises up to see — it can see so far and no more; but Lord Kṛishṇa's stature is like that of an ocean on which the whole of space is reflected. Thus the Lord knows 'them all' and Arjuna knows 'them not'.

Arjuna had challenged Lord Kṛishṇa's words, and the expression 'you know them not' shows that the Lord is obliged to use His authority. But at the same time He addresses Arjuna as 'scorcher of enemies', so as to prevent his morale from sinking. Lord Kṛishṇa uses His authority with love.

The next verse further explains the Lord's nature.

VERSE 6

अजोऽपि सन्नव्ययात्मा भूतानामीश्वरोऽपि सन्
प्रकृतिं स्वामधिष्ठाय संभवाम्यात्ममायया

Ajo 'pi sann avyayātmā bhūtānām Īshwaro 'pi san
prakṛitiṁ swām adhishthāya saṁbhavāmyātmamāyayā

Though I am unborn and of imperishable nature,
though Lord of all beings, yet remaining in My own
Nature I take birth through My own power of creation.

At this point there is an illustration of an important psychological technique. As the Lord has earlier affirmed the authenticity of this system of Yoga, declaring that it is ancient and has a great tradition, He must also make clear to Arjuna that He who is giving out this eternal wisdom is great in Himself, is one whose word alone can be taken as authoritative.

The direction of the discourse is such that it makes Arjuna question the Lord on the very point about which He wants to speak next. Had the Lord spoken the words of this and the preceding verse in a different context and not in reply to Arjuna's question (verse 4), then they would not have been so effective and convincing. It is the greatness of the teacher that brings out the right question from the pupil. In answering it, the teacher freely develops his own theme and at the same time keeps the interest of the pupil more actively engaged than it would be if only the teacher spoke.

Although manifest creation, which includes men and other creatures, springs from the unmanifest, its manifestation is by virtue of *Prakṛiti*. But the divine manifestation of the unmanifest Being, which comes to re-establish the forgotten wisdom of life, is by virtue of '*Līlā-shakti*', which is the very power of the Absolute, an integral part of Its transcendent divine Nature.

Surgery is the inseparable power of the surgeon. Sometimes it is active, as when the surgeon works at the operating table, but at other times it is latent, as when he is resting at home. *Līlā-shakti* (the play-power of *Brahman*) functions in an analogous way, and by virtue of this the unmanifest, ever remaining in its absolute state, manifests into creation. The almighty nature of the eternal Being thus maintains Reality in both Its aspects, absolute and relative.

The Lord says: 'remaining in My own Nature I take birth'. Just as the sap in a tree appears as a leaf and a flower without losing its quality as sap, so the unmanifest Being, remaining unmanifest, imperishable, and eternal, takes birth. Nothing happens to the Absolute, and yet the Incarnation of the Absolute springs up, by virtue of Its own Nature.

Here the Lord is saying: While remaining in My own Nature I take birth through My power of creation, and through that I function; that is how I remain unbound and at the same time am able to restore law and order in creation.

This principle is developed in the following verse.

VERSE 7

यदा यदा हि धर्मस्य ग्लानिर्भवति भारत
अभ्युत्थानमधर्मस्य तदात्मानं सृजाम्यहम्

Yadā yadā hi dharmasya glānir bhavati Bhārata
abhyutthānam adharmasya tadātmānaṁ sṛijāmyaham

Whenever Dharma is in decay and adharma flourishes, O Bhārata, then I create Myself.

'*Adharma*': the opposite to *Dharma*.

'*Dharma*' is derived from the root *dhṛi*, meaning 'that which upholds'. *Dharma* is that which upholds or sustains all that is. What is this that sustains creation? Charak and Sushrut, the ancient Indian exponents of Āyurveda, the doctrine of health, hold that it is the equilibrium of the three *Guṇas* — *Sattwa*, *Rajas*, and *Tamas* — that sustains all things. Creation gains in integrity with the rise of *Sattwa* and disintegrates with the rise of *Tamas*. The equilibrium of the three *Guṇas* is maintained automatically, just as law and order are automatically maintained by a government. But whenever a crisis arises, the head of state has to exercise his special power. Whenever *Dharma* is in decay, the balance of the three *Guṇas* is disturbed, the equilibrium in Nature is lost, the path of evolution is distorted, and chaos prevails. At such special times the Lord incarnates. The Incarnation of Lord Kṛishṇa is such a special manifestation of *Brahman*, the eternal immutable Being.

Life has two phases, relative and absolute. Both are full: the Absolute is full in its eternal never-changing nature, and the relative is full in its eternally ever-changing nature. This eternally ever-changing nature of relative life is maintained in all its aspects of creation and evolution by virtue of the enormous power of Nature called *Dharma*, which is at the basis of the smooth functioning of the three *Guṇas*. It is like a powerful current which forcibly carries with it all that comes in its path.

Dharma upholds evolution; but when, as a result of the wrong-doing of a large majority of people on earth, the power of *Dharma* becomes greatly overshadowed, the natural force of evolution in Nature becomes weak. A situation is created whereby the ever-changing world of relative existence begins to lose its natural pattern. This endangers the fullness of the relative aspect of life. The almighty power that holds intact the fullness of the Absolute together with the fullness of the relative phase of life is stirred. And that almighty power incarnates.

The decay of *Dharma* — the distortion of the path of evolution, the decline of righteousness in society — brings about a need for the restoration of the true principles of life; the Incarnation comes, the whole of Nature rejoices in that coming, *Dharma* is restored, and evil is brought to an end.

The righteous, therefore, feel obliged to the wicked because, as wickedness increases and dominates the world, the need is created for the Almighty to take form and be enjoyed by the righteous.

The full purpose of Incarnation is made clear in the following verse.

VERSE 8

परित्राणाय साधूनां विनाशाय च दुष्कृताम्
धर्मसंस्थापनार्थाय संभवामि युगे युगे

Paritrāṇāya sādhūnāṁ vināshāya cha dushkṛitām
dharmasaṁsthāpanārthāya saṁbhavāmi yuge yuge

To protect the righteous and destroy the wicked, to establish Dharma firmly, I take birth age after age.

The Lord says that He has a twofold purpose: to protect the righteous and destroy the wicked. The protection of the righteous is implied in the destruction of the wicked; but when the Lord here speaks of protecting the righteous, He means something more than merely removing the thorns from their path.

The righteous continue to uphold *Dharma* and they succeed in this, even in times when unrighteousness dominates society, by virtue of the great strength that they receive when, during their daily meditations, they come into communion with the Divine.

As their minds grow in divine consciousness, the purity of their lives increases until they eventually begin to feel a strong need for the abstract bliss of God Consciousness to be materialized, to be brought to the level of the senses, where it will become the object of all the senses and be enjoyed by them. Their hearts are more and more filled with love, and the need for divine revelation in some form becomes increasingly intense. When Nature can no longer resist it, then the Lord takes birth and fulfils the desire of the righteous. This is how the righteous are protected by the Lord.

The Lord says: 'I take birth age after age'. This shows that in every age there are those ardent, loving devotees of God for whose sake He takes form; and when He comes to satisfy them, He also purifies the earth by destroying the negative forces which contaminate the atmosphere by opposing righteousness.

Destruction of the wicked, although a reason for the Lord's Incarnation, is not His main purpose. He comes to satisfy and protect the righteous. He comes on earth moved by the righteous, for the love of the righteous, for the fulfilment of the righteous; and to come on earth in order to give His love to His devotees is a joy for Almighty God. He comes on earth, and the light comes; it brings extinction to the darkness of ignorance and destruction to the wicked. Equilibrium in Nature is restored, and the forces of evolution become stronger. *Dharma* becomes firmly established in the world.

The establishment of *Dharma* in God's creation is His own work. He does it. He does it again and again, either through the automatic arrangement of His government, He Himself remaining behind the scenes, or by taking a body and coming to be active in the affairs of the world.

VERSE 9

जन्म कर्म च मे दिव्यमेवं यो वेत्ति तत्त्वतः
त्यक्त्वा देहं पुनर्जन्म नैति मामेति सोऽर्जुन

Janma karma cha me divyam evaṁ yo vetti tattwataḥ
tyaktwā dehaṁ punarjanma naiti mām eti so 'rjuna

My birth and My activity are divine. He who knows this in very essence, on leaving the body is not reborn. He comes to Me, O Arjuna.

'My birth': the birth of the Lord is not the same as the birth of man. It is divine in the sense that He, the Divine, ever remaining in His cosmic state of transcendental Being, takes a body and comes on earth. The divine birth needs no period of transition and involves no process of physical birth: the divine Being does not become non-divine and non-Being; remaining divine and remaining Being, He appears as man to save human life on earth and re-establish the path of righteousness.

'My activity': the unmanifest transcendental Divine, assuming human form, remains in His divine nature and He acts. The divine nature is all Being, eternal, unchanging, and non-active, even though it is the infinite source of life-energy. Because the Lord acts while remaining in His divine nature, His actions also are divine.

In order to understand the divine birth and the activity of the divine Incarnation, man has to rise to the state of Divinity. Having risen to this state, having become established in the eternal Being of the Absolute, he rises above the bondage of time, space, and causation. For him there is no question of birth or death. He has life eternally, and he has it in the timeless unbounded omnipresence of the Lord; his life is in His life. 'He comes to Me', says the Lord. There is no question of his rebirth in the world.

Verse 10

वीतरागभयक्रोधा मन्मया मामुपाश्रिताः
बहवो ज्ञानतपसा पूता मद्भावमागताः

Vītarāgabhayakrodhā manmayā mām upāshritāḥ
bahavo gyānatapasā pūtā madbhāvam āgatāḥ

Freed from attachment, fear, and anger, absorbed in Me, taking refuge in Me, purified by the austerity of wisdom, many have come to My Being.

The sequence of expressions is highly significant: 'Freed from attachment, fear, and anger' is a prerequisite to 'absorbed in Me'.

'Freed from attachment, fear, and anger': attachment,[9] fear, and anger[10] find fertile ground in the soil of ignorance, where the self has not discovered its meaning in the Self. Transcendental Meditation, as explained in Chapter II, verse 45, takes the mind to the field of Bliss Consciousness, supreme contentment, and infinite energy, leaving no room for any kind of weakness. It brings the mind to the state of Being, which forms the basis of God Consciousness, expressed in the words 'absorbed in Me' and 'taking refuge in Me'.

'Purified by the austerity of wisdom': austerity means denial of the pleasures of the senses, or coming out of the field of sensory activity and enjoyment. The purpose of austerity is to purify by freeing the mind from the impact of the objects of sense. Likewise knowledge separates the Self from the whole field of activity. This is the significance of the expression: 'austerity of wisdom'. It should not be understood to mean that, as the practice of austerity involves hardship, so does the path of knowledge. On the contrary, gaining knowledge is joyful from beginning to end: from the state of Transcendental Consciousness, through Cosmic Consciousness, to God Consciousness. As the mind proceeds towards the Transcendent, it becomes more and more free from the gross fields of experience and this brings it nearer and nearer to a state of purity. Eventually, when the mind transcends the subtlest state of experience, it is left to itself, and then it reaches the state of absolute purity.

This state of absolute purity, gained during Transcendental Consciousness, becomes permanent in Cosmic Consciousness and finds its purpose and consummation[11] in the state of purity born of knowledge of the ultimate oneness of life in God Consciousness. In this state of knowledge man finds that Union with God of which the Lord says: 'many have come to My Being'.

By the use of the word 'many', the Lord extends the hope of Union with God to any man.

9 See III, 7, 28, 31.
10 See III, 41, 43.
11 See verse 38.

Having now described the direct way of attaining the ultimate knowledge in God Consciousness, the Lord, in the following verse, speaks about His reaction to the method of approach adopted by the seeker.

VERSE 11

ये यथा मां प्रपद्यन्ते तांस्तथैव भजाम्यहम्
मम वर्त्मानुवर्तन्ते मनुष्याः पार्थ सर्वशः

Ye yathā māṁ prapadyante tāṁs tathaiva bhajāmyaham
mama vartmānuvartante manushyāḥ Pārtha sarvashaḥ

As men approach Me, so do I favour them;
in all ways, O Pārtha, men follow My path.

'As men approach Me, so do I favour them': it is an established natural law that action and reaction are equal to one another. In the fullness of Divinity, God is ever full, and like the water of a great lake, so does this fullness remain. The water has a tendency neither to flow away nor to resist flowing; it just remains as it is. If a farmer wants to take water to his field, he brings a pipe up to the level of the water. The water does not refuse to flow once the pipe is raised to its level.

Furthermore, the Lord says: 'in all ways, O Pārtha, men follow My path'. This has different meanings at different levels. First, the nature of man is like the nature of God in that man behaves to others as others behave to him.

Secondly, learning that the nature of the Lord is such that He Himself does not take any initiative, that He only responds, people try to derive the maximum benefit from surrendering themselves completely to Him through meditation, which is the direct way to God Consciousness. One who reaches this state, truly losing his limited identity, gains the status of unbounded eternal Being in God Consciousness. The Lord's purpose in disclosing this essential characteristic of His nature is that thereby all men should reach this state of divine existence. Here is the exposition of a technique by which the limited personality of man is enabled to rise to the unlimited status of eternal existence in God Consciousness. It is open to all.

Thirdly, the natural tendency of every man is to turn towards greater happiness, and therefore to proceed towards the eternal happiness of God Consciousness. This is another reason why the Lord says: 'in all ways, O Pārtha, men follow My path'.

Finally, 'in all ways, O Pārtha, men follow My path' indicates that God's own consciousness is the sole guiding factor of man's consciousness. It underlies all life in the cosmos and is the basic motivating intelligence of all beings. Cosmic intelligence upholds man's intelligence.

VERSE 12

काङ्क्षन्तः कर्मणां सिद्धिं यजन्त इह देवताः
क्षिप्रं हि मानुषे लोके सिद्धिर्भवति कर्मजा

Kānkshantaḥ karmaṇāṁ siddhiṁ yajanta iha devatāḥ
kshipraṁ hi mānushe loke siddhir bhavati karmajā

Those who desire fulfilment of actions here on earth
make offerings to the gods, for success born of action
comes quickly in the world of men.

Success is certainly gained by effort. Those who know how to contact the Vedic gods do so through specific sacrificial ceremonies and, having contacted these higher powers in Nature, receive their goodwill and achieve greater success in life. When the Lord says here: 'success born of action comes quickly in the world of men', He means to bring home to Arjuna that whereas in the lower species the evolution of the soul depends upon the upward moving currents of evolution in Nature, in the human species the soul has freedom of action, and that therefore the development of man depends upon how he acts and what he does.

This verse establishes the necessity of action as such for success in the world and at the same time shows the direction in which the activity must proceed.

Verse 13

चातुर्वर्ण्यं मया सृष्टं गुणकर्मविभागशः
तस्य कर्तारमपि मां विद्ध्यकर्तारमव्ययम्

Chāturvarṇyaṁ mayā sṛishtaṁ guṇakarmavibhāgashaḥ
tasya kartāram api māṁ viddhyakartāram avyayam

The fourfold order was created by Me according to the division of Guṇas and actions. Though I am its author, know Me to be the non-doer, immutable.

The entire creation is the interplay of the three *Guṇas*. When the primal equilibrium of *Sattwa*, *Rajas,* and *Tamas* is disturbed, they begin to interact and creation begins. All three must be present in every aspect of creation because, with creation, the process of evolution begins and this needs two forces opposed to each other and one that is complementary to both.

Sattwa and *Tamas* are opposed to each other, while *Rajas* is the force complementary to both. *Tamas* destroys the created state; *Sattwa* creates a new state while the first is being destroyed. In this way, through the simultaneous processes of creation and destruction the process of evolution is carried on. The force of *Rajas* plays a necessary but neutral part in creation and destruction; it maintains a bond between the forces of *Sattwa* and *Tamas*. Thus all three *Guṇas* are necessary for any state of manifested life.

'The fourfold order': mathematically, the three *Guṇas* may combine with each other in six possible ways:

1. *Sattwa* dominates, *Rajas* is secondary
2. *Sattwa* dominates, *Tamas* is secondary
3. *Rajas* dominates, *Sattwa* is secondary
4. *Rajas* dominates, *Tamas* is secondary
5. *Tamas* dominates, *Sattwa* is secondary
6. *Tamas* dominates, *Rajas* is secondary.

Combinations 2 and 5 are not possible because of the contrast in the nature of *Sattwa* and *Tamas*. Thus the three *Guṇas* have only four possible combinations.

This is the fourfold order in creation. Every species, whether vegetable, animal, or human, is divided into four categories according to the four divisions of the *Guṇas*, which determine the natural mode of activity of each category.

'Non-doer': activity in all fields of life is caused by the three *Guṇas*.[12] The ultimate universal Being is the basis of the *Guṇas*; therefore it is said that the 'I' of the unmanifested omnipresent immutable Being is the Creator. He is the Creator and at the same time, ever remaining established in His own Being, is uninvolved, 'the non-doer'.[13]

This may be further clarified by an example. Oxygen and hydrogen ions combine to give rise to the properties of water. The water freezes, giving rise to the properties of ice. In these different states of gas, liquid, and solid, the basic elements — oxygen and hydrogen — remain the same. In as much as they are the fundamental material from which gas, water, and ice are formed, oxygen and hydrogen could be said to have created these different substances. But because they remain oxygen and hydrogen through their various stages, they could be said to be non-doing. Such is the state of ultimate Being. Lying at the base of all creation, it is the 'author' and, remaining unchanged, it is the 'non-doer' and 'immutable'.

When the Lord says: 'know Me to be the non-doer', He is asking Arjuna to take his mind to the transcendental state of consciousness, beyond the field of the three *Guṇas*, and gain first-hand knowledge of the source of creation; to see for himself that absolute silence is the creative energy and intelligence of eternal Being, the fountainhead of all creative energy and intelligence in the relative field.

In this verse, the Lord takes upon Himself the authorship of creation, at the same time declaring His absolute immutable Nature. Being almighty, He is able to maintain His non-involved status even while giving rise to creation. The next verse further clarifies this idea.

12 See III, 27.
13 See verse 6.

VERSE 14

न मां कर्माणि लिम्पन्ति न मे कर्मफले स्पृहा
इति मां योऽभिजानाति कर्मभिर्न स बध्यते

Na māṁ karmāṇi limpanti na me karmaphale spṛihā
iti māṁ yo 'bhijānāti karmabhir na sa badhyate

Actions do not involve Me, nor have I any longing for the fruit of action. He who truly knows Me thus is not bound by actions.

Anyone who has God Consciousness, constant awareness of the source of creation, will know by his own experience that it is transcendental in nature. That is why the Lord says: 'He who truly knows Me thus is not bound by actions.' 'Truly knows Me thus' means knows Me completely. Complete knowledge means knowledge on the basis of experience as well as understanding.[14]

'Actions do not involve Me': it will be recalled from verse 28 of Chapter III that 'it is the *Guṇas* which act upon the *Guṇas*' while Being remains uninvolved. Again, it will be recalled from verse 9 of the present chapter that the activity of the Lord is not worldly, not within the field of the *Guṇas*; it is divine and takes place in His eternal freedom. The nature of the Lord as absolute has been brought out in verse 6. The uninvolved nature of the Lord is therefore perfectly clear.

'Nor have I any longing for the fruit of action': the Lord has already expressed His eternal state of contentment in Chapter III, verse 22.

'He who truly knows Me thus' means he who has thoroughly known My nature as absolutely uninvolved with actions as well as with their fruits. The word 'truly' is highly important. It means knowing by participation, indicating that a man has gained God Consciousness.

The expression: 'nor have I any longing for the fruit of action' brings out by implication a feature common to the manifested and unmanifested spheres of life. Both eternally continue to be

14 See verse 38, commentary.

by virtue of the eternal nature of the almighty and supreme Lord. Precise knowledge of the non-involvement of the Supreme in the midst of the vast activity of unlimited creation can only dawn on the basis of one's own experience of the Self as uninvolved with the field of activity.

Here is the sequence of realization of the true nature of the Lord: first, one realizes one's own Self as separate from activity and thus, gaining knowledge of the true nature of one's Self, surrenders all activity to the Lord and takes refuge in Him (verse 10). Then, in Unity with Him, one knows Him in His true nature as uninvolved with activity and without any longing for the fruits of action. This knowledge of the true nature of God results in eternal freedom from the binding influence of action. That is why the Lord says: 'He who truly knows Me thus is not bound by actions.'

This verse presents one of the most important teachings of Sāṁkhya. It reveals the non-involved nature of the Lord and, simply through the knowledge of this fact, promises liberation from bondage. This is the strength of Sāṁkhya, which offers liberation through the path of knowledge.

A similar teaching was contained in verse 28 of Chapter III. But there the argument was in terms of the knowledge of the three *Guṇas*, the knowledge of the relative field of activity; whereas in this verse it springs from the knowledge of the essential nature of the divine Being, personified by Lord Kṛishṇa, who is beyond the relative and the Absolute, beyond the Unity of Being and the diversity of creation, but holds within Himself the fullness of both.

VERSE 15

एवं ज्ञात्वा कृतं कर्म पूर्वैरपि मुमुक्षुभिः
कुरुकर्मैव तस्मात्त्वं पूर्वैः पूर्वतरं कृतम्

Evaṁ gyātwā kṛitaṁ karma pūrvair api mumukshubhiḥ
kuru karmaiva tasmāt twaṁ pūrvaiḥ pūrvataraṁ kṛitam

Having known this, even the ancient seekers of liberation performed action; therefore, do you perform action as did the ancients in olden days.

'Having known this' refers to the teaching of the two previous verses.

In order to bring home to Arjuna that there could be a state of life in which the greatest activity would not disturb the eternal status of absolute Being, the Lord, in the two previous verses, gave an example of this state by referring to His own case. Seeing thus before him a living embodiment of the ideas which were being taught to him, Arjuna might then become convinced that he also could rise to this state in his own life.

'Ancient seekers of liberation': this expression refers to 'Janaka and others' (III, 20). The use of the phrase 'seekers of liberation' makes it clear that action is necessary even for those who have devoted their lives to the pursuit of Truth and are not interested in anything other than liberation. But, as the expression 'Having known this' shows, knowledge about the real nature of the Lord is a prerequisite for the activity of 'seekers of liberation'.

When the seeker of liberation has attained Cosmic Consciousness and realized himself as separate from activity, he has reached his goal. He will be liberated from the bondage of action and, if he has no greater ideal before him, he will feel fulfilled. But if one feels fulfilled in the state of Cosmic Consciousness and does not aspire to God Consciousness, then one has missed the chance of the supreme attainment that is Union with God. For this reason, knowledge about the real nature of the Lord is essential even for the seekers of liberation. There is no doubt as to its necessity for the seekers of God.

In this verse, the Lord wants to make clear that knowledge of the three *Guṇas* and their interplay[15] should be supplemented by knowledge of the essential nature of the supreme Lord[16] in order that it may bring fulfilment to the state of liberation.

'Ancients in olden days': by this expression the Lord gives authority to His statement. The teaching is that the path of evolution that has withstood the test of time should not be doubted, because only that which is in accordance with the laws of evolution can last. Anything that does not conform to these laws is thrown off by Nature.

15 See III, 28; IV, 13.
16 See verse 14.

In the following verses the argument turns to a close analysis of action.

VERSE 16

किं कर्म किमकर्मेति कवयोऽप्यत्र मोहिताः
तत्ते कर्म प्रवक्ष्यामि यज्ज्ञात्वा मोक्ष्यसेऽशुभात्

Kiṁ karma kim akarmeti kavayo 'pyatra mohitāḥ
tat te karma pravakshyāmi yaj gyātwā mokshyase 'shubhāt

What is action, what inaction? Even the wise are bewildered here. I shall expound to you that action, knowing which you will be freed from evil.

In the previous verse the Lord gave Arjuna reasons for action; so it is natural that in this verse He should bring out the gravity and far-reaching influence of action in order to prepare Arjuna's mind for the details of that action which will be useful to him and deliver him from all 'evil'.

Ignorance of one's own blissful divine nature as non-involved and independent of activity keeps one under the binding influence of action, causing the complications and sufferings of life.

The Lord says that 'even the wise are bewildered' over the issue of action and inaction. The wise man is he who has understood that action is by virtue of the three *Guṇas* and that he himself remains uninvolved because his true nature is transcendental. But such understanding, says the Lord, is not sufficient, for even the wise continue to be bewildered.

The 'wise' have known the Self as separate from activity and thereby they have attained liberation. The Lord says that even the wise are bewildered over action and inaction. Gaining freedom from action is one thing: gaining full knowledge about action and inaction is quite another. The Lord says in the next verse: 'Unfathomable is the course of action.' It is impossible to know the full range of action on the level of intellectual understanding. That is why the Lord says: 'Even the wise are bewildered'.

It may be recalled that while enlightening Arjuna with the

wisdom of Sāṁkhya in verse 38 of Chapter II the Lord said: 'Having gained equanimity … you will not incur sin'; in the present verse He says: 'I shall expound to you that action, knowing which you will be freed from evil.' A careful study of these expressions unfolds the ascending order of the Lord's teaching; as the capacity for understanding increases, the teaching is imparted in subtler yet simpler forms. In the earlier verse it is implied that something has to be done to gain the equanimity which will result in freedom from sin. In the present verse, the Lord shows that nothing has to be done, that simply by the knowledge of activity Arjuna will be freed from evil. The teaching has shifted from the level of doing to the level of knowing. It may well be that, as the teaching advances, even knowing will be replaced by a simpler process on the common sensory level of hearing or seeing. This is the technique of teaching Sāṁkhya — a series of arguments will eventually culminate in some simple spoken word which will revolutionize the whole understanding of life and will once and for all raise a man to the state of eternal freedom from bondage.

It is also of interest to note that the two preceding verses proclaimed liberation from bondage through knowledge of the non-involved nature of the transcendent Lord, whereas this verse promises freedom through knowledge even of the relative field, the knowledge of activity and non-activity. This knowledge is given in the following five verses.

VERSE 17

कर्मणो ह्यपि बोद्धव्यं बोद्धव्यं च विकर्मणः
अकर्मणश्च बोद्धव्यं गहना कर्मणो गतिः

Karmaṇo hyapi boddhavyaṁ boddhavyaṁ cha vikarmaṇaḥ
akarmaṇash cha boddhavyaṁ gahanā karmaṇo gatiḥ

Action, indeed, should be understood, wrong action should also be understood, and inaction should be understood as well. Unfathomable is the course of action.

'Action': to understand action it is necessary to know the different states of consciousness of the actor, because the value of action depends mainly upon the level of consciousness of the one who acts. The possible states of consciousness are: waking, dreaming, sleeping, Transcendental Consciousness, Cosmic Consciousness, and God Consciousness.

Action is here used to mean right action, which produces life-supporting effects for the doer and for the entire creation, action which helps the evolution of the individual and simultaneously serves the cosmic purpose. Such action is possible only when man's mind is in complete harmony with the transcendent Being, which underlies all creation and is the basis of all life and all the Laws of Nature. This is the case in Cosmic Consciousness. God Consciousness is another state where such action is automatically carried out. In Cosmic Consciousness, a man established in cosmic life performs action as an individual; in the state of God Consciousness, the individual's activity, set in the Light of God, is on a level which corresponds to the level of cosmic activity. He lives the eternal Unity of life through all activity.

'Unfathomable is the course of action': one's natural activities in the three relative states of consciousness — waking, dreaming, and sleeping — are governed by the *Dharma* of one's level of evolution. *Dharma* differs at different levels of evolution. Moreover, even on the same level *Dharma* differs in different circumstances and in different spheres of life. In all these differences there is the additional complexity that in each case *Dharma* refers not only to activity as it affects the individual, but also as it affects the family, society, the nation, and the world. Every thought, word, or act sets up waves of influence in the atmosphere. These waves travel through space and strike against everything in creation. Wherever they strike they have some effect. The effect of a particular thought on any particular object cannot be known because of the diversity and vast extent of creation. This complexity goes beyond the possibility of comprehension. That is why the Lord says: 'Unfathomable is the course of action.'

'Wrong action' can be of many kinds: actions that harm the doer in the present or the future; those that do not succeed; those that hinder evolution; those that lead to dissolution; those that bind the doer to the cycle of birth and death; those that produce life-damaging influences upon the surroundings and upon others; those that are against the Laws of Nature. Even the field of wrong action is thus found to be 'unfathomable'.

Such wrong actions are possible so long as the doer is in a state of ignorance about his own *Dharma*, so long as he is unaware of the essential nature of his own self, the nature of activity, and the nature of God, and so long as his waking state of consciousness is not supported by transcendental pure consciousness.

'Inaction': absence of activity. Deep sleep is a state of inaction, but it is not the only such state. The state of inaction is also found in Transcendental Consciousness. Furthermore, inaction is an essential constituent of Cosmic Consciousness and also of God Consciousness, the highest state of human evolution. On the one hand inaction is the inertia of sleep, while on the other it becomes the basis of the living Reality of the whole cosmos. This is what the Lord means when He says: 'inaction should be understood as well'. This shows not only action but also inaction to be unfathomable.

'Indeed': by this word the Lord emphasizes the need for knowledge of action. Life means action — no one can escape activity. This being so, it is wise to know not only what one is going to do, but where, as a result, one is going to end up.

It will be interesting to observe closely how the Lord, having admitted that the course of action is unfathomable and having emphasized that it has to be understood, manages to steer a fine course between these opposing facts. To justify His expression 'unfathomable', wisdom demanded that He did not enter upon an examination of the course of action. But the word 'indeed' demands that whatever way He adopts, whether He enters into detail or not, knowledge of action must be conveyed. The Lord adopts a mode of instruction whereby, without knowledge of the whole field of action, one can acquire every benefit that such knowledge could bestow. He brings to light the art of action whereby, without having to gain knowledge of action, one can enjoy the blessings which such knowledge would give. This art of action is like the art of a gardener who, by watering the root, makes the sap rise to every part of the tree without having to know anything about the mechanics of rising sap.

Such is the marvel of perfection of this discourse. The Lord has said that knowledge of action is necessary and yet, the course of action being unfathomable, knowledge of it must remain incomplete. He therefore brings to light a technique by which the effects of knowledge will be gained without the necessity for gaining the knowledge. This is because the Lord's teaching is not for the sake of knowledge as such; it is solely to produce a specific effect in practical life. What is important is the effect, not the knowledge. This is the discourse of *Yoga Shāstra*, the most practical philosophy of Divine Union. Its purpose is to give the practical wisdom whereby any man may naturally gain the highest good through his activity.

The following verses clarify this teaching.

VERSE 18

कर्मण्यकर्म यः पश्येदकर्मणि च कर्म यः
स बुद्धिमान्मनुष्येषु स युक्तः कृत्स्नकर्मकृत्

Karmaṇyakarma yaḥ pashyed akarmaṇi cha karma yaḥ
sa buddhimān manushyeshu sa yuktaḥ kṛitsnakarmakṛit

He who in action sees inaction and in inaction sees action is wise among men. He is united, he has accomplished all action.

'In action sees inaction': this means that while the mind is engaged with the senses and through them in the process of action, it is anchored to the silence of the inner Being. This anchorage provides the experience of silence in the midst of all activity.

For the man who 'in action sees inaction', the permeation of the whole field of action by the non-active ever-silent Being is a living reality. Action for him does not overshadow the state of inaction, or Being, that underlies it. He lives the ever-silent Being that permeates all activities of senses, mind, and body; he sees silence in activity and activity in silence.

Here is a teaching which enables a man to enrich the liberation attained by the knowledge that 'it is the *Guṇas* which act upon the *Guṇas*'.[17] It connects the active world of the three *Guṇas* with the silence of Being and thus, on the level of silence, establishes the coexistence of the ephemeral and the eternal. It confirms the ultimate teaching of the Upanishads: '*Pūrṇam adaḥ pūrṇam idam*' — this manifested world of activity is full (*Pūrṇa*), That life of absolute Being is full.

Realization of this truth comes in the state of Cosmic Consciousness, but the teaching of this verse extends even to God Consciousness.

The realization of complete Reality establishes a state of life lying beyond the Unity of the Absolute and the multiplicity of the relative and produces the wholeness of vision that holds this and That both together in the Light of God, in God Consciousness. One who has achieved it is 'wise among men'. According to this phrase, 'men' are those who have realized either the truth of activity[18] or the truth of silence.[19] But 'wise' is he who has realized the truth of both, either in the state of their separation in Cosmic Consciousness or in the state of their Union in God Consciousness.

The definition of man given in this verse points to the conclusion that one who has not realized the truth of activity or the truth of silence does not deserve to be called a man. It is therefore an essential feature of man's life that he should be established either on the path of knowledge or on the path of action. And if he wants to be 'wise', then he must also rise to embrace the goal of both.

'He has accomplished all action' means that in his individual life he has performed the whole range of activity, gross and subtle. Moreover, he has performed activity on the level of cosmic life as well. Activity on the individual level includes not only ordinary mental and physical activity but also the subtlest activity of transcending and gaining Union with divine Being. Activity on the cosmic level is of two types: first, activity in Cosmic Consciousness, which is fully in accordance with the process of

17 See III, 28.
18 See III, 28.
19 See II, 45.

evolution, and secondly, activity in God Consciousness, which is on the level of the ultimate Unity of life.

'He has accomplished all action' also means that he has attained perfection. Action is a way of fulfilling one's desires. To have 'accomplished all action' means to have accomplished all desires, indicating that one has gained fulfilment. It should be noted that the accomplishment of an action does not lie in gaining the fruit of action alone. It lies in gaining the fruit of action along with freedom from the binding influence of action and its results. The cognition of inaction in action and of action in inaction is the result of the fulfilment gained through the direct experience of absolute bliss, and of the eternal freedom from bondage that lies in the state of Cosmic Consciousness, where the Self is experienced as separate from activity.

In this verse the sequence of expressions is highly important. In order to convey that 'he who in action sees inaction and in inaction sees action' is not insane, the Lord adds that such a man has better understanding than other people: he is 'wise among men'. Further, in order to indicate that this wise man is not just a theorizing man engaged in mere idealistic thinking, the Lord says: 'He is united', implying that he is a practical man, who has gained fulfilment in life.

There are four expressions in this verse, each containing distinct and independent ideas:

1. In action sees inaction
2. In inaction sees action
3. Wise among men he is united
4. He has accomplished all action.

It is interesting to observe that each of these thoughts is developed successively in the next five verses. The first thought of this verse is developed in the first thought of each of the other verses. The second, third, and fourth thoughts of this verse likewise find their development in the corresponding second, third, and fourth thoughts of the other five verses.

The comparative study of these five verses presenting the science of action has been summarized at the end of the commentary on verse 23.

The Lord gave Arjuna a vision of activity in inactivity and of inactivity in activity when, in verses 13 and 14, He referred to Himself as an example. That is why it is sufficient for this verse to make a statement of fact without entering into details and explanations.

The following verses, however, discuss this point from the more concrete considerations of practical life.

VERSE 19

यस्य सर्वे समारम्भाः कामसंकल्पवर्जिताः
ज्ञानाग्निदग्धकर्माणं तमाहुः पण्डितं बुधाः

Yasya sarve samārambhāḥ kāmasaṁkalpavarjitāḥ
gyānāgnidagdhakarmāṇaṁ tam āhuḥ paṇḍitaṁ budhāḥ

He whose every undertaking is free from desire and the incentive thereof, whose action is burnt up in the fire of knowledge, him the knowers of Reality call wise.

This verse presents the thought of the previous verse in a more developed form. In order to see inaction in action it is necessary to undertake action and yet to remain free from desire within oneself. A man's inner state 'free from desire' is a field of 'inaction'. This is how he 'whose every undertaking is free from desire' 'in action sees inaction' (verse 18).

The Lord mentions the special qualities of the action of an enlightened man. The action must certainly have impetus and an effective start, but the 'wise' man is not motivated by personal attachment in beginning the action any more than during its process or at its completion. Nor does he depend upon its fruits. Thus through the whole range of action he is involved yet not involved. That is why the Lord says: 'whose action is burnt up in the fire of knowledge, him the knowers of Reality call wise'.

The realized man does undertake activity but, by virtue of the knowledge that the Self is separate from activity, he remains free from the binding influence of action. This knowledge is compared here to a blazing fire which burns up all his action, in the sense that the action is set completely free from the binding influence of action or its fruits.

'Undertaking is free from desire': commonly a man begins an action only when he has become aware of the desire for it. The level at which a desire is appreciated differs according to the level of the conscious mind of the individual. Men of purer mind appreciate thought and desire at a much subtler level during the process of thinking.[20] It should be understood that a thought starts from the deepest level of consciousness and develops into a desire when it reaches the conscious level of the mind. A man for whom the level of Transcendental Consciousness has become the level of the conscious mind appreciates the thought at its very start before it actually develops into a desire. His thought becomes transformed into action without expressing itself as a desire.[21] This explains how, when a man succeeds in harmonizing his mind with Transcendental Consciousness, his 'every undertaking is free from desire'.

This state of non-attachment is more advanced than that described in the previous verse, in which one sees inaction in action and action in inaction. As the practice of Transcendental Meditation advances, Being begins to become established in the nature of the mind and one begins to feel oneself as separate from activity. Activity is then found on the quiet level of inner awareness. This is how one naturally begins to appreciate silence and activity simultaneously.

As the practice of meditation advances further, the silence of Being becomes appreciable even at the start of activity, so that a natural situation arises for every action to be 'free from desire and the incentive thereof'. It should be noted that the start of action engages the mind more deeply than action in progress. This is why the Self is first experienced as uninvolved during the process of action, and only when the practice is fairly well advanced does It begin to be appreciated as uninvolved at the start of action. Thus, with the growth of Being in the nature of the mind, a natural situation arises in which 'every undertaking' is on the level of the silence of Being, which in Its essential nature is Bliss Consciousness. This Bliss Consciousness provides a level

20 See Appendix: The *Transcendental Meditation* Technique.
21 See III, 7.

of eternal contentment on the basis of which 'every undertaking is free from desire and the incentive thereof'.

At this stage of the growth of Being into the nature of the mind, one feels unattached to the action both at its start and during its progress. But because every action is begun to accomplish some end, the purpose of an action engages the mind more deeply than does its start and progress; therefore non-attachment to the fruit of action demands a much fuller infusion of Being into the nature of the mind. By the time Cosmic Consciousness is gained, one has completely 'cast off attachment to the fruit of action' (verse 20). This, the most advanced state of non-attachment,[22] eventually finds its fulfilment in God Consciousness, in which 'you will see all beings in your Self and also in Me' (verse 35).

Every action depends upon the state of consciousness of the actor. Therefore if it is desired that all actions shall have a particular quality, it is necessary to produce a state of consciousness which will allow that quality of action to arise.

The word 'every' is very important in this context. It includes the whole range of sensory and mental activity. It suggests that the state of man's consciousness should be such that any action undertaken by him at any time is naturally free from desire and its incentive. Such a state of consciousness is found in Cosmic Consciousness and God Consciousness.

A man for whom the level of Transcendental Consciousness has become the level of the conscious mind has gained Cosmic Consciousness, and in this state he experiences Being as separate from action. This experience creates a natural condition in which there is action on the surface and a state of inaction within. Desire is a link between the doer and the action. But when a natural state of separation is established between the doer and action, there exists no link between them. In such a situation between the doer and his actions, desire has no place. This is how it is possible for 'every' undertaking to be free from desire.

'Free from ... the incentive thereof': in order to understand the incentive of desire, we must analyse the process of the formation of a desire. Experience results when the senses come in contact with their objects and an impression is left on the mind.

22 This is dealt with in the commentary on the following verse.

The impulse of this new impression resonates with an impression of a similar past experience already present in the mind and associates itself with that impression. The coming together of the two gives rise to an impulse at the deepest level of consciousness, where the impressions of all experiences are stored. This impulse develops and, rising to the conscious level of the mind, becomes appreciated as a thought. This thought, gaining the sympathy of the senses, creates a desire and stimulates the senses to action. In principle, the incentive of desire is due to the feeling of want. In the state of Cosmic Consciousness, where one finds eternal contentment within oneself and the field of activity is naturally separate from oneself, the Self is self-sufficient — It can have no want. In this state, therefore, every undertaking is free from the incentive of desire.

The question may then be asked: What is responsible for initiating action in such a man?

The answer is the almighty power of Nature,[23] which is the cause of the vast and incessant activity of creation and evolution throughout the cosmos.

Being forms the basis of Nature. When the mind comes into full unison with Being, it gains the very status of Being and thus itself becomes the basis of all activity in Nature. Natural Laws begin to support the impulses of such a mind: it becomes as if one with all the Laws of Nature. The desire of such a mind is then the need of Nature, or, to put it in another way, the needs of Nature are the motive of such activity. The Self has nothing to do with 'desire and the incentive thereof'. This is how it becomes possible for 'every undertaking' to be naturally 'free from desire and the incentive thereof'.

We must remember that the development of such a state of consciousness comes about through the presence of Being on the level of the conscious mind, the surface mind. There is no way to develop it through any process of thinking or understanding. The purpose of this verse is to give an explanation of this state; it does not describe the way to accomplish it. It would be quite wrong to imagine that, by trying to eliminate desire and to reduce one's wants in order to lessen the incentive of desire, one

23 See III, 27–8.

could gain this natural state of non-attachment, which makes a man 'wise' in the eyes of the knowers of Reality.

'Fire of knowledge': awareness of Being as separate from the field of action.

The actions of such an enlightened man are, therefore, not his actions; they are the actions of the three *Guṇas* (III, 28). He remains unattached, contented (IV, 20), his heart and mind disciplined (21), beyond the pairs of opposites (22), and liberated (23).

VERSE 20

त्यक्त्वा कर्मफलासङ्गं नित्यतृप्तो निराश्रयः
कर्मण्यभिप्रवृत्तोऽपि नैव किंचित्करोति सः

Tyaktwā karmaphalāsangaṁ nityatṛipto nirāshrayaḥ
karmaṇyabhipravṛitto 'pi naiva kiṁchit karoti saḥ

Having cast off attachment to the fruit of action,
ever contented, depending on nothing, even though
fully engaged in action he does not act at all.

In the commentary on the previous verse it was explained how, with the growth of Cosmic Consciousness, non-attachment becomes so profound that a man casts off even 'attachment to the fruit of action'.

The present verse can be considered from another angle. When pure honey comes on the tongue, the taste of great sweetness surpasses in degree all the sweet tastes experienced up to then. If the tongue continues to cherish the taste of honey, then there will be no chance for a previous sweet taste to recur. This is what happens when the mind lives permanently in the experience of transcendental bliss in the state of Cosmic Consciousness; there then remains no chance for impressions of past experiences to capture it. This is how the enlightened man has 'cast off attachment to the fruit of action' performed in the past.

If one has the taste of concentrated sweetness on the tongue and then tastes other sweets, these tastes do not leave any significant impression. When a man, established in the bliss of the absolute

Being, acts in the relative field of life, his experiences will not leave on the mind any deep impression which could give rise to future desires. In this way the cycle of action-impression-desire-action is broken. It is thus that, in an enlightened man, activity and experience in the world are debarred from sowing the seed of future action. This will be further clarified in the following verse.

'Even though fully engaged': his organs of action[24] continue to perform their duties motivated by Nature, and his senses of experience likewise remain engaged; in this way he is found acting.

'He does not act at all': his mind, established in the fullness of Being, remains uninvolved in activity. This is his state of life — outwardly engaged in activity, inwardly established in eternal silence.[25]

VERSE 21

निराशीर्यतचित्तात्मा त्यक्तसर्वपरिग्रहः
शारीरं केवलं कर्म कुर्वन्नाप्नोति किल्बिषम्

Nirāshīr yatachittātmā tyaktasarvaparigrahaḥ
shārīraṁ kevalaṁ karma kurvan nāpnoti kilbisham

Expecting nothing, his heart and mind disciplined,
having relinquished all possessions, performing action
by the body alone, he incurs no sin.

'Expecting nothing': the cause of anxiety and expectation is desire. The actions of the enlightened man have been declared to be 'free from desire and the incentive thereof' (verse 19). That is why he acts 'expecting nothing'.

'His heart and mind disciplined': see Chapter III, verse 43.

'Having relinquished all possessions': this expression runs parallel with 'depending on nothing' (verse 20). The word 'possessions' indicates all that one has gathered around oneself, everything other than one's own Self; relinquishing everything that is outside one's own Self means abandoning the whole field of

24 See III, 7.
25 See III, 7, 27; IV, 14.

relative existence, being 'without the three *Guṇas*'.[26]

'Performing action by the body alone': it has been explained in the commentary on verse 19 how the mind of the enlightened man remains unattached, even when he is performing actions on the level of the senses,[27] so that 'every undertaking is free from desire and the incentive thereof'. The mind of an enlightened man does not register deeply any impressions of actions performed by the body on the level of the senses; through all activities his mind remains ever fixed in Being. Established in the absolute purity of Being, he is out of the field of ignorance, out of the field of 'sin'.

Verse 22

यदृच्छालाभसंतुष्टो द्वन्द्वातीतो विमत्सरः
समः सिद्धावसिद्धौ च कृत्वापि न निबध्यते

Yadṛichchhālābhasaṁtushto dwandwātīto vimatsaraḥ
samaḥ siddhāvasiddhau cha kṛitwāpi na nibadhyate

Satisfied with whatever comes unasked, beyond the pairs of opposites, free from envy, balanced in success and failure, even acting he is not bound.

This verse presents the picture of one who is liberated.

'Satisfied with whatever comes unasked': the enlightened man lives a life of fulfilment. His actions, being free from desire, serve only the need of the time. He has no personal interest to gain. He is engaged in fulfilling the cosmic purpose and therefore his actions are guided by Nature. This is why he does not have to worry about his needs. His needs are the needs of Nature,[28] which takes care of their fulfilment, he being the instrument of the Divine.

'Beyond the pairs of opposites': beyond the three *Guṇas*.[29] This expression applies equally to Transcendental Consciousness,

26 See II, 45.
27 See III, 7.
28 See verse 19, commentary.
29 See II, 45, 50, 56–7.

Cosmic Consciousness, and God Consciousness. Transcendental Consciousness is absolute in nature, without any trace of duality. Cosmic Consciousness accepts 'the pairs of opposites', but as completely separate from the Self. God Consciousness also accepts 'the pairs of opposites', but as inseparable from the Self, which in Its turn is inseparable from God.

'Free from envy': envy is a quality which disturbs one's equilibrium and allows one to be invaded by the *Dharma* of a level of consciousness different from one's own.[30] This is a great danger, for it is apt to throw a man off the path of his own evolution. One who is free from envy is free from this danger. Such a man is not tempted by anything, because he has risen to absolute freedom. To what more could he aspire? Having risen to the state of Cosmic Consciousness he could aspire to God Consciousness, and this might be thought to leave open a possibility for envy. But if a man of Cosmic Consciousness were to see a man of God Consciousness, he would be filled with love and devotion for him rather than envy his state.

'Balanced in success and failure': see Chapter II, verses 38, 48, 50.

'Even acting he is not bound': see Chapter III, verse 28.

When the mind, through meditation, has become contented in the bliss of the Self, there is no possibility of discontent. Then there is evenness of mind both in pleasure and in pain. Such is the state of a liberated man.[31]

VERSE 23

गतसङ्गस्य मुक्तस्य ज्ञानावस्थितचेतसः
यज्ञायाचरतः कर्म समग्रं प्रविलीयते

Gatasangasya muktasya gyānāvasthitachetasaḥ
yagyāyācharataḥ karma samagraṁ pravilīyate

He who is freed from attachment, liberated, whose mind is established in wisdom, who acts for the sake of Yagya, his action is entirely dissolved.

30 See III, 35, commentary.
31 See II, 71; III, 17, 28.

This verse demonstrates that when, through constant practice of meditation, a man has gained Cosmic Consciousness, when pure Transcendental Consciousness is grounded in the very nature of his mind, he becomes 'liberated' from the field of action and 'freed from attachment'. In this state, every action produces life-supporting influences in creation and thus helps cosmic evolution; therefore every action is 'for the sake of *Yagya*'.

Thus the actions of one who practises Transcendental Meditation are worthy of being ranked as *Yagya*.

The four expressions of this verse conclude the development of the four expressions contained in each of the previous five verses.[32] To illustrate this development, they are set out below:

I. 'He who in action sees inaction' (18)
'He whose every undertaking is free from desire' (19)
'Having cast off attachment to the fruit of action' (20)
'Expecting nothing' (21)
'Satisfied with whatever comes unasked' (22)
'He who is freed from attachment' (23)

II. 'In inaction sees action' (18)
(He whose every undertaking is free from) 'the incentive thereof' (19)
'Ever contented' (20)
'His heart and mind disciplined' (21)
'Beyond the pairs of opposites, free from envy' (22)
'Liberated' (23)

III. 'Is wise among men. He is united' (18)
'Whose action is burnt up in the fire of knowledge' (19)
'Depending on nothing' (20)
'Having relinquished all possessions' (21)
'Balanced in success and failure' (22)
'Whose mind is established in wisdom' (23)

IV. 'He has accomplished all action' (18)
'Him the knowers of Reality call wise' (19)
'Even though fully engaged in action he does not act at all' (20)
'Performing action by the body alone, he incurs no sin' (21)

32 See verse 18, commentary.

'Even acting he is not bound' (22)
'Who acts for the sake of *Yagya*, his action is entirely dissolved' (23)

It is by reason of the teaching contained in these six verses that this fourth chapter is the chapter of wisdom — the wisdom of *Karma Yoga* and Sāṁkhya at the same time. It reveals the state of a realized man on the level of action and behaviour, thus presenting the practical aspect of the abstract metaphysical quest which confronts man on the path of his evolution.

VERSE 24

ब्रह्मार्पणं ब्रह्म हविर्ब्रह्माग्नौ ब्रह्मणा हुतम्
ब्रह्मैव तेन गन्तव्यं ब्रह्मकर्मसमाधिना

Brahmārpaṇaṁ Brahm havir Brahmāgnau Brahmaṇā hutam
Brahmaiva tena gantavyaṁ Brahmakarmasamādhinā

Brahman is the act of offering. Brahman the oblation poured by Brahman into fire that is Brahman. To Brahman alone must he go who is fixed in Brahman through action.

This verse does not teach that during the performance of ritualistic *Yagya*, or any other type of action, one should hold in the mind the idea that everything is *Brahman*. The teaching here concerns far deeper levels of life than the surface level of thinking and making moods.

In the preceding verse it was said: 'who acts for the sake of *Yagya*, his action is entirely dissolved'. These words are further explained in the present verse, which considers different aspects of action performed by the enlightened man. It speaks of that state of consciousness which realizes oneness of existence in all the diversity of action.

In this verse and those following the Lord enumerates different aspects of the action of *Yagya* and says that all aspects are *Brahman*. Certainly offering is offering, oblation is oblation, fire is fire, and the performer is the performer — on the level of relative life duality prevails. Everything is *Brahman* only on the level of consciousness of the performer who is established in Cosmic Consciousness.[33] What has been said in verses 19 to 23 leads to the conclusion that the enlightened man, established in Bliss Consciousness at all times, irrespective of the engagement of the mind and senses in action, is intent on *Brahman*, while at the same time everything that action entails proceeds naturally at the level of the senses,[34] through the agency of the *Guṇas*.[35]

When the mind becomes infused with Being, then no thought, word, or act can take the mind out of Being. This is the state of Cosmic Consciousness.[36] The purpose of the present verse is to describe clearly the relationship of action to Cosmic Consciousness in which all actions form an integral part of that consciousness and are therefore appreciated as none other than that consciousness, none other than *Brahman*.

The verse also implies that fixity in *Brahman* constitutes mastery over action and is at the same time the fulfilment of action.

The Lord speaks of *Yagya* in order to explain that the different parts of an action and the various modes of their performance do not leave any trace of bondage for the enlightened man. Ever established in the state of pure consciousness, or eternal Being, he is simply a silent and innocent witness of what is happening through him; he is a means through which Nature fulfils its purpose of evolution. His actions are a response to the needs of the time. Quite naturally he performs actions which result in every kind of good.

'To *Brahman* alone must he go': *Brahman* is the Reality which embraces both the relative and absolute fields of life. Having gained the state of *Brahman*, a man has risen to the ultimate Reality of existence. In this state of enlightenment he has accomplished eternal liberation, and once a man has risen to this state there is no falling away from it. That is why the Lord says: 'To *Brahman* alone must he go who is fixed in *Brahman* through action.'

The expression 'must he go' does not mean that on leaving the

33 See II, 71–2.
34 See III, 7.
35 See III, 28.
36 See II, 72.

body he departs to some other place. The word 'go' here finds its meaning in the fact that, with the destruction of the body, the realized man is no longer found as an individual, and when someone is not to be found he is said to have gone. Where then has he gone? In order to explain his position in terms of going, it must be said that he has gone to *Brahman*; but in fact there is no question of going for him who is already 'fixed in *Brahman*', who has risen to the omnipresent Reality: He remains what he was — *Brahman* — but without the individual body.

'Who is fixed in *Brahman* through action': one rises to the state of *Brahman* in Cosmic Consciousness. *Brahman* is reached by the performance of activity after gaining the state of Being through the activity of meditation — the inward activity of meditation followed by the outward activity of daily life. Thus it is clear that it is 'through action' that one 'is fixed in *Brahman*'. This verse therefore not only describes the state of *Brahman* but also shows a direct way to Its realization.

VERSE 25

दैवमेवापरे यज्ञं योगिनः पर्युपासते
ब्रह्माग्नावपरे यज्ञं यज्ञेनैवोपजुह्वति

Daivam evāpare yagyaṁ yoginaḥ paryupāsate
Brahmāgnāvapare yagyaṁ yagyenaivopajuhwati

Some Yogīs perform Yagya merely by worshipping the gods,
others by offering the Yagya itself into the fire that is Brahman.

'Worshipping the gods' is said to be the performance of *Yagya*. The Lord says that when this worship of the gods is offered to *Brahman*, such an offering is also performance of *Yagya*.

An analysis of how 'worshipping the gods' is offered to *Brahman* and how the offering to *Brahman* is the performance of *Yagya* may make this clear.

Cosmic Consciousness is the state of *Brahman*.[37] Since it is transcendental Self-consciousness that develops into Cosmic Con-

37 See II, 72.

sciousness, in order to achieve Cosmic Consciousness through worshipping, one has to transcend through worshipping. This necessitates entering into the subtle phases of the act of worship. And this is most successfully done in a systematic manner by taking the name or form of the god and experiencing it in its subtler states until the mind transcends the subtlest state and attains Transcendental Consciousness. Those who are highly emotional, however, may even transcend through an increasing feeling of love for the god during the process of making offerings.

Transcending the act of worship is said to be the offering of the worship to *Brahman*. It has the advantage of receiving the blessings of the god and at the same time of helping to develop Cosmic Consciousness.

By transcending, a worshipper arrives at the ultimate fulfilment of *Yagya* and thereby develops Cosmic Consciousness, the state where his every action will prove to be *Yagya*. All that concerns him will be helpful to evolution and, established in his Being, he will fulfil the purpose of life. That is why transcending the field of *Yagya* to arrive at the state of *Brahman* also ranks as *Yagya*. When a man has gained Cosmic Consciousness, all his actions assume the status of *Yagya*. Because such action is performed in the state of *Brahman*, it is already on the level of *Brahman*. This is offering the *Yagya* itself into the fire that is *Brahman*.

VERSE 26

श्रोत्रादीनीन्द्रियाण्यन्ये संयमाग्निषु जुह्वति
शब्दादीन्विषयानन्य इन्द्रियाग्निषु जुह्वति

Shrotrādīnīndriyāṇyanye saṁyamāgnishu juhwati
shabdādīn vishayān anya indriyāgnishu juhwati

Some offer hearing and other senses in the fires of control;
some offer sound and other objects of the senses in the fires
of the senses.

'Fires': the plural is to indicate that there are different methods for controlling different senses.

There are two types of people: those who keep their senses active, enjoying objects in the world, and those who practise different methods of control. The Lord refers to the second when He says the senses are offered in 'the fires of control'.

The word 'control' has been interpreted by most commentators as implying restraint, and consequently they advocate forcible subjugation of the senses. But it is certainly not possible to put an end to the activities of the senses through the practice of refraining from feeding them. This has already been made clear by the Lord in verse 59 of the second chapter. Therefore it is obvious that the word 'control' means something other than restraint, something which will indeed have the strength to calm the senses. This is explained in two ways: first, as the proper use of the senses, which is the interpretation given in this verse; secondly, as the process of allowing all the senses to converge naturally upon one point and to remain there in the state of contentment. This second path[38] is described in the next verse.

'Some offer sound and other objects of the senses in the fires of the senses': some people have their senses active in the outside world. This is using the senses rightly, for the experience of objects, excepting only those that are forbidden, is also considered to be the performance of *Yagya*.

Thus the meaning of this verse is clear. Some turn their senses inwards through the practice of Transcendental Meditation and thus create a situation in which their senses automatically converge to Being, thereby naturally fulfilling the very purpose of control. Others do not meditate but keep their senses controlled by righteous action; by not allowing their senses to experience forbidden things, they too follow the path of *Yagya* and evolve to reach the Supreme. This is a slow and difficult process — difficult because the basis of right action is pure consciousness. Right action without a proper basis is very hard, if not impossible. By Transcendental Meditation, however, it is easy to gain pure consciousness[39] and thereby automatically to perform right action.

38 See also III, 43.
39 See II, 40.

VERSE 27

सर्वाणीन्द्रियकर्माणि प्राणकर्माणि चापरे
आत्मसंयमयोगाग्नौ जुह्वति ज्ञानदीपिते

Sarvāṇīndriyakarmāṇi prāṇakarmāṇi chāpare
ātmasaṁyamayogāgnau juhwati gyānadīpite

Others offer all the activities of the senses and of the life-breath in the fire of Yoga, which is self-control kindled by enlightenment.

It is generally understood that the practice of self-control is necessary to bring enlightenment; this is clearly contrary to the Lord's teaching, which states specifically that 'self-control' is the result of the state of enlightenment.[40]

During the process of Transcendental Meditation, when the mind enters the subtler levels of experience, the activity of all the senses decreases and finally stops; the breath also becomes more refined and eventually comes to a standstill. This is the offering of 'all the activities of the senses and of the life-breath in the fire of Yoga'.

'Self-control kindled by enlightenment': self-control means the self remaining within itself without any deviation into the outer world. Control of the mind in its perfect state means the mind remaining within itself without any deviation into the outer world. A lesser degree of control of the mind would be deviation into the outer world in a desired direction. Similarly, control of the senses in its perfect state means the senses remaining in themselves without any deviation into the outer world. A lesser degree of sense-control would be deviation into the outer world in a desired direction.

'Self-control kindled by enlightenment' means a perfect state of control of the self, the mind, and the senses. It means that in the state of enlightenment, or pure consciousness, in the state of Being, the mind and senses are set within themselves without any deviation into the outer world. This takes place in the transcendental state devoid of any activity. When, however, this

40 See II, 59.

transcendental state of consciousness becomes permanent and is transformed into Cosmic Consciousness, then the mind remains anchored to the state of Being and entertains activity in the outer world in the desired direction.

This is how the mind, even while active, remains within the range of self-control. The senses always follow the pattern of the mind, so when the mind is in this state of self-control, the activity of the senses also remains quite spontaneously within the boundaries of self-control. This means that the senses automatically function in the right direction.

This is how, by means of gaining the state of enlightenment, the 'activities of the senses and of the life-breath' are offered 'in the fire of Yoga'. It is clear therefore that the 'fire of Yoga' has to be lit first, and only then the control follows.

It should be noted that by virtue of this state of self-control on the cosmic level, the activity of the creation and evolution of cosmic life is spontaneously carried out by the nature of the three *Guṇas*, while cosmic Being, God, remains uninvolved with activity. This is a picture of the inner functioning of cosmic life; it shows with what spontaneity and precision, based on self-control, the activity of cosmic life is carried on.

Here Yoga has been defined as the state of self-control spontaneously created by enlightenment, by the realization of the Self in Transcendental Consciousness, and therefore in the state of Cosmic Consciousness as well.

God Consciousness is the supreme state of enlightenment. As this state is gained, self-control on the level of the individual life rises to self-control on the level of cosmic life.

VERSE 28

द्रव्ययज्ञास्तपोयज्ञा योगयज्ञास्तथापरे
स्वाध्यायज्ञानयज्ञाश्च यतयः संशितव्रताः

Dravyayagyās tapoyagyā yogayagyās tathāpare
swādhyāyagyānayagyāsh cha yatayaḥ saṁshitavratāḥ

Some likewise perform Yagya by means of material possessions, by austerity, and by the practice of Yoga; while other aspirants of rigid vows offer as Yagya their scriptural learning and knowledge.

Here the Lord describes material, bodily, and mental methods of purification for the sake of evolution, for the sake of gaining freedom in Cosmic Consciousness and its fulfilment in God Consciousness.

'*Yagya* by means of material possessions' denotes giving away wealth to the deserving. It also means the performance of Vedic rituals by offering sacrificial fires.[41]

To perform *Yagya* 'by austerity' means subjecting the body to heat, cold, and other such sufferings for the sake of purification.

'By the practice of Yoga': see II, 45, 50; III, 7.

'Offer as *Yagya* their scriptural learning and knowledge': sit and meditate and transcend the field of learning; experience the transcendent Being, which is the goal of all learning.[42]

Verse 29

अपाने जुह्वति प्राणं प्राणेऽपानं तथापरे
प्राणापानगती रुद्ध्वा प्राणायामपरायणाः

Apāne juhwati prāṇaṁ prāṇe 'pānaṁ tathāpare
prāṇāpānagatī ruddhwā prāṇāyāmaparāyaṇāḥ

Others again, who are devoted to breathing exercises, pour the inward into the outward breath and the outward into the inward, having restrained the course of inhalation and exhalation.

Here the Lord explains to Arjuna that there is a class of seekers of Truth who try to realize through the process of breathing exercises. They induce 'the inward into the outward breath and the outward into the inward', thus restraining 'the course of inhalation and exhalation'. This results in the suspension of breathing, which brings the mind to stillness in the silence of

41 See III, 12–13; IV, 25.
42 See II, 52–3.

Bliss Consciousness, simultaneously culturing the nervous system[43] to maintain this state of consciousness. That is why the practice of breathing exercises is included here as *Yagya*.

Transcendental Meditation also fulfils the requirements of this verse, for during its practice the outgoing and ingoing breaths quite spontaneously begin to become more shallow. The flow of the outgoing breath becomes less, and the flow of the ingoing breath becomes less. This phenomenon of the simultaneous diminution of both has been described as the pouring of one into the other. This is how, through the practice of Transcendental Meditation, in a very easy manner, one pours 'the inward into the outward breath and the outward into the inward'.

VERSE 30

अपरे नियताहाराः प्राणान्प्राणेषु जुह्वति
सर्वेऽप्येते यज्ञविदो यज्ञक्षपितकल्मषाः

Apare niyatāhārāḥ prāṇān prāṇeshu juhwati
sarve 'py ete yagyavido yagyakshapitakalmashāḥ

Yet others, restricting their food, offer breaths into breaths.
All these indeed are knowers of Yagya, and through Yagya
their sins are cast away.

When a man restricts his food, less oxygen is needed for metabolism, and therefore his breathing becomes more shallow.

'Restricting their food' means not feeding the senses with their objects, not engaging in the activity of action or even thought. This non-engagement in activity requires a reduction in metabolism, which in turn requires a reduction of respiratory activity. This, as has been explained in the previous verse, is what the Lord means by 'offer breaths into breaths'.

All these are different ways of purifying[44] oneself; that is why they are called *Yagya*. Through their practice 'sins are cast away'. The Dhyānbindu Upanishad declares that a huge mountain of sins extending for miles is destroyed by Union brought about

43 See verse 38, commentary.
44 See verse 38, commentary.

through Transcendental Meditation, without which there is no way out.[45]

VERSE 31

यज्ञशिष्टामृतभुजो यान्ति ब्रह्म सनातनम्
नायं लोकोऽस्त्ययज्ञस्य कुतोऽन्यः कुरुसत्तम

Yagyashishtāmṛitabhujo yānti Brahm sanātanam
nāyaṁ loko 'styayagyasya kuto 'nyaḥ Kurusattama

Eating the remains of the Yagya, which is nectar, they reach the eternal Brahman. This world, O best of Kurus, is not for him who offers no Yagya, much less the world hereafter.

Having described the various types of *Yagya* in the previous verses (24–30), the Lord, in this verse, explains their result. *Yagya* is the process of purification. Every such process leaves the mind finer and thus more capable of transcending. When *Yagya* is over,[46] the mind is purified and gains a higher level of consciousness. This eventually results in Bliss Consciousness, which the Lord calls 'nectar'. The bliss remains,[47] as it were, when the *Yagya* is over. Those who enjoy this bliss, says the Lord, 'reach the eternal *Brahman*', because it is this transcendental Bliss Consciousness that, through continued practice, develops into Cosmic Consciousness and eventually into God Consciousness.

The Lord says further that if a man does not perform *Yagya* he will be successful neither in this world nor hereafter. Unless the arrow is fully drawn back on the bow, it does not gain sufficient energy to shoot forward with great force; unless the mind is drawn inwards and brought to the extreme limit of its inward march, it does not become dynamic. And unless the mind becomes active and powerful, it certainly will not achieve success

45 यदि शैलसमं पापं विस्तीर्णं बहुयोजनम्
भिद्यते ध्यानयोगेन नान्यो भेदः कदाचन
Yadi shailasamaṁ pāpaṁ vistīrṇaṁ bahuyojanam
bhidyate dhyānayogena nānyo bhedaḥ kadāchana
(Dhyānbindu Upanishad, 1)

46 See verse 33.

47 See III, 13, commentary.

in the world. The Lord shows that the process of purification, or *Yagya*, is necessary both for success in this world and to gain strength for success in the world hereafter.

Of all the *Yagyas*, the *Yagya* of Transcendental Meditation[48] is the most[49] effective, for it is a direct means of bringing the mind to absolute purity and enabling it to contact the source of limitless life-energy and intelligence.

VERSE 32

एवं बहुविधा यज्ञा वितता ब्रह्मणो मुखे
कर्मजान्विद्धि तान्सर्वानेवं ज्ञात्वा विमोक्ष्यसे

Evaṁ bahuvidhā yagyā vitatā Brahmaṇo mukhe
karmajān viddhi tān sarvān evaṁ gyātwā vimokshyase

In this way Yagyas of many kinds are set forth in the
words of the Veda. Know them all as born of action.
Thus knowing you will find release.

The Vedas speak of various kinds of *Yagya* which help the process of the evolution of man at different levels of life. The Lord means that the knowledge of the various *Yagyas*, as found in the Vedas, is complete in itself; it has only to be adopted. To convey this, He says: 'Know them all as born of action.' Action is necessary to perform *Yagya*: unless they are performed, *Yagyas* will not yield any result. Theoretical knowledge of them has its value but does not in itself carry the fruits of *Yagya*. The importance of action is emphasized here.

The phrase 'Know them all as born of action' suggests another point. The Lord wants to make it very clear to Arjuna that the knowledge of *Yagya*, which He has been teaching in the previous verses and which has the authority of the Vedas, is essential for success in this world and hereafter. But at the same time He indicates that this is not the final knowledge which will free him from bondage; something more has to be known. While continuing in the activity of *Yagya*, Arjuna should bear in mind that it

48 See Appendix: The *Transcendental Meditation* Technique.
49 See verse 33.

is all in the field of activity and that Reality is transcendental. So one has not to remain permanently in the field of the activity of *Yagya*. The knowledge that *Yagya* is activity and that Reality is transcendental will certainly free a man.

Here is an important point for the practice of Transcendental Meditation. The medium of attention must enable the mind to reach the Transcendent and realize the absolute state of Being. If the aspirant is not aware of this fact then, during his practice of meditation (*Yagya*) when he finds that the medium of attention has disappeared, he will feel confused. To save him from such confusion, the Lord says that all the practices which bring enlightenment (*Yagyas*) are in the field of activity, and that the goal is to transcend that field, to arrive at Transcendental Consciousness, gain Cosmic Consciousness, and ultimately rise to the consummation of all action in the state of Unity in God Consciousness.

The following verse throws more light on this point.

VERSE 33

श्रेयान्द्रव्यमयाद्यज्ञाज्ज्ञानयज्ञः परंतप
सर्वं कर्माखिलं पार्थ ज्ञाने परिसमाप्यते

Shreyān dravyamayād yagyāj gyānayagyaḥ Paraṁtapa
sarvaṁ karmākhilaṁ Pārtha gyāne parisamāpyate

Better than the Yagya through material means is the Yagya of knowledge, O scorcher of enemies. All action without exception, O Pārtha, culminates in knowledge.

'*Yagya* through material means': see verse 28.

'*Yagya* of knowledge' means action that leads to knowledge.[50] *Yagya* of 'material means' is performed through material offerings, whereas *Yagya* of knowledge is performed through mental activity — mental activity leading to the state of Transcendental Consciousness, and also the mental activity of understanding of the Transcendent. Knowledge[51] in its content is God Conscious-

50 See verse 38, commentary.
51 See verse 38.

ness, which develops from the state of Cosmic Consciousness, which in its turn develops from the knowledge (understanding and experience) of Transcendental Consciousness.

Action is a means of evolution, and evolution gains its highest peak when man has attained Unity with God, God Consciousness. In this state of fulfilment there is nothing that he need do.[52] He has arrived at the goal of all actions.

All means come to an end as a matter of course when the goal is reached. Any form of *Yagya* aims at a certain degree of purification. When pure consciousness has been permanently achieved, when the Self has been realized as separate from activity, and when God Consciousness has been gained, then the extreme limit of purification has been achieved. Having achieved it, a man naturally feels fulfilled in eternal freedom. This state of fulfilment is the goal of all action, the goal of all *Yagya*. That is why the Lord says that knowledge is a field towards which all actions converge and in which they finally become merged: 'All action without exception, O Pārtha, culminates in knowledge.'

The Lord's discourse is an example of great psychological skill. Gradually (from verse 23 to this verse) He builds up the importance of *Yagya*, the path to enlightenment. When He has established the greatness of it, He suddenly says that this is all in the field of action,[53] thereby implying first that it is within the reach of every man, and secondly that no man should remain held up within the field of action, or *Yagya*, for it is not the final goal of life. Having pointed this out, the Lord, in this verse, immediately concludes His account with the statement that knowledge is the goal of all actions. *Yagya* through material means can at best raise the level of consciousness in the relative field of life. *Yagya* of knowledge transforms the entire human mechanism into a means by which the Divine expresses[54] Itself in the world. Because there could be no state of evolution greater than this, 'the *Yagya* of knowledge', leading as it does to this state, is better than '*Yagya* through material means'.

When the Lord lays stress on knowledge as against action, He

52 See III, 17.

53 See verse 32.

54 See verse 38, commentary.

addresses Arjuna as 'scorcher of enemies', as one engaged in vigorous activity. This is to show him that it is through knowledge that life can be made most dynamic. In the verse which follows, the Lord indicates a direct way to search for this 'knowledge'.

VERSE 34

तद्विद्धि प्रणिपातेन परिप्रश्नेन सेवया
उपदेक्ष्यन्ति ते ज्ञानं ज्ञानिनस्तत्त्वदर्शिन:

Tad viddhi praṇipātena pariprashnena sevayā
upadekshyanti te gyānaṁ gyāninas tattwadarshinaḥ

Know this: through homage, repeated inquiry, and service, the men of knowledge who have experienced Reality will teach you knowledge.

Here is the process of gaining enlightenment from the enlightened. By 'homage' is meant submission or surrender. This serves to produce a state of receptivity. In the state of submission, the heart and mind set aside their own ways of feeling and thinking; they become free from all that overshadows their potentiality and become fully receptive to the enlightened man, the embodiment of knowledge.

Submission is a means of depriving the seeker quite naturally of his limited individuality and overcoming in him any resistance that prevents him from opening himself to the cosmic Being. In this verse the seeker of Truth is advised to submit to the enlightened man and not merely to have a sense of submission to cosmic Being. This is because submission to omnipresent Being, having no concrete point of focus, remains abstract and indefinite and does not crystallize into concrete results. Direct submission of the individual intellect to the cosmic intelligence takes place only in the state of transcendence. In the field of relativity, submission on the level of thinking and understanding demands a specific point of focus if it is to be valid and productive of results.

The second point in the process of reaching enlightenment is that the intellect should be alert, so that discrimination, or the ability to understand different aspects of Reality, is sharp. This is necessary because the state of full enlightenment includes a clear understanding of Reality, and this again can only be accomplished by an intellect which is alert and sharp, discriminating and decisive. The state of intellectual alertness conflicts with the state of submission. This conflict is resolved by what the Lord calls 'service'.

'Service' means action in accordance with the desire of the master. A sense of service has little to do with the nature of the work itself, but is primarily concerned with the fulfilment of the master's desires; if the master is pleased, service is successful. If he is pleased by the accomplishment of the work, then the service is done and the work has accomplished its purpose. If, in the middle of the work, the master wants it undone, then the success of the service will demand obedience. This art of service covers those states of submission and alertness of intellect which are necessary for enlightenment.

A right sense of service trains the mind of the seeker to adjust itself to the status of the integrated mind of the enlightened man. In order to be successful in the art of service, one has to adjust one's mind, one's likes and dislikes, to bring them into accord with the mind of the master. One does something and then closely watches to see whether he is pleased or displeased. Then one adjusts one's actions accordingly. This does more than merely hold together submission and alertness of intellect. By adjusting itself to the likes and dislikes of the enlightened cosmic mind of the master, the ignorant mind of the seeker gradually gains that same status. Thus we find submission, questioning, and service, all these three, are complementary and create a situation favourable to enlightenment.

Commenting on this verse, Shankara says: 'Know by what means it is gained. Having approached the teachers humbly, fall down and prostrate yourself before them, paying them prolonged homage. Ask them what is bondage and what liberation, what is wisdom and what ignorance. Perform service for the master. Pleased by these and other signs of reverence, the teachers, who know the Truth from the scriptures and have also realized It through direct personal experience, will declare to you this knowledge.'

The result of this knowledge is shown in the next verse.

VERSE 35

यज्ज्ञात्वा न पुनर्मोहमेवं यास्यसि पाण्डव
येन भूतान्यशेषेण द्रक्ष्यस्यात्मन्यथो मयि

Yaj gyātwā na punar moham evaṁ yāsyasi Pāṇdava
yena bhūtānyasheshena drakshyasyātmanyatho mayi

Knowing this, O son of Pāṇdu, you will no more fall into such delusion; for through this you will see all beings in your Self and also in Me.

'Knowing this': having gained the knowledge given in the preceding verses.

'You will no more fall into such delusion': here the Lord gives Arjuna the technique of rising above the possibility of delusion. The field of the duality of life alone can be the field of delusion. When, in the state of Cosmic Consciousness, one has realized the Self as separate from activity, and when this state has developed to the eternal Unity of God Consciousness, then you see 'all beings in your Self and also in Me'. In this state of oneness of life, oneness of God Consciousness, there is no trace of duality and therefore there is no possibility of any delusion. The teaching is: cultivate the state of Unity in God Consciousness; cultivate this state of knowledge so that you will no more fall into such delusion.

The word 'such' is highly significant. It indicates a special state of delusion — Arjuna's delusion in particular — delusion in the state of *Sattwa*. Thereby the Lord silently educates Arjuna in the philosophy of delusion: any delusion experienced in the state of *Tamas* can be overcome with the increase of *Rajas*; likewise, delusion experienced in the state of *Rajas* can be overcome with the rise of *Sattwa*; but a delusion in the state of *Sattwa*, as in Arjuna's case, cannot be overcome unless one transcends the field of *Sattwa* and gains Transcendental Consciousness. Here the qualities of the heart and mind find a common goal, thereby dissolving the duality of their separate existences and rising above the possibility of delusion.

It is not physically possible, however, to remain in the Transcendent at all times. Therefore it is necessary to make this Transcendental Consciousness permanent and to rise to the state of Cosmic Consciousness. In this state of Cosmic Consciousness one experiences one's Self as separate from activity. It might appear that in this state one was living a duality, the duality of Being and activity; but this type of duality, in which the Self remains detached from everything, is free from the possibility of delusion. But the Lord wishes Arjuna to rise above duality even of this nature. In order that he may do so, He emphasizes the importance of gaining knowledge of Unity in God Consciousness which results from devotion in the state of Cosmic Consciousness.

By the practice of the teaching in the previous verse the heart and mind of the seeker are automatically refined to become capable of devotion; this devotion develops God Consciousness, in which Unity becomes a living reality of life, and the possibility of any kind of duality is completely eliminated.

'You will see all beings in your Self and also in Me': when one sees through green spectacles, then everything looks green. When, through knowledge, the Self is realized as separate from activity and Self-consciousness becomes permanent in the state of Cosmic Consciousness, then everything is naturally experienced in the awareness of the Self; and when this permanent state of Self-consciousness, or Cosmic Consciousness, has been transformed through devotion into God Consciousness, then everything is naturally experienced in the awareness of God, every experience is through God Consciousness, everything is experienced and understood in the Light of God, in terms of God, in God.

Seeing 'all beings' includes knowledge of the whole field of the universe constituted by the three *Guṇas*; and seeing 'Me' means seeing the Lord presiding over both the Absolute and the relative. Thus seeing 'all beings in your Self and also in Me' implies having a complete knowledge of both the absolute and relative fields, of the relationship between them, and of God presiding over them both.

Seeing all beings in the Self is the start of the transformation of Cosmic Consciousness into God Consciousness, and this transformation comes to completion when all beings are seen in God. First, all beings are seen in the Self, and then the Self is seen in God. That is why the Lord says: 'you will see all beings in your Self and also in Me'. The two ideas in one phrase not only describe the two states but also the sequence in which they develop.

In the state of Cosmic Consciousness, the Self is experienced as separate from activity. This state of life in perfect non-attachment is based on Bliss Consciousness, by virtue of which the qualities of the heart have gained their most complete development. Universal love then dominates the heart, which begins to overflow with the love of God; the silent ocean of bliss, the silent ocean of love, begins to rise in waves of devotion. The heart in its state of eternal contentment begins to move, and this begins to draw everything together and eliminate the gulf of separation between the Self and activity. The Union of all diversity in the Self begins to grow. The intensity of this Union cultures man's consciousness, which begins to find everything inseparable from the Self; and this is how, in the most natural manner, the Self, which held Its identity as separate from all activity in the state of Cosmic Consciousness, finds everything in Itself. This happens on the way to God Consciousness, which in its completeness absorbs even the Self, containing all things.

Beings separate themselves from the supreme Being by means of *Prakṛiti*, but this veil is removed when life is dominated by the light of knowledge, the light of the awareness of life's Unity in God Consciousness, which establishes eternity in the ephemeral world.

This seeing of everything in God is not restricted to the limitations of vision; it is on the level of life as a whole; it is on that high level of life which corresponds to the Life of God Himself. Fortunate is man that he can rise to the Life of God.

VERSE 36

अपि चेदसि पापेभ्यः सर्वेभ्यः पापकृत्तमः
सर्वं ज्ञानप्लवेनैव वृजिनं संतरिष्यसि

Api ched asi pāpebhyaḥ sarvebhyaḥ pāpakṛittamaḥ
sarvaṁ gyānaplavenaiva vṛijinaṁ saṁtarishyasi

Even if you were the most sinful of all sinners, you would cross over all evil by the raft of knowledge alone.

Having, in the preceding verse, extolled knowledge for its effectiveness in destroying delusion, the Lord now speaks of its effectiveness in destroying sin. The special value of this knowledge lies in the fact that it eliminates the necessity[55] for gaining knowledge about wrong action. The silent teaching here is that knowledge of the Divine is necessary and not knowledge of action, wrong action, and inaction as referred to in verse 17. This becomes all the more apparent in the light of the following verse, where the Lord explains that all actions are burned to ashes by the fire of knowledge.

'You would cross over all evil by the raft of knowledge alone': the word 'alone' indicates that nothing other than knowledge is necessary for a man to 'cross over all evil'. How one goes beyond evil in the state of enlightenment should be properly understood.

It has been said in verse 35 that knowledge takes a man beyond delusion and moulds his life in the oneness of God Consciousness. In this state one's life is on the supreme level of existence, being united with the Lord of all. All the Laws of Nature respond favourably to such a life, for it is in tune with the almighty invincible force of Nature, which is working out the evolution of everything in creation. In such a state a man's every thought, word, and action produce a life-supporting influence for himself and for the whole universe. This is a state of life where no wrong action is possible. In this state one has crossed over all evil by the raft of knowledge.

'Knowledge' is irresistible, for no one can resist himself. The state of knowledge at one level is the state of one's own Self,

55 See verse 17.

Transcendental Consciousness. At another, it is the state of the Self in the midst of activity, Cosmic Consciousness. At yet another, it is the state of God Consciousness. Enlightenment is irrespective of anything in the relative field; nothing can be an obstacle[56] to enlightenment. However dense the darkness and however long it may have existed, one ray of the rising sun is enough to dispel the darkness, though it takes time to reach the brightness of the midday sun. Even a momentary flash of Transcendental Consciousness is enough to dispel the delusion of ignorance, though it takes time to gain full enlightenment in God Consciousness, where one has crossed over all evil by the raft of knowledge. This brings hope even to a man whose life may be full of wrong-doing.

Sin produces coarseness in the nervous system, preventing it from functioning normally and obstructing its ability to give rise to pure consciousness. Such an impaired state of the nervous system prevents Being from directly influencing the field of activity.

This is how, by attacking the physical structure of the nervous system and thus preventing pure consciousness from being lived in daily life, sin causes sorrow and suffering. Knowledge, in eliminating this possibility, at the same time roots out all possibility of sorrow and suffering. This verse recommends taking refuge in knowledge in order to rise above the possibility of any sin in life and promises redemption even to the worst sinner in the world.

While in this verse the Lord promises release from the bondage of any wrong action through knowledge, in the following verse He promises the actual annihilation of all action in the fire of knowledge.

VERSE 37

यथैधांसि समिद्धोऽग्निर्भस्मसात्कुरुतेऽर्जुन
ज्ञानाग्निः सर्वकर्माणि भस्मसात्कुरुते तथा

Yathaidhāṁsi samiddho 'gnir bhasmasāt kurute 'rjuna
gyānāgniḥ sarvakarmāṇi bhasmasāt kurute tathā

As a blazing fire turns fuel to ashes, so does the fire of knowledge turn all actions into ashes.

56 See II, 40.

'Knowledge': that by which all 'sins are cast away' (verse 30), and that by which 'you will see all beings in your Self and also in Me' (verse 35). Knowledge means awareness, which in its nature is pure consciousness; this state of knowledge is devoid of any activity. That is why the Lord says that 'the fire of knowledge' turns 'all actions into ashes'. When this state[57] has become permanently established in the nature of the mind, the Self is experienced as separate from activity and its fruits (verse 19). This is how the fire of knowledge, the fire of Cosmic Consciousness, turns 'all actions into ashes'. When this state of consciousness, the state of knowledge, reaches its consummation in God Consciousness, the separation of the Self from activity dissolves into oneness of the Self and activity. Thus in its supreme state also the fire of knowledge turns 'all actions into ashes'.

When the Lord said in verse 33 that 'all action ... culminates in knowledge', He explained that once knowledge has been gained actions have come to an end — they have fulfilled their final purpose. In this situation man has risen to a state of consciousness above the reach of activity; all activity, mental and physical, is carried out under the direct influence of the forces of Nature, which are unconcerned with the consciousness of the doer. The doer finds himself established on a level of life which has nothing in common with the field of action. In this state, the action that is performed ceases to be, ceases to engage the consciousness of the actor. This is what the Lord means when He says that 'the fire of knowledge' turns 'all actions into ashes'.

'All actions': this expression has both a qualitative and a quantitative meaning and also includes the range of time — past, present, and future. The impressions of past actions, which serve as the seed for future actions, become like roasted seeds, losing their potency. This is how the actions of the past are burnt in 'the fire of knowledge'. Actions performed in the present remain on the level of the mind and senses; they do not touch the depths of the mind anchored to Being, and therefore no deep impressions are created to be stored as the seed for future actions. This is how actions performed in the present are burnt in 'the fire of knowledge', completely eliminating the basis of future actions.

57 See verse 36, commentary.

This puts an end to the cycle of cause and effect in the field of action; and this in turn puts an end to the cycle of birth and death, bringing eternal freedom to life.

VERSE 38

न हि ज्ञानेन सदृशं पवित्रमिह विद्यते
तत्स्वयं योगसंसिद्धः कालेनात्मनि विन्दति

Na hi gyānena sadṛishaṁ pavitram iha vidyate
tat swayaṁ yogasaṁsiddhaḥ kālenātmani vindati

Truly there is in this world nothing so purifying as knowledge; he who is perfected in Yoga, of himself in time finds this within himself.

'Nothing so purifying as knowledge': the work of a purifier is first to purify the different ingredients or components and then, having freed the components from impurities, to present the whole compound in its pure state.

Knowledge is the purifier of life. It purifies life in the sense that it analyses the different aspects of existence and distinguishes and separates the eternal aspects from the transient. It acts like a filter to clear the mud from muddy water. The real nature of life is absolute Bliss Consciousness; this crystal water of life has been polluted by becoming mixed with the activities of the three *Guṇas*. This has resulted in masking the eternity of life behind its transient and ever-changing aspects.

The pure state of Being is realized by knowing the relative and the absolute components of life. This knowing comes to perfection when the knower gains perfect intimacy with Being and becomes fully aware of the basic activity of life, the activity of the three *Guṇas* as separate from Being. Perfect intimacy with Being is gained when the mind gains the transcendental state of consciousness. This is the absolute state of knowledge, which can be described as the state of knowingness. When knowledge becomes perfect, it arrives at the state of knowingness and brings life to perfect purity. In this way knowledge removes ignorance, which is the greatest impurity of life, and takes life out of the cycle of birth, death, and suffering.

The superficial aspect of knowledge is knowing and understanding; the real nature of knowledge is the state of knowingness, the state of pure consciousness, or Being. Considering knowledge in this way, we find that Transcendental Consciousness represents the real nature of knowledge. Another phase of knowledge is where Transcendental Consciousness coexists with the activity of the waking state of consciousness. In this state, when Transcendental Consciousness becomes permanently established in the very nature of the mind, the absolute and relative phases of life begin to be appreciated simultaneously: the Self is experienced as separate from activity. There is yet another state of knowledge in which the separateness of the Self and activity dissolves into the Unity of God Consciousness, which is the most purified state of life, free from any stain of impurity. Such a life in absolute purity represents the supreme state of knowledge, about which the Lord says: 'he who is perfected in Yoga, of himself in time finds this within himself'.

It may be added that only through Transcendental Meditation, which is the direct way to gain pure consciousness and rise finally to God Consciousness, can absolute purity be lived in daily life.

When the state of Yoga, the state of Transcendental Consciousness, becomes permanent so that it maintains itself throughout all activity, one has reached the state of Cosmic Consciousness. Such perfect infusion of the Absolute into relativity takes place by degrees, through the regular practice of going to the Transcendent and coming back to the field of action in daily life. A balanced alternation of meditation and activity results in full realization. One analogy will make this clear: we dip a white cloth in a yellow dye and let it remain in the dye to be coloured for a few minutes. Then we take it out and expose it to the sun till the colour begins to fade. We repeat the same process, again putting the cloth into the sunlight till the colour fades. Similarly, we meditate for about half an hour and follow this by coming out to act in practical life for about ten hours, by which time we begin to feel that we are out of the influence of the morning meditation. We meditate again in the same way and again let the influence fade by coming out into practical life; we keep repeating the process of gaining the state of universal Being in transcendence (*Samādhi*) during meditation and of coming out to regain individuality in the field of relative existence. This allows more and more infusion of Being into the nature of the mind even when it is engaged in activity through the senses.

When the full infusion of Being has been accomplished, then the state of Cosmic Consciousness has been gained.

The state of Cosmic Consciousness provides the basis for the development of the state of perfected Yoga in God Consciousness. The development of Cosmic Consciousness into God Consciousness requires that the separation found to exist between the Self and activity be transformed into a fusion of these two separate identities, resulting in the eternal Unity of God Consciousness.

This transformation of the state of separation takes place by virtue of the most refined activity of all, the activity of devotion to God.

In order to analyse the way in which the act of devotion effects this transformation and produces the state of eternal Unity in God Consciousness, it is necessary to examine closely how, in the state of Cosmic Consciousness, the Self is experienced as separate from activity; how the eternal silence of transcendental Self-consciousness becomes compatible with the incessant activity of the waking state of consciousness. Those practising Transcendental Meditation experience a slowing down of the metabolism during the inward stroke of meditation; they experience that the nervous system comes to a state of restful alertness when the mind transcends thought and gains Transcendental Consciousness. Again, they experience that the nervous system becomes active when it engages itself in the activity of thought or action.

Any state of consciousness is the expression of a corresponding state of the nervous system. Transcendental Consciousness corresponds to a certain specific state of the nervous system which transcends any activity and is therefore completely different from that state of the nervous system which corresponds to the waking state of consciousness.

Now, for Transcendental Consciousness to become permanent and to coexist with the waking state of consciousness, it is necessary that the two states of the nervous system corresponding to these two states of consciousness should coexist. This is brought about by the mind gaining alternately Transcendental Consciousness and the waking state of consciousness, passing from one to the other. This gradual and systematic culture of the physical nervous system creates a physiological situation in which the two states of consciousness exist together simultaneously. It is well known that there exist in the nervous system many autonomous levels of function, between which a system of coordination also exists. In the state of Cosmic Consciousness, two different levels of organization in the nervous system function simultaneously while maintaining their separate identities. By virtue of this anatomical separation of function, it becomes possible for Transcendental Consciousness to coexist with the waking state of consciousness and with the dreaming and sleeping states of consciousness.

In the early stages of the practice of Transcendental Meditation, these two levels of function in the nervous system are unable to occur at the same time; the function of the one inhibits the function of the other. That is why, at this stage, either Transcendental Consciousness or the waking state of consciousness is experienced. The practice of the mind in passing from one to another gradually overcomes this physiological inhibition, and the two levels begin to function perfectly at the same time, without inhibiting each other and still maintaining their separate identities. The function of each is independent of the other, and that is why this state of the nervous system corresponds to Cosmic Consciousness, in which Self-awareness exists as separate from activity. Silence is experienced with activity and yet as separate from it.

In order to develop Cosmic Consciousness to God Consciousness, the nervous system needs to be cultured further so that these two levels, which function independently, come to function in an integrated manner. This will give rise to a state of consciousness in which the sense of separation between the Self and activity is dissolved, and this duality constituting Cosmic Consciousness is subsumed into the Unity of God Consciousness.

This integration of functions on the physiological level is brought about by a mental activity of ultimate refinement. In order to define activity of this quality, we must analyse the whole range of activity. The activity of the organs of action is the most gross, the activity of the senses of perception is more refined, the mental activity of thought is finer still, and the activity of feeling and emotion is the finest of all. One could further classify different levels of quality in emotional activity, such as anger, fear, despair, happiness, reverence, service, and love.

The activity of devotion comprises the feelings of service, reverence, and love, which are the most refined qualities of feeling. It is through the activity of devotion that Cosmic Consciousness develops into God Consciousness.

When the nervous system is constantly exposed to this most refined activity of devotion, the physiological integration of functions that has been described takes place. And it is the permanent state of this condition of the nervous system that enables a man to live God Consciousness in his daily life; acting in the midst of all sorts of circumstances, fulfilling the purpose of cosmic life, he carries the totality of existence within himself and moves in the Unity of God.

From this it is clear that to develop God Consciousness, which represents the supreme state of knowledge, it is necessary to culture the physical nervous system. This requires regular and sustained practice, which obviously needs time. That is why the Lord says 'in time finds'.

'Within himself': by this expression the Lord wishes it to be clearly understood that the supreme state of knowledge is not gained from outside. It is gained within oneself, when one has lived for some time the perfected state of Yoga in God Consciousness. The element of time indicates here that during the early stages of God Consciousness life is full of such overwhelming experience of Unity in diversity that one lives deeply lost in it. Gradually as time passes one begins to appreciate this Unity in terms of other things and activities in the world. It is then that one has realized God, that one has the knowledge of God. Thus it becomes clear why the Lord speaks of the necessity for time in gaining supreme knowledge.

VERSE 39

श्रद्धावाँल्लभते ज्ञानं तत्परः संयतेन्द्रियः
ज्ञानं लब्ध्वा परां शान्तिमचिरेणाधिगच्छति

Shraddhāvāṁllabhate gyānaṁ tatparaḥ saṁyatendriyaḥ
gyānaṁ labdhwā parāṁ shāntim achireṇādhigachchhati

He gains knowledge who is possessed of faith, is active of purpose, and has subdued the senses. Having gained knowledge, swiftly he comes to the supreme peace.

'Knowledge': awareness of Unity in the midst of the diversity of life. When this awareness has become complete, it is said to be God Consciousness.

To rise from the waking state of consciousness to God Consciousness, one has to pass through the states of Transcendental Consciousness and Cosmic Consciousness. In the sequence of development, one state leads to another in the order of waking, Transcendental, Cosmic, and God Consciousness. They are as different one from another as spectacles of different colours through which the same view looks different. When the same object is cognized in different states of consciousness, its values are differently appreciated. Life is appreciated differently at each different level of consciousness.

As the mind passes through all these states, it has to undergo various new experiences which, in the absence of faith, can easily be misunderstood at any step. That is why the Lord names faith as a prerequisite to knowledge.

There are three fields of faith: faith in oneself, faith in the teacher, and faith in God. Faith in oneself is necessary so that one does not begin to doubt one's own experience. Faith in the teacher enables one to accept the fundamentals of the teaching; if in the absence of faith the basic principles of the teaching are rejected, one can neither derive any benefit from it nor verify its truth, since the truth of the teaching can be verified only by personal experience which arises from the practice given by the teacher. Faith in God protects man's heart and mind and ensures that steady progress which is so important in the life of a seeker.

Faith provides an anchor in life, not only for the seeker of Truth but for any man. It is needed for any accomplishment in life; for greater accomplishment it is needed in greater measure; for ultimate fulfilment in God Consciousness the greatest faith is needed.

Meditation is a process which provides increasing charm at every step on the way to the Transcendent. The experience of this charm causes faith to grow. Moreover, the regular practice of meditation brings the great blessings of harmony and joy to life; this too helps the heart and mind to grow in faith and keeps a man 'active of purpose' on the path to enlightenment, and thus stability is gained on the way. The activity of the senses also becomes balanced and natural. Thus, when a man begins the practice of Transcendental Meditation, he fulfils the conditions necessary for enlightenment.

The first ray of the rising sun is enough to dispel the darkness of the night, and yet it takes some time for the sun to become fully risen. Through meditation, the mind reaches Transcendental Consciousness quickly and is enlightened by the first ray of the Divine; yet to allow this transcendental divine consciousness to shine forth through all circumstances, through waking, dreaming, and dreamless sleep, regular practice of meditation is absolutely essential.

Meditation takes the mind to transcendental Self-consciousness, and a natural and balanced activity infuses the transcendental divine nature into the mind, where it is not lost even when the mind is engaged in the field of activity. In this way, Self-consciousness grows to Cosmic Consciousness — *Ātmānanda* to *Brahmānanda*, *Savikalpa Samādhi* to *Nirvikalpa* — and eventually this state of Yoga, Cosmic Consciousness, attains its fulfilment in God Consciousness; the first ray of enlightenment reaches its full glory.

This verse emphasizes the need for a man to be 'active of purpose' and to have a natural balanced activity of the senses and the mind in addition to faith. All these, combining harmoniously, help to produce devotion, that highest quality in a seeker by which he accomplishes the final stage of his evolution. These taken together create a situation for the unfolding of the supreme

Reality in its all-embracing nature, raising the limited status of the individual to the unbounded status of Cosmic Consciousness and eventually to that Unity of life in God Consciousness which eternally satisfies the mind and heart. Having gained this, a man in time gains knowledge,[58] through which he becomes free from any doubt or delusion.[59] This is that state of 'supreme peace' where the heart rests in eternal contentment and the mind is filled with the Unity of life, where there is no trace of duality and therefore peace is abiding.

VERSE 40

अज्ञश्चाश्रद्दधानश्च संशयात्मा विनश्यति
नायं लोकोऽस्ति न परो न सुखं संशयात्मनः

Agyash chāshraddadhānash cha saṁshayātmā vinashyati
nāyaṁ loko 'sti na paro na sukhaṁ saṁshayātmanaḥ

But the man who is without knowledge, without faith, and of a doubting nature perishes. For the doubting mind there is neither this world nor another nor any happiness.

The sequence of expressions is highly important in giving insight into the teaching. Lack of knowledge is the basis of lack of faith, which in turn is the basis of 'a doubting nature'. Therefore it is lack of knowledge, or the state of ignorance, which is at the root of all failure in material advancement and spiritual development. Ignorance is the source of all weakness and suffering in life. The teaching is that one must cast off ignorance and rise to the state of knowledge in order to win all happiness and progress in this world and hereafter.

In view of what has been said about the preceding verse, the significance of this verse is obvious. Yet one must remember that it is the ignorant who become enlightened, for meditation is a process which reveals Reality to the ignorant. One thing may be added here: no man could ever be completely devoid of faith

58 See verse 38.
59 See verse 35.

and completely full of doubt, and no man could be completely ignorant of Reality. Moreover, the practice of Transcendental Meditation is such that it can be started from whatever level of faith a man may have, for it brings faith to the faithless and dispels the doubts in the mind of the sceptic by providing direct experience of Reality.

The previous verse demanded faith for the sake of gaining knowledge. This verse says that lack of faith results from ignorance. This apparent contradiction establishes the principle that faith and knowledge are interdependent from the most elementary to the most advanced stage, each deriving inspiration from the other while at the same time helping the other's growth.

VERSE 41

योगसंन्यस्तकर्माणं ज्ञानसंछिन्नसंशयम्
आत्मवन्तं न कर्माणि निबध्नन्ति धनंजय

Yogasaṁnyastakarmāṇaṁ gyānasaṁchhinnasaṁshayam
Ātmavantaṁ na karmāṇi nibadhnanti Dhananjaya

He who has renounced action by virtue of Yoga, O winner of wealth, whose doubts are rent asunder by knowledge, who is possessed of the Self, him actions do not bind.

'He who has renounced action by virtue of Yoga': 'he who in action sees inaction' (18); 'whose every undertaking is free from desire' (19); 'having cast off attachment to the fruit of action' (20); 'expecting nothing' (21); 'satisfied with whatever comes unasked' (22); 'freed from attachment, liberated ... his action is entirely dissolved' (23).

Here 'Yoga' means *Karma Yoga*. When, by the practice of *Karma Yoga* — the practice of Transcendental Meditation[60] supplemented by activity — one begins to live Being together with activity, one experiences It as separate from activity, and this experience of separation of one's Self from activity is called renunciation. Renunciation is thus gained automatically

60 See II, 45.

through the practice of Yoga. It may be noted that this state of renunciation is not limited to the mental level of thinking or the intellectual level of understanding: it is on the level of Being, on the level of life itself. It is a living reality for the realized man in Cosmic Consciousness.

'Whose doubts are rent asunder by knowledge': 'he … is wise among men … he is united' (18); 'whose action is burnt up in the fire of knowledge' (19); 'ever contented' (20); 'his heart and mind disciplined' (21); 'balanced in success and failure' (22); 'whose mind is established in wisdom' (23); 'so does the fire of knowledge turn all actions into ashes' (37).

Having stated that renunciation is achieved through the practice of *Karma Yoga*, the Lord here clarifies a very practical point on the path of enlightenment. As the practice of *Karma Yoga* advances, one begins to feel one's Self as separate from activity. This experience brings with it a feeling of confusion. One finds oneself active and yet inwardly one feels somewhat aloof from activity. Doubts begin to arise in the mind, and the intellect seeks for some explanation of the situation. Right understanding about the ultimate Reality is provided by the teaching of the preceding forty verses; when a man attains Cosmic Consciousness, the knowledge that Being is independent and separate from activity confirms that his experience is valid. It is this knowledge that removes all doubt about the nature of Reality. Without proper understanding, even the direct experience of eternal freedom may be found to create confusion and fear. The glory of knowledge is extolled here.

'Possessed of the Self': this is said of him 'who has renounced action by virtue of Yoga' and 'whose doubts are rent asunder by knowledge'. Someone who experiences himself as uninvolved with activity but has no clear understanding of this experience remains confused by it; in this state he fails to live Being fully, fails to possess the Self in Its full glory and grace. 'Possessed of the Self' indicates fixity in the Self for all time, the state of Cosmic Consciousness. Of such a man the Lord says: 'him actions do not bind'; because he is no more involved with actions, he ceases to identify himself with his activity. He has identified himself with eternal Being, he is 'possessed of the Self'.

Various implications of the expression 'possessed of the Self' have been explained in previous verses of this chapter: 'he has accomplished all action' (18); 'him the knowers of Reality call wise' (19); 'depending on nothing' (20); 'performing action by the body alone' (21); 'balanced in success and failure' (22); 'who acts for the sake of *Yagya*' (23).

VERSE 42

तस्मादज्ञानसंभूतं हृत्स्थं ज्ञानासिनात्मनः
छित्त्वैनं संशयं योगमातिष्ठोत्तिष्ठ भारत

Tasmād agyānasaṁbhūtaṁ hṛitsthaṁ gyānāsinātmanaḥ
chhittwainaṁ saṁshayaṁ yogam ātishthottishtha Bhārata

Therefore, having cut asunder with the sword of knowledge
this doubt of yours born of ignorance and rooted in the heart,
resort to Yoga. Stand up, O Bhārata!

The state of Union is full even in Transcendental Consciousness. But it is not considered to be the mature state of Union unless Transcendental Consciousness has become permanent in the state of Cosmic Consciousness. Thus we find that the Union gained in the state of Transcendental Consciousness reaches maturity in Cosmic Consciousness, which in turn finds fulfilment in God Consciousness.

'Yoga' here again means *Karma Yoga*, which requires a man to gain Transcendental Consciousness and engage in activity. When *Samādhi*, the state of Yoga, begins to be experienced, nothing more need be done for full enlightenment — for Cosmic Consciousness, or *Jīvan-mukti* — except regular practice of *Samādhi*, alternating with normal activity in practical life. For this reason the Lord urges Arjuna to 'resort to Yoga', to gain Transcendental Consciousness and be engaged in action. This, He says, will free Arjuna from all doubts. The Lord brings home to him that all misery is due to ignorance of the state of separation of Being from activity.

'Sword of knowledge': as the sharp edge of a sword is capable of cutting whatever it meets, so the state of knowledge, the awareness of Being as separate from activity, cuts asunder all doubts about the true nature of life and activity. Until this knowledge dawns, doubts are certain to remain. All doubts are due to 'ignorance' of this Reality, says the Lord.

'Born of ignorance and rooted in the heart': the doubt born of ignorance should belong to the mind, but the Lord says: 'rooted in the heart'. The heart is concerned with experience and the mind with understanding. When the Lord speaks of doubt as 'rooted in the heart', He means that even though the doubt is in the mind, it has its roots in the heart, which is devoid of the experience of Being and of the experience of Being as separate from activity.

The teaching is that it is necessary to experience Being and to understand clearly the separateness of Being from activity; thus enlightened, one should perform one's duty.

It should be stressed that the state of renunciation is not exclusive to either *Karma Yoga* or Sāṁkhya. It is a state that develops on both these paths. Whether one is following *Karma Yoga*, the practice of Transcendental Meditation supplemented by physical activity, or the path of Sāṁkhya, the practice of Transcendental Meditation supplemented by the mental activity of contemplation, one is sure to arrive at the experience of the state of renunciation.

Here is the essence of the teaching of this chapter: remove all doubts about Reality by means of the knowledge of Sāṁkhya, and engage yourself in the practice of *Karma Yoga*.

ॐ तत्सदिति श्रीमद्भगवद्गीतासूपनिषत्सु ब्रह्मविद्यायां योगशास्त्रे
श्रीकृष्णार्जुनसंवादे ज्ञानकर्मसंन्यासयोगो नाम चतुर्थोऽध्यायः

Oṁ tat sad iti Shrīmad Bhagavadgītāsūpanishatsu Brahmavidyāyāṁ Yogashāstre Shrīkṛishṇārjunasaṁvāde Gyānakarmasaṁnyāsayogo nāma chaturtho 'dhyāyaḥ

Thus, in the Upanishad of the glorious Bhagavad-Gītā, in the Science of the Absolute, in the Scripture of Yoga, in the dialogue between Lord Kṛishṇa and Arjuna, ends the fourth chapter, entitled: The Yoga of Knowledge of Renunciation of Action.

Chapter V

A Vision of the Teaching in Chapter V

Verses 1–3. Liberation is gained both through action and renunciation; but the path of action is superior, even though renunciation easily brings liberation from bondage.

Verses 4–10. The two paths are not considered separate by the wise. The seer of Truth sees them both as one; for renunciation is difficult to attain without Union with the Divine, which also brings freedom from the bondage of action.

Verses 11–13. Man established in Divine Union performs actions on the levels of the senses, mind, and intellect for the purification of his soul. Remaining in bliss within himself, he is uninvolved with action and its fruits.

Verses 14–16. In reality, authorship of action does not belong to the doer. All action is performed by the force of Nature. Under the spell of ignorance, the doer assumes authorship of action and becomes bound to its fruits. Knowledge brings the light of Truth and dispels the darkness of ignorance.

Verses 17–21. Established in that knowledge, wholly purified, in that state of profound equanimity, a man lives eternal freedom in the perpetual bliss of Divine Union.

Verses 22–3. The joys of the senses are sources of sorrow; the enlightened man does not delight in them. The ability to resist the excitement of desire and anger is the criterion of a man in Union.

Verse 24. Delighted in the Self, freed from desire and anger, man finds abiding freedom in Cosmic Consciousness and rises to eternal peace in God Consciousness.

Verses 25–9. The principle of renunciation comprehends the same height of human perfection as is achieved by the path of action.

IN the second chapter Lord Kṛishṇa enlightened Arjuna on the understanding of Sāṁkhya and Yoga so that he might be clear about the perishable and imperishable aspects of life and thereby, casting off his ignorance about the nature of life and its relationship with the field of action, realize his true divine nature in eternal freedom.

The Lord's inspiring words created in Arjuna's mind an urge to follow them. The third chapter brought to light the practice of *Karma Yoga*, action in the state of Union with the Divine, or action in order to make this Divine Union permanent, thus raising the dignity of both the doer and the action.

Continuing the teaching in the fourth chapter, Lord Kṛishṇa gave Arjuna a deeper understanding of the relationship of one's self with the field of action, making clear to him the state of separation that exists naturally between the inner Being and the outer phase of life in activity. This gave him insight into the reality of life and activity, and revealed to him that the inner Being is completely independent of action. Arjuna then perceived that activity does not belong to what life essentially is — Being in eternal freedom.

The fourth chapter has been called 'The Yoga of Knowledge of Renunciation of Action'. The title is significant. It tells us that according to this teaching Yoga, or Union, is gained through the knowledge of renunciation, through the knowledge of the Self as completely detached from activity. It establishes that the state of renunciation is natural on the levels both of cosmic and of individual life: on the cosmic level God remains uninvolved with the activities of creation and evolution; on the level of individual life the Self remains uninvolved with activity. A natural state of renunciation is the true basis of all life, and proper knowledge of it brings freedom from bondage. This is the essential teaching of the fourth chapter.

It might seem that the fourth chapter was challenging the doctrine of *Karma Yoga* taught in the third. But in fact this is not so. If the chapter had proclaimed enlightenment through renunciation of action, then it would have been contrary to the principle of *Karma Yoga*. But it proclaims enlightenment through the *knowledge* of renunciation of action. This makes it clear that the principle of renunciation is only to be understood; it is not to be practised. The state of renunciation is produced through *Karma Yoga* (IV, 41); there is no way of *practising* renunciation. Knowledge of renunciation is extolled here, not the practice of renunciation.

When we state that renunciation is not to be practised we are aware of the recluse way of life. But the renunciation of the recluse is renunciation of external things and is relevant only to a particular way of living; it is not in itself a way to God. It is not the practice of renunciation but the knowledge of it that helps on the way to God.

The knowledge of renunciation expounded in the fourth chapter is necessary for those on the path of *Karma Yoga* as well as for those on the path of Sāṁkhya. The state of renunciation is experienced on both paths, and unless the intellect is clear about the significance of this experience, doubts will remain and will impede further progress.

Karma Yoga and Sāṁkhya each start on the common ground of Transcendental Meditation. This leads directly to transcendental Self-consciousness, where even the most refined field of thought has been renounced and the Self stands alone in Its pure state of Being (verse 2). This is a state of complete renunciation, but it is reached only during meditation; it is not permanent. Through the regular and continued practice of meditation, alternating with activity — mental activity on the path of Sāṁkhya and physical activity on the path of *Karma Yoga* — transcendental Self-consciousness develops into Cosmic Consciousness, wherein one experiences the Self as separate from activity and lives the natural state of renunciation in daily life. The state of renunciation has become permanent. This state of Cosmic Consciousness develops further so that the separation between the Self and activity, which already presented the complete state of renunciation, dissolves into the ultimate Unity of God Consciousness. The state in which this separation has been resolved would seem to be beyond the range of renunciation, but it is, in fact, renunciation in its full perfection. Nothing now remains except pure life. The fourth chapter brings out the principle of renunciation in each of these states: Transcendental Consciousness, Cosmic Consciousness, and God Consciousness.

The knowledge given in that chapter has enriched the teachings about the paths of Sāṁkhya and *Karma Yoga* given in the second and third chapters. It has silently established the state of renunciation as common ground, a common milestone, and the common goal on both paths. The fifth chapter, taking advantage of the knowledge given in the fourth, explicitly places Sāṁkhya and *Karma Yoga* together, presenting them as equally useful in bringing eternal liberation in the midst of every activity.

It establishes a philosophy of Yoga, or Divine Union, through renunciation of action. This might be expected to contradict the philosophy of Yoga through action, *Karma Yoga*. But the Lord's theme is so marvellous that, far from offering any sense of contradiction with *Karma Yoga*, it succeeds in drawing together *Karma Yoga* and Sāṁkhya. Gloriously, it places them both on the same level of renunciation and, by showing the principles of these two paths to be in close proximity, it uses them both together to evolve a new philosophy of Yoga: the Yoga of renunciation.

Renunciation as such is plainly a state of loss. Yoga of renunciation thus means Yoga of loss: Union through loss. It is the glory of the Lord's discourse that loss becomes a means to perfection — renunciation comes forward to save life and bring fulfilment to it.

Without the philosophy of renunciation, the philosophy of action will always remain incomplete, because the renunciation of action lies at the opposite extreme to the performance of action. Just as separation contrasts with Union, so renunciation of action contrasts with the Yoga of action. Unless these two extremes, Union and renunciation, are taken into account the philosophy will be incomplete.

The philosophy of renunciation is not merely complementary

to the philosophy of action, nor just an essential part of that philosophy. Indeed, it can be considered as a complete philosophy of action in itself. The philosophy of renunciation is so complete that by remaining strictly within the boundaries of renunciation, and without having to consider the field of action at all, it is capable of upholding the philosophy of action. The whole philosophy of *Karma Yoga* can be explained through this philosophy of renunciation, because the basis of *Karma Yoga* is Transcendental Consciousness. And as the way to Transcendental Consciousness is through the withdrawal of the mind from the field of outside experience, it does not matter whether we consider the process of gaining Transcendental Consciousness in terms of activity towards the Transcendent or in terms of activity away from the field of outside experience. The first would express the principle in terms of *Karma Yoga*, the second in terms of renunciation. But one should not lose sight of the fact that renunciation does not offer any practice. The practical aspect of the philosophy of renunciation is to be found in the techniques of Sāṁkhya and *Karma Yoga*. The doctrine of renunciation does not provide an independent practice, and renunciation is therefore not a path in itself — it presents a theory based on the practices of other paths.

The principle of action having been brought out in Chapter III, and knowledge of renunciation in Chapter IV, Chapter V now expounds the compatibility of these two. The marvel is that it does so from the standpoint of renunciation, which is abstract, rather than from that of action, which is concrete. While combining the two extremes of action and renunciation, it combines the two different paths of Yoga and Sāṁkhya, and thus it gives expression to a complete philosophy of the integrated life. Here is a call to every man: Come by any path, and liberation will be yours.

This is what makes the Bhagavad-Gītā the Scripture of Divine Union. With ease it proclaims both the Yoga of action and the Yoga of renunciation of action. This is the perfection of the discourse from the lips of the Yogīshwara, Kṛishṇa, the Lord of the *Yogīs* of all time.

The most extreme contradictions are harmonized and unified in this chapter. It presents the state of eternal freedom in divine consciousness on the level of action based on renunciation. Moreover, it establishes the necessity of gaining divine consciousness for the sake of successful activity in daily life, and at the same time emphazises the need for activity to gain divine consciousness. By bringing into harmony the material and spiritual aspects of life, it opens a way both to success and to salvation for man, whether householder or recluse, in any age. It enables any man to glorify his world by the light of the Divine — and also to attain divine freedom in a most natural way through the daily activity of life.

Inexhaustible wisdom is contained in the twenty-nine verses of this chapter. It stands as a beacon not only for those who are miserable and confused, but also for seekers, and even for those who are well advanced on the path.

VERSE 1

अर्जुन उवाच
संन्यासं कर्मणां कृष्ण पुनर्योगं च शंससि
यच्छ्रेय एतयोरेकं तन्मे ब्रूहि सुनिश्चितम्

Arjuna uvācha
Saṁnyāsaṁ karmaṇāṁ Kṛishṇa punar yogaṁ cha shaṁsasi
yach chhreya etayor ekaṁ tan me brūhi sunishchitam

Arjuna said:
Thou praisest, O Kṛishṇa, renunciation of action and Yoga (of action) at the same time. Tell me decisively which is the better of these two.

Here is the proof of what the Lord has said: 'Even the wise are bewildered'[1] about the problem of action and inaction. Through all his utterances so far, Arjuna has shown himself to be wise, to have great foresight and to have knowledge of *Dharma*.[2] He will not act until he is sure of all the implications of his action.

1 See IV, 16.
2 See I, 23, 31, 36, 39–45.

This is the third question,[3] in the same spirit, that Arjuna has asked about the best course of action to follow for his own good and that of others. These repeated questions arise from his sincere desire to know the Truth; they are in keeping with a character that is without blemish and spring naturally from the state of one who seeks the Truth[4] and has surrendered himself to his master.[5]

If it had not been for these questions of Arjuna's, the great wisdom of this chapter and the next would not have been revealed, and the discourse of the Lord would not have been complete. For this reason those who seek the Truth will always be indebted to Arjuna. Commentators who have portrayed him as confused have missed the depth of his understanding. Arjuna asks profound questions again and again because, being a practical man of great intelligence, he does not wish to take anything for granted. He wants every detail of the plan to come from the Lord, because he knows that any small mistake on his part will prejudice the destinies of many generations to come.

The Lord has said: 'Unfathomable is the course of action.'[6] When such is the nature of action, there can be numberless flaws in any exposition of it, there can be an unlimited number of viewpoints about any one situation. That is why, to resolve the riddle of action for all time, the Lord told Arjuna: 'I shall expound to you that action, knowing which you will be freed from evil'.[7] He then went on to expound that eternal wisdom[8] which presents the solution to all problems of action and behaviour for all men of every age.

The Lord advocates the performance of action from that level of life where the mind is established in a state of freedom. This state can be lived without difficulty, but to describe it adequately in words is difficult. That is why the Lord asked Arjuna to 'Be without the three *Guṇas*'.[9] He would then actually come to experience the state of non-attachment described to him by

3 See II, 7; III, 2.
4 See IV, 34.
5 See II, 7.
6 See IV, 17.
7 See IV, 16.
8 See IV, 17–42.
9 See II, 45.

the teaching of Sāṁkhya.[10] The aspirant can be shown the path to follow, but it is hard to give him a definite picture of that state because it lies in the field which transcends all speech.

Because the very nature of action in freedom includes the states of action, inaction, and renunciation of action simultaneously, the Lord, in His exposition, has to speak sometimes in terms of action and sometimes in terms of inaction — sometimes of the Yoga of action and sometimes of the renunciation of action. It is the need to clarify these opposing statements that has given rise to Arjuna's present question. It does not spring from any inadequacy of his understanding.

The immediate reason for the question can be found in two expressions at the end of the fourth chapter: 'renounced action by virtue of Yoga' (verse 41) and 'resort to Yoga' (verse 42). The first presents Yoga as a means to renunciation, the second emphasizes the practice of Yoga after knowledge of renunciation has been gained. In one statement Yoga is the means and renunciation the goal; in the other renunciation is the means and Yoga the goal. Arjuna, noticing this apparent contradiction, raises the question which opens this chapter. His question is responsible for the flow of great wisdom from the Lord and not only presents the essence of the Lord's teaching so far, but also gives added momentum to the theme of the Lord's discourse.

VERSE 2

श्रीभगवानुवाच
संन्यासः कर्मयोगश्च निःश्रेयसकरावुभौ
तयोस्तु कर्मसंन्यासात्कर्मयोगो विशिष्यते

Shrī Bhagavān uvācha
Saṁnyāsaḥ karmayogash cha niḥshreyasakarāvubhau
tayos tu karmasaṁnyāsāt karmayogo vishishyate

The Blessed Lord said:
Both renunciation and the Yoga of action lead to the supreme good. But of the two, the Yoga of action is superior to the renunciation of action.

10 See II, 11–38.

'The renunciation of action' (*Sanyāsa*) may be interpreted in four ways. According to the first and more common understanding, a man detaches himself from all the activity of worldly life. According to the second, he takes to the practice of Transcendental Meditation[11] in order to renounce even the most refined state of thought and thus reach Self-consciousness. This is the whole concern of *Sanyāsa* — the renunciation of everything in the field of relativity and detachment from all aspects of life, gross and subtle. According to the third, entertaining activity after gaining Transcendental Consciousness, he rises to Cosmic Consciousness, in which he experiences the Self as completely separate from activity. Thus he attains a state of life in perfect renunciation. According to the fourth, entertaining the activity of the finest quality, devotion, he rises to God Consciousness, where the state of renunciation experienced in Cosmic Consciousness as separation of the Self from activity is transformed into a living link to unite the Self and activity. The two merge in the Unity of God Consciousness.[12]

'The Yoga of action' has been defined in the third chapter.[13] When the mind has retired from the field of activity and has reached the state of transcendental Self-consciousness, it comes back again into the field of activity. As the mind returns, the Self-consciousness infused into its nature enables the transcendental absolute Being to become harmonized with the field of activity. This bringing of the Divine into the world is the purpose of *Karma Yoga*. It reaches maturity in the state of Cosmic Consciousness and finds its fulfilment in God Consciousness.

In the state of Cosmic Consciousness the Self is realized as separate from activity, and this makes renunciation a living reality of daily life, bringing the blessings of eternal freedom. Thus we find that *Sanyāsa* and *Karma Yoga* run parallel. The Lord says: 'of the two, the Yoga of action is superior to the renunciation of action', because the process of renunciation is one of losing and the process of Yoga, or Union, is one of gaining; and gain is more acceptable to the mind than loss, all the more so when, in the process of Union, the mind experiences increasing charm

11 See II, 45.
12 See IV, 38.
13 See III, 3, 7, commentaries.

at every moment. Thus it is clear that to engage in the process of gaining Divine Union is easier for the mind than to engage in the process of renunciation of the world. This is what makes *Karma Yoga* superior to *Sanyāsa*. Moreover, the process of *Karma Yoga* automatically gives rise to the state of renunciation. When the mind proceeds towards the Transcendent, the state of Divine Union, it automatically recedes from the world, simultaneously producing the state of renunciation. Considered from this point of view, *Karma Yoga* is found to be the cause of renunciation. This in itself is a sufficient reason for the Lord to say that 'the Yoga of action is superior to the renunciation of action' even though both, running parallel and simultaneously, 'lead to the supreme good'.

The following verse considers the real *Sanyāsī*, the man who is established in the state of renunciation.

VERSE 3

ज्ञेयः स नित्यसंन्यासी यो न द्वेष्टि न कांक्षति
निर्द्वन्द्वो हि महाबाहो सुखं बन्धात्प्रमुच्यते

Gyeyaḥ sa nityasaṁnyāsī yo na dweshti na kāṁkshati
nirdwandwo hi Mahābāho sukhaṁ bandhāt pramuchyate

Know him to be ever a man of renunciation who neither hates nor desires; free from the pairs of opposites, he is easily released from bondage, O mighty-armed.

In this verse, the Lord brings out the essential qualities of 'a man of renunciation', a *Sanyāsī*. He is free from desire while at the same time he rejects nothing; he takes life easily as it comes, creating no tensions. His life flows freely in harmony with the Laws of Nature governed by the Cosmic Law.[14]

Such a carefree state of life in freedom is only possible when a man is contented. And contentment is possible only when the mind is established in Bliss Consciousness, the state of the transcendental Absolute, because in the relative field there is no happiness so intense that it could finally satisfy the thirst of the mind for joy.

Having gained this state of Transcendental Consciousness

14 See Appendix: Cosmic Law, The Basic Law of Creation.

permanently, a man is freed from bondage and lives a life in the eternal freedom of Cosmic Consciousness. In this state he lives eternal Being as completely separated from the field of activity. This is the state of perfect detachment, or *Sanyāsa*, described by the Lord as freedom 'from the pairs of opposites'. Such freedom prevails in Transcendental Consciousness, Cosmic Consciousness, and God Consciousness.

The word 'easily' is of great significance. Freedom from bondage is 'easily' gained by rising above 'the pairs of opposites' to the state of Being, by rising to that state of *Sanyāsa*, that state of separation which naturally exists between Being and activity.

The state of freedom from bondage can be reached either through the wisdom of Sāṁkhya or the practice of Yoga, as shown in the following verse.

Verse 4

सांख्ययोगौ पृथग्बालाः प्रवदन्ति न पण्डिताः
एकमप्यास्थितः सम्यगुभयोर्विन्दते फलम्

Sāṁkhyayogau pṛithag bālāḥ pravadanti na paṇḍitāḥ
ekam apyāsthitaḥ samyag ubhayor vindate phalam

The ignorant, and not the wise, speak of the path of knowledge (Sāṁkhya) and the path of action (Yoga) as different. He who is properly established even in one gains the fruit of both.

The teaching of Sāṁkhya brings to light the separation that exists between the imperishable and perishable aspects of life, between Being and activity. The practice of Yoga, by bringing Being into direct experience, also brings to light the separation that exists between Being and activity. This is how Sāṁkhya and Yoga both lead to freedom from bondage.

The phrase 'properly established' is of importance for a true understanding of the teaching of this verse. In order to be 'properly established' in the teaching of Sāṁkhya or Yoga, both understanding and experience are of vital importance. Sāṁkhya and Yoga are each sufficient in themselves to bring liberation. Therefore it does not matter whether the one or the other is given first importance.

'The wise' are those who have risen to the state of freedom. They do not see Sāṁkhya and Yoga as different, not only because both lead to the same goal, but also because the main feature of both is the same practice of Transcendental Meditation. The only difference is that on the path of *Karma Yoga* Transcendental Meditation alternates with activity on the level of the senses and on the path of Sāṁkhya with mental activity. But for this small difference Sāṁkhya and Yoga are the same. That is why the wise do not look upon them as different.[15]

This verse and the next present the whole purpose of the fifth chapter, which is to place Yoga and Sāṁkhya on the same footing as far as their results are concerned.

VERSE 5

यत्सांख्यैः प्राप्यते स्थानं तद्योगैरपि गम्यते
एकं सांख्यं च योगं च यः पश्यति स पश्यति

Yat sāṁkhyaiḥ prāpyate sthānaṁ tad yogair api gamyate
ekaṁ sāṁkhyaṁ cha yogaṁ cha yaḥ pashyati sa pashyati

The state attained by men on the path of knowledge is also reached by those on the path of action. He who sees Sāṁkhya and Yoga to be one, verily he sees.

This is the verse that promises liberation for both the ways of life, that of a householder and that of a recluse. It establishes the basic unity of Sāṁkhya and Yoga. Eternal liberation is their common goal, and the seer of Truth sees it to be so.

It is evident that the path of Sāṁkhya does not apply to the life of the householder and that *Karma Yoga* does. But Lord Kṛishṇa says here that the difference between the two paths is resolved when the goal is reached. Only an undeveloped intellect dwells on the differences between them. The wise man sets out upon one or the other and reaches the goal. He does not waste his time and energy in a scrutiny of distinctions.

15 See verse 5 and VI, 2.

The verse shows that Sāṁkhya and Yoga are designed to satisfy different kinds of people. But so far as their goal is concerned, they are the same.

This understanding of the matter finds further justification in verses 24 and 25, which describe the attainment of eternal liberation through Yoga and Sāṁkhya respectively, and in verse 21, which speaks of the attainment of immeasurable happiness through both paths.

Furthermore, by studying the details of the path of knowledge and that of action one finds that even the paths themselves are basically the same. The single process of Transcendental Meditation brings fulfilment to both.[16] That is why 'He who sees Sāṁkhya and Yoga to be one, verily he sees.'

The two paths start from and proceed on the common ground of Transcendental Meditation, and as they advance both give rise to the same experience of renunciation in Cosmic Consciousness. But having reached a common milestone in this direct realization of the separateness of Being from activity, they still have not attained their final goal. For complete fulfilment they must proceed further to merge in one goal, in the great Unity in God Consciousness.

Chapter V dwells mainly on the experience of renunciation common to both paths. Chapter VI will give details of their common practice of Transcendental Meditation and Chapters VII to XII will unfold the nature of their ultimate goal — God Consciousness — as well as the path to it.

VERSE 6

संन्यासस्तु महाबाहो दुःखमाप्तुमयोगतः
योगयुक्तो मुनिर्ब्रह्म नचिरेणाधिगच्छति

Saṁnyāsas tu Mahābāho duḥkham āptum ayogataḥ
yogayukto munir Brahm nachireṇādhigachchhati

Renunciation is indeed hard to attain without Yoga,
O mighty-armed. The sage who is intent on Yoga
comes to Brahman without long delay.

16 See III, 28, commentary.

This verse makes it quite clear that the state of renunciation 'is indeed hard to attain', that the separateness of Being from activity is hard to realize, unless the mind is firmly established in Being.

Here the word 'Yoga' does not mean either *Karma Yoga* or the practice of gaining Transcendental Consciousness;[17] it means the state of Union itself, Transcendental Consciousness.

The state of *Brahman*, which is the fullness of the relative and the Absolute both together, is best appreciated on the level of Union made permanent, Transcendental Consciousness made permanent. This state of Cosmic Consciousness gives the experience of *Sanyāsa*, the separateness of the Self from activity; the separateness of the relative and the Absolute here becomes a living reality.

The Lord is referring to this process of making the Union permanent when He says: 'without long delay'. This is because the state of Union, or Transcendental Consciousness, being blissful in its nature, is always inviting to the mind. The mind arrives at it drawn by its own nature, which is always to want to enjoy more. Thus the attainment of Union becomes easy, without resistance.[18]

The natural process of gaining this state need only be alternated with the natural activity of daily life to bring it to permanency. Thus it is clear that the whole process is a natural one; that is why it does not take a long time.

A man who has attained Cosmic Consciousness is always established in the Self, even while engaged in activity. This state of consciousness is the mature state of *Sanyāsa*, a state of complete non-attachment of the Self with activity, even while activity continues in the relative field of life. Such complete non-attachment is not possible unless the mind is established in eternal contentment. The constant practice of gaining Yoga, or Union with divine consciousness, brings the mind to the state which gives eternal contentment, thereby establishing a natural state of *Sanyāsa* or renunciation.

With growth towards Cosmic Consciousness, contentment grows, and with the growth of inner contentment, appreciation

17 See II, 40, 45.
18 See II, 40.

of the separation between Being and activity increases until the mind becomes rooted in the nature of Being. It has then achieved Cosmic Consciousness. By showing the difficulty of attaining renunciation without Yoga, the Lord indicates the simplicity of rising to a state where Yoga and *Sanyāsa* will become the daily habit of life.

This verse sings the glory of Union. It is the basis of true renunciation and gives rise to the state of *Brahman* in man's daily life.

The next verse shows how, by means of this Union, a man rises above the binding influence of action and lives a life of eternal freedom.

VERSE 7

योगयुक्तो विशुद्धात्मा विजितात्मा जितेन्द्रियः
सर्वभूतात्मभूतात्मा कुर्वन्नपि न लिप्यते

Yogayukto vishuddhātmā vijitātmā jitendriyaḥ
sarvabhūtātmabhūtātmā kurvann api na lipyate

Intent on Yoga, pure of spirit, he who has fully mastered himself and has conquered the senses, whose self has become the Self of all beings, he is not involved even while he acts.

Here, as in the previous verse, the word 'Yoga' does not mean either *Karma Yoga* or the practice of transcending; it is used in the sense of Unity of the mind with Being.

'Intent on Yoga': one who is never out of the Self, whether waking, dreaming, or in the state of deep sleep. Such a man is established in himself, and no experience of relativity is able to overshadow his status of absolute Being.

'Pure of spirit': one who has reached the state of Being, absolute consciousness, which is ever the same in its eternal purity, and who has established that state in the very nature of his mind. Action is a veil which hides this essential nature of the Self. Meditation is a process of diving through all the subtle levels of activity; when the subtlest level is transcended, the mind gains the state of pure Being. When the mind, being That, comes out into the field of activity, then the Self is said to shine forth in Its purity. When, through constant practice, complete integration of the Self with the mind is achieved, the pure status of Being gained by the mind is not in any way overshadowed even though the mind occupies itself with activity in the relative field. This is the state of Cosmic Consciousness, where the Self has separated Itself completely from the field of activity. In this state, where absolute Being and the relative world of activity are lived simultaneously, the self is said to have been permanently freed from all stain; it has achieved absolute purity.

'He who has fully mastered himself.' Self has two connotations: lower self and higher Self. The lower self is that aspect of the personality which deals only with the relative aspect of existence. It comprises the mind that thinks, the intellect that decides, the ego that experiences. This lower self functions only in the relative states of existence — waking, dreaming, and deep sleep. Remaining always within the field of relativity, it has no chance of experiencing the real freedom of absolute Being. That is why it is in the sphere of bondage. The higher Self is that aspect of the personality which never changes, absolute Being, which is the very basis of the entire field of relativity, including the lower self.

A man who wants to master himself has to master the lower self first and then the higher Self. Mastering the lower self means taking the mind (mind, intellect, ego) from the gross fields of existence to the subtler fields, until the subtlest field of relative existence is transcended and transcendental absolute unmanifested Being is reached in divine consciousness. This robs the lower self of its individuality bound by time, space, and causation and sets it free in the state of universal existence.

When the lower self has been mastered by the higher Self in this way and the higher Self has accepted it completely, then the two become one. And then a state develops in which each is found intimately within the realm of the other in complete cohesion of existence. When the divine consciousness of transcendental absolute Being is found in coexistence with the mind in relative existence, in the field of time, space, and causation, then the mastery of the higher Self is accomplished. The Absolute has been as it were brought out from the transcendental field of existence to serve and support the field of relativity. The never-changing is brought into the life of the ever-changing. The relative states of existence — waking, dreaming, and sleeping — are infused with the absolute state of Being. Eternal freedom has become infused into the field of bondage. The Unity of the divine nature is lived in the multiplicity of diversified creation. This enables a man to live a life of eternal freedom in a world of transitory existence. Thus the master of the Self, enjoying the whole field of relativity, lives the life of absolute Being in divine consciousness.

It is interesting to discover how the process of Transcendental Meditation succeeds in mastering both the self and the Self. The inward stroke of meditation takes one to a state where the mind, freed from individuality, surrenders itself to the higher Self. This is the mastery of the lower self. The outward stroke of meditation brings the mind out infused with Being. As a result of constant practice, the mind then lives absolute Being in all fields of relative life. This is mastery of the higher Self.

Thus mastery of the self and of the Self is accomplished by means of the inward and outward strokes of a single technique of Transcendental Meditation.

'Has conquered the senses': has mastery over them. In actual fact the senses are always under the command of the mind. Everyone knows that the eyes will see only if and when a man wishes to see. If he does not wish to see, he will not do so even with open eyes. Therefore victory over the senses seems to have no obvious meaning. The inner meaning of this expression is that, when Being first begins to be infused into the nature of the mind, the mind becomes as if intoxicated with a feeling of self-sufficiency. When the mind in this state acts through the senses, it behaves in a rather carefree manner, which may be thought of as akin to indifference.

In a more advanced state of enlightenment this peculiar sense of indifference diminishes, and the behaviour of the mind becomes more natural. Activity in the outer sphere of life becomes harmonized with the natural state of inner silence. Activity goes on as a result of the coordination between the mind and the organs of action. At the same time, coordination between the mind and the senses of perception enables the senses to register experience. With the infusion of Being into the mind, the senses of perception, while engaged in the process of experiencing, do not register deep impressions of experiences. The impressions they receive are just sufficient to enable them to experience, but are not deep enough to form the seed of future desires. This happens more and more effectively as the mind becomes more established in Being. Such, then, are the inner mechanics of mastering the senses.

A real conquest is that where the enemy ceases to be an enemy; he is left free to do as he likes, but is not in a position to attack or do any harm. The conquest of the senses is so fully accomplished through the mastery of the Self that the senses are left free to function and, notwithstanding all the experiences of the relative field, life is firmly established in the eternal freedom of divine consciousness.

Once the Self is experienced as separate from the senses and their activity, in the state of Cosmic Consciousness, a man sees within himself the state of unbounded Being on one side and involvement in the world of forms and phenomena on the other. He sees every living being as supported by that Being which is his own Self.

Thus he naturally experiences his Self as 'the Self of all beings', and in this state 'he is not involved even while he acts'.

This non-involvement can also be understood from another point of view. The light of a lamp is invisible in the light of the sun. The glory of the drop has no effect on the glory of the ocean. The joy of an action leaves no lasting impression upon the bliss of Cosmic Consciousness. Therefore once a man is established in this state, he naturally enjoys so great a fullness of Being that he never feels he is out of It. For him action does not involve coming out of the Self; there is, indeed, never any chance of his doing so. That is why the Lord says that 'he is not involved even while he acts'. He is firmly secured in cosmic existence which, though the very basis of all action, is without activity. For him it is as if everything were going by itself. This state is further described in the next two verses.

VERSES 8, 9

नैव किंचित्करोमीति युक्तो मन्येत तत्त्ववित्
पश्यञ्शृण्वन्स्पृशञ्जिघ्रन्नश्नन्गच्छन्स्वपञ्श्वसन्

Naiva kiṁchit karomīti yukto manyeta tattwavit
pashyan shriṇvan sprishan jighrann ashnan gachchhan swapan shwasan

प्रलपन्विसृजन्गृह्णन्नुन्मिषन्निमिषन्नपि
इन्द्रियाणीन्द्रियार्थेषु वर्तन्त इति धारयन्

Pralapan visrijan grihṇann unmishan nimishann api
indriyāṇīndriyārtheshu vartanta iti dhārayan

One who is in Union with the Divine and who knows the Truth will maintain 'I do not act at all'. In seeing, hearing, touching, smelling, eating, walking, sleeping, breathing, speaking, letting go, seizing, and even in opening and closing the eyes, he holds simply that the senses act among the objects of sense.

'One who is in Union with the Divine': the divine nature is completely separate from the field of activity. When this has been realized, the Self is experienced as independent of activity. Then the teaching of this verse becomes a living reality of daily life.

'One … who knows the Truth' is one who knows that life has two aspects, relative and absolute, and that the field of relative life is governed by the three *Guṇas*.[19] He knows through understanding and experience that the Self is separate from the field of activity.

This basic knowledge about the Self and the nature of activity creates a situation in the mind where the realized man is automatically established in the truth of the expression: 'I do not act at all'. It is not that he holds on to this thought artificially but that the very structure of his mind is based on this natural non-attachment. He lives this state. To him non-attachment is a living reality in daily life. He acts and experiences, making use of his senses, but within himself he is fixed in Being. He lives fullness

19 See III, 28.

of Being while fully engaged in the field of the senses. He lives twofold: the stability of changeless Being constitutes the inner core of his life, and on the periphery is found the activity of the sensory level — the senses engaged in the experience of their objects.[20] This is what the Lord means when He says: 'the senses act among the objects of sense'.

These two verses develop the idea expressed in the previous one. When, through the practice of Transcendental Meditation, Cosmic Consciousness has been gained, and the individual ego has expanded to cosmic status, the mind automatically functions from the level of its full potentiality and the senses, having reached their maximum development, function at their highest capacity. The objects of sense, however, remain in their unchanged state. That is why the senses, acting from their raised level, experience objects more completely, resulting in an even greater appreciation of the objects and thus providing experience of greater happiness on the sensory level. This creates a situation in which the objects of sense are enjoyed more thoroughly than before, but because Being is more fully grounded in the very nature of the mind, the impressions of sensory experience fail to capture the mind. The enlightened man thus naturally remains in a state where the senses continue to experience their objects while he remains free.

This is merely a comparative statement; it does not in any way imply that such a man becomes incapable of experience. It only means that, whereas before enlightenment experience in the world used to overshadow his Being, now his Being shines forth through all experience. Before enlightenment, if he saw a flower, the flower overwhelmed the mind so completely that only the flower remained and the experiencer was lost in the experience. The subject was as if annihilated by the object.

Life in which objects predominate, where matter alone is found and the values of the spirit or soul are overshadowed, is called material life. After enlightenment the flower is still seen, but the experience of the flower does not overshadow Being, because Being has been realized as separate from the field of activity, and thus the subject and the object are both separately

20 See III, 7.

maintained; both, so to speak, alive in their fullness. The flower fails to overshadow Being and at the same time the light of Being does not diminish the validity of the flower. Through the light of Being the flower is appreciated infinitely more, and this brings about the integration of spirit and matter. This is the glory of Transcendental Meditation: it brings enlightenment that integrates all the material values of life with the Divine.

VERSE 10

ब्रह्मण्याधाय कर्माणि सङ्गं त्यक्त्वा करोति यः
लिप्यते न स पापेन पद्मपत्त्रमिवाम्भसा

Brahmaṇyādhāya karmāṇi sangaṁ tyaktwā karoti yaḥ
lipyate na sa pāpena padmapattram ivāmbhasā

He who acts giving over all actions to the universal Being, abandoning attachment, is untouched by sin as a lotus leaf by water.

'Universal Being': *Brahman*, the ultimate Reality, the Absolute and the relative together at the same time.

The inward stroke of meditation leads the mind to Self-consciousness and infuses the state of Self-consciousness, Being, into the nature of the mind. The outward stroke of meditation brings such a mind into the field of action, where it acts with a certain degree of Being. This practice of meditation and the activity that follows it — morning and evening meditation and activity during the day — develop a state in which the nature of the mind becomes transformed into the state of Being, while the ability to act in all fields of practical life is fully maintained. Only when the mind, thus established in the Self, acts from that state of universal Being, is it possible to act 'giving over all actions to the universal Being'; in that state one has gained Cosmic Consciousness, which is the level of universal Being.

These words do not mean that a man should act while holding in his mind the thought of the universal Being. This verse does not teach an intellectually conceived surrender to the universal Being, or cherishing the thought of It, or making a mood of the Divine, or remembering God while working. It does not teach that any such attempts on the level of the mind or intellect can lead a man to a sinless state. All actions are given over naturally to the divine Being and all attachments are abandoned[21] naturally when, through the practice of Transcendental Meditation, the mind rises to the level of divine consciousness and maintains it permanently. When the self has completely separated itself from activity, then a situation is created in which the authorship of action becomes automatically transferred to the universal Being.

'Untouched by sin' means free from any wrong,[22] a life that is completely harmless, being in accordance with the Laws of Nature.[23] This state is gained in Cosmic Consciousness, in which the Self is completely separate from activity. It is in this state that actions are motivated by the power of Nature responsible for all creation and evolution. That is why they all produce life-supporting effects and no wrong is possible.

VERSE 11

कायेन मनसा बुद्ध्या केवलैरिन्द्रियैरपि
योगिनः कर्म कुर्वन्ति सङ्गं त्यक्त्वात्मशुद्धये

Kāyena manasā buddhyā kevalair indriyair api
yoginaḥ karma kurvanti sangaṁ tyaktwātmashuddhaye

By means of the body, by the mind, by the intellect,
and even by the senses alone, Yogīs, abandoning attachment,
perform action for self-purification.

Here the Lord makes clear the necessity of action for self-purification. Towards what state of self-purification does a *Yogī* aim when he performs action? Through the practice of *Samādhi*,[24] does not a *Yogī* already have a pure state of consciousness? Is not

21 See IV, 20; III, 30.
22 See II, 38.
23 See Appendix: Cosmic Law, The Basic Law of Creation.
24 See II, 53.

the practice of *Samādhi* sufficient to purify the soul? It seems not, for here the Lord is clearly expressing the need for performance of action for that degree of self-purification which is not gained by *Samādhi* alone.

'*Yogīs*': they who are united with the Divine in Transcendental Consciousness, Cosmic Consciousness, or God Consciousness.

When a *Yogī* has attained Cosmic Consciousness and has realized the Self as separate from the field of activity, he is able, by virtue of this realization, to entertain activity[25] while yet remaining in the eternal freedom of the Self. Because performance of action in this state of realization does not involve the Self, it naturally remains on the level of the 'body', 'mind', 'intellect', and 'senses'.[26]

The word 'alone' in this context is highly significant. It establishes without doubt and with all possible emphasis the separateness of the Self from the field of activity in the life of a realized man. Moreover, it also means that in this state of realization the body, the mind, the intellect, and the senses are capable of acting quite independently.[27]

During the practice of Transcendental Meditation, as the mind gains Transcendental Consciousness, the metabolism of the body is reduced to a minimum and the entire nervous system gains a state of restful alertness.[28] This is the physical condition corresponding to the state of Being. In this state, the mental and physical levels of the individual life come to the level of the cosmic life of omnipresent Being — the individual mind is held by cosmic intelligence and individual physical existence sustained by cosmic existence — they become Its instrument and begin to respond to the cosmic need.

When Cosmic Consciousness has been gained, this situation is made permanent. 'Body', 'mind', 'intellect', and 'senses' remain the instrument of the divine will, irrespective of their mode of activity. In this state the main motivating force of their activity is the divine will, the almighty cosmic intelligence, responsible for the creation and evolution of the entire cosmos. Just as

25 See VI, 1.
26 See III, 7.
27 See III, 7.
28 See IV, 38, commentary.

everything in nature responds to the need of cosmic purpose, so man's body, mind, intellect, and senses, brought to the level of cosmic intelligence, respond to the need of cosmic life. This is what the Lord means when He says: 'By means of the body, by the mind, by the intellect, and even by the senses alone, *Yogīs*, abandoning attachment, perform action'.

The significance of the expression 'abandoning attachment' in this context is that, in coming under the direct influence of the divine intelligence, the whole field of activity leaves the realm of the individual self, which then gains freedom from the binding influence of action. Because a man has risen to the level of divine Being, 'abandoning attachment' automatically becomes a living reality of his daily life, without the need to cultivate non-attachment at any time.

'Self-purification': pure consciousness is the pure state of the Self; it is of transcendental nature. The mind arrives at it by transcending even the subtlest experience of the relative field. When this state is alternated with activity, the mind gains pure consciousness permanently. Pure consciousness is then naturally maintained in spite of engagement in activity. In this state, the duality of life becomes a living reality — the two aspects of life, Self and non-Self, absolute and relative, become separated, and the Self is lived as pure Being unallied with anything.

This experience of the complete separateness of the Self and activity should mean the culmination of the process of 'self-purification'. But still the process continues, finally to give rise to that state of Unity which does not accept activity even as separate from the Self. Here the separateness responsible for giving rise to a sense of duality in the state of Cosmic Consciousness is transformed into the Light of God, allowing the duality of the Self and activity to merge into the homogeneity of divine existence in the oneness of God Consciousness. This state of the eternal Unity of life is the real culmination of the process of 'self-purification'.

The process of purification of the Self thus has three stages: first, from the waking state of consciousness to Transcendental Consciousness; second, from Transcendental Consciousness to Cosmic Consciousness; third, from Cosmic Consciousness to

God Consciousness. In all three stages it is necessary to 'perform action for self-purification'. Performance of action on the subtler levels of life enables one to transcend the field of activity and gain Transcendental Consciousness. By the alternation of Transcendental Consciousness with the normal, natural activity of daily life — the mental activity of discrimination in the life of a recluse and physical activity in the life of a householder — Transcendental Consciousness becomes permanent and gains the status of Cosmic Consciousness. Again, Cosmic Consciousness develops into God Consciousness by virtue of the most highly refined type of activity, the activity of devotion.

This is how the process of purification is carried on to its ultimate conclusion through the performance of action.

This verse brings out a technique for the performance of action in the state of Cosmic Consciousness, for it says: 'By means of the body, by the mind, by the intellect, and even by the senses alone, *Yogīs* ... perform action'. It has already been shown, in explaining the significance of the word 'alone', that action on this level is action in the state of Cosmic Consciousness, and this helps to transform Cosmic Consciousness into God Consciousness.

VERSE 12

युक्तः कर्मफलं त्यक्त्वा शान्तिमाप्नोति नैष्ठिकीम्
अयुक्तः कामकारेण फले सक्तो निबध्यते

Yuktaḥ karmaphalaṁ tyaktwā shāntim āpnoti naishthikīm
ayuktaḥ kāmakāreṇa phale sakto nibadhyate

He who is united with the Divine, having abandoned the fruit of action, attains to lasting peace. He who is not united with the Divine, who is spurred by desire, being attached to the fruit of action, is firmly bound.

Gaining Unity with the Divine is the key to gaining freedom[29] from the bondage of the fruits of action, and this in turn is the key to gaining lasting peace. Unity with the Divine is found in

29 See IV, 20.

three states: in Self-consciousness, which is of transcendental nature; in Cosmic Consciousness, which includes both the absolute and relative states of consciousness simultaneously — transcendental Self-consciousness together with the consciousness of the waking, dreaming, or sleeping state; and in God Consciousness, which holds together as one both the Self and the field of activity.

'Having abandoned the fruit of action': this expression runs parallel to the expression 'giving over all actions to the universal Being, abandoning attachment'.[30]

In the state of lasting peace, the inner and outer phases of life both grow so strong that ultimately they become completely independent of each other. Inner Being is experienced as wholly separate from activity, while activity grows so strong as to become completely independent of Being. Being and activity both rise to their full stature.

This is the state in which one lives in the Divine and in the world simultaneously, in which activity is carried on spurred by Nature and without a spur of desire in the self, in which one enjoys freedom from the bondage of action. This is the ideal of *Sanyāsa* — life in complete detachment from the world of action.

'Who is spurred by desire': who is not firmly established in the Self, or the Divine. Because he lacks such firmness, he remains attached to the fruits of action and, because of this, 'firmly bound' to the whole process of action from beginning to end.[31]

The present verse not only describes the state of one who is united with the Divine, but also of one who is not so united. It points out the mechanics of bondage: when a man is not united with the Self, or the Divine, the attachment to the fruits of action caused by desire is responsible for binding together the self and activity. It should not be lost to sight that this bondage is not real; for the self in its essential nature being eternally free, can never be bound. Only so long as he has not[32] realized this eternally free status of the self, does a man feel attached to activity and therefore remain in bondage. How he can come out of the bondage of desire is explained in the following verse.

30 See verse 10.
31 See IV, 18–20.
32 See verse 16.

Verse 13

सर्वकर्माणि मनसा संन्यस्यास्ते सुखं वशी
नवद्वारे पुरे देही नैव कुर्वन्न कारयन्

Sarvakarmāṇi manasā saṁnyasyāste sukhaṁ vashī
navadwāre pure dehī naiva kurvan na kārayan

Having renounced all action by the mind, the dweller in the body rests in happiness, in the city of nine gates, neither acting nor causing action to be done.

Mind is the link between the action and the actor, the self. As long as the mind is one-sided, subjected only to activity and without the direct influence of Being, it fails to be a successful mediator. It fails to safeguard the freedom of the self from the influence of action, and at the same time fails to safeguard action from the limitations of individuality, so that activity remains without the direct support of the almighty power of Nature.

This verse explains how the mind can become a successful mediator and bring strength, grace, and glory to action and freedom to life. The mind has to become as familiar with Being as it is with activity, and for this to happen it has first to come out of the field of activity and enter the sphere of Being. The present verse describes how, once out of the field of action,[33] the mind finds itself as the Self, completely unattached to activity, ever remaining in the absolute state, 'in happiness', a silent witness (*Sākshi-kūtastha*) of all events, 'neither acting nor causing action to be done'.[34]

'In happiness': happiness lies beyond the range of activity, where the 'self is untouched by external contacts'.[35] Once it has reached this state, the mind knows the truth of the relationship of the doer with his actions and with their fruits, which is proclaimed in the next verse.

33 See II, 55.
34 See verse 14.
35 See verse 21.

VERSE 14

न कर्तृत्वं न कर्माणि लोकस्य सृजति प्रभुः
न कर्मफलसंयोगं स्वभावस्तु प्रवर्तते

Na kartṛitwaṁ na karmāṇi lokasya sṛijati prabhuḥ
na karmaphalasaṁyogaṁ swabhāvas tu pravartate

The Lord creates neither the authorship of action nor the action of beings; nor does He create the link between (the doer), the action, and its fruits. Nature carries this out.

'Nor the action of beings': this makes it clear that beings create their own actions.

'Nor does He create the link between the doer, the action, and its fruits': the teaching is that the doer himself creates the link between himself and his action, while the link between the fruit of action and the doer is created by Nature.

'Nature carries this out': the nature of the doer creates action, and the nature of action creates the quality of the fruit. The fruit of an action is linked with the doer by the nature of the doer and his action.

This verse establishes emphatically the complete separateness of the inner divine Being and the outer field of action. It enlightens us about the state of perfect renunciation that naturally subsists between the inner and outer phases of life; for life is composed of activity on the outer surface together with the stability of Being within. In their essential nature there exists no[36] link between them. Just as a coconut has two different aspects, the outer hard cover and the inner milk within, one solid, the other liquid, without any link between them, so life has two aspects, one unchanging and eternal, the other ever-changing and relative, without any link between them.

The previous verse explained how the dweller in the body is unaffected by action. In the present verse, the Lord intends to convince Arjuna of the truth that action and the relation 'between (the doer), the action, and its fruits' belong solely to the

36 See IV, 18–20.

relative field of life, they belong to Nature; they have no bearing on the absolute status of Being.[37]

The purpose of creation is the expansion of happiness. The three *Guṇas*, born of Nature, are responsible for creation and its evolution; they are responsible for all the various divisions — the doer, the action, and the fruits. They alone underlie and are responsible for the creation, the maintenance, and the dissolution of everything in the universe, the subjective aspects of the inner life and the objective aspect of the outer world.

The authorship of action does not in reality belong to the 'I'. It is a mistake to understand that 'I' do this, 'I' experience this, and 'I' know this. All this is basically untrue. The 'I', in its essential nature, is uncreated; It belongs to the field of the Absolute, whereas action, its fruits, and the relationship between the doer and his action belong to the relative field, to the field of the three *Guṇas*.[38] Therefore all action is performed by the three *Guṇas* born of Nature. The attribution of authorship to the 'I' is only due to ignorance of the real nature of the 'I' and of action.

The theme of the Lord's teaching about the knowledge of action is developed in a remarkable way. In Chapter II, verse 48, the teaching was to abandon attachment, and the glory of such abandonment was sung in verses 64 and 71. The idea of abandoning attachment led to the teaching of non-attachment in Chapter III, verse 7. In the same chapter, verses 17 and 18 explained that non-attachment is attained by realizing the Self. Verse 19 established the dignity of action in this state of non-attachment gained through realization of the Self. Verse 25 gave a new turn to this theme by introducing the element of natural action. Verse 26 extolled natural action according to a man's level of evolution. Verse 27 explained that in reality all actions are performed by Nature, and that only the deluded assume the authorship of action; the enlightened man knows that the *Guṇas* interact amongst themselves, that the whole field of activity belongs to the field of the *Guṇas,* and that the Self remains uninvolved in their activity. Verse 30 introduced the element of God, to whom all actions of the three *Guṇas* may be surrendered

37 See IV, 18–20.

38 See III, 27–8.

as a means of separating the field of activity from the Self. Verse 33 refuted the need for control in bringing about such surrender of action to God and again extolled action according to a man's nature, free from any control. Verse 39 introduced the idea that ignorance of the Self is responsible for bondage. Verse 43 raised the sword of knowledge to cut asunder this ignorance.

The development of the teaching thus far led to the principle that action is necessary for coming out of the field of bondage. The fourth chapter began to expound the nature of the Lord as separate from the incessant activity of the universe. This introduced the exposition of the knowledge of the renunciation of action, which is developed throughout the fourth chapter and in the earlier verses of this chapter until the present verse proclaims that there exists absolutely no relationship 'between the doer, the action, and its fruits'. This is true on both levels of life — the level of cosmic life and the level of individual life. The present verse puts the point clearly when it says that 'the Lord creates neither the authorship of action nor the action of beings', meaning that He does not create anything; He remains completely aloof from the incessant activity of creating.

This is the situation on the cosmic level. The same situation is found on the level of individual life, because there exists no real link 'between the doer, the action, and its fruits'. This eliminates all need for any doing, for any attempt at Self-realization. Abandoning all attempts at realization and living in the state of fulfilment is that high state, renunciation, which finds its consummation in the state of knowledge,[39] in God Consciousness. This is the glory of renunciation.

The most evolved state of life in eternal freedom is readily available in a most natural way to everyone. The sufferings and the joys of life come to man through the ignorance of this, says the next verse, and the glory of knowledge is extolled in the verse that follows it.

39 See IV, 38.

VERSE 15

नादत्ते कस्यचित्पापं न चैव सुकृतं विभुः
अज्ञानेनावृतं ज्ञानं तेन मुह्यन्ति जन्तवः

Nādatte kasyachit pāpaṁ na chaiva sukṛitaṁ vibhuḥ
agyānenāvṛitaṁ gyānaṁ tena muhyanti jantavaḥ

The all-pervading Intelligence does not accept the sin or even the merit of anyone. Wisdom is veiled by ignorance. Thereby creatures are deluded.

'The all-pervading Intelligence' is the absolute Being. Because It is all-pervading, It is of transcendental nature, and because It is transcendent, It lies out of the influence of action. It is the silent witness of the whole of relative life.

The previous verse made it clear that the authorship of action truly belongs to the three *Guṇas*. Therefore no agency other than that of the three *Guṇas* is involved in creating good or bad results.

The state of enlightenment is obscured by ignorance, and 'Thereby creatures are deluded.' The knowledge of the Divine as uninvolved with the field of action, and the knowledge of one's own Self as divine Being, bring freedom to life, whereas ignorance of this truth is responsible for the delusion that it is the Divine which bestows the fruits of one's actions. Here the Lord intends to show that the unrealized state is the cause of the bondage of action and involvement in sin and virtue.

Reality is known in two ways: with reference to the Absolute[40] and with reference to the relative.[41] The *Guṇas* are responsible for action and for everything in the field of relative existence, and the Lord, 'the all-pervading Intelligence', remains completely uninvolved.[42] This is how It, the divine Intelligence, or He, the Lord, remains in eternal freedom. Those who rise to this supreme knowledge[43] gain eternal freedom; others remain in bondage.

The following two verses throw more light on this.

40 See II, 45.
41 See III, 27–8.
42 See verse 14.
43 See IV, 38.

VERSE 16

ज्ञानेन तु तदज्ञानं येषां नाशितमात्मनः
तेषामादित्यवज्ज्ञानं प्रकाशयति तत्परम्

Gyānena tu tad agyānaṁ yeshāṁ nāshitam Ātmanaḥ
teshām ādityavaj gyānaṁ prakāshayati tat param

But in those in whom that ignorance is destroyed by wisdom, wisdom, like the sun, illumines That which is transcendent.

'Ignorance': about the separateness of the inner and outer aspects of life, about Being as uninvolved with activity, about the real nature of the 'I' and the world, about the permanent and the ever-changing aspects of life, about the nature of freedom and bondage.

'That ignorance': the use of the word 'that', and not 'this', conveys the idea that ignorance is away from oneself. In its nature it is foreign to the Self.

In depicting wisdom as destroying ignorance, this verse shows that the destruction of ignorance and the illumination of the transcendent Being by wisdom go hand in hand. The sun removes the darkness and spreads the light at the same time. This indicates that when ignorance has been destroyed by wisdom, nothing more need be done to realize the Transcendent. It is omnipresent, veiled only by ignorance, and when this veil has been destroyed by knowledge, It shines forth in Its own light. That is why wisdom is attributed to the nature of the Absolute, the transcendent Being — wisdom is the Absolute; as the Upanishads have proclaimed: '*Pragyānaṁ Brahm*'.

This verse makes it clear that ignorance is destroyed by gaining knowledge, and not that knowledge is gained by destroying ignorance. Therefore the seeker has not to try to come out of ignorance; rather, he should try to gain knowledge through direct experience.[44]

It may be interesting to mention here that life, held as one

44 See IV, 38.

by ignorance, is torn apart by the analysis of Sāṁkhya into two different components, the changing and the unchanging.[45] These are cognized as two different fields of life by direct experience through Yoga.[46] The understanding gained through Sāṁkhya is confirmed by Yoga: when, in Cosmic Consciousness, one begins to live life in a state where the Self remains uninvolved with activity,[47] then the truth of the teaching of Sāṁkhya becomes significant in practical life. This enables man to live in the awareness that the two phases of life, relative and absolute, are separate from one another, and that even in the relative field, sin and virtue, which result in suffering and joy, each arise from attachment of the self to activity, which in turn arises from lack of knowledge.

VERSE 17

तद्बुद्धयस्तदात्मानस्तन्निष्ठास्तत्परायणाः
गच्छन्त्यपुनरावृत्तिं ज्ञाननिर्धूतकल्मषाः

Tadbuddhayas tadātmānas tannishthās tatparāyaṇāḥ
gachchhantyapunarāvṛittiṁ gyānanirdhūtakalmashāḥ

Their intellect rooted in That, their being established in That, intent on That, wholly devoted to That, cleansed of all impurities by wisdom, they attain to a state from which there is no return.

This verse unites Yoga and Sāṁkhya in their common goal of absolute purity and eternal liberation. It supports the truth of verses 4 and 5, which proclaim the theme of this chapter.

The words 'intellect' and 'being' are of great significance, and so is the sequence in which they are used. It teaches that when the intellect is rooted in That, the whole of one's being also becomes 'established in That'. Moreover, when, during meditation, the intellect becomes 'rooted in That', on coming

45 See II, 11–38.
46 See II, 45.
47 See II, 48.

out of the Transcendent it remains 'intent on That'. When the intellect becomes 'intent on That', one's being becomes 'wholly devoted to That'.

The word 'being' has been chosen here to translate the Sanskrit word '*Ātmā*', which is variously used to mean the Self, the intellect, the mind, the breath, and the body. Therefore the expression 'being' becomes 'wholly devoted to That' means that the mind, the breath, and the body all become orientated[48] towards 'That'.

The Lord shows that unless the intellect and the whole of one's being are established in the transcendent Reality, they are not pure; they remain in the realm of temporary existence, unconnected with the state of eternal freedom whence 'there is no return'. Unless the transcendent absolute phase of life is realized, the scope of the individual phase of life remains insignificant and its purpose is not fulfilled; bondage continues and the cycle of birth and death meets no end.

This verse makes it clear that purity of life, which is the basis of all success in the world and at the same time the basis of eternal freedom, is gained by wisdom — realization of the Transcendent. It also states the principle that, unless a man has stabilized this absolute state of purity in his life by rising to the state of Cosmic Consciousness, there may always be the possibility of his stepping down to a lower level of life. This means that as long as Transcendental Consciousness has not become permanent, the effect of morning meditation does not persist in its full intensity throughout the day. As the hours go by, the intensity of the effect diminishes, and with this the level of purity in life falls, until the evening meditation restores it.

'Be without the three *Guṇas*', as explained by the Lord in the 45th verse of the second chapter, is the key to realizing the teaching of this verse in daily life.

Life finds its goal in the state of the eternal freedom of the Transcendent, spoken of here as 'That': Knowledge Itself.[49] The use of the word 'That' makes it clear that the goal of life does not lie in the sphere of phenomenal existence; it lies beyond it.

48 See IV, 38.
49 See IV, 38.

The real life is not this which is commonly referred to as life; beyond this is That Reality of life. This is a teaching of life from the standpoint of renunciation.

The Upanishads declare: '*Tat Twam Asi* — That Thou Art', implying that this obvious phase of phenomenal existence, which you take as your self, is not your real nature — you, in fact, are That transcendent Reality.

'Cleansed of all impurities by wisdom': refer to verses 35 to 38 of Chapter IV.

'From which there is no return': as long as the self is not embedded in the eternity of life, as long as the mind has not permanently gained absolute purity in Transcendental Consciousness, life remains within the relative field of existence. In this situation the cycle of birth and death continues within the various strata of the evolution of life.[50] When one has gained Cosmic Consciousness, life goes beyond the sphere of birth and death. For being eternal it is changeless; it cannot partake of change. It should be clearly noted that this situation can only be created during man's life on earth. It is as a man that one rises to that 'state from which there is no return'. The way to it lies in the principle described in the 45th verse of Chapter II.

The following verse also is concerned with transcending the diversity of form in creation, and it portrays the oneness of life everywhere. It continues the teaching of the renunciation of this to find That.

VERSE 18

विद्याविनयसंपन्ने ब्राह्मणे गवि हस्तिनि
शुनि चैव श्वपाके च पण्डिताः समदर्शिनः

Vidyāvinayasaṁpanne Brāhmaṇe gavi hastini
shuni chaiva shwapāke cha paṇḍitāḥ samadarshinaḥ

In a Brāhmaṇa endowed with learning and humility,
in a cow, in an elephant, in a dog, and even in one who
has lost his caste, the enlightened perceive the same.

50 See VI, 41.

This verse provides a criterion of vision in the state of enlightenment. Those who have realized the Reality of life 'perceive the same' oneness through all the diversity of experience.

'*Brāhmaṇa*': a man born in a *Brāhmaṇa* family, whose life is dedicated to the study of the Veda and spiritual learning. The use of this word in conjunction with cow, elephant, and dog indicates that the Lord wants to emphasize that the Being of an evolved man and that of the animals is the same; and that, established in the oneness of Being, and having realized the Unity of the Transcendent underlying all diversity, he gains evenness of vision.

'Learning and humility': wisdom brings humility. Just as the wise man sees the distinctions and differences in creation as only temporary, with one ultimate Reality underlying them all, so he does not insist that things should happen in any particular way. He takes things lightly, for he knows they all have their common end. This natural quality of Being in the wise is interpreted as humility. Indeed, humility is the criterion of wisdom, arising as it does out of the increased sense of the oneness of life, of the basic Unity of all beings.

Humility is commonly understood to be the honest recognition of one's personal limitations, one's ignorance and insignificance; but true humility lies in the quality of Being and not in any attitude of mind.

The mind of the realized man is fully infused with the state of Being — the oneness of life — and such a mind naturally has oneness of vision irrespective of what it sees. The apparent distinctions of relative existence fail to create division in its view.

This does not mean that such a man fails to see a cow or is unable to distinguish it from a dog. Certainly he sees a cow as a cow and a dog as a dog, but the form of the cow and the form of the dog fail to blind him to the oneness of the Self, which is the same in both. Although he sees a cow and a dog, his Self is established in the Being of the cow and the Being of the dog, which is his own Being. The Lord stresses that the enlightened man, while beholding and acting in the whole of diversified creation, does not fall from his steadfast Unity of life, with which his mind is saturated and which remains indelibly infused into his vision.

'A *Brāhmaṇa* endowed with learning and humility' represents all that is dominated by the influence of *Sattwa*. 'A cow' represents all that is dominated by the mixed influence of *Rajas* and *Sattwa*. 'A dog' represents all that is dominated by *Rajas* and *Tamas*. 'An elephant' represents all that is dominated by the influence of *Tamas*. 'One who has lost his caste' represents the lowest in human life, a man living in complete ignorance, who has lost the path of his evolution. The meaning is that one who has realized the Self as separate from the field of relative existence is steadfast in himself and quite untouched by the influence of *Sattwa*, *Rajas*, or *Tamas* and tendencies that arise from them. He has evenness of vision everywhere.

The following verse shows the primary importance of such oneness of vision.

VERSE 19

इहैव तैर्जितः सर्गो येषां साम्ये स्थितं मनः
निर्दोषं हि समं ब्रह्म तस्माद् ब्रह्मणि ते स्थिताः

Ihaiva tair jitaḥ sargo yeshāṁ sāmye sthitaṁ manaḥ
nirdoshaṁ hi samaṁ Brahm tasmād Brahmaṇi te sthitāḥ

Even here, in this life, the universe is conquered by
those whose mind is established in equanimity. Flawless,
indeed, and equally present everywhere is Brahman.
Therefore they are established in Brahman.

When the mind, through the practice of Transcendental Meditation, rises to the state of Cosmic Consciousness, absolute Being becomes permanently established in the nature of the mind, and it attains the state of *Brahman*, the universal Being. Then the mind finds itself on a level of life from which all the gross and subtle levels of creation can be stimulated, controlled, and commanded. It is like a gardener who knows how to work at the level of the sap and can influence the whole tree in any way he likes. Someone who is acquainted with the atomic or sub-atomic level of an object, by working on that level could easily bring about a desired change in any stratum of the object's existence. This is what the Lord means when He says: 'Even here, in this life, the universe is conquered by those whose mind is established in equanimity', in the serenity, the calmness,[51] which is the ultimate level of life.

This verse reveals the status of the established intellect, described here as the state in which 'the universe is conquered'. Contentment, power, wisdom, and the ability to support all things are obvious qualities of a conqueror of the world. These qualities, and many more besides, are found in the nature of a man who, while living in the world, has gained equanimity of mind. That stable state of evenness of mind in the eternal oneness of Reality belongs to the field of pure consciousness, or omnipresent Being, which is the very source of life-energy, the reservoir of eternal wisdom, the origin of all power in Nature, and the fountainhead of all success in the world.

As long as the mind has not risen permanently to the state of Being and cognized the field of activity as separate from itself, so long does it continue to be involved with activity. Indeed, it is like a slave to activity, a slave to the universe. But when it gains stability in Being and acquires a natural state of equanimity, then it finds the universe as separate from itself, responding quite automatically, like a servant, to its every need. This state of separateness of Being from activity, which is the basis of equanimity of mind, is gained through both Yoga[52] and Sāṁkhya.[53]

VERSE 20

न प्रहृष्येत्प्रियं प्राप्य नोद्विजेत्प्राप्य चाप्रियम्
स्थिरबुद्धिरसंमूढो ब्रह्मविद्ब्रह्मणि स्थित:

Na prahṛishyet priyaṁ prāpya nodwijetprāpya chāpriyam
sthirabuddhir asaṁmūdho Brahmavid Brahmaṇi sthitaḥ

He who neither greatly rejoices on obtaining what is dear to him, nor grieves much on obtaining what is unpleasant, whose intellect is steady, who is free from delusion, he is a knower of Brahman, established in Brahman.

51 See VI, 3.
52 See II, 48.
53 See II, 38.

This verse describes the nature of the enlightened man's mind. He stands for full Reality, the relative and the Absolute together. Such a man certainly has his own likes and dislikes, he has his own joys and sorrows in the relative field, but they do not take him out of himself; this meaning is clear from the words 'greatly', qualifying 'rejoices', and 'much', qualifying 'grieves'. It shows that a realized man, even though established in divine consciousness, keeps his feet on the ground. Remaining on the human level, he is divine.

When the mind is deeply rooted in the Bliss Consciousness of the Self, it naturally remains unaffected by the attachment or aversion present[54] in the objects of the senses. This is the reason why the enlightened man neither 'rejoices' nor 'grieves'. It is a common experience even in worldly life that when the mind is deeply rooted in one thing it fails to register deeply experiences of other matters. If the idea of catching an aeroplane on time engages the mind fully, none of the many objects that are seen and sounds that are heard while one is driving through the streets will deflect the mind from the air terminal. In such circumstances the experience of the other things remains on the surface level of sensory perception and makes only a very faint impression on the mind. If this can happen within the waking state of consciousness, how much more so when another state of consciousness overtakes the mind.

The mind of an enlightened man is active in the manifested world, but fails to register deeply the experience of that world. His intellect is steady in its own inner light, the light of the Self. He is awake in himself and yet is awake in the outer world. He lives the Divine in the world; he lives the Absolute and the relative together. Therefore 'he is a knower of *Brahman*, established in *Brahman*'.

Consider a man in the waking state of consciousness, engaged in the experience of the outside world, while at the same time he carries the experience of the dreaming state of consciousness in his mind. For him the experiences of the waking state are certainly more concrete than those of the dreaming state, but the two types of experience coexist. This makes it clear that it

54 See III, 34.

is possible for a man to be in one state of consciousness and yet accept the experience of another state of consciousness at the same time. When, through meditation, one gains Transcendental Consciousness, its self-sufficiency is so overwhelming that even in the waking state of consciousness one maintains within oneself the influence of Being. Moreover, when the maintenance of Being in the active mind becomes full and permanent, the entire activity of the waking state is found only on the very surface of the mind. This is the state of Cosmic Consciousness, in which activity is experienced as separate from Being.

It will be noticed that the Lord describes two conditions that have to be fulfilled if a man is to become realized. The first is that he should be a 'knower of *Brahman*', that is, he should have a clear intellectual understanding of Reality. This condition belongs to the sphere of Sāṁkhya. The second condition is that he should be 'established in *Brahman*', that is, he should have direct experience of divine nature so that his daily life becomes its expression. This condition belongs to the field of Yoga.

Therefore this verse too upholds the teaching of verses 4 and 5 of the present chapter and also that of the last verse of Chapter IV in that it satisfies both Sāṁkhya and Yoga on the level of renunciation. It describes the inner state of renunciation of a realized man, whether he has realized through Yoga or through Sāṁkhya.

Because he has realized the independent nature of the Self, such a man is without delusion about his own identity; this makes the intellect steady. This steadiness of intellect is the state of life in which he 'neither greatly rejoices on obtaining what is dear to him, nor grieves much on obtaining what is unpleasant'.

The present verse brings to light the natural state of renunciation in the life of a realized man, who does not rejoice in anything external. The following verse explains the reason for his renunciation: he is fixed in the bliss of his own Being.

Verse 21

बाह्यस्पर्शेष्वसक्तात्मा विन्दत्यात्मनि यत्सुखम्
स ब्रह्मयोगयुक्तात्मा सुखमक्षयमश्नुते

Bāhyasparsheshwasaktātmā vindatyātmani yat sukham
sa Brahmayogayuktātmā sukham akshayam ashnute

He whose self is untouched by external contacts knows that happiness which is in the Self. His self joined in Union with Brahman, he enjoys eternal happiness.

'Self is untouched by external contacts': in order to gain the experience of the inner Self in the transcendental state of consciousness, the experience of outside objects has to be eliminated. Through constant experience, the Self becomes so familiar to the mind that the very nature of the mind is transformed into the nature of the Self. Then Transcendental Consciousness is maintained together with the waking state of consciousness, which continues to support all activity as it did before. By virtue of the permanent maintenance of Transcendental Consciousness, the Self is always experienced as Self. And simultaneously, by virtue of the waking state of consciousness, activity continues to be experienced. This is how the Self is experienced as separate from activity. In this state the self is lost forever; it has become the Self.

With the loss of the self, the contact of the self with objects through the agency of the mind and senses, which was responsible for giving rise to experience, becomes non-existent. What remains is the Self in Its pure nature of Bliss Consciousness, devoid of any contact with the objects that were held by the self. This is what the Lord means when He says: 'He whose self is untouched by external contacts'. Now that the Self is forever established in Its own essential nature, Bliss Consciousness has become permanent. When this Bliss Consciousness comes in contact with objects, it produces a state described by the expression 'self joined in Union with *Brahman*'. This is because *Brahman* is the state of Cosmic Consciousness, which embraces activity and Bliss Consciousness.

'Joined in Union with *Brahman*': this expression, together with 'self is untouched by external contacts', presents a criterion whereby a seeker can know when he has gained '*Brāhmī-sthiti*',[55] or the state of *Brahman* — Cosmic Consciousness. While the mind is experiencing objects through the senses, he is awake in the awareness of his self as separate from the field of experience and action. This then is the state of Cosmic Consciousness, in which he is awake in the world and awake in himself.

Many commentators have done great injustice to the teaching of this verse by suggesting that it describes a technique of enjoying the bliss of the Self by means of constructing a mood of remaining unaffected while experiencing joy through the objects of the senses. Many translations have treated the original text in a way which, while consistent with the grammar of the verse, presents a false picture of its teaching and is contrary to the essential principle of action and of renunciation.

It is the permanency of Bliss Consciousness gained through the Yoga of action, and again it is the state of renunciation gained through the Yoga of renunciation based on Bliss Consciousness that keep the Self unaffected during the experience of joy; it is not the intellectual practice of trying to hold the mind back and keep it unaffected during the process of experience that brings one to Bliss Consciousness and to the state of renunciation, where the Self is experienced as separate from activity. It is because the Self is joined in Union with *Brahman* that a man enjoys eternal happiness.

The reason why the joys of the senses cannot make a deep impression on the enlightened man is that his self has become Self, which is wholly blissful in nature. Being wide awake in cosmic intelligence, his natural stand is at the fountainhead of all the joys of all the senses. Being permanently established in absolute bliss, the temporary joys of relative existence fail to fascinate his self. Even when sensory objects come into contact with his senses, the joys of such contacts are not so powerful as to distract the self from its natural state of Bliss Consciousness. This is why his self remains unaffected while his senses are fully

55 See II, 72.

in contact with their objects.

The expressions 'self is untouched by external contacts', 'knows that happiness which is in the Self', and 'his self joined in Union with *Brahman*' place Sāṁkhya and Yoga on a common basis, thus upholding verses 4 and 5, which contain the essence of the teaching of this chapter.

Verse 22

ये हि संस्पर्शजा भोगा दुःखयोनय एव ते
आद्यन्तवन्तः कौन्तेय न तेषु रमते बुधः

Ye hi saṁsparshajā bhogā duḥkhayonaya eva te
ādyantavantaḥ Kaunteya na teshu ramate budhaḥ

All pleasures born of contact are only sources of sorrow;
they have a beginning and an end, O son of Kuntī.
The enlightened man does not rejoice in them.

This verse contrasts with the previous one in that it explains the principle of the unattached state of the Self, and at the same time complements it by clarifying the principle of happiness and suffering.

'Contact': as in the previous verse, this means contact of the self with the field of activity or experience. It depicts the state in which the self does not remain untouched, the state in which the self remains involved with the field of experience and joys of the senses. Such joys are 'sources of sorrow' by virtue of the self being involved with them. If, however, the Self remains untouched, then the joys of the senses are not sources of sorrow, for in that state the Self is established in eternal happiness.

When the mind begins to take delight in the objects of the senses, this shows that its delight is not within; the mind is not anchored to the bliss of the Self, it is absorbed in the outer direction away from bliss. If the mind no longer faces in the direction of bliss, and if it is not neutral, then it is obviously turned towards sorrow. Therefore when the mind is absorbed in outer joys, then it is absorbed in the field of sorrow. Anything that leads the mind in an outward direction becomes a source of sorrow.

This truth about the enjoyments of the world is valid when considered from the level of Cosmic Consciousness and from that of God Consciousness, the ultimate Reality of life. Seen from the ordinary level of the consciousness of man, to say that the 'pleasures born of contact are only sources of sorrow' seems absurd. Yet even on this level of consciousness the same principle applies: they 'are only sources of sorrow', the reason being that 'they have a beginning and an end'.

'The enlightened man does not rejoice in them': established in the state of eternal happiness, in *Brāhmī-sthiti*, and experiencing the Self as separate from activity, he has by nature risen above the phenomenal phase of life, above the fleeting joys of the relative field, and so he is not in a state where he can rejoice in temporary joys. When a retailer becomes a wholesale merchant he no longer deals in the retail field, which requires more effort and produces less profit.

The experience of the objects of the senses in the waking state differs from that in the state of Cosmic Consciousness. It may be likened to the experience of objects through glasses of different colours, whereby the same object is experienced differently. The enlightened man is simply not in a position to 'rejoice in them' as he did before realization, because of the difference in his state of consciousness.

'Sources of sorrow': the intensity of happiness that one can enjoy depends on the level of one's consciousness. At every level of consciousness there is a corresponding intensity of happiness. This principle applies also to intelligence and power.

The difference between the consciousness of the enlightened man and that of the unenlightened is as great as that between the Absolute and the relative, between light and darkness. For this reason the joys of the senses, which delight the ignorant, are looked upon as sources of sorrow by the wise. In comparison with the eternal bliss of the Absolute, in which the enlightened are naturally established, the fleeting joys of the world 'are only sources of sorrow'. When the Lord uses these words, it is to express the truth and at the same time strike hard at the minds of those who are engrossed in such joys and whose vision is thus blinded.

If the self delights in the experience of objects, since the objects are changing, the delight will soon be lost. This loss of pleasure will give rise to suffering. That is why the Lord says: 'they have a beginning and an end... The enlightened man does not rejoice in them.' He who lacks contact with inner Being becomes engrossed in external pleasures.

'They have a beginning and an end': this expression presents a contrast with 'eternal happiness' in the previous verse. When one joy comes to an end, the self is subjected to a state without joy which, in contrast with the experience of joy, is suffering. But if the Self has gained a state of perpetual happiness, then It is left with no possibility of suffering. Absence of Bliss Consciousness is the source of sorrow.

VERSE 23

शक्नोतीहैव यः सोढुं प्राक्शरीरविमोक्षणात्
कामक्रोधोद्भवं वेगं स युक्तः स सुखी नरः

Shaknotīhaiva yaḥ sodhuṁ prāk sharīravimokshaṇāt
kāmakrodhodbhavaṁ vegaṁ sa yuktaḥ sa sukhī naraḥ

He who is able, even here, before liberation from the body, to resist the excitement born of desire and anger, is united with the Divine. He is a happy man.

'Even here': remaining within the limitations of the relative field of daily life in the world. The ability 'to resist the excitement born of desire and anger' has its basis in the state of supreme contentment which results from Union with the Divine and from the knowledge of the Self as separate from the field of activity in the state of Cosmic Consciousness, which is the result of such Union.[56] In this state of lasting contentment there is no possibility of any excitement. Excitement can only arise in a discontented mind ever seeking something more.

'Desire and anger' belong to the realm of the mind. For

56 This principle was presented in verse 66 of Chapter II; verses 50 and 51 of that chapter described the advantages of the established intellect.

any mental activity to take place there must of necessity be a corresponding activity in the physical structure of the nervous system. The mental activity of desire and anger produces very powerful 'excitement' in the nervous system. It is this physical excitement that stirs the nervous system to activity. In the case of a non-realized man this excitement is immediately expressed as speech and action; but in the case of a realized man, it is anchored to eternal silence as a ship is anchored to the sea-bed. His nervous system permanently maintains that state of restful alertness which corresponds to pure awareness of the Self, and this state of restful alertness prevents the stir of desire and anger in the nervous system. This is how the state of his nervous system does not allow excitement to arise in a realized man.

Self-awareness acts as a shock-absorber on the mental level, while the state of restful alertness of the nervous system acts as a shock-absorber on the physical level. This is the natural state of life in Cosmic Consciousness.

Life flows through desire. As long as desire is present, the possibility of anger will always exist, and therefore the stir produced by desire and anger is an essential feature of life. This is why the Lord does not advocate the elimination of desire, but only says that it is necessary to create a situation in which 'the excitement born of desire and anger' is automatically resisted, in the sense that it does not overpower life.

This situation is created by culturing both the mental and physical aspects of life through the practice of Transcendental Meditation, which produces the necessary refinement in the mind and the nervous system simultaneously.[57] In the state of Cosmic Consciousness, which is the state described by 'united with the Divine', this refinement is such that it does not allow the excitement of desire and anger to arise. But the Lord says: 'before liberation', before gaining Cosmic Consciousness. This is because the knowledge that the Self is divine in Its nature and is completely unattached to the field of activity grows as the practice of gaining Transcendental Consciousness advances, so that long before a man has actually gained Cosmic Consciousness the infusion of Being into the nature of the mind becomes intense

57 See IV, 38, commentary.

enough to give him the ability to resist 'the excitement born of desire and anger'. The need for resisting this excitement arises only when there is a chance for the excitement to arise. This happens only before Cosmic Consciousness is actually gained.

Nevertheless, it is clear from this teaching that the ability to resist excitement should be considered as one criterion of being united with the Divine. This is because there is no direct way of measuring the degree of infusion of Being into the mind and ascertaining whether or not full and final infusion of Being has taken place. The second criterion that the Lord gives is: 'He is a happy man'; he is free from the 'sources of sorrow', as shown in the previous verse.

'Before liberation from the body': this expression shows that the present teaching is for an aspirant engaged in the practice of gaining the state of Unity with the Divine. It means before having gained release from the binding influence of action, before having gained the state of Cosmic Consciousness, in which the Self is permanently experienced as separate from activity, before identification of the self with the body is dissolved, before the state of renunciation has been achieved.

This verse has been generally misunderstood to mean that resisting desire is a way to Union with the Divine, and this has given rise to all sorts of ascetic practices and exhortations to abandon desire for the sake of coming to Union. It is wrong to suppose that this verse offers a path to Union through attempting to resist desire. It merely places Union with the Divine parallel to the natural ability to resist desire. This ability in the relative field is the expression of the Union in the absolute field. Of the two, Union with the Divine is easier to attain.[58] It forms the basis of the ability to resist.

Having declared in this verse that the mind of a *Yogī* remains unshakeable in the field of activity, the Lord, in the following verse, goes on to describe the inner state of such a mind.

58 See II, 40, 45; VI, 28.

VERSE 24

योऽन्तःसुखोऽन्तरारामस्तथान्तर्ज्योतिरेव यः
स योगी ब्रह्मनिर्वाणं ब्रह्मभूतोऽधिगच्छति

Yo 'ntaḥsukho 'ntarārāmas tathāntarjyotir eva yaḥ
sa yogī Brahmanirvāṇaṁ Brahmabhūto 'dhigachchhati

He whose happiness is within, whose contentment is within, whose light is all within, that Yogī, being one with Brahman, attains eternal freedom in divine consciousness.

This verse is the crest of the teaching of this chapter on renunciation. It presents a state in which life is wholly converged upon its innermost aspect, and declares that state to be eternal freedom. Furthermore, it brings to light the sequence of stages on the way to realization: as the practice of Transcendental Meditation advances, inner happiness grows; with this, contentment grows, and at the same time the experience of Being becomes clearer — the inner light grows. With this, inner awareness grows, and with it the ability spontaneously to maintain Being during activity. When one naturally begins to maintain the state of Being in all states of waking, dreaming, and deep sleep, then one has attained eternal freedom in divine consciousness.

'He whose happiness is within': this expression is a development of the argument in the two preceding verses. First, 'All pleasures born of contact are only sources of sorrow ... The enlightened man does not rejoice in them' (verse 22). This implies that the outside world is not the field of happiness for a realized man. Second, 'He is a happy man' (verse 23). If his happiness does not lie in the outside world and yet he is happy, his happiness can only be within himself. The mind wanders in search of happiness but when, through Union with the Divine,[59] the mind is transformed into Bliss Consciousness, it finds the goal of its search within itself.

By virtue of Bliss Consciousness, even the relative aspect of man's existence is wholly permeated by bliss. So, experiencing the relative field of happiness outside and absolute bliss within,

59 See verse 21.

his whole life is naturally anchored to inner happiness, and therefore to 'contentment' also.

'Whose light is all within'; who dwells in the light of the Self, whose inner being is illumined by the light of the inner Divine. The word 'all' is important: it means that he is totally absorbed in the inner light, that his whole life is permeated by the light of inner Being. He is awake within himself and remains so in spite of any activity in the outside world. He is established on that absolute level of existence which is deep within everything, that field of unbounded Bliss Consciousness which is self-sufficient and self-illuminating.

This does not mean that he is not active in outer life. It simply means that even though his mind, intellect, ego, senses, and body are functioning on their respective levels, and he has the whole phenomenal world around him, his Self remains completely unattached. It is only superficially affected by this outer field of life. This is that integrated state of existence in which every level of life is self-sufficient and all the different levels progressively function together in harmony.

'Eternal freedom in divine consciousness': this translates the Sanskrit, *Brahmanirvāṇa*, the freedom born of the state of *Brahman*.

The present verse speaks of 'that *Yogī*' who does not require anything in the outside world to make him happy. Nothing in the outside world attracts him. He does not need an external light, for he is awake in his own light. Established in the freedom of Cosmic Consciousness, he is always free. The experience of variety in the world in no way takes him out of his liberation; no external light, or knowledge of the relative world, can in any way deprive him of his state. Once Self-consciousness is established in the nature of the mind, the mind cherishes it in all conditions.

The Lord is saying that nothing in the world will be able to overshadow the perpetual freedom of a *Yogī* in this resolute state. While he acts in the relative field of life, he is yet established in his own Self. Divine consciousness is not opposed to life in the world, nor is consciousness of the relative world opposed to the divine consciousness of absolute existence.

The following verse brings out other features of the state of enlightenment.

VERSE 25

लभन्ते ब्रह्मनिर्वाणमृषयः क्षीणकल्मषाः
छिन्नद्वैधा यतात्मानः सर्वभूतहिते रताः

Labhante Brahmanirvāṇam Ṛishayaḥ kshīṇakalmashāḥ
chhinnadwaidhā yatātmānaḥ sarvabhūtahite ratāḥ

The seers, whose sins are destroyed, whose doubts are dispelled, who are self-controlled and take delight in doing good to all creatures, attain eternal freedom in divine consciousness.

It should be noted that when the Lord presents the state of eternal freedom through the principle of renunciation, as He does in the previous verse, He does not lose a moment before adding that in such a state a man takes 'delight in doing good to all creatures'. In the state of renunciation a man becomes devoted to all creatures and capable of doing good not only to himself but to all other beings. It is this teaching that places the philosophy of renunciation parallel to that of the Yoga of action.

'Seers': the knowers of Reality, established in the realization of the Self as separate from activity, who see life as the drama of the Divine while themselves remaining uninvolved.

'Whose sins are destroyed': sins are destroyed by both Yoga[60] and Sāṁkhya.[61]

'Doubts are dispelled' by both Yoga[62] and Sāṁkhya.[63]

'Self-controlled': this state is gained by both Yoga[64] and Sāṁkhya.[65]

'Delight in doing good to all creatures': this state is reached by both Yoga[66] and Sāṁkhya.[67]

The Lord here describes certain prerequisites for one who is to 'attain eternal freedom in divine consciousness'. It is fortunate

60 See II, 65; III, 13, 41.
61 See II, 38; IV, 21, 30, 36.
62 See II, 72; V, 20.
63 See IV, 35, 40–1.
64 See II, 61; III, 7.
65 See IV, 18, 20–1, 23, 28, 41.
66 See III, 20.
67 See III, 25.

for aspirants that all these conditions are fulfilled quite naturally and automatically through the teaching of Sāṁkhya, which is inclusive of the method described by the Lord in the 45th verse of the second chapter: 'Be without the three *Guṇas*'. The simple technique of achieving this state 'without the three *Guṇas*' is the practice of Transcendental Meditation, for it readily[68] brings the mind from the field of gross experience to the state of Transcendental Consciousness.

When the mind transcends during meditation, it reaches the state of pure consciousness, free from all diversity. Once it becomes permanently established in Being, knowledge becomes complete and all its doubts,[69] whatever they may be, quite naturally disappear. Having risen above the egocentricity and selfishness of individuality, abiding in Bliss Consciousness and fully connected with the source of energy, a man can but move about compassionately doing good to all beings.

Verse 26

कामक्रोधवियुक्तानां यतीनां यतचेतसाम्
अभितो ब्रह्मनिर्वाणं वर्तते विदितात्मनाम्

Kāmakrodhaviyuktānāṁ yatīnāṁ yatachetasām
abhito Brahmanirvāṇaṁ vartate viditātmanām

Disciplined men, freed from desire and anger, who have
disciplined their thoughts and have realized the Self,
find eternal freedom in divine consciousness everywhere.

It should be noticed that verse 24 promises eternal liberation through Yoga, that verse 25 promises it through Sāṁkhya, and that this verse translates the same promise of eternal liberation into terms of renunciation. The sequence of these three verses mirrors the sequence of the theme of Chapters III, IV, and V. Thus the Lord brings completeness to the philosophy of renunciation.

This verse describes a man in eternal freedom. He is 'disciplined' because he is established in the knowledge of Reality, which gives

68 See II, 40.
69 See IV, 41.

him a clear understanding of the state of renunciation, or the separation that lies between the Self and activity. By gaining that state he is freed from desire and anger and has disciplined his thoughts. He has 'realized the Self', for he is permanently established in the pure state of Being, or Self-consciousness — he has gained Cosmic Consciousness. Thus established in divine consciousness he finds eternal freedom everywhere.

The state described in this verse is higher than that described in verse 23, for it has arisen out of the destruction of sins and the dispelling of doubts specified in verse 25.

Verse 23 presented a happy man in Union with the Divine as one 'who is able ... to resist the excitement born of desire and anger'. This implies that it is still possible for the excitement of desire and anger to bubble up in such a happy man united with the Divine, but that he will be able to resist this excitement. The present verse shows that those 'who have disciplined their thoughts and have realized the Self' are freed from any possibility of the excitement of desire and anger arising in them. Such men of fulfilment live eternal freedom in divine consciousness.

'Who have disciplined their thoughts': a disciplined thought is that which is in harmony with the process of evolution of the thinker and of everything around him. It is in accordance with all the Laws of Nature. When, during meditation, the mind gains the state of transcendental divine consciousness, it becomes the basis of all the Laws of Nature that govern the process of evolution on every level of creation. On coming out into the field of relative life, its thoughts naturally receive the support of all the Laws of Nature. Therefore 'have disciplined their thoughts' means living the Being in daily life; it does not mean controlling thoughts.

'Everywhere' means during life here on earth and hereafter.

Arjuna is shown that, to become liberated, it is not necessary to die or to leave the body. If one has known the Self and the mind is inseparably established in It, if the Self is appreciated as separate from activity, then whatever desires or anger arise, the Self remains completely uninvolved and therefore free from them. This is how, when the mind is disciplined in terms of the Self, it remains unconcerned with all activity, even the activity of desire or anger. Naturally, in such a state a man is liberated during his lifetime here on earth and subsequently after death.

It may be recalled that a disciplined life,[70] freedom from desire and anger,[71] discipline of thoughts,[72] and realization of the Self[73] are achieved by both Yoga[74] and Sāṁkhya.[75] Therefore it may be inferred from this verse that Yoga and Sāṁkhya are the same so far as these results are concerned. This inference is in keeping with verses 4 and 5, which present the purpose of this chapter.

This verse, together with the three previous verses, establishes the possibility of divine life in the world either through the practice of Yoga or the wisdom of Sāṁkhya. In the following verse, the Lord begins a precise description of the practice which leads a man to achieve that state of Cosmic Consciousness (*Jīvan-mukti*) during his lifetime. This will complete the teaching of the chapter and will provide a sound basis for the wisdom of Chapter VI.

VERSE 27

स्पर्शान्कृत्वा बहिर्बाह्यांश्चक्षुश्चैवान्तरे भ्रुवो:
प्राणापानौ समौ कृत्वा नासाभ्यन्तरचारिणौ

Sparshān kṛitwā bahir bāhyāṁsh chakshush chaivāntare bhruvoḥ
prāṇāpānau samau kṛitwā nāsābhyantarachāriṇau

Having left external contacts outside; with the vision within the eyebrows; having balanced the ingoing and outgoing breaths that flow through the nostrils,

The first point is that the attention has to shift away from the external field of sensory perception. 'Having left external contacts outside' means closing the gates of the senses to any outside experience and at the same time not thinking about objects of sensory impression.

The second point is that the vision is 'within the eyebrows'. This means that vision is directed outwards from within the

70 See III, 7, 17.
71 See III, 43.
72 See III, 43.
73 See III, 43.
74 See IV, 23, 38.
75 See IV, 19.

eyebrows — it is directed from behind the eyebrows, and this is done with closed eyes. It is the most relaxed and effortless state of the ocular muscles. It is soothing to the entire system and also has the simultaneous effect of leaving 'external contacts outside' and balancing 'the ingoing and outgoing breaths'. This point has been widely misunderstood and the verse misinterpreted as advocating concentration of the vision between the eyebrows. Such a practice may have its value in other systems which depend on effort. Concentrating the vision in this manner involves great strain even with the eyes closed; such a practice has no place in the Bhagavad-Gītā, which teaches a simple and effortless method.

The third point is that a state of balance should be established between the outward and inward breaths. This balance means that they should flow evenly, and should cease flowing, in alternating directions, finally coming to a state of suspension.

There are many ways of accomplishing these three aims. In some practices, control of the senses predominates, in others control of thought, in others control of breath. But the practice to which the Lord refers in this verse is one which works on all these aspects simultaneously and results in the state described in the following verse.[76]

Verse 28

यतेन्द्रियमनोबुद्धिर्मुनिर्मोक्षपरायणः
विगतेच्छाभयक्रोधो यः सदा मुक्त एव सः

Yatendriyamanobuddhir munir mokshaparāyaṇaḥ
vigatechchhābhayakrodho yaḥ sadā mukta eva saḥ

The sage, whose senses, mind, and intellect are controlled, whose aim is liberation, from whom desire, fear, and anger have departed, is indeed forever free.

'The sage' (*Muni*): see II, 56, 59.

'Senses, mind, and intellect are controlled' by 'having known him who is beyond the intellect' (III, 43).

'Whose aim is liberation' means that all his efforts are directed

76 See also commentaries on VI, 13–14.

one-pointedly towards liberation. He follows unswervingly the sure path trodden by 'the ancient seekers of liberation' (IV, 15). The whole routine of his life is dedicated to the practice of meditation and balanced activity.[77]

As a result of this constant practice, he becomes quite naturally free from desire, fear, and anger. 'From whom desire, fear, and anger have departed' indicates that he has not done anything to drive them away — they have of themselves departed from him.[78]

The present verse describes an even more perfect state of realization than that portrayed in verse 26. There the expression 'freed from desire and anger' indicates that a man has abandoned them; the expression in the present verse, 'from whom desire, fear, and anger have departed', indicates that they have abandoned him.

The reason is that he has arrived at a state where the Self is experienced as separate from activity, and thus he finds himself 'indeed forever free'. This is the state of perfect renunciation that is gained in Cosmic Consciousness. Here is the fulfilment of the philosophy of renunciation — everything has been separated from the Self, which has gained in liberation a perfect state of non-attachment.

This apparently marks the peak of renunciation. But the question arises: Is this all that the philosophy of renunciation can offer? If it is, then the philosophy is not complete, because an existence aloof from everything could not possibly be the fulfilment of life. This anxious inquiry is answered in the next verse, which provides for the desired fulfilment of life and shows that fulfilment to be the real pinnacle of the philosophy of renunciation.

VERSE 29

भोक्तारं यज्ञतपसां सर्वलोकमहेश्वरम्
सुहृदं सर्वभूतानां ज्ञात्वा मां शान्तिमृच्छति

Bhoktāraṁ yagyatapasāṁ sarvalokamaheshwaram
suhṛidaṁ sarvabhūtānāṁ gyātwā māṁ shāntim ṛichchhati

77 See commentaries on II, 45; IV, 18, 21.

78 See commentaries on verse 26 and II, 40, 45.

Having known Me as the enjoyer of Yagyas and austerities, as the great Lord of all the world, as the friend of all beings, he attains to peace.

Here is the real glory of renunciation. It discovers the great 'enjoyer': it develops into Union with God.

'Me': whose birth and actions are divine (IV, 9); who am the refuge of those freed from attachment, fear, and anger, unto whose Being have come those purified by the austerity of wisdom (IV, 10); who show men favour in the same manner as they approach Me (IV, 11); who am the author of the fourfold order of creation, yet remain the non-doer, immutable (IV, 13); whom actions do not involve and who am without longing for the fruit of action; knowledge of whom liberates men from the bondage of action (IV, 14).

'*Yagyas*': actions supporting life and evolution. These have been dealt with in detail in Chapter IV, verses 24 to 33.

'Austerities': means of purification. The performance of *Yagya* is also considered to be austerity. Verse 10 of Chapter IV describes wisdom in terms of austerity, purified by which one participates in the consciousness of the Supreme.

'Having known Me as the enjoyer of *Yagyas* and austerities': he sees Me as accepting his *Yagya* and austerity; having separated himself from the field of activity, his activity has been given over to Nature, which is the Lord's. This is why the Lord says: 'Having known Me as the enjoyer of *Yagyas* and austerities'.

'Having known me ... as the great Lord of all the world':[79] having raised his consciousness to the level of My consciousness; that is, having attained God Consciousness. Knowledge of God is possible only when one has reached the state of God Consciousness. This has been made clear in the commentary on verse 38 of Chapter IV.

'As the friend of all beings': a friend is a source of joy. He brings life-supporting happiness. The purpose of the Lord's creation is the expansion of happiness. Men enjoy His love expressed in creation, each at his own level of consciousness. This is how 'the great Lord of all the world' is also the life-supporting friend, the

79 See III, 22, 30; IV, 6, 13.

bestower of happiness on all beings. One who knows Him thus and finds himself close to Him, gains fulfilment: 'he attains to peace', says the Lord.

So that Arjuna's mind may not escape from the present realities of life to an abstract conception of a far-distant friend of all beings, so that he can see the great Lord of all the world close at hand, speaking to him, Lord Kṛishṇa shows that He Himself is that Lord. It is only because of Arjuna's complete surrender that He reveals Himself so completely.

This chapter, which lays open the wisdom of the renunciation of action, ends with an exposition of the divine nature of Lord Kṛishṇa, so full, friendly, and peaceful. This is the glory of the wisdom of renunciation that is uniquely the Bhagavad-Gītā's. It does not leave a man in dry detachment, barren, and without support. It carries renunciation to the direct realization of the supreme authority, the supreme good, the supreme happiness that are found in rising to the level of the Godhead, to direct communion with God. This humanly inconceivable accomplishment in man's life is the blessing of renunciation. Here is the Lord's invitation to humankind: Enter into the Kingdom of Heaven through the path of action or through the path of renunciation of action. Make your choice.

ॐ तत्सदिति श्रीमद्भगवद्गीतासूपनिषत्सु ब्रह्मविद्यायां योगशास्त्रे श्रीकृष्णार्जुनसंवादे कर्मसंन्यासयोगो नाम पञ्चमोऽध्यायः

Oṁ tat sad iti Shrīmad Bhagavadgītāsūpanishatsu Brahmavidyāyāṁ Yogashāstre Shrīkṛishṇārjunasaṁvāde Karmasaṁnyāsayogo nāma panchamo 'dhyāyaḥ

Thus, in the Upanishad of the glorious Bhagavad-Gītā, in the Science of the Absolute, in the Scripture of Yoga, in the dialogue between Lord Kṛishṇa and Arjuna, ends the fifth chapter, entitled: The Yoga of Action and Renunciation of Action, Karma-Sanyāsa Yoga.

Chapter VI

A Vision of the Teaching in Chapter VI

Verse 1. The performance of right action in the state of non-attachment mirrors the outer and inner life of a realized man.

Verses 2–10. A difference of path is not significant so long as Divine Union is gained. What is important is to know that each path starts from the level of activity and ends in the eternal silence of absolute Being, which develops into God Consciousness. This process is divided into three stages: from the waking state to Transcendental Consciousness, from Transcendental Consciousness to Cosmic Consciousness, from Cosmic Consciousness to God Consciousness.

Verses 11–28. The practice for rising from the waking state of consciousness to Transcendental Consciousness.

Verse 29. The practice for rising from Transcendental Consciousness to Cosmic Consciousness.

Verses 30–2. The practice for rising from Cosmic Consciousness to God Consciousness.

Verses 33–4. How can the mind, which is wavering, be steady on the path?

Verses 35–6. It is difficult to control the mind directly, but through practice and non-attachment it becomes subdued.

Verses 37–9. The principle of renunciation comprehends the same height of human perfection as is achieved by the path of action.

Verses 40–5. Death is no barrier to evolution. In his next life a man continues to evolve from the level gained in this life. If he fails to gain perfection in one life, he will gain it in another; for once set on this path, no one can miss the goal.

Verses 46–7. The seeker is exhorted to set himself on the path of Transcendental Meditation, gain Union of the mind with the divine Self in Transcendental Consciousness, realize that Self as separate from activity in Cosmic Consciousness, rise to God through devotion, and finally attain complete Union with Him.

THIS chapter stands as the keystone in the arch of the Bhagavad-Gītā. It explains in detail what may be called the Royal Yoga of Lord Kṛishṇa, which readily brings enlightenment to any man in any age.

The greatness of the theme of these six chapters lies first in the explanation of life in its manifold aspects and then in the synthesis of all these aspects in the Unity of God Consciousness.

It is a divine theme expounding Reality, which assumes newer and newer meanings as man's consciousness grows. It gives significance to life at every level of consciousness and brings fulfilment at every step of man's evolution until eternal fulfilment is gained.

The first chapter showed a great hero overcome by a profound state of suspension, which rendered him unable to act. Presenting this extreme case, it silently demanded a master-cure for all sufferings and sorrows in man's life at any time.

Chapter II gave the vision of the full life by bringing to light the relative and the absolute phases of existence. It suggested a practice by which all problems in the relative phase of life could be solved by adding the value of absolute consciousness to the consciousness of the relative state.

Chapter III expounded the validity of action to make permanent the state of Union experienced in the state of absolute consciousness gained in the transcendental state.

Chapter IV brought knowledge of the state of non-attachment, or renunciation, experienced when the state of Union becomes permanent.

Chapter V showed this state of non-attachment to be common to the paths of both Sāṁkhya and *Karma Yoga*.

Chapter VI describes the practice that brings about this state of non-attachment, thus fulfilling the teachings on action and on renunciation contained in the third and fifth chapters.

This sixth chapter serves as a commentary[1] on the 45th verse of Chapter II, which contains the central teaching of the Bhagavad-Gītā: 'Be without the three *Guṇas*'. It develops a simple technique of Transcendental Meditation leading to a state of consciousness which at all times spontaneously maintains Being and thereby equanimity of mind and behaviour in the field of activity. This technique provides the practical basis for both Sāṁkhya and Yoga and for the very different ways of life associated with these paths, that of the recluse and that of the householder. They virtually cease to be two different paths. But even if they are regarded as different, it can still be said that they develop on a common ground and arrive at a common goal. This is the glory of the practical teaching of the sixth chapter.

VERSE 1

श्रीभगवानुवाच
अनाश्रितः कर्मफलं कार्यं कर्म करोति यः
स संन्यासी च योगी च न निरग्निर्न चाक्रियः

Shrī Bhagavān uvācha
Anāshritaḥ karmaphalaṁ kāryaṁ karma karoti yaḥ
sa saṁnyāsī cha yogī cha na niragnir na chākriyaḥ

The Blessed Lord said:
He who performs action that ought to be done, without depending on the fruit of action, he is a Sanyāsī and he is a Yogī; not he who is without fire and without activity.

The first two expressions of this verse, 'performs action that ought to be done' and 'without depending on the fruit of action', summarize the teaching of the whole discourse thus far. At the same time they indicate that the practice which is going to be explained in this chapter will enable man to live the teachings

1 It also clarifies the teaching contained in II, 48; III, 2, 7, 9, 30, 34, 43; IV, 27, 41–2; V, 1, 4, 6–7, 11.

they contain. This practice will enable all men to cultivate that high state of divine consciousness which should be normal to man and which forms the basis of the life of a *Sanyāsī* and of a *Yogī*.

It is obvious from the theme of the discourse that what brings fulfilment to life is not a specific way of life, either that of a recluse or of a householder, but experience of Reality and knowledge about It. This again is obvious from the expressions in the present verse, which describe the state of consciousness common to a *Yogī* and a *Sanyāsī*: 'He who performs action that ought to be done, without depending on the fruit of action'.

This verse is a continuation of Lord Kṛishṇa's answer to Arjuna's question, in the first verse of Chapter V, about the relationship of renunciation of action to the Yoga of action.

In the early stages of His answer, the Lord showed that both ways have an identical end in the state of liberation, that in their aim they are the same. He then made clear the supremacy of the Yoga of action (*Karma Yoga*) over the renunciation of action (*Sanyāsa*), and this brought out the fact that the two are distinct paths. In the present verse, the Lord establishes that, while there may be certain points of difference between the path of a *Sanyāsī* and that of a *Karma Yogī*, there is at least one common factor which brings them together: the unattached state of the mind in relation to the fruits of action during activity. The Lord holds this to be the criterion both of a *Sanyāsī* and of a *Yogī*, both of the state of renunciation and of the state of Union.

To say that the state of Union is equivalent to the state of renunciation may sound contradictory, but the truth of this statement becomes clear in the state of Cosmic Consciousness. In this state the mind's Union with Being, Self-consciousness, has become permanent; this is the state of perfect Union. In this state also the Self is experienced as separate from activity; this is the state of perfect renunciation. This is how renunciation and Union coexist in the same state of life.

The state of mind which is unattached to the fruits[2] of action is a result of the experience of the Self as separate from activity. This in turn results from the Union that comes from the

2 See IV, 19–20, commentaries; V, 12.

practice of gaining transcendental Bliss Consciousness through the method which the Lord has already given to Arjuna in the 45th verse of Chapter II.

The Lord says to Arjuna: 'action that ought to be done'. By this He intends to save from misinterpretation His teaching about action in the light of non-attachment. Otherwise a misguided man might commit murder or theft and claim that he acted without attachment to the fruits of action.

The doctrine of *Karma Yoga* is not based on the manner in which a man thinks. It is based upon a state of consciousness, the state of Being. Its purpose is to allow the infusion of Being into the nature of the mind and to make It permanent there. Then It becomes permanent in the whole field of thought, speech, and action, in the whole field of man's life. This is brought about very naturally by the practice of Transcendental Meditation followed by activity that is unforced and without strain.

The purpose of both *Karma Yoga* and *Sanyāsa* is to establish a man in the state of complete integration of life. Non-attachment to the fruits of action, described here as characteristic both of a *Sanyāsī* and of a *Yogī*, is a particular state of mind, not on the level of thought but on the level[3] of Being.

It would be a mistake to make a mood of non-attachment to the fruits of action during activity. It would be sheer hypocrisy to try to hold intellectually, on the level of thought or by mood-making, the idea or feeling: 'I am doing this action for the sake of God, or for the sake of duty, and have no desire[4] for its fruits; I am indeed doing the action, but actually I am not doing it; I am *Brahman*, and action is also *Brahman*, and the fruit of action is also *Brahman*, so even the fruit is nothing but my own Self, and that Self I am already. What need, therefore, to think about the fruit of action?' This way of thinking has nothing to do with the doctrine of non-attachment in *Karma Yoga* or *Sanyāsa*, and anyone who tries to live non-attachment on the basis of such thinking is only deluding himself. Yet for many centuries the doctrines of *Karma Yoga* and *Sanyāsa* have been misunderstood in just this way.

Sanyāsa and *Karma Yoga* are neither of them based on any

3 See IV, 19–20, commentaries.
4 See IV, 19–20, commentaries.

manner of thinking, nor on making moods at the conscious level of the mind; they are based on the inner stability of the mind in the state of enlightenment. The way to this is through Transcendental Meditation. Without right meditation and the attainment of the state of Transcendental Consciousness, and eventually of Cosmic Consciousness, one's action will always be a means of bondage; no amount of thinking will help to free a man from the binding influence of action.

It is a matter for regret that at the present time a man who is active in the world, but without having gained Transcendental Consciousness, should consider himself a *Karma Yogī* simply because he leads a life of activity, performing certain kinds of action and thinking about them in terms of God or in some other special way. To be a *Karma Yogī*, one has first to be a *Yogī*. It is the state of transcendental pure consciousness going hand in hand with activity that constitutes *Karma Yoga*. Through the practice of Transcendental Meditation the mind is so steeped in pure consciousness, or Being, that this cannot be overshadowed, however numerous a man's actions, however intense his experience in life. The state of Being together with activity makes him a *Karma Yogī*.

The experience of Being is the first prerequisite of *Karma Yoga*, as it is of *Sanyāsa*. So far as the state of consciousness is concerned, *Sanyāsa* and *Karma Yoga* are the same.

'Without fire': fire cooks food. By tradition, a *Sanyāsī* is not expected to cook food lest it bind him to the needs of the body. Therefore being without fire symbolizes the life of a *Sanyāsī*. Again, fire is that which destroys. What destroys the eternal calmness of the ocean? A wind that sets up waves. Eternal unmanifested Being appears as waves of individual life through the instrumentality of desire. That is why desire is considered to be fire for one who chooses the life of silence.

In this verse, the Lord pictures the life of a *Sanyāsī* not in terms of non-attachment or desirelessness, but in terms of activity in freedom.

VERSE 2

यं संन्यासमिति प्राहुर्योगं तं विद्धि पाण्डव
न ह्यसंन्यस्तसंकल्पो योगी भवति कश्चन

Yaṁ saṁnyāsam iti prāhur yogaṁ taṁ viddhi Pāṇḍava
na hyasaṁnyastasaṁkalpo yogī bhavati kashchana

That which they call Sanyāsa, know it to be Yoga,
O son of Pāṇḍu, for no one becomes a Yogī who
has not relinquished the incentive of desire.

'Incentive[5] of desire' translates the Sanskrit word '*Sankalpa*', which conveys the idea of a seed which sprouts into desire.

Lord Kṛishṇa here makes a most essential point for the student of Yoga: *Sankalpa* has to be rooted out in order that one may become a *Yogī*.

The Lord has already established *Sanyāsa* and *Karma Yoga* on an equal footing with regard to their results: 'Both renunciation and the Yoga of action lead to the supreme good' (V, 2); 'He who is properly established even in one gains the fruit of both' (V, 4). In this, as in the preceding verse, He puts the two paths themselves on the same basis, and He does so with great emphasis: 'That which they call *Sanyāsa*, know it to be Yoga'. The Lord proves this by bringing to light the single quality which makes a man a *Sanyāsī* or a *Karma Yogī*. He says: 'no one becomes a *Yogī* who has not relinquished the incentive of desire'. A *Yogī* is he whose mind is united with the Divine, and in that state of Transcendental Consciousness the incentive of desire is rooted out.

The question arises: If abandonment of *Sankalpa* is necessary before a man can become a *Yogī* and is also the characteristic of a *Sanyāsī*, how in practice is it possible for anyone to become a *Sanyāsī* or a *Yogī*? For life, whether lived in the household or in seclusion, is full of *Sankalpa* and desires. The answer is that a man has to create a state of mind in which there is no *Sankalpa*; and seeing that the Lord's discourse is for the man in the world, it must be possible for everyone to create such a state of mind.

5 See IV, 19, commentary.

The principle of the technique to make the mind free from *Sankalpa* was given to Arjuna by the Lord in the 45th verse of Chapter II and will be further expounded in this chapter. During meditation, the mind goes through states of experience which become progressively finer until the finest is transcended. In this way the mind is led to the state of Transcendental Consciousness and comes completely out of the realm of *Sankalpa*. This is the state of Yoga. It is also the state of *Sanyāsa*, where the mind has renounced everything and is left alone by itself. Thus the technique of Transcendental Meditation, which helps the mind to transcend *Sankalpa*, is the technique of becoming a *Yogī* or a *Sanyāsī*.

As the practice advances, Transcendental Consciousness becomes permanent in the state of Cosmic Consciousness, and in this state one has permanently relinquished the incentive of desire.

The following verse considers the activity of an aspirant and the serenity of an accomplished *Yogī* in relation to the state of mind without *Sankalpa*.

VERSE 3

आरुरुक्षोर्मुनेर्योगं कर्म कारणमुच्यते
योगारूढस्य तस्यैव शमः कारणमुच्यते

Ārurukshor muner yogaṁ karma kāraṇam uchyate
yogārūdhasya tasyaiva shamaḥ kāraṇam uchyate

Action is said to be the means for the man of thought wishing to ascend to Yoga; for the man who has ascended to Yoga, and for him alone, calmness is said to be the means.

'Means': course, path, way.

'Man of thought': this translates the Sanskrit '*Muni*'. A *Muni* is one whose path of fulfilment is through thought. His practice is in the field of the mind as opposed to the field of bodily activity. In order to make this clear, it must be explained that for the mind to register any experience a corresponding activity in the nervous system is necessary. It follows from this relationship of the mind with the nervous system that any experience can be stimulated either by the one or by the other. *Hatha Yoga* is an approach to realization which trains the physical nervous system and thereby conditions the mind to gain the state of Transcendental Consciousness and eventually to gain Cosmic Consciousness. On the other hand, the practice of meditation, referred to in these verses, is an approach to realization which trains the mind and thereby conditions the nervous system to give rise to the state of Transcendental Consciousness and eventually to Cosmic Consciousness. This mental approach is the way of the *Muni*.

By using the word '*Muni*', the Lord wants to make it clear that action is not the means for a man of action only, but also for the man whose way of approach is through knowledge.

'Wishing to ascend to Yoga' means that he has not yet attained the state of mind without *Sankalpa*, described in the previous verse.

'Action is said to be the means': action is the means of cultivating the state of mind without *Sankalpa*. This appears to be a paradox similar to the one in verse 18 of Chapter IV. The Lord said there: 'who in action sees inaction'. Here He seems to be saying: Create calmness through action. There is deep meaning in the Lord's expression: 'Action is said to be the means'. It reveals the whole secret of the path of Yoga, the way to create the state of mind without *Sankalpa*.

This expression may be considered on different levels. First, it means that the Lord wants the aspirant to perform right action according to his *Dharma*, thus purifying himself and, through the increase of purity, maintaining steadiness of mind. This consideration belongs to the surface of life and should be valued for the inspiration which it gives to a righteous way of living.

The consideration which follows reveals a deeper meaning of the Lord's words. He wants the aspirant to involve himself in subtler forms of activity; He wants him to bring the mind from more gross levels of activity on the common sensory level of action and experience to the finer levels of thinking and, eventually transcending the finest level of thinking, to arrive at Transcendental Consciousness, the state of mind without *Sankalpa*, the state where one 'has ascended to Yoga'.

Thus it is through activity that Transcendental Consciousness is gained. Moreover, the mind, travelling as it were on the ladder of activity from the relative state of waking consciousness to the silence of the transcendental field of absolute consciousness, and again from there to the activity of the waking state, establishes eternal harmony between the silence of the Absolute and the activity of the relative. This is Cosmic Consciousness,[6] in which Transcendental Consciousness, the state where one 'has ascended to Yoga', becomes permanent. This expression of the Lord's also has its meaning therefore on the level of Cosmic Consciousness. Cosmic Consciousness in turn forms the basis for the supreme state of Yoga in God Consciousness, where the eternal Unity of life prevails in the Light of God. One who has reached this state has ascended to Yoga in the highest sense of the expression.

Having defined activity as the means of ascending to Yoga, the Lord turns to the importance of that 'calmness' which serves as a means when one has 'ascended to Yoga'.

'The man who has ascended to Yoga': a man whose mind has risen from the waking state of consciousness to the transcendental state of consciousness, in which his mind is in full Union with the Divine. This state of Yoga in Transcendental Consciousness becomes permanent in Cosmic Consciousness through increase of calmness, or the infusion of Being into the nature of the mind. That is why the Lord says that calmness is the means when ascent to Yoga in Transcendental Consciousness has been gained. Again, calmness is the means of ascent from Yoga in Cosmic Consciousness to Yoga in God Consciousness. In the state of Cosmic Consciousness, calmness gives the experience of the Self as separate from activity. In God Consciousness, this calmness is transformed into the Light of God, in which the experience of the duality of the Self and activity is dissolved.

This eternal silence of God Consciousness is the advanced stage of the silence experienced in the state of Cosmic Consciousness. It is the living silence of that Unity of life which forms the basis

6 See III, 20.

of cosmic activity and at the same time completely separates God from cosmic activity. The silence which is experienced in Cosmic Consciousness, and which separates the Self from activity, is on an infinitely smaller scale, for it is on the level of individual existence. The one forms the basis of the activity of the whole of creation, the other the basis of individual activity. The essential difference between the two lies in this: in Cosmic Consciousness silence and activity coexist on the same level, whereas the level of God Consciousness is completely free from duality — it is all the living silence of eternal life, and Unity pervades all activity as water every wave. God Consciousness is pure awareness in the oneness of Being. When the awareness of the Self in Cosmic Consciousness develops into the awareness of God in God Consciousness, it develops on the level of silence; the whole process is one of the transformation of silence. At every step of development the quality of the silence changes. This is the reason why the Lord says: 'for the man who has ascended to Yoga, and for him alone, calmness is said to be the means'.

Thus there are three states of silence: in Transcendental Consciousness, in Cosmic Consciousness, and in God Consciousness. In Transcendental Consciousness, silence is devoid of any trace of activity. In Cosmic Consciousness, the silence of Self-awareness coexists with activity. In God Consciousness, the coexistence of activity and silence is transformed into oneness of awareness of God. This silence of God Consciousness is the most highly developed state of silence. It is all life on the almighty level of existence. It is the omnipresent, omnipotent, omniscient silence of Godhead. It is a completely different state of silence, which has nothing in common with the silence of Cosmic Consciousness or Transcendental Consciousness.

Any achievement by an accomplished *Yogī*, established in Cosmic Consciousness or God Consciousness, is brought about by the power of silence, the eternal silence of absolute Being, which is the source of all the innumerable Laws of Nature creating and maintaining life in the cosmos. The individual life of a *Yogī* being one with That, he finds that that omnipresent silence works out everything for him.

By using the phrase 'for him alone', the Lord makes it clear that everything will happen without doing[7] — silence will work as a means for him 'who has ascended to Yoga', but only for him and for none other. When a man gains Transcendental Consciousness, his nervous system gains the state of restful alertness which corresponds with, and is able to reflect, life eternal on the level of that silence of the Omnipresent. That is why, in this state, the divine intelligence does everything for him. When Transcendental Consciousness becomes permanent and gains the state of Cosmic Consciousness, the nervous system permanently remains the instrument of the Divine: Self-awareness is permanently established throughout life. This blessed state exists in a much deeper sense in God Consciousness.

In the next verse, the Lord further explains the expression: 'Action is said to be the means'. He shows how the state of non-action is gained through the means[8] of action. Then, in the verse which follows, He explains the expression: 'calmness is said to be the means', showing that the elevation of the self by the Self is brought about by 'calmness'.

VERSE 4

यदा हि नेन्द्रियार्थेषु न कर्मस्वनुषज्जते
सर्वसंकल्पसंन्यासी योगारूढस्तदोच्यते

Yadā hi nendriyārtheshu na karmaswanushajjate
sarvasaṁkalpasaṁnyāsī yogārūdhas tadochyate

Only when a man does not cling to the objects of the senses
or to actions, only when he has relinquished all incentive
of desire, is he said to have ascended to Yoga.

Here the Lord describes to Arjuna the state of the mind established in Yoga, the state of Divine Union. When, during meditation, the mind retires from the field of sensory perception, it becomes disconnected[9] with the outside world. It is turned

7 See IV, 38.
8 See III, 4.
9 See III, 4, commentary.

inwards, away from the field of 'the objects of the senses', away from the sphere of 'actions'. As the mind advances in an inward direction, so it retreats further from the field of gross experience. It continues through increasingly subtle fields of thinking, until it eventually transcends even the subtlest state of thought and reaches the transcendental state of Being. Here it does not in any way 'cling to the objects of the senses or to actions'.

The state of Being is one of pure consciousness, completely out of the field of relativity; there is no world of the senses or of objects, no trace of sensory activity, no trace of mental activity. There is no trinity of thinker, thinking process, and thought; doer, process of doing, and action; experiencer, process of experiencing, and object of experience. The state of transcendental Unity of life, or pure consciousness, the state of Yoga, is completely free from all trace of duality. In this state of Transcendental Consciousness a man is 'said to have ascended to Yoga'.

Here the Self stands by Itself, Self-illuminant, Self-sufficient, in the fullness of Being. Here one 'has relinquished all incentive[10] of desire', for where there is no duality there cannot be even the seed of desire. But the state of Yoga in Transcendental Consciousness is not permanent. When the mind comes out of meditation, it will once more cling to the objects of the senses and to actions, even if not so firmly as before, and the incentive of desire will once more play its part. Only when a man has reached the state of Cosmic Consciousness, where he is ever contented and forever firmly established in the Self, will the conditions which this verse sets for one who has 'ascended to Yoga' be permanently fulfilled. Naturally these conditions are also satisfied in God Consciousness, which is the fulfilment of Cosmic Consciousness. Thus, as the previous verse has already shown, the expression 'is ... said to have ascended to Yoga' applies not only to Transcendental Consciousness but also to Cosmic Consciousness and God Consciousness.

10 See IV, 19; VI, 2.

VERSE 5

उद्धरेदात्मनात्मानं नात्मानमवसादयेत्
आत्मैव ह्यात्मनो बन्धुरात्मैव रिपुरात्मनः

Uddhared Ātmanātmānaṁ nātmānam avasādayet
Ātmaiva hyātmano bandhur Ātmaiva ripur Ātmanaḥ

Let a man raise his self by his Self, let him not debase his Self; he alone, indeed, is his own friend, he alone his own enemy.

Here is a single teaching to show the basic principle of development in any sphere of life, spiritual, mental, or material. Every individual is responsible for his own development in any field.

In the previous verse Arjuna was shown the meaning of realization; now the Lord commands him to reach that state.

'Raise his self': the word used in the original Sanskrit is '*uddhared*'. It means to raise, uplift, elevate, glorify, to free from bondage. By using the word, the Lord inspires Arjuna to raise himself from the level of sensory perception and the field of thought and activity to the state of Self-realization. He not only inspires Arjuna to cultivate the state of transcendental Self-consciousness, but instructs him in the direct way of doing so: 'raise his self by his Self'. No help from outside is required. A man has in himself everything he needs to rise to any height of perfection. Nothing of the world is needed to elevate the self; no method is to be adopted, no means to be sought. The self is elevated by the Self alone.

The question may then arise: How can a man 'debase his Self' when he has been declared as beyond the reach of anything outside himself? Do not verses 13 to 30 of Chapter II pronounce the dweller in the body as beyond any influence of time and space?

To understand this one must recall the previous verse. When the mind attains to Transcendental Consciousness, it is in the state of perfect purity; it achieves cosmic status. In the present verse, the Lord encourages Arjuna to rise to that state, and at the same time wants him not to fall from it once it has been achieved, for when the mind comes out of the transcendental state to experience once more the objects of the senses in the world, it regains its limited individual status and falls from that height of universal existence. In order to warn him against this, the Lord says: 'let him not debase his Self', meaning that, once having attained the state of Self-consciousness, he should go on to rise to the state of Cosmic Consciousness, as explained in the commentaries on verses 3 and 4.

The expression, 'he alone, indeed, is his own friend', indicates that only in its pure state of Transcendental Consciousness is the mind helpful to itself. When it comes out of that state of Being, it acts as its own enemy to deprive itself of its cosmic status; but when it continues the practice and rises to Cosmic Consciousness, then it acts as its own friend to maintain that cosmic status.

This teaching illuminates the whole area of the search for Truth. Nothing in the outside world is relevant to this search. For, the Lord says, there is no friend of the self other than the Self. No particular culture or way of life is especially conducive to Self-realization; no sense of detachment or attachment is conducive or opposed to Self-realization. Renunciation of the world, or a recluse way of life, is not especially helpful to the unfolding of the Self, for It unfolds Itself by Itself to Itself. Through meditation a situation is created where the Self is found uncovered, unfolded in Its pure and essential nature with no shadow cast upon It by anything.

Meditation does not unfold the Self — the Self, it must be repeated, unfolds Itself by Itself to Itself. The wind does nothing to the sun; it only clears away the clouds and the sun is found shining by its own light. The sun of the Self is self-effulgent. Meditation only takes the mind out of the clouds of relativity. The absolute state of the Self ever shines in Its own glory.

The Lord's teaching in this verse applies to every level of evolution. This is obvious from the two preceding and the two following verses. It may be interesting to note at this point that the fullest development of the self is through three stages: from the waking state of consciousness to Transcendental Consciousness, from Transcendental Consciousness to Cosmic Consciousness, and from Cosmic Consciousness to God Consciousness. The teaching of this verse is equally applicable to all these stages of one's development. In the first stage, the self evolves by means of the activity of Transcendental Meditation and realizes the Self. In the second stage, from Transcendental Consciousness to Cosmic Consciousness, the state of Self is supplemented by the activity of the self in order to maintain the Self in Its true nature even in the midst of activity. In the third and final stage, from Cosmic Consciousness to God Consciousness, the Self has to go all by Itself and on the level of silence devoid of any activity. That is why the Lord said in the third verse: 'calmness is said to be the means'. And in the present verse, He says: 'Let a man raise his self by his Self'.

VERSE 6

बन्धुरात्मात्मनस्तस्य येनात्मैवात्मना जितः
अनात्मनस्तु शत्रुत्वे वर्तेतात्मैव शत्रुवत्

Bandhur Ātmātmanas tasya yenātmaivātmanā jitaḥ
anātmanas tu shatrutwe vartetātmaiva shatruvat

He who has conquered his self by his Self alone is himself his own friend; but the Self of him who has not conquered his self will behave with enmity like a foe.

The acquisition by the mind (the self in its relative aspect) of the state of Self-realization, or Transcendental Consciousness, is described here as a conquest: the lower self has conquered the higher Self. Through this conquest, the individual mind has gained the status of cosmic mind, or pure consciousness. This cosmic intelligence then becomes the basis of the whole of practical life; it supports and gives strength to all fields of relativity.

The mind, during meditation, reaches the state of transcendental Being and, coming out of the Transcendent into the field of relative life, remains saturated with Being. With constant practice of Transcendental Meditation, there comes a point where the saturation of the mind with Being becomes permanent and continues without interruption throughout all experiences in the relative world, with the result that the Self is experienced as separate from activity, and the binding influence of action is neutralized. The conscious mind of man, acting in the world, then acts in freedom, supported and protected by Being. This is how the Self, having been conquered by the self, befriends the self.

The lower self and the higher Self belong to the one indivisible Reality, which is inclusive of both the transcendental and relative aspects of life. Like brothers bound by the natural affinity of blood, they support each other in every way. This is one aspect of their relationship. But there is another: when a difference arises between brothers, they can become deadly enemies. This happens when the self has not conquered the Self.

If a man has not begun to meditate and has not consciously realized the Self, if his mind has not reached the realm of transcendental Being, then it will not have attained the status of cosmic intelligence either temporarily or permanently. This means that his lower self is not familiar with the higher Self, and there is no coordination between the two. The one has not accepted the other. They stand opposed to each other in their essential nature, for one is relative and the other transcendental. In the field of relativity they exist as enemies. The lower self is always acting through the senses, encouraging them and enjoying the variety of objective experience, thus preventing the higher Self from being effective in the relative field of existence and allowing It to remain as it were confined in the field of the Transcendent. In return, the higher Self also behaves as an enemy to the lower self. It does not save the self from the fast grip of the ever-changing life of relative existence, but allows it to remain within the cycle of birth and death. The higher Self does not provide the unlimited energy, wisdom, creativity, and happiness which alone will give peace and abundance to the lower self.

Conquest of the self by the Self and conquest of the Self by the self amounts to the same thing. It can be understood in either way so long as the conquest denotes the Union of the two, or merger of the one into the other. The merger of the self into the Self takes place in the state of Transcendental Consciousness and becomes permanent in Cosmic Consciousness. The self finds itself one with the Self. This is that state where the self and the Self support each other so intimately that they do not exist independently of each other.

The next verse elaborates the inner and outer condition of the realized man, of one who has 'conquered'.

Verse 7

जितात्मनः प्रशान्तस्य परमात्मा समाहितः
शीतोष्णसुखदुःखेषु तथा मानापमानयोः

Jitātmanaḥ prashāntasya paramātmā samāhitaḥ
shītoshṇasukhaduḥkheshu tathā mānāpamānayoḥ

For him who has conquered his self, who is deep in peace,
the transcendent Self is steadfast in heat and cold, in
pleasure and pain, in honour and disgrace.

In verse 4 of this chapter, the Lord made a distinction between the realm of worldly activity and that of Being. In verses 5 and 6, He showed the way to establish coordination between the two. In the present verse, He describes the condition of the mind in this state, how one feels within when coordination between outer life and inner Being is established. The Lord says that one feels eternally peaceful, being immersed in the glory of the Supreme. In this state the whole of life, with all its pairs of opposites, is permeated with the glory of the transcendent Being. This state of eternal peace in Bliss Consciousness cannot be shaken by anything whatsoever.

This verse emphasizes the resolute nature of the established intellect.[11] In the following verse, the idea is developed and is elaborated into a description of the *Yogī* who is united.

11 See II, 56.

VERSE 8

ज्ञानविज्ञानतृप्तात्मा कूटस्थो विजितेन्द्रियः
युक्त इत्युच्यते योगी समलोष्टाश्मकाञ्चनः

Gyānavigyānatṛiptātmā kūtastho vijitendriyaḥ
yukta ityuchyate yogī samaloshtāshmakānchanaḥ

That Yogī is said to be united who is contented in knowledge and experience, unshakeable, master of the senses, who is balanced in experiencing earth, stone, or gold.

The Lord brings out the two aspects of realization, the two aspects of becoming a *Yogī*. The first is that of gaining a clear intellectual conception of the Truth through a proper understanding of Reality reached by listening, thinking, contemplating, and discriminating intellectually between Its various aspects. This, however, satisfies only the mind. The other aspect is that of knowing Reality by direct experience, which satisfies the heart. This is gained through Transcendental Meditation.

The Lord says that when the mind is satisfied by a completely clear intellectual conception of Reality, and the heart is satisfied by the direct experience of Its blissful and eternal nature, then a man gains eternal contentment. Then only does he become firm in his own state of life. Such an 'unshakeable' nature always behaves in the field of the senses as a 'master of the senses' and never as their slave. He 'is said to be united', and he is a *Yogī* whose life is marked by a balanced state of mind throughout all experience in the field of diversity.

This idea of balance in life will recur many times during the discourse. The repetition of this principle at short intervals indicates not only its intrinsic importance, but its relevance to Arjuna's situation. At the same time it brings home to him that, whatever method the mind adopts in order to become established in Reality — be it the path of action or that of renunciation — once it becomes established, the infusion of Being into the nature of the mind is the same and brings with it the same balanced vision. Although they may differ in mode of life and manner of activity, those who are realized have this in common: they always possess balanced understanding and vision.

Having spoken of the realized man's inner state of mind and of his nature during experience of the outer world, the Lord, in the following verse, describes his behaviour towards others in society.

VERSE 9

सुहृन्मित्रार्युदासीनमध्यस्थद्वेष्यबन्धुषु
साधुष्वपि च पापेषु समबुद्धिर्विशिष्यते

Suhṛinmitrāryudāsīnamadhyasthadweshyabandhushu
sādhushwapi cha pāpeshu samabuddhir vishishyate

Distinguished is he who is of even intellect among well-wishers,
friends, and foes, among the indifferent and the impartial,
among hateful persons and among kinsmen, among the
saintly as well as the sinful.

'Even intellect': because of this inner state of eternal contentment, the mind of a *Yogī* abides in silence. Based on this silence, his intellect is even. This does not mean that he behaves to everyone in like manner. A *Yogī* does not create confusion in the various fields of relationship by failing to recognize due differences. But among all the variety of relationships his understanding, based on the oneness of life, does not waver. He remains 'of even intellect'.

A man who has balanced vision while experiencing objects has been declared a *Yogī* in the previous verse. The balanced vision described in that verse belongs to a *Yogī*, whether he has reached his state through the path of Sāṁkhya or *Karma Yoga*. The present verse sets the standard for a *Yogī* who is 'distinguished'.

Having so far devoted this chapter to describing all that the practice of meditation can accomplish for man, the Lord, in the following verses, explains the details of the practice.

VERSE 10

योगी युञ्जीत सततमात्मानं रहसि स्थितः
एकाकी यतचित्तात्मा निराशीरपरिग्रहः

Yogī yunjīta satatam Ātmānaṁ rahasi sthitaḥ
ekākī yatachittātmā nirāshīr aparigrahaḥ

Let the Yogī always collect himself remaining in seclusion, alone, his mind and body subdued, expecting nothing, without possessions.

'Collect himself' means meditate. The manner in which the *Yogī* collects himself is mentioned in verse 27 of Chapter V and is detailed in the following five verses of the present chapter.

'*Yogī*' does not here mean an accomplished *Yogī*. An accomplished *Yogī* no longer has any need to continue the practice necessary for reaching the higher state, for he has already attained it. Because the necessity of practice is being explained, '*Yogī*' in this context means an aspirant to Yoga. At the same time the word '*Yogī*' indicates one who has reached a state of Union. The word, therefore, is best understood here as referring to a man who has realized the state of Self-consciousness, or *Samādhi*, but has not yet attained Cosmic Consciousness — *Nitya-samādhi*, or *Jīvan-mukti*. Such a *Yogī* has to be intent on practice so that Self-consciousness may become continuous and established in the nature of the mind to such a degree that even when the mind is out in the field of relative experience it is never out of the state of Being. This is the state of Cosmic Consciousness, the state of an accomplished *Yogī*. To arrive at Cosmic Consciousness, the *Yogī* has to meditate in silence and then come out into activity.[12] In the present verse, the Lord wants to emphasize that when a *Yogī* meditates he should always do so under the following conditions:

1. remaining in seclusion
2. alone
3. his mind and body subdued

12 See V, 11.

4. expecting nothing
5. without possessions.

'Seclusion' is essential because the process of Transcendental Meditation, which is a direct way for the mind to arrive at transcendental Bliss Consciousness, is a delicate one. It must be allowed to go its way unhindered. If the place of meditation is not secluded, there is more possibility of disturbance. During meditation the mind engages itself in the deeper levels of the thought-process; if it is disturbed and suddenly made to come out into the gross levels of sensory perception, it will experience a great contrast between the subtle and the gross fields of perception. This sudden contrast will damage the mind's serenity and will upset the nervous system.

'Alone': if a man does not meditate alone, then the feeling of someone being around him or watching him may impede the smoothness of the process of transcending. Any such influence, slowing down the march of the mind towards Bliss Consciousness, may bring undue strain to the mind and produce a corresponding stress in the nervous system.

'Mind and body subdued': the word 'subdued' is of special interest. The mind is 'subdued' by the experience of happiness.[13] As the mind, during meditation, experiences ever subtler states of thought, it experiences increasing charm at every step. This increasing happiness keeps the mind unwaveringly on the process of meditation. When the mind is subdued in this manner, the nervous system, following the pattern of the mind, remains unwavering. This is how 'his mind and body' are 'subdued' in a most natural manner.

It would be wrong to conclude here that the *Yogī* has to make constant and strenuous efforts of control in order to have 'his mind and body subdued'.

'Expecting nothing': when the Lord says that the aspirant should 'always collect himself remaining in seclusion', He wants at the same time to warn him against any tendency to expect. This process of collecting oneself should not contain any element of expectation of some further step in the process or, indeed, of

13 See III, 43; V, 21; VI, 21.

any particular experience. It should be free from any expectation of success in arriving at the goal. This expression brings out the meaning of verse 47 of Chapter II as applied to meditation: 'You have control over action alone, never over its fruits.'

The warning against 'expecting' is very significant. When, during meditation, the mind is engaged in experiencing subtler states of the thought-process on the way to transcending, it is set on the path of increasing charm. Any tendency to expect or hope only serves to pull the mind away from this path. The mind, by nature, does not cherish this deviation from the path of increasing happiness and is put to strain. 'Expecting', therefore, will only tend to make the mind miserable, with the result that the body too will be strained. That is why the principle of 'expecting nothing'[14] during meditation is brought out here.

'Without possessions':[15] meditation is a process which takes the mind from the consciousness of possessions to the consciousness of Being. In terms of possessions, it is a process of becoming possessionless: the Self is left by Itself. The mind loses consciousness of the surroundings and the body, leaving the *Yogī* quite naturally without any consciousness of possessions. The Lord speaks of being 'without possessions' to indicate that nothing is helpful for meditation, because it proceeds on the basis of the mind's natural tendency to go to a field of greater happiness, and that at the same time the process leaves one in a state where everything is abandoned of itself.

This expression also conveys that one should sit in meditation prepared to lose everything. When consciousness of outside objects begins to be lost, one should not begin to mourn its loss. The *Yogī*, when he starts his meditation, should not try to hang on to anything. With a free mind he should go to Being and *be* — awake in himself and lost to the world. As a result, he will be possessed of the Self in the midst of the possessions of the world. The phrase 'without possessions' expresses the state of Being.

When the Lord says: 'expecting nothing, without possessions', it is to show Arjuna what actually happens to the mind during meditation. It would be wrong to try not to have any expectations

14 See IV, 21.
15 See II, 45.

or desires, not to long for possessions when one sits in meditation; for while trying, the mind would be engaged in the thought of possessions and other objects of desire in order to forget them. Trying to forget amounts to remembering what one aims to forget. This should not be done because the process of meditation does not advance on the basis of forgetting the gross material objective world of possessions, but on the basis of entertaining finer fields of experience. The attempt to forget is based on hatred and condemnation, whereas the spontaneous experience of finer fields of thought during meditation is based on that willing acceptance which is the natural tendency of the mind on the way to greater happiness, on the path of God-realization.

This verse brings out the essentials of meditation — the practice which easily leads the mind to Transcendental Consciousness and from there, through the spontaneous infusion of Being into activity, to Cosmic Consciousness. It must not be mistaken as teaching a mode of conduct for life as a whole. This verse does not advocate a monkish withdrawal from life for a *Yogī*. It should not be understood as teaching that a *Yogī* must always remain away from society, by himself, aspiring to nothing, and possessing nothing.

If the distinction is not made between the time of meditation itself and the time spent out of meditation, then this verse and the succeeding ones may well be misunderstood.

The following verses give further details of the practice.

VERSE 11

शुचौ देशे प्रतिष्ठाप्य स्थिरमासनमात्मनः
नात्युच्छ्रितं नातिनीचं चैलाजिनकुशोत्तरम्

Shuchau deshe pratishthāpya sthiram āsanam Ātmanaḥ
nātyuchchhritaṁ nātinīchaṁ chailājinakushottaram

In a clean place, having set his seat firm, neither very high nor very low, having placed sacred grass, deerskin, and cloth one upon the other;

'A clean place' means either that the place is naturally clean or has been made clean and free from dust and insects; that it is, if possible, in surroundings that are pleasant, or at least not unsightly and unpleasant. Both the place and the seat should be conducive to meditation. The meditator should feel comfortable and pleasant.

Verse 12

तत्रैकाग्रं मनः कृत्वा यतचित्तेन्द्रियक्रियः
उपविश्यासने युञ्ज्याद्योगमात्मविशुद्धये

Tatraikāgraṁ manaḥ kṛitwā yatachittendriyakriyaḥ
upavishyāsane yunjyād yogam ātmavishuddhaye

Seated there on the seat, having made the mind one-pointed,
with the activity of the senses and thought subdued,
let him practise Yoga for self-purification.

The first point the Lord wants to make clear is that meditation should be performed in the sitting position and not lying down or standing. Lying down makes the mind dull; standing produces a fear of falling when the mind is drawn deep within. A normal state of mind is needed for starting meditation. The mind should neither be dull nor very active. When it is dull, tending to sleepiness, it loses the capacity for experience. When it is very active, it remains in the field of gross experience, and, as it were, refuses to enter into the field of subtle experience, just as someone very active on the surface of the water does not sink. To meditate is to let the mind sink into the Self. The process of sinking does not start if the mind is too active, as it has to be when the body is standing. The Lord therefore tells Arjuna that he should sit in order to start meditation.

'Having made the mind one-pointed': one-pointedness is most effectively brought about by allowing the mind to become drawn to more and more subtle states of the thought-process.

'With the activity of the senses and thought subdued': all experience arises out of the association of the mind with the objects of experience through the senses. During meditation the mind begins to associate itself with the subtler realms of the senses and in this way goes on experiencing more and more subtle aspects of the object of experience until eventually, associating itself with the subtlest level of the senses, it perceives the subtlest state of the object and then, transcending it, becomes established in the state of Being. In this way the activities of the mind and senses are gradually subdued.

In the state of absolute consciousness, the mind is free from all modes of the relative order and thus gains its most purified state. This is the state of Yoga. The Lord says: 'practise Yoga for self-purification'. Thereby He means that the practice of gaining this state is a means of gaining purification of body, mind, and spirit.

When the mind experiences subtle states of the object of meditation, it becomes very sharp and refined. At the same time the breath becomes correspondingly refined, and this soft, fine breathing tends to return the nervous system to its normal functioning order; any abnormal functioning is restored to normality. When the mind gains Transcendental Consciousness, it reaches its most purified state. At the same time the whole nervous system gains a state of restful alertness. In this state the body becomes a living instrument tuned to the divine nature.[16] This is the most purified state of the body.

As for the purification of the spirit, or self, the pure state of the spirit is Being, which is unbounded universal pure consciousness. When, through the practice of meditation, the mind reaches this consciousness, the individual spirit bound by time, space, and causation finds its unbounded cosmic nature. With practice, this state becomes permanent and the Self is experienced as completely separate from activity. This is the most purified state of the self, or the spirit.

This is how the practice of Yoga — that is, Transcendental Meditation — results in self-purification.

It is interesting to notice that in verse 11 of Chapter V the effect of self-purification was attributed to action performed by a *Yogī*. This teaching becomes significant through the practice of Yoga.

16 See IV, 38.

VERSE 13

समं कायशिरोग्रीवं धारयन्नचलं स्थिरः
संप्रेक्ष्य नासिकाग्रं स्वं दिशश्चानवलोकयन्

Samaṁ kāyashirogrīvaṁ dhārayann achalaṁ sthiraḥ
saṁprekshya nāsikāgraṁ swaṁ dishash chānavalokayan

Steady, keeping body, head, and neck upright and still, having directed his gaze to the front of his nose, without looking in any direction;

The art of being steady is described here. When the neck and head are upright, in line with the spine, the path of the breath is clear; inhalation and exhalation are smooth and unrestricted. This eliminates the possibility of any unnatural movement of the body.

Having shown the method of stilling the body, the Lord explains how to still the senses. Sight is the most active of the senses, and if this is stilled the other senses will quite naturally follow it. The sense of sight, like all the senses, functions through the mind. Activity of the mind involves breath. So in order to coordinate the mind, the senses, and the breath, the attention is brought 'to the front of his nose', the point where the breath and the normal line of vision meet. The effect of this is to establish coordination between the activities of the mind, the senses, and the breath and to remove any abnormalities of these functions. It calms the mind and makes it one-pointed; it quietens the senses and refines the breath.

'Having directed his gaze' means directing it and releasing it, not continuing to gaze.

'Without looking in any direction' means first, not looking here and there; and secondly, not fixing one's look sharply even in the direction of the front of the nose; and thirdly, closing the eyes.

The teaching given here is generally misunderstood in terms of concentration on the tip of the nose. Shankara says that if fixing the gaze on the tip of the nose were meant here, the mind would be left with the nose but without God.

The posture described is free from any strain on the body, mind, senses, or breath.

This verse prepares the platform from which the mind plunges into Being. It gives a technique whereby one gathers the attention from the multiplicity of the outside world to a calm and quiet state, while yet remaining in the field of outside experience. From here the process of meditation leads the mind inwards.

Verse 14

प्रशान्तात्मा विगतभीर्ब्रह्मचारिव्रते स्थित:
मन: संयम्य मच्चित्तो युक्त आसीत मत्पर:

Prashāntātmā vigatabhīr brahmachārivrate sthitaḥ
manaḥ saṁyamya machchitto yukta āsīta matparaḥ

With his being deep in peace, freed from fear, settled in the vow of chastity, with mind subdued and thought given over to Me, let him sit united realizing Me as the Transcendent.

'With his being deep in peace' means that the mind is set on the path of increasing charm, bringing greater contentment at every step and filling one's being with ever deeper silence and peace. This is a state where there is no disturbing element. It is not the state of deep sleep because there the sense of being is lost. It is a state where peace is profound and the sense of being is not lost. It is a state of pure awareness. The mind has shifted from the field of sensory experience to the state of the Self, the state of profound peace.

'Freed from fear': on the path of increasing happiness during meditation there is no chance of fear. The Upanishads declare that fear comes with the sense of duality. Freed from fear means freed from the field of duality. The previous verse has seen the mind collected from the field of diversity; in this verse, it is gaining freedom from the sense of duality. The mind, during the inward stroke of meditation, begins to lose the sense of duality, begins to move away from the field of fear. Once begun, this process puts an end to duality and gives rise to Transcendental

Consciousness, in which there is no possibility of fear.

'Settled in the vow of chastity': this does not mean that the practice here prescribed is only for those who have taken a vow of chastity. In the present context, the Lord is not dwelling on any gross aspect of the aspirant's way of life, on whether or not he may have taken any vow of chastity. Every expression in this verse gives deep insight into the state of the mind during the inward stroke of meditation, and it is in this sense that the words 'settled in the vow of chastity' should be understood.

All the energies of a man who has taken a vow of chastity are ever directed upwards, the whole stream of body, mind, and senses being channelled towards the higher levels of evolution, with no chance for his energy to flow downwards. Likewise, when the mind of the meditator goes deep within, this too has the effect of directing upwards the life-energy in the different spheres of his body, senses, and mind towards the highest level of evolution, at the same time allowing no chance of a downward flow of any mental, sensory, or bodily energy. Every aspect of his individuality converges upon universal consciousness in the transcendental field of Being. Because Transcendental Meditation brings with it a continuous rise of the mind towards the consciousness of eternal Being, it may be compared to the vow of chastity, by virtue of which the whole life-stream of a celibate ever rises towards this supreme consciousness.

It is not, therefore, the act of taking a vow that is emphasized here; rather, it is the secure and safeguarded upward flow of one's energies on the road of the divine quest. This takes place during the process of Transcendental Meditation and also in the life of a celibate — one becomes '*ūrdhwaretas*', meaning that one's energies flow only in an upward direction.[17]

'With mind subdued': having brought the mind under the influence of eternal Being. This happens in Transcendental Consciousness and therefore also in Cosmic Consciousness and God Consciousness. This is the central point of the present verse; all its other expressions follow from this one.

The expression 'with mind subdued' does not mean that the

17 The glow appearing on the face during meditation is due to this upward flow of energy.

mind has to be controlled against its natural inclination and forced to go in the direction of the Transcendent. To discipline the mind by trying to control it is not the way to establish the mind in the Self. This verse gives a simple method for the realization of Truth and does not make it in any way complicated or difficult. 'Mind subdued' here signifies both the mind's natural state of calmness in Transcendental Consciousness and its natural tendency to flow freely in the single channel leading to transcendent bliss because it experiences greater charm at every inward step during meditation. The mind becomes subdued quite naturally, drawn to the Transcendent by increasing charm and not forced by will, pressure of discipline, or control.

'Thought given over to Me' means thought surrendered to Me, who am the supreme Lord of all creation.[18] 'Thought given over to Me'[19] does not mean thinking of 'Me'. It means surrendering one's authorship of thoughts. This in turn does not mean that one stops thinking. It means entertaining thoughts in the state of non-attachment, where the Self remains unattached to the process of thinking, remains in Its eternal freedom, while all activity is naturally given over to God, who is the basis of the entire life of the cosmos.

In the present context, however, 'thought given over to Me' is best seen as referring to the time of meditation. The Lord's words indicate that when thoughts appear one should not fight them, should not try to control the mind against them, or try to run away from them; one should deal with them innocently. Let it be according to the Will of God. Proceed on your meditation in a relaxed way and unconcerned with thoughts, as though you had already given them over to God.

During meditation one should not make a mood of surrendering thoughts to God — one should treat them as though they had already been surrendered to Him and did not belong to one any more; one remains completely indifferent to them.

'Let him sit united': let him be in Transcendental Consciousness, or let his mind be firmly established in Cosmic Consciousness or in God Consciousness. The expression 'sit united' has no

18 See V, 29.
19 See also IV, 19–20.

reference to activity or inactivity; it only means that in the states of Transcendental Consciousness and Cosmic Consciousness, the infusion of Being into the nature of the mind is so complete that the mind is totally fixed and embedded in it, and that in the state of God Consciousness, the mind is completely taken over by the Unity of life. In the states of Cosmic Consciousness and God Consciousness this Union remains the same whether the mind is active or inactive.

'Realizing Me as the Transcendent': this expression makes clear the whole meaning of the present verse, for it brings to light the state of surrender. Surrender has to be on the level of pure consciousness, on the level of life itself, on the level of Being — not on the level of thinking, feeling, or understanding.

VERSE 15

युञ्जन्नेवं सदात्मानं योगी नियतमानसः
शान्तिं निर्वाणपरमां मत्संस्थामधिगच्छति

Yunjann evaṁ sadātmānaṁ yogī niyatamānasaḥ
shāntiṁ nirvāṇaparamāṁ matsaṁsthām adhigachchhati

Ever thus collecting himself, the Yogī of disciplined mind
attains to peace, the supreme liberation that abides in Me.

'Ever thus collecting himself': this expression refers to the practice explained in the four preceding verses. When the *Yogī* sits to meditate, he continues to collect his mind, that is, he leads it back to the 'subdued' state described in the previous verse.

The Lord's use of the words 'collecting himself', rather than 'collecting the mind', is significant. 'Collecting himself' means collecting all aspects of his being: body, breath, senses, mind. This happens when the mind enters the realm of subtler experience on the way to gaining pure consciousness. All the senses begin to converge and collect themselves in the silent ocean of Being, the activity of the body's inner mechanism begins to sink into that silence, and the breath collects itself on that silent level of cosmic breath. All the different constituents of oneself begin to lie together on that level of pure Being. This comes about automatically and simultaneously for mind, senses, breath, and body.[20] The expression 'collecting himself' thus indicates the process of Transcendental Meditation which results directly in the state referred to in the Lord's command: 'Be without the three *Guṇas*'.[21]

'Ever' means that the *Yogī's* only concern during meditation is to remain collected or engaged in the process of collecting himself. Either he remains collected in the state of pure Being mentioned in the previous verse, or if at any moment the whole structure of collectedness loosens, he has to collect himself again. He has always to be engaged in this manner. The significance of the word 'ever' is restricted to the time of meditation. It does not extend to the whole twenty-four hours of the *Yogī's* day.

'The *Yogī* of disciplined mind': this expression placed immediately after 'collecting himself' gives insight into the technique of 'collecting'. How does a *Yogī* collect himself when he loses the state of collectedness during meditation? By the 'disciplined mind', by a mind which is orderly, smooth, and harmonious in its functioning, so that its actions are easy and quiet. The mind is easy and naturally disciplined between 'collecting' and collectedness and again between the state of collectedness and 'collecting'. This means that when the mind goes off the path of meditation, the *Yogī* quietly brings it back without any jerk, without causing strain. The practice, during meditation, of handling all situations in a delicate manner develops discipline in the mind, which then ceases to wander unreasonably and unnecessarily in the outer field of activity.

'Attains to peace': when, during meditation, the mind is collected, it enters into the experience of subtler states of thought. Experiencing increasing charm at every step, it becomes more and more contented, and this brings peace to the mind.

'The supreme liberation': having used the word 'peace', the Lord wants to make clear the nature of this peace in order to distinguish it from such peace as a man may gain through sleep, when the burden of thought has been lifted for a while, or through

20 See IV, 38.
21 See II, 45.

satisfaction in the various fields of life. He therefore adds that this peace is the supreme liberation. One who begins meditation in the right manner, under the guidance of a qualified[22] person, certainly develops in himself the state of abiding peace and eternal liberation while leading an active life in the world.

'That abides in Me': the supreme liberation does not lie in any sovereign power, or power of Nature, but in Me, the great Lord of all creation. By virtue of My Being, this mighty universe of huge and contrasting elements eternally and spontaneously exists, while I remain uninvolved. This is 'the supreme liberation that abides in Me', says the Lord, and this uninvolved state of mind is developed by the 'disciplined mind' as it grows in 'peace'[23] and attains God Consciousness.

It may be noted that this verse declares the result of practice to be peace and liberation, whereas verse 28 declares it to be infinite joy. Here no reference is made to this joy because, as verse 28 will show, it is the outcome of a life 'freed from blemish', and this comes about through the practice described in the present verse.

VERSE 16

नात्यश्नतस्तु योगोऽस्ति न चैकान्तमनश्नतः
न चातिस्वप्नशीलस्य जाग्रतो नैव चार्जुन

Nātyashnatas tu yogo 'sti na chaikāntam anashnataḥ
na chātiswapnashīlasya jāgrato naiva chārjuna

Yoga, indeed, is not for him who eats too much nor for him who does not eat at all, O Arjuna; it is not for him who is too much given to sleep nor yet for him who keeps awake.

'Eats' and 'eat': these words indicate feeding the senses with their objects. The senses should not be provided with the objects of their enjoyment so excessively as to overfeed them, nor should they be completely deprived of their experience.[24]

22 See Appendix: The *Transcendental Meditation* Technique.
23 See verse 3, which says 'calmness' is the means.
24 See II, 64, 67.

'Sleep' means a state where the senses of experience are not active, while 'awake' denotes the opposite state. It is implied here that if a man is 'too much given to sleep' or too much given to keeping awake, then he will find it difficult to rise above the states of waking and sleeping; and rising above them is absolutely essential for Yoga.[25]

It is a common axiom that anything in excess is bad. Even food, which is the source of energy, creates dullness and inefficiency when too much or too little of it is taken. Here the Lord cautions against excess in either direction. In both cases the mind becomes dull and fails to reach finer states of experience during meditation. Remaining in the field of gross experience, it tends to passivity. This is a waste of precious human existence, which is meant for the expansion of happiness and the realization of an integrated state of life, the state of supreme liberation referred to in the previous verse.

The present verse advocates a normal and comfortable routine in daily life for success in the practice of Yoga.

Verse 17

युक्ताहारविहारस्य युक्तचेष्टस्य कर्मसु
युक्तस्वप्नावबोधस्य योगो भवति दुःखहा

Yuktāhāravihārasya yuktacheshtasya karmasu
yuktaswapnāvabodhasya yogo bhavati duḥkhahā

For him who is moderate in food and recreation, moderate of effort in actions, moderate in sleep and waking, for him is the Yoga which destroys sorrow.

Here is the broad principle to be followed by one who wishes to live a life of inner peace and happiness integrated with successful activity in the outside world. The body should be given the rest it needs, and one should engage in activity, but not to a state of exhaustion. Recreation should be taken in due proportion, so that it is neither too little nor too much. The Lord means that life

25 See II, 69, commentary.

should flow in a regular way, with a proper measure of activity and with each thing given its just value. One should avoid excess in all things and be regular in meditation, for this will result in the state of inner peace and freedom from bondage described in the 15th verse.

'Yoga', Union, is not only a state where the mind is fixed in divine consciousness. It is at the same time a state of individual life where every aspect of being is in perfect harmony with divine life and with life in Nature. This state can only become permanent when the physical nervous system is sufficiently cultured to maintain it. The mind, as stated in the commentary to verse 15, is in tune with the cosmic mind, or intelligence of God, while the functioning of the body sets itself in tune with the functioning of cosmic nature. The senses rise to the full height of their capability, in order to experience and enjoy objects on the level of the divine play. But for body, organs, and senses to function in their most natural way, in full accord with the Laws of Nature, it is absolutely essential that the routine of life be moderate, that everything connected with food and activity remain within the limits of moderation, that the happy medium be maintained.

'Moderate in sleep and waking': in its higher sense this expression indicates that one is only moderately involved[26] in the states of sleeping and waking. This means that the waking state, the state of knowing and experiencing the objective world, is primarily maintained by the senses, while the mind is primarily held in Being. And in the sleeping state, the body and the senses are completely withdrawn from activity but the mind is not overtaken by sleep: although detached from all activity it is awake in its awareness. Thus one is 'moderate in sleep and waking' in the sense of not being wholly engrossed in them.

'Moderate in food': in order to be moderate in food it is necessary to keep the whole system functioning normally. With regular meditation morning and evening, the functioning of the inner mechanisms is maintained in a normal condition,[27] and one becomes by nature 'moderate in food and recreation'.

'Recreation' means re-creation of the normal functioning of

26 See II, 69.

27 See verse 14, commentary.

the entire system so that it is capable of operating to its maximum capacity. When certain mechanisms of the body have been put to one specific type of activity, they become tired and a man loses efficiency in that activity. When he engages in another type of activity, other mechanisms become active and the tired ones take rest, thereby regaining their efficiency. This is said to be recreation. Those forms of recreation which are based on a change of activity in the outer field of life do not re-create the whole system at one time and therefore do not renew efficiency to the maximum extent. Transcendental Meditation re-creates, in that it produces a state of restful alertness for the entire system and rejuvenates it, thus fulfilling the purpose of recreation.

'Moderate of effort in actions' means that one has not to over-exert when working. This implies first, that one should be strong enough not to get tired — in other words, one should be energetic, alert, and free from laziness; and secondly, that the undertaking should be in accordance with one's own *Dharma*,[28] consistent with the Laws of Nature,[29] otherwise Nature offers its silent protest against the effort, and one is compelled to make unduly great 'effort in actions'. The regular practice of Transcendental Meditation fulfils both these needs because it provides greater energy and produces harmony in Nature.

It should not be understood that being 'moderate of effort in actions' is a prerequisite for Yoga. This quality grows as the practice advances. It is not something which can be achieved without transforming the very nature of the man and his surroundings. As the practice of meditation advances, it effortlessly transforms both his inner nature and the influence of his surroundings. This automatically makes him 'moderate of effort in actions'.

Each condition given in this verse lays emphasis on moderation, which is most effectively brought about through the regular practice of Transcendental Meditation. Therefore Transcendental Meditation can be regarded as the most effective form of recreation.

'Yoga which destroys sorrow': it has been said earlier that the transcendental state of consciousness is the state of Yoga. This

28 See I, 1, commentary.

29 See Appendix: Cosmic Law, The Basic Law of Creation.

is undoubtedly a state of bliss, but how does the bliss that lies in the transcendental state help to end sorrow and suffering in the relative field of life? By taking the transcendental bliss and bringing it back to the field of relative existence, bliss begins to dominate the sphere in which sorrows and suffering prevailed. The expression 'Yoga which destroys sorrow' makes it clear that the different points which this verse brings out regarding conduct form an essential part of the practice designed to transform transcendental pure consciousness into Cosmic Consciousness.[30]

The present verse explains the general mode of conduct which alone will allow the bliss experienced in meditation to be infused into the relative phase of existence. Its entire purpose is to warn the aspirant against laying too much importance on any one aspect of relative life. If only he takes things in their due proportion, every aspect of his life will remain without strain. It is this harmonious level of existence which provides the basis on which the divine Being can be lived in the world. This is further explained by the word 'united' in the following verse.

VERSE 18

यदा विनियतं चित्तमात्मन्येवावतिष्ठते
निःस्पृहः सर्वकामेभ्यो युक्त इत्युच्यते तदा

Yadā viniyataṁ chittam Ātmanyevāvatishthate
niḥspṛihaḥ sarvakāmebhyo yukta ityuchyate tadā

When his mind, completely settled, is established
in the Self alone, when he is free from craving for
any pleasure, then is he said to be united.

This is a description of the state of mind reached through the practice described in the previous verses.

'His mind completely settled': this refers to Transcendental Consciousness, where the mind has become an unlimited and silent ocean of pure consciousness without a single wave of thought. It may also be said to refer to Cosmic Consciousness,

30 See verse 25.

where the calm of the ocean is not disturbed in spite of waves of thought and experience.

It may be argued that it is the very nature of the mind to become completely settled in any object of experience, for was it not said in the 67th verse of Chapter II that a man's intellect is carried away by the senses 'as a ship by the wind on water'? This being the case, does not the mind, drawn by the force of the senses, become completely settled at the contact of the senses with their objects and enjoy the happiness to be derived therefrom?[31]

In order to give no room for such arguments and to avoid misunderstanding, the Lord says: 'established in the Self alone'. This expression has its meaning on two levels: on the level of Transcendental Consciousness and on that of Cosmic Consciousness. On the transcendental level there is nothing but the Self alone. The nature of the Self is pure consciousness, cosmic intelligence, cosmic existence, cosmic life, eternal Being, absolute bliss. It is transcendent, ever the same, imperishable. It is 'smaller than the smallest'. It is the silence. The word 'Self' expresses the inexpressible transcendental Truth of life. The mind, coming to this field, loses its individuality and gains its true nature as pure Being.

On the level of Cosmic Consciousness, the expression 'established in the Self alone' means that in the midst of all behaviour, in the activity or the silence of the waking, dreaming, and sleeping states, a man realizes the Self as completely separate from the field of activity and thus remains established in the Self alone. The varied experiences of life fail to overshadow this state of cosmic existence and complete fulfilment which the mind has gained.

Having explained the steadfast and unshakeable character of the mind in the state of eternal contentment, the Lord turns to the practical value of such a state of mind; for a principle or a state of mind which has no practical use in daily life is of little importance in the world. The Lord has told Arjuna that the Yoga which He is expounding here was given to the first rulers of the world,[32] thereby placing it on a very practical level. Moreover,

31 See II, 14.
32 See IV, 1–2.

throughout the discourse, at the end of any exposition of a highly spiritual and abstract nature, the Lord says something to tie it down to practical life. Here He says: 'free from craving for any pleasure'.

'Free from craving for any pleasure' means fulfilled. Craving for pleasure arises from lack of contentment, which may be due to the objects of the senses not being available, or to the inability of the senses to experience the joy that is available.[33] But once a man is established in the state described in this verse, he is eternally contented, and this state of lasting contentment leaves no room for any craving for pleasures.[34]

This state of freedom 'from craving for any pleasure' is on the level of that complete fulfilment of life where the individual being is one with the cosmic Being. It is on the level of 'eternal freedom in divine consciousness';[35] on the level of 'maintaining your consciousness in the Self;[36] on the level of Union and knowledge.[37] It fulfils the aspirations expressed by verse 55 of Chapter II and verse 38 of Chapter IV, and satisfies the level of attainment given in verse 8 of Chapter V.

This state is on the level where the paths of Sāṁkhya and *Karma Yoga* meet to find fulfilment in a common goal, as brought out by verse 5 of Chapter V.

'United': in verse 8, this word was used to denote evenness of vision; here, as in verse 14, it is given a much wider meaning. It is used in terms of the whole being, encompassing the entire field of the mind, its silence and its desires and activities, the whole field of life that lies between the two extremes of bondage and eternal freedom, between the individual man and the cosmic Divine. It denotes life in Cosmic Consciousness, which is inclusive of the relative and the Absolute.

33 See II, 59.
34 See III, 17–18; VI, 2.
35 See V, 24–6; II, 55–72.
36 See III, 30.
37 See IV, 10, 18–24, 35, 41; V, 7, 19–21, 23; VI, 4, 8.

VERSE 19

यथा दीपो निवातस्थो नेङ्गते सोपमा स्मृता
योगिनो यतचित्तस्य युञ्जतो योगमात्मनः

Yathā dīpo nivātastho nengate sopamā smṛitā
yogino yatachittasya yunjato yogam Ātmanaḥ

A lamp which does not flicker in a windless place —
to such is compared the Yogī of subdued thought
practising Union with the Self.

This verse may be compared with verse 69 of Chapter II, which says that in the night of all beings the self-controlled man is awake. But the simile in the present verse is more profound, for whereas the expression in the second chapter is in the context of the senses and their control,[38] the lamp in the windless place represents 'thought', standing by itself, freed from the influence of the senses.

This illustrates the reason for the difference between the discourses of enlightened men at different times. When such men come out to explain the Truth, their manner of expression and depth of thought depend upon the time and surrounding circumstances. Their discourse depends upon the purity of consciousness of those listening to it. At this stage, Arjuna's consciousness has become pure enough to understand with exactness the state of 'the *Yogī* of subdued thought practising Union with the Self'.

It may be noted that any objective experience is due to the mind's association with the object through the senses. For example, if one is meditating on a thought, the experience of the gross and subtle states of that thought are due to the mind's association with the sense of speech.

During meditation the object of experience continues to be perceived in its diminishing states, but when the subtlest state of experience has been transcended, then the mind is free from the influence both of the object and of the sense through which it has been experiencing. As long as the mind is influenced by the

38 See II, 68.

senses and their objects, so long is it like a lamp flickering in the wind, but once out of their influence it becomes steady, like 'a lamp which does not flicker in a windless place'.

As long as the mind is associated with the object, so long is it the experiencing mind; but when the object of experience has diminished to the point where it has disappeared, the mind ceases to be the experiencing mind. Conscious mind becomes consciousness. But during this process of transformation, it first gains the pure state of its own individuality.

It is interesting to see that the verse does not speak of the mind but of 'thought' as being steady. The Sanskrit word used is '*Chitta*', which signifies that aspect of mind which is a quiet and silent collection of impressions, or seeds of desires. *Chitta* is like water without ripples. It is called '*Manas*', or mind, when ripples arise.

When the mind gains this state of *Chitta*, or 'thought', then it stands steady, like 'a lamp which does not flicker in a windless place'. It holds its individuality in the void — the abstract fullness around it — because there is nothing for it to experience. It remains undisturbed, awake in itself.

Imagine a silent wave on a silent ocean, ready to expand and merge into the silence of the deep. The state of the pure individuality of the mind, the pure individuality of the 'I', expressed by this verse, directly merges into transcendental Self-consciousness; this is expressed by the Lord as 'Union with the Self': the mind is united with divine Being.

This state of Divine Union, or Yoga, is defined in its different aspects in the four following verses, after which six verses are devoted to the transformation of Transcendental Consciousness into Cosmic Consciousness. Then three verses bring to light the essence of the path from Cosmic Consciousness to God Consciousness, in which a *Yogī* reaches the pinnacle of achievement.

VERSE 20

यत्रोपरमते चित्तं निरुद्धं योगसेवया
यत्र चैवात्मनात्मानं पश्यन्नात्मनि तुष्यति

Yatroparamate chittaṁ niruddhaṁ yogasevayā
yatra chaivātmanātmānaṁ pashyann Ātmani tushyati

That (state) in which thought, settled through the practice of Yoga, retires, in which, seeing the Self by the Self alone, he finds contentment in the Self;

This verse describes a further step in the practice. The previous verses have taken the mind to the state where thought — the resolute intellect — stands by itself, steady and unmoved. The present verse says that when, with continued practice, this steady intellect gains a clear experience of its individuality, it begins to retire. The process of retiring begins with the expansion of individuality, and when this happens the intellect, losing its individuality, begins to gain universality, begins to gain the unbounded status of Being. While merging into Being, it cognizes Being as its own Self and gains Bliss Consciousness — the *Yogī* 'finds contentment in the Self'.

The Self, as was said in the commentary on verse 18, is of transcendental nature; until the mind transcends all experience, it does not realize the Self. In the process of transcending all experience, the mind retires from the experience of multiplicity and gains the experience of Unity in its own individual nature. Then, transcending its individual status, it expands into cosmic Being. This state of Being, the state of Transcendental Consciousness, is referred to by the words, 'seeing the Self by the Self alone'.

The word 'alone' is significant, for it emphasizes that the transcendental Self Itself forms the content of Its Being and that nothing which is of relative existence can possibly cognize It. Its purity, eternal and supreme, is such that even the finest aspect of individual life, the resolute intellect, is foreign to It and is denied entry into It. The intellect has to surrender its existence in order to find its place in the eternal Being of the Self.

This is the glory of the nature of the Self. Having come back home, the traveller finds peace. The intensity of happiness is beyond the superlative. The bliss of this state eliminates the possibility of any sorrow, great or small. Into the bright light of the sun no darkness can penetrate; no sorrow can enter Bliss Consciousness, nor can Bliss Consciousness know any gain greater than itself. This state of self-sufficiency leaves one steadfast in oneself, fulfilled in eternal contentment.

The present verse forms the beginning of a long sentence that culminates in verse 23. Nowhere else in the Bhagavad-Gītā do we find a sentence of this extended nature. This is because these four verses present Yoga, the state of Divine Union, in its complete glory. The present verse brings to light the state of Divine Union in Transcendental Consciousness. The following verse depicts it in Cosmic Consciousness, the third in terms of the supreme gain that is God Consciousness, and the fourth in terms of the elimination of suffering.

VERSE 21

सुखमात्यन्तिकं यत्तद्बुद्धिग्राह्यमतीन्द्रियम्
वेत्ति यत्र न चैवायं स्थितश्चलति तत्त्वतः

Sukham ātyantikaṁ yat tad buddhigrāhyam atīndriyam
vetti yatra na chaivāyaṁ sthitash chalati tattwataḥ

Knowing that which is infinite joy and which, lying
beyond the senses, is gained by the intellect, and
wherein established, truly he does not waver;

In order to know why the senses cannot experience 'infinite joy', it is necessary to understand the origin of the senses and their objects. Creation begins with *Prakṛiti*, or Nature, which expresses itself in the three *Guṇas: Sattwa, Rajas,* and *Tamas*. As the process of creation continues, the three manifest as *Mahat Tattwa*, the principle of intellect. This further manifests as *Ahaṁ Tattwa*, the principle of mind, which in its turn manifests as the five *Tanmātras*, from which arise the five senses. Then, as the process of manifestation continues, the five *Tanmātras* manifest into the five elements, which combine to constitute the entire objective creation.

The range of sensory experience is limited to the field of creation resulting from these five elements. The senses only enable one to experience the joys of the objective world. The bliss of eternal life lies far beyond the senses and immediately beyond the intellect. It can be appreciated by the intellect but cannot be appreciated by the senses.

The Lord says that infinite joy is of transcendental nature; it is known only when the subtlest aspect of relativity, the intellect, surrenders itself to the transcendental Self, as was explained in the previous verse. Once it is known, one is so captivated by it that one can never again be completely out of its influence.

'Gained by the intellect': although infinite joy comes with the surrender of the intellect, it is even then said to be 'gained by the intellect'. When the crown prince becomes king, the crown prince ceases to exist, but even then it can be said that the crown prince has 'gained' kingship. It is in this sense that the state of transcendental Self is 'gained by the intellect'.

'Does not waver': in the state of Transcendental Consciousness there is no possibility of activity, but continued practice of transcending the field of relativity cultures the mind so that it remains established in bliss, unwavering even in the field of activity.

This verse brings out the essential characteristic of Yoga in Cosmic Consciousness: 'infinite joy', 'lying beyond the senses', 'gained by the intellect', 'wherein established, truly he does not waver'.

Details of this state are given in verses 24 to 29.

VERSE 22

यं लब्ध्वा चापरं लाभं मन्यते नाधिकं ततः
यस्मिन्स्थितो न दुःखेन गुरुणापि विचाल्यते

Yaṁ labdhwā chāparaṁ lābhaṁ manyate nādhikaṁ tataḥ
yasmin sthito na duḥkhena guruṇāpi vichālyate

Having gained which he counts no other gain as higher,
established in which he is not moved even by great sorrow;

This is the glory of the supreme state of Yoga; the supreme state of Divine Union in God Consciousness, the blessed oneness of life in which 'he counts no other gain as higher'. This is that state in which the separation of the Self from activity, as experienced in Cosmic Consciousness, finds its consummation in Unity of life, in the Light of God, which knows no duality. Life becomes so at home with this state that 'he is not moved' by all the sorrows and sufferings that go on in the relative aspect of life.

The glory of this discourse of the Lord is found in the words 'established in which he is not moved even by great sorrow'. Even when the Lord here presents the supreme state of life, 'having gained which he counts no other gain as higher', He keeps it within the range of the human heart, which is exposed to sorrow. Indeed, He extends the very definition of this most blessed state of Divine Union, or Yoga, to the level of human suffering. This is to indicate how even those phases of life in most extreme contrast to Divinity are intimately embraced by this blessed state of Divine Union. The following verse develops this point.

The details of the state of God Consciousness are dealt with in verses 30 to 32.

Verse 23

तं विद्याद्दुःखसंयोगवियोगं योगसंज्ञितम्
स निश्चयेन योक्तव्यो योगोऽनिर्विण्णचेतसा

Taṁ vidyād duḥkhasaṁyogaviyogaṁ yogasaṁgyitam
sa nishchayena yoktavyo yogo 'nirviṇṇachetasā

Let that disunion of the union with sorrow be known by the name of Yoga (Union). This Yoga should be practised with firm resolve and heart undismayed.

This verse brings out the spiritual teaching of the Lord in terms of Union in 'disunion'. He shows that Yoga is universal; it is found even in the field of 'disunion'. He says that even the disunion of the mind with sorrow is Union, and that this Union (Yoga) must be practised with determination and firmness of mind. The Lord wants everyone to practise this: those who can practise it in the name of Union should do so; those who cannot should do so in the name of disunion. The word 'Union' is for those who can conceive of absolute bliss and wish to possess it even to the extent of being it. The word 'disunion' is for those who cannot conceive of this bliss, or cannot think themselves capable of aspiring to it. But these latter are certainly familiar in their lives with sorrow and will wish to come out of its reach. Let them therefore begin this practice in order to put an end to sorrow. The mind must be taken out of the realm of suffering, for there is no need to suffer in life when there is this centre of happiness within oneself.

How one may continue to practise this Yoga which puts an end to all one's suffering is explained in the five verses that follow.

Verses 20 to 23 have been devoted to the definition of Yoga. The purpose of defining Yoga in four verses is to show that Yoga is sufficient to fulfil all the four aims of life prescribed by the scriptures. These declare the purpose of life to be the fulfilment of 1. *Dharma*, 2. *Artha*, 3. *Kāma*, and 4. *Moksha*.

1. *Dharma* is one's natural duty, which includes all moral goodness, right action, freedom, justice, and lawfulness — all the principles that uphold and support life. All these are completely satisfied once a man has realized himself. For in the knowledge and experience of the Self, a man attains a level of life which is the basis of all morality, virtue, and right action, and from which he is able to fulfil the Laws[39] of Nature and do justice to all creation. Verse 20, describing the Unity of the mind and Being, shows all aspirations of *Dharma* fulfilled.

2. *Artha* is fulfilled in verse 21. *Artha* means wealth, business, advantage, utility, reward, and gain. With the experience of eternal bliss, all such aspirations are completely satisfied, for to store more and more means of happiness is the only purpose of *Artha* in all its aspects.

3. *Kāma* is desire. Desire naturally aims at happiness and the removal of suffering. All aspirations on this level are satisfied when man realizes the eternal bliss of the Self. When one

39 See Appendix: Cosmic Law, The Basic Law of Creation.

seeks no more and desires no greater happiness, then one is fulfilled from the point of view of *Kāma*. Describing such fulfilment, verse 22 presents the summit of the realization of *Kāma*. It provides security even against great sorrow and offers supreme happiness.

4. *Moksha* is liberation. Verse 23 proclaims liberation from all pain and sorrow through Yoga, or Union with the Supreme, as described in verse 20.

These verses, 20 to 23, form the four pillars of the edifice of Yoga. They stand to remind men of every generation that it is not necessary to suffer in life, that life's goal is easy to attain and that all aspirations are easy to fulfil. The way is by the inward march of the mind, by quietly locating the hidden universal Being, a ray of whose eternal light is sufficient to dispel all the darkness of ignorance and shower down the blessings of almighty God.

These verses, in giving the definition of Yoga, provide a royal road to fulfilment at every level[40] of human life. Fortunate are those who take this highway, who practise Transcendental Meditation.

It must be made quite clear at this point that the purpose of Yoga does not end in realizing the Self in the transcendental state (verse 20). Although this is the final attainment of the inward stroke of meditation and although it gives a full meaning to Yoga in that it brings complete Union with divine consciousness, it is not complete. The overall purpose of Yoga is not yet satisfied. Unless the divine consciousness, gained in the transcendental state, continues to maintain itself at all times, in a natural manner, irrespective of the different states of waking, dreaming, or sleeping, and irrespective of the mind's engagement in activity or in silence, the purpose of Yoga is not fulfilled. Yoga, or Divine Union, attained in the state of Self-consciousness, or *Ātmānanda*, has to develop into Cosmic Consciousness, or *Brahmānanda*, which again is a state of Yoga. This eventually gives rise to God Consciousness, the pinnacle of Yoga, where there is no trace of sorrow or suffering.

40 Refer to: Maharishi Mahesh Yogi, *Science of Being and Art of Living* (New York: Plume Publications, 2001). (Original work published in 1963.)

VERSE 24

संकल्पप्रभवान्कामांस्त्यक्त्वा सर्वानशेषत:
मनसैवेन्द्रियग्रामं विनियम्य समन्तत:

Saṁkalpaprabhavān kāmāṁs tyaktwā sarvān asheshataḥ
manasaivendriyagrāmaṁ viniyamya samantataḥ

Abandoning without reserve all desires from which the incentive (to action) is born, controlling the village of the senses on every side by the mind alone;

Having thus far defined three states of Yoga, the Lord, in this and the following four verses, describes how the state of Yoga in Transcendental Consciousness is transformed into the state of Yoga in Cosmic Consciousness.

Such is the marvel of the Lord's expression that in each of these five verses[41] in sequence He is able to develop not only the theme of gaining Transcendental Consciousness, but side by side with this a second theme: that of the development of Cosmic Consciousness when Transcendental Consciousness has already been gained. The parallel presentation of these two themes is a teaching in itself. It shows first that the path to Cosmic Consciousness comprehends the path to Transcendental Consciousness, and secondly that Cosmic Consciousness develops simultaneously with the growth of Transcendental Consciousness in the mind.

'The incentive (to action)': the stimulus that a desire produces in the nervous system, bringing into action the senses of perception and the organs of action. This stimulus is opposed to the process of gaining that state of restful alertness of the nervous system which corresponds with Transcendental Consciousness. That is why, when the Lord is explaining the whole process of making Transcendental Consciousness permanent, He emphasizes the need for preventing the opposing process from interfering. It should be borne in mind, however, that even though the Lord gives this caution He is not advocating a practice of

41 Verses 24–8.

controlling desire. He states as a principle that desires are not helpful[42] on the path because they stimulate the nervous system to external activity and this is opposed to its internal activity, which gives experience of subtle states of thought as the mind proceeds towards the state of Transcendental Consciousness.

When the Lord says: 'Abandoning without reserve all desires from which the incentive (to action) is born, controlling the village of the senses on every side by the mind alone', He means engage the mind in the process of Transcendental Meditation and let it enter into the experience of subtle fields of thinking.

Having become familiar with Bliss Consciousness in the field of the Transcendent, the mind is very naturally and automatically drawn in that direction if allowed to proceed without distraction. The Lord says: 'by the mind alone', meaning that one does not use any austerity or forcible control to close the gates of the senses. The senses will automatically set themselves quietly to follow the mind as it proceeds to the Transcendent. In the quiet inward stroke of the mind during meditation, desires are automatically abandoned. Here the Lord is only saying that one should let the mind follow its familiar path to the Transcendent in the most natural and normal manner.

'The village of the senses': the place where the senses are housed. This is the structure of the nervous system. The whole nervous system is the village, the individual senses are the villagers, and the mind the landlord. Thus, when the Lord says: 'controlling the village of the senses on every side by the mind alone', the principle He wants to bring out is this: control the landlord to influence the villagers, in order to reorientate the village so that its activity, the activity of the nervous system, proceeds in accordance with the Laws of Nature, while the awareness of the Self maintains its natural state in eternal Being. This places the whole of life in its most natural state: absolute Being and the relative field of activity remain separate and yet integrated in the individual life in the state of Cosmic Consciousness.

The practice is entirely mental, but it directly influences the whole nervous system, through which the senses function. It should be noted that when the Lord begins the teaching about

42 See III, 37.

gaining Cosmic Consciousness, He speaks of the nervous system, the physical aspect of life, and emphasizes the need for its reorientation. But the human nervous system is of such extreme complexity and refinement that it is not possible to reorientate it through a physical approach. This difficulty is solved by the emphasis that the Lord places on the words 'the mind alone'. Thereby He warns the aspirant against making any attempt to control the senses directly, or to influence the nervous system by any physical means. The reorientation of the nervous system is essential in order to make permanent the state of Transcendental Consciousness,[43] but it must be brought about by a mental process. If the aspirant tries to control the senses on their own level, or if he attempts to control them by a mental process which goes against their natural tendencies, the result will be strain. The practice taught in this verse is absolutely free from any possibility of strain.

'Controlling the village of the senses on every side': this expression indicates the technique of controlling all the senses at one and the same time, without offering them any resistance individually on the level of the senses themselves, and without attacking their natural tendency to lead the mind towards their objects. This aspect of the teaching is of the utmost value. When the senses are turned inwards during the inward stroke of meditation, and outwards during the outward stroke of meditation, then they are becoming reorientated in a most natural way so that their every activity is spontaneously in accordance with the Laws of Nature.

This process of reorientation will be strained if the senses are restricted. Only if a situation is created in which the senses have a free inward and outward activity motivated by their own nature to enjoy is it possible for man to realize that the greater intensity of happiness lies in the inward direction. And with this realization, the habit of remaining under the influence of the bliss of Being is built up, to give rise to Cosmic Consciousness.

43 See IV, 38.

VERSE 25

शनैः शनैरुपरमेद्बुद्ध्या धृतिगृहीतया
आत्मसंस्थं मनः कृत्वा न किंचिदपि चिन्तयेत्

Shanaiḥ shanair uparamed buddhyā dhṛitigṛihītayā
Ātmasaṁsthaṁ manaḥ kṛitwā na kiṁchid api chintayet

Let him gradually retire through the intellect possessed of patience; having established the mind in the Self, let him not think at all.

This verse clarifies the words 'retires' (verse 20) and 'abandoning' (verse 24). It emphasizes that the process of retiring should be gradual and adds 'possessed of patience' to make quite clear that nothing should be done to hasten or modify this process. Once begun, it should be allowed to proceed by itself.

The points about patience and gradualness are highly important. If a man becomes impatient and tries to push the mind into the Transcendent, then many disadvantages arise. The intensity of thought is very great at that subtle level of thinking where the mind is slipping out of thought and is about to lose the experience of the relative field. If the process is not disturbed and is allowed to go by itself in a very innocent manner, then the mind slips into the Self. If, on the other hand, pressure or force is applied in any way to check the mind or to control the process, the mind will be thrown off the course on which it is naturally set and off-balance into agitation and a feeling of discomfort. That is why the process has to be allowed to take place quietly and patiently, without any anxiety or hurry.

One must not exert oneself in order to transcend. Exertion of any kind only retards the process of transcending. The mind naturally proceeds towards the Self because in that direction it is attracted by ever-increasing happiness. So the Lord says it should be allowed to come in that direction naturally and innocently.

'Intellect possessed of patience' has an inner meaning, apart from the obvious one of advocating patience on the part of the intellect. It is that the intellect should not function during the process. What is happening should not be watched and analysed or scrutinized by the intellect. No critical scrutiny of the process is needed. The intellect only needs to be receptive and appreciative and not in any way discriminative or on its guard. It has only to accept experience as it comes.

'Let him gradually retire': so that the mind, as it fathoms the deeper levels of the thought-process, may simultaneously become refined in order to experience further subtler states and may proceed onward in an innocent manner. If a man standing in bright light suddenly rushes into a dark cave, his eyes may not be able to see what is there inside the cave; but if he enters slowly, his eyes become used to the lesser intensity of light, and then he is able to see. The mind, when it retires deep within, goes from the more gross to the subtler levels of experience. Therefore it is essential for the mind not to rush in suddenly but to go gradually and patiently.

Again, when the individuality of the intellect begins to gain the state of Being, it is absolutely necessary that the process be slow. Only then will the bliss be within the range of experience.

'Let him not think at all': the Lord says that when the mind is established in the Self one should not try to think, because the transcendental state of consciousness lies beyond the mind's ability to think. Any attempt to think in that state will not succeed. This is the state where one just enjoys being there. It is not on a level where thought can find a place. The Lord informs the aspirant of its nature so that he may not expect some good thoughts to come in that state.

The Lord says: 'Do not think at all.' This state of not thinking is a natural consequence of the mind's being established in the Self; and it holds good only during meditation. It does not mean that a man should not think of anything when he is out of meditation, for a habit of not thinking will make his life dull and useless.

The mind, coming out of the Self, out of the state of transcendence during meditation, alights on a thought; what is then to be done is explained in the following verse.

'Let him gradually retire through the intellect possessed of patience': this expression also presents a teaching which is important on the way to Cosmic Consciousness when Transcendental Consciousness has already been gained. When, through the practice of Transcendental Meditation, the mind gains familiarity with the state of Being, one begins to feel as if uninvolved while engaged in activity. This experience of non-attachment grows in intensity with practice. This is what the Lord means by 'gradually retire', in the context of gaining Cosmic Consciousness. He adds that during this process the intellect should be 'possessed of patience' so that it may not hurriedly and wrongly interpret the experience. It should be noted that when this sense of non-attachment is appreciated by the intellect, activity becomes much more effective and fruitful in the outer world. In the absence of a proper interpretation of this expression of non-attachment, one might become bewildered, and this great blessing of life might become a liability.

'Having established the mind in the Self, let him not think at all': when the mind has permanently gained transcendental Self-consciousness, then it is no longer required to embark upon any mental activity, the necessity of which was implied by the previous verse. When the mind is permanently established in the Self, the purpose of the teaching of the previous verse has been accomplished: Cosmic Consciousness has been gained.

The expression, 'let him not think at all', brings out the essential features of Cosmic Consciousness. First, this state of life is not maintained on the basis of thinking or feeling: it is lived naturally on the level of Being. Secondly, the Self in this state has separated Itself so completely from the field of activity that, even when the mind entertains thoughts, the Self remains completely free[44] from the process of thinking. This is that state of life referred to in verse 3: 'for the man who has ascended to Yoga, and for him alone, calmness is said to be the means'.

The previous verse described the value of mental activity during the inward stroke of meditation. The following verse shows how to direct mental activity when the mind comes out of the transcendental state of consciousness.

44 See V, 7–9.

VERSE 26

यतो यतो निश्चरति मनश्चञ्चलमस्थिरम्
ततस्ततो नियम्यैतदात्मन्येव वशं नयेत्

Yato yato nishcharati manash chanchalam asthiram
tatas tato niyamyaitad Ātmanyeva vashaṁ nayet

Whatever makes the fickle and unsteady mind
wander forth, from that withdrawn, let him
bring it under the sway of the Self alone.

'Withdrawn': the word in the text is '*niyamya*', which means having regulated or disciplined. Here it means having turned back to the Self.

This is the art of successful meditation. It is natural that when the mind has taken a dive into the Self and comes out to the relative field again, it should be brought back to the medium of meditation in order to begin a second dive. In the early stages of meditation, however, it is generally found that with the outward stroke of meditation the mind comes on to some thought. The Lord therefore says that the mind should be brought back from a foreign thought to the medium of meditation, so that it comes once more to the established channel and, experiencing the finer states of the medium in a natural way, comes again to the Transcendent.

The Lord says: Turn the mind towards the Self. This in no way suggests difficulty. Unfortunately for the student of the Bhagavad-Gītā, commentators have stated that the mind needs to be controlled and disciplined, which implies that the whole approach is strenuous and difficult. There is, however, no idea of control or discipline of the mind in the Lord's teaching. True, He has used two adjectives to qualify 'mind': 'fickle' and 'unsteady'. But we have to remember that the Lord is here describing the process of leading the mind to the Self, whereas these adjectives apply to the mind when it is subjected to the outward stroke of meditation. It is quite right for the mind to enter a wavering state when it comes out of the field of transcendental Unity, like waves beginning to appear on the still surface of the ocean. So when at times the mind is found on a foreign thought during meditation, this should be regarded — if the process of meditation is a right one — as the outward stroke of meditation. It should not be taken as evidence that the mind is by nature 'fickle' and 'unsteady', though commentators have supposed it to be so.

If one notices that the mind is going out into thoughts even when it has not reached the transcendental Being but is only on the way to It during the inward stroke of meditation, this again should not be ascribed to the innate weakness of the mind. It may be due to the nervous system being under strain, or it may be due to lack of proper guidance. It can be the result of inefficiency either on the part of the teacher or of the pupil, but usually the inadequacy is found to be on the part of the teacher.

The Lord, then, teaches that if it happens that the mind is distracted by something external, one should quietly bring it back to the channel which leads to the Self. It is the nature of the mind to go to a field of greater happiness. When, during meditation, the mind begins to experience the finer states of the object of attention, it begins to experience increasing charm at every step. There is then no chance for it to go anywhere except in the direction which leads to the Transcendent.

This is true of the system of Transcendental Meditation, which is the main concern of these verses.

The significance of this verse in relation to Cosmic Consciousness lies in its emphasis on the necessity of alternating the inward and outward march of the mind. This is to allow the infusion of Being into the nature of the mind so that all its activity may become supported and enriched by divine value, and so that finally the whole of life may become divine in Cosmic Consciousness.

The following verse brings to light the nature of Cosmic Consciousness in terms of supreme happiness and summarizes the essential features of the way.

VERSE 27

प्रशान्तमनसं ह्येनं योगिनं सुखमुत्तमम्
उपैति शान्तरजसं ब्रह्मभूतमकल्मषम्

Prashāntamanasaṁ hyenaṁ yoginaṁ sukham uttamam
Upaiti shāntarajasaṁ Brahmabhūtam akalmasham

For supreme happiness comes to the Yogī whose mind is deep in peace, in whom the spur to activity is stilled, who is without blemish and has become one with Brahman.

The Lord made a similar statement about supreme happiness in the 21st verse; but from the 24th verse He has been intent upon describing the method by which supreme happiness is to be attained. During meditation the mind, as it experiences the finer aspects of the object of meditation, eventually transcends even the subtlest experience, and then there is no activity. This is what the Lord means when He says that the 'spur to activity' (*Rajas*) 'is stilled'. This is the field of the Transcendent, the state of pure consciousness, stainless, sinless. Here the individual mind ceases to be; it gains the status of divine intelligence. Having gone beyond the limits of an individual mind's wanting and desiring, it is fully established in deep peace and attains supreme happiness.

The faculty of experience becomes extinct when the mind loses its individuality. The state of Being knows no knowing; it is a state that transcends all knowing or experiencing. But if this is so, how can it be said that the mind experiences supreme happiness? First, it should be noted that the Lord uses the word '*upaiti*', which means 'comes to'; the word 'experiences' is not used. However, even if the word 'experiences' were used, it could be regarded as valid. The mind does have the ability to experience when it is on the verge of transcending, at the junction of relativity and the Absolute. It is at this point that the mind experiences the nature of absolute Bliss Consciousness. This has been brought out in the Upanishads, where it is stated specifically that Reality is experienced by the mind alone.

Experience of Reality by the mind is always at the junction-point: while it is about to transcend at the end of the inward stroke of meditation, and while coming out of transcendence at the start of the outward stroke of meditation.

'Deep in peace': see verses 7, 14, and 15 of this chapter and verses 70 and 71 of Chapter II. The Lord means peace that is not overshadowed even by activity — the eternal peace that is gained when one 'in action sees inaction' (IV, 18); 'the supreme peace' (IV, 39); 'lasting peace' (V, 12).

The nature of the 'spur to activity' (*Rajas*) was explained in the commentary on verse 45 of Chapter II.

'Who is without blemish': who is established in the absolute purity of Being, completely separate from the field of activity. His actions being completely in accordance with the Laws of Nature,[45] they are free from blemish.

'Has become one with *Brahman*': has gained Cosmic Consciousness.

It is interesting to see how this one verse describes both the state of Cosmic Consciousness itself and the path by which it is reached. It makes clear that supreme happiness is gained in Cosmic Consciousness and that there are three prerequisites to gaining it: the mind must be 'deep in peace', 'the spur to activity' must be 'stilled', and one must be 'without blemish'.

The teachings of the three previous verses, which have defined in detail the nature of the path to Cosmic Consciousness, are represented by individual phrases in this verse. 'Mind is deep in peace' refers to verse 24; 'in whom the spur to activity is stilled' refers to verse 25; 'who is without blemish' refers to verse 26.

The flower of divine wisdom of this verse comes to full bloom in the following five verses.

45 See V, 25.

Verse 28

युञ्जन्नेवं सदात्मानं योगी विगतकल्मषः
सुखेन ब्रह्मसंस्पर्शमत्यन्तं सुखमश्नुते

Yunjann evaṁ sadātmānaṁ yogī vigatakalmashaḥ
sukhena Brahmasaṁsparsham atyantaṁ sukham ashnute

Ever thus collecting himself, the Yogī, freed from blemish,
with ease attains contact with Brahman, which is infinite joy.

Here the Lord brings out quite clearly that realization of Cosmic Consciousness is not at all difficult. It is easily attained.

'Ever thus collecting himself' gives expression to the points brought out in the previous four verses.

'Ever' here does not signify continuity of time. It means regularly, as part of the daily routine. It is directly connected with 'thus', which indicates that whenever the *Yogī* collects himself he should do so in this particular manner.

'Freed from blemish': for any experience there must be a corresponding state of the nervous system.[46] The most normal state of the human nervous system is that which can support 'contact with *Brahman*', the omnipresent Reality. It must necessarily be a state of extreme refinement and flexibility, and this is possible only when the nervous system is entirely pure. Such purity demands that the functioning of the nervous system should be in no way contradictory to the Laws of Nature. The influence that it produces should support all life, fulfilling the cosmic purpose.

It is interesting to note that the first half of verse 15 has the same text as the present verse, except that the *Yogī* is 'of disciplined mind', whereas here he is 'freed from blemish'. This important difference brings correspondingly different results: in the earlier instance the outcome is 'peace' and 'liberation'; in the present it is 'infinite joy'.

It is clear from this comparison that if the nervous system is not freed from blemish, even though it may give the experience of peace and freedom it cannot give rise to infinite joy.

46 See IV, 38.

The repeated practice of 'collecting' oneself and arriving at Transcendental Consciousness continues to refine the nervous system until it becomes so pure that it is capable of giving rise to a state of consciousness described as 'contact with *Brahman*'.

'With ease attains': because the practice is easy and the way of life that is prescribed is also easy and comfortable. The practice is easy because it represents the movement of the mind in a direction which it follows quite automatically, that is, towards bliss. This teaching of a way that is easy both recalls and supplements the teaching in verse 40 of Chapter II, where the Lord declared this method to be free from any resistance.

It has been made clear that the practice of Transcendental Meditation, by leading the mind to Transcendental Consciousness, also brings purity to all aspects of life and sets it in tune with Nature. One practice accomplishes all this.[47] The practice itself is in accordance with the very nature of the mind, and this is what makes 'contact with *Brahman*' easy.

'Contact with *Brahman*': it was stated in the commentary on verse 20 that in the transcendental state of consciousness the mind becomes Being. When Being is retained in a natural manner even while the mind is out in the relative field, then 'contact with *Brahman*' is realized. Such contact means harmony between the absolute and the relative states of consciousness. With the practice described in the previous verses, and with an easy manner of life, this highly developed state of consciousness, says the Lord, is attained 'with ease'. The result is 'infinite joy'.

It should be noted that it is the 'contact' that is infinite joy, and not *Brahman* Itself. *Brahman*, which is an all-pervading mass of bliss, does not exhibit any quality of bliss. It may be likened to a mass of energy — matter — which does not exhibit any quality of energy. This verse emphasizes the glory of 'contact'; it does not set forth the nature of *Brahman*.

Brahman is that which cannot be expressed in words, even though the Upanishads use words to educate us about Its nature. In the field of speech, *Brahman* lies between two contrary statements. It is absolute and relative at the same time. It is the eternal imperishable even while It is ever-changing. It is said to be both

47 See Appendix: The *Transcendental Meditation* Technique.

this and That. It is spoken of as *Sat-chid-ānanda* but includes what is not *Sat*, what is not *Chit*, and what is not *Ānanda*.[48] It is beyond speech and thought, yet the whole range of thought and speech lie within It. 'Within It' and 'without It' are just expressions, and like any other expressions about *Brahman* they do justice neither to *Brahman* nor to the speaker nor to the listener. *Brahman* is lived by man with ease but cannot be spoken of, in the sense that words are inadequate to encompass That which is the unlimited fullness of transcendental Being and the fullness of active life at the same time. Verse 29 of Chapter II speaks of It as a 'wonder', for it is not anything that can be conceived of intellectually; it is not anything that can be appreciated by emotion.

This verse and its expression 'with ease' give added meaning to earlier verses about *Brahman*: 'This is the state of *Brahman*, O Pārtha. Having attained it, a man is not deluded. Established in that, even at the last moment, he attains eternal freedom in divine consciousness';[49] 'his self joined in Union with *Brahman*, he enjoys eternal happiness';[50] 'being one with *Brahman*, attains eternal freedom'.[51]

Brahman is the value of our life, and the truth about It is that It is lived 'with ease'.

The glory of this verse is also the glory of the Bhagavad-Gītā. The eternal glory of the goal of human endeavour is that one 'with ease attains contact with *Brahman*, which is infinite joy'.

VERSE 29

सर्वभूतस्थमात्मानं सर्वभूतानि चात्मनि
ईक्षते योगयुक्तात्मा सर्वत्र समदर्शनः

Sarvabhūtastham Ātmanaṁ sarvabhūtāni chātmani
īkshate yogayuktātmā sarvatra samadarshanaḥ

He whose self is established in Yoga, whose vision everywhere is even, sees the Self in all beings, and all beings in the Self.

48 *Sat*, eternal; *Chit*, consciousness; *Ānanda*, bliss.
49 II, 72.
50 V, 21.
51 V, 24.

This verse portrays the state of *Brahman* and at the same time gives a practical meaning to the 'contact' of which the previous verse speaks.

The nature of *Brahman* is expressed in two phrases placed together: 'Self in all beings' and 'all beings in the Self'[52] — the Absolute and the relative, one within the other. This makes *Brahman* seem incomprehensible. Even taken separately, the relative and the Absolute, the diversity of creation and the Unity underlying it, are each too much for the mind to grasp; how much more so when they are found integrated in *Brahman*! It is the glory of the Lord's discourse that we are enabled to comprehend the incomprehensible so clearly and are shown how to live it 'with ease'.

The quality of experience depends upon the state of one's consciousness. If the mind is cheerful, everything is found to be cheerful; if the mind is sad and miserable, one's outlook is gloomy. When the state of Being becomes infused into the nature of the mind during meditation, then this infusion makes the mind divine. And when this infusion becomes permanent, the mind begins to live Unity throughout the whole field of diversity. The whole field of diversity is then appreciated in the light of the inner divine Unity. When the mind becomes filled with divine Being, the vision is naturally full and even. It is steady and undistorted by the diversity of life in the world. This is the vision of a man who has gained 'contact' with *Brahman*.

It must not be lost to sight that evenness of vision is the result of 'contact with *Brahman*'. It should not be regarded as a path to realization of *Brahman*. If an unrealized man tries to cultivate evenness of vision in life, he will only create confusion for himself and for others. Such attempts result in strange moods and stranger behaviour. And responsibility for this lies with those commentators who have deduced from this verse the value of mood-making in the name of understanding the Reality and living It.

The glory of this verse is beyond description. Most lucidly, it expresses the inexpressible *Brahman* and at the same time lays It

52 See also IV, 35.

open to the level of human vision. It is this that has made the Bhagavad-Gītā the 'milk' of the Upanishads.

The following three verses take this blessed vision to its consummation in God Consciousness.

VERSE 30

योो मां पश्यति सर्वत्र सर्वं च मयि पश्यति
तस्याहं न प्रणश्यामि स च मे न प्रणश्यति

Yo māṁ pashyati sarvatra sarvaṁ cha mayi pashyati
tasyāhaṁ na praṇashyāmi sa cha me na praṇashyati

He who sees Me everywhere, and sees everything in Me,
I am not lost to him nor is he lost to Me.

When a man has gained the oneness of vision described in the previous verse, when the fullness of Being overflows through the mind into the fields of perception, when spiritual Unity prevails even on the level of the senses, when the oneness[53] of God overtakes life, then is that state attained where perception of anything whatsoever is perception of the Being made manifest. Then his consciousness finds a direct relationship with the Lord, with Being made manifest, who becomes a living Reality for him on that supremely divine level of consciousness. Then he and his Lord are not lost to one another.

This direct relationship of man with God is first established on the level of Being and then comes to be on the level of feeling; from there it enters the field of thinking and then finds its way on to the sensory level of experience. God thus overtakes all the levels of man's life. Man lives in the sanctuary of God. His life is in love, in bliss, in wisdom, in God Consciousness. He lives in the realm of universal existence. He moves on earth and he lives in the land of God, in the divine ground of Being far above human vision and far beyond human thought.

The way to cultivate this blessed state is to transcend thought. Continuing to think about it has its own value — it fills the mind

53 See IV, 35.

with a pleasant thought — but fails to create the desired state. Transcending thought is infinitely more valuable than thinking.

Therefore let the mind transcend thought and enter that realm of absolute purity which is the abode of God. Thinking about it is wasting time on the surface of life. A thought keeps the mind away from that blessed realm. A thought of bread neither gives the taste of bread nor fills the stomach. If you want bread, go to the kitchen and get it instead of sitting outside thinking about it. We remain thinking of God, or trying to feel Him, only so long as we lack knowledge of Him, so long as we do not know how to break through the phenomenal field of experience and enter the realm of transcendental bliss, the pure kingdom of the Almighty.

The records that history has brought us of the direct communion of saints and sages with God reveal their blessed lives, but the secret of the success of such lives lay in their transcending the fields of thought, emotion, and experience. The secret of God-realization lies in transcending the thought of God. Thought that remains thought obscures God Consciousness. Emotions likewise hide the blessed bliss. The thought of God finds fulfilment in its own extinction. And emotion too has to cease in order to let the heart be full in the unbounded love of God.

The state of consciousness that knows the glory of the great Lord of all beings is divine. It is developed through constant and regular practice of meditation and the experience of transcendental Being, which eventually brings Cosmic Consciousness, the state in which the heart and mind are fully matured. This full development of the capacities of heart and mind enables a man to understand and live the divine Being. The relationship that exists between the unmanifested Absolute and the manifested Being unfolds itself. The personal God comes to be experienced on the sensory level. He becomes the living Reality of daily life. Every object in creation reflects the Light of God in terms of one's own Self.

Philosophers call this a mystical experience, but it is no more mysterious than is the working of a clock for a child. On one level of consciousness it is normal, on another it is mysterious, and again on another it is impossible. The intensity of God-realization in its personal and its impersonal aspects depends upon the level of Being, or the purity of consciousness (verse 28). It is not possible to conceive of God Consciousness through any state of consciousness that is not God Consciousness itself; but it is possible for everyone, at any level of human consciousness, to rise to the realization of God Consciousness through the practice of Transcendental Meditation which is a simple and direct way of developing pure consciousness.

The overpowering sweetness of the Lord's assurance in this verse gives expression to the glory of life. It has been, it is, and it will continue to be the source of inspiration and the guiding light to many an ardent seeker of Truth, to many an ardent devotee of God. It is given to such men to enjoy the love of the Almighty and the protection that He offers. This is their good fortune; they share their life with God. The oneness that they live from moment to moment is the Union of the oneness of the Absolute, the oneness of eternal life in the multiplicity of creation — the great oneness symbolized in the Divine made manifest, the almighty personal God.

The Lord's assurance in this verse is restated in the following verses with even deeper truth and greater glory.

VERSE 31

सर्वभूतस्थितं यो मां भजत्येकत्वमास्थितः
सर्वथा वर्तमानोऽपि स योगी मयि वर्तते

Sarvabhūtasthitaṁ yo māṁ bhajatyekatwam āsthitaḥ
sarvathā vartamāno 'pi sa yogī mayi vartate

Established in Unity, he who worships Me abiding in all beings, in whatever way he lives, that Yogī lives in Me.

To live through the various phases of man's life on earth while abiding in the worship of God is the character of a particular level of consciousness. In order to make clear that its basis is not thought about God, the Lord says: 'in whatever way he lives'. This is that fullness of life in God which knows no variation, however the mind or senses may be engaged, whatever the different modes of activity. When a man looks at things through green spectacles, no matter what he sees the green is there. For a devotee, no matter what he is doing God is there in his consciousness; He is there in his vision and in his being.

The word 'worships' is of great significance. It expresses devotion, dedication, dependence, and surrender. From the ordinary level of consciousness this is hard to understand, and to explain the nature of God Consciousness is still harder. But some idea may be gained by making clear the difference between levels of consciousness.

A child takes delight in toys; his consciousness grows and books take their place; as he develops farther his career in the world begins to interest him. As his consciousness grows, so does he rise to different levels of interest and understanding. Similarly, when a man's consciousness has grown to cosmic status, the supreme level of creation becomes his normal field of interest. God, the manifested Being on the supreme level of creation, begins to draw him to Himself; he begins to rise to God Consciousness. Remaining in the world of his fellow men, he begins to live in the world of God. And when he is permanently established in this blessed state, he is included within this loving expression of the Lord's: 'in whatever way he lives, that *Yogī* lives in Me'.

In order to make clear the nature of worship, the Lord adds to the words 'worships Me' the phrase 'abiding in all beings'. The sense of worship holds the devotee to his God; it expresses a personal relationship. What is impersonal and universal from the point of view of ordinary human consciousness becomes intimate and personal in this state of consciousness, for it is at the level of harmony between the unmanifested Absolute and the manifested Being, the Lord of all creation. It would be wrong to understand from the Lord's words here that the *Yogī* tries to see the personal God in all things. This would not only be impractical but would result in strain, to say the least. The divine Being is worshipped through the most natural way of living, based on God Consciousness. Trying to see one's God here, there, and everywhere is an act of the imagination which is far from the truth of this verse, and farther still from the practicalities of life.

When the individual consciousness has developed into Cosmic Consciousness, then this state of fullness of divine consciousness develops into God Consciousness. It is in this established state of God Consciousness that the Lord is worshipped 'abiding in all beings'. Every thought is then a flower at the feet of God, every word a prayer, and every action an offering to Him. The scriptures sing the glory of God in the glory of such a devotee, of whom the Lord says he 'lives in Me'.

Having shown that the realized man attains His level of existence, the Lord, in the following verse, establishes the evenness of such a man's vision in life.

Verse 32

आत्मौपम्येन सर्वत्र समं पश्यति योऽर्जुन
सुखं वा यदि वा दुःखं स योगी परमो मतः

Ātmaupamyena sarvatra samaṁ pashyati yo 'rjuna
sukhaṁ vā yadi vā duḥkhaṁ sa yogī paramo mataḥ

He who sees everything with an even vision by
comparison with the Self, be it pleasure or pain,
he is deemed the highest Yogī, O Arjuna.

This verse brings out the practical value of God Consciousness and extends the dignity of this enlightenment to everything around the realized man.

Verse 29 expressed the state of realization in terms of impersonal Being; verse 30 expressed it in terms of the personal. Verse 31 brought the personal God into intimate contact with the realized man and kept alive the bond of devotion in order to maintain that blessed state of Union with Him. The present verse dissolves the bond of devotion, for this can no longer exist when intimacy becomes complete. While devotion served as a link to maintain Union, this remained in some degree on the level of formality. The formality of worship is a pleasure which overtakes the devotee's heart and his whole being, which gives meaning to his life and glorifies it on all levels; but the joy of such devotion is the joy of Union at a distance. As the Union grows more complete, the link of worship, of adoration and devotion, finds fulfilment in its own extinction, leaving worshipper and worshipped together in perfect oneness, in the oneness of absolute Unity. Then he and his God are one in himself. Then himself has become Himself; his vision is in terms of Himself, his pleasure and pain are in terms of Himself.

'By comparison with the Self': in terms of his own Self.[54] In the state described in the previous verse, the Unity of the devotee with God has reached such fullness that his life is the life of God. Everywhere and in everything he lives God. He sees everything in terms of God. This exalted state of Union with God becomes yet more glorious in the present verse, where the Lord says: 'with an even vision by comparison with the Self'. Here the difference between the devotee and God, which was alive in the state described by the previous verse, is found no more. His Union with God, which was of an order that still permitted worship of Him, has become a Union of much greater intensity. Now his God is one with himself; the supreme divine Unity prevails in him. In his individuality, the eternal glory of the Divine shines brightly and in such fullness that It exists not only on the level of his Being but is infused into his feeling, his thinking, his vision, his whole field of experience. His vision, which before was coloured by his devotion to the Lord, now stands clear in terms of his own Self, permeated by his own eternal Being; in that Being the glory of God resides, sustaining It and maintaining the eternal freedom that His beloved devotee has gained in Him.

In that perfect liberation he leads the life of fullness and abundance. His vision is such that it quite naturally holds alike all things in the likeness of his own Self, because he himself and the vision that he has are the expression of the Self.

The Lord uses the words 'pleasure or pain' to show that the pairs of opposites — and indeed the whole diversity of creation which his individuality offers him — fail to present their differences to the *Yogī's* vision. His is a vision of life in totality.

54 See IV, 35.

The pairs of opposites, such as pleasure and pain, which present great contrasts on the lower levels of evolution, fail to divide the evenness of his vision. To make such a vision more comprehensible to the ordinary level of consciousness, it may be compared to a father's even vision towards a variety of toys which, to the vision of his child's undeveloped consciousness, will present great differences.

This verse shows the height of realization, which is to realize the supreme oneness of life in terms of one's own Self. No diversity of life is able to detract from this state of supreme Unity. One who has reached It is the supporter of all and everything, for he is life eternal. He bridges the gulf between the relative and the Absolute. The eternal Absolute is in him at the level of the perishable phenomenal world. He lives to give meaning to the paean of the Upanishads: '*Pūrṇam adaḥ pūrṇam idam*' — That Absolute is full, this relative is full. One who lives this supreme Reality in his daily life 'is deemed the highest *Yogī*', says the Lord. Yoga in this state has reached its perfection; there is no level of Union higher than this that he has gained. He stands established on the ultimate level of consciousness.

It may be of interest to those who like to dwell on the metaphysics of Union with God that two states of Union have been clearly portrayed in the present context. That described in this verse is only a more advanced state of Union than that of the preceding verse. The Union where the devotee still holds to the supremacy of his God passes very naturally into a much more intimate Union with Him. The principle of Union is not affected. This is not a matter which can be decided by metaphysical speculation or theological understanding. Unless one's consciousness is actually raised to that level of God Consciousness, any description or understanding of the difference between the two states of Union will always fall far short of truth for, as has already been said, the truth about a more advanced state of consciousness cannot be rightly evaluated from a lower level.

Fortunate are they who live in Union with God. They are man's guides on earth, furthering the evolution of all creation. They are above the limitations of religion or race. Whether they play with God or hold Him as one with their own Being is a point to be settled between them and God. They live as devotees of God or they become united, become one with their Beloved — it is a matter between them. Let it be decided on that level of Union. One view need not exclude the other. It is a sin against God to raise differences over the principle of Union. Let the followers of both schools of thought aspire to achieve their respective goals and then find in that consciousness that the other standpoint is also right at its own level.

Verse 33

अर्जुन उवाच
योऽयं योगस्त्वया प्रोक्तः साम्येन मधुसूदन
एतस्याहं न पश्यामि चञ्चलत्वात्स्थितिं स्थिराम्

Arjuna uvācha
Yo 'yaṁ yogas twayā proktaḥ sāmyena Madhusūdana
etasyāhaṁ na pashyāmi chanchalatwāt sthitiṁ sthirām

Arjuna said:
This Yoga described by Thee as characterized by evenness, O Madhusūdana, I do not see its steady endurance, because of wavering.

Arjuna has understood the Lord's teaching concerning the cultivation of God Consciousness. Now he brings up a point which arises out of the Lord's exhortation in verse 26 about 'the fickle and unsteady mind'. The question is that if the mind is indeed 'fickle and unsteady', as the Lord Himself has said, then how is it possible to maintain 'an even vision'[55] in the oneness of God Consciousness?

Arjuna's question does not imply any doubt about the possibility of cultivating God Consciousness, even with a wavering mind. What he doubts is its steady endurance when the mind is wavering.

That has been the story of many seers and devotees of God. Having felt occasional flashes of divine radiance, they become miserable because it is not there all the time. But they miss it

55 See verse 32.

when their attention wavers only because they have cultivated it on the level of attention. It is wrong to think that the steady endurance of God Consciousness is based on attention. If it does not endure, this is only due to lack of Being. For the basis of God Consciousness is that oneness of life which develops on the solid foundation of Cosmic Consciousness. This the Lord is going to explain in answer to Arjuna's question. The following verse completes that question.

VERSE 34

चञ्चलं हि मनः कृष्ण प्रमाथि बलवद्दृढम्
तस्याहं निग्रहं मन्ये वायोरिव सुदुष्करम्

Chanchalaṁ hi manaḥ Kṛishṇa pramāthi balavad dṛidham
tasyāhaṁ nigrahaṁ manye vāyor iva sudushkaram

For wavering is the mind, O Kṛishṇa, turbulent, powerful, and unyielding; I consider it as difficult to control as the wind.

The nature of the senses has already been accepted by the Lord in Chapter II[56] as 'wavering', 'turbulent', 'powerful and unyielding'. It is in the nature of things that the mind, on the level of the senses, is never steady. Arjuna reminds the Lord of this fact.

There is no reason to think that Arjuna missed the Lord's essential teaching that it is easy[57] to cultivate God Consciousness, irrespective of the wanderings of the mind in the field of the senses and regardless of the dragging influence of the senses on the mind. He is only afraid of losing it when the mind is drawn by the senses. So he wants to know some method which can bring the mind under control and thus enable him to cultivate and enjoy evenness of mind in God Consciousness. His question is really about the control of the mind on the level of the senses, and it is in regard to this level that the Lord's answer is given.

Arjuna's question in these two verses has been widely misunderstood to mean that God Consciousness is difficult of attainment because of the wavering nature of the mind. This

56 See II, 60, 67.
57 See II, 40.

has resulted either in restraining enthusiasm for cultivating God Consciousness or in leading seekers to practise strenuous methods of controlling the mind and steadying the attention. This pitiable state of affairs in the exalted field of God-realization has come about only because one essential principle has been missed: that God Consciousness is based on the level of Being in Cosmic Consciousness and not on any thinking, understanding, or fixity and continuity of attention.[58]

It should be noted that when the Lord, in answer to Arjuna's question, emphasizes the need for practice, such practice is for the purpose of developing Transcendental Consciousness into Cosmic Consciousness and then into God Consciousness, and not at all for gaining the ability to maintain the attention.

VERSE 35

श्रीभगवानुवाच
असंशयं महाबाहो मनो दुर्निग्रहं चलम्
अभ्यासेन तु कौन्तेय वैराग्येण च गृह्यते

Shrī Bhagavān uvācha
Asaṁshayaṁ Mahābāho mano durnigrahaṁ chalam
abhyāsena tu Kaunteya vairāgyeṇa cha gṛihyate

The Blessed Lord said:
No doubt, O mighty-armed, the mind is hard to control,
it is wavering, but by practice and non-attachment
it is held, O son of Kuntī.

The Lord accepts the difficulty of controlling the mind on the level of its wandering, because the nature of life is such that the mind has to attend to a variety of things. If the mind is channelled only in one direction, other phases of life will suffer. It wanders of necessity, and this is what makes it difficult for the mind to remain steady at any one place. It is unnatural to try to keep it steady. Steadiness does not belong to the relative field of life. That is why the Lord accepts that 'the mind is hard to control'.

58 See II, 45; III, 43.

It should not be lost to sight, however, that even when the mind is wavering and wandering 'it is held' by the experience of happiness. This fact about the nature of the mind enables the Lord to show Arjuna a way of keeping the mind 'held' wherever it may be, to show him something which will give the mind steadiness even when it continues to waver.

By saying that the mind 'is held' through practice and non-attachment, the Lord does not mean that the mind will cease its wandering and will always remain fixed and steady, for this would be impractical in daily life. He only means that practice and non-attachment will provide a steady field of omnipresent Being, by virtue of which the mind will be permanently held in the bliss of its own essential nature.

'Practice and non-attachment' means regular practice of Transcendental Meditation and an easy comfortable routine of daily life after meditation. Practice is not recommended for gaining the ability to keep the mind fixed and steady. It is for cultivating Being. The state of non-attachment helps Being to be infused into the nature of the mind.

'Non-attachment' signifies a simple, easy, and unstrained way of life with a proper sense of values, giving no undue importance to anything; for attachment restricts life by laying stress on one particular aspect. Non-attachment does not mean refraining from the responsibilities of life, but rather giving all aspects of practical life their due, while spontaneously maintaining the Self as separate from activity. This happens as Transcendental Consciousness grows into Cosmic Consciousness. The state of non-attachment is meant here and not the practice of gaining that state.

'Practice' brings the mind in contact with transcendental Being, while the unstrained life of 'non-attachment' helps Being to be lived in the field of activity, eventually giving to God Consciousness that steady endurance which was Arjuna's main concern in verse 33 and which is the goal of all Yoga.

Cosmic Consciousness is the complete state of non-attachment. Practice has to be continued in that state of non-attachment in order to gain and maintain God Consciousness. Practice at this stage means devotion.

VERSE 36

असंयतात्मना योगो दुष्प्राप इति मे मतिः
वश्यात्मना तु यतता शक्योऽवाप्तुमुपायतः

Asaṁyatātmanā yogo dushprāpa iti me matiḥ
vashyātmanā tu yatatā shakyo 'vāptum upāyataḥ

For an undisciplined man, Yoga is hard to achieve, so I consider; but it can be gained through proper means by the man of endeavour who is disciplined.

'Yoga' in this verse refers to the state of Yoga in God Consciousness, for Arjuna's question, here answered by the Lord, concerns this state.

'An undisciplined man' in this context is he who has not disciplined himself according to the teaching of verses 24 and 25; he who has not gained Cosmic Consciousness.

The Lord here names three prerequisites for success in Yoga: 'proper means',[59] 'endeavour',[60] and a 'disciplined'[61] life.

'Through proper means' refers to 'practice and non-attachment' in the previous verse.

The expression 'man of endeavour' indicates that the state of Yoga in God Consciousness is not for dull and lazy people: it is for men of responsibility and of a dynamic nature. Thereby the Lord dismisses Arjuna's fear of losing God Consciousness when the mind is engaged in different fields of life (verse 33).

'Who is disciplined': this means a man who has a proper sense of values, who does not confuse the activity of relative life with the Self, or absolute Being. It means the man who has realized Cosmic Consciousness.

It should not be thought that one has to strain in order to keep life disciplined. There are two ways of disciplining a dog. One way is difficult, the other easy. Run after the dog, try to catch it, and then tie it down at the door — this is one way of controlling the dog. Do not run after it, do not try to catch it,

59 See verse 3.
60 See verse 1; III, 8–9.
61 See V, 26.

do not try to tie it at the door; rather, leave the dog quite free to go anywhere it wants, only put some food outside the door, just what the dog likes to eat. The dog will be found always at the door and as often as you wish. This is a simple way of gaining control over the dog without controlling it. We want to discipline the mind, and the easy way is not to try to put restraint upon it. It is attracted by fields of greater happiness; then lead it towards some field of greater happiness in life and it will be found to stay there through its own desire to enjoy that happiness. The practice of Transcendental Meditation, bringing contentment through the experience of Being, naturally establishes Cosmic Consciousness and thus gives a disciplined pattern to life. This is the simple way of gaining a disciplined state of mind.

In this verse, the Lord is not advocating any particular way, either simple or difficult; He is only bringing out the principle of success in Yoga: the need for discipline in life. The principle which the Lord sets out is indisputable: 'For an undisciplined man, Yoga is hard to achieve'. The mind is undisciplined when it is not contented and at the same time has the whole field of the senses laid open for it to explore. It becomes disciplined when it gains contentment through the permanent experience of transcendent absolute bliss[62] in Cosmic Consciousness. The word 'disciplined' indicates that, even if the mind associates itself with the senses to enjoy their objects, it does not lose the equanimity which has become permanent through the realization of the Self as separate from activity.

VERSE 37

अर्जुन उवाच
अयतिः श्रद्धयोपेतो योगाच्चलितमानसः
अप्राप्य योगसंसिद्धिं कां गतिं कृष्ण गच्छति

Arjuna uvācha
Ayatiḥ shraddhayopeto yogāch chalitamānasaḥ
aprāpya yogasaṁsiddhiṁ kāṁ gatiṁ Kṛishṇa gachchhati

62 See II, 59.

Arjuna said:
What goal does he reach, O Kṛishṇa, who is not perfected in Yoga, being endowed with faith, yet lacking effort, his mind strayed from Yoga?

The roots of this question lie in the Lord's teaching in verses 24 to 28, which proclaim attainment of Cosmic Consciousness through practice, through 'effort'.

The immediate stimulus to the question, however, is given by the words of the previous verse: 'It can be gained through proper means by the man of endeavour who is disciplined'. The three conditions thus set out for gaining supremely divine evenness of mind[63] make it seem to Arjuna as if he had a long way to go. The Lord has told him earlier that 'In this (Yoga) no effort is lost and no obstacle exists. Even a little of this *Dharma* delivers from great fear.'[64] So when He now puts three conditions upon it, Arjuna wants to make sure whether or not there will be any advantage in starting on this path, bearing in mind that one may not be able to arrive at the goal in this life.

There is yet another implication in this verse. When Arjuna hears about the three prerequisites for the attainment of the state of Yoga in God Consciousness, he wants to know if there is any shortcut. He wants to know how far faith can help a man on this path, for he probably thinks that it may be easier to succeed in God-realization through faith alone. Such a question from Arjuna, a very practical man, comes as no surprise. It does not arise from any wish on his part to avoid effort: it arises from the very practical quality of his understanding. Wise are those who understand the nature of a path from beginning to end before they enter upon it, and wiser still are they who take a shortcut to accomplish the goal. Arjuna's question reflects his seriousness and the great alertness with which he is following the Lord's discourse.

Arjuna asks: 'What goal does he reach?' What is his destiny, where does he go? His concern with this problem springs from his knowledge of the universe. His statements at the beginning

63 See verse 32.
64 See II, 40.

of the discourse about *Dharma*, about his ancestors, about hell and heaven, and about the structure of society have revealed his precise knowledge about life and the world. A man of such learning will naturally be anxious to understand the goal of an aspirant on the path of Yoga. And he has all the more reason to ask because the Lord is speaking to him about attainments in those abstract regions of consciousness which seem very far removed from practical everyday life in the world — or the urgency of a battlefield.

In the following verse he makes his question clearer.

VERSE 38

कच्चिन्नोभयविभ्रष्टश्छिन्नाभ्रमिव नश्यति
अप्रतिष्ठो महाबाहो विमूढो ब्रह्मणः पथि

Kachchin nobhayavibhrashtash chhinnābhram iva nashyati
apratishtho Mahābāho vimūdho Brahmaṇaḥ pathi

Deluded on the path to Brahman, O mighty-armed, without foothold and fallen from both, does he not perish like a broken cloud?

'Deluded on the path to *Brahman*' means fallen from the regular practice of Transcendental Meditation which develops Cosmic Consciousness. The question is about a man who starts the practice[65] but who for various reasons is unable to continue it. The word 'deluded' indicates that the reason for giving up the practice lies with the aspirant. There exists nothing on the side of God or on the path to Him that might encourage or impel the aspirant to stop his practice. If he does so, it can only be as a result of his own delusion. This, in turn, may be due to lack of knowledge about the goal or to doubt about his own ability to reach it; or it may be due to lack of proper estimation of its worth. All this may be due to lack of proper guidance. Whatever the cause, if a man stops the practice it can only be because he is deluded. Arjuna's use here of the word 'deluded' reveals the

65 See II, 45.

depth of his understanding of the Lord's teaching. Even though he is asking a question about the man who falls from practice, he wishes to show that he already regards such a man as deluded.

'Without foothold': Arjuna is aware of different levels of consciousness and of the different states of life that correspond to them. He is also aware that when a man's consciousness evolves from one level to another, the life of the previous level becomes useless to him. His question is about one who, as the result of a certain amount of practice, has risen above the level of ordinary human consciousness but who has not yet attained Cosmic Consciousness, which ensures liberation and is the foundation of God Consciousness. Such a man has lost ground on the human level but has as yet no foothold on the divine level. He is neither here nor there. This is what Arjuna expresses with the words 'fallen from both', and he thereupon presents a terrible picture of destruction with the words 'perish like a broken cloud'.

Arjuna wants to understand the destiny of the deluded man who has fallen from practice. The question sounds simple but is, in fact, extremely complex, because there can be innumerable levels of consciousness between that of the ignorant and that of a fully liberated, realized man. As Arjuna recognizes in the next verse, the precise answer can come only from Him who knows the whole range of life and all the possibilities that exist between ignorance and the realized state of consciousness.

VERSE 39

एतन्मे संशयं कृष्ण छेत्तुमर्हस्यशेषतः
त्वदन्यः संशयस्यास्य छेत्ता न ह्युपपद्यते

Etan me saṁshayaṁ Kṛishṇa chhettum arhasyasheshataḥ
twadanyaḥ saṁshayasyāsya chhettā na hyupapadyate

Thou art able to dispel this doubt of mine completely, O Kṛishṇa. Truly, there is none save Thee who can dispel this doubt.

Having listened to the Lord, Arjuna is by now convinced of the immeasurable depth of His wisdom. The words 'there is none save Thee' indicate that Arjuna, even while raising the question, feels that this is not the right moment for it, the battlefield being no place for metaphysical discussion. But he justifies his question by pointing out that if he does not ask it now he may never have another chance, since no one else can answer it. It appears that the discourse in verses 28 to 32 has convinced Arjuna of the limitless wisdom that lies at the feet of Lord Kṛishṇa.

When the disciple expresses appreciation of the wisdom of the master, then the wisdom flows from the master in a more delicate atmosphere of kindness and love. This is clear from the first word of Lord Kṛishṇa's answer in the following verse and from the great flood of knowledge that He pours out in response to this question of Arjuna's.

VERSE 40

श्रीभगवानुवाच
पार्थ नैवेह नामुत्र विनाशस्तस्य विद्यते
न हि कल्याणकृत्कश्चिद्दुर्गतिं तात गच्छति

Shrī Bhagavān uvācha
Pārtha naiveha nāmutra vināshas tasya vidyate
na hi kalyāṇakṛit kashchid durgatiṁ tāta gachchhati

The Blessed Lord said:
O Pārtha, there is no destruction for him in this world or hereafter; for none who acts uprightly, My son, goes the way of misfortune.

If someone has begun to wash a cloth and for some reason can rinse it only once, he has at least succeeded in removing some of the dirt, even though the cloth is not completely clean. Certainly he has not made it more dirty. A man begins the practice of meditation and, even if he meditates only a few times and transcends only once or twice, whatever purity the mind has gained thereby is his.

Verse 41

प्राप्य पुण्यकृतां लोकानुषित्वा शाश्वतीः समाः
शुचीनां श्रीमतां गेहे योगभ्रष्टोऽभिजायते

Prāpya puṇyakṛitāṁ lokān ushitwā shāshwatīḥ samāḥ
shuchīnāṁ shrīmatāṁ gehe yogabhrashto 'bhijāyate

Having attained the worlds of the righteous and dwelt there for countless years, he that strayed from Yoga is born in the house of the pure and illustrious.

'He that strayed from Yoga' means either he who could not complete the practice of meditation during his lifetime and has therefore not been able to attain Cosmic Consciousness, which ensures liberation, or he who has lost interest and has abandoned the practice of Yoga after some time.

Purity follows from meditation in proportion to practice. Increased purity leads to a better and happier level of consciousness here, which continues hereafter.

During meditation the mind reaches the state of Transcendental Consciousness and becomes free from any shadow of relativity. It attains to its real status of cosmic existence, unstained by any shadow of ignorance. This is the purified state of the mind, which is completely free from the influence of sin. Having attained it, the mind gains the status of universal Being so perfectly that, on returning to the field of relativity, it brings contentment into the whole realm of thought, speech, and action. This quite naturally makes a man's behaviour righteous in every aspect of life, and as a result he attains to the worlds of the righteous, which are said to comprise different planes of existence above the human.

When righteous people who have not been able to gain Cosmic Consciousness die, they enter one or other of these planes, for human life is regarded as the gateway to them all. Here life is longer and very much happier because these planes correspond to higher levels of consciousness. The highest level of consciousness is absolute Being, which has eternal life. At the other end of the scale, where purity is least, life is infinitely short. The level of purity determines the span of life on each plane and also the degree of happiness.

The Taittirīya Upanishad describes the various degrees of happiness enjoyed by the different beings in creation. All the different planes of life are gained in accordance with the principle of action and its results. The degree of righteousness in this world is the criterion for determining which of these higher planes of life is reached.

The worlds of the righteous are therefore the worlds of greater happiness, where beings enjoy much greater harmony and freedom than man enjoys on earth. But they no longer engage in the practice of Yoga. For that they have to come back to earth. Coming back here they are born 'in the house of the pure and illustrious', which provides a congenial atmosphere for Yoga. They resume their practice and attain final liberation.

VERSE 42

अथवा योगिनामेव कुले भवति धीमताम्
एतद्धि दुर्लभतरं लोके जन्म यदीदृशम्

Athavā yoginām eva kule bhavati dhīmatām
etad dhi durlabhataraṁ loke janma yad īdṛisham

Or he is born in an actual family of Yogīs
endowed with wisdom, though such a birth as
this on earth is more difficult to attain.

The Lord wishes to impress upon Arjuna that to be 'born in the house of the pure and illustrious' is easier than to be born into a 'family of *Yogīs* endowed with wisdom'. There are two reasons for this: not only are such families of *Yogīs* scarce in the world, but one also needs to attain a great degree of purity before one can be born into the holy atmosphere of a *Yogī's* family. For having been born into that atmosphere one gains a chance of quickly realizing God Consciousness.

VERSE 43

तत्र तं बुद्धिसंयोगं लभते पौर्वदेहिकम्
यतते च ततो भूयः संसिद्धौ कुरुनन्दन

Tatra taṁ buddhisaṁyogaṁ labhate paurvadehikam
yatate cha tato bhūyaḥ saṁsiddhau Kurunandana

There he regains that level of Union reached by the intellect in his former body, and by virtue of this, O joy of the Kurus, he strives yet more for perfection.

'There': in the atmosphere of the 'family of *Yogīs* endowed with wisdom' (verse 42), or 'in the house of the pure and illustrious' (verse 41).

'He regains': he starts his life from 'that level of Union reached by the intellect in his former body'. This may be understood from an example. Suppose that a cloth needs dipping a hundred times in dye before it is fully coloured, and that after it has been dipped ten times the factory closes. The cloth will then be taken to another factory. The second factory can only start from the eleventh dipping. Thus, even though the cloth could not be fully coloured by a continuous process in one factory, the degree of colour attained in the first factory determines the starting-point in the second. When a man begins to meditate, Being begins to grow into the nature of his mind. If, after a certain degree of infusion, he stops the practice in this life, or if his body perishes, whenever he again resumes his practice he will do so at that level of purity of consciousness which he had obtained through his former practice. The degree of purity gained in this life is not lost because of the death of the body.

VERSE 44

पूर्वाभ्यासेन तेनैव ह्रियते ह्यवशोऽपि सः
जिज्ञासुरपि योगस्य शब्दब्रह्मातिवर्तते

Pūrvābhyāsena tenaiva hriyate hyavasho 'pi saḥ
jigyāsur api yogasya shabdabrahmātivartate

By that former practice itself he is irresistibly borne on.
Even the aspirant to Yoga passes beyond the Veda.

'By that former practice itself': by the practice of meditation in the life that is past. The word 'itself' indicates that the strength of that former practice is in itself sufficient to set a man on this path of Yoga. Nature becomes favourable to him, and circumstances mould themselves in favour of his resuming the practice.

'Irresistibly borne on' means that, whether he makes a conscious effort to start the practice or is unconsciously drawn by the accumulated effect of the practice performed in his previous life, he resumes meditation.

The Lord means that no temptation held out by any other aspect of life is able to keep him from resuming his path. He is not held back by anything, not even by the promise of various gains through Vedic rites and rituals.[66] One-pointedly he sets himself on the path of Yoga and, being intent on it, quickly attains the goal.

'Passes beyond the Veda': transcends the field of relativity and arrives at Transcendental Consciousness. The Lord means that even 'the aspirant', the beginner in Yoga, transcends the field of relative life because, as has already been brought out in verse 40 of Chapter II, there is no difficulty for the mind in reaching absolute Transcendental Consciousness. Here is a great hope for the student of Yoga, whether learned or otherwise.

66 See II, 42–3.

VERSE 45

प्रयत्नाद्यतमानस्तु योगी संशुद्धकिल्बिषः
अनेकजन्मसंसिद्धस्ततो याति परां गतिम्

Prayatnād yatamānas tu yogī saṁshuddhakilbishaḥ
anekajanmasaṁsiddhas tato yāti parāṁ gatim

But the Yogī who strives with zeal, purified of all sin and perfected through many births, thereupon reaches the transcendent goal.

The present verse has been the cause of great misunderstanding and discouragement, for many people have inferred that the Lord here enunciates the principle that attainment requires many lifetimes. This comes from a failure to understand the true meaning of the word 'birth'. Birth means taking a new body. If we analyse what happens when the individual mind gains cosmic status in Transcendental Consciousness, we find that the individual ceases to exist — he becomes pure Existence. On coming out from the Transcendent, individual life is regained. Birth means this regaining of individual existence. Failure to understand the language of the Scripture of Yoga is due to lack of experience of the state of Yoga and to lack of knowledge of the details concerning the practice of Yoga. In this situation misinterpretations are bound to arise.

Three states of Yoga[67] have already been referred to: Yoga in Transcendental Consciousness, in Cosmic Consciousness, and in God Consciousness. The expression 'perfected' shows that the present verse refers to God Consciousness. The Lord says: 'perfected through many births'. By this He means perfected through the continued practice of repeatedly gaining Transcendental Consciousness and thus being re-born to the world many, many times until Cosmic Consciousness is gained. This state of Cosmic Consciousness, which the Lord says is attained 'with ease',[68] forms the solid foundation upon which God Consciousness grows.

67 See verse 3, commentary.
68 See verse 28.

Of this growth of God Consciousness from the state of Cosmic Consciousness, the Lord says: 'in time finds this within himself'.[69] It should be noticed that the Lord's expression 'in time' contains no suggestion whatever of many lifetimes. Thus there is absolutely no reason to suppose that the expression 'many births' means many lifetimes. The teaching is that by the practice of Transcendental Meditation one readily gains Transcendental Consciousness, and that through constant practice of gaining Transcendental Consciousness, one rises to Cosmic Consciousness 'without long delay',[70] and then to God Consciousness.

We may interpret 'many births' in the superficial sense of the expression as many lives, but it is clear that this meaning will apply only to those who are 'not perfected in Yoga' in this life through 'lacking effort' and because their 'mind strayed from Yoga'.[71] Even they, the Lord says, attain the transcendent goal by gradually purifying themselves through practice in many lives.[72] This is the glory of Yoga, that once it has been started it will have its effect. If it does not bring complete fulfilment in this life, owing to lack of practice, then it will have its influence in future lives, bringing a man back to its practice and eventually to liberation.

'Transcendent goal': the goal of Transcendental Consciousness. When Transcendental Consciousness becomes permanent in Cosmic Consciousness, the goal that lies ahead is God Consciousness.

VERSE 46

तपस्विभ्योऽधिको योगी ज्ञानिभ्योऽपि मतोऽधिकः
कर्मिभ्यश्चाधिको योगी तस्माद्योगी भवार्जुन

Tapaswibhyo 'dhiko yogī gyānibhyo 'pi mato 'dhikaḥ
karmibhyash chādhiko yogī tasmād yogī bhavārjuna

---

69 See IV, 38.
70 See V, 6.
71 See verse 37.
72 See verses 43–4.

A Yogī is superior to the austere; he is deemed superior even to men of knowledge. A Yogī is superior to men of action. Therefore be a Yogī, O Arjuna.

In this verse the Lord denies the value of all doing, of all straining, and of all effort for the sake of enlightenment. The man of austerity strains both body and mind. The practice of Yoga refines the nervous system in a gentle way and, removing all strain, leads to Transcendental Consciousness. Therefore austerity is inferior to Yoga from every point of view.

The man of knowledge in this context is one who has theoretical knowledge about the three *Guṇas*, the Self, and God, but has not directly experienced them. Certainly he is inferior to the *Yogī*, who knows their nature through direct experience.

The path through activity is taken by one who strives for purification of the body, mind, and soul by the ritualistic performance of righteous action, by charity, and by the exercise of a proper sense of duty, by any kind of action aimed at refining his mind and reaching enlightenment. This path again is inferior to Yoga, which enlightens the mind in an easy and direct way.

It is certainly true that all such practices have a purifying effect, thus helping the mind to grow in *Sattwa*. Becoming more pure in this way, the mind will eventually reach the status of the Self. The theory of all these paths is right, but they are inferior to Yoga. Not only do they take a very long time, but they are confined within the field of which the Lord has said 'action is … the means';[73] whereas the *Yogī* is established in the field of which the Lord has said 'calmness is … the means'.[74] This is a very much more advanced state of life.

The superiority of a *Yogī* lies not only in his realizing the Supreme quickly and easily but also in his realization of Its fullest glory, the glory of the manifested Being in the absolute existence of God. This is the glory of God Consciousness in man's life, a glory beyond the excellence reached through austerity or knowledge or action.

73 See verse 3.

74 See verse 3.

VERSE 47

योगिनामपि सर्वेषां मद्गतेनान्तरात्मना
श्रद्धावान्भजते यो मां स मे युक्ततमो मतः

Yoginām api sarveshāṁ madgatenāntarātmanā
shraddhāvān bhajate yo māṁ sa me yuktatamo mataḥ

And of all Yogīs, I hold him most fully united who worships Me with faith, his inmost Self absorbed in Me.

Here is an exposition of the highest state of evolution. The Lord says: 'of all *Yogīs*'. By this He means that there are various types of *Yogī*, the *Hatha Yogī*, *Gyān Yogī*, *Karma Yogī*, and so on. All these have four levels of attainment: the first is realization of Self-consciousness (verses 10–18); the second, realization of Cosmic Consciousness (verses 24–9); the third, realization of God Consciousness (verses 30–2), and the fourth, realization of all creation in God Consciousness (verse 32). When the Lord says: 'of all *Yogīs* ... his inmost Self absorbed in Me', He is referring to the man who has established within himself a natural and permanent bond of Union with the Lord of all beings and with the whole creation. This happens on the level where devotion is fulfilled.

Infusion of the state of Being into the nature of the mind, in such fullness and so permanently that no experience of relativity can overshadow it, characterizes Cosmic Consciousness. One who has reached this state is ever contented in himself. But though this contentment is positive and actual, it is wholly abstract in its essential nature, for it is, after all, a sign of the infusion of transcendental Being into the nature of the mind. This infusion does not cause Being to be experienced on the level of the senses. The eyes cannot see Being, the tongue cannot taste It, the ears cannot hear nor the hands touch It. It is the process of devotion in faith which brings this about.

Devotion is always on a personal level. So, when the Lord says: 'of all *Yogīs*' he 'who worships Me with faith', He means one who, established in Cosmic Consciousness, attaches himself to the manifest expression of cosmic existence, to cosmic existence made individual in God, for the sake of devotion and worship. Then the eyes enjoy the abstract eternal Being made manifest — all the senses enjoy It as their object of experience. This is the way of devotion which glorifies even one who has gained Cosmic Consciousness and enables him to enjoy the Transcendent, the Supreme, on the level of the senses. Religious history records individuals — men like Shukadeva, King Janaka, and others — who, established in Reality, were devoted to the Lord and enjoyed Him by every means of experience, by the senses, by the mind, by the intellect, and by the soul. Such fortunate beings, the Lord says, are 'most fully united'.

This is the verse which puts an end to any misunderstanding about the highest state of Union. The Lord shows that in Him rests 'absorbed' the 'inmost Self of the highest *Yogī*'. This is an explanation from His side, but the expression which He gives to that state from the side of the devotee is different: the devotee worships Him 'with faith'. This is the glory of Union with the Lord. The Lord embraces the devotee and makes him one with Himself, and the devotee holds fast to the Lord in worship. This is the state of oneness where each upholds the other.

This is the duality and the Unity in the Great Union.

ॐ तत्सदिति श्रीमद्भगवद्गीतासूपनिषत्सु ब्रह्मविद्यायां योगशास्त्रे श्रीकृष्णार्जुनसंवादे आत्मसंयमयोगो नाम षष्ठोऽध्यायः

Oṁ tat sad iti Shrīmad Bhagavadgītāsūpanishatsu Brahmavidyāyāṁ Yogashāstre Shrīkṛishṇārjunasaṁvāde Ātmasaṁyamayogo nāma shashtho 'dhyāyaḥ

Thus, in the Upanishad of the glorious Bhagavad-Gītā, in the Science of the Absolute, in the Scripture of Yoga, in the dialogue between Lord Kṛishṇa and Arjuna, ends the sixth chapter, entitled: The Yoga of Meditation, Dhyān Yoga.

JAI GURU DEV

Appendix

The Holy Tradition

The following verse records the cherished names of the great Masters of the Holy Tradition of Vedic Wisdom:

Nārāyaṇaṁ Padmabhavaṁ Vasishthaṁ
Shaktiṁ cha tatputra Parāsharaṁ cha
Vyāsaṁ Shukaṁ Gaudapādaṁ mahāntaṁ
Govinda Yogīndram athāsya shishyam

Shrī Shankarāchāryam athāsya Padma-
Pādaṁ cha Hastāmalakaṁ cha shishyam
Taṁ Trotakaṁ Vārtikakāram anyān
Asmad Gurūn santatam ānato 'smi

Shruti-Smṛiti-Purāṇānām
Ālayaṁ Karunālayam
Namāmi Bhagavat-pādaṁ
Shankaraṁ loka-shankaram

Shankaraṁ Shankarāchāryaṁ
Keshavaṁ Bādarāyaṇam
Sūtra-Bhāshya-kṛitau vande
Bhagavantau punaḥ punaḥ

Yad-dwāre nikhilā nilimpa-parishad
Siddhiṁ vidhatte 'nisham
Shrīmat-Shrī-lasitaṁ Jagadguru-padaṁ
Natwātmatṛiptiṁ gatāḥ

Lokāgyān payod-pātan-dhuraṁ
Shrī Shankaraṁ Sharmadam
Brahmānanda Saraswatīṁ Guruvaraṁ
Dhyāyāmi jyotirmayam

The *Transcendental Meditation*® Technique: The Main Principle

When a wave of the ocean makes contact with deeper levels of water, it becomes more powerful. Likewise, when the conscious mind expands to embrace deeper levels of thinking, the thought-wave becomes more powerful.

The expanded capacity of the conscious mind increases the power of the mind and results in added energy and intelligence. Man, who generally uses only a small portion of the total mind that he possesses, begins to make use of his full mental potential.

The technique may be defined as turning the attention inwards towards the subtler levels of a thought until the mind transcends the experience of the subtlest state of the thought and arrives at the source of the thought. This expands the conscious mind and at the same time brings it in contact with the creative intelligence that gives rise to every thought.

A thought-impulse starts from the silent creative centre within, as a bubble starts from the bottom of the sea. As it rises, it becomes larger; arriving at the conscious level of the mind, it becomes large enough to be appreciated as a thought, and from there it develops into speech and action.

Turning the attention inwards takes the mind from the experience of a thought at the conscious level (B) to the finer states of the thought until the mind arrives at the source of thought (A). This inward march of the mind results in the expansion of the conscious mind (from W_1 to W_2).

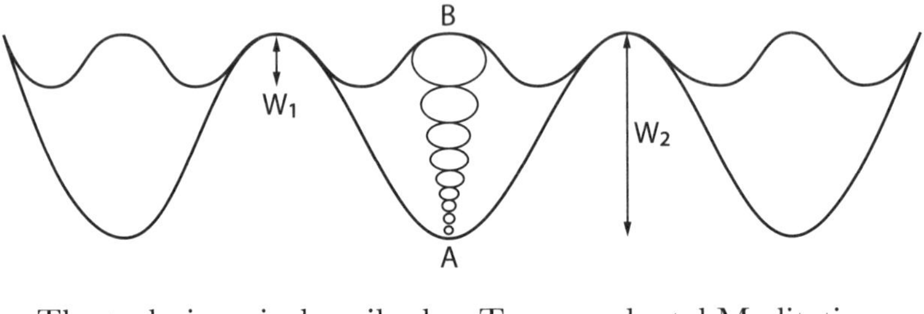

The technique is described as Transcendental Meditation.

Its practice is simple. There are no prerequisites for beginning the practice, other than receiving instructions personally from a qualified teacher.

It should be noted that the Transcendental Meditation technique is neither a matter of contemplation nor of concentration. The process of contemplation and concentration both hold the mind on the conscious thinking level, whereas Transcendental Meditation systematically takes the mind to the source of thought, the pure field of creative intelligence.

Cosmic Law, The Basic Law of Creation

The ever-changing creation of infinite variety seems to be grounded on some stable plane of existence. The rhythm of Nature seems to conform to a definite pattern. The infinite number of the galaxies in the vast structure of cosmic space seem to move according to a definite plan. The creation, evolution, and dissolution of all things seem to follow a definite procedure. Things change, but the incessant change itself seems to have some unchanging basis.

Hydrogen and oxygen are gases. They combine to form water, H_2O. The qualities of gas change to the qualities of water, but hydrogen and oxygen remain H and O. Again, when water freezes and is transformed into ice, the qualities of water change to those of ice, but hydrogen and oxygen, the essential constituents, remain the same. This means that, while there are certain laws responsible for changing the qualities of gas to water and water to ice, there is some force, some law, which maintains the integrity of hydrogen and oxygen.

The law that does not allow hydrogen and oxygen to change into anything else is itself the unchanging basis of the laws responsible for changing gas into liquid and liquid into solid. The Cosmic Law is that law which maintains the integrity of the essential and ultimate constituent of creation — absolute Being. Being remains Being by virtue of the Cosmic Law, which gives rise to different laws responsible for different strata of creation. Although these varied Laws of Nature are directly responsible for the maintenance and evolution of the universe, their basis is the eternal Cosmic Law at the plane of Being.

When, during Transcendental Meditation, the mind transcends the subtlest state of thought and attains the state of Self-consciousness, or pure Being, it attains the level of Cosmic Law. Coming out of that state, its position is like that of a man entering the office of the President and coming out endowed with his goodwill; all the subordinates begin to be in sympathy with him and give him their full support by directing his activities towards a successful end.

When the mind comes out from the field of Being, the plane of Cosmic Law, into the relative field of activity, which is under the influence of innumerable Laws of Nature, it automatically enjoys the support of the Cosmic Law, and this makes possible the accomplishment of any aspiration and the ultimate fulfilment of life.

This is how the life of a man who has risen to Cosmic Consciousness is eternally established on the level of Cosmic Law and receives spontaneous support from all the Laws of Nature.

The Six Systems of Indian Philosophy

Knowledge is true only when it is acceptable in the light of each of the six systems of Indian philosophy. The truth of every statement in the Bhagavad-Gītā can be tested and proved in this way. The second[1] verse of Chapter I is analysed below to illustrate this perfection of Vyāsa's exposition. The systems are presented in their classical sequence.

The first system, Nyāya, analyses the correctness of the procedure of gaining knowledge. Having arrived correctly at the object of investigation through Nyāya, one turns to the second system, Vaisheshik, which sets forth the criteria for analysing the special qualities which differentiate the object from other objects. When Vaisheshik has identified the object of inquiry beyond any doubt, the third system, Sāṁkhya, enumerates the different components of the object. Yoga, the fourth system, then offers a way for the direct cognition of the object. Knowledge of the

1 The first verse presents a question. The truth of a question does not need to be verified as does the truth of a statement which presents the answer. That is why the first verse has not been analysed here. The answer begins from the second verse and its validity is open to verification in the light of the six systems of Indian philosophy.

modes of activity of the object and of its components is provided by the fifth system, Karma Mīmāṁsā. These five systems having analysed the different aspects of the object of inquiry from the point of view of relative existence, the sixth system, Vedānt, shows that the ultimate Reality of the object, which underlies all its different phases, is absolute in nature. Thus it is clear that the six systems taken together make knowledge complete by considering every possible aspect of the object.

It should be noted that each system is so thorough in itself that it appears to be sufficient to give complete knowledge for liberation. Many scholars have thus been dazzled by one particular system and blinded to the value of the others. It therefore seems that the very perfection of each system has robbed Indian philosophy of its wholeness and made it weak. In order to be complete, knowledge requires the support of all six systems.

The following analysis illustrates how the various words of the second verse of Chapter I give expression to each of the six systems in detail.

It will be recalled that the verse runs as follows:

Then Duryodhana the prince, seeing the army of
the Pāṇdavas drawn up in battle array, approached
his master and spoke these words

Nyāya

Nyāya, the science of reasoning expounded by Gautama, presents sixteen points by which to test the procedure of gaining knowledge:

1. THE MEANS OF VALID KNOWLEDGE (*PRAMĀṆA*)

There are four means of valid knowledge:

i. *Perception* (*Pratyaksha*). The lesson on perception[2] is given by the word 'seeing'.

ii. *Inference* (*Anumāna*). 'Seeing ... battle array': seeing the army in battle array, Duryodhana inferred that it was time to fight, and this made him approach his master.

2 The *Transcendental Meditation* technique, which forms the central teaching of the Bhagavad-Gītā, is a means of direct perception, a direct means of gaining knowledge.

iii. *Comparison* (*Upamāna*). This is a means of gaining knowledge of something by comparing it with another well-known object. Here the word 'prince' is used with reference to Duryodhana.

iv. *Verbal testimony* (*Shabda*). 'These words': the words of a prince are authentic.

2. THE OBJECT OF VALID KNOWLEDGE (*PRAMEYA*)

The object of knowledge is that about which the inquiry is made, or that which is approached, in this case the 'master'.

A point to be noted here is that when Vyāsa teaches the lesson of *Prameya*, he presents as the object of knowledge the master, who is the source of all knowledge.

3. DOUBT (*SAṀSHAYA*)

The 'approach' to a 'master' is made in order to remove doubts and gain clarity.

4. PURPOSE (*PRAYOJANA*)

The words 'drawn up in battle array' demonstrate the purpose of the army.

5. EXAMPLE (*DṚISHTĀNTA*)

'Duryodhana' gives the lesson on *Dṛishtānta*. In the previous verse, Dhṛitarāshtra asked about the actions of his sons. Duryodhana being the eldest, his actions may be taken to exemplify the actions of all the hundred sons of Dhṛitarāshtra.

6. ESTABLISHED PRINCIPLE (*SIDDHĀNTA*)

It is an established principle that the master is always approached by the disciple. Duryodhana 'approached his master'.

7. PARTS OF A LOGICAL ARGUMENT (*AVAYAVA*)

'Seeing ... approached ... spoke.'

8. THE PROCESS OF REASONING (*TARKA*)

Duryodhana 'approached his master' in order to gain an authoritative decision which would leave no possibility of error or supposition. The lesson on reasoning given here is highly practical.

9. THE ART OF DRAWING CONCLUSIONS (*NIRṆAYA*)

Seeing the army, Duryodhana judged the situation and immediately acted upon the conclusion he had drawn: he 'approached his master'.

10. DISCUSSION (*VĀDA*)

Discussion consists of the interplay of two opposing sides for the purpose of arriving at a decisive conclusion. The lesson on discussion taught by this verse is of a very perfect nature. One man seeing both sides 'approached' the 'master', the knower of Reality, to find a solution. In teaching the lesson of discussion, of the interplay of two opposing sides, this verse at the same time teaches the lesson of harmony.

11. POLEMICS (*JALPA*)

Polemics is argument for the sake of victory, as opposed to discussion for the sake of arriving at the truth. In the present verse, the lesson on polemics is given by 'spoke these words'. The battlefield is the place for action, but instead of taking action Duryodhana engages in speech. Further, the opposing army is silent, and against that silence Duryodhana 'spoke these words'. Therefore in this verse action is pitted against speech and speech challenges silence. Here is a lesson on polemics in its most extreme form.

12. CAVIL (*VITAṆḌĀ*)

This verse places 'the army' on one side and 'words' on the other and thereby lowers the dignity of the army. This is the purpose of cavil — to lower the dignity of the other side. It is the beauty of this verse that it teaches a lesson on cavil without using the language of cavil.

13. FALLACIES (*HETWĀBHĀSA*)

Fallacies are of five types:

i. *The inconclusive* (*Savyabhichāra*) — reasoning from which more than one conclusion can be drawn. This verse leaves us in uncertainty about what Duryodhana said, even though it uses the word 'these', which indicates definiteness.

ii. *The contradictory* (*Viruddha*) — where the reasoning contradicts the proposition to be established. In the face of 'the army of the Pāṇdavas ... in battle array', the reasonable thing to be established by Duryodhana was that the fighting should begin. But instead of starting to fight, Duryodhana 'approached his master'.

iii. *The equivalent to the question* (*Prakaraṇasama*) — where the reasoning is such that it provokes the very question that it is designed to answer. The lesson on this fallacy is found in 'these words'. The word 'these' is definite in its character, but here its use is such that it provokes a question about the definiteness of the 'words'.

iv. *The unproved* (*Sādhyasama*) — where the reason given in order to establish a conclusion is not different from what is to be proved and itself stands in need of proof. The reason for Duryodhana's approach to his master needs proof or justification, because at the time of battle Duryodhana could have had a reason for going to the commander-in-chief but not for going to his master.

v. *The belated* (*Kālātīta*) — where the reason is advanced when the time for it is past. The master is consulted in order that he may give his judgement on the correctness of an action. The reasonable thing would have been for Duryodhana to approach his master before coming on the battlefield.

14. EQUIVOCATION (*CHHALA*)

Equivocation is of three types:

i. *Verbal* (*Vākchhala*) — assuming a word to have a meaning other than that intended by the speaker. The sequence of words in the original text is such that the word 'prince' (*Rājā*) can also be taken to qualify 'words'. It would then mean that Duryodhana spoke princely words, that he spoke like a king — implying that he was not a king but spoke like one. This use of 'prince' with reference to 'words' gives the teaching on verbal equivocation.

ii. *Generalizing* (*Sāmānyachhala*) — challenging the possibility of a statement because of the impossibility of the whole situation. Duryodhana's words had never been as responsible as those of a prince, so the use of the word 'prince' could be taken ironically. It would then mean that Duryodhana is being ridiculed here. This is a teaching on the second type of equivocation.

iii. *Figurative* (*Upachārachhala*) — misinterpreting a word which is used figuratively by taking it literally. As Duryodhana was not a true ruler, the use of the word 'prince' (*Rājā*) with reference to him may be regarded as figurative. When it is taken literally, it gives a lesson on this type of equivocation.

15. FUTILE ARGUMENT (*JĀTI*)

This means argument based merely on similar and dissimilar characteristics. There is similarity of nature between 'Duryodhana' and 'prince'. There is dissimilarity of nature between 'the Pāṇdavas' and their 'army ... in battle array', because the Pāṇdavas are by nature peaceful.

16. DISAGREEMENT ON FIRST PRINCIPLES (*NIGRAHASTHĀNA*)

This arises from mistaken ideas or from a complete lack of understanding. A master is approached when one needs some clarification, and clarification is needed to eliminate error or misunderstanding. The lesson with regard to disagreement on first principles is exemplified by the 'master', in whom all disagreements are dissolved.

This is the perfection of the teaching of Gautama's Nyāya in the Bhagavad-Gītā: even the lesson on disharmony is taught from the centre of all harmony, so that the student of Nyāya is not left on the dry plains of reason.

VAISHESHIK

Vaisheshik, the system expounded by Kaṇāda, analyses the special qualities (*Vishesha*) which distinguish an object from other objects. In the present verse, the word 'prince' brings out a special quality which distinguishes Duryodhana from other men. 'His' specifying 'master' and 'these' specifying 'words' serve a similar purpose. Here we have a general lesson on the Vaisheshik philosophy.

According to Vaisheshik, there are nine substances which form the basis of all creation. The special qualities of these substances are responsible for the varying qualities of the multitude of objects in creation. The nine ultimate substances are: earth (*Pṛithivī*), water (*Āpas*), fire (*Tejas*), air (*Vāyu*), space (*Ākāsha*), time (*Kāla*), direction in space (*Dik*), soul (*Ātmā*), mind (*Manas*).

The first four ultimate substances are distinguished from one another by the special qualities of their *Paramāṇus*, or atoms. There are four such special qualities: odour (*Gandha*), taste (*Rasa*), form (*Rūpa*), touch (*Sparsha*). Earth possesses all four of these qualities; water possesses flavour, form, and touch; fire possesses form and touch; air possesses touch only.

1. EARTH (*PṚITHIVĪ*)

The lesson on the earth element is given by the word 'Duryodhana'. As odour is inseparable from earth, so a princely fragrance is inseparable from Duryodhana, the prince, or master of the earth.

2. WATER (*ĀPAS*)

Taste is the essential quality of the water element. The sense of taste dwells in the tongue, which is also the organ of speech. Therefore the word 'spoke' may be said to give the lesson on the water element.

3. FIRE (*TEJAS*)

'Seeing' gives the lesson on the fire element, because the sense of sight relates to the fire element.

4. AIR (*VĀYU*)

'Approached' gives the lesson on the air element, because touch is the inseparable quality of the air element. The process of approaching culminates in touch.

5. SPACE (*ĀKĀSHA*)

The fifth ultimate substance, space, is characterized by sound. Therefore the lesson on space is given by 'words'.

6. TIME (*KĀLA*)

Time is indicated by such concepts as sequence, simultaneity, speed, and slowness. 'Seeing ... approached ... spoke' gives a lesson on all these concepts.

7. DIRECTION IN SPACE (*DIK*)

Direction in space is indicated by expressions such as here, there, far, near, above, below. The lesson on direction in space is given by 'army ... in battle array' and 'approached'.

8. SOUL (*ĀTMĀ*)

According to the Vaisheshik Sūtras, the existence of the eighth ultimate substance, soul, is indicated by the ascending life-breath (*Prāṇa*), the descending life-breath (*Apāna*), the closing of the eyelids (*Nimesha*), the opening of the eyelids (*Unmesha*), life (*Jīvana*), mental activity (*Manogati*), the inner changes in the field of the senses (*Indriyāntara-vikāra*), pleasure (*Sukha*), pain (*Duḥkha*), desire (*Ichchhā*), and effort (*Prayatna*).

The lesson on soul is given by:

i. The ascending and descending life-breaths join to bring forth speech: 'spoke these words'.
ii. The closing and opening of the eyelids relate to vision: 'seeing'.
iii. Life is indicated in Duryodhana by the words 'seeing ... approached ... spoke'.
iv. Mental activity is inherent in the sequence of 'seeing ... approached ... spoke'.
v. Pleasure is inherent in 'approached his master'.
vi. Pain is inherent in 'seeing the army of the Pāṇḍavas ... in battle array'. The lesson on pain is taught without recourse to any obvious reference to pain.
vii. Duryodhana's desire is indicated by the word 'these'. Vyāsa, in giving a lesson on desire, uses an expression which indicates the principle of desire without specifying any particular

desire lest the mind be drawn away from the central point under consideration. Here is an example of Vyāsa's great precision of language in his teaching on the different systems of Indian philosophy.

viii. The lesson on effort is given by the word 'approached'. For any man the process of approaching involves effort; all the more so for a prince, who wields the power to summon anyone at any time.

It is clear that in order to verify the special qualities of the soul, the soul must be 'approached'. In the verse under consideration, 'approached' is the result of some mental activity following upon the sensory activity of 'seeing'. Likewise, in order to approach the soul, it is necessary to go from the experience of the field of sensory activity to that of mental activity until, transcending the subtlest mental activity, one approaches the field of pure Being, which is pure consciousness, the basis of all activity. Only through this process, known as Transcendental Meditation, can the mind realize intimately the subtle fields of relative existence, which Kaṇāda indicates as constituting the special qualities of the soul, and this fulfils the purpose of the Vaisheshik teaching.

9. MIND (*MANAS*)

The ninth ultimate substance, mind, is the faculty responsible for giving knowledge to the soul upon the soul's contact with the senses and their objects. The lesson on mind is given by the thought that lies between 'seeing' and 'approached' and 'spoke'.

SĀṀKHYA

Sāṁkhya means 'pertaining to number'. This system of philosophy, expounded by Kapila, holds that knowledge of an object will not be complete without the knowledge of its components. In its analysis of life and creation, Sāṁkhya establishes twenty-five categories as lying at the basis of the entire creation and of the process of cosmic evolution. The teaching concerning these categories can be verified by direct experience through the practice of the Transcendental Meditation technique, in which the mind travels through all the gross and subtle levels of creation to the state of pure Transcendental Consciousness.

1. *PURUSHA*

Purusha, or Cosmic Spirit, is the transcendental Reality which comes into direct experience during Transcendental Meditation at the point where even the subtlest level of creation is transcended and pure Transcendental Consciousness alone remains. *Purusha* forms the basis of the subjective aspect of life. He is the eternal silent witness of all that was, is, and will be.

In the verse under consideration, the teaching about *Purusha* is found in the word 'Pāṇdavas'. The expression 'army of the Pāṇdavas' indicates that while the army belongs to the Pāṇdavas, the Pāṇdavas themselves may not necessarily form a part of the army; they may remain, as it were, uninvolved. Even though the whole of Nature functions under His will, *Purusha* remains a silent witness to its activity.

2. *PRAKṚITI*

Prakṛiti, or Nature, is the primal substance out of which the entire creation arises. Its constituents are the three *Guṇas*,[3] *Sattwa*, *Rajas*, and *Tamas*. They are responsible for all change and form the basis of evolution.

Whereas in the present verse 'the Pāṇdavas' represent *Purusha*, 'the army' represents *Prakṛiti*. Furthermore, the phrase 'army ... drawn up in battle array' represents *Prakṛiti* laid out in its different constituents, ready to be active. Without specifically mentioning the three *Guṇas*, Vyāsa fully conveys the nature of *Prakṛiti*. As long as the three *Guṇas* are in equilibrium, they do not present themselves as three, they do not demonstrate any activity, and there is no process of creation and evolution; when they have begun to be active, they appear in a whole multitude of permutations and combinations.

3. *MAHAT*

Mahat is that first state of evolution where the previously undifferentiated primal substance, *Prakṛiti*, begins to move towards manifestation, begins to take a specific direction. It is the Cosmic Will in operation, satisfying the urge for manifestation that has been created by the disturbance of the perfect equilibrium

3 See II, 45, commentary.

of the three *Guṇas*.

The lesson on *Mahat* is given by the word 'approached', which depicts the first stir in the situation presented by the verse — a movement in a specific direction.

4. *AHAṀKĀRA*

Ahaṁkāra is the principle responsible for the individuation of *Mahat*.

The teaching of *Ahaṁkāra* is to be found in the word 'his', which presents an example of the principle of individuation, the individuation of the general term 'master'.

5. *MANAS*

Manas is the cosmic mind which provides the object for the individuating principle, *Ahaṁkāra*. In the state of *Manas*, the urge of *Prakṛiti* towards manifestation becomes clearly defined.

The lesson on *Manas* is given by the phrase 'these words', which gives definite shape to the situation created by the first stir, *Mahat*, indicated by the word 'approached'.

6–15. THE *INDRIYAS*

The next ten principles are called *Indriyas*, or senses: five senses of perception (*Gyānendriya*) and five organs of action (*Karmendriya*). They connect the mind with the manifested world of objects.

The lesson on the senses of perception is given by the word 'seeing', taking the sense of sight as representative of the five senses of perception.

The lesson on the organs of action is given by the word 'spoke', the organ of speech being taken as representative of the five organs of action.

16–20. THE *TANMĀTRAS*

The *Tanmātras* constitute the five basic realities, or essences, of the objects of the five senses of perception. They express themselves in the five elements which go to make up the objects of the senses and which provide the material basis of the entire objective universe. Thus the essence of sound (*Shabda Tanmātra*) expresses itself in space, the essence of touch (*Sparsha Tanmātra*) in air, the essence of form (*Rūpa Tanmātra*) in fire, the essence of taste (*Rasa Tanmātra*) in water, and the essence of smell (*Gandha Tanmātra*) in earth.

The lesson on the *Tanmātras* is provided by the Sanskrit word '*tu*', omitted in the translation, meaning 'only after' seeing. This expression draws a dividing line in the sequence of events. Likewise the *Tanmātras* mark the dividing line between the subjective and objective creation. In the process of evolution, as the influence of *Tamas*[4] increases, the subjective creation comes to an end and the objective creation begins. The *Tanmātras*, forming as they do the basis of the five elements, lie in the grossest field of the subjective aspect of creation.

21–5. THE *MAHĀBHŪTAS*

The five *Mahābhūtas*, or elements out of which material creation is constituted, are space (*Ākāsha*), air (*Vāyu*), fire (*Tejas*), water (*Āpas*), and earth (*Pṛithivī*).

The lesson on the *Mahābhūtas* has already been made clear while dealing with Vaisheshik.

It may be noted that the whole teaching of Kapila's can be verified by direct experience through Transcendental Meditation, because in order to reach the state of Transcendental Consciousness the mind has to traverse all the gross and subtle levels of creation.

YOGA

The purpose of Yoga is to gain knowledge by direct perception. Yoga is a practical science of life which lays open to direct experience not only the field of absolute Being but all the different levels of relative creation as well.

The very first word of the verse in the original text, '*dṛishtwā*' (literally 'having seen'), gives a lesson both on the purpose of Yoga and the way to its fulfilment.[5]

4 See II, 45, commentary.
5 The phrase 'a little of this *Dharma*' in verse 40 of Chapter II gives expression to the principle of direct perception.

Patanjali, in his exposition of Yoga, divides life into eight spheres in order to deal thoroughly and completely with the subject of Yoga:

1. The entire field of creation lying outside the individual but constantly influenced by his thoughts and actions. The state of Yoga, or perfect harmony, is found established in this field when man's life is naturally upheld by the five qualities of observance (*Yama*):

i. Truthfulness (*Satya*)
ii. Non-violence (*Ahiṁsā*)
iii. Non-covetousness (*Asteya*)
iv. Celibacy[6] (*Brahmacharya*)
v. Non-acceptance of others' possessions (*Aparigraha*)

These qualities are represented by 'the Pāṇḍavas', the five virtuous sons of Pāṇḍu.

2. The physical structure of the individual body and nervous system. The state of Yoga is found established in the field of the body and nervous system when man's life is naturally upheld by the five rules of life (*Niyama*):

i. Purification (*Shaucha*)
ii. Contentment (*Santosha*)
iii. Austerity (*Tapas*)
iv. Study (*Swādhyāya*)
v. Devotion to God (*Īshwara-praṇidhān*)

These five qualities again are represented by 'the Pāṇḍavas'.

3. The different limbs of the body, the sphere of posture (*Āsana*). The state of Yoga is found established in the sphere of the limbs of the body when there is a perfect functioning of all the limbs in good coordination with each other. In this state, the body is capable of remaining in a steady posture for any length of time.

The lesson on *Āsana* is given by 'drawn up', for in the state of Yoga, the state of Transcendental Consciousness, all the limbs of the body are in perfect accord with each other, fully alert, but not yet set in action.

6 A state of the individual where the life-force is always found directed upwards.

4. The sphere of the individual breath, the sphere of breathing exercises (*Prāṇāyāma*). In the state of Yoga, the activity of breath comes automatically to rest.

The lesson on *Prāṇāyāma* is given by 'the army of the Pāṇdavas, drawn up in battle array'. 'The Pāṇdavas', or five sons of Pāṇdu, represent the five breaths — *Prāṇa, Apāna, Vyāna, Udāna,* and *Samāna* — functioning in different parts of the body. 'The army of the Pāṇdavas drawn up in battle array' represents the steadiness of all the five breaths in the state of Yoga.

5. The sphere of life which lies between the senses and their objects. The state of Yoga in this sphere is marked by complete self-sufficiency on the part of the senses so that they are no longer projected outwards towards their objects. Yoga here means retirement from the field of the objects of the senses.

The lesson on the turning away of the senses from their objects (*Pratyāhāra*) is given by the word 'seeing' (literally 'having seen'), which shows that Duryodhana's vision, having fallen on the army of the Pāṇdavas, was thereupon withdrawn.

6. The sphere of life that lies between the senses and the mind. The state of Yoga in this sphere is marked by the withdrawal of the mind from the realm of the senses.

The lesson on steadiness of mind (*Dhāraṇā*) is given by the expression 'drawn up', which indicates that the mind is steady, that it is no longer associated with the senses.

7. The sphere of life that lies between the mind and Being. The state of Yoga in this sphere is marked by the refining of the mental impulses until the most refined state of mental activity is transcended and the mind gains the state of pure consciousness, absolute existence, or eternal Being.

The lesson on this process of meditation (*Dhyān*) is given by the words 'approached his master', the master representing the state of Being.

A close scrutiny of Patanjali's exposition of Yoga reveals that the actual process of attaining the state of Yoga belongs not only to *Dhyān*, or meditation, which alone appears to result directly in *Samādhi*, or Transcendental Consciousness, but also to all the other limbs of his eightfold Yoga. Each limb presents the principle underlying the practices that bring about the state of Yoga in the sphere of life pertaining to that limb.

For hundreds of years these different limbs of Yoga have been mistakenly regarded as different steps in the development of the state of Yoga, whereas in truth each limb is designed to create the state of Yoga in the sphere of life to which it relates. With the continuous practice of all these limbs, or means, simultaneously, the state of Yoga grows simultaneously in all the eight spheres of life, eventually to become permanent.

It seems necessary to point out here that even *Samādhi*, which is already the state of Yoga in the sense of Transcendental Consciousness, serves as a means to the ultimate state of Yoga, Cosmic Consciousness. In the state of Cosmic Consciousness, Transcendental Consciousness has become permanently grounded in the nature of the mind or, to speak in Indian terms, *Kshaṇika* (momentary) *Samādhi* has become *Nitya* (perpetual) *Samādhi*. It is in this sense that Maharishi Patanjali has placed *Samādhi* along with the other seven limbs, or means, of Yoga.

In order to connect the principle of *Dhyān* with practice it may be mentioned that the most valuable practice in the sphere of *Dhyān* is the simple system of Transcendental Meditation. Transcendental Meditation belongs to the sphere of *Dhyān*, but at the same time transcends that sphere and gives rise to the state of Transcendental Consciousness, *Samādhi*. After this state has been gained the attention returns to the sphere of *Dhyān*, which is a sphere of activity. This regular passing of the attention from one sphere to the other enables Transcendental Consciousness to be maintained even during activity, first at a very subtle level and later in the gross activity of daily life, so that it may eventually become permanent. In this way the simple system known as Transcendental Meditation, which is a specific type of practice, forms the most effective working tool of these two spheres of life, *Dhyān* and *Samādhi*.

8. The sphere of absolute Being, the state of Transcendental Consciousness (*Samādhi*).

The lesson on *Samādhi* is given by the word 'Pāṇḍavas'. In

this verse, the use of the word 'Pāṇdavas' indicates that the Pāṇdavas possess the army and, as its masters, are separate from it. Similarly, in the state of *Samādhi* the Self is experienced as the Transcendent, uninvolved with anything.

Karma Mīmāṁsā

Mīmāṁsā means investigation, close consideration. Karma Mīmāṁsā is concerned with the close study of action, because action forms the basis of the existence and evolution of the individual. The very first sūtra of Jaimini's Karma Mīmāṁsā begins an inquiry into *Dharma*, the invincible force of Nature which upholds the entire creation. The main quest of Karma Mīmāṁsā is for that action which will be spontaneously in accord with *Dharma*. The influence of every action is so far-reaching[7] as to be beyond human understanding. Therefore the criterion by which the rightness of an action should be judged can be no other than the verbal testimony (*Shabda*) of the Vedas.

Jaimini establishes the eternal nature of *Shabda* by logical argument and removes all doubts concerning it. The lesson on this is given by the expression 'approached his master', because the master is approached to remove all doubts.

Having established the eternity of *Shabda*, it was necessary for Jaimini to establish that the Veda is divine revelation at the time of creation. The lesson on this is found in the word 'then' — at the time of creation.

Jaimini also proves that the words of the Veda, even though impulses of the Divine, are not meaningless notes or rhythms. They have a meaning and therefore a specific purpose just like any spoken sound (word) in any language. Every word and every phrase of the verse under consideration offers a lesson on this point.

Because he held the Veda to be the final authority on *Dharma*, it was necessary for Jaimini to devise a definite method of investigation of the Vedic text. This he did by analysing the contents of the Vedas as follows:

7 See IV, 17, commentary.

1. *VIDHI* (PRECEPTS OR INJUNCTIONS)

The lesson on this is given by the sequence 'seeing . . . approached . . . spoke'.

2. *MANTRA* (KEY-WORDS)

Mantras are key-words which help one to remember the different steps of the *Yagyas*.[8]

The 'master' (*Āchārya*) is the custodian of the knowledge of the *Mantras* and is there to answer all objections raised against them. The *Mantras* exist to help the performance of the *Yagya*: there is a different *Mantra* at every step. During the process of the *Yagya*, the master speaks the *Mantra*, and in accordance with that others perform actions. Duryodhana 'approached his master' in order to receive the right word (*Mantra*) of action from him.

3. *NĀMADHEYA* (PROPER NOUNS)

The lesson on *Nāmadheya* is given by 'Duryodhana' and 'Pāṇdavas'.

4. *NISHEDHA* (PROHIBITIONS)

Nishedha is the opposite of *Vidhi*.

The lesson on *Nishedha* is given by 'approached his master' and 'spoke these words'. The procedure in accordance with precept (*Vidhi*) is that after approaching the master one should at once prostrate oneself. But instead of prostrating himself, Duryodhana began to speak.

5. *ARTHAVĀDA* (EXPLANATORY PASSAGES)

'The prince' gives a lesson on *Arthavāda*.

The Mīmāṁsākas, following the Sanskrit grammarians, divide Vedic substantives into three types:

i. *Rūdhi*, a simple non-compound word with a conventional acceptation which we learn from a teacher or other authority.

   The lesson on *Rūdhi* is given by 'words'.

ii. *Yaugika*, a compound word made up of two or more words, each of which has its independent meaning and contributes to the meaning of the whole.

8 See III, 9, commentary.

The lesson on *Yaugika* is given by 'army of the Pāṇḍavas' (Pāṇḍava-Anika).

iii. *Yogarūdhi*, a word which, though compound, has its own conventional meaning.

The lesson on this is given by the word 'Duryodhana' (Dur-yodhana).

Jaimini points out that substantives are not self-sufficient but require a verb to convey the purpose of speech. Verbs introduce the element of action, which is classified by Jaimini according to whether its effects are mainly visible or invisible. Those actions with mainly invisible effects (*Apūrva*) are called principal (*Pradhāna*), and those with mainly visible effects are called secondary (*Gauṇa*).

The lesson on actions which are *Pradhāna* is given by the word 'spoke', because the effects of Duryodhana's speech are not visible in this verse. The lesson on actions which are *Gauṇa* is given by the word 'seeing', because the effect of seeing is immediately apparent in 'approached his master and spoke these words'.

In order to permit a thorough scrutiny of the Vedic texts in accordance with the principles of interpretation laid out above, the Vedas are considered in two sections: (i) The Saṁhitās — those parts which deal with the *Mantras*; (ii) The Brāhmaṇas — those parts which deal with ritualistic performances and explanatory passages.

1. THE SAṀHITĀS

These are divided into three sections:

i. Ṛk — verses collected in a group and marked by their metrical arrangement. The lesson on this is given by the metrical quality of the present verse.

ii. Sāma — verses sung at the conclusion of the *Yagya*. The lesson on Sāma is given by the word 'then'. This word places the situation portrayed in the verse at the end of some other happening.

iii. Yajus — *Mantras* in prose. They are of two types:

a. those which are spoken aloud (*Nigada*). The lesson on this type of *Mantra* is given by all the words of this verse since they are spoken aloud.

b. those which are pronounced silently (*Upaṁshu*). 'These words' refer to words that are not pronounced in this verse. This gives a lesson on the *Mantras* which are pronounced silently.

2. THE BRĀHMAṆAS

Shabara, in his commentary on the Mīmāṁsā Sūtra, mentions ten ways of analysing the Brāhmaṇas:

i. *Hetu — motive*. The lesson on this is given by the word 'seeing'. It was 'seeing' which caused Duryodhana to approach his master and speak.

ii. *Nirvachana — explanation or expression*. The lesson on this is given by 'drawn up in battle array', an expression which explains what is seen.

iii. *Nindā — deprecation*. The lesson on deprecation is taught by the fact that the word 'Pāṇdavas' remains unqualified, whereas Duryodhana is called a prince.

iv. *Prashaṁsā — praise*. The lesson on this is taught by the phrase 'drawn up in battle array', which expresses the dignity of the army.

v. *Saṁshaya — doubt*. 'Approached his master' gives a lesson on doubt, because the master is always approached in order to remove doubt.

vi. *Vidhi — precept*. As explained earlier, the lesson on this is given by 'seeing ... approached ... spoke'.

vii. *Parakriyā — the action of an individual*. The whole verse is concerned with Duryodhana's action: 'seeing ... approached ... spoke'.

viii. *Purākalpa — past events*. The lesson on this is given by 'army drawn up in battle array'.

ix. *Vyavadhāraṇa Kalpana — meaning according to context*. The word 'then' teaches this lesson.

x. *Upamāna — comparison*. This helps to gain knowledge of a thing by comparison with another well-known object. The lesson on *Upamāna* is given by the word 'prince', used with reference to Duryodhana.

It is important to note that the practice of Transcendental Meditation spontaneously fulfils the quest of Karma Mīmāṁsā for action in accordance with *Dharma*. Transcendental Meditation brings the mind to the state of Being. Being is eternal; It forms the basis of creation and therefore upholds the entire universe. When the mind gains the state of Being, it simultaneously gains the level of *Dharma*. Therefore action by a mind held in Being is automatically in accordance with *Dharma*. Transcendental Meditation thus brings fulfilment to the teaching of Karma Mīmāṁsā.

Vedānt

Vedānt means 'end of the Veda', 'final knowledge of the Veda'. The system of Vedānt is also known as Uttara Mīmāṁsā, meaning that it is an investigation into the last chapter of the Veda, the Upanishads. Whereas Jaimini's Karma Mīmāṁsā, or Pūrva (earlier) Mīmāṁsā as it is sometimes called, considers that portion of the Veda which is concerned with action, Vyāsa's[9] Uttara (later) Mīmāṁsā, or Vedānt, considers that portion of the Veda which is concerned with knowledge. The main purpose of Vedānt is to educate man in the truth that complete knowledge of life is no other than life itself as it is lived naturally on the level of Being.

From a cosmic standpoint, Vedānt explains the relationship of the unmanifested absolute Reality (*Brahman*) with the manifested relative aspect of life by introducing the principle of *Māyā*. The word '*Māyā*' means literally that which is not, that which does not exist. This brings to light the character of *Māyā*: it is not anything substantial. Its presence is inferred from the effects that it produces. The influence of *Māyā* may be understood by the example of sap appearing as a tree. Every fibre of the tree is nothing but the sap. Sap, while remaining sap, appears as the tree. Likewise, through the influence of *Māyā*, *Brahman*, remaining *Brahman*, appears as the manifested world.

On the individual level, Vedānt explains the relationship of

9 Vyāsa, who recorded Lord Kṛishṇa's discourse to Arjuna in the Bhagavad-Gītā, also expounded the system of Vedānt.

the absolute Self (*Ātmā*) and the relative aspect of individual life by the principle of *Avidyā*. *Avidyā*, or ignorance, is nothing but *Māyā* in a coarser form. If *Māyā* can be likened to clear water, then muddy water is *Avidyā*.

Under the influence of *Māyā*, *Brahman* appears as Īshwara, the personal God, who exists on the celestial level of life in the subtlest field of creation. In a similar way, under the influence of *Avidyā*, *Ātmā* appears as *Jīva*, or individual soul.

The lesson on *Brahman* is given by the word 'master'. The master, possessing the whole wisdom of life, is established in *Brāhmī-sthiti*, the state of *Brahman*, or Cosmic Consciousness.

The lesson on *Māyā* is given in this verse by the word '*Rājā*', which means 'prince' or 'king'. A rightful king Duryodhana was not.

The lesson on Īshwara also is given by the word '*Rājā*', or king. The king wields the highest authority on the human level.

The lesson on *Ātmā* is given by the word 'Pāṇdavas'. The phrase 'army of the Pāṇdavas' expresses that the Pāṇdavas are not necessarily part of the army even though they are the masters of it. Likewise, *Ātmā* is separate from and not involved with the world of activity.

The lesson on *Avidyā* is given by 'seeing ... approached ... spoke'. *Avidyā*, or ignorance, is at the basis of all the activity of individual life.

The lesson on *Jīva* is taught by 'Duryodhana', of whom it is said that he saw, approached, and spoke. It is the *Jīva* which participates in activity.

The exposition of knowledge about life in Vedānt is so perfect that the ordinary level of human intelligence is unable to comprehend it. Therefore, as a necessary prerequisite for gaining knowledge of Vedānt, the level of consciousness must be raised. In order to become capable of understanding Vedānt, one's life must be lived on the level of the four qualities:

1. *VIVEKA* (DISCRIMINATION)

The lesson on this is taught by 'seeing the army' and 'approached his master'. It was through the power of discrimination that Duryodhana, on seeing the army, decided to approach the master and present to him the situation before finally plunging into battle.

2. *VAIRĀGYA* (NON-ATTACHMENT)

The lesson on this is found in the word 'Pāṇdavas'. The Pāṇdavas were on the battlefield, yet the expression 'army of the Pāṇdavas' depicts them as separate from the army, as though uninvolved with it. This makes it clear that the teaching of *Vairāgya*, according to this verse, does not involve abandonment of the activities and responsibilities of life. It is enough to remain uninvolved with one's possessions. Abandonment of possessions is no criterion of non-attachment.

3. *SHATSAMPATTI* (THE SIX TREASURES)

i. *Shama — control of mind.* The lesson on this is given by 'seeing the army' and 'approached his master'. Had Duryodhana not possessed this quality of *Shama*, he could not have had the presence of mind to approach and consult his master.

ii. *Dama — control of senses.* The lesson on this is given by the expression 'army ... drawn up in battle array'. The army of the senses is drawn up, capable of functioning but not yet active. This indicates that the alertness of the senses does not discredit the principle of control of the senses.

iii. *Uparati — abstinence.* 'Approached his master' gives a lesson on abstinence. It suggests that the path to the state of enlightenment is true abstinence — abstinence from ignorance and bondage. This word has commonly been misunderstood to mean abstinence from activity.

The practical aspect of abstinence is Transcendental Meditation, because this practice is a direct way to Transcendental Consciousness, the state of enlightenment. After gaining Transcendental Consciousness by the inward stroke of meditation, the mind comes out to engage in activity. This process of repeatedly gaining Transcendental Consciousness and then engaging in activity results in making permanent the state of enlightenment. It is therefore clear that the teaching on *Uparati*, or abstinence, in no way involves falling into inactivity or abandoning activity altogether.

iv. *Titikshā — endurance.* The lesson on this is given by 'army ... drawn up in battle array'. The army, whose function it is to fight, endures non-activity. The essence of endurance is to take all things as they come.

v. *Shraddhā — faith.* The lesson on faith is given by 'approached his master'.

vi. *Samādhāna — mental equilibrium.* The unmoved state of the 'master' presented in this verse gives a lesson on mental equilibrium.

4. *MUMUKSHUTWA* (DESIRE FOR LIBERATION)

The lesson on this is taught by 'approached his master'.

This analysis of the second verse of Chapter I serves as an illustration showing that every verse of the Bhagavad-Gītā is valid and its truth verifiable in the light of the six systems of Indian philosophy. At the same time it has been shown that the aims of each system are fulfilled through the practice of Transcendental Meditation.

JAI GURU DEV

Shankarāchārya Nagar,
Rishikesh, U.P.

Mahāshivarātri
18 February 1966

INDEX

Absolute
- attributeless, 102–3
- experience of, 213, 249
- incarnation of, 261
- is bliss, 132, 144, 161, 169, 333, 367
- mind/intellect established in, 118–19
- same from any angle of reasoning, 103–4
- shines forth in Its own light, 355
- wisdom of, 11, 25, 75, 125, 177, 195, 251
- *Yagya* and, 205
- *See also* Being

Absolute and God, 446–47

Absolute and relative
- Bliss Consciousness at junction point of, 437–38
- as imperishable and perishable, 115, 128, 179–80
- Kṛishṇa and, 162, 210, 260, 272, 305–7, 441–47
- *Māyā* explains relationship of, 491–92
- play-power of *Brahman*, 261
- *Pūrṇam adaḥ pūrṇam idam*, 79, 250–51, 279, 449
- realizing truth of both, 279
- remaining in My own Nature I take birth, 259–64
- Sāṃkhya is all about nature of, 90–116
- *Shākhās* related to, 195–96
- this and That held together, 279
- This covered by that, 238
- unchanging as basis of ever-changing, 471
- Vedānt on, 491–92
- *See also Brahman*; relative existence; two fullnesses; Upanishads

absolute state
- of *Dharma*, 64
- of intellect, 140
- of knowledge, 311–12
- of Self, 396
- *See also* established intellect

abstinence
- doer remains separate from field of activity, 186–89
- from activity of experience, 231
- misunderstanding about, 170–71
- Transcendental Meditation as practical aspect of, 493
- from war, 110
- *See also* non-action; non-attachment; restraint

accomplished *Yogī*, 389, 392, 402

action
- abstaining from, 186–89
- accomplishment of an, 153, 153*n*29, 272, 280
- aim of any, 61–62, 132, 302
- all, culminates in knowledge, 301–2
- art of, 134, 136, 226–28
- authorship of, 199–200, 220–24, 235, 269–70, 351–56, 411
- beginning of, 282
- code of, 123, 186
- devotion as most highly refined, 193, 313, 348
- divided mind and weakness of, 185
- Divine pervades all, 134–35
- for enlightenment, 377–78
- entirely dissolved, 288–89
- in every case performed by *Guṇas*, 220–21
- family *Dharmas* and complexity of, 276
- fixed in *Brahman* through, 290–92
- fundamental principle of, 69
- he who in, sees inaction, 278–81
- if I did not engage in, these worlds would perish, 217
- incentive to, 429–31
- is born of Brahmā, 205–7
- is said to be means, 389–93

Karma Kāṇda prescriptions for, 67, 123–24
knowledge as superior to, 178–80
natural, in accord with Laws of Nature, 191–92, 242, 308, 333, 345, 438
no one can exist without, 188
philosophy of, 10, 327–28
quality of, helpful for higher states of consciousness, 212
reputation based on, 111–12
for sake of *Yagya*, 288–90
science of, 245, 280
seed of, 142, 158, 286, 310, 388
for self-purification, 323, 345–56
of Self-realized man, 207–14
in sequence of subtler aspects, 213–14
skill in, 141–43, 147–48
as superior to inaction, 191, 192
surrendered to God, 225–27
that ought to be done, 384–86
transcending as, required for all paths, 389, 390–91
as unfathomable, 275–78
Vedas expound theory of, 205–6
which carries divine consciousness, 205–8
wrong, 50, 62–64, 141–43, 220, 275–77, 308–9
See also bondage of action; fruit of action; *Karma Yoga*; non-action; organs of action; right action; spontaneous right action

action, in Cosmic Consciousness
has status of *Yagya*, 198, 293
mainly from force of habit, 174
See also separation from activity; spontaneous right action

action–impression–desire cycle, 142–44, 163, 283–86
See also desire(s); impressions

action–reaction
always equal each other, 63, 85
collective *Karma*, 44
killing is sin, 55–71, 108
as men approach Me, so do I favour them, 267–68
See also action; bondage of action; *Karma Yoga*

activity
according to level of consciousness, 230, 232, 283
basis of all, 220
Creator uninvolved in His own, 269–73
devotion as most refined, 193, 313, 348
eternal freedom while engaged in, 220–24
from force of habit, 174
gauging influence on future generations, 65
God pervading whole field of, 211–12
Guṇas driving all, 188
for householder and recluse, 185–86, 345–48, 388–89
householder's, for self-purification, 345–48
integration of life through, 173, 185–86, 194
Karma Yoga as Transcendental Meditation alternated with, 319, 321
Kṛishṇa remains neutral yet engages in, 215–20
in Light of God, 288–303
mental, as means to Yoga, 389–90
mental, of discrimination, 345–48
mind uninvolved in, 137–38
moderate of effort, 416–17
My birth and My activity are divine, 265
not he who is without fire and without, 384, 387
physical, in life of householder, 322, 326, 348
silence of Being at very start of, 282–83
steady intellect maintained in, 135, 138–39, 154
Transcendental Consciousness imbues contentment into, 460
after Transcendental Meditation, 184, 312–14, 321, 326, 335–37, 347–48, 436
two paths (knowledge and action) start with, and end in silence, 388–89
See also alternation, of Transcendental Meditation and activity; separation from activity; *Yagya*; *specific state of consciousness*

activity, God's, 188, 211–12, 265–73, 288–303

remaining in My own Nature I take birth, 259–64
though I am its author, know Me to be the non-doer, 269–70
activity and silence. *See* action, in Cosmic Consciousness; separation from activity; silence
adharma, 64–68
aggression, 36–37
Ahaṁ Tattwa, 424
Ahaṁkāra, 482
air element, 101–2, 478
Ākāsha, 478–79
alien to honourable men, 78–79
allotted duty, 191, 193
alternation, of Transcendental Meditation and activity, 184, 312–14, 326, 335–37, 347–48
'abstinence' develops from, 493
by action alone Janaka and others gained perfection, 212–14
'action worthy of performance' resulting from, 210, 211
Cosmic Consciousness brought about by, 435–36
Karma Yoga as, 319, 321
senses reorientated by, 431
See also Transcendental Meditation
amnion-and-embryo analogy, 238
analysis, intellectual
inadequacy of, 63, 152
for problem-solving, 78–79, 89–90
See also established intellect; Sāṃkhya
Ānanda, 187, 441, 441*n*48
ancestors, 457
Piṇdodaka ceremonies for, 66–67
anchor-and-ship analogy, 19, 129, 369
ancients, 259, 273
chronological ordering of history, 251–54
oldest tradition as nearest to life eternal, 65
See also time
angels, 123
anger
departure of, 154–55
destroys expansion of happiness, 236–37
as enemy, 236–37
equanimity versus excitement of, 235–44, 366–70
excitement born of, 369
flares from obstruction of desire, 163, 236, 369
freed from attachment, absorbed in Me, 265–67
impels to commit sin, 236–37
in sequence of subtler aspects, 315
as sign of weakness, 45–46
steady intellect compared to, 154
by virtue of *Rajo-guṇa*, 236
See also desire(s)
animals, 270, 358–59
lower species compared to human, 268
annihilation
of all action, 308–9
of subject by object, 343
anticipation, of fruit of action, 134–35
you have control over action alone, 133
See also fruit of action
anxiety, desire as cause of, 286
Aparigraha, 484
Āpas, 101–2, 478
See also water (element)
appreciation
disciple's, 459
in higher states, 343
arguments
Arjuna's, 61, 64–65, 78–79, 90
futile, 477
Krishṇa's, 103, 107–10
as method of teaching, 419, 474–75
as technique in Sāṃkhya, 275
Arjuna
arguments of, 61, 64–65, 78–79, 90
asks about shortcuts to enlightenment, 456–57
asks for signs of steady intellect, 148–49
asks what impels us to commit sin, 235
as 'best of Kurus', 299
as 'Bhārata', 89, 105, 107, 217, 241, 261
bow of, 41, 53–54, 71–72
caught between love and duty, 52–69, 76–77, 85
concern about mind's wavering, 450–52
consciousness of, 59, 64–65, 83, 89, 180–81, 421
on family and caste *Dharmas*, 64–69

greatness of heart and mind of, 57–64, 76–77, 85
as 'Gudākesha', 45–46, 88
Kṛishṇa becomes charioteer of, 38
not confused, 76–77
as 'Pārtha', 46–48, 80, 99, 109, 150, 172, 216, 267–68, 301, 459
question about deluded on path, 457–63
as 'scorcher of enemies', 48, 80–81, 255, 257, 259, 260
silence of, 87, 89
as son of Kuntī, 452
as son of Pāṇdu, 28, 388
sorrow and compassion of, 49, 71–72, 76–78
surrenders to Kṛishṇa, 84–88
wave of love fills, 25, 47–55, 58, 76–77, 80–81
art of action, 134, 136, 226–28
'water the root' as, 277–78
Artha, Yoga as fulfilment of, 427
ascetic practices, 370
See also austerity
Ātmā, 98, 357
Brahman and, 491–92
Vaisheshik on eighth ultimate substance, 478, 479
Vedānt on relationship of *Brahman* and, 491–92
See also Being; Self; soul
Ātmānanda, 317, 428
attachment
to action, 217–18
aversion and, 230–31, 236, 362
equanimity and contentment versus, 154–55
freed from, fear and anger, 265–67
holds him imprisoned, 172
is located in object of sense, 230–31, 236, 362
love overshadowed by, 58
to objects of senses, 163
as seat of bondage, 230
'wise' not motivated by, 281
See also non-attachment
attainment, four levels of, 467–68
See also states of consciousness
attention
effortlessly goes towards bliss, 117–19
greater charm draws, 121, 169, 317, 432, 455
from gross to subtle planes during Transcendental Meditation, 129
music analogy about shift of, 118
object of, during Transcendental Meditation, 223, 436
attraction
aversion and, 230–31, 236, 362
free from, to object of senses, 159
principle of increasing charm, 121, 169, 317, 432, 455
attributeless Absolute, 102–3
austerity
no forcible control or, 430
perform *Yagya* by means of, 297
purified by, of wisdom, 265–66, 379
strenuous, 244
Tapas, 484
Yogī is superior to the austere, 466
See also control; misinterpretation/misunderstanding
authenticity
ancients in olden days, 273
from generation to generation, 255–58
Holy Tradition, 256–57, 256*n*5, 469
survival through ages shows nearest to Truth, 65
this same age-old Yoga, 258
author of creation, while remaining uninvolved, 269–73
See also Creator, the
authorship
assuming, of action, 220–24
does not belong to doer, 351–56
surrendering all actions to Me, 225, 351
thief analogy, 199–200, 235
though I am its author, know Me to be the non-doer, 269–70
of thoughts, 411
See also non-attachment; separation from activity
aversion, to objects of senses, 230–31, 236, 362
Avidyā, 492
Ayodhyā, 252
Āyurveda, 262

balance in life
balance of mind is called Yoga, 135, 138–39, 154
balanced in experiencing earth, stone, or gold, 400–401

description of life in equanimity, 150–74
in eating and sleeping, 414–15
from infusion of Being, 400–401
moderate of effort, 415–18
universe conquered by state of equanimity, 360–61
See also established intellect; steady intellect

balanced breath, 377

balanced intellect, 138–41
See also established intellect; resolute intellect; steady intellect

balancing force of Nature, 9
See also equilibrium

battlefield of life
basis of all conflicts, 23, 78
conflict between love and duty, 52–69, 76–77, 85
evil rejoices in challenging good, 23, 35–36
forces that support evil, 23, 32–34
good responds to challenge of evil, 23, 36–41
light-to-remove-darkness analogy, 126–28, 244, 355
as one's own creation, 23, 30
opposing forces as core of life itself, 48–52
principle of second element, 78–79, 126–28
righteousness rises to neutralize evil, 23, 41–42
seeker of Truth takes stand on, 23, 34–46
solution to any conflict, 78

Be without the three *Guṇas,* 126
brings fulfilment to Sāṁkhya and *Karma Yoga*, 251
'cleansed of all impurities by wisdom' realized via, 357
completeness of practical wisdom in, 126–38
to experience state of non-attachment, 330–31
frees mind from *Sankalpa*, 389
Transcendental Meditation as technique to, 374, 384, 413
as way of knowing truth at subtlest level, 223

Being
as all-pervading Intelligence, 354
Ātmā, 98
attributeless, 102–3
bliss of absolute, 166
bliss of contacting, 132, 144, 161, 166, 169–70, 333
Cosmic Law, 63–64, 133, 233–34, 333, 471–72
divine Incarnation of, 259–65
dweller in body as eternal, 97–99
as eternal peace, 368–70
field of three *Guṇas* enlivened by, 131–32
imperishable, 128, 179–80
mind transforms into state of, 144, 210, 344, 359, 370, 413, 442
omnipresent, 270, 278–79, 392–93
same from any angle of reasoning, 103–4
senses converge in silent ocean of, 412–13
shines forth in Its own light, 355
silence of, at start of activity, 282–83
state of, transcends all knowing or experiencing, 437–38
unchanging, 471
weapons cannot cleave Him, 101–2
See also Ātmā; established in Being; infusion of Being; silence

benefits. *See* holistic benefits

Bhagavad-Gītā
Brahma Vidyā expounded in, 75, 85, 177
keystone in arch of, 383
as 'milk' of Upanishads, 443
misinterpreted, 152
need for twenty-four commentaries, 20
outlives time, 20
presents understanding and direct experience, 116–17
reason for new commentary on, 19–21
records wisdom of life and technique of living, 50
Shankara's commentary on, 21, 152, 256–57, 304, 408
significance of, in span of time, 252–58
six systems of Indian philosophy applied to, 472–94
undertakes solution to suffering, 50–52

Bhakta, 86*n*4, 131
cow-and-calf (devotion and affection) analogy, 86

Bhārata
  Arjuna as, 89, 105, 107, 217, 241, 261
  Arjuna's ancestor, 93
  therefore, O, fight!, 97
Bhīma, 30, 34
Bhīshma, 33, 34–35, 46–48
binding influence. *See* bondage of action
birth and death
  born in family of *Yogīs*, 461–62
  born in house of pure and illustrious, 460–61
  certain indeed is death for born, 102
  to establish *Dharma* firmly I take birth age after age, 259–64
  experiencing Transcendental Consciousness as many births, 464
  liberated from bonds of birth, 143–44
  many births have passed for Me, 259
  My birth and My activity are divine, 265
  See also body; death; divine Incarnation
bliss
  Absolute is, 132, 144, 161, 166, 169–70, 333, 367
  awake in light of absolute, 169–70
  Brahman as all-pervading mass of, 440
  direct experience of transcendental, 116, 137
  effortlessly attention goes towards, 117–19
  eternally content in Cosmic Consciousness, 157, 161–63
  'in this Yoga' indicates path to, 121
  omnipresence of, 166, 169
  principle of increasing charm, 117–19, 121, 169, 317, 432, 455
  Sat-Chid-Ānanda, 187, 441, 441*n*48
  Transcendental Meditation practice infuses, 156, 418
  See also happiness
Bliss Consciousness, 223
  absence of, is source of sorrow, 368
  brings end to all sorrows, 164–65
  corresponds to state of restful alertness, 173
  desires are as rivers to ocean of, 170–71
  eternal freedom in, 371–72
  his self joined in Union with *Brahman*, 364–66
  increasingly positive forces bring, 27–28
  at junction of relative and Absolute, 437–38
  knowing that which is infinite joy, 414, 424–25
  Kṛishṇa symbolizes, 89
  lies immediately beyond intellect, 425
  as nectar of *Yagya*, 298–99
  as purpose of recluse and householder, 186
  Transcendental Meditation practice develops, 154–56
  See also Transcendental Consciousness; *Yogī*
boat
  -in-fast-current analogy, 66
  -of-life analogy, 164, 182
body
  cells (levels of life) analogy, 197–98
  -chariot, 36–37
  dweller in the, 92, 97–99, 100, 103, 107, 350
  even survival of your, requires action, 191–92
  gods as analogous to, 197–98
  as instrument tuned to divine, 407
  before liberation from, 368, 370
  like worn-out garment, 100–101
  limbs and, analogy, 68
  performing action by, alone, he incurs no sin, 286–87
  purity not lost at death of, 462–63
  wise not taken aback by changes of, 92–93
  See also birth and death; divine Incarnation; nervous system
body-and-limbs analogy, 68
bondage of action
  cycle of impression–desire–action, 142–44, 163, 283–86
  God Consciousness as end to, 247
  he is firmly bound, 348–49
  he who truly knows Me is not bound by actions, 271–72
  him actions do not bind, 319–21
  ignorance as cause of, 274
  liberated from bonds of birth, 143–44
  technique to cast away, 115–17, 140, 189, 194, 203
  See also Cosmic Consciousness; separation from activity

bow and arrow
analogy, 139, 140, 141–42, 300
Arjuna's, 41, 53–54, 71–72
Brahmā, the Creator
know action to be born of, 205–7
life-span of, 253
remaining uninvolved, 269–73
Veda as first manifestation of, 205–6
Brahma Sūtra, 256
Brahma Vidyā, 75, 85, 177
Brahman
all aspects of *Yagya* are, 290–91
as all-inclusive, 172–74, 337, 344
as all-pervading mass of bliss, 440
Ātmā and, 491–92
attained at last moment, 172–74
attained in this life, 360
cannot be expressed in words, 440
contact with, is infinite joy, 439–41
with ease attains contact with, 439–40
as equally present everywhere, 358–61
evenness of vision is, 441–50
fixed in, through action, 291–92
his self joined in Union with, 364–66
as inclusive of all that lies between two extremes of life, 172–74
Līlā-shakti as play-power of, 261
no outer signs of, 153, 174
offering *Yagya* itself into fire that is, 292–93
one sees him as a wonder, 106–7, 441
one who has reached It is life eternal, 449
as relative and Absolute; this and That, 337, 344, 440–42
remaining on human level he is divine, 361–63
sage intent on Yoga comes to, without delay, 336–38
Upanishads for education about, 440–41
Upanishads show way of contacting, 195
See also integrated life; Kṛishṇa; Unity
Brāhmaṇa, 32, 132–33, 358–60
Brahmānanda, 317, 428
Brahmananda Saraswati, Shankaracharya of Jyotir Math, 16–17
Brāhmaṇas, 490–91
Brahma-nirvāṇa, 372
Brāhmī-sthiti, 172, 365, 367, 492
branches-and-trunk analogy, 256
breathing
comes automatically to rest, 485
goal of, exercises, 297–98, 407
life-breaths join as speech, 479
Bṛihad-Āraṇyak Upanishad, 140
bubble analogy, 470
Buddha
revived knowledge of integration of life, 10
teachings distorted by followers, 10–11
Buddhi Yoga, 138–39
See also resolute intellect
businessman (above loss and gain) analogy, 117, 137, 142

calmness, is said to be means, 389–93, 397, 466
caste *Dharmas*
Arjuna's concern for, 64–69
lost his caste, 358, 360
as open door to heaven, 109, 113
See also Dharma
cause and effect
influence cause to modify effect, 126–27, 243, 430
Laws of Nature governing all, 123
See also action–reaction; *karma*; time, space, and causation
cave analogy, 433
cells-of-body (levels of life) analogy, 197–98
ceremonies
Karma Kāṇda's practical rites and, 67, 123–24
Piṇdodaka, 66–67
'twice-born' indicates, of purification, 32
Yagya of knowledge better than, 301–3
See also Yagya
certain indeed is death for born, 102
Charak, 262
chariot
metaphysical connotation of, 36–37
Vyāsa's description of, 46
charity, 466
charm, principle of increasing, 121, 169, 317, 432, 455
chastity/celibacy, 410*n*17, 484
life-stream rises during Transcendental Meditation, 409, 410
Chaturyugī, 254

Chit, 187, 441, 441*n*48
Chitta, 422
city of nine gates, 350
civilization
  historical accounts of highest, 254
  at time of Bhagavad-Gītā, 45
cloth
  dyeing analogy, 312–13, 462
  washing analogy, 459
cloud analogy (perish like broken cloud), 457–58
coarseness, due to sin, 207, 309
coconut analogy, 351
code of action, 123, 186
code of thinking, for recluse, 186
cold and heat, 93
  See also pairs of opposites
collecting himself, 412–13, 439
  See also Transcendental Meditation
come out to fight, 113–14
comfort, for Transcendental Meditation practice, 405–6
community
  calamities, crises, and catastrophes in, 27–28
  collective *Karma*, 44
  See also family *Dharmas*
compassion
  Arjuna's grief and, 49, 71–72, 76–78
  distressed by misfortunes of others, 72
  doing good to all creatures, 373
  looking to welfare of world, 212–14, 217–18
complete knowledge
  requires experience and understanding, 271
  state of knowingness is Transcendental Consciousness, 311–12
  Yoga alone is not enough without Sāṃkhya, 103–4
concentration, 471
conch blowing
  impact of, 40–41
  significance of, 37–39
condemnation, forgetting involves, 405
conflicts, basis of all, 23, 78
consciousness
  activity according to level of, 230, 232, 283
  Bhagavad-Gītā and reader's level of, 383, 421
  Chit, 187, 441, 441*n*48
  conscious mind becomes, 422
  God's, as sole guiding factor, 268
  influence of one state while living another, 363
  innumerable levels between ignorance and enlightened, 458
  intensity of happiness and level of, 367
  Kauravas', 39
  nervous system and, 173, 226, 298, 313–15
  personal *Dharma* and level of, 288
  quality of experience based on state of, 442
  resolute, 127
  'senseless' and devoid of, 228
  this system of Yoga awakens, 256
  thought starts from deepest level of, 282
  three relative states of, 187, 314
  vibrates and becomes mind, 236
  worlds of righteous and levels of, 460–61
  See also pure consciousness; states of consciousness; *specific state*
contemplation, 184–85, 322, 471
contentment
  eternal fullness, 157, 161–63, 179, 262–63, 272
  Santosha, 484
  in Self, 423–24
  in senses, 207–8
  as status of established intellect, 361
control
  mind subdued by experience of happiness, 402–4
  of mind without using restraint, 451–55
  negation of sense-control principle, 189, 229, 241
  no austerity or forcible, 430
  organs of action subdued, 190
  self-, at level of cosmic life in God Consciousness, 296
  self-, kindled by enlightenment, 295–96
  senses subdued, 160–63, 189–90, 242–45, 316–22, 429–30
  some offer sound and other objects of senses in fires of, 293–94
  you have, over action alone, 133
  See also restraint
cooking
  purpose of, 203
  Sanyāsī does not engage in, 387

See also food
Cosmic Consciousness
activity and silence in, 314
all actions appreciated as *Brahman*, 291
by alternation of inward and outward, 435–36
anatomical separation of function, 314
anchored to eternal silence, 369
destination of those not able to attain, 460–61
duality of Self and activity in, 211, 250, 306, 314, 347
essence of path from, to God Consciousness, 443–50
'established in Yoga' means established in, 135–36
eternally contented in bliss, 157, 161–63
gives disciplined pattern to life, 454–55
inner freedom along with outer activity, 274–88
joys of senses leave no lasting impression, 341, 365
as liberation from bondage, 144
life in, 162–63
without long delay, 336–37, 465
as *Nītya-samādhi*, 150–51, 402, 486
only one step on path to, 145
perceptions do not register deep impressions, 190, 340–41, 365
as remains of *Yagya*, 200–203, 299
silence of, 392–93
as stage of purification of Self, 347–48
Transcendental Consciousness into, 429–43
See also alternation, of Transcendental Meditation and activity; bondage of action; infusion, of Being; separation from activity
Cosmic Law, 63–64, 333
attunement with, 133, 233–34
as basic law of creation, 471–72
See also Absolute; Laws of Nature; support of Nature
cosmic/divine plan
instruments of, 36, 172, 209, 218, 393
See also divine Incarnation; revival of knowledge
cow
in a, enlightened perceive the same, 358–60
-and-calf (devotion and affection) analogy, 86
craving. *See* desire(s)
creation
battlefield of life as one's own, 23
constant awareness of source of, 271–72
expansion of happiness as purpose of, 352, 379–80
fourfold order created by Me, 269–70
happiness varies in different states of, 167
of human beings along with *Yagya*, 196
sequentially subtler aspects of, 204, 242–43, 315, 372
silence of Being at start of activity, 282–83
Taittirīya Upanishad on higher planes of, 461
Veda as first manifestation of, 206
See also manifestation, process of
Creator, the, 196, 225, 247, 253, 355
know action to be born of, 205–7
remaining uninvolved, 269–73
cycle of action–impression–desire, 142–44, 163, 283–86
cycle of action–*Yagya*–rain–food–creatures, 204–5

dark-cave analogy, 433
darkness-of-ignorance analogy, 119–20
See also second element, principle of
death
better is, in one's own *Dharma*, 231–34
better is, than to commit sin, 70–71
beyond influence of, 94–95
certain indeed is, 104
die for others, 57, 111
does he not perish like a broken cloud?, 457–58
for one in *Brahman*, 291–92
Piṇḍodaka ceremonies for departed, 66–67
purity not lost at, of body, 462–63
for those of doubting nature, 318–19
of those through whom vice enters world, 42
wise grieve neither for dead nor living, 90–91
See also birth and death; relative existence
debase his Self, 395–96

delight in doing good to all creatures, 373–74
delusion, 146–48
  desire overshadows Self, 240–41
  destruction of intellect due to, 163–64
  fever of, 225
  finding fault and speaking ill as signs of, 227–29
  of one fallen from regular Transcendental Meditation practice, 457–58
desire(s)
  anger due to thwarted, 163, 236, 369
  as communication between heart and mind, 51–52
  cycle of action–impression–, 142–44, 163, 283–86
  disciplined men freed from, 374–75
  every undertaking free from, 281–84
  formation of, 283–84
  he whom all, enter as waters enter unmoved sea, 170–71
  impels to commit sin, 235–37
  insatiable flame of, 238–40
  is vibrating consciousness channeled in particular direction, 236
  Kāma, 427–28
  machinery which gives rise to, 240–41
  misunderstanding about, 244, 370
  relinquished all, 171–72
  rising above binding influence of, 239–42
  seeds of, 310, 341, 388, 394, 422
  slay enemy in form of, 243–45
  subdue, 243–45
  transcending, to bring its fulfilment, 245
  from which incentive to action is born, 429–31
  See also control; *Yagya*
destruction
  collective *Karma* threatening, of nation, 44
  equilibrium of creative and destructive forces, 27, 264
  of family and social order, 66
  indestructibility of inner Reality, 95–99
  of intellect due to delusion, 163–64
  love without righteousness becomes means of, 54
  war as Nature's breaking point, 35–36
  women impacted by war, 82
  See also killing; war
detachment
  distorted understanding of, 15
  overshadows love, 58
  practice of, unnecessary, 244
  rising above, 157
  sense of, not conducive to enlightenment, 396
  two understandings of, 322
devotee
  Bhakta, 86, 86*n*4, 131
  entitled to receive supreme secret, 258
  he who worships Me with faith, 467–68
  must first be purely himself, 131
  sees all beings in Self and also in God, 305–7, 441–47
  that *Yogī* lives in Me, 445–47
  two states of Union with God, 449–50
  Union with Lord, 447–48, 467–68
  wants abstract bliss to be materialized, 264
  for whose sake God takes form, 264
  Yoga of action declared to My, 258
  you are My, and friend, 258
  See also God Consciousness; Light of God; *Yogī*
devotion
  brings Being to sensory level, 447–50, 467–68
  cow-and-calf analogy, 86
  Hanumān symbolizing, 41–42
  Īshwara-praṇidhān, 484
  from level of pure consciousness, 161–63
  misunderstanding about, 13–14
  as most refined activity, 193, 313, 348
  on path from Cosmic to God Consciousness, 314–15
  in sequence of subtler aspects, 315
  as stage of self-purification, 348
  transcendental basis of, 12–14
  universal love and, 11–14
  See also faith; God Consciousness
devotional sects, 13–14
Dhananjaya, 37–8
Dhāraṇā, 485
Dharma
  absence of, 64–68
  all moral codes based on, 110
  of another brings danger, 231–35
  ascending current of, 179
  from attunement with Cosmic Law,

133, 233–34
better is death in one's own, 231–34
caste, 64–68, 109, 113, 358–60
casting away reputation and, 78–79, 109–12
deviation from, 66
different powers upholding different *Dharmas*, 64–68
each successive stage is of vital importance, 231–32
to establish, I take birth age after age, 259–64
even a little of this, delivers from great fear, 117–18, 456
family, 64–69, 276
God's re-establishment of, 262–64
invincible power of, as basis of cosmic life, 26–28
Karma Mīmāṁsā for action in accord with, 491
'killing is sin' versus *Kshatriya's*, 55–71, 108
Laws of Nature and, 417
level of consciousness and personal, 288
maintains equilibrium, 26–28
natural action in accord with, 191–92
one's own, though lesser in merit is better, 231–34
overshadowed on earth, 262–63
positive and negative forces on field of, 26–28
practice of this Yoga as, of everyone, 118
of Self, 233–34
understood through Sāṃkhya, 108–10
Yoga as fulfilment of, 427
See also evolution
Dharmakshetra, 28
Dharmarāj, 28
dhṛi, 262
Dhṛishtadyumna, 30
Dhṛitarāshtra, 26, 28–29, 33, 474
addressed as Lord of earth, 40, 42, 44
sons not educated in transcending, 44–45
sons of, 28, 41, 60–61, 70
Dhyān, 485, 486
See also Samādhi
Dhyān Yoga, 468
Dhyānbindu Upanishad, 298–99, 299*n*45
Dik, 478, 479
disciplined men freed from desire and anger, 374–75
disciplined mind, 412–14, 439, 454–55
discrimination
as activity of recluse life, 348
anger causing loss of, 164
Gyān Yoga and, 183–86
necessary for full enlightenment, 303–4
between Reality and non-Reality, 60, 152
senses rob a man of, 167–68
service requires, 304
as *Viveka*, 152*n*27, 492
when established in Self, 165
See also established intellect; resolute intellect; steady intellect
distraction, fruit of action as, 134
during Transcendental Meditation, 436
disunion of union with sorrow, 426–27
See also sorrow; Yoga
divided mind, weakness of action due to, 185
Divine, the
body as instrument tuned to, 407
instrument of, 36, 172, 209, 218, 393
My birth and My activity are divine, 265
pervades all action, 134–35
problems do not exist for, 73
simplicity of approach to, 120
sin destroyed by knowledge of, 308–10
See also God; Light of God
divine Incarnation, 25
many births have passed for Me, 259
My birth and My activity are divine, 265
reason for, 264
remaining in My own nature I take birth, 259–64
See also equilibrium; God; Kṛishṇa; revival of knowledge
Divine Mother, 253
diving analogy, 119, 136, 145
doctrine of liberation, 249
dog
in a, enlightened perceive the same, 358–60
discipline analogy, 454–55
doubts
born of ignorance and rooted in heart, 321–22

dispelled, 373–80
about falling from Transcendental Meditation practice, 458–59
freedom from, 316–22
rent asunder by knowledge, 319–21
Self-realized man is above, 146–48
Draupadī, 31, 40
dreaming state of consciousness, 340
never out of Self even in, 338, 371
outward and inward activity continues in, 188
dṛishtwā, 483
Droṇāchārya, 29–30, 81–82
Drupada, 30
duality
Being and activity as, 250
fear is born of, 50, 409
freed from, ever firm in purity, 126–38
as fundamental cause of suffering, 51–52
of life, 291, 305
Reality is devoid of, 101, 288, 305
of Self and activity, 211
subsumed into Unity, 314
See also Cosmic Consciousness
Duryodhana, 28–30, 32–35, 44, 56
in analysis of six systems of Indian philosophy, 473–93
chooses Kṛishṇa's army, 38
desires material possessions, 130
dice match with, 31
dust-and-mirror analogy, 238
duty
allotted, 191, 193
caught between love and, 52–69, 76–77, 85
See also Dharma
Dwāpara-yuga, 254
dweller in body, 92, 103
as distinct from body, 97–99
as *Jīva*, 100
permanent nature of, 107
rests in happiness, 350
dyeing-cloth analogy, 312–13, 462

earth (element)
balanced in experiencing, stone, or gold, 400–401
essence of smell expresses as, 483
as one of five *Tanmātras*, 483
as Pṛithivī, 101–2, 478
earth (planet)
conches reverberate through, 41
desire and anger as enemies here on, 236–37
Dhṛitarāshtra addressed as Lord of, 40, 42, 44
eternal liberation gained only on, 358, 461
as gateway to other planes, 460–61
God's Kingdom on, 32, 70, 380, 444
offerings to gods for success on, 268
as one of three worlds, 59
power of *Dharma* overshadowed on, 262–63
victorious you will enjoy, 113
easiness
actions are easy and quiet, 413
of being what you are, 244
effortlessly attention goes towards bliss, 117–19
of flow of wisdom from teacher to student, 86
no obstacle in Transcendental Meditation process, 117–20
of performing right action, 294–96
principle of increasing charm, 121, 169, 317, 432, 455
slow and difficult versus easy path to reach the Supreme, 294
of transcending, 432–34
eating
food first offered to God, 203
moderation in, 414–15
remains of *Yagya*, 200–203, 299
See also food
education, leaders organize, to cultivate consciousness, 45
See also teaching
effort
concentration and strain, 377
endowed with faith yet lacking, 456–59, 465
moderate of, 415–18
no, is lost, 117–19
retards transcending, 432–34
skill in action as least, 141–43
success by, 268
See also misinterpretation/misunderstanding
effortlessness
of attaining freedom, 210
attention goes towards bliss, 117–19

greater charm draws attention, 121, 169, 317, 432, 455
music analogy about shift of attention, 118
no obstacle exists, 117–20
of wisdom's flow from teacher to student, 86
ego, 98, 172, 219, 221, 223, 339
as early manifestation, 206
expanded to cosmic status, 343
in sequence of subtler aspects, 204, 242–43, 315, 372
eightfold *Prakṛiti*, 221
elephant, 358–60
embryo analogy, 238
emotion
Brahman is beyond appreciation by, 441
enrichment of feelings, 448
has to cease to be in unbounded love of God, 444
no room for negative, 155
on path from Cosmic to God Consciousness, 314–15
universal love and devotion, 11–12, 157
while making offerings, 293
See also heart; *specific emotion*
endurance
mind of steady, 450–51, 453
'take all things as they come' as essence of, 493–94
enemy
ceases-to-be-, analogy, 341
desire and anger as, 236–37
desire as, 238–45
even intellect among friends and foes, 401
he alone is his own friend/his own, 395–99
righteousness neutralizes excess evil, 41–42
energy
arrow analogy, 136, 299
balanced intellect and absolute life-, 140–41
directed upward, 409, 410, 410*n*17, 484*n*6
food as source of, 415
of gods, 197–98
Hṛishīkesha's, 37, 45–46, 88, 89
life-, 140–41, 265, 300, 361
limitless source of, 126, 266, 270, 300
mass of, does not exhibit quality of, 440
modern physics on, 105
no effort is lost, 117–20
Rajo-guṇa responsible for motion and, 236
at source of creation, 206, 374
enlightened *Brāhmaṇa*, 132–33
enlightenment
cannot be gained through restraint, 230
enjoyed during life on earth, 174, 244–45, 443–61
enlightened *Brāhmaṇa*, 132–33
gaining, from the enlightened, 303–5
God Consciousness as supreme state of, 296
innumerable levels between ignorance and, 458
intellectual preparation for, 103
as liberation from bonds of birth, 143–44
misunderstanding about desires and, 244, 370
Moksha, 368, 370, 377–78, 427–28
self-control kindled by, 295–96
Transcendental Meditation fulfils conditions necessary for, 317
wholly purified in state of profound equanimity, 356–66
wisdom like sun illumines That, 355–56
Yagya as path to, 302
See also Light of God; *Yogī*; *specific state of consciousness*
envy, 287–88
equanimity
cannot be faked, 156
description of life in, 150–74
gained by path of knowledge or action, 183–86
in pleasure and pain, 113–15
in success and failure, 135–36, 139, 249, 287–89, 320–21
universe conquered by state of, 360–61
wholly purified in state of profound, 356–66
See also Samādhi
equilibrium
between creative and destructive forces, 27, 264
family *Dharmas* and, of Nature, 64–69, 276
Nature's breaking point, 35–36

restored by God, 264
righteousness rises to neutralize excess evil, 41–42
Samādhāna, 494
of three *Guṇas*, 269–70
See also divine Incarnation
essence
of Bhagavad-Gītā, 117
of Bhagavad-Gītā missed, 20
indestructibility of human essence, 95–100
of *Karma Yoga*, 243
My birth and My activity are divine: He who knows this in, 265
of path from Cosmic to God Consciousness, 443–50
of Sāṃkhya, 91–95
Shankara revives, of Vedic Literature, 256
'take all things as they come' as, of endurance, 493–94
Tanmātras as, of objects of perception, 424–25, 482–83
of Yoga, 126–38
established in Being
action when, is called *Karma Yoga*, 144
Buddha's message of action while, 10
doubts disappear when, 374
impressions no longer create seed of desires, 341
intellect becomes, 166
renunciation is hard to attain unless, 337
Shankara's message of action while, 11
wise are, 218, 224
wise are not bound by fruit of action, 144
See also Karma Yoga
established in Yoga perform actions, 135–36, 177–78, 182, 210, 249
established intellect
awake in light of absolute bliss, 169–70
based in natural state of non-attachment, 158–59
behaves as master of senses, 160
belongs to field of pure consciousness, 361
free from sense of 'I' and 'mine', 171–72
he who is not established has no intellect, 165–66
misunderstanding about, 156–57
only then mind ceases to wander, 160
as self-illuminant effulgence: Veda, 206
See also resolute intellect; steady intellect
eternal freedom. *See* freedom, eternal
eternal fullness, 157, 161–63, 179, 262–63, 272
See also Life Eternal
even a little of this *Dharma* delivers from great fear, 117–18, 456
even if you were most sinful of all sinners, 308–9
even intellect, 401
See also steady intellect
evening meditation, purity restored by, 312–13, 357
evenness of vision, 441–50
evil
atmosphere, 64
forces that support, 23, 32–34
good responds to challenge of, 23, 36–41
raft of knowledge crossing over all, 308
rejoices in challenging good, 23, 35–36
righteousness rises to neutralize, 23, 41–42
seeker of Truth takes stand between good and, 23, 34–46
those through whom vice enters world, 42
See also good and evil; sin
evolution
'age-old' represents genuine path of, 65
Arjuna's concern to preserve, 64–68
cow-and-calf (devotion and affection) analogy, 86
through creative and destructive forces, 27, 264
each successive stage is of vital importance, 231–32
gods working for purpose of, 197–98
ill fame impairs one's, 111
right action only possible with knowledge of divine nature, 274–88
of those fallen from Transcendental Meditation practice, 461–63

wheel of, 27
See also Dharma; states of consciousness
excitement, from desire and anger, 235–44, 366–70
expectations
desire as cause of, 286
having no, during Transcendental Meditation, 402–5
you have control over action alone, 133
eyebrows, within, 376–77

failure
equanimity in success and, 135–36, 139, 249, 287–89, 320–21
lack of knowledge as root of all, 318
unseen working of Nature behind, 63–64
faith
endowed with, yet lacking in effort, 456–59, 465
he who worships Me with, 467–68
light of knowledge kindled in man of, 316–22
for readiness to receive wisdom, 86
those possessed of, 227–29
three fields of, 316
See also devotion
fame
this blemish alien to honourable men, 78–79
vibrations of one's reputation, 109–12
whatsoever a great man does, 214–15
family *Dharmas*
complexity of action and, 276
equilibrium of Nature influencing, 64–69, 276
work in family profession, 69
family of *Yogīs*, 461–63
fault-finding, 227–29
fear, 154–55, 265–66
certainly, is born of duality, 50, 409
departure of, 154–55
due to improper understanding, 320
even a little of this *Dharma* delivers from great, 117–18, 456
freed from, 409–10
freed from attachment, and anger, absorbed in Me, 265–67
in sequence of subtler aspects, 315
of spiritual life, 156
steady intellect versus, 154
fight. *See* battlefield of life; war
finest aspect, of relative existence, 164, 169, 219, 222, 315, 389–91, 423
finest intellect, 151
See also intellect
finest relative, 164, 169, 219, 222, 315, 389–91, 423
fire
as, is covered by smoke, 238
as blazing, turns fuel to ashes, 309
of knowledge, 281, 285, 289, 308–11, 320
not he who is without, and without activity, 384, 387
offering *Yagya* itself into, that is *Brahman*, 292–93
as *Tejas*, 101–2, 478
five elements, 424–25, 482–83
five senses, 190, 190*n*12, 340–41, 482
origin of, 482–83
See also senses
fondness, 'has no undue fondness', 149
See also attachment; friend(s); heart; love
food
cooked to offer to God, 203
in dog-disciplining analogy, 454–55
eating remains of *Yagya*, 200–203, 299
mind influenced by quality of, 203
in moderation, 414–16
restricting, 298
Sanyāsī not expected to cook, 387
Self-realization influencing rhythms of Nature, 204–5
forces of Nature
absolute Being present between opposing, 43
constructive and destructive, 27, 237
coordination with, 123
equilibrium of *Guṇas*, 262, 269–70
higher, 200, 205
opposing, 23, 26–28, 38
power of love and, 54
war and, 108
See also nature
forgetting
trying to forget amounts to remembering, 231, 405
willing acceptance rather than, 405
See also loss of knowledge
fourfold order, 269–70

free will, 27, 268
inevitability of change influencing, 104–5
master of own destiny, 63–64
freedom, eternal
attained even at last moment, 172–74
beyond influence of relative existence, 94–95
Brahma-nirvāṇa, 372
Cosmic Consciousness as state of, 145
from craving for any pleasure, 418–20
disciplined men freed from desire and anger, 374–75
in divine consciousness, 371–72
from doubts, 316–22
effortlessness of attaining, 210
he is indeed forever free, 316–22, 377–78
he who is freed from attachment, 288–89
he who truly knows Me (completely), 271–72
as life's goal, 357–58
naturalness of living, 170–72
with outer activity, 274–88
prerequisites for, 371–75
in state of profound equanimity, 356–66
supreme liberation that abides in Me, 412, 413–14
Transcendental Meditation creates, from relative influences, 198
while engaged in activity, 220–24
See also bondage of action; Cosmic Consciousness; liberation; separation from activity; *Yogī*
friend(s)
bring life-supporting happiness, 379
evenness of intellect among, and foes, 401
God as friend of all beings, 379–80
he alone indeed is his own, 395–99
Kṛishṇa and Arjuna, 31
viewed on battlefield, 48, 62
you are My devotee and, 258
fruit of action
attached to, he is firmly bound, 348–49
carries out links between doer, action, and, 351–53
having abandoned, attains to lasting peace, 348–49
infusion of Being and non-attachment to, 283
non-anticipation of, 133–35
pitiful are those who live for, 138–41
Sanyāsa and *Karma Yoga* as non-attachment to, 384–87
you have control over action alone, 133
See also bondage of action; established in Being

Gāṇḍīva slips from my hand, 53–54
garment, worn-out, analogy, 100–101
Gautama, 473, 477
Gītā-Bhāshya (Shankara), 21, 257
glasses, coloured, analogy, 306, 316, 367, 446
goal
of all action, 302
of breathing exercises, 297–98, 407
eternal freedom as life's, 357–58
heaven as, 124
Samādhi as, of all paths/all Vedic Texts, 147
same, for recluse or path of action, 373–80
transcending as, of *Yagya*, 300–303
Yoga as, 453
God
Absolute and, 446–47
actions do not involve Me, 271–72
activity of, 188, 259–73, 288–303
all beings seen in, 305–7, 441–47
in all ways, O Pārtha, men follow My path, 267–68
of all Yogīs I hold him most fully united, 467–68
as author of creation while remaining uninvolved, 269–73
creation comes out of, 196
as Creator, 196, 205–7, 253
even so I am engaged in action, 215–16
as expounded by Me of old, 183–84
faith in self, teacher, and, 316–18
freed from attachment, fear, and anger, absorbed in Me, 265–66
as friend of all beings, 379–80
government of, 262–64
he who truly knows Me (completely), 271–72
he who worships Me abiding in all beings, 445–47
I am not lost to him nor is he lost to Me, 443–45

Kingdom on earth, 32, 70, 380, 444
know Me to be the non-doer, 269–70
let him sit united looking to Me as Supreme, 161–63
many births have passed for Me, 259–60
as men approach Me so do I favour them, 267–68
My birth and My activity are divine, 265
offering food to, 203
omnipresent, omnipotent, omniscient silence of, 392–93
pervading whole field of activity, 211–12
realizing Me as the Transcendent, 409–12
remaining in My own nature I take birth, 259–64
supreme liberation that abides in Me, 412–14
surrendering all actions to Me, 225–27
this teaching of Mine, 227–28
thought given over to Me, 409–12
Transcendental Consciousness as link to, 196
two states of Union with, 449–50
whole field of action pervaded by, 211–12
Will of, 108, 411
See also Divine, the; divine Incarnation; Light of God

God and humanity
action–reaction between, 247, 267–68
in all ways men follow My path, 267–68
difference in scale between, 391–92
direct relationship of, 443
established intellect as instrument for divine plan, 209
ever-full-lake analogy, 267
having known Me as friend of all beings, 379
individual actions surrendered, 225–27
inmost Self of *Yogī* absorbed in Divine, 467–68
Kingdom of God on earth, 32, 70, 380, 444
many births have passed for Me, 259–65
as men approach Me, I favour them, 267–68
re-establishment of *Dharma*, 262–64
revival of knowledge, 247, 262–65
right action through knowledge of divine, 274–88
secret of saints' communion, 444
See also devotion; faith

God Consciousness
all activity in Light of God, 288–303
calmness transforms, into Unity, 389–91, 397, 466
constant awareness of source of creation, 271–72
devotion dissolves into Union with God, 447–50, 467–68
duality subsumed into Unity, 314
essence of path from Cosmic Consciousness to, 443–50
holds together Self and field of activity, 349
mind of steady endurance in, 450–51, 453
puts end to all bondage of action, 247
quality of silence in, 391–93
as remains of *Yagya*, 200–203, 299
seeing all beings in oneself and oneself in God, 305–7, 441–47
self-control rises to level of cosmic life, 296
as stage of purification of Self, 347–48
state of non-action rises to state of God's action, 188
in time finds this within himself, 311–12, 465
Transcendental Meditation and attainment of, 443–45, 465
two states of Union with God, 449–50
wants abstract bliss to be materialized, 264
whole of life immersed in glory of, 399
worships Me abiding in all beings, 445–47
See also Unity

gods, 194–95
acting for purpose of evolution, 197–98
body as analogous to, 197–98
energy and intelligence of, 197–98
offerings to, for success on earth, 268
as powers of Nature, 200
Yagya and, 197–200
See also Laws of Nature; *Yagya*

good and evil
casting off of, 141–43, 154–56, 354
seeker of Truth takes stand between, 23, 34–46
good to all creatures, 373–74
government
Bhagavad-Gītā's message heeded by, 45
God's, 262–64
philosopher-kings, 255
Govinda, Kṛishṇa as, 56–57, 88
grace, 164–65
See also God
greed
blinding from right and wrong, 62–64
for pleasures of a kingdom, 70
green-spectacles analogy, 306, 316, 367, 446
grief. *See* sorrow
Gudākesha, 45–46, 88
Guṇa(s)
as agents of Lord, 225–26
all actions performed by, 220–21
born of/constitute *Prakṛiti*, 128, 188, 206, 220–21, 424, 481
defined, 126–29
deluded by, 224–25
Dharma of three, brings danger, 233–35
equilibrium of, 262, 269–70
everyone helplessly driven to activity by, 188
field of three, enlivened by Being, 131–32
fourfold order created by Me, 269–70
Guṇas act upon *Guṇas*, 221
one *Guṇa* cannot exist without other two, 128
truth about, at subtlest level of creation, 222–23
untouched by influence of, 358–61
See also Be without the three *Guṇas*; Nature
Gyān, 12
See also separation from activity
Gyān Kāṇda, 123–24, 132, 195
Gyān Yoga, 131–32, 244, 467
equanimity gained via, 183–86
Karma Yoga differs only in type of activity, 184
as Transcendental Consciousness and discrimination, 183–86
Gyānendriya, 190, 482
Gyānī, 86, 86*n*5, 131, 467

Hanumān, 41–42
happiness
as aim of every action, 61–62, 132
all sorrow due to lack of, 154–56
eternal, 157, 161–63, 179, 262–63, 272, 364–66
expansion of, as purpose of life, 352, 379–80
friends bring life-supporting, 379
he is a happy man, 368–70
he rests in, 350
killing versus potential, 60–62
mind subdued by experience of, 402–4
mind's wavering versus experience of, 452–55
natural tendency towards, 229, 404–5, 411
principle of increasing charm, 121, 169, 317, 432, 455
in sequence of subtler aspects, 315
steady thought and, 165–67
supreme, for *Yogī* deep in peace, 437–38
Taittirīya Upanishad on degrees of, 461
Transcendental Consciousness is limitless, 126
See also Bliss Consciousness
Hastināpur, 26, 28
Hatha Yoga, 390, 467
having directed his gaze, 408
hearing
even on seeing, speaking, and, some do not understand, 106–7
flowery words, 125
functioning in organized/controlled manner, 190
some offer sound, 293–94
about Truth gains fulfilment in direct experience, 146
tumultuous sound of Duryodhana's army, 35
worthy of, contemplating and realizing, 9
heart
anger's influence, 163–64
communication between mind and, 25, 51
conflict between love and duty, 52–69, 76–77, 85

doubts born of ignorance and rooted in, 321–22
future's image on sanctuary of pure, 55
as machinery which gives rise to desires, 240–41
Shankara exemplifies full development of, 12–14
they alone have fullness of, 157
undismayed, 426–28
See also emotion; *specific emotion*
heaven
Arjuna's knowledge of, 456–57
caste *Dharma* as open door to, 109, 113
Kingdom of God, 32, 70, 380, 444
Nirvāṇa, 10–11
as purpose of *Yagyas'* ritualistic aspect, 197–98
slain you will reach, 113–14
whence this blemish . . . opposed to, 78–79
in which beings no longer practise Yoga, 461
with, as their goal, 124
worlds of righteous, 460–61
hell
doomed and senseless due to ignorance, 228
intermixture of castes as path to, 65–66, 68–69
knowledgeable statements about, 456–57
highest good, 198
his action is entirely dissolved, 288–89
history, purpose of studying, 252–54
holistic benefits
cross over all evil by raft of knowledge, 308
of divine Incarnation on earth, 25, 259–65
ease in performing right action, 294–96
family *Dharmas* keep stream of life in harmony, 64
grace and, 164
harmony in nature from Self-realization, 204–5
mental and physical are cultured, 369, 430–31
stream of life flows in ascending current of *Dharma*, 179
stream of life in accord with Laws of Nature, 192, 416
Transcendental Meditation cultures mental and physical, 369, 430–31
Transcendental Meditation's life-supporting influences, 201, 214
'water the root' for, 19, 78, 87, 245, 277–78
whole life-stream rises towards supreme consciousness, 409, 410
Yogī does good to all creatures, 373–80
See also support of Nature; Transcendental Meditation
Holy Tradition, 256–57, 256*n*5, 469
homage, repeated inquiry, and service, 303–5
honey (concentrated sweetness) analogy, 285
householder
daily activities for self-purification, 345–48
gains of spiritual life available to, 152–53
Karma Yoga of, 149
physical activity of, 322, 326, 348
purpose is same as recluse, 186, 245, 249, 335
renunciation is same as recluse, 326–29
steady intellect attained by, 151–52
as valid way of life for spiritual growth, 157, 184–85
in whatever way he lives that *Yogī* lives in Me, 445–47
See also Karma Yoga
Hṛishīkesha, Kṛishṇa as, 37, 45–46, 88, 89
humility, 358–59
hypocrisy, 94, 139
of he who sits restraining organs of action, 189
See also misinterpretation/misunderstanding; mood-making

ignorance
about authorship of action, 199–202, 220–24, 235, 269–70, 351–56, 411
Avidyā, 492
as cause of grief/sorrow, 79, 154–55
causes bondage of action, 274
doomed and senseless due to, 228
doubts born of, and rooted in heart, 321–22
God Consciousness puts end to all, 247
has no material substance, 81

of Self as basis of all problems, 78–79
that which is night for all beings, 169–70
Unity shattered on rocks of, 13
veils wisdom, 354–55
ignorant
innumerable levels between enlightened and, 458
Self-realized help raise consciousness of, 225–34
speak of two paths as different, 334–35
wise do not confuse/disturb, 218–19, 244
Ikshwāku, 252
ill fame. *See* reputation
immortality, fitness for, 94
See also freedom, eternal
Imperishable, the, 205–7
imperishable phase of life
dweller in body as, 97–99
perishable and, 115, 128, 179–80
weapons cannot cleave, 101–2
See also Absolute
imperishable Yoga, 251–55
impressions
Chitta and past, 422
cycle of action–impression–desire, 142–44, 163, 283–86
like roasted seeds in fire of knowledge, 310–11
that do not form future desires, 190, 340–41
See also desire(s)
inaction
action is indeed superior to, 191, 192
he who in action sees, 278–81
sleep as state of, 277, 406
what is action, what inaction?, 274–75
See also non-action
incarnation. *See* divine Incarnation
increasing charm, principle of, 121, 169, 317, 432, 455
independent of possessions, 126, 129–30
indestructibility, of human essence, 95–100
Indian culture
Āyurveda on equilibrium of *Guṇas*, 262
concept of history, 252–54
receptivity to Truth, 17
Shankara misinterpreted, 13–15, 152–53, 171, 257
Shankarāchārya tradition, 256–57, 256*n*5, 469
six systems of Indian philosophy, 21, 23, 116, 472–94
Indra, 38
Indriyas, 482
inertia
sinful actions lead to, 207
sleep as, 277, 406
infinite joy, 414, 424–25
contact with *Brahman* is, 439–41
infinite life, 90–98
infinite life-energy, 78, 265
infusion, of Being
balance in life from, 400–401
complete, 412
dyeing-cloth analogy, 312–13, 462
equanimity through, 175
into ever-changing relative states, 340–41
gives ability to resist 'excitement born of desire and anger', 370
impressions no longer form seed of desires, 341
integration of life through, 173
as *Karma Yoga*, 386–87
makes mind divine, 144, 210, 344, 359, 370, 413, 442
non-attachment demands fuller, 283
Samādhi represents complete, 144
as solution to suffering, 52
spontaneous, during Transcendental Meditation, 404–5
spontaneous right action through, 175–76
strain and tension as hindrances to, 191
by virtue of action, 211, 332
wealthy-man (above loss and gain) analogy, 117, 137, 142
whole life-stream rises during, 409, 410
See also alternation, of Transcendental Meditation and activity; inward stroke, of Transcendental Meditation
infusion, of Transcendental Consciousness, 141–43
changes field of bondage into eternal freedom, 340
does not bring Being to sensory level, 467
dyeing-cloth analogy, 462

enriches feelings and vision, 448
enriches mind with divine value, 436
as infusion of calmness, 389–91, 397, 466
Karma Yoga based on, 386
as mechanics of mastering senses, 341
mind transforms into state of Being, 144, 210, 344, 359, 370, 413, 442
moderation and, 418
requires alternation of Transcendental Meditation and activity, 317, 332
stopping, 457–63
straining interferes with, 191, 453
takes place by degrees, 312–13
into waking, sleeping, and dreaming, 340–41
See also infusion, of Being

innocence, during Transcendental Meditation, 411, 432–33

innocent field of life, 58
See also love

instrument, of Divine, 36, 172, 218, 393
established intellect as, 209

integrated life, 212–14, 249
activity on both paths brings, 173, 185–86, 194
through infusion of Being, 173
Kṛishṇa revives knowledge of, 9–10
of spirit and matter, 343–44
Yoga as basis of, 135–36
See also Brahman; revival of knowledge; Unity; Yoga

intellect
Brahman is beyond appreciation by, 441
deluded by anger and desire, 240–41
destruction of, due to anger, 163–64
happiness and, 165–68
he who is beyond, 242–43, 377
is denied entry to transcendental Self, 423–24
as *Mahat Tattwa*, 424
Pragyā, 151, 151*n*23
as seat of desire and anger, 235–44
in sequence of subtler aspects, 204, 242–43, 315, 372
take refuge in, 138–39
See also balanced intellect; established intellect; resolute intellect

intelligence
all-pervading, 197–98, 354
individual mind is held by cosmic intelligence, 346
omniscient silence of God, 392–93
student submits to teacher not abstract, 303
Veda as first in process of manifestation, 206
See also manifestation, process of

intermixture of castes, 65–66, 68–69

inward stroke, of Transcendental Meditation, 193, 214, 225, 312, 435–36
bliss at junction point of relativity and Absolute, 437–38
desires automatically abandoned during, 430
life-stream rises during, 409, 410
mastery of self from, 340
mind moves away from field of duality/fear, 409–10
outward and, 340, 344, 435–36
quietly bring mind back to, 435–36

Īshwara-praṇidhān, 484

Jaimini, 487, 489, 491
Janaka, 212–13, 468
Janārdana, Kṛishṇa as, 69
Jīva, 98–100, 492
Jīvan-mukta, 132–33
Jīvan-mukti, 144, 223, 321, 376, 402
See also Bliss Consciousness
joy, 220–24, 414, 424–25, 439–41
See also bliss; contentment; happiness
junction point, of Absolute and relativity 437–38

Kāla, 478, 479
See also time
Kali-yuga, 254
Kalpa, 253–54
Kāma
Yoga's fulfilment of, 427–28
Kaṇāda, 477, 480
Kāṇda, 67, 122–23, 132, 195
Kapila, 480, 483
Karma, 15, 142
bow-and-arrow analogy, 141
collective, 44
influence cause to modify effect, 126–27, 243, 430
is in field of diversity, 178
Karma-Sanyāsa Yoga, 380
philosophy of, 139

release from bondage of, 244
See also action; bondage of action; *Karma Yoga*
Karma Kāṇda, 67, 132
for relative joys, 123–25
Karma Mīmāṁsā
for action in accord with *Dharma*, 491
as one of six systems of Indian philosophy, 21, 487–91
Karma Yoga
based on inner stability of mind, 387
based on Yoga rather than action, 15
defined, 325
Divine Union gained through, 332–33
equanimity gained through, 183–86
established in Being, action is, 144
first step of, 131
Gyān Yoga differs only in phase of activity, 184
as householder's path, 149
influence cause to modify effect, 243
infusion of Being through, 386–87
is superior to *Sanyāsa* path, 329–34
Janaka and others' use of, 212–13, 468
misunderstanding about, 386–87
non-attachment to fruits of action, 384–87
as perfect Union and perfect renunciation, 384–87
renunciation naturally achieved through, 320, 322, 326
Sāṁkhya and, 223, 251–52, 290, 327–28, 335, 337–38
Transcendental Meditation alternated with activity is path of, 319, 321
Transcendental Meditation as necessity on path of, 177–78, 185, 190, 326
Yogasthaḥ kuru karmāṇi doctrine of, 135–36, 177–78, 182, 249
See also householder; Yoga of action
Karma Yogī, 131, 190, 385, 387–88, 467
Karma-Sanyāsa Yoga, 380
Karmendriya, 190, 190*n*11, 482
Kauravas, 28–29, 33, 36, 38–39, 41, 45, 59
Keshava, Kṛishṇa as, 55, 148–49, 178
killing
is sin, 55–71, 108
Self cannot slay or be slain, 98–102
slay enemy in form of desire, 243
See also destruction; war
king analogy, 94–95, 425
Kingdom of God on earth, 70
knowingness, state of, 311–12
knowledge
all action culminates in, 301–2
complete, requires experience and understanding, 271
cross over evil by raft of, 308
doubts rent asunder by, 319–21
experience and, 116–17, 427
fire of, 281, 285, 289, 308–11, 320
Gyān Kaṇda, 123–24, 132, 195
handed from generation to generation, 255–57
he gains, who is possessed of faith, 316–18
is irresistible, 308–9
is superior to action, 178–80
man without, 318–19
nothing so purifying as, 311–15
Nyāya's sixteen points for valid approach to, 21, 473–77
scriptural, 50, 132, 146–48, 157
scriptural, offered as *Yagya*, 297
sin destroyed by, 308–10
state of knowingness is Transcendental Consciousness, 311–12
sword of, analogy, 322
Transcendental Meditation as direct means of gaining, 473, 473*n*2
understanding and experience, 116–17, 249, 302
validity substantiated by six systems, 21
Vedānt, 16, 79, 256–57, 473, 491–94
wise do not confuse/disturb ignorant, 218–19, 244
Yagya of, 301–2
Yoga alone is not enough without Sāṃkhya, 103–4
See also revival of knowledge; Sāṃkhya; six systems of Indian philosophy; teaching; wisdom; Yoga
knowledge with devotion
Bhakta, 86, 86*n*4, 131
Shankara's, 12–13
See also devotion
Kṛishṇa, 28–29
as 'Achyuta', 42
in all ways ... men follow My path, 267–68
Arjuna surrenders to, 84–88
author of creation while remaining

uninvolved, 270
becomes Arjuna's charioteer, 38
breathes out through Pānchajanya, 37–39
describes life in equanimity, 150–74
educates Arjuna in philosophy of delusion, 305–6
entirety of Vedānt expressed in first word, 79
to establish Dharma I take birth age after age, 259–64
fourfold order was created by Me, 269–70
as 'Govinda', 56–57, 88
as head of Yādava clan, 28–29
holds within Himself fullness of Absolute and relative, 272
as 'Hṛishīkesha', 37, 45–46, 88, 89
as 'Janārdana', 69
as 'Keshava', 55, 148–49, 178
as 'Mādhava', 36–37, 61
as 'Madhusūdana', 37, 59, 76, 81–82, 450
as ocean on which whole of space is reflected, 260
petitioned for freedom from suffering, 25
remains neutral, 38, 43
remains neutral yet engages in activity, 215–20
restored direct contact with Being, 9–10
Royal Yoga of Lord, 383, 428
seeing all beings in Self and also in Me, 305–7, 441–47
sequence of words of, 102
smilingly spoke, 89
supreme liberation that abides in Me, 412, 413–14
surrendering all actions to Me, 225–27
symbolizing Bliss Consciousness, 89
teaching gradually forgotten, 9–10
in three worlds there is no action I need do, 215, 216
Transcendental Meditation taught by, 44–45
as 'Vārshṇeya', 65–66, 235
on wavering mind, 452–55
worship Me abiding in all beings, 445–47
See also Brahman; *specific topic*

Kshatriya
ancient wisdom given to, 252, 252*n*2
Arjuna as, 191
do battle in accord with *Dharma*, 108
as upholders of law/protectors, 85, 109, 113
Kuntī, 39, 80
See also Pṛithā
Kurukshetra, 26, 28
Kurus
Arjuna as 'best of', 299
Arjuna as 'joy of the', 121, 462
Bhīshma as grandsire of, 33, 34–35, 46–48
Duryodhana, 28–35, 38, 44, 56, 473–93
eager to fight, 26
field of, 26, 28
Pārtha! behold these, gathered together, 46–48
See also Dhṛitarāshtra
Kūtastha, 151, 151*n*24, 350
See also silent witness

lake-and-pipeline analogy, 267
lamp
invisible in light of sun, 341
which does not flicker, 421–22
Laws of Nature, 133
Cosmic Law underlying, 63, 276
Dharma and, 191–92, 417
govern all cause and effect, 123
mind becomes one with, 284, 375
natural action in accord with, 191–92, 242, 308, 333, 345, 438
pure nervous system and, 438–39
react to doer's action, 197
senses reorientated to activity in accord with, 431
stream of life in accord with, 192, 416
Yagya and, 195, 197–98, 204
See also gods; *Guṇa(s)*; Nature; support of Nature
laziness, 454
See also moderation
leaf analogy, 78
let a man raise his self by his Self, 395–97
let him not debase his Self, 395–96
let that disunion of union with sorrow, 426–28

liberation
from bonds of birth, 143–44
doctrine of, 249
eternal, enjoyed during life on earth, 174, 244–45, 443–61
he who is freed from attachment, 288–89
Moksha, 368, 370, 377–78, 427–28
supreme, that abides in Me, 412–14
wholly purified in state of profound equanimity, 356–66
See also freedom; Self-realized man
life, purpose of
Dharma, Artha, Kāma, and *Moksha* as, 427
eternal freedom as, 357–58
expansion of happiness, 352, 379–80
restored to humanity, 9–10, 16, 156–57
See also subtle fields, of subjective life
Life Eternal
oldest tradition as nearest to, 65
one who has reached Unity is, 449
Life of God, 307
See also God
life-span
Brahmā's, 253
Divine Mother's, 253
level of purity and, 461
Shiva's, 253
Vishṇu's, 253
life-supporting influence
friends bring, 379
killing never produces, 60–61
right action's, 276
Transcendental Meditation's global, 201, 214
when established in Being, 201–3
Yagya's, 204–5
See also spontaneous right action; support of Nature
light
awake in, of absolute bliss, 169–70
Being shines forth in Its own, 355
from bright, into-dark-cave analogy, 433
bring, to remove darkness, 126–28, 244, 355
celestial, 89
of knowledge kindled in man of faith, 316–22
lamp's, invisible in light of sun, 341
therein self-controlled is awake, 169–70
whose, is all within, 371–72
See also second element, principle of; sun
Light of God
all activity in, 288–303
everything understood in, 306
inner kingdom of human opens to, 32
living in, 175, 193, 247, 276
as state of eternal Unity, 347, 391, 426, 444
this and That held together in, 279
See also devotee; God Consciousness; *Yogī*
Līlā-shakti, 261
limbs-and-body analogy, 68
Lord of Creation, 175, 196
See also God
Lord of senses, 89
loss of knowledge
Buddha's teachings distorted, 10–11
due to long lapse of time, 255–57
Kṛishṇa's teaching forgotten, 9–10
power of *Dharma* overshadowed, 262–63
Shankara's teaching misunderstood, 14, 152–53, 171, 257
See also misinterpretation/misunderstanding; revival of knowledge
love
Arjuna's wave of, 25, 47–55, 58, 76–77, 80–81
brings strength, 81
caught between duty and power of, 52–69, 76–77, 85
for everyone in like manner, 157
heart filled with universal, 214
as innocent field of life, 58
without righteousness becomes destructive, 54
in sequence of subtler aspects, 315
sorrow due to lack of, 154–56

Mādhava, Kṛishṇa as, 36–37, 61
Madhusūdana, Kṛishṇa as, 37, 59, 76, 81–82, 450
Mahābhārat, 31, 45, 254
Mahābhūtas, 483
Mahārathī, 30, 31
Mahat Tattwa, 424
Manas, 422, 478, 482

manifestation, process of
finest relative, 164, 169, 219, 222, 315, 389–91, 423
first manifestation, 206–7
intellect as *Pragyā*, 151, 151*n*23
junction point of Absolute and relativity, 437–38
Mahat Tattwa, 424
origin of senses and their objects, 424–25
Prakṛiti begins, 261, 424
pure consciousness vibrates, 236
Rajo-guṇa overshadows pure consciousness, 236–37
See also creation; relative existence
Manu, 251–52, 252*n*3, 254
Manwantara, 253–54
master–disciple relationship. *See* teaching
Masters of Holy Tradition, 256–57, 256*n*5, 469
mastery of senses, 160
See also established intellect; senses
material gains
aspiration beyond, 200
balanced in experiencing earth, stone, or gold, 400–401
established in Yoga, O winner of wealth, 135–36
lack of knowledge as root of failure in, 318
mind entangled only in, 124–25
misinterpretation regarding, 171
victorious you will enjoy earth, 113
Yagya for, 204–5
See also possessions
material life
defined, 343
entertaining finer fields of experience, 405
spiritual life brought into, 329, 343–44
See also body; nervous system
Māyā, 491–92
Māyāvāda, 13
meditation. *See* misinterpretation/misunderstanding; Transcendental Meditation
memory
trying to forget amounts to remembering, 231, 405
unsteadiness of, 163–64
millionaire analogy, 136–37, 154
mind
anger and desire influencing, 163–64, 240–41
Arjuna's concern about wavering, 450–52
balance of, 135–36, 139
becomes basis of all Laws of Nature, 375
beyond pairs of opposites' influence, 94–95
as collection of seeds of desires, 422
conscious, 422, 470–71, 470*f*
controlling of senses by, 242–45
divided, 185
fickle and unsteady, 435–36
food's influence, 203
gains status of absolute Being, 144, 210, 344, 359, 370, 413, 442
held by experience of happiness, 452–53
individual, is held by cosmic intelligence, 346, 369, 393, 407, 417, 429
as machinery giving rise to desires, 240–41
natural tendency of, towards happiness, 229, 404–5, 411
orderly, smooth, harmonious, 413
as seat of desire and anger, 235–44
seems to whirl, 54
in sequence of subtler aspects, 204, 213–14, 242–43, 315, 372
of steady endurance, 450–51, 453
Transcendental Consciousness cultures equanimity of, 188–207
Transcendental Meditation activates deeper levels of, 136
Transcendental Meditation frees, from *Sankalpa*, 389
uninvolved in activity, 137–38
unshaken in midst of sorrow, 154–55
village of senses controlled by, 429–30
weakness of, as basis of all problems, 78–79
wins automatic control over senses, 162
See also control; equanimity; infusion, of Being; restful alertness; specific emotion
mirror-and-dust analogy, 238
misinterpretation/misunderstanding
about abstaining from enterprise, 170–71

about Arjuna, 47, 178
about art of action, 136, 139
ascetic practices based on, 370
about desires, 244, 370
disinterest versus natural contentment, 209
of *Karma Yoga*, 139, 386–87
'many births' and 'rebirth', 464–65
of 'non-attachment', 155–57, 386–87, 434
of Patanjali's Yoga, 15, 486
about recluse way of life, 13, 15, 113, 151–53, 257
about religion and philosophy, 16
about restraint, 241, 294
of *Sanyāsa* and 'renunciation', 16, 386–87
about Shankara's teaching, 152–53
about spiritual practice, 120
about state of established intellect, 156–57
about 'vision within eyebrows', 376–77
about wandering mind, 160
'without possessions', 402, 404–5
about *Yagya* and offerings, 199–200
See also desire(s); loss of knowledge; mood-making
moderation, 400–401
in eating and sleeping, 414–15
moderate of effort, 415–18
towards objects of senses, 414–18
See also energy
Moksha, 368, 370, 377–78, 427–28
as Union with the Supreme, 427–28
mood-making
devotion as, 14
divided mind resulting from, 185
of equanimity and unaffectedness, 94, 114, 135, 137, 139, 365
of evenness of vision, 441–47
of non-attachment to fruits of action, 386–87
of surrender to God, 226, 345
of surrendering during Transcendental Meditation, 411
unnatural and warped personality from, 156
while making offerings, 199–200
about *Yagya* and *Brahman*, 290–91
See also loss of knowledge; misinterpretation/misunderstanding
moral codes
basis of all, 110
basis of morality, 257, 427
greed blinding us from, 62–64
Samādhi not gained by secular virtues, 15–16
See also Dharma; scriptures; virtue
mother
-and-child analogy, 95
–child bond, 47
Divine Mother, 253
as expression of Nature's creative power, 66
See also women
mountain
-peak analogy, 122
-of-sins analogy, 298–99
Muni, 154, 377–78
mental activity as means to Yoga for, 389–90
not necessarily recluse, 169
music analogy (no effort to shift attention), 118

Naishkarmya, 186–87
nation
collective *Karma* threatening destruction of, 44
destruction of social order as greatest loss to, 66
Dharma affects, 276
tender mother/child bond influencing, 47
natural behaviour
deviation from *Dharma* brings suffering, 66
increasing-charm principle, 121, 169, 317, 432, 455
mood-making is un-, 156
of righteous people, 36–37
to turn towards happiness, 268
undisturbed by selfish desires or shortcomings, 209
when in one's own *Dharma*, 230–31
Yoga as fulfilment of personal *Dharma*, 427
See also social behaviour
natural tendency, towards happiness
no effort is lost, 117–20
Nature
balancing force of, 9
Being as basis of, 284

breaking point of, 35–36
carries out links between doer, action, fruits, 351–53
emergence of three *Guṇas*, 206
family *Dharmas* and equilibrium of, 64–69, 276
gods as powers of, 200
invincible force/power of, 9, 26
mind becomes basis of Laws of, 375
mother as expression of creative power of, 66
Prakṛiti, 206, 307, 424
Rajo-guṇa as basis of all forces of, 237
rhythms of, 204–5
Self-realization influencing harmony in, 204–5
unseen working of, behind success and failure, 63–64
war as breaking point of, 35–36
See also forces of Nature; *Guṇa(s)*; Laws of Nature; support of Nature
nectar, as remains of *Yagya*, 299
nervous system
consciousness and, 173, 226, 298, 313–15
culturing of, 173, 298, 314–15, 369
free from blemish attains infinite joy, 439–41
refined in gentle way, 466
refinement of, takes its own time, 173
reorientation of, through mind, 431
sin produces coarseness in, 207, 309
two styles of functioning in Cosmic Consciousness, 314
See also body; purification; restful alertness; senses
night for all beings, 169–70
Nirvāṇa, 10–11
Nirvikalpa Samādhi, 317
Nistraiguṇyo bhava-Arjuna. See Be without the three *Guṇas*
Nitya-samādhi, 150–51, 402, 486
See also Cosmic Consciousness
Niyama, 484
misunderstanding of, 15–16
niyamya, 241, 435
no effort is lost, 117–20
no obstacle exists, 117–20
nobility of character, 28, 32, 49–51
understanding Reality and, 116
non-action
experience of Being as basis of, 187
know Me to be the non-doer, 269–70
as *Naishkarmya*, 186–87
participation without becoming involved, 137–38
state of, rises to state of God's action, 188
as unfathomable as action, 275–77
See also inaction; renunciation; separation from activity
non-anticipation, 133–35
non-attachment
without depending on fruit of action, 384–87
engage in action free from attachment, 193–94
engaging in action truly unattached, attain Supreme, 210–11
every undertaking free from desire, 278–81
has no undue fondness, 155, 157
I do not act at all, 342–44
infusion of Transcendental Consciousness and, 283
inner condition of, 158–59
is as untouched by sin as lotus leaf by water, 344–45
is called Yoga, 135–36, 139
mind's wavering solved by experience of happiness, 452–55
misunderstanding about, 155–57, 386–87
as silent witness, 98–99, 291, 350, 481
thoughts in state of, 411
untouched by external contacts, 364–66
Vairāgya, 493
See also mood-making; separation from activity
Nyāya, 21, 472–77

object of attention, during Transcendental Meditation, 223, 436
objects of perception, 342–44
attachment to, 163
attraction and aversion located in, 230–31, 236, 362
essence of *Tanmātras* constitutes, 424–25, 482–83
freedom from craving for, 418–20

moderation towards, 414–18
senses withdrawn from, 153, 158–59, 168
some offer sound and other, in fires of senses, 293–94
steady intellect and, 159–60
See also senses
ocean
-of-eternal-Being analogy, 21
of eternal freedom, 250
he whom all desires enter as water enters unmoved sea, 170–71
Kṛishṇa as, of life, 260
of lasting peace, 170–71
life and love full as, 58, 157
-of-mind analogy, 136, 145, 470
non-involvement of, 341
rising waves of devotion, 307
rivers entering, analogy, 94
senses converge in silent, of Being, 412–13
Transcendental Consciousness analogous to, 418–19, 422, 436
waves and, analogy, 63, 392, 422
waves-of-bliss analogy, 162–63, 240
wind of desire stirs, analogy, 387
-of-wisdom analogy, 19, 75
offerings
to gods for success on earth, 268
of material possessions, 296–97
misunderstanding about *Yagya* and, 199–200
technique of transcending as process of, 194, 198, 201
See also Yagya
officer analogy, 243
omens, 55
omnipresence
of Being, 270, 278–79, 392–93
of bliss, 166, 169
of God, 392–93
one sees him as a wonder, 106–7, 441
one-pointedness, of resolute intellect, 121–25, 406–7
opposed statements, 182–83
opposed to heaven, 78–79
orange-juice analogy, 77–78, 206–7
organs of action
engaged in Yoga of action, 189
Karmendriya, 190, 190*n*11, 482
restraining of, as straining, 189
in sequence of subtler aspects, 242–43, 315
technique for control and organization of, 190
though fully engaged in action he does not act at all, 285–86
See also action
outward and inward breaths, 376–77
outward stroke, of Transcendental Meditation, 344, 435–36
mastery of higher Self from, 340
See also alternation, of Transcendental Meditation and activity; inward stroke, of Transcendental Meditation
oxygen-and-hydrogen analogy, 270

pairs of opposites, 129, 333
attraction and aversion, 230–31, 236, 362
beyond, 287–88
fail to present differences to *Yogī*, 448–49
friends and foes, 401
pleasure and pain, 92–95, 113–14, 399, 447–49
real and unreal, 95–96
success and failure, 135–36, 139, 249, 287–89, 320–21
transient they come and go, 93
See also good and evil
Pāṇdavas, 28, 39–40, 484
Pāṇdu, 28, 388
Parā Bhakti, 12
Paramāṇus, 478
Pārtha, 80, 99, 109, 150, 172, 216, 267–68, 301, 459
spoken creates divinely inspired wave of love, 46–48
See also Arjuna; Pṛithā
Patanjali, 15, 484–87
path of action. *See Karma Yoga*
path of knowledge. *See Gyān Yoga*
patient-and-surgeon analogy, 85
peace
basic principles of, 43
without delay, 316–22
eternal, 368–70
happiness of *Yogī* deep in, 437–38
he whom all desires enter as waters enter sea, 170–71
with his being deep in, 399, 409–10
permanent world, 19

without steady thought, 165–66
supreme, 316–18
Transcendental Consciousness as limitless source of, 126
traveller finds, 424
of disciplined mind attains to, 412–13
See also silence
perfection of life, *Yagya* as means to, 197
philosopher–kings, 251–55
philosophy of action, 10, 327–28
See also action
physics, 105
Piṇdodaka ceremonies, 66–67
pipeline-and-lake analogy, 267
pitiful are those who live for fruits of action, 138–41
pleasing-melody analogy, 118
pleasure(s), 56–57, 70, 82, 130, 154, 366–68
freedom 'from craving for any pleasure', 418–20
Sukya, 479
pleasure and pain, 92–95, 113–14, 399
evenness of vision in both, 447–49
possessions
having relinquished all, 286–87
independent of, 126, 129–30
non-acceptance of others', 484
non-realized man as thief, 199–200, 235
perform *Yagya* by means of material, 296–97
possessed of Self, 126, 130–31
'without possessions', as state of Being, 402, 404–5
See also material gains
Pragyā, 151, 151*n*23
Pragyānaṁ Brahm, 355
Prakṛiti
eightfold, 221
emergence of, 206
Guṇas and, 128, 188, 206, 220–21, 424, 481
manifestation by virtue of, 261, 424
in Sāṃkhya, 481
as veil separating from Being, 307
See also Guṇa(s); Nature
pratyavāya, 117–18
principle of second element. *See* second element, principle of
Pṛithā, 39, 47, 48, 80
See also Kuntī
Pṛithivī, 478
problems
Arjuna presents fundamental, of life, 23, 49, 66
Dharma of another brings danger, 231–34
do not exist for the Divine, 73
inner state of no, 235–44
light-to-remove-darkness analogy, 126–28, 244, 355
love as innocent field of life without, 58
not solved on level of, 78–79
principle of second element to alleviate, 78–79, 126–28
sixteen fundamental, 23, 78
solution to all, 23, 330
when attachment/detachment overshadows pure love, 58
proper action. *See* right action
psychology theories, 126
pure consciousness, 295–96
as basis of right action, 294
devotion from level of, 161–63
established intellect belongs to field of, 361
grace resulting from, 164
Karma Yoga and, 190–93, 387
manifests as vibration, 236
as mind's most purified state, 407
Rajo-guṇa overshadows, 236–37
Samādhi, 15–16, 144, 147, 150–51, 402, 485, 486
secret of arriving at, 129
surrender must be on level of, 412
Yagya and, 291
See also Being; infusion, of Being
pure of spirit, 338–41
purification
any form of *Yagya* aims at, 302
cleansed of all impurities by wisdom, 356–57, 356–58
Dhyānbindu Upanishad on destroying mountain of sins, 298, 299n45
finding fault and speaking ill causes impurity, 227–29
nothing so purifying as knowledge, 311–15
perform action for self-, 345–48
practice of Transcendental Meditation for, 406–7

refinement of nervous system, 173, 193, 313, 348, 466
Shaucha, 484
'twice-born' indicates ceremony of, 32
washing-of-cloth analogy, 459
Yagya as process of, 299
purity
free from blemish, 439–41
freed from duality ever firm in, 126–38
future casts its image on sanctuary of pure hearts, 55
is not lost due to bodily death, 462–63
life-span and, 461
Sattwa, 36–37, 128, 237, 269–70
seeing all beings in oneself and oneself in God, 305–7, 441–47
Transcendental Meditation and state of absolute, 266, 312, 407
worlds of righteous correlated to, 460–61
Pūrṇam adaḥ pūrṇam idam, 79, 250–51, 279, 449
Purusha, 481
Pūrva Mīmāṁsā. *See* Karma Mīmāṁsā

raft of knowledge, 308
rain, 204–5
raise his self by his Self, 395–97
Rajo-guṇa, 128
in fourfold order, 269–70
impels committing sin, 236–37
See also Guṇa(s); spur to activity
real and unreal, 95–96
See also pairs of opposites
realizing Me as the Transcendent, 409–12
recluse
engages in mental discrimination, 345–48
Gyān Yoga for, 184–86
householder's purpose same as, 186, 245, 249, 335
misunderstanding about, 13, 15, 113, 151–53, 257
Muni is not necessarily, 169
as one of two ways of life, 149, 157
performs mental activity for self-purification, 345–47
renunciation is same for householder and, 326–29
Sanyāsī, 257, 384–89
Shankara misinterpreted, 13–15, 257
Transcendental Meditation as basis for, 384
in whatever way he lives that *Yogī* lives in Me, 445–47
See also Gyān Yoga; Sāṁkhya
recreation
moderation in, 415–17
purpose of, is re-creating entire system, 417
refinement, of nervous system
devotion as most refined activity, 193, 313, 348
in gentle way, 466
takes its own time, 173
See also purification
reflection analogy, 166
regularity, of Transcendental Meditation practice, 439
delusion of one fallen from, 457–58
fallen from, 461–63
relative and Absolute. *See* Absolute and relativity
relative existence, 215, 216
beyond influence of, 94–95
ever-changing, 471
finest aspect of, 164, 169, 219, 222, 315, 389–91, 423
ignorance has no material substance, 81
knowledge of, gains fulfilment in realization of the Supreme, 225–26
Paramāṇus, 478
sequence of subtler aspects, 204, 242–43, 315, 372
Taittirīya Upanishad on higher planes of, 461
take life/things as they come, 93, 493–94
as unmanifest to manifest to unmanifest, 105
whole field of action pervaded by God, 211–12
See also Absolute and relativity; time, space, and causation
remembering, trying to forget amounts to, 231, 405
renunciation
comprehends same goal as path of action, 373–80
without depending on fruit of action, 384–87

doer remains separate from field of activity, 187–88
hard to attain without Yoga, 336–38
is naturally achieved through *Karma Yoga*, 320, 322, 326
state of Union is equivalent to state of, 385–86
See also non-action; *Sanyāsa*; separation from activity
repeated inquiry, 303–5
reputation
put to shame, 111–12
this blemish alien to honourable men, 78–79
vibrations from one's, 109–12
what a great man does is followed by others, 214–15
reservoir analogy, 132
resolute intellect
Arjuna's forthcoming, 86
one-pointedness of, 121–25, 406–7
as refuge, 138–41
Shankara defines man of, 152
skill in action from, 141–43, 147, 148
technique for instantaneous, 126–32
See also established intellect; intellect; steady intellect
restful alertness
body becomes instrument tuned to divine, 407
corresponds to Bliss Consciousness, 173
corresponds with silence of Omnipresent, 393
as cosmic existence sustains individual physical existence, 346
nervous system permanently maintains, 369
in Transcendental Meditation rejuvenates system, 417
when activity of senses ceases, 168
when mind transcends thought, 313, 429–30
restraint
breathing exercises, 297–98, 407
gaining control without, 451–55
he who sits restraining organs of action, 189
misunderstanding about, 241
non-attachment never gained by, 229–31
sense-control principle negated, 189, 229, 241, 431
See also control
retail-merchant analogy, 367
revival of knowledge, 9, 17
God's appearance for, 247, 262–65
I take birth age after age, 259–64
righteousness rises to neutralize excess evil, 41–42
Shankarāchārya tradition, 256–57, 256*n*5
this same age-old Yoga, 256–58
by virtue of play-power of *Brahman*, 261
See also divine Incarnation; Transcendental Meditation
right action, 10–11, 15, 192, 208–14, 219
born of inner state of no problems, 235–44
ease of performing, 294–96
life-supporting effects of, 276
only possible with knowledge of divine, 274–88
pure consciousness as basis of, 294
in state of non-attachment, 384–87
See also Cosmic Consciousness; spontaneous right action; wrong action
righteousness
forces that support, 23, 31–32
God's appearance re-establishes, 262–65
Kingdom of God on earth, 32, 70, 380, 444
love without, becomes destructive, 54
seeker of Truth takes stand between good and evil, 23, 34–46
worlds of, 460–61
roasted-seeds analogy, 311
Royal Yoga of Lord Kṛishṇa, 383, 428
See also Transcendental Meditation

Sākshi-kūtastha, 350
See also silent witness
Samādhāna, 494
Samādhi
cannot be gained by secular virtues, 15–16
as converging point of innumerable radii, 147–48
Dhyān and, 485, 486
as goal of all paths and all Vedic Texts, 147
as limb of Yoga, 485–87

Nitya-, 150–51, 402, 486
practice of Yoga begins with, 15–16
Savikalpa to *Nirvikalpa*, 317
as Transcendental Consciousness, 144
See also equanimity
Sāṃkhya
all about nature of Absolute and relative, 90–116
Dharma understood through, 108–10
equanimity gained on path of, 183–86
essence of, 91–95
he who sees, and Yoga to be one, 335
Karma Yoga and, 223, 251–52, 290, 327–28, 335, 337–38
as one of six systems of Indian philosophy, 116, 480–83
results of action understood through, 112–13
social relationships understood through, 109–12
as teaching technique, 275
Transcendental Meditation as common ground of Yoga and, 335–36, 384
Transcendental Meditation provides verification of, 326, 480
on uninvolved nature of doer, 113–15
unreal has no being; real never ceases to be, 95–96
wisdom of perishable and imperishable phases of life, 115
Yoga alone is not enough without, 103–4
and Yoga as knowledge and experience, 116–17
See also recluse
Sanjaya, 26, 29, 45–46
Sankalpa
abandoning desires from which, is born, 429–31
Muni has not yet rooted out every, 390
Sanyāsa as state of no, 388–90
Santosha, 484
Sanyāsa, 386, 386*n*3
based on inner stability of mind, 387
can refer to aspirant or one in divine Union, 402
direct relationship with God, 443
family of *Yogīs*, 461–63
four interpretations of, 332
has evenness of vision, 441–50
for him alone calmness is means, 389–91, 397, 466
incentive of desire has been rooted out, 388–89
inmost Self of highest, absorbed in God, 467–68
Karma-Sanyāsa Yoga, 380
mature state of, 337
mind of, abides in silence, 401
misunderstanding about, 16, 386–87
non-attachment to fruits of action, 384–87
not he who is without fire and without activity, 384, 387
pairs of opposites fail to present differences to, 448
performs action for self-purification, 345–48
performs action in state of non-attachment, 384–87
perpetual freedom of, 372
power of silence works out everything for, 392–93
renunciation and Union coexist in, 385
as seer, 373–80
as state of no *Sankalpa*, 388–90
superiority of, 466
supremacy of *Karma Yoga* over, 329–34, 385–87
that which they call, know it to be Yoga, 388–89
two aspects of becoming, 400–401
two states of Union with God, 449–50
unshakeable mind of, 368–70
whose happiness is within, 371–72
See also Light of God; Self-realized man; Unity
Sanyāsī, 257
he is a, and he is a *Yogī*, 380
incentive of desire must be rooted out, 388–89
not he who is without fire, 384, 387
performs action in state of non-attachment, 384–87
sap analogy, 277–78, 360
every fibre of tree is sap, 261, 491
for *Māyā*, 491–92
Sat, 441, 441*n*48
Sat-Chid-Ānanda, 187, 441, 441*n*48
See also Bliss Consciousness
satisfied with whatever comes unasked, 287–88
Sattwa, 36–37, 466
in fourfold order, 269–70

Rajo-guṇa responsible for functioning of, 237
Sato-guṇa, 128
See also Guṇa(s); purity
Sātyaki, 30, 31
Sat-yuga, 254
Savikalpa Samādhi, 317
science of action, 245, 280
'scorcher of enemies', 48, 80–81, 255, 257, 259, 260
scriptures, 146–48
beyond need of, 132
misguided interpretations of, 157
save from falling into error, 50
state of suspension despite, 146
See also moral codes
seclusion, 402, 403
second element, principle of, 78–79
light-to-remove-darkness analogy, 126–28, 244, 355
seeds
of action, 142, 158, 286, 310, 388
of desire, 310, 341, 388, 394, 422
roasted, analogy, 310–11
sees all beings in Self, 305–7, 441–47
Self
cannot slay or be slain, 98–102
conquest of self by Self, 397–99
Dharma of, 233–34
his inmost, absorbed in Me, 449–50
let a man raise his self by his, 395–97
mastery of both self and, 340
possessed of, 126, 128, 130–31
satisfied in, 150–51
seeing, by, alone, 423–24
three stages of purification of, 347–48
unfolds Itself by Itself to Itself, 396
Vedānt on relationship of *Ātmā* and *Brahman*, 491–92
See also separation from activity; states of consciousness
self-deception, 139
See also mood-making
Self-realized man
actions spontaneously effective and right, 208–14
arrives at state devoid of suffering, 143–45
cannot be judged by outer signs, 153
characteristics of, 150–74
delighted in Self alone, 207–8
disciplined mind does not lose, 454–55
freedom even while engaged in activity, 220–24
has no undue fondness, 157
for him there is no action that he need do, 208
is above doubt and delusion, 146–48
is balanced in success and failure, 135–36, 139, 249, 287–89, 320–21
not finding fault/speaking ill as prerequisites, 227–29
should help raise consciousness of ignorant, 225–34
skill in action of, 141–43, 147, 148
state of mind of, 373–80
that which is night for all beings, 169–70
See also resolute intellect; separation from activity; wise, the; *Yogī*; *specific state of consciousness*
sense-control principle, negated, 189, 229, 241, 431
sense(s)
balanced in experiencing earth, stone, or gold, 400–401
Being brought to level of, 447–50, 467–68
city of nine gates, 350
closing gates of, 376
contentment in, 207–8
controlling village of, 429–30
dries up my, 87
as enemy no longer, 340–41
five, of perception, 190, 190*n*12, 482
impressions of, no longer form seed of desires, 341
Indriyas, 482
under influence of desire and anger, 240–41
inner mechanics of conquering, 336–41
joys of, as sources of sorrow, 367–70
Lord of, 89
mastery of, 160, 162
niyamya as having organized/withdrawn, 241, 435
origin of, and their objects, 424–25
perceptions do not register deep impressions, 190, 340–41, 365
pleasures born of contact as sources of sorrow, 366–68
reorientated from alternation of Transcendental Meditation and

activity, 431
as seat of desire and anger, 235–44
in sequence of subtler aspects, 204, 242–43, 315, 372
some offer sound and other, in fires of control, 293–94
spontaneously more natural and useful to evolution, 188–207
subdued, 160–63, 189–90, 242–45, 316–22, 429–30
Supreme lived/appreciated on sensory level, 153, 159–60
Tanmātras, 424–25, 482–83
taste for objects of, ceases, 159–60
transcending naturally controls, 242–45
untouched by external contacts, 364–66
wandering, 167–68
Yoga is not for him who eats too much, 414–15
See also control; objects of perception

separation from activity
'calmness' as, 389–91, 397, 466
Gyān as, 12
having left external contacts outside, 376–77
he is not involved even while he acts, 336–41
'I do not act at all', 342–44
inner freedom with outer activity, 274–88
mind uninvolved, 137–38
Self's, 180, 187–88, 344–45, 434
Transcendental Meditation brings natural state of, 223, 226
truly unattached man, 210–11
untouched by external contacts, 364–66
untouched by *Guṇas'* influence, 358–61
See also Cosmic Consciousness

service
as alertness and submission, 303, 304–5
Hanumān symbolizes, 41–42
homage, repeated inquiry, and, 303–5
as subtler emotional activity, 315

Shākhā, 195–96

Shankara
Bhagavad-Gītā commentary by, 21, 257
description of 'steady intellect' misinterpreted, 152–53
on 'directed his gaze to front of his nose', 408
established four seats of learning, 12
lifetime of, 256, 256*n*5
lived/taught fullness of heart and mind, 12–13
misinterpreted, 13–15, 152–53, 171, 257
revival of Vedānt by, 256–57
revival of Vedic wisdom by, 11–16
on steady intellect, 152–53
on 'through homage, repeated inquiry, and service', 304
transcendental devotion of, 12–14

Shankarāchārya tradition, 256–57, 256*n*5, 469

Shaucha, 484

Shiva, 253

shortcut, to enlightenment, 456–57

Shreyas, 55

Shukadeva, 468

sight
functioning in organized/controlled manner, 190

silence
of absolute omnipresent Being, 270, 278–79, 392–93
of Being at very start of activity, 282–83
both paths start in activity and end in, 388–89
different in Cosmic and God Consciousness, 391–93
God's and humanity's compared, 391–92
mind of *Yogī* abides in, 401
power of, works out everything for *Yogī*, 392–93
restful alertness corresponds with, of Omnipresent, 393
against that, Duryodhana speaks, 475
three states of, 392–93
of Transcendental Consciousness, 226, 313, 391, 392–93
true surrender leads to, 87, 89
See also peace; separation from activity

silent witness, 98–99, 291, 354, 481
Sākshi-kūtastha, 350

sin(s)
all-pervading Intelligence does not accept, 354
better to die than to commit, 70–71

of casting away *Dharma* and reputation, 78–79, 109–12
creates suffering, 59–60, 110
cross over all evil by raft of knowledge, 308
desire impels committing of, 235
eating without offering to God, 203
even if you were most sinful of all sinners, 308–9
gets destroyed by knowledge of Divine, 308–10
killing is, 55–71, 108
mountain of, analogy, 298–99
produces coarseness of nervous system, 207, 309
technique for rising above all, 200–202, 308
untouched by, as lotus leaf by water, 344–45
you will not incur, 113–14
sitting
in any style, 153
how does he sit, how does he walk?, 148
in order to start meditation, 406–7
restraining the organs of action, 189
sit united looking to Me as Supreme, 161–63
sit united realizing Me as the Transcendent, 409–12
six systems of Indian philosophy, 23, 116
Bhagavad-Gītā's truth to analysed by, 472–94
Transcendental Meditation fulfils, 494
validity of knowledge in light of, 21, 472
See also Karma Mīmāṁsā; Nyāya; Sāṃkhya; Vaisheshik; Vedānt; Yoga
sixteen fundamental problems, 23, 78
sixteen points for valid knowledge, Nyāya's, 21, 473–77
skill in action, 141–43, 147, 148
sleep state of consciousness
established in bliss during, 135, 151, 157, 371
governed by *Dharma* of one's level of evolution, 276
Gudākesha as Lord of, 45–46, 88
inertia of, 340
moderation in sleep and waking, 416
of one in Union with Divine, 342
outward and inward activity continues in, 188
peace of liberation as different from, 409, 412–14
Self maintained during, 170, 173–74, 183–84, 187, 208, 249, 419
sense of being is lost in, 409
as state of inaction/inertia, 277, 406
too much or not enough, 414–16
smaller than smallest, 419
smell, 478, 482
does not register deep impressions, 190
smilingly spoke, 89
smoke, as fire is covered by, analogy, 238
social behaviour
all moral codes based on *Dharma*, 110
caste *Dharmas*, 64–68, 109, 113, 358, 360
code of action, 123, 186
complexity of action and its consequences, 276
gauging influence of, on future generations, 65
mother/child tender bond influencing future, 47
Nature's equilibrium influencing family *Dharmas*, 64–69, 276
others will follow one's example, 214–15
protectors of society, 85, 109, 113
See also natural behaviour
sorrow
absence of Bliss Consciousness is source of, 368
Arjuna's, 49, 71–72, 76–78
Bliss Consciousness brings end to all, 164–65
disunion of union with, 426–28
ignorance as cause of, 79, 154–55
joys of senses are sources of, 366–70
lack of fulfilment causes, 154–56
pleasures born of contact as sources of, 366–68
unshaken in midst of, 154–55
Yoga which destroys, 417–18
soul
actions for purification of, 323, 345–56
as *Ātmā*, 478–79
engage in activity for evolution of, 214–15
evolution of, based on one's choices, 268
evolution of, in species, 268

lower species compared to human, 268
material life overshadows, 343–44
as real Self, 103
See also Ātmā
sources of sorrow, 366–68
space, 478
Kṛishṇa as ocean on which whole of, reflected, 260
See also time, space, and causation
species, four categories of every, 270
spectacles analogy, 306, 316, 367, 446
speech
anger/excitement in, 369
apparently opposed statements, 182–83
Brahman lies between two contrary statements, 440–41
imbued with contentment, 460
Jaimini on verbs and purpose of, 489
Kṛishṇa's, to shock Arjuna, 78–81
Kṛishṇa's, transforms Arjuna's mind, 149
life-breaths join to bring forth, 479
polemics, 475
repeated inquiry, 303–4
sequence of Kṛishṇa's words, 102
Shankara's, 12
speaking ill of others, 227–28
tongue as organ of, 478
words inadequate to express realization, 146, 331
spontaneous right action, 10–11, 15, 219
art of, 175–76, 192, 296, 431
born of inner state of no problems, 235–44
ease of, 294–96
only possible with knowledge of divine, 274–88
pure consciousness as basis of, 294
of Self-realized man, 208–14
in state of non-attachment, 384–87
See also Dharma; right action; support of Nature
spur to activity, 128, 178, 236, 349, 437–38
starting an action, 282
states of consciousness, 276
action as blessing leading to higher, 193
'ascends to Yoga' applies to several, 393–94
different as wearing different coloured glasses, 316, 367
let a man raise his self by his Self, 395–97
life is appreciated differently in different, 316, 444–46, 449
more advanced, cannot be evaluated from lower, 449
quality of action worthy for higher, 212
refining of nervous system takes its own time, 173
three states of silence differentiating higher, 391–93
in time finds this within himself, 311–12, 465
Transcendental into Cosmic Consciousness, 429–43
'worlds of righteous' corresponds to, 460–61
'Yoga' applies to development of all higher, 428
See also Self; *specific state*
steady intellect, 150–51
balance of mind naturally maintained in activity, 135, 138–39, 154
cannot be judged by outer signs, 153
consequences of not having, 163–67
intellect anchored to Immovable, 151, 151*n*24
senses' taste for objects vanishes, 159–60
Shankara on, 152–53
when senses withdraw, 155–57
See also established intellect; resolute intellect
steady thought, happiness and, 165–67
straining
comfort during Transcendental Meditation versus, 408–9
concentration practices, 377
he who sits restraining organs of action is, 189
practice of Yoga removes all, 466
unnatural actions produce tension and, 191
See also mood-making; natural behaviour
stress, 229, 403
student–teacher relationship. *See* teaching
subtle fields, of subjective life
are more powerful, 214
ever thus collecting himself, 412–13, 439
first manifestation of creation, 206–7
process of manifestation, 424–25

sequence of, 242–43, 315
truth about *Guṇas* at subtlest level, 222–23
wheel of origin returning back to origin, 207–8

success
balanced in failure and, 135–36, 139, 249, 287–89, 320–21
is born of action, 267–68
prerequisites for, in Yoga, 454–55
unseen working of Nature behind, 63–64

suffering
Bhagavad-Gītā undertakes solution to, 50–52
deviation from one's natural course brings, 66
duality as fundamental cause of, 51–52
ignorance of Self as basis of all, 78–79
increasingly negative forces brings, 27–28
infusion of Being as solution to, 52
love without righteousness creates, 54
scriptures prescribe means to avoid, 50
Self-realized man arrives at state devoid of, 143–45
sin causes, 59–60, 110
Yoga which destroys sorrow, 417–18

sun
-dispels-darkness analogy, 119–20
light of, analogies, 355–56, 396, 424
wind-and-, analogy, 396
wisdom like, illumines That, 355
See also light

superiority
of action to inaction, 191, 192
Karma Yoga to *Sanyāsa*, 329–34
of knowledge to action, 178–80
of *Yogī* to men of action, 466
of *Yogī* to men of knowledge, 466

support of Nature, 50–51, 272, 472, 487
from attunement with Cosmic Law, 133, 233–34
by his Self alone is his own friend, 397–99
by living in Being in daily life, 375
for Pāṇdavas, 28, 43
power of silence works out everything for *Yogī*, 392–93
satisfied with whatever comes unasked, 287–88
Yagya and, 194, 198, 379
See also life-supporting influence

Supreme, the
engaging in action truly unattached, man attains to, 210–12
knowledge of relativity gains fulfilment in realization of, 225–26
let him sit united, looking to Me as, 161–62
lived/appreciated on level of sensory perception, 153, 159–60
Moksha as Union with, 428
one participates in consciousness of, 279
precise knowledge of, dawns on basis of one's own experience, 272
realization of, is within your reach, 244
realization of Its fullest glory, 466
slow and difficult versus easy path to reach, 294
whole of life immersed in glory of, 399

supreme action, 210–11
supreme consciousness, 409, 410
supreme happiness, 437–38
supreme liberation, 412, 413–14
supreme peace, 316–18
supreme secret, 258
supreme state of enlightenment, 296
supreme state of Yoga, 391, 447–50
surgeon analogy, 85
surrender, 131
action surrendered to God, 225–27
Arjuna's, to Kṛishṇa, 84–88
as men approach Me, I favour them, 267–68
realizing Me as the Transcendent, 409–12
true, 87, 89, 412
Sushrut, 262
suspension, of outward and inward breaths, 376–77
swimming analogy, 136
sword-of-knowledge analogy, 322

Taittirīya Upanishad, 461
take life/things as they come, 93, 493–94
take refuge in intellect, 138–41

Tamas
in fourfold order, 269–70
Rajo-guṇa responsible for functioning of, 237
Tamo-guṇa, 128
See also Guṇa(s)
Tanmātra, 424–25, 482–83
Tapas, 484
taste, 478, 482
does not register deep impressions, 190
Tat Twam Asi, 9, 81, 358
teaching
alertness to pupil's reactions, 102
authority with love, 260
cow-and-calf analogy, 86
to cultivate divine consciousness, 44–45
five to ten minutes transforms Arjuna's mind, 149
good teacher is encouraged by questions, 259
of history, 252–53
through homage, repeated inquiry, and service, 303–5
imparted in increasingly subtle yet simpler forms, 275
initial upliftment, 111
intellectual preparation before direct experience, 103
introducing new topic, 116
mountain-peak analogy, 122
noble way of enlightening aspirant, 120
about philosophy of delusion, 305–6
readiness to receive wisdom, 47
repeated questions to know Truth, 330
Sāṃkhya as technique of, 275
Shankara lived/taught highest development of heart and mind, 12–13
speaking to startle/shock, 78–81
student submits to teacher not abstract intelligence, 303
student's faith in self, teacher, and God, 316–18
teach me for I have taken refuge in Thee, 84–86
teacher and pupil relationship, 90–91
two qualities entitling one to receive wisdom, 258
Upanishads for, about *Brahman*, 440–41
Upanishads show way of contacting *Brahman*, 195
use of negation and affirmation, 102
Vedānt on relationship of *Ātmā* and *Brahman*, 491–92
wise do not confuse/disturb ignorant, 218–19, 244
See also knowledge; wisdom
Tejas, 101–2, 478
that which is night for all beings, 169–70
thief, non-realized man as, 199–200, 235
This covered by that, 238
thought
authorship of, 411
bubble analogy, 470
given over to Me, 409–12
God is beyond appreciation by, 444
happiness and steady, 165–67
as lamp which does not flicker, 421–22
let him not think at all, 432–34
more subtle levels of, in Transcendental Meditation, 470
restful alertness when mind transcends, 313, 429–30
retires, 421–22
in sequence of subtler aspects, 213–14
source of, in Transcendental Meditation, 470–71
starts from deepest level of consciousness, 282
state of realization beyond, 146
Transcendental Consciousness imbues contentment into, 460
See also mind
three fields of faith, 316
three worlds
in, there is no action I need do, 215, 216
sovereignty over, 59
time
arrives without delay, 336–38
Bhagavad-Gītā outlives, 20
cannot be recaptured, 15
distinction between, in and out of Transcendental Meditation, 405, 413
epochs of, 254
I take birth age after age, 259–64
in, finds this within himself, 311–12, 465
Indian concept of, 251–54

Kāla, 478–79
loss of knowledge due to long lapse of, 255–57
mechanics of Nature pictured on screen of, 43
omens of future, 55
one day of Brahmā, 253–54
peace without delay, 316–22
refinement of nervous system takes its own, 173
Savikalpa to *Nirvikalpa Samādhi*, 317
there never was, when I was not, 91–92
time, space, and causation
beyond bondage to, 145, 157, 265, 407
eternal freedom within limitations of, 173–74
lower self bound by, 339
Self beyond limits of, 99
See also relative existence
tortoise analogy, 158–59
touch, 478, 482
does not register deep impressions, 190
toys analogy, 15, 446, 449
tradition(s)
of age-old family *Dharmas*, 64–69
complexities of today's mixed civilizations, 192
Holy Tradition, 256–57, 256*n*5, 469
Shankara's, misunderstood, 14, 152–53, 171, 257
survival through ages shows nearest to Truth, 65
this same age-old Yoga, 258
of Yoga of action, 251–55
Transcendental Consciousness
brings contentment into activity, 460
into Cosmic Consciousness, 429–43
is state of knowingness, 311–12
for *Karma Yogī* or *Bhakta* or *Gyānī*, 131
as link between humanity and God, 196
realizing Me as the Transcendent, 409–12
as release from field of activity, 300–301
repeatedly gaining, interpreted as many births, 464–65
Samādhi is, 15–16, 144, 147, 150–51, 402, 485, 486
Self maintained during sleep, 170, 173–74, 183–84, 187, 208, 249, 419
silence of, 226, 313, 391, 392–93
as stage of self-purification, 347–48
See also infusion, of Transcendental Consciousness
transcendental devotion, 12–14
Transcendental Meditation
activates deeper levels of mind, 136
advantages of, 73
allotted duty unfolds from practice of, 193
aspirants start from any level, 319
charm increases at every step, 121, 169, 317, 432, 455
collectedness during, 412–13, 439
comfort for practising, 405–6
conditions for practising, 402–4
delivers from great fear, 117–18, 456
details of practice, 402–41
for direct experience of inner divine nature, 14
as direct means of gaining knowledge, 473, 473*n*2
distraction during, 436
easiness of, 432–34
evening meditation, 312–13, 357
exertion retards transcending, 432–34
expands conscious mind, 470–71, 470*f*
fulfils conditions for enlightenment, 317
fulfils six systems of Indian philosophy, 480, 491, 494
gives rise to *Samādhi*, 485, 486
innocence is key, 411, 432–33
inward stroke, 435–36
Kṛishṇa teaches, 44–45
let a man raise his self by his Self, 395–97
life-stream rises during, 409, 410
mind held by experience of happiness, 452–53
neither contemplation nor concentration, 471
no effort is required, 117–20
no expectations during, 402–5
no obstacle exists in process of, 117–20
outward stroke, 340, 344, 435–36
as practical aspect of abstinence, 493
practice of, infuses bliss, 156, 418
quietly bring mind back to inward direction, 435–36

regularity of practice, 439, 457–58, 461–63
as Royal Yoga of Lord Kṛishṇa, 383, 428
Sāṃkhya and, 326, 335–36, 384, 480
for self-purification, 406–7
sequential stages as practice advances, 371
in sitting position, 406
at start of creation, 252
stopping practice of, 457–63
taught to Arjuna, 44–45
as *Yagya*, 198, 201
See also alternation, of Transcendental Meditation and activity; infusion, of Being; *specific analogy; specific topic*
transcending
as action required for all paths, 389, 390–91
as basis of non-action, 187
Dhṛitarāshtra's sons not educated in, 44–45
disadvantages of exertion, 432
established in, perform actions, 135–36, 177–78, 182, 210, 249
as going beyond act of worship, 292–93
on level of senses, 447–50, 467–68
mind's status in, 144, 210
to omnipresence of Being, 270, 278–79, 392–93
Prakṛiti and, 307
as prerequisite of *Karma Yoga* and *Sanyāsa*, 387
Transcendental Meditation for direct, 144, 210
'without possessions' and, 402, 404–5
Yagya goal is, 300–303
See also pure consciousness
tree analogies
branches and trunk, 256
every fibre of tree is sap, 261, 491
tree of life, 245
See also water-the-root analogy
Tretā-yuga, 254
true surrender, 87, 89, 412
Truth
direct experience of, 146–48
distorted by interpreters, 257
established in, 90, 96
oldest traditions as nearest to, 65
repeated question to arrive at, 330
of Vedic Wisdom, 9
Turīya, 187
twice-born
Transcendental Consciousness as rebirth, 464–65
Vedic ceremony of *Brāhmaṇa*, 32
two fullnesses, 157, 161–63, 179, 262–63, 272
Pūrṇam adaḥ pūrṇam idam, 79, 250–51, 279, 449
two paths (knowledge and action)
both start in activity and end in silence, 388–89
muddled understanding of, 185–86
See also Gyān Yoga; *Karma Yoga*
two types of people, 183–84
See also householder; recluse

Ultimate, the, 85, 95, 244
undisciplined state of life, 454–55
unfathomable is course of action, 275–78
uninvolved intellect, 138–39, 175
See also established intellect; resolute intellect
uninvolvement
closing gates of senses, 376
in Cosmic Consciousness, 341
with one's possessions, 493
precise knowledge of Supreme's, dawns on basis of one's own, 272
See also separation from activity
Unity
of all *Yogīs* I hold him most fully united, 467–68
calmness transforms to, of God Consciousness, 389–91, 397, 466
devotion to God dissolves in, 447–50, 467–68
duality subsumed into, of God Consciousness, 314
Light of God as state of eternal, 347, 391, 426, 444
living silence as basis of cosmic activity, 391–92
omnipresent, omnipotent, omniscient silence of God, 392–93
one who has reached, is life eternal, 449
Pūrṇam adaḥ pūrṇam idam, 79, 250–51, 279, 449

silence of, 392–93
as supreme state of Yoga, 391, 447–50
this and That held together in, 279
See also Brahman; devotee; God Consciousness; Yoga; *Yogī*
universe
conquered by those in equanimity, 360–61
five elements, 424–25, 482–83
ignorance has no material substance, 81
physics on, 105
Tanmātras, 424–25
See also creation; relative existence
Upanishads
Bhagavad-Gītā as 'milk' of, 443
Bṛihad-Āraṇyak, 140
'certainly fear is born of duality', 50, 409
Dhyānbindu, on destroying mountain of sins, 298–99, 299*n*45
elucidate nature of *Brahman*, 440–41
in *Gyān Kāṇda*, 195
on happiness in different states of creation, 167
Pragyānaṁ Brahm, 355
Pūrṇam adaḥ pūrṇam idam, 79, 250–51, 279, 449
Shākhās and, 195–96
Shankara's commentary on, 257
show way of contacting *Brahman*, 195
Taittirīya, on degrees of happiness, 461
'That Thou Art', 9, 81, 358
See also Vedānt
Uparati, 493
Upāsana Kāṇda, 123, 132
ūrdhwaretas, 409, 410, 410*n*17
Uttara Mīmāṁsā. *See* Vedānt

vacuum analogy, 220
Vairāgya, 493
Vaisheshik, 21, 477–80
Vaivaswat Manu, 252*n*3
Vāyu, 101–2, 478
Veda
concern is with three *Guṇas*, 126–32
eternal, 9
expound theory of action and all pertaining to action, 205–6
Holy Tradition, 256–57, 256*n*5, 469
know action to be born of Brahmā, 205–7
of no more use than well in flooded place, 132–33
'passes beyond', 463
qualification for study of, 32
as self-illuminant effulgence of life, 206
Shākhās of, 195–96
those engrossed in letter of, 122–25
Yagya as subject of, 195–96
See also Yagya; *specific branch*
Vedānt
on *Ātmā* and *Brahman*, 491–92
on *Māyā*, 491–92
as one of six systems of Indian philosophy, 257, 473, 491–94
prerequisites for, 492
Shankara's revival of, 256–57
Vyāsa as seer of, 491, 491n9
whole, in Kṛishṇa's first word, 79
Vedic Literature
different perspectives within, 147
Samādhi as goal of all, 147
Shankara revived essence of all, 256
vibrations
consciousness vibrates and becomes mind, 236
individual reputation emanates, 109–12
See also manifestation, process of
villager-and-landlord analogy, 430
virtue
Arjuna's concern to safeguard, 44
basis of all moral codes, 110
in evil atmosphere, 64
five Pāṇdavas', 484
happiness from, 61
as primary consideration, 114
Samādhi not gained by secular, 15–16
suffering despite adherence to, 50
unrealized state as cause of sin and, 354–56
Tamas as secular, 15
See also Dharma; moral codes
Vishṇu, 253
Vivaswāt, 251–52, 252*n*3
Viveka, 152*n*27, 492
Vyāsa
enlightened vision of, 39, 46, 472, 480–81
as seer of Vedānt, 491, 491*n*9
as Vedic sage, 9, 252–53
See also Bhagavad-Gītā

waking state of consciousness, 226, 276, 317
  details of Transcendental Meditation practice, 402–41
  moderation in sleep and, 416
  outward and inward activity continues in, 188
  as undisciplined state of life, 454–55
walking analogy, 129
war
  abstinence from, 110
  basis of all conflicts, 23, 78
  come out to fight, 97, 113–14
  die for others, 57, 111
  forces of nature and, 108
  Kshatriya's duty, 85, 108, 109, 113, 252*n*2
  as Nature's breaking point, 35–36
  women impacted by, 82
  See also battlefield of life
washing-of-cloth analogy, 459
water, as element, 101–2, 478
water analogies
  boat of life, 164, 182
  boats in fast current, 66
  lake and pipeline, 267
  for *Māyā*, 491–92
  of no more use than well in flooded place, 132–33
  oxygen and hydrogen in various forms, 270
  underground currents' outlet, 242
  untouched by sin as lotus leaf by, 344–45
  See also ocean
water-the-root analogy, 19, 87
  as art of action, 277–78
  as solution to any problem, 78
  transcending desire to bring its fulfilment, 245
wavering, mind's
  Arjuna's concern about, 450–52
  solved by experience of inner bliss, 452–55
wealthy man
  businessman (above loss and gain) analogy, 117, 137, 142
  poor man and, analogy, 156
  son of, analogy, 137
weapons cannot cleave him, 101–2
welfare of world, 212–14, 217–18
whatsoever a great man does, 214–15
wheel
  revolving from origin back to origin, 207–8
  spinning, of evolution, 27
  See also birth and death
whence has this blemish, 78–79
whirlpool analogy, 236
white horses, 36–37
Will of God, 108, 411
  See also God
wind-and-sun analogy, 396
windless place, 421–22
wisdom
  cannot be imparted unless asked for, 46–47
  cleansed of all impurities by, 356–58
  established intellect has, 361
  freed from attachment . . . mind established in, 288–89
  Holy Tradition of Vedic Wisdom, 256–57, 256*n*5, 469
  humility and, 358–59
  illumines That which is transcendent, 355
  is veiled by ignorance, 354–55
  like sun illumines That which is transcendent, 355–56
  purified by austerity of, 265–66, 379
  two qualities entitling one to receive, 258
  See also Absolute; knowledge; teaching
wise, the
  are established in Being, 144, 218, 224
  are not taken aback by changes of body, 92–93
  constant enemy of, 238–40
  do not confuse/disturb ignorant, 218–19, 244
  do not find fault/speak ill of others, 227–29
  grieve neither for dead nor living, 90–91
  him knowers of Reality call, 281–85
  view path of knowledge and path of action as same, 334–36
  see all beings in Self and also in Me, 305–7
  see Self in all beings, 441–47
  See also knowledge; *Yogī*
without possessions, 402, 404–5

See also possessions
without problems, 66
See also problems
without suffering, 52
See also suffering
without the three *Guṇas*. *See* Be without the three *Guṇas*
women
Adharma causes corruption of, 65–66
mother–child bond influencing all relationships, 47
mother's life as expression of Nature's creative power, 65
purity of mother influencing next generation, 65–66
war impacting, 82
See also family *Dharmas*
worlds of righteous, 460
in, no longer engage in Yoga, 461
See also heaven
worn-out-garment analogy, 100–101
worship
going beyond, 292–93
Me abiding in all beings, 445–47
Me with faith, 467–68
wrong action, 62–64, 141–43, 220, 308–9
Dharma overshadowed, 262–63
scriptural guidance to avoid, 50
should also be understood, 275–77
See also right action; sin

Yādava clan, 28–29
Yagya
action for sake of, 288–90
action which carries divine consciousness, 205–8
activity of transcending as, 194, 198, 201
advantages of, 196–98
all aspects of, are *Brahman*, 283–84, 290–91
austerity and, 297
as born of action, 300–301
Bliss Consciousness as nectar of, 298–99
breathing exercises as, 297–98
Cosmic and God Consciousness as remains of, 200–203, 299
cycle of action–*Yagya*–rain–food–creatures, 204–5
defined, 196–200
every action as, in Cosmic Consciousness, 198, 293
gods and, 197–200
importance of, as path to enlightenment, 302
of knowledge, 301–3
for material gain, 204–5
through material means alone, 301–2
by means of material possessions, 296–97
misunderstanding about offerings, 199–200
offering, itself, 292–93
as subject of Veda, 195–96
Transcendental Meditation as, to gain higher than highest, 198
Transcendental Meditation as most important, 201
transcending as goal of all, 300–303
See also Transcendental Meditation
Yama
five qualities of observance in Yoga, 484
as secular virtues, 15
Yoga
action is said to be means for, 389–93
alone is not enough without Sāṃkhya, 103–4
applies to development of all higher states of consciousness, 428
'ascends to Yoga' applies to several states of consciousness, 393–94
attaining, without renunciation, 336–38
austerity inferior to, 466
balance of mind is, 135, 138–39, 154
as basis of integrated life, 135–36
begins with *Samādhi*, 15–16
defined, 137–38, 296, 423–28
essence of, 126–38
established in, perform actions, 135–36, 177–78, 182, 210, 249
fulfils *Dharma*, *Artha*, *Kāma*, and *Moksha*, 427–28
goal of all, 453
imperishable, proclaimed to Vivaswāt, 251–55
'in this Yoga' indicates path to bliss, 121
intent on, 336–41
is skill in action, 141–43, 147, 148
Karma-Sanyāsa Yoga, 380

knowledge of, given to philosopher-kings, 251–55
moderation in eating and sleeping, 414–15
once started will have its effect, 465
as one of six systems of Indian philosophy, 21, 483–87
Patanjali's eight spheres/limbs of, 484–87
Patanjali's eightfold path reversed, 15
as path of Union, 116
prerequisites for success in, 454–55
qualities naturally present in state of, 484
Royal, of Lord Kṛishṇa, 383, 428
Samādhi as limb of, 485–87
same age-old, 258
as Sāṃkhya and *Karma Yoga*, 223, 251–52, 290, 327–28, 335, 337–38
for self-purification, 406–7
as Transcendental Consciousness, 183, 483
Transcendental Meditation as common ground of Sāṃkhya and, 335–36, 384
understand '*Sanyāsa*' as, 388–89
for undisciplined man, hard to achieve, 454–55
which destroys sorrow, 417–18
worlds of righteous no longer practice, 461
See also Gyān Yoga; *Karma Yoga*; *specific type*

Yoga of action
bow-and-arrow analogy, 139, 140, 141–42, 300
declared to My devotee and friend, 258
defined, 183–89
dyeing-cloth analogy, 312–13, 462
is superior to renunciation of action, 331–33
lost due to long lapse of time, 255–57
perceptions do not register deep impressions, 190, 340–41, 365
take refuge in the intellect, 140–41
tradition of, 251–55
See also Karma Yoga

Yoga Shāstra, 199, 233, 278
Yogasthaḥ kuru karmāṇi, 135–36, 177–78, 182, 210, 249
Yogī, 86*n*3
of all *Yogīs* I hold him most fully united, 467–68
can refer to aspirant or one in divine Union, 402
cow-and-calf (devotion and affection) analogy, 86
family of *Yogīs*, 461–63
has direct relationship with God, 443
has evenness of vision, 441–50
for him alone calmness is means, 389–91, 397, 466
incentive of desire has been rooted out, 388–89
mind of, abides in silence, 401
not he who is without fire and without activity, 384, 387
pairs of opposites fail to present differences, 448
performs action for self-purification, 345–48
performs action in state of non-attachment, 384–87
perpetual freedom of, 372
power of silence works out everything for, 392–93
as seer, 373–80
superiority of, 466
two aspects of becoming, 400–401
whose happiness is within, 371–72
See also Light of God; Self-realized man; Unity

Yogīshwara, 328
Yudhishthira, 28, 40
Yuga, 254
Yuyudhāna, 30, 31

Contact Information for Maharishi's Global Programs

For information on Maharishi's programs and contact details for Transcendental Meditation introductory talks and courses in your country, see the websites below. If your country is not listed, go to **www.tm.org** or **www.uk.tm.org** and enter your country name on the contact page.

ALBANIA www.al.tm.org

ALGERIA www.mt-algerie.org

ANDORRA www.meditacionmt.es

ANGOLA www.tm-africa.org

ANGUILLA www.uk.tm.org

ANTIGUA AND BARBUDA www.ag.tm.org

ARGENTINA www.ar.meditacion.org

ARMENIA www.armenia.tm.org

ARUBA www.meditacion.org/web/aruba

AUSTRALIA www.tm.org.au

AUSTRIA www.meditation.at

AZERBAIJAN www.tm.org.az

BANGLADESH www.uk.tm.org

BARBADOS www.uk.tm.org

BELGIUM www.transcendentemeditatie.be

BELIZE www.uk.tm.org

BENIN www.mt-afrique.tm.org/web/benin

BERMUDA www.uk.tm.org

BHUTAN www.tm.org

BOLIVIA www.meditacion.org/web/bolivia

BOSNIA AND HERZEGOVINA www.uk.tm.org

BOTSWANA www.tm-africa.org

BRAZIL www.meditacaotranscendental.com.br

BULGARIA www.tm-bg.org

BURKINA FASO www.mt-afrique.tm.org/web/burkina-faso

BURUNDI www.meditation-transcendantale.fr

CAMBODIA www.kh.tm.org

CAMEROUN www.mt-afrique.tm.org/web/cameroun

CANADA www.ca.tm.org

CAPE VERDE www.meditacaotranscendental.blogspot.com

CHILE www.cl.meditacion.org

CHINA www.cn.tm.org/en

COLOMBIA www.co.meditacion.org

COSTA RICA www.meditacion.org/web/costa-rica

COTE D'IVOIRE www.mt-afrique.tm.org/web/cote-d'ivoire

CROATIA www.tm-savez.hr

CUBA www.meditacion.org

CYPRUS www.intl.tm.org/web/cyprus

CZECH REPUBLIC www.cz.tm.org

DENMARK www.dk.tm.org

DOMINICA www.dm.tm.org

DOMINICAN REPUBLIC www.meditacion.org/web/republica-dominicana

ECUADOR www.meditacion.org/web/ecuador

EGYPT www.eg.tm.org

EL SALVADOR www.meditacion.org/web/el-salvador

ESTONIA www.tmkeskus.ee

ETHIOPIA www.tm-africa.org

FIJI www.fiji.tm.org

FINLAND www.meditaatio.org

FRANCE www.meditation-transcendantale.fr

FRENCH GUIANA www.meditation-transcendantale.fr

GABON www.meditation-transcendantale.fr

GAMBIA, THE www.tm-africa.org

GAUDELOUPE www.meditation-transcendantale.fr

GEORGIA www.meditation.ge

GERMANY www.de.tm.org

GHANA tmeditationghana.org

GREECE www.yperbatikosdialogismos.tm.org

GREENLAND www.dk.tm.org

GRENADA www.tm.org

GUATEMALA www.meditacion.org/web/guatemala

GUINEA mt-afrique.tm.org/web/guinee

GUINEA-BISSAU www.tm-africa.org

GUYANA www.meditacion.org/web/guyana

HAITI www.tm.org

HONDURAS www.meditacion.org

HONG KONG www.hk.tm.org

HUNGARY www.hu.tm.org

ICELAND www.ihugun.is

INDIA www.in.tm.org

INDONESIA www.tmindonesia.org

IRELAND www.tm-ireland.org

ISRAEL www.meditation.org.il

ITALY www.meditazionetrascendentale.it

IVORY COAST *See* Cote d'Ivoire

JAMAICA www.uk.tm.org

JAPAN www.tm-meisou.jp

KAZAKHSTAN www.tm-meditation.kz

KENYA www.ke.tm.org

KIRIBATI www.tm.org.au

KOSOVO www.al.tm.org

KYRGYZSTAN www.kg.tm.org

LATVIA www.tmlatvija.wordpress.com

LEBANON www.maharishitm.net/tm

LESOTHO www.za.tm.org

LIBERIA www.tm.org

LITHUANIA www.elori.lt

LUXEMBOURG www.meditation-transcendantale.fr

MACAU www.hk.tm.org

MACEDONIA www.mk.tm.org

MALAYSIA www.malaysia.tm.org

MALI www.mt-afrique.tm.org/web/mali

MALTA www.uk.tm.org

MARTINIQUE www.meditation-transcendantale.fr

MAURITANIA www.mt-afrique.tm.org/web/mauritanie

MAURITIUS www.intl.tm.org/web/mauritius

MEXICO www.mx.meditacion.org

MOLDOVA www.md.tm.org

MONACO www.monaco.tm.org

MONGOLIA www.uk.tm.org

MONTENEGRO www.me.tm.org

MOROCCO www.tm-africa.org

MOZAMBIQUE www.tm-africa.org

MYANMAR www.mm.tm.org

NAMIBIA www.tm-africa.or

NEPAL www.nepal.tm.org

NETHERLANDS www.nl.tm.org

NETHERLANDS ANTILLES www.nl.tm.org

NEW CALEDONIA www.meditation-transcendantale.fr

NEW ZEALAND www.tm.org.nz

NICARAGUA www.meditacion.org/web/nicaragua

NIGER www.mt-afrique.tm.org/web/niger

NIGERIA www.nigeria.tm.org

NORTHERN MARIANNA ISLANDS www.tm.org

NORWAY www.no.tm.org

PAKISTAN www.tm.org

PANAMA www.meditacion.org

PARAGUAY www.meditacion.org/web/paraguay

PERU www.meditacion.org/web/peru

PHILIPPINES www.tm.org

POLAND www.tm.net.pl

PORTUGAL www.meditacaotranscendental.blogspot.com

PUERTO RICO www.meditacion.org/web/puerto-rico

REPUBLIC OF KOREA www.intl.tm.org/web/republic-of-korea

REUNION www.tm-africa.org

ROMANIA www.ro.tm.org

RUSSIA www.maharishi-tm.ru

RWANDA www.tm-africa.org

SAINT KITTS AND NEVIS www.uk.tm.org

SAINT VINCENT AND THE GRENADINES www.uk.tm.org

SAN MARINO www.meditazionetrascendentale.org

SAO TOME AND PRINCIPE meditacaotranscendental.blogspot.com

SENEGAL www.mt-afrique.tm.org/web/senegal

SERBIA www.stm.rs

SEYCHELLES www.tm-africa.org

SIERRA LEONE www.tm-africa.org

SINGAPORE www.sg.tm.org

SLOVAKIA www.cz.tm.org

SLOVENIA www.atma.si

SOLOMON ISLANDS www.tm.org.au

SOUTH AFRICA www.za.tm.org

SPAIN www.meditacionmt.es

SRI LANKA www.lk.tm.org

ST LUCIA www.lc.tm.org

SURINAME www.meditacion.org/web/suriname

SWAZILAND www.za.tm.org

SWEDEN www.transcendental-meditation.se

SWITZERLAND www.schweiz.tm.org; suisse.tm.org; switzerland.tm.org

TAIWAN www.tw.tm.org

TANZANIA www.intl.tm.org/web/tanzania

THAILAND www.rajapark.ac.th

TOGO www.mt-afrique.tm.org/web/togo

TRINIDAD AND TOBAGO www.trinbago.tm.org

TUNISIA www.tm-africa.org

TURKEY www.tr.tm.org

TUVALU www.tm.org.au

UGANDA www.uganda.tm.org

UKRAINE www.tm.org.ua

UNITED ARAB EMIRATES www.tm.ae

UNITED KINGDOM www.uk.tm.org

UNITED STATES OF AMERICA www.tm.org

URUGUAY www.meditacion.org/web/uruguay

U.S. VIRGIN ISLANDS www.tm.org

VANUATU www.tm.org.nz

VENEZUELA www.meditacion.org/web/venezuela

VIETNAM www.vietnam.tm.org

ZAMBIA www.zambia.tm.org

ZIMBABWE www.zimbabwe.tm.org

Transcendental Meditation Program for Women

AUSTRALIA www.meditationforwomen.org.au

AUSTRIA www.gmdo.at

CANADA www.tm-women.org

GERMANY www.tmfuerfrauenundfamilien.de

GREECE tm-gmdo.gr

HUNGARY www.gwo.hu

ISRAEL www.tmwomen.org.il

LUXEMBOURG www.meditation.lu

MEXICO organizacionglobaldemujeres.org.mx/wp

NEW ZEALAND www.tmforwomen.co.nz

SLOVENIA www.gwo.si

UNITED STATES OF AMERICA
www.tm-women.org
www.tmwomenprofessionals.org
www.tmforwomenshearthealth.org

Architecture and City Planning

Maharishi Sthapatya Veda

Architecture in Accord with Natural Law

International Institute of Maharishi Sthapatya Veda www.maharishivastu.org

Institute of Vedic City Planning www.vediccityplanning.com

Australia www.vastuarchitecture.com.au

Canada www.vastu.ca

France www.vastu.fr

Italy www.vastumaharishi.it

Russia www.maharishi-vastu.ru

Switzerland www.rajabuilders.ch/fr

Health

Maharishi AyurVeda Health Products

Australia, Maharishi AyurVeda Products www.mapi.com.au

Europe, Maharishi AyurVeda Products Europe B.V. (MAP) www.ayurveda.eu

India www.maharishiayurvedaindia.com

Netherlands, Maharishi Technology Corporation B.V. www.ayurveda-produkte.de

New Zealand, Maharishi AyurVeda Products www.getbalance.co.nz

Switzerland www.ayurveda-products.ch www.veda.ch

United Kingdom www.maharishi.co.uk

United States of America, Maharishi AyurVeda Products International, USA www.mapi.com

Maharishi AyurVeda Health Programs

Maharishi College of Perfect Health, USA www.mum.edu/premed

Institute of Natural Medicine and Prevention www.mum.edu/inmp

Maharishi Vedic Vibration Technology www.vedicvibration.com

Maharishi AyurVeda Health Centres

Maharishi AyurVeda Health Spa: *The Raj*, Fairfield, Iowa, USA www.theraj.com

Maharishi AyurVeda Health Centre, Skelmersdale, Lancashire, UK www.maharishiayurveda.co.uk

Maharishi AyurVeda Health Centre, Bad Ems, Germany www.ayurveda-germany.com

Maharishi AyurVeda Health Centre, Seelisberg, Switzerland www.ayurveda-seelisberg.ch

Education

International Foundation of Consciousness-Based Education www.consciousnessbasededucation.org

Maharishi University of Management, Fairfield, Iowa, USA www.mum.edu

Maharishi School of the Age of Enlightenment, Fairfield, Iowa, USA www.maharishischooliowa.org

Maharishi University of Enlightenment, USA www.maharishiuniversityofenlightenment.com

Maharishi School, UK www.maharishischool.com www.consciousnessbasededucation.org.uk

Maharishi School, Australia www.maharishischool.vic.edu.au

Maharishi Invincibility Institute, South Africa www.cbesa.org

Stress-Free Schools Program for Latin America www.escuelasinestres.org

Publications

Maharishi University of Management Press, USA www.mumpress.com

Other Programs

Global Country of World Peace www.globalcountry.org

Maharishi Vedic Organic Agriculture Institute www.mvoai.org

Maharishi Gandharva Veda *The Eternal Music of Nature* www.maharishi-gandharva.com

Maharishi Purusha Program www.purusha.org

Mother Divine Program www.motherdivine.org

Maharishi Vedic Pandits www.vedicpandits.org

David Lynch Foundation www.davidlynchfoundation.org